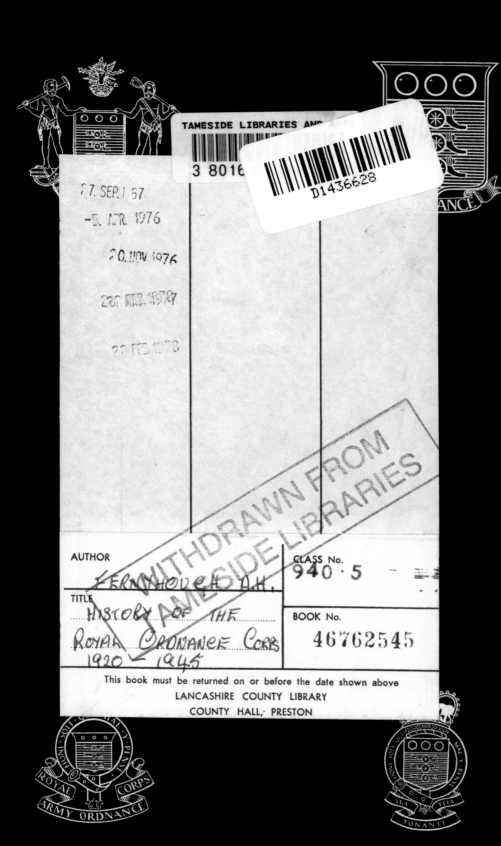

HISTORY OF THE
ROYAL ARMY ORDNANCE CORPS 1920–1945

Her Majesty the Queen
Colonel-in-Chief of the Royal Army Ordnance Corps

History of the

Royal Army Ordnance Corps

1920–1945

BRIGADIER A. H. FERNYHOUGH CBE MC

ASSISTANT AUTHOR

MAJOR H. E. D. HARRIS

ROYAL ARMY ORDNANCE CORPS

Made and printed in Great Britain by
William Clowes and Sons, Limited, London and Beccles

Contents

List of Maps

Foreword

This book tells the story of the Royal Army Ordnance Corps during the period between the two wars and in the Second World War, when the Corps was called upon to make the greatest effort in its history.

It describes how the Corps expanded from a very small nucleus and achieved in the shortest possible time the creation of an efficient and virile organization to deal with the enormously complex and vital task of supplying the great war-time Army with its stores, vehicles and ammunition.

It was an extremely difficult story to write because of its wide range and many ramifications and the necessity of giving a balanced picture in as few words as possible. We were fortunate, therefore, that Brigadier Alan Fernyhough, CBE, MC, should have undertaken the task of writing this momentous history. The son of a senior officer in the Corps, he himself had a most distinguished career and his wide experience, knowledge and ability made him an admirable choice as author. He has been greatly helped by another Corps officer, Major H. E. D. Harris, who carried out a tremendous amount of valuable research work for this history.

This is a story full of important lessons, and in this respect perhaps the failures are of more account than the successes. Both should be taken to heart.

As the head of the Corps from 1942 to 1946, I am honoured to have been asked to write this short Foreword. I am confident that the book will commend itself to a wide body of readers, and I know it will be read with pride and interest by all those who are or have been connected with the Corps.

Major-General Sir Leslie Hamlyn Williams,
KBE, CB, MC.
Controller of Ordnance Services, 1942–46, and
Colonel Commandant, RAOC, 1943–58.

ACKNOWLEDGEMENTS

THE scope of RAOC activity in the Second World War was so great that a reasonably complete history could not be produced without the active assistance of very many people.

The late Major-General Sir Leslie Williams, KBE, CB, MC, as Colonel Commandant RAOC and Chairman of the Corps History Committee was the moving spirit behind the whole enterprise and, as head of the Corps from 1942 to 1946, he had exceptional knowledge of the events of this period.

Colonel R. H. A. P. Finney, OBE, has been kind enough to read the drafts and advise on the method of presentation of the various chapters.

Major-General Sir Lancelot Cutforth, KBE, CB, Major-General Sir John Hildreth, KBE, and Major-General E. G. Brown, CB, CBE, have devoted much time and trouble to the screening and editing of the final drafts of all chapters.

I gratefully acknowledge the assistance of those who have first-hand knowledge of the various events described and in particular Brigadier R. L. Allen, OBE, Colonel R. P. Bridge, Brigadier L. A. Coates, OBE, Brigadier W. T. Cobb, CBE, MC, Brigadier C. H. Cooper, CBE, Brigadier C. E. de Wolff, CB, CBE, Lieutenant-Colonel A. Duncan, OBE, Major V. S. Ebbage, MBE, BEM, Brigadier G. C. Evelegh, CBE, Major-General C. H. Geake, CB, CBE, Lieutenant-Colonel W. H. J. Gillow, MBE, Brigadier B. A. Goldstone, CBE, Lieutenant-Colonel E. J. Longstaff, MBE, Major-General L. L. Hoare, DSO, Lieutenant-Colonel J. W. Lupton, MBE, Colonel G. T. Meadows, MBE, Lieutenant-Colonel M. Nicol, ERD, Brigadier J. S. Omond, MBE, MC, Colonel S. Preston, CBE, Major General E. P. Readman, CBE, TD, Brigadier D. S. Robinson, OBE and Brigadier H. C. Whitaker, CBE.

My thanks are due to the Survey Production Centre RE for providing the outline maps and L/Cpl R. Bumstead, RAOC, of the School of Ordnance, for the art work on them.

Much valuable information on the Middle East Theatre and Western Desert campaigns was obtained from the papers of the late Major-General W. W. Richards, CB, CBE, MC, access to which was kindly granted by Mrs. Richards.

Cassell and Company Ltd have been kind enough to give permission for the quotation from the Memoirs of Lord Woolton which appears in Chapter 2.

There have been frequent references to and quotations from the various volumes of the *History of the Second World War*, United Kingdom Military Series, and official despatches published in the *London Gazette*. Permission to quote these sources has been granted by the Controller H.M. Stationery Office.

Finally I should like to thank Mr. V. Lyen, whose long hours of patient work on the typing and production of the various drafts and the considerable correspondence associated with all this work have made publication of the history possible.   A.H.F.

Historical Introduction

The Ordnance Department goes back into older history than the Army of which it has since become a part. There were Master-Generals and Boards of Ordnance centuries before there were Secretaries of State for War or Commanders-in-Chief.

The Board of Ordnance was the predecessor of the RAOC. It built forts and barracks wherever these were required, supplied war material for the armies which were formed and equipped the artillery and engineers, the technical arms which came under the Master-General of Ordnance. The organization was set forth in great detail in a Warrant issued in 1683 and remained almost unchanged until 1855, when it fell in the panic that followed the disasters of the Crimean War.

The Board of Ordnance was replaced by the Military Store Department, whose officers held the Queen's Commission, and soon afterwards, in 1865, a Royal Warrant authorized an establishment of soldiers under the title of the Military Store Staff Corps. In time the Military Store Department was renamed the Ordnance Store Department and then, before the end of the century, the Army Ordnance Department. The Military Store Staff Corps became the Army Ordnance Corps.

From 1855 to 1870 the new Department flourished. The officers were of a high educational standard, were given thorough technical training and received a high rate of pay. In 1870 a system known as Control was introduced with the idea of merging all supply and transport branches. The two main elements were the Military Store Department (Ordnance) and the Commissariat and Transport Department. The differential in pay was abolished and an intermediate rate adopted. Apart from the loss of pay the Ordnance suffered from being much the smaller of the two branches, and the Commissariat obtained almost all the higher posts. The smaller and weaker Ordnance, about which controllers cared little and knew less, was under-officered and under-manned at a time when the Army was consuming equipment at a rate which increased in compound ratio, while its consumption of food remained a constant.

After a time the Control system was dropped and the two main branches separated again. But the old advantages of the Military Store Department were not restored. Commanders and staff understood neither the nature nor the importance of the technical work for which Ordnance was responsible. For more than 20 years the Department was neglected and suffered a sad decline in efficiency. The Department did not even have its own chief but came under the Director of Artillery, who was inclined to regard it as a poor relation.

By 1893 the need for the complete reorganization and regeneration of the Department was realized. A high rate of Corps pay was introduced so as to attract the right type of officer whose training was improved and made more scientific. The Ordnance officer's responsibility, both for the stores in his charge and as adviser to the local Commander on the supply of war material, was clearly defined.

These changes had an immediate effect. A number of energetic and efficient young officers transferred to the AOD, and it was largely due to their influence that the Ordnance Services earned a reputation for initiative and the ability to overcome all difficulties both in the South African War and the Great War.

Unfortunately the Department was still no man's child at the seat of war. The staff knew little of its functions and methods, and Ordnance was not integrated into the field force in the same way as the Army Service Corps. The officers were not eligible for administrative staff appointments.

Presumably it was felt that the number of such technically trained and highly paid officers must be kept to a minimum, and this could only be achieved by classing them as specialists, permanently engaged on Ordnance work. This classification was given the unfortunate misnomer of "non-combatant status", which effectively isolated Ordnance Officers from the rest of the Army and ensured that they could exercise no influence over logistic concepts.

In 1904 the Esher reforms led to the creation of the Army Council. The QMG was made responsible for the Army Ordnance Department and Corps, which at last had its own chief, the Director of Equipment and Ordnance Stores with staff branches (QMG 7, 8 and 9) under him. At the same time Ordnance Officers were appointed on the headquarters of formations (divisions, corps and armies).

In the Great War the supply of stores, equipment and ammunition was a far more important factor than ever before. General Sir Travers Clarke (the QMG in France for a large part of the war) stated: "Ordnance was the ever-present help of the British soldier in an ordeal of unexampled severity. The devoted and skilful work of its officers and men kept the Army equipped to a point near perfection." Immediately after the Great War the Army Ordnance Department and Corps was re-named the Royal Army Ordnance Corps.

This introduction is a summary of the History of the Army Ordnance Services by the late Major-General A. Forbes. The present history carries the story on from 1920 to the end of the Second World War.

Code Words

ANVIL   The landing in the south of France after a bridgehead had been established in Normandy. The aim was to accelerate the re-occupation of France and increase the Allied forces on the Continent for the attack on Germany. The troops mainly came from Italy, and this tended to weaken the forces available to Field-Marshal Alexander.

AVALANCHE   A combined operation on the coast of Italy, involving a landing in the Bay of Salerno by a combined United States/British force —the Fifth Army.

BATTLEAXE   An attack on General Rommel launched by General Wavell in 1941 with the object of raising the siege of Tobruk and re-occupying Cyrenaica. It failed.

BAYTOWN   An attack on Italy by the Eighth Army across the Straits of Messina after the occupation of Sicily.

BOLERO   The plan for the accommodation in the United Kingdom of American forces assembling for operations in Europe. Its effect on the RAOC was that storage accommodation in the south of England had to be handed over to the Americans.

BUTTRESS   The occupation of the "toe" of Italy by 10 Corps after the capture of Sicily. This operation never took place.

BRIMSTONE   The capture by the Fifth U.S. Army of Sardinia. A possible alternative to the assault on Sicily and later to the attack on the Italian mainland. It never materialized and in the end Sardinia surrendered without a fight.

COSSAC   Stands for "Chief of Staff Supreme Allied Commander" and was the code name for the Planning Staff under General Sir Frederick Morgan which did all the early planning for OVERLORD.

CRUSADER   The campaign in the Western Desert from November 1941 to February 1942 in which the Eighth Army defeated Rommel, raised the siege of Tobruk and occupied Cyrenaica.

DYNAMO   The successful naval operation in which the BEF and many French soldiers were withdrawn across the Channel from Dunkirk in May and June 1940.

FLAMBO   The name for the Advanced Administrative Echelon of Allied Forces Headquarters. For many months after the landings in Italy AFHQ had to remain in Algiers. An advanced administrative headquarters (FLAMBO) was therefore established in Italy, at Naples.

FORTBASE   An Eighth Army organization. It was an administrative organization which moved forward with the Army and opened up new ports as they were captured. For the campaigns in Sicily and the south of Italy this organization was known as FORTBASE. It lapsed with the creation of FLAMBO.

FORCE EMU   A force sent from India to reinforce Malaya Command in anticipation of a Japanese invasion.

GOBLET   A plan for 5 Corps to land in the south of Italy at Crotone after the occupation of Sicily. It supplemented BUTTRESS and like that operation never materialized.

GOLDFLAKE   The transfer of units from the Central Mediterranean Force to 21 Army Group after ANVIL.

HABFORCE   An improvised force formed in Palestine to move across the desert into Iraq and raise the siege, by Rashid Ali, of Habbaniya.

HUSKY   The Anglo-American operation for the capture of Sicily.

MARKET GARDEN   The operation to establish a bridgehead over the Rhine by occupying Arnhem with 1st Airborne Division and linking 30 Corps with them across the Nijmegen Bridge. It failed.

MULBERRY   The construction of an artificial harbour which was towed in sections across the Channel and established off the Normandy beaches. It greatly facilitated the build-up of stores in the Rear Maintenance Area.

OVERLORD   The Anglo-American combined operation for the invasion of Europe over the Normandy beaches in June 1944.

SHINGLE   The landing by an Anglo-American force under American command at Anzio with the object of outflanking the German "Winter Line" and forcing a withdrawal. Tactically it failed but had important strategic effects.

TIGER   The name for a convoy carrying considerable reinforcements of tanks to General Wavell to enable him to undertake the BATTLEAXE operation.

TORCH   The Anglo-American landings in French North Africa in November 1942. The allied forces were under General Eisenhower as Supreme Commander.

GOLD, JUNO, SWORD   The invasion beaches in Normandy used by 21 Army Group in the OVERLORD operation.

BLACKCOCK, VERITABLE, GRENADE   The various operations undertaken by 21 Army Group to clear the left bank of the Rhine in preparation for the crossing of the river and the advance across Germany.

ABBREVIATIONS

AA	Anti-Aircraft
AAD	Advanced Ammunition Depot
AAG	Assistant Adjutant-General
AAI	Allied Armies in Italy
AAOD	Anti-Aircraft Ordnance Depot
AASF	Advanced Air Striking Force
ADGB	Air Defence Great Britain
ADOS	Assistant Director of Ordnance Services
ADOS(P)	Assistant Director of Ordnance Services (Provision)
ADST	Assistant Director of Supplies and Transport
AE	Ammunition Examiner
AFHQ	Allied Forces Headquarters
AFV	Armoured Fighting Vehicle
AFW	Army Field Workshop
AG	Adjutant-General
AIA	Assistant Inspector of Armourers
AMPC	Auxiliary Military Pioneer Corps (later Royal Pioneer Corps)
AOD	Advanced Ordnance Depot
AOER	Army Officers Emergency Reserve
AOME	Assistant Ordnance Mechanical Engineer
AOW	Advanced Ordnance Workshop
AP	Armour Piercing
AQMG	Assistant Quartermaster-General
ARH	Ammunition Railhead
ASD	Ammunition Sub-Depot
ASE	Ammunition Section En Cas Mobile (Ammunition held on rail)
ATS	Auxiliary Territorial Service (now WRAC)
BAD	Base Ammunition Depot
BAS	British Army Staff (North America)
BEF	British Expeditionary Force (France, 1939)
BIGU	Base Industrial Gas Unit
BMP	Beach Maintenance Pack
BOD	Base Ordnance Depot
BOW	Base Ordnance Workshop
BPC	British Purchasing Commission (U.S.A.)

CAD	Central Ammunition Depot
CAO	Chief Administrative Officer
CCD	Civilian Clothing Depot
CIA	Chief Inspector of Armaments
CMF	Central Mediterranean Force
COD	Central Ordnance Depot
COME	Chief Ordnance Mechanical Engineer
COO	Chief Ordnance Officer
COPO	Central Ordnance Provision Office (Middle East)
COS	Controller of Ordnance Services
CPR	Canadian Pacific Railway
CRD	Central Repair Depot
DADOS	Deputy Assistant Director of Ordnance Services
DAQMG	Deputy Assistant Quartermaster-General
DCIGS	Deputy Chief of the Imperial General Staff
DCOS	Deputy Controller of Ordnance Services
DCS	Director of Clothing and Stores
DDOS	Deputy Director of Ordnance Services
DEOS	Director of Equipment and Ordnance Stores
DGAE	Director-General of Army Equipment
DME	Director of Mechanical Engineering
DMS	Department of Munitions and Supply (Canada)
DMT	Director of Military Training
DOS	Director of Ordnance Services
DOS(E)	Director of Ordnance Services (Engineering)
DOS(W)	Director of Ordnance Services (Weapons)
DQMG(AE)	Deputy Quartermaster-General (Army Equipment)
DSD(W)	Director of Staff Duties (Weapons)
DST	Director of Supplies and Transport
DWS	Director of Warlike Stores
DUKWS	American amphibious lorries
EAAOC	East African Army Ordnance Corps
EAASC	East African Army Service Corps
EAEME	East African Electrical and Mechanical Engineers
EAM	Equipment Ammunition Magazine
FMA	Forward Maintenance Area
FMAS	Forward Maintenance Ammunition Section
FMC	Field Maintenance Centre
FOD	Forward Ordnance Depot
FSD	Field Supply Depot
FTS	Forward Trailer Section
GHQ	General Headquarters
G(SD)	General Staff (Staff Duties branch)
HKVDC	Hong Kong Volunteer Defence Force
IAD	Intermediate Ammunition Depot
IAOC	Indian Army Ordnance Corps

IAOS	Inspector of Army Ordnance Services
IAOWS	Inspector of Army Ordnance Workshop Services
ICC	Indent Clearing Centre
IOO	Inspecting Ordnance Officer (Ammunition)
IOM	Inspector of Ordnance Machinery
LAD	Light Aid Detachment
LCT	Landing Craft (Tank)
LDV	Local Defence Volunteers (later Home Guard)
L of C	Lines of Communication
LR	Landing Reserve
LST	Landing Ship (Tank)
LRS	Light Repair Section
MARU	Mobile Ammunition Repair Unit
MBSTD	Main Base Stores Transit Depot
MEF	Middle East Forces
MGA	Major-General in charge of Administration
MGO	Master-General of Ordnance
MIGU	Mobile Industrial Gas Unit
MLBU	Mobile Laundry and Bath Unit
MNBDO	Mobile Naval Base Defence Organization
MPI	Master Parts Index
MT	Mechanical Transport
NAAFI	Navy, Army and Air Force Institutes
NCR	National Cash Register (Machine accounting system)
OBD	Ordnance Beach Detachment
OC	Officer Commanding
OCTU	Officer Cadet Training Unit
OFP	Ordnance Field Park
OME	Ordnance Mechanical Engineer
OO	Ordnance Officer
OTU	Officer Training Unit
PAD	Port Ammunition Detachment and Passive Air Defence
PIAT	Projector Infantry Anti-Tank
POD	Port Ordnance Detachment
POME	Principal Ordnance Mechanical Engineer
POO	Principal Ordnance Officer
QMG	Quartermaster-General
RACD	Royal Army Clothing Department
RAOS	Regulations for Army Ordnance Services
RCASC	Royal Canadian Army Service Corps
RCOC	Royal Canadian Ordnance Corps
RIASC	Royal Indian Army Service Corps
RD/GD	Regimental Duties and General Duties Branch
REME	Royal Electrical and Mechanical Engineers
RMA	Rear Maintenance Area
RPC	Royal Pioneer Corps

RSD	Returned Stores Depot
RTC	Royal Tank Corps (later Royal Tank Regiment)
SOCR	Signal Officer in Chief's Reserve
SOME	Senior Ordnance Mechanical Engineer
TA	Territorial Army
VRD	Vehicle Reserve Depot
VRS	Vehicle Reception Store or Section
WAAOC	West African Army Ordnance Corps
WD	War Department
WEO	Workshop Executive Officer

CHAPTER ONE

FROM WAR TO PEACE, 1920–1927

The Army of 1920

By 1920 the Army of the Great War had been drastically reduced and the shape of the peace-time Regular Army was beginning to emerge. The experiences of the last war were not particularly helpful as a guide to the future. In the main theatre of operations, France and Flanders, the war had been won by infantry masses supported by powerful artillery concentrations. But this type of battle, with its appalling loss of life for such meagre results, was not expected to be repeated.

However, in the subsidiary theatre of Palestine, Allenby's cavalry had achieved spectacular successes. Brilliant generalship and magnificent fighting troops had combined to deliver a knock-out blow to an opponent already "softened up" by a war of attrition for which he was ill-prepared.

Thus a feeling persisted in some quarters that cavalry had not yet had its day, and although a considerable degree of mechanization had been introduced during the war, the tank was sadly neglected. The lesson of Cambrai—that the use of tanks in mass can be decisive if success is exploited—had not been absorbed, and the tank was relegated to the position of a supporting weapon.

As war on a large scale was "unthinkable", meaning that it was forbidden to think about it, little was done to modernize the equipment of the Army. Some new weapons were devised but they rarely passed beyond the design stage. Money was not available for the complex and expensive paraphernalia of a modern war, and it was considered that future military activity would be limited to the protection of an Empire which was larger than ever, owing to the additional responsibilities for certain territories under League of Nations mandate. This concept envisaged small wars, euphemistically described as Imperial Policing, and Duties in Aid (or more often in default) of civil power.

Nevertheless many post-war problems remained. Occupation forces had to be found for Germany. Fighting continued in Russia and there was trouble in Egypt, Iraq, Turkey and the Black Sea area.

Consequently the Army was still 484,000 strong and widely dispersed. The RAOC had to supply the equipment to sustain all these activities, and

1

do so in the atmosphere of economy and retrenchment which inevitably followed a world war. There was also the very heavy task of disposing of large surpluses and sorting and re-deploying the stocks of stores and ammunition still required. The strength of the Corps at this time was 1,365 officers and 9,434 other ranks.

THE HIGHER DIRECTION OF THE CORPS

In 1920 Ordnance Services came (as they do now) under the Quartermaster-General to the Forces. At this time the QMG was Lieutenant-General Sir Travers E. Clarke, KCMG, CB, a great friend and admirer of the Corps, having been QMG in the British Expeditionary Force for the greater part of the war and seen Ordnance Services fully tested in the field. He is remembered in the Corps to this day by the annual Travers Clarke Athletic meeting between units of the Corps for a trophy he presented.

Ordnance Services at the War Office were headed by the Director of Equipment and Ordnance Stores, whose responsibilities were defined as— "The supply of clothing, arms, ammunition, stores and equipment and also for mobilization in connection with these services. Also the duties and administration of the RAOC." The holder of this appointment was Major-General Sir Harold Parsons, KCMG, CB, an officer particularly qualified to be at the head of the Corps. He had over 30 years' service in the Army Ordnance Department, had been on active service in the South African War and had been Director of Ordnance Services in France for over 3 years of the war. He had also been "Officer Commanding" Army Ordnance Corps and in charge of Records for 5 years before the war. The small Directorate comprised some 11 officers and was divided into 3 branches each under an ADEOS. QMG 7 dealt with clothing, QMG 8 with personnel matters and QMG 9 with stores.

Also at the War Office was the Inspector Army Ordnance Services. He was responsible, not to the DEOS, but directly to the QMG—a sort of official spy on his own Corps. This rather odd arrangement, which did not apply only to the RAOC, apparently caused no embarrassment in practice.

At Woolwich, the Principal Ordnance Officer (Major-General Sir J. G. Butcher, KCMG), assisted by a DDOS, controlled the Ordnance store-keeping activities at the Arsenal and Dockyard Depots and also had certain responsibilities for the Ordnance "main" depots, as Didcot, Chilwell, Georgetown and Aintree were then called.

The important duties of Inspection of Stores were divided between the MGO and the QMG's branches. The RAOC, as part of the QMG's Department, staffed only the Inspectorate of Stores (at Woolwich) and Clothing (at Pimlico). In January 1920 there were separate RAOC Inspectorates for Equipment and Stores, and for Clothing; but by September 1920 these had been combined under a Chief Inspector of Stores and Clothing at Woolwich, which continued up to 1926, when the separate inspectorates were reintroduced. Also at Woolwich was the Assistant Director of Ordnance Services (Provision), and in Red Barracks the Depot and School of Instruction commanded by Colonel H. S. Bush.

The making of clothing was the only manufacturing process entirely in Ordnance hands, and this together with its inspection and storage was located at Pimlico, London, in the Royal Army Clothing Department. The senior Ordnance Officer there was known at first as Chief Ordnance Officer, but in 1920 this title was changed to Deputy Director of Clothing.

With one or two minor changes this top structure of the Corps remained until 1923, but it derived from war-time expansion and the aftermath tasks of dealing with large post war surpluses of stores and ammunition held in temporary depots.

In early 1923 the higher direction was reorganized to accord with the peace-time situation. To begin with the title Principal Ordnance Officer was removed from the senior Ordnance appointment at Woolwich and became the secondary title of the DEOS. At the same time the DDOS Woolwich was re-designated Directing Ordnance Officer. He now became responsible to the DEOS for all Central Ordnance Depots (as "main" depots were now called), Ammunition Depots, the Small Arms Depot, the Royal Army Clothing Depot and Factory and for Provision Duties. The office of ADOS Ammunition was abolished. The Chief Inspector of Stores and Clothing was now directly responsible to the DEOS.

Central Ordnance Depots in 1923 were—Bramley (Ammunition), Chilwell (Surpluses, general stores and some clothing), Purfleet (Ammunition), Didcot (General stores and some clothing), Hereford (Ammunition), Pimlico (Clothing factory and depot), Royal Arsenal, Woolwich (Gun stores and ammunition), Weedon (Small arms).

The Structure of the Corps

OFFICERS

The 1,365 officers serving in January 1920 were grouped into the following categories:

1. Directing Staff Officers. Officers in this category filled the higher appointments in the Corps, represented the Ordnance Services on formation and static headquarters, and were in charge of stores and ammunition depots. Notwithstanding the presence of other Ordnance Officers of various ranks in any depot or branch, an officer of the Directing Staff was always in command.

These officers had transferred after several years' service in other regiments or corps. It was considered that this gave them the necessary maturity and "user experience". Designation was by class as well as rank, an Ordnance Officer 1st Class being a Colonel or above and an Ordnance Officer 4th Class being a Captain (or Subaltern until Captain became the junior rank in this category). A Subaltern on transfer to the RAOC drew the pay of a Captain plus 5s. per day Corps pay.

This incentive, which was considerable in those days, had to be earned, after a period of attachment to a unit in the Corps, by passing the Ordnance Course, most of which was held at the Artillery College, Woolwich, which has now become the Royal Military College of Science, Shrivenham.

An officer who passed this course had the letter "o" after his name in the Army List. This also qualified him as an Inspecting Ordnance Officer, which meant that his duties could include the inspection, proof and repair of ammunition in RAOC hands and the inspection of unit ammunition.

2. Workshops Branch. Officers in this branch were designated Inspectors of Ordnance Machinery (IOM). An IOM 1st Class was a Lieutenant-Colonel. The title was changed in 1924 to Ordnance Mechanical Engineer (OME). Although in 1920 a number of these officers had transferred from other arms, recruiting thereafter was mainly by direct entry. Basic technical qualifications were necessary, followed by a course and a period of military training. These officers were in charge of Ordnance workshops and advised the Directing Staff on workshops matters.

3. Officers commissioned from warrant rank. Then, as now, they formed a significant proportion of the RAOC officer strength. They were known in 1920 as Commissaries of Ordnance and are now known as Ordnance Executive Officers. Their military background and long practical experience of Ordnance work were invaluable, particularly in war. This category included a number of workshop officers known as Assistant Inspectors of Armourers, commissioned from other ranks of the Armourer Section and subordinate to the Inspectors of Ordnance Machinery.

4. Temporary Officers. There were some of these in all categories except AIA. They represented the difference between the Regular officer establishment and the numbers required to cope with the post-war RAOC task. A few became Regular officers, and in due course the remainder retired into civilian life.

Although, 40 years later, this officer structure may appear strange, it was adequate to the circumstances of the time. A more significant question is whether the individuals had the knowledge and ability to carry the Corps through a difficult period of transition. The answer is provided, in part at least, by a summary of the awards shown against the names of RAOC officers in the 1920 Army List. This shows: Knights, 7; CB, 20; CSI, 1; CMG, 34; CIE, 1; CBE, 15; OBE, 27; DSO, 51; DSC, 1; MC, 4.

OTHER RANKS

The other ranks of the Corps were divided into three branches of tradesmen, the Store, Armament Artificer, and the Armourer Branches.

The Store Branch consisted of clerks, storemen and artisans, the latter embracing some 20 trades ranging from blacksmith to welder. From the clerks and storemen ranks a number were trained as laboratory foremen (the forerunner of ammunition examiners) for ammunition duties; however, this was not regarded as a separate trade but rather as a subsidiary qualification and the individuals were not remustered. The Store Branch entrants were obtained normally through Recruiting Offices as privates on a 3 to 6 year engagement after sitting educational tests and submitting several references as to character. There was also in 1920 a small number of boy trainee clerks and storemen.

Armourers were enlisted as boys, and after training and passing examinations at Enfield were promoted to NCO ranks and sent to regiments or to Ordnance workshops. Armament Artificers were obtained by transfer of suitable NCOs from other Arms or enlisting qualified civilians. Their training included a course divided between the School of Instruction and the Artillery College, at the end of which they were promoted to Staff-Sergeant. For the directly enlisted civilian an intensive course of regimental training at the Depot was included.

Ranks and appointments conformed to those of the rest of the Army with some exceptions. The most notable of these were the appointments of Conductor and Sub-Conductor held by Warrant Officers Class I of the Store Branch. This ancient title of Conductor goes back to the days of the Board of Ordnance and is exclusive to the RAOC—it took precedence with Master Gunners 1st Class and Staff-Sergeant-Majors 1st Class over all Warrant Officers in the Army.

Up to May 1920 the Corps had a rank of Second Corporal, but this was then abolished and all the holders absorbed as Corporals, Corporals on that date all being appointed Lance-Sergeants. Warrant Officers of the Armourer Branch were known as Armourer Sergeant-Majors and those of the Armament Artificer Branch as Armament Sergeant-Majors.

Lower ranks of these two branches also had the prefixes "Armourer" or "Armament Artificer" before their rank. The Store Branch ranks had no prefixes until it was decided that Artisan Warrant Officers should be known as Artisan Sergeant-Major instead of Conductor, this latter title being historically more appropriate to store work.

There was no Regimental Duties Branch and only one non-tradesman was borne on the roster of the Corps, the Regimental Sergeant-Major at the Depot. Drill and weapon training instructors for the Depot and Company Sergeant-Majors for outstations were found by the simple method of selecting tradesmen NCOs with smart bearing and aptitude for the duties. There was no lack of suitable men for such posts. Orderly Room Sergeants and Company Quartermaster-Sergeants were similarly selected from tradesmen. This system of selection for regimental duties had several advantages, notably that efficiency at regimental duties was expected of all tradesmen, and the Corps was not split into two mutually exclusive groups—tradesmen and non-tradesmen.

All ranks of the Corps were distributed throughout the Army much as they are today. At each of the seven Home Command Headquarters (which in 1920 included the Aldershot and Irish Commands) there was an ADOS with a very small staff and each Depot had a Section or Detachment. The basis of this organization was the pre-war one of allotting a Company to each Command, sub-divided into Station Sections. The effect of the war was to make the Sections autonomous and they in turn had a number of detachments. The Company organization disappeared. Sections varied greatly in size from those in Guernsey (No. 16 Section) and Jersey (No. 17 Section), each with only a few officers and men, to several hundreds at No. 1 Section, Aldershot, and No. 2 Section, Tidworth. Whilst Armourers were on the establishments of their Regiments or Battalions, Armament Artificers working in Forts and Coast Defences were on the strength of Sections at home.

In theatres overseas and expeditionary forces there was an ADOS with a staff at each Headquarters to advise on Ordnance Services. Depots were manned initially by Ordnance companies, one or more being combined according to the size of the task. The workshops were found by combining the standard light or medium mobile workshops of the type used in the war. As the overseas theatres crystallized into permanent stations, the static "section" organization adopted at home was gradually applied so that by the mid 1920's all RAOC units were known by this form of designation.

THE TASK OF THE RAOC

The work of the Corps in 1920 was broadly the same as today, but there were several interesting exceptions.

The following duties are not now undertaken:

1. The inspection of stores other than armament and engineer stores.
2. The manufacture of clothing.
3. Workshop Services, now the responsibility of a separate Corps, the Royal Electrical and Mechanical Engineers.

On the other hand the supply and repair of wheeled MT vehicles was the responsibility of the RASC, at that time the main, almost the only, user. The RAOC was responsible for tanks and armoured cars.

In an army which was not yet mechanized the supply of harness and saddlery, horseshoes and nails, wagons and limbers, was a considerable commitment, as important then as the supply of MT vehicles and their spares is today. In 1920 the animal strength (horses and mules) was 108,000.

TRAINING AND RESPONSIBILITIES OF ORDNANCE OFFICERS

The duties of Ordnance Officers were defined in *Regulations for Army Ordnance Services* (RAOS), in those days a relatively slim volume of 130 pages.

The old pre-war "O" Course, suspended during the war, was replaced in 1921 by the new Ordnance Officer's Course, the scope of which should give the modern Ordnance Officer some cause for reflection. The subjects taught included mathematics, physics, electricity, chemistry, metallurgy, weapons and optical work as well as instruction in organization, store accounting and practical instruction in inspection and testing of ammunition, explosives, general stores and clothing. In addition, there were visits to factories and business firms to see their methods. The course lasted a year with periods at the Artillery College, Bramley, and the School of Instruction. It was something of an endurance test.

At this time the length of training and other aspects of Corps work came under the basilisk eye of the Geddes Committee.[1] In point of fact the Committee found very little to complain of as far as Ordnance Services were concerned. It was noted that the increase over the 1914 strength of the Corps was "largely accounted for by the vastly increased equipment of the Army and of its reserves of material". It also noted that the cost of civilians was five times more than pre-war and that much of their work could be done by military labour from existing units. It also recommended that the reserves of mobilization equipment and armaments were costly to store, guard and maintain and that such holdings resulted in heavy indirect costs. At this time the Mobilization Reserves held in store were for a force of 6 Regular Infantry and 1 Regular Cavalry Divisions and 14 Territorial Divisions, but they were by no means complete.

In addition to the Ordnance Course there were many other measures to train Ordnance Officers. Within Corps resources there were courses at the Small Arms Factory at Enfield Lock, on cinematography stores at the Field Stores, on new artillery equipments at Hilsea and on ammunition at Bramley. Outside the Corps, vacancies were obtained on courses at the Artillery College on such subjects as Inspection and Repair of Wireless Telegraphy and Sound Ranging Apparatus, Anti-Gas Respirators at Porton and Tank Stores at the Tank Training Centre, Wool.

High on the list of outside courses for RAOC officers was the 6 months' Administrative Training Course at the London School of Economics. The subjects studied were accounting methods, transportation, economic geography, British Government systems, industrial and social institutions, international affairs, economic problems of war and Army finance and administration. A number of Ordnance Officers were fortunate in attending this course, which brought them into contact with economists and political figures of the time. Officers who attended this course obtained the symbol (e) after their name in the Army List.

[1] The Geddes Committee on National Expenditure was set up by the Government to "recommend forthwith all possible reductions in National Expenditure on Supply Services". It carried out a rapid review of 8 Government Departments, and in the case of the Army, basing its findings on the official policy of "no great war for 10 years", recommended a reduction of 50,000 officers and men (subsequently reduced to 30,000 by the Government) as well as the points pertaining to Ordnance Services quoted above. It was undoubtedly one of the most unpopular post-war measures ever introduced and much bitterness was felt towards the operators of the "Geddes Axe" wherever it fell.

The Corps also participated in the teaching at the London School of Economics. In 1925 and 1926 Lieutenant-Colonel B. A. Hill gave three important lectures: (1) The organization and functions of the RAOC with details of provision work; (2) The duties of COs of units with regard to Ordnance stores; and (3) The duties of the RAOC on mobilization and in the field. Model lectures of their kind, there is no doubt that they were invaluable in explaining Ordnance work and problems to an important group of civilians representing trade, industry and the professions.

This forerunner of what is now known as "management training" was taken further by the arrangement for visits by officers to the Home Office Permanent Industrial Museum in London, where the latest "methods", arrangements and appliances for promoting safety, health and welfare of industrial workers could be studied.

CIVILIAN STAFF

The welfare of civilian employees was emphasized in the *Regulations for Army Ordnance Services* in the 1920s. It was laid down that in recruiting civilian subordinates "preference was to be given to men who had served with credit in the forces", and this was not difficult in a period of large-scale demobilization.

Under this system civilians remained for the whole of their time in the Ordnance Department, often in one depot. The Corps had the services of workers who had been employed "man and boy" on Ordnance duties for many years, and the soldier approaching the end of his military career could look to the civilian complement of the Ordnance Services as a means of continued employment under the Crown in an environment which he knew and understood. It did much to unite the energies and loyalties of officers, soldiers and civilians who thought of themselves as one unit.

This is in marked contrast to the present system in which, for certain activities at certain levels, movement from one department to another is normal and frequent. This may be in the national interest but from the point of view of RAOC efficiency the disadvantages are many.

The civilian employee who never left the Ordnance Service may have been set in his ways and reluctant to accept new methods, but he did know his job and depots could be run efficiently with remarkably small numbers of such men. To an increasing extent vacancies, including those for supervisory posts, now tend to be filled by civilians who have no previous experience of Ordnance work, and are therefore learners. The man who is exceptionally gifted will learn quickly, but he is on that account the more likely to be moved quite soon to other work "in his own interest". If the Ordnance Officer sighs for the good old days it is not in a spirit of reactionary nostalgia, but because he regrets the loss of that continuity, knowledge and team spirit which the old system engendered.

An example of the interest taken by Ordnance Officers in their civilian employees is provided by the Staff Suggestion Scheme which originated in a proposal by the DEOS in 1924 to reward employees who made useful suggestions, as distinct from awards for inventions. The recommendation was approved and a small sum was provided in Vote 8. Powers of award were vested in the DEOS. In 1926 the War Office decided to extend the scheme to all WD establishments.

The keystone of this civilian structure in Ordnance Services was the Storeholder. To him much of the detailed instruction in RAOS was addressed.

STORE DEPOT ORGANIZATION AND METHODS

Indents for ordnance stores were passed to the DADOS for approval. He was usually located in the depot and acted in a dual capacity, as RAOC representative in the area and senior officer in the depot.

Management of the depot was the responsibility of the Ordnance Officer, but indents went straight from the DADOS to the Group. The Group was largely self-contained, a sort of depot within a depot. RAOS stated: "At all Ordnance Depots a Storeholder will be in charge of one or more Vocabulary Sections and these will be stored in the same or contiguous buildings. The Storeholder is responsible that all stores held by him are correct according to the quantity in the books, are kept in good order and precautions taken to preserve and maintain them from deterioration."

The "books" referred to were loose leaf Tally Sheets, kept in the Group office. There was a sheet for each item showing transactions and stock. Behind it was a record of Dues In and Dues Out. An Issues Progress Record was kept on a copy of the indent. Pads of vouchers were kept and a set was made out in the Group for each issue. When stock fell to a certain level a Provision Review Form was made out in the Group showing assets, liabilities, total normal issues, etc., and passed to the Provision Office, who returned it with information of provision action taken and the new provision stock level (Provision Action Figure). However, the Tally was not the official audited record of stocks. This was the Ledger, kept in the central office under the immediate supervision of the Ordnance Officer.

The Ledger Office was a sort of Holy of Holies—forbidden ground for the storehouse staff. All entries were made by hand and checked by another clerk. When a new ledger sheet was opened it had to be initialled by the head clerk to give it legitimacy.

This stately minuet of a procedure might well be described as the auditor's delight. The main purpose was to take extreme precautions to ensure that honest men did not cheat. The staff who manned the Ordnance depots of those days were selected for reliability and integrity rather than exceptional brain power, and it seems odd that so much trouble should have been taken to prevent them from doing something for which, on the whole, they had neither the inclination nor the aptitude.

The procedure was so cumbersome that the increase in receipt or issue activity which followed an emergency created a formidable list of outstanding ledger entries, the tallies and ledgers differed enormously and the account was worthless as a record of actual stocks in the depot.

Later on, when the mechanization of the Army imposed a system appropriate to the issue and receipt of fast moving MT spares, it was found that the elaborate devices for preventing collusion between the accounts and storehouse staff had always been completely unnecessary.

PROVISION

The principles of provision do not alter and the method of collecting the essential information, and consolidating it centrally so that the requirements of the Army may be calculated was in essence the same in the 1920s as it is now under the Global Provision procedure.

In those days a complicated form of many columns was compiled by all depots and submitted to ADOS(P) at Woolwich. This form was known as the Annual Demand and it gave the requirements for a specified period —normally 2 years from the date of the demand.

The work was compressed into a few weeks as all demands had to be with ADOS(P) at roughly the same date. The period was therefore one of peak activity in every depot, although the range of items affected was only about 20,000 then compared with well over 500,000 now.[1] With experienced staff, few technical items, a reliable source of supply and a reasonably steady policy it was possible to study all aspects of usage and provision thoroughly and decisions were usually sound.

In its detailed application the system would break down in the conditions which prevail today, so that it has been found necessary to spread the load over the year by phased provision reviews, to plan expenditure well ahead by means of Long Term Equipment Programmes and by other devices iron out the jerky and spasmodic effect of rigid application of the Annual Parliamentary Estimate system.

In one respect things have changed very much for the worse since the 1920s. At that time there was no such thing as a bad contractor. He would be black listed at once. Stores were up to specification and delivery dates were met. Although unit entitlements of stores were strictly controlled and by no means generous, a unit could rely on receiving equipment to which it was entitled. This is indeed a contrast with the present day when an army of officials is needed to persuade some contractors to meet their contractual obligations. They usually fail because penalty clauses are considered to be unworkable or unethical. In such circumstances, the most painstaking work on provision may be ineffective.

---

[1] This is, however, not a true comparison of Ordnance activity. The Annual Demand was not comprehensive. It excluded many items for which the usage in peace was so low that provision could be done centrally without gathering annual information from outstations.

COMMAND AND CAMP DEPOTS

Command Depots issued direct to units. There were no Field Parks or Stores Sections in those days and military as well as civilian staff were on the establishments of Command Depots.

This provided a good opportunity for training RAOC soldiers in their primary duty of supplying equipment. Some Ordnance Officers took considerable trouble to train their soldiers and give them responsibility; and the benefits were felt in 1939 as these men were commissioned or promoted to warrant rank, forming an invaluable nucleus for the rapid expansion which came with the war.

Another most practical form of training and one which was very popular was the Camp Depot. A number of these were formed at practice camps such as Okehampton, Watchet and Barry. They remained open for 6 or 7 months and were staffed by men selected from the Central or Command Depots issuing the stores. The role of these depots was to receive, issue and exchange camp equipment, weapons and stores for the series of units which came to the camp for training.

Conditions at the camps varied. Some were in well-found huts and others under canvas. The work was always interesting and sometimes heavy, particularly at the beginning and end of the camp. Most of the other ranks were given promotion for the period of the camp, and it was normal to appoint a Warrant Officer as acting Ordnance Officer with a special increase in pay.

MOBILIZATION DUTIES

The work of mobilization groups in depots was very systematic even though there was the "no major war for ten years" policy at the time. Some equipments were assembled and these were inspected every 6 months and stock taken at least every 2 years. Vehicles (wagons, limbers and gun carriages) were inspected every 3 years by artificers. Gun carriages, limbers and ammunition wagons were kept packed with their stores. To avoid stress on any one spoke "the wheels of these were to be revolved one spoke in a pre-determined direction every month". Shrapnel and plugged high explosive ammunition was to be stored in all the vehicles in which it was to be carried unless in dangerous proximity to inhabited houses or possible causes of fire. Other mobilization equipments were not assembled but held in bulk in Central Depots "to be sent on mobilization to the Command Depot nearest the place of mobilization". There were similar arrangements for Territorial Army units. Command Depots were to hold enough consumable stores to complete the war entitlement of Regular units in the area. Reserves for maintenance of the Army in the field were held in Central Depots. The Command Defence, "Home" Mobilization Scheme and the like, were covered by Command Depots in their "normal" holdings.

To achieve this degree of readiness with the small staffs on depot establishments for that purpose was possible only because plans for mobilization were reasonably stable, and amendments infrequent. The modern tendency towards complete flexibility means that firm planning is absent, the equipment cannot be made ready for an emergency which is undefined and mobilization becomes another word for improvisation.

COST ACCOUNTING

The Army Lists of this period show two top-level Civil Servants as Joint Secretaries and members of the Army Council. One of these was responsible for financial matters and was designated the Accounting Officer.

For many years, during and after the 1914–18 war, the financial appointment was held by Sir Charles Harris. He was a man of strong character with a brilliant financial brain who made a special study of Army Finance.

He advocated a form of cost accounting in which the system of recording expenditure by "subject" headings such as food, stores and transport was replaced by grouping under "objects", for example the complete cost of an infantry battalion, a hospital or a stores depot. "Complete" cost included that of buildings, fuel, light, etc. Impetus was given to the scheme by the criticism by the Public Accounts Committee of the fact that no exact money value could be attached to the stores in Ordnance depots.

The RAOC view was that commerce and the War Department were not strictly comparable, and that in commerce the primary object was profit and to make sure of it accurate figures of the value of stocks in hand were essential. The kinds of goods handled were to a large extent immaterial provided that they sold well. The successful buyer purchased only these goods and did not attempt to provide for every out-of-the-way demand. He welcomed extravagance on the part of his customers and whilst wishing to please them had no responsibility for their complete equipment. What it did not pay him to sell they could do without or buy elsewhere.

The RAOC had a completely different aim. They did not and could not work to a commercial profit or loss. Their object was the equipment of the Army with each and all of its needs and equally with no more than its needs. Their aim was to ensure that all requisite articles were available and also that capital was not tied up in any article in excess of requirements. This was work which must be done on a quantitative basis. It was for this reason that records of the quantities of stock available and required were of primary importance. Although the Army Council supported this answer to the Public Accounts Committee the Cost Accounting Scheme continued.

The purpose of costing was to keep the Accounts showing the full cost of each unit so that Commanding Officers would be able to exercise control and be held responsible for reasonable economy. The Corps of Military Accountants, formed for this purpose, was distributed among some units and establishments to maintain these accounts showing, as well as the above, depreciation of assets, rental value of WD properties and services rendered by one Department of the Army to another and between the WD and other Government Departments. Command Accountants also had to keep accounts for each unit. Ordnance depots had to price all vouchers for stores issued to units and keep accounts of their own establishments on the lines mentioned above. These latter were prepared by the Corps of Military Accountants staff, signed as accepted by the DADOS or COO and sent to Woolwich. From them the War Office circulated half yearly statements of comparative total cost of all depots and workshops showing in each case the ratio cost of administrative personnel to that of operating personnel.

Being superimposed on the existing system of cash and store accounts the scheme was expensive and involved very great additional work. It was reviewed by a number of important War Office committees (who disagreed with one another) and several modifications were made.

The controversy which ensued effectively obscured the most important factor which was that an Army must always be ready for war and that, to put it mildly, all this costing activity left little capacity for achieving the state of readiness expected.

Matters came to a head with the Chanak affair. Troops from Aldershot Command had to be mobilized at short notice, and it was soon evident to the ADOS that either mobilization or costing must be suspended. The obvious decision was made and the troops sailed fully equipped on time.

Very soon the ADOS was "on the mat" in front of Sir Charles Harris and a number of distinguished people. His explanation that mobilization was more important than cost accounting carried very little conviction in that company, particularly as Sir Charles Harris was very deaf, and the hearing aids of those days were remarkably selective in the information which they passed on. Luckily the MGA Aldershot Command strongly supported the action of the ADOS and the matter was allowed to drop.

Like most peace-time schemes which have the effect of spending a pound to save sixpence this one dragged on and was only finally discarded in 1926. By then its chief supporter was no longer there to keep the faint pulse stirring, and the death of the project was regretted by few. Nevertheless, to this day a phoenix occasionally rises from the ashes.

ORDNANCE WORKSHOPS

Ordnance workshops were in the charge of the Inspectors of Ordnance Machinery but under the control of the Chief Ordnance Officer. The most important development was in the repair of tanks and armoured cars. This was shared with the Tank Corps, who had their own workshop organization at the time for repairs up to a certain capacity. The Tank Corps Central Workshop at Bovington had an Inspector of Ordnance Machinery as workshop manager, and to facilitate the spread of tank technology RAOC armament artificers and some other tradesmen attended courses at the Tank Corps Training Centre. Tank Corps crews accompanied their vehicles into Ordnance workshops to assist in the repairs.

Apart from this and a growing amount of repairs to instruments the activity was as in 1914, namely: repairs to carriages and wagons and limbers, re-wheeling, spoking, sweating on of iron tyres, harness and saddlery repairs and in certain workshops repairs to guns. With the end of the war the heavy artillery was taken into store and most of this work dealt with the 18 pounder guns and 4·5-inch howitzers of the Field Artillery. Workshops at ports of call of WD vessels were authorized to carry out incidental repairs to them when this was preferable to contract repair.

The IOM's duties included annual inspection of all artillery equipment in the possession of units, visits to forts, attendance at trials of guns and mountings and firing of test rounds and attendance at Artillery practice camps.

Armament Artificers RAOC could be posted for permanent duty to definite forts or Fire Commands but carried out their work under supervision of an IOM. They too were to be available at Artillery practice camps to repair or make adjustments to equipment.

The need for the most efficient workshop service possible was constantly before both Directing Staff and Workshop Officers. The respective merits of local and centralized workshops and other organizational matters were the subject of prolonged and intensive study. It was found that work for which the RAOC had become responsible exceeded that of the other two services (RE and RASC) and that special measures were necessary. The situation was due to an increase in tanks and mechanized artillery, extra guns with the TA and extra machine guns. New central workshops at Aldershot, Tidworth and Catterick were proposed.

A further recommendation was that first line repair in units should be done on a "hand tools only" basis, the second line repair of unit equipment or vehicles to be in Ordnance workshops. These should be divided into light local shops analogous to mobile workshops in war, and central shops on the scale of one per Command to carry out periodic overhauls on a programme and to undertake modifications. The retention of 8 existing workshops was recommended with the reconstruction of 2 and the building of a further 2.[1]

A further important aspect of Ordnance work was carried out within units. To every Regiment of Cavalry and Battalion of Infantry was attached an Armourer and to Artillery units there were one or more

---

[1] Existing workshops were at Plymouth (Devonport), Bovington, Hilsea, Lydd, Dover, Chatham, Aldershot and Catterick (the last only just completed).

Armament Artificers. These men were very expert at their trades and carried out all the inspection, servicing and repair of small arms, machine guns, and bicycles and, in the case of Artificers, gun and'range-finding equipment. Their services were greatly valued by the units to which they were attached.

AMMUNITION DUTIES

In each area in the United Kingdom or station overseas an Ordnance Officer was appointed, among his many other duties, as Inspecting Ordnance Officer. The work involved inspection, proof, sentencing and minor repair of ammunition both in RAOC and unit hands.

In the United Kingdom, CAD Bramley was the only central depot holding ammunition, although small stocks, mainly for training issues to Commands, were held at places such as Tipnor (near Hilsea) and Selby in Yorkshire.

Normally units held their own first line ammunition. Coast artillery was a big item, both first and second line ammunition being held in the various forts. Coast Defence storage was normally good, although safety distances were practically unknown, but the other ammunition held by units was stored in a rough and ready way. Field Artillery ammunition was often stored in a compartment next to the gun park or even in the gun park itself. In other units a small store forming part of the guard room building was used, and here the ammunition was held irrespective of group. In overseas stations units normally held their own ammunition, small replenishment stocks being stored by the RAOC.

The ultimate authority on technical ammunition matters was the Chief Inspector of Armaments (CIA). This department produced RAOS, Volume 2, which was the "bible" for all inspection and proof. Inspection, proof and heat test created a mass of paper work, complicated Army forms having to be filled in for each process. After all details had been completed, including recommendations and sentencing, one copy of each form was sent to CIA, Woolwich, through Command Headquarters, for confirmation or otherwise. Confirmation was usually received by letter after considerable further correspondence on trivialities. CIA as a branch was remote and olympian, and it was seldom that officers or other ranks in the RAOC saw any member of the CIA staff.

Ammunition Examiners. In 1920 a proportion of other ranks, who had previously volunteered, were selected for training as Laboratory Foremen. Candidates had to have at least 2 years to serve and be willing at the end of that time to extend for further service, this condition being imposed owing to the cost of training.

The course was held at Woolwich and lasted 6 months. It included chemistry, chemical and heat tests of explosives and propellants, lectures and practical instruction on ammunition and proof, the practical work being done in the filling factories and proof yards on Plumstead marshes. The course was run by the Artillery College.

Those who passed the course with a mark of 70% or more were graded Laboratory Foreman (Group C) and, with the generosity typical of those days, rewarded for their efforts by the grant of the rank of Lance-Corporal (unpaid). This qualification made no change in their basic trade of clerk or storeman, which continued to be the basis for trade tests and promotion examinations for laboratory foremen.

In 1923 the significance of the work of Laboratory Foreman was recognized by the change of classification to a Group A trade, the name being changed to Ammunition Examiner. Existing Laboratory Foremen were re-mustered to the new trade. Qualified other ranks received an increase of a shilling a day up to and including the rank of Lance-Sergeant, Sergeants and above were no better off than clerks and storemen.

Half yearly promotion examinations covered all aspects of RAOC procedure and only two out of the six questions were based on the work of an Ammunition Examiner. The highest rank in which an Ammunition Examiner was employed was SQMS. Thus, before being placed on 3 months' probation for promotion to Sub-Conductor, Ammunition Examiners had to re-muster in the grade of Clerk Class 1.

On the face of it the advantages of becoming an Ammunition Examiner were nicely balanced by the disadvantages. The reasons why there was no shortage of volunteers were the slight increase in pay for the lower ranks, the interest and responsibility of the work and the fact that Ammunition Examiners were given preference for extension of service. This was a big factor between 1925 and 1931, when retrenchment was causing a strict quota to be imposed on the numbers allowed to extend their service while unemployment was high and jobs for ex-soldiers difficult to obtain.

Bramley. In 1920 Bramley was developed as a central holding of ammunition reserves and stocks for training. The depot had been built towards the end of the war but it was far from complete. Accommodation for military staff was lacking and labour was brought in by special train from Basingstoke and Reading. Large quantities of ammunition were dumped in the depot and had to be sorted and stored correctly.

The work of creating an organization to run this depot fell to Lieutenant-Colonel W. H. McN. Verschoyle-Campbell. He found a number of ex-officers who had served in ammunition depots overseas during the war. He managed to have them appointed as storeholders and their work at Bramley between the wars and in the 1939–45 war was invaluable.

He then turned his attention to the training of Laboratory Foremen, starting a school which became "B" Branch of the School of Instruction. In 1923 the branch gave preliminary tests to potential Ammunition Examiners to weed out those who lacked the aptitude to pass the course at Woolwich. In 1925 Ammunition Examiners who passed the course at Woolwich received further practical training of 4 to 6 weeks at "B" Branch before posting to their new stations.

OVERSEAS STATIONS

Overseas there were no big depots, each Command having one general depot and workshops with an adjacent magazine or fort for storing ammunition and sometimes a separate location for clothing. These places varied very much in local detail and were valuable practical training grounds for young NCOs of the Corps who assumed duties several grades higher than at home. A typical example of such a depot is that described by a young NCO called Hewett who in 1920 was posted to Freetown, Sierra Leone. "I was a storeholder in charge of a group. The depot consisted of three main single storey sheds, a workshop and a two storey office block all surrounding a small compound on Tower Hill. The Magazines were situated on the opposite side of the Hill. The force maintained consisted of one Battalion West Africa Regiment and detachments, two Coast Defence Batteries, RGA, and the Sierra Leone Artillery.

"The RAOC Detachment consisted of 1 Officer, 1 Conductor, 1 Armourer Sergeant Major, 5 other Artificers and Armourers and 10 Store Branch personnel. The detachment lived with personnel of other Corps in joint barrack accommodation on top of Tower Hill. No families were allowed but the tour was for 1 year and counted as double for pension. The range of stores covered clothing, personal weapons and equipment, barrack and hospital stores, oils and paints, ironmongery, metals and artillery stores for maintenance of 9·2 inch, 6 inch and 2·75 inch guns.

"The civilian staff consisted of two classes of natives—educated and tribal. The former were descendants of the slaves freed by Wilberforce. They staffed the offices and such posts as traffic foreman on the dockside. The latter could neither read nor write, but had exceptional memories. The man in my Group covering barrack, hospital, oil and paint stores knew the position of each tally board and after the boards had been collected for the annual balance would replace each one in the correct place.

"There was no transport other than the railway and a native carrier corps, native carriers having a load limit of 50 lb per man. If loads of over 50 lb had to be carried, civilian carriers were hired by the RASC. The usual transport for personnel on tour was by hammock carried by four natives."

The Regimental Life of the Corps

THE CORPS DEPOT, WOOLWICH, 1920–1921

No serving man today knows Red Barracks, Woolwich, but to the smaller AOC of the twentieth century and to the thousands of the Great War it meant as much as Hilsea came to mean between the two world wars. Here were to be found the Records Office, the training centre for recruits, the holding unit for men proceeding to and returning from overseas, the mobilization centre for the Corps.

In 1920 the most urgent requirement was that of technical training for both officers and men. The lessons of the war, both at home and abroad, had to be gathered and studied and the result of experience put into effect by teaching and practice and by embodiment in Regulations.

General Parsons therefore asked Brigadier-General C. C. Wrigley to form a Committee to study how best all this could be done. His members were Colonels Forbes and Bush, and Lieutenant-Colonels F. S. Exham, D. Paul and W. N. Stokes. This Committee has now passed into history as the Wrigley Committee, and it made a number of wise and far-reaching recommendations, including the institution of a School of Instruction and the founding of a Corps Headquarters. It was realized that Red Barracks would be too small for all these requirements but in the meantime one of the proposed measures, the founding of a School of Instruction, was put into effect late in 1920, "for the purpose of training officers and other ranks of the RAOC in the special duties of the Corps". A few barrack rooms were misappropriated as classrooms and in these Colonel Bush, Lieutenant-Colonel Wethered and Conductor Jones hammered out a syllabus, taught the rudiments of ordnance duties to recruits, received the First Ordnance Officers' Course and set them to work on the first part of their course at the Artillery College nearby.

COLONEL-IN-CHIEF AND COLONEL COMMANDANT

In January 1921 there occurred an event of great significance to the Corps. His Majesty the King appointed HRH The Duke of York Colonel-in-Chief of the Royal Army Ordnance Corps. From the beginning the new Colonel-in-Chief took a great personal interest in all RAOC activities and achievements.

At the wedding of HRH on April 26th 1923, Generals Sir John Steevens, Sir Harold Parsons and Sir Charles Mathew and Colonels H. S. Bush and H. C. Fernyhough were among the guests in the Abbey and a detachment of the Corps formed a Guard of Honour outside.

Another important event was the appointment of a Colonel Commandant. During 1921 the Army Council had been considering the question of Colonels Commandant for the Administrative Corps and in April it was agreed in principle that the RAOC should have one. The appointment was to be "a titular one and unpaid" and the duties were defined as—"To occasionally visit the Corps Headquarters and head-quarters of the RAOC at principal Ordnance Depots. He will also visit London occasionally in connection with Corps business."

Under the existing rules RAOC Major-Generals either on the active or retired list were eligible in order of seniority, and following precedent the first appointment was offered to Major-General Sir John Steevens on the retired list, who accepted it as "a great honour" on August 12th. The proposal was submitted to the Colonel-in-Chief who wrote that he had much pleasure in concurring with the recommendation. A Submission was made to the King who assented on August 23rd.

Commissioned into the Ordnance Store Department in 1874, Sir John Steevens had taken part in a number of colonial wars of the late nineteenth century and was the first Ordnance Officer ever to have gone to Tel-el-Kebir, being there in the Egyptian campaign of 1882. During the South African War he had been Principal Ordnance Officer at Woolwich Arsenal and responsible for the supply of stores from what was the only main depot of that day. During the major part of the Great War, he had been DEOS at the War Office controlling and guiding an Ordnance Service which had expanded beyond all recognition. His return to deal with Corps affairs in this new capacity was noted with gratification by all who knew him.

CORPS MOTTO

In March 1920 the King was graciously pleased to approve a motto for the Corps. It was decided to adopt that of the old Board of Ordnance— SUA TELA TONANTI. This motto is none the less impressive for having no precise meaning at all, being three words extracted from a sentence of Latin poetry. Much learned argument has been devoted to attempts to find a translation which would be acceptable to classical scholars, make sense and be appropriate to the purpose of the Corps. It is doubtful whether a solution could ever be found which satisfied all these requirements, but the generally accepted translation "To the Thunderer his Weapons" is at any rate an ingenious compromise.

DOMINION CORPS

At the end of 1920 His Majesty the King was also pleased to approve alliance with the Ordnance Corps of Australia, Canada, New Zealand and South Africa. All the Dominion Corps welcomed the alliance as warmly as the RAOC did and it was put to practical use, especially in Canada and Australia, where much personal effort was made to assist ex-RAOC emigrants who went to those Dominions in the 'twenties'.

MOVE OF THE CORPS HEADQUARTERS TO HILSEA

The Wrigley Committee had recommended that a new location be found to replace Red Barracks. In September a working party visited Hilsea, Portsmouth, to report on the suitability and adaptability of the RA Barracks there to accommodate RAOC Records, a School of Instruction and the Depot. It was considered that with the use of the Hilsea Hutments sufficient accommodation existed but that certain reappropriation would be essential to bring it up to the standard required.

On October 20th 1921 the RAOC left Red Barracks. Before the train left, General Sir Denis O'Callaghan, Colonel Commandant Royal Artillery, and himself formerly of the AOD, together with the Garrison Commander and Garrison Adjutant, came up to wish them good-bye and good luck.

The Woolwich Sub-Area Commander published a Special Order of the Day.

"The Depot RAOC has been established at Woolwich for more than 40 years and the severance of this connection will be regretted by all ranks of their comrades in the Garrison. In bidding them good-bye the Colonel Commandant desires to express his personal regret at their departure and wishes them the best of luck in their new station."

HILSEA

Although Hilsea was a suitable site for development the immediate facilities were far from satisfactory and much improvisation was necessary until works services could be put in hand. A pleasantly situated country house, Gatcombe House, was taken over as the Headquarters Officers Mess and served the purpose well until the move of Corps Headquarters in 1940.

VISIT OF THE COLONEL-IN-CHIEF

On May 2nd 1922 the Colonel-in-Chief visited the Corps at Hilsea. He was accompanied by Lieutenant-General Sir Travers Clarke, Major-General Sir John Steevens and Lieutenant-Colonel H. L. Wethered, who acted as ADC for the day.

After the normal ceremonial parade the Colonel-in-Chief watched a drill display by a recruit squad under RSM Cook. In a speech HRH commented on the proud tradition of the Corps and its great achievements in the last war.

After lunch at the Officers' Mess and an inspection of the barracks the Colonel-in-Chief inspected the adjacent stores depot (Ordnance Depot, Hilsea Lines) where Lieutenant-Colonel J. Baker showed him various aspects of storage and repair work.

THE SCHOOL OF INSTRUCTION

The School of Instruction soon settled down at Hilsea and continued the work begun at Woolwich, but it was some years before all the desired improvements in accommodation were realized.

The School set the standards for trade training and testing throughout the Corps, and also overhauled the syllabus for other ranks promotion examinations, thus establishing a proper basis for guaranteeing a high standard of senior NCO and Warrant Officer.

A valuable piece of work undertaken by the School was the publication of *Notes on RAOC Duties and Procedure*, which became known as the

Pink Book. It was in fact an explanatory supplement to RAOS and other regulations governing Ordnance duties.

WAR MEMORIALS

An RAOC War Memorial Committee was formed in 1919 and there was a very generous response to an appeal for funds. It was decided to build a permanent memorial at Hilsea. A large stone reredos was erected on the east side of the parade ground,[1] and a brass tablet was placed in Hilsea Garrison Church. They were unveiled on November 11th 1922 by Sir John Steevens at a large Armistice Day parade.

THE ASSOCIATION

The Old Comrades Association was formed in May 1923. The idea of an association had originated at one of the "Boulogne Dinners", an annual event held by those who had served in the ammunition organization in France. Over 200 past and present members of the AOD, AOC and RAOC came to London and "unanimously resolved to form an Association, to be known as the Royal Army Ordnance Corps Old Comrades Association, to promote and maintain comradeship between past and present members of the Royal Army Ordnance Corps, and to render assistance to past members of the Corps who may fall on adverse days".

TERRITORIAL RAOC UNITS

The Corps had no Territorial Army units until 1920 when Divisional Ordnance Companies were formed for each of the TA Divisions. Ex-officers and men who had served with the Corps in the war, including a number of civilians in the depots, were quick to respond. Pride of place must be given to Major E. Williams, who is recorded as the first RAOC TA officer in the Army List, serving with the Northumbrian Ordnance Company on May 31st 1920. He was quickly followed by other officers joining the 1st and 2nd London, Highland, Welsh, Essex and West Riding Companies.

Great energy and enthusiasm, the characteristics of the Territorial, brought most of the Companies quickly up to strength, but as part of the national economy drive the establishments were cut. This meant the discharge of many keen men and was disheartening, but those that were left continued to train hard and were able to give valuable assistance to the Regular Corps at the times of the annual manœuvres.

---

[1] When after the Second World War, Corps Headquarters was moved to Blackdown the Memorial was transferred there. It was extended to include the names of the fallen in the recent war. The South African War Memorial was also moved from Woolwich to Blackdown. It is generally known as "Private Barry" from the name of the RAOC soldier who was the model for the statue.

21

Officers had to undergo attachments and courses for promotion purposes. For Lieutenant to Captain this was a course of 12 working days at the School of Instruction, followed by an examination; and for Captain to Major an attachment of 4 working days to a Command Headquarters followed by an 8 day course at the School, also with an examination.

By 1923 the Companies were sufficiently cohesive and well trained to assist in the issue of stores to their formations. 56 London Division, with a strength of only 27 other ranks, trained for a camp period spread over 4 weeks during which they handled over 200 tons of stores. During the first weekend they drew the stores from Hilsea and set up a Divisional dump at East Boldre in the New Forest. The next week issues and return of surpluses occupied their time, and during the last week they received all their stores back, checked, sorted and loaded them on to rail wagons for return to Hilsea by the Friday night.

In 1924 the 49th (West Riding) Company had the unusual experience of receiving over 400 tons of stores in the docks at Douglas, Isle of Man, for the Divisional Camp at Ramsey. Persistent rain fell, but the timetable was adhered to and all stores transferred in good order, with a strength of only 17 men.

RECRUITING

By 1920, one of the most pressing problems was the recruitment of suitable men for the Corps. The pre-war system of careful selection, testing and training had provided an other rank strength of 2,272 in 1914, but few of these now remained owing to war casualties, promotion to commissioned rank or discharge to pension. The war-time expansion had been met by "Duration of War" engagements, and in January 1920 there was a need for 2,000 men.

To offset the rapid demobilization in 1919 a scheme of recruiting on a short-term bounty basis had been adopted. This was successful in producing numbers but quality and technical capacity were lacking. The conditions of Army Service at that time were not good enough to attract the right type of man in sufficient numbers and in competition with industry and commerce.

In an attempt to get suitable men from young soldier battalions, Captain Skinner and Sub-Conductor Redfearn went from Corps Headquarters as part of an "all arms" recruiting mission to Germany in 1920 but with little success, mainly because the young soldiers were away from home for the first time and disliked this above all else, their sights being set on demobilization. As a further attempt, Colonel Bush suggested to the War Office that a number of RAOC recruiters be sent to the various Recruiting Centres. This was done and 2,000 men were obtained in under 3 months. Only 460 were obtained on normal engagements (6 years' Colour Service and 6 years on Reserve) the remainder being, 1, 2 and 3 year men. Some of the figures for 1 year engagements make interesting reading. In 1 month 105 men joined from Aberdeen and 91 from Exeter.

This suggests that persuasive Ordnance recruiters induced practically whole companies of Infantry in process of disbandment to join the Corps.

The effect of these measures was still largely to sacrifice quality for quantity. Many of the men who joined only did so to avoid unemployment and to provide a temporary job until conditions improved in civilian life. Such men had neither the educational standards nor the disciplinary qualities required in the Corps.

In addition to this the age structure was out of balance. Of a total strength of 9,000 men only 450 were between the ages of 19 and 21. Very large numbers were in the older age groups. To offset this General Parsons warmly supported a Corps Headquarters plan to enlist 500 boys between the ages of 15 and 17 who could be given fairly long training and be almost fully fledged tradesmen by the time they were 18.

Ultimately, all these efforts bore fruit and they illustrate the principle that the worst possible thing to do in any circumstances is to lower standards.

RAOC GAZETTE

Apart from a break of a few months in 1923 on his retirement from the Service, Major Asser steered the *Gazette* through 19 difficult years, during which his pride in the Corps allied to a remarkable business acumen combined not only to make the *Gazette* a reflection of the life of the Corps but to raise it to a position of eminence among its contemporaries.

Under Asser the pages of the *Gazette* were not confined to recording social activities and successes in sport. A series of full page photographs has given us a valuable collection of individuals and groups for the period immediately following the war and no major event in or affecting the Corps went unnoticed. In addition to station letters there was a planned series of articles on Ordnance stations and reviews of new equipment which came into the Service.

Having been through the war himself, Asser was intensely sympathetic to the ex-serviceman, and championed the various organizations which were doing something to alleviate hardship and find work in that bleak period.

RAOC BAND

In January 1921 it was decided that the Corps should have a band. This decision was put into effect in April 1922. The Bandmaster was Mr. R. T. Stevens, who had formerly been bandmaster of the 3rd Battalion, The Rifle Brigade. He suggested the adoption of the "Village Blacksmith" as the Corps march on the grounds that the melody had a marching lilt, that the theme was appropriate and that many regimental marches were based on traditional airs. Accordingly, "The Village Blacksmith" became the RAOC Regimental March. The tune undeniably had a lilt of sorts but it lacks that indispensable feature of martial music—a brisk and lively tempo; a defect aggravated by the fact that it used habitually to be played with religious unction and in the manner of a processional hymn. But no really good alternative has yet been suggested and as time goes on tradition will increase the resistance to change.

The Corps Band continued for many years in a state of being "recognized but not authorized", which meant that it was supported by officers' subscriptions and had no establishment. The bandsmen were borne on the Corps Roster as tradesmen and had to pass normal trade tests. It was not until 1938 that approval for a Staff Band was given.

RAOC Activities

IRELAND, 1920–22

At the beginning of the period covered by this history, there was a rebellion in Ireland which necessitated the employment of a force totalling some 50,000 officers and men. They were in large concentrations like Dublin and the Curragh and also dispersed over the country in many small detachments. Their role was to support the civil power and aid the police, the Royal Irish Constabulary. They were largely young soldiers with little training. The RIC had been greatly weakened and its morale lowered by rebel attacks on small police posts, the murder of constables when off duty and boycotting of families. New reinforcements to the RIC had perforce to be issued by the RAOC with a mixture of khaki service dress jackets and trousers, but they wore black RIC forage caps and it was this mixture of dress that gave them the nickname of "Black and Tans".

The Ordnance Services consisted of an ADOS at Headquarters Irish Command in Dublin, and 440 other Ordnance men in two "regimental units", Nos. 14 and 15 Sections. The supply of stores to the Army was hampered at first by the fact that units were on peace scales of equipment until February 1920, when sanction was obtained for the issue of Ordnance stores for "defence" purposes on presentation of an indent countersigned by a Brigade Commander. This enabled the Corps to issue stores and equipment speedily when required.

A truce was arranged in July 1921 and soon after this civil war broke out between the Provisional Government of the Irish Free State and the Irish Republican Army which then became an illegal body even in Irish eyes. The Provisional Government asked for assistance in fighting the republican forces, and arms, clothing and transport valued at £458,000 altogether were handed over between then and the evacuation in December 1922.

With the creation of the Irish Free State, Ireland was divided into two, that part that remained in the United Kingdom becoming ultimately Northern Ireland District. Located therein was the other Irish Depot at Carrickfergus Castle, which had enjoyed comparative peace during the "troubles" in the South. This became a detachment of No. 10 Section, Burscough, but with its own DADOS and IOM. The Ordnance requirements of the Coast Defences of Spike Island and Berehaven were looked after also by Western Command and supplied by the ubiquitous WD vessel.

BRITISH ARMY OF THE RHINE, 1920–29

Although it was officially regarded as an Army of Occupation and was there to enforce the Allied decisions on a beaten enemy, the British Army of the Rhine had the characteristics of a static command and was in fact treated as one for Ordnance Services.

In the first part of the 1920s the force to be supplied varied considerably. Early in 1920 the British Zone had 38,000 British troops, 71,000 Indians and a Chinese Labour Corps of 25,000. The administrative troops and the labour were engaged on a vast clearing-up programme, and by the end of 1920 nearly half a million tons of stores of all sorts had been shipped home. The strain on the Army to find forces for Ireland and the Black Sea was so great that in 1922 the strength fell temporarily to 2 Squadrons of Cavalry, 3 Batteries of Artillery and some Infantry details; and the French supplied an Infantry Brigade to assist in guard duties. For the RAOC soldier, paid in sterling with the Mark at 1,000 to the £1, with good married quarters, and on cordial terms with the local population, life could be said to be good. Eventually, the British Army of the Rhine strength was fixed at 8 Infantry Battalions, but this bore no relation to the possible requirements of any situation in which it might become involved.

The RAOC Organization in the British Army of the Rhine consisted of an ADOS with the usual staff at Headquarters, and Stores Depots and Workshops at Nippes, Cologne and an Ammunition Depot at Longerich. The RAOC were formed into companies, of which originally there were four, Nos. 8, 13, 14 and 17, but eventually these came down to two.

At the end of 1925 in accordance with the provisions of the Peace Treaty the Allies moved from Cologne southwards, the British to the Wiesbaden Bridgehead. In the opinion of the Official Historian "the position assigned to the British Army of the Rhine was strategically bad . . . wedged in between French Corps on right and left and with a demilitarized zone in front". The move was ordered abruptly in the middle of winter at only a fortnight's notice. Although the distance was only 100 miles the British Army of the Rhine was not a mobile formation of 8,000 but a static garrison with transport cut to the minimum. Nevertheless, it was done, stores were sent by train and barge and the depots at Longerich and Nippes were sold to civilians.

The accommodation in the Wiesbaden area which we took over from the French forces was found to offer no room for Engineer, Supply or Ordnance Services. So whilst an ammunition depot was located at

Schierstein, a temporary stores depot was set up in a furniture factory at Wiesbaden and it was not until the following summer and by working much overtime that regrouping of stores into the main depot took place.

THE BLACK SEA AND CHANAK, 1920–22

The purpose of the Army of the Black Sea was to keep peace in the neutral zone around Constantinople. In 1920 the situation was very confused. In South Russia there were missions to the anti-revolutionary forces at Novorossik and a garrison of 2 battalions and supporting arms at Batoum, and in Thrace and Asia Minor there were considerable forces. The chief problem for the Army was to keep the Turks and Greeks apart as well as keeping an eye on the Bolshevik forces in the North. However, during 1920, the anti-Bolshevik forces were defeated, and by November the Crimea was evacuated. Bolshevik forces entered Baku in May compelling British forces to retire from Enzeli, and in July we withdrew from Batoum. The Ordnance Mission which had gone to Novorossik under Colonel de Wolff and Major Donovan in 1919, and done splendid work under extraordinary difficulties, departed from there in March 1920 and finally from Theodosia in June.

Up to February 1919 the Army had been supplied from Salonika Base Depots but as these could not be retained indefinitely some stocks were transferred to Constantinople, some sent to the British Military Mission in South Russia to re-equip anti-revolutionary troops and the balance shipped home or disposed of locally. The ADOS at GHQ was Colonel P. W. H. Wortham.

During 1921 the Greeks had some success against the Turks in Asia Minor but operations had ceased in the winter. In early 1922 the Paris Peace Conference suggested armistice terms which were unacceptable to Greek public opinion and their troops began to threaten Constantinople. In Asia Minor in September, Turkish forces drove the Greeks into the sea at Smyrna and these activities led to a British warning that violation of the Neutral Zone or attempts to cross the straits would be opposed. Some re-deployment of our Army took place and to supply the troops a new depot was hastily formed at Kilia on the Gallipoli side of the Dardanelles Straits, opposite Chanak.

To help staff this a draft of 150 officers and men under Major M. Meares was assembled at Hilsea. They entrained for Avonmouth and there boarded the SS *Ekaterinoslav*. The ship had been laid up for 15 months and was in a very dirty condition. Apart from the RAOC draft there was only a small party of Cavalry conducting 640 horses and mules. On the somewhat prolonged voyage, the RAOC groomed and fed these animals. Among the officers in this draft was Captain J. S. Omond. He kept a diary of his years at Kilia from which the following account of the depot has been reconstructed.

KILIA DEPOT, 1922–23

Captain Omond disembarked with 100 RAOC men. The arrival of the party was unexpected and on the first night the men slept in a nearby General Hospital.

The depot consisted of lines of tents on half-finished roads on a site near the beach. The receipt of stores, which had to come in over the beach, presented considerable difficulties. Ordnance stores had to be sorted from mixed loads of RE stores, NAAFI supplies, etc., and advice of receipts was often lacking. Stores had also been moved back from Constantinople in great hurry and confusion. On top of this the depot had to meet a continuous series of urgent demands from Chanak, the other side of the "straits".

Inevitably, the depot account soon ceased to be an accurate record of stocks held. There was, however, no relaxation of the cumbersome rules for peace-time accounting—a completely unsuitable system for the emergency conditions which existed. Investigations of alleged discrepancies, courts of inquiry on trivial losses (e.g. loss of soap worth 8s. 6d.) and long written reports enormously and unnecessarily added to the burden of those who were already working under conditions of extreme difficulty.

Ships arrived which had been loaded in great haste and without reference to the situation at the receiving end, where they had to be unloaded with equal haste. Inevitably the result was an unsorted dump of miscellaneous stores on the beach and in the depot.

The stores were there. This was satisfactory as far as it went, which was practically no distance at all, for they were not assets until every item had been discovered, identified and was fit for issue. Even in good conditions it would have needed far more than 150 RAOC staff at Kilia to do the work in reasonable time. In the event a war did not take place, so the initial supply arrangements were never fully tested.

Although the forces at Chanak were only intended to remain there while the emergency lasted, the depot at Kilia was steadily improved with hutting, roads, railways and workshops. This was a case not of "too little and too late" but "too much and too late"—unnecessary expenditure on a project, which had only a limited life, when the real emergency had passed.

INDIA, 1920–22

The full range of RAOC activities did not extend to India, which had its own separate Ordnance organization, the Indian Ordnance Department (later the IAOC). From time to time a number of liaison visits were made, and of course the RAOC Armourers accompanied British regiments to India, and RAOC workshop officers and other ranks were seconded to Indian Ordnance Arsenals.

Following on the successful operation of Ordnance Services in Mesopotamia (Iraq) by the Corps, the Indian Government asked for and obtained the services of Major-General Sir Hugh Perry as DEOS India, and a number of RAOC officers accompanied him together with a party of 20 from France at the end of 1918. These officers were distributed through the Ordnance appointments of GHQ India and the lower head-quarters and a number saw active service as DADOS of Divisions in the Afghan War in 1919.

General Perry was able to render valuable service to the Indian Army by bringing not only his own experience to bear on India's Ordnance problems but also that of the other RAOC personnel who came to India during his tenure as DEOS. In addition to giving India up-to-date information on the layout of depots and procedure during this time, better pay and conditions were inaugurated for personnel and a system of clothing depots introduced. It was hoped among other matters to standardize equipment in both Armies and even eventually to combine the two Ordnance organizations to some degree. It was a great disappointment to all those who had worked so hard for this aim when the two Governments decided not to proceed with complete assimilation, and at the end of 1922 only a small party was left attached to Rawalpindi Arsenal.

IRAQ (MESOPOTAMIA), 1920–23

In early 1919 the Indian Government took a high proportion of their stores away for the Afghan campaign, asked for the return of IOD personnel then remaining, and also requested the loan of the RAOC there for service in India.

In July 1919 a rebellion broke out. The 6th Division was sent in August to assist in quelling the rising, and in subsequent operations British control was established by the end of the year.

The force was distributed in a number of districts with GHQ at Baghdad. Operations consisted of defence against the Arab raids on the L of C (from Basrah to Mosul was 600 miles as the crow flies, much more by river transport) and of punitive columns. To meet this situation the RAOC had to extend, and in addition to Basra and Baghdad, an advanced depot and workshop was opened at Mosul and a number of small depots elsewhere. To staff these there were about 350 of the RAOC organized in 6 under-strength companies and 2 mobile workshops.

During 1922, the Kingdom of Iraq began to emerge and the State forces were built up. Ordnance representatives were attached, an IAOC man to the King's Army and Conductor Morris RAOC to the Levies. In May of that year King Feisal held his first levee and the ADOS (Colonel Davidson) attended on behalf of the Corps.

In 1923 the plan for the Royal Air Force to take over defence responsibility under the treaty with Iraq was brought into effect. A large number of RAOC men were free to leave, and the remainder were attached to the new RAF Stores Organization which they helped to found. The Magill Depot was renamed "Ordnance Group RAF", but soon became known to all as "O" Squadron. Excellent relations existed between the new Service and the Corps.

EGYPT, 1920–27

In 1920 there was an Egyptian Expeditionary Force consisting of 2 Divisions with smaller formations at Sollum and Kantara. There were also detachments in Palestine, Khartoum and Cyprus.

The Ordnance Services comprised an ADOS with staff at GHQ Cairo and 4 Companies and 2 Mobile Workshops distributed in the depots and workshops. By the middle of the "twenties" the Ordnance Organization had taken on a static form with general stores depots at Alexandria (Mex) and Cairo (Abbassia) and a clothing depot at Alexandria (Mustapha). Ammunition was stored in Cairo Citadel and there was a small detachment in Cyprus. The depot at Sarafand was closed after 2 years in mid-1924. The Nationalist disorders of the first years of this period imposed extra tasks on the Ordnance Services. Stores were constantly being got ready for "eventualities" as well as actual issues to the formations which underwent reorganization several times.

To help deal with disturbances in Cairo and Alexandria the RAOC were formed into fighting units for local defence schemes. They were armed and trained with Lewis guns in addition to their rifles. Various other forms of depot security forces were also used including a body of Russians enrolled as depot police at Mex.

When mechanization began there were requirements of a new sort. The first tanks had to have their cooling fans reversed in the workshops as they were blowing sand into the engines. In accordance with Egyptian law all mechanical vehicles on the streets had to have bulb horns so the law-abiding British Army had these fitted to the tanks and armoured cars by Ordnance workshops. When large quantities of surplus stores were being disposed of by auction the prices being obtained were so high that serious consideration was given to shipping unserviceable canvas from the United Kingdom for sale in Egypt but to the relief of the local RAOC this idea did not materialize.

THE FAR EAST

As far as Ordnance Services were concerned the Far East was an uneventful part of the world up to 1926. A small depot was maintained in Colombo principally to supply the Coast Defences in Ceylon.

In the Malaya Command there was an Ordnance depot on an island off the extreme south of the Malay peninsular, almost on the equator, called Pulau Brani, the "Island of the Brave". The depot was on sea level surrounded by hills which in that climate made it very hot. The main buildings presented a mosque-like appearance from the distance, and the Corps practically "owned" the island having workshops, instrument repair shops and messes distributed around. The COO, OO and the Storehouse staff were all located on Pulau Brani with the majority of the

Artificers on Pulau Blakang Mati, a nearby island with the Artillery. The Storehouse staff of 20 other ranks was supplemented by local native labour speaking a diversity of tongues.

China was a separate Command with Ordnance depots at Hong Kong and Tientsin. This latter was notable as being the only British Army Station in the world where fur clothing was a routine issue for winter wear. In theory, the Tientsin Depot came under the DADOS Hong Kong but as they were over 1,000 miles apart most of the powers were delegated to the OO at Tientsin. Although small, Tientsin Depot carried a wide range of stores and was ideal for the junior ranks to obtain personal experience of many aspects of Ordnance duties. There was also a small sub-depot for ammunition and defence stores in Peking with 2 other ranks stationed there.

In December 1926 the situation in China became very threatening to British subjects and interests, so Hong Kong Garrison was reinforced, and a special force was despatched to Shanghai, for the defence of the International Settlements there. This force totalled 16,000 all ranks and was known as the Shanghai Defence Force. The RAOC contingent comprised 4 officers under Major A. G. B. Stewart, 2 WOs and 39 other ranks.

The force landed in Shanghai in February and March 1927 and in order to accommodate them buildings were hired and adapted and a great deal of hutting erected. A state of emergency was declared in Shanghai on March 21 1927. The defence measures included manning a defensive line around the International Settlement and some patrolling as a result of which fire was drawn from the Chinese Nationalist troops and casualties were incurred.

The RAOC were joined by some Indian Army Ordnance Corps personnel and the combined Corps built up a small but all-embracing Ordnance service for the force. A Bulk Depot under Captain Genders was established at West Point outside the city and an advanced depot in the city itself under Sub-Conductor Howes.

MT vehicles accompanied the Force, the Royal Artillery having 18 Burford-Kegresse and 8 Citroen-Kegresse half-track vehicles and 6 Crossley trucks; and the Armoured Car Company having 16 Rolls-Royce armoured cars. For these and other tasks an Ordnance workshop was opened. Finally, to complete the Ordnance Services of the force, there was a small ammunition depot located near the workshops. Accommodation was in "go-downs", large buildings and around the wharves and here during the first 6 months of the emergency, this small RAOC contingent operated in improvised conditions, for a force 23,000 strong with several hundred animals and MT vehicles.

In May 1927 a further 5,300 troops, consisting of another Infantry Brigade and supporting units had arrived from England. Later in the year, as the Chinese Civil War moved northwards, 2 Infantry Battalions were sent to Tientsin and Wei-Hai-Wei and the mixed Brigade from India was released and returned to that country. The IAOC also withdrew and some re-organization of the RAOC took place to enable officers and senior WOs and NCOs to take on duties previously done by the IAOC.

The despatch of the force entailed a great deal of hard work in the depots at home. To complete the force, reservists had to be called up and the requirements for these, together with the issue of large quantities of stores and equipment to bring the units up to establishment, made heavy calls on the depots.

It must be remembered that this was done in a period of severe financial stringency when stocks were scarce and depots were under-staffed. All that was required was done well enough for the QMG to send a personal message to the DOS expressing his warm appreciation of the extraordinarily good work in connection with the preparation and despatch of this force.

SIBERIA 1920

In 1918 one officer (Lieutenant-Colonel T. A. Robertson) and two men of the RAOC from Hong Kong went as part of a military mission to the White Russian Forces in Vladivostock. In January 1920 after many exertions and trials only Colonel Robertson and Sub-Conductor Brooks were left. The former left at the end of January and Brooks shortly afterwards. In his despatch Major-General Sir Alfred Knox of the British Military Mission said, "It was only the British Ordnance who could have worked and carried out such hard duties so successfully."

CHAPTER TWO

UNDER THE MGO 1928–1939

Mechanization and the Corps

Much has been written about the impact of the tank on the Army, the story of its appearance on the battlefield in 1916, and the hopes entertained for its future by its advocates. But the tank was only one part of the revolution in warfare brought about by the internal combustion engine of which General Maurice wrote:

"The internal combustion engine revolutionized road transport and demanded better roads. The lorry could carry a load three or four times the size of that carried by a horse-drawn wagon, it only occupied similar space on the road and it travelled six times as fast. It could bring supplies from convenient depots at a safe distance from the front. Transport ceased to be the limiting factor on the size of armies."

The logistic implications of this statement were, however, not widely understood by the public then nor by a great part of the Army, in which horse transport was still accepted as the normal conveyance.

The RAOC regarded the tank and the armoured car as no more than additional weapons of war; certainly they were specially complex weapons but nevertheless such as could be absorbed into the existing stores and workshops structure with some slight adjustment. In the 1920's this was a valid viewpoint. No continental war was envisaged; the Tank Corps, the sole users of these weapons, had shrunk to some 6 battalions and 4 armoured car companies; the only operational use of armoured vehicles was by the latter units in India and then only in very small numbers (their maintenance was not the responsibility of the RAOC in that country), and in 1925 the total armoured vehicle strength of the Army including vehicles with units, in store and under repair was:

Medium tanks, post-war type   94
Obsolete tanks of the war   233
                             ———
                              327

In addition there were 58 half-track vehicles and 46 Dragons. The latter was a lightly armoured tracked vehicle for towing field and medium artillery. In the Rhine Army tanks were carefully nursed and after manœuvres the problem of replacing worn-out vehicles was evaded by bringing the unit home.

Provision of AFV's was in the hands of branches of the MGO's Department at the War Office, who advised the DEOS (whose directorate was under the QMG) what was being ordered. The consequent receipt, storage, issue and maintenance, including the provision of spares, was the responsibility of the RAOC. Storage of AFV's and their spares was centred at Woolwich Arsenal, where the bulk of repairs was done apart from what the Tank Corps carried out in their workshop at Bovington, which was supervised by an OME.

At this time the Corps had nothing to do with load- and passenger-carrying MT vehicles, which were the responsibility of the Royal Army Service Corps. In the post-1918 period the RASC was in fact the only part of the Army operating vehicles on a world-wide scale, with some 2,000 in use, backed by its own organization for supply and repair. The RASC had pioneered the use of MT in the Army, and it trained its officers and artificers to a high professional standard in their work. For the supply of vehicles and spares it relied on commercial types and did what it could to influence design through the medium of the MT Advisory Board. The 6-wheeled load carrier of the period was a typical example.

By the middle of the 1920's it was becoming clear that modernization of the Army, when it came, would mean mechanization and that this would affect the whole of the Army. When MT vehicles began to be issued to units various anomalies of the dual system became apparent.

When a unit, which had both AFV's and MT vehicles on its charge, wanted replacement or spares there were two different channels of supply and the line of demarcation between them was not always apparent. In one case, if it was an AFV provided by the MGO, it was maintained and repaired by the RAOC (a QMG Corps) and in the other, if it was an MT vehicle provided by the QMG, it was maintained by the RASC (also a QMG Corps). The addition of a weapon or some light armour to one of the latter vehicles often withdrew it from the RASC range and in some cases the distinction was arbitrary and bordered on the ridiculous.

The War Office, in the next few years, devoted a great deal of time to the question of the best organization for the new mechanized Army. A number of tentative proposals were made. They were not put into effect at the time but illustrate the ideas from which policy eventually emerged. Among these recommendations were:

1. That all internal combustion-engined vehicles should be under one authority, the MGO.
2. That the RAOC should become a Corps of Mechanical Engineers, and be responsible to the MGO for all warlike stores including MT but not for clothing and general stores, which did not involve engineering knowledge.

3. Clothing and general stores and laundries to be transferred to the RASC.
4. The MT Heavy Repair Workshop at Feltham to be transferred to the RAOC.
5. The RAOC engineering officers of the future should be regarded in their own sphere as of equal importance to officers of the RE, highly paid, highly qualified and eligible for the highest appointments connected with the production and maintenance of war material.

Although these recommendations were not accepted at the time, some changes were needed, and in October 1927 there was a major reorganization of War Office branches concerned with mechanization. The MGO took over from the QMG the responsibility for all wheeled MT vehicles except those on the establishment of RASC units and MT sections of medical units. These duties included research, design, experiment, provision, inspection, storage and repair. The duties of receipt, storage, issue and repair were allotted to the RAOC, which was moved from the QMG's to the MGO's Department. The title of the Directorate was changed to the Directorate of Ordnance Services and the branches QMG 7, 8, 9 and 10 renamed MGO 7, 8, 9 and 10. It was announced as official policy that the Government did not intend to manufacture any wheeled vehicles but were going to rely on the trade as before.

A new nomenclature was given to the vehicles to be maintained by the Corps. "A" vehicles were all those incorporating full or part tracks; Rolls-Royce armoured cars, Peerless armoured cars; petrol electric lorries, and Peerless anti-aircraft lorries. These were to be provisioned by MGO 5. Tanks were renamed as heavy, medium and light. Armoured cars were to continue to be known by their maker, and it was announced that a new type of "A" vehicle, a "carrier", was to be introduced for machine guns. "B" vehicles were all 6-wheeled lorries (medium and light), all other lorries excluding the Peerless; all vans, cars and motor cycles; tractors and trailers. These were to be provisioned by MGO 6.

In 1928 the first two cavalry regiments were converted to armoured car regiments, the 11th Hussars at Aldershot and the 12th Lancers in Egypt, each with an establishment of 34 armoured cars and 15 "B" vehicles. The Corps did what it could to assist by training and advice and by emphasizing the importance of unit inspection and maintenance of vehicles. In 1928 Lieutenant-Colonel E. J. J. Britton, then SOME Aldershot Command, gave a series of lectures to cavalry officers on the inspection and repair of vehicles.

Special training courses in mechanization were also given in the Corps. Many Ordnance Officers attended lectures, demonstrations and films, and visited such places as London General Omnibus Company garages, the Tank Training Centre and the Experimental Establishment at Farnborough.

Major-General C. D. R. Watts succeeded Major-General Scott on January 1st 1928, the date mechanization policy was implemented, and assumed the new title of Director of Ordnance Services. General Watts brought a wide experience to the post, having been DDOS Third Army in the BEF, IAOS and DDEOS at the War Office and ADOS (P). His fixity of purpose and charm of manner were the ideal blend with which to get results at this time.

When he visited Corps Headquarters later in the year he stressed the need for all ranks to study the problems of mechanization: "Whilst the exact shape and organization of the forces of the future might be hard to visualize at present, it is clear that the RAOC will be greatly affected."

In 1929 the new type of mobile workshop took part in the divisional manœuvres and the lessons learnt confirmed the remarks of the DOS. The chief feature about the workshop, in comparison with its predecessors of the war, was that it was really self-contained and mobile. Basically it consisted of a headquarters and a number of sections which could be detached to serve the units in the formation. Among the duties of this unit was the recovery of vehicles, and for this recovery sections were included.

The workshop went into camp at Blackdown as an independent unit and in the course of the exercise carried out several moves which demonstrated the difficulty of keeping touch with units when all were on the move at the same time. The work carried out was exclusively on MT, and it was realized that no training was provided in dealing with battle casualties to vehicles, which somewhat limited the value of the exercise. Some recovery work was carried out mostly under a neutral flag in the enemy lines which, though unreal, gave good technical experience.

In 1930 the Finance Member of the Army Council, Mr. E. Shinwell, carried out a personal investigation into the repair organization for mechanically propelled vehicles. It was conducted for the purpose of reducing expenditure on maintenance. It was also made the opportunity by some of the War Office directors to propose certain alterations to the organization created by the 1927 changes and in this field extended beyond the terms of reference. Mr. Shinwell's enquiry revealed the striking fact that the Corps had been placed at a grave disadvantage for workshop capacity as a result of the take-over of the RASC vehicles without the corresponding repair facilities; viz.:

	RASC	*RAOC*	*TOTAL*
Capacity (expressed in lorry units)	1,740[1]	2,085	3,825
Liability	470	3,527	3,997

[1] This figure excluded the Heavy Repair Shop, Feltham, which was stated to have a further capacity of 3,000 lorry units. The lorry unit was a measure of repair load. A motor cycle was one-third of a lorry unit, a tank equalled 3 lorry units.

The investigation led to a decision not to extend existing workshop accommodation for the present, and to establish the principle of reciprocity in the repair of vehicles between the RASC and the RAOC, including the use of Feltham which appeared to be out of scale.

Although the regrouping, as between the QMG and MGO, had only been in operation for 2 years it did not give complete satisfaction. Further proposals continued to be submitted. Reciprocity was clearly more of an expedient than the final answer, and there was considerable argument between two schools of thought, one stating that each supply service should repair the equipment it supplied, the other advocating the creation of a Corps of Mechanical Engineers to undertake all repair work.

An extension of the second theory was that the RAOC should be regarded as the skilled storekeepers for the whole Army, attaching men to units of other arms and services to handle their stores problems. It is interesting to note that this idea has now been adopted by the Canadian Army.

The RASC pressed strongly for the retention of control over the supply and repair of its own vehicles, on the grounds that the delivery of essential supplies and petrol to the troops could not otherwise be guaranteed. It was argued less convincingly that there were fundamental differences between the problems of repair of fighting vehicles and transport vehicles.

The RAOC comments stressed the danger of treating the problems of repair in isolation. It was pointed out that repair, as distinct from manufacture, was only one of the many functions of maintenance which comprised general management, provision, receipt, storage, issue and repair. Not all these functions required the services of professional engineers, whose activities should be confined to workshops, inspection and technical advice.

The point was also made that units must be well trained in the technical details of their own equipment so that they could keep it in running order to the maximum extent without assistance. From time to time this principle tends to be forgotten and units become helpless unless continually "wet nursed" by experts.

Attention was also drawn to other anomalies in the existing grouping such as the supply of general stores by the RAOC and the existence of a Barracks Service under the RASC which introduced an intermediate supply service for a certain range of these same stores.

In peace-time, violent and frequent changes in organization are not normally to be expected, and none immediately followed these various proposals, but active minds were at work and the results are reflected in the organization at the present day, which also reflects the British genius for, or alternatively obsession with, compromise.

FARNBOROUGH

Some 1,500 vehicles were transferred to RAOC responsibility with the expectation of a big increase as mechanization progressed. The effective date was January 1st 1928, and meanwhile the appropriate stocks of spares had to be taken over from the RASC. The only accommodation immediately available was at the Field Stores, Aldershot.

However, it was soon found that the Field Stores was inadequate, and a new "B" vehicle depot was created at Farnborough, which had previously been used for storing mobilization equipments, and for various miscellaneous purposes not all of which were the province of the RAOC.

The immediate requirement was to house the stores and pending the introduction of modern methods various expedients were adopted such as the use of empty ammunition boxes as bins and the replacement of the storehouse tally by bin cards. There is always a danger in peace-time that expedients, because they appear to serve the purpose, will be accepted as the final answer. This was not allowed at Farnborough and the use of ammunition boxes led to investigation and research into the best methods of storage and the adoption a few years later of the three types of adjustable binning which are still in use. By then Chilwell had become the Central Depot for MT stores.

The traditional procedure was radically altered and streamlined. Indents were retained in the main office as a permanent record of unit requirements and vouchers were centrally prepared off approved indents. Stores were selected from the bin card which was also a location index.

The Account was mechanized, all transactions being posted on National Cash Register accounting machines which showed not only the stock but also provision data, e.g., dues in and dues out. When stock fell to the Provision Action Figure stores were ordered, frequently off running contracts, and further part vouchers were made out to await receipt of stores when issues could not be made from existing stocks.[1]

A useful Exchange Indent system was adopted. It was based on the system used by General Motors at Hendon and in the RAF. The only requirements were production of the worn-out item and information that the vehicles for which the part was required was shown on the Census as on charge to the unit. This was a true over-the-counter service.

Cataloguing was carefully studied. Although the Maker's Part Number was the basis, many stores, notably proprietary items such as electrical fittings, were common to two or more makes of vehicle. "Commonality" sections were created and the holdings of the same items under a variety of part numbers was avoided. In 1928 the Vehicle Reception Centre was established at Farnborough. It will be seen that at Farnborough much useful pioneering work was done, which paved the way for the MT organization to be developed at Chilwell.

CHILWELL

Chilwell had been an Ordnance depot from 1919 until 1925 when it was closed down. The site remained unused, although several times in

---

[1] These machines were operated by other ranks who had aptitude for this type of work. The Group held 30,000 items and had 2 National Cash Register machines.

the interval the question of using it as a depot was considered. In September 1927 a working party which included Colonel H. B. Warwick and Colonel C. D. R. Watts, as he then was, considered its suitability as an alternative site for the Royal Army Clothing Department. They found the site too large for the Clothing Department to operate economically on its own and recommended the closure of the depots at York and Selby and the transfer of stocks and activities to Chilwell. In the event nothing came of this, but the working party half realized other possibilities as they mentioned that Chilwell might possibly be required as a storage depot for mechanical transport.

Towards the end of 1934 Major (Brevet Lieutenant-Colonel) L. H. Williams was selected as COO designate of a future MT depot, to replace Farnborough, and was told to inspect Chilwell. He went to the top of a hill (on which now stand Williams Barracks) and surveyed an area of 235 acres of empty shells of buildings, with roads and railway tracks overgrown with weeds. He returned to Catterick and thought about it and wrote a paper to clear his mind. To make Chilwell into an MT depot there appeared to be three main problems:

1. The layout of the new depot, the storage methods and types of racks to be used.
2. The best methods of meeting demands and continuing services to Command Depots during the move.
3. The system of accounting and provision to be used.

It seemed to him that the latest methods of the industrial firms in the motor industry should be studied and assimilated where they applied. He submitted his proposals to the War Office and it was agreed that he would proceed to Farnborough to study racking methods, Didcot to examine machine accounting systems in operation, and to eight of the principal motor manufacturers. He also paid return visits to Chilwell and began to examine critically the provisional plans for the layout of the depot. At this time, the plan only envisaged the use of Chilwell as a depot for "B" vehicles with "A" vehicles remaining at Woolwich. Colonel Williams came to the conclusion that Chilwell should become the centre for all the vehicles supplied by the Corps. The two main reasons for this conclusion were that greater efficiency and economy would result in centralized accounting, storage and repair in one location, and from the point of view of user units it was obviously unsound and confusing to demand on Chilwell for certain MT items and on Woolwich for others.

In the meantime, arrangements for the transfer from Farnborough were pressed forward. A formidable reconstruction and building programme confronted the Royal Engineers and the contractors. Only one building (Shed 157) could be used at once for storage of vehicles and this was earmarked as the Vehicle Reception Section, workshop and component stores. It needed little alteration. All the others required repair and alteration to make them suitable for use. There was also extensive demolition and removal and relaying of railway tracks. The Royal Engineers gave every assistance at Chilwell but were handicapped by a shortage of trained men. Works progress was slow and a lot of improvisation had to be accepted, as it was in the very early days of the rearmament programme and a number of people had still to shake off the effect of the stringency of the last decade. Colonel Williams, however, continued to plan on the grand scale and to press for whatever he considered was wanted. He made his tour of the motor firms to study their methods and ask their advice. It is pleasant to record that without exception these firms took willing and endless trouble to demonstrate how they solved their problems of storage and maintenance. As a result of this he was able to prepare and revise plans for every aspect of the scheme, set up a number of working committees among the officers and civilians detailed for Chilwell and prepare a transfer programme.

On May 1st 1935 the small advance party arrived, and Chilwell could be said to have begun its second life as an Ordnance depot. The development of Chilwell was planned in two stages, first the move of "B" vehicles from Farnborough and secondly the move of "A" vehicles from Woolwich. The Vehicle Reception Section move was planned to begin in September during the height of the training season when the majority of vehicles would be out with units who could return them direct to Chilwell. The move of the workshops followed so that repair programmes could be put in hand to have all vehicles ready for the next season's training. The last part of the Farnborough move took place between March and July 1936 when Major E. Tankard and Captain F. Journeaux brought up the stores section less an MT Group left behind for Aldershot Command.

Life at Chilwell was not easy for those early Vehicle Depot pioneers. Living conditions had to be accepted as they found them, and their work was subjected to upheavals to make way for the building contractors. However, the COO succeeded in infusing into all his own enthusiasm and the feeling that they were playing a leading part in a new era in Ordnance history, as indeed they were.

Those who were posted to or visited Chilwell at that time noted a striking contrast between it and other central depots. At Chilwell there was a great sense of urgency, a search for new ideas and methods, the realization that the depot was expanding and that it was essential to plan ahead. The most significant impression of all was that there seemed to be unlimited money available for the new project.

By contrast the other depots seemed to be less dynamic. In fact, they merely illustrated the stultifying effect of 15 years of retrenchment, of "managing somehow", of "doing without", of arguing over every penny, all the inevitable result of the world depression of the late twenties and early thirties. No more than any other machine can a depot switch immediately from reverse to top gear.

Chilwell suffered from no such disadvantage. The depot started from scratch at a time when the nation was beginning to recover from the depression. Moreover, Hitler had been in power for more than a year and the war clouds were beginning to build up on the horizon.

Colonel Williams saw at once the extent of the problem, its importance to the Army and the opportunities which now existed for obtaining the means to fulfil the task which had been entrusted to him. But if recognizing the problem is half the battle, the other half is the fight, and Colonel Williams possessed to a marked degree the gift of persuading other people to have the courage of his convictions. It must not be thought that this was easy. Money was not there just for the asking. The shock of the depression had by no means worn off. If the war clouds were there for those who had eyes to see, many politicians and a fair proportion of ordinary citizens were looking steadfastly in the other direction. The speed and efficiency of the development of Chilwell was a fine achievement by any standards, and in the long run contributed to the high standard attained by other depots under the stress of war.

Although the principles of Ordnance work were unaltered, the procedure and systems were new, the best that could be obtained from the applied knowledge of commercial firms. The stores at Chilwell were representative of the machine age, so, too, were the methods of storing and accounting. Floor conveyors and belts were installed. Machine Accounting was started in March 1936, the first civilian women employees being trained in these duties by Sub-Conductor A. J. Hunt. By 1937, 2,500 transactions a day were being recorded on the mechanical ledger posting machines, and there were over 50,000 items of MT spares and assemblies on the account. At a later date machine accounting was replaced by the Visidex system of hand-posting using carbon-backed slips to provide an independent check.

The COO did not allow technical reconstruction, urgent though it was, to become the only consideration. He pressed for, and obtained, amenities for both military and civilian when he felt they were due. A social club for the latter was opened in March 1936 and a Sergeants' Mess in March 1937. The former soon became the centre of the depot social life with both local amateur and professional entertainers taking part.

Many other social and sporting activities were fostered, yet the programme of storage and supply of MT stores and repair of vehicles, planned on a scale never before attempted in peace, remained up to schedule. In July 1936, the DOS made a visit of inspection and stayed on to an evening entertainment.

As well as perfecting a growing system Chilwell had to make its new methods known to the rest of the Army. New expressions were appearing in the Ordnance vocabulary, "Schedules", "Makers' Part Lists", MT publications, which tended to confuse. The COO wrote a paper which was distributed, stating the principles of supply for MT.

He explained that "MT Groups in Command Depots are in effect branches of the central organization at Chilwell. The aim is to stock these with items in common demand by units and workshops and give an 'over the counter' service. Demands for items not stocked are forwarded to Chilwell for direct issue to units." In reply to the suggestion that units could obtain spares from the trade he pointed out that "parts held by local agents or obtained quickly from the makers are the common parts of which Chilwell holds good stocks . . . makers do not generally hold stocks for the older vehicles and we have to press them hard to make enough. A close personal liaison is now being established."[1]

The use of the various publications was explained. "The ordinary small unit needs only the maker's parts list as issued by Chilwell in order to prepare indents. This list is the foundation of the whole system. Our policy is to purchase and issue all maker's parts under the maker's catalogue number and description. But as these do not include 'proprietary' items, dynamos, starters, carburettors, etc., special lists of these are prepared and printed at Chilwell and bound into the maker's lists. There are also special lists of tools, where issued, and the whole gives the unit a complete record of only those parts which form part of their vehicles." It was more complicated for major units and workshops dealing with vehicles of different ages, and for these there were Schedules and Key Lists which gave the necessary cross-references.

This use of Maker's Parts Lists as the basis for unit demands for spares was a new and somewhat revolutionary system, allied as it was to the special list of common items which was bound into each Maker's List. It enormously simplified things for the units, and avoided the unnecessary creation of new "Army" part numbers for items which would always remain peculiar to a particular vehicle. A pioneer in this work of cataloguing and the creation of a "commonality" list was Captain C. G. Reynolds. Others who helped to lay the foundations of the new system were Captain E. Tankard and Conductor A. J. Hunt, who was expert in converting a new process into a precise, workable, written procedure which was easy to follow. The transfer of "A" vehicles from Woolwich began in March 1937 and was completed with the move of key personnel by the following July.

One aspect of reorganization was noted by Colonel Williams among the "three main problems of Chilwell", namely, "the system of provisioning to be used". At the end of 1935 the matter of provision was being studied by the DDOS, Brigadier L. L. Hoare. The organization of provision branches at that time was found to be defective in certain respects such as their physical locations *vis-à-vis* the stores and their size which tended to make them unwieldy.

---

[1] The origin of the MT Liaison Officer who visited makers and suppliers to explain the Army's urgent requirements and press for various priorities. The concept was based on a similar function in commercial life.

To Colonel Williams it appeared that these defects could only be remedied by dividing provision functions into:

1. Those that should obviously be carried out in close contact with the Store Depot, i.e., normal replacement of stores, placing of orders other than through a War Office contracts branch, central records, inspection and bill clearance.
2. Those involving various War Office branches and other departments, e.g., introduction of new vehicles or equipment, and special provision due to changes in scales and policy. Such work must be done at the War Office.

He therefore proposed that Provision Branches should be split into two on these lines, the former to remain in the depots for the duties suggested, and the latter to be centralized under the DDOS at the War Office. In addition to the duties noted above, the DDOS Provision Branches would issue instructions to the branches in the depots as to how detailed provision would be conducted. To illustrate his point, Colonel Williams drew comparisons between his proposal and the systems followed by a large commercial concern with a central London office and several factories or depots. In such a system, the policy was centralized where it could be dealt with at high level, and then executive instructions were sent out to the several depots. In this proposal we have the seeds of the system today.

One of the complexities of provision work on MT spares was that of "scales", a requirement to review proposed demands from the technical standpoint and to work out scales required for all new types of vehicles, as well as investigating all aspects of inter-changeability. The work called for a high degree of technical knowledge which normally provision personnel did not possess and so led to a new branch, "Scales", being formed with a special staff for this purpose.

Chilwell came in for a good deal of attention and a succession of visitors ranging from senior officers and officials concerned with mechanization to experienced industrialists. In February 1937 the DOS brought the MGO to see the organization because, as he said, "any original doubts he had about the move from Farnborough had been banished by the sight of the smoothness and speed with which it had been done". He wanted the MGO to see this important part of army mechanization in the process of being developed so that he too could see and appreciate the problems and know how they were being tackled.

The GOC in C Eastern Command, General Sir Edmund Ironside, visited Chilwell in April 1937. He wrote a letter of thanks to the COO in which he said, ". . . You can be proud of your baby and despite the disadvantages it had you have done wonders in such a short time. It puts my mind much more at rest to think we have such a centre of mechanization. . . ."

In November 1937 some 40 members of a Management Research Group from London spent a whole day touring the depot. For such a visit a certain amount of special organizing had to be done and this included an information service to provide quick answers to questions. Shorthand typists were attached to each party as they were conducted round and took down the questions raised by the visitors. These questions were quickly passed back to an Information Bureau presided over by Captain Reynolds where the appropriate answer with its question was typed out on a slip of paper and brought back to the group within a few minutes.

They praised the layout and system to the extent of asking for further details with a view to embodying some features in their own methods. In a speech, Brigadier Hoare expressed the indebtedness of the Ordnance Services to industry in providing so much information when Chilwell was re-opened. In a reply on behalf of the visitors, Mr. H. S. Burn, Chief Engineer of the Imperial Tobacco Company, said that although he had been asked to criticize, he felt he was unable to do so in view of the large amount of work done so quickly. As taxpayers, as well as business men, they were all satisfied that their money was being spent most efficiently.

One of the most important visitors to come to Chilwell was Lord Nuffield, who came to inspect the layout and methods in June 1939. Apart from his favourable comments on what he saw, his visit demonstrated to the hard-working Chilwell Depot staff the status the MT organization had acquired in little more than four years.

In April 1938, the press, BBC and the news reels came to Chilwell to record and show to the public the achievement of this acknowledged centre of army mechanization, "Where in two years 650 derelict acres had been transformed into the most modern depot with 40 acres of covered storage, a range of 75,000 spare parts held in the largest installation of steel bins and racks in the country and with an establishment of 3,000 officers, soldiers and civilians, all working together as one team."

Some idea of the load which Chilwell had to carry while the depot was still being built is given by the progress of mechanization during that period. In just over two years (1936–39) the Army's holding of vehicles had increased from 4,000 to 22,500. All of these had passed through Chilwell where they had been inspected, serviced, kitted and accounted for in order that their subsequent repair and maintenance would be assured.

There were now enough vehicles coming into the Service for a small reserve to be held, and accommodation for this had to be considered. The Sinfin Lane Site at Derby was acquired in 1937 and factory premises at Harlescott (Shrewsbury) and Handforth, near Manchester, in 1938.

The supply of vehicles at that time included delivery by Chilwell drivers to destinations in the United Kingdom and there were daily scenes of convoys leaving for Southampton docks and other parts. In emergencies, clerks and others who had learned to drive were employed in vehicle delivery and did this work very satisfactorily.

DIDCOT

Most of the non-technical items in the rearmament programmes were supplied by Didcot. Examples were increased scales of furniture, new types of tentage, new pattern web equipment and camouflage stores.

At the beginning of this period, Didcot was under command of Colonel J. H. Stone, who took a lively interest in modern methods, and it was largely due to his influence that the additional stocks were handled and stored efficiently. Internal transport was modernized in 1935 by the introduction of light tractors, trailers and stillages which could enter the sheds. Time-studies of this type of transport were made by Lieutenant Ailwood and a speeding up of internal movement resulted.

Half the depot's holdings of stores and clothing was put on to machine accounting in 1934 using the National Cash Register system, and the term "control" was first heard about this time relating to a new section of the office established under Major B. A. Goldstein.

In 1936, the Hollerith punched-card system was on trial in parallel with the National Cash Register machines and much valuable data was obtained. It was realized that the old ledger and tally systems would have to be replaced by something more suitable for the great increase in activity. Brigadier Hoare pointed out that compared with 1913, activity had increased sixfold in the central depots. The pioneer work on machine accounting proved of great value to those who studied and introduced these methods in the 1950's. But the Didcot system was not adopted for war, the vote going in favour of the hand-posting Visidex method, studied and used at Chilwell.

The main reason for the decision was that a simple, universal system was required, one that could be used in the field and in newly created installations. The Visidex system was ideal in these circumstances, being compact and incorporating an independent check through the use of carbon-backed posting slips.

Another possible point of criticism of the Didcot scheme was that it was over-centralized. The accounts of Command Depots were to be maintained at Didcot. The responsibility of the man on the spot for maintaining an accurate record of stock was to be taken away. It was realized that this was unsound in principle.

Problems of storage space were solved by the decision to move all the clothing to a new central depot site in 1938, and by the building of "S" Shed—a large building giving 6 acres of covered accommodation which was completed shortly before the war began.

COMMAND DEPOTS IN THE UNITED KINGDOM

By the standards of the time, Catterick was one of the best of the Command Depots for accommodation. Originally, it consisted of only two large sheds used to hold surplus stores for York, but between 1926 and

1929 the whole garrison area was replanned to replace the Curragh and as a centre for mechanized units. On the withdrawal from the Rhine, most of the units went there and formed the 5th Division. New store buildings and workshops had been started in 1925 and in 1936 a large storehouse was added. The following year, two large sheds for camp equipment and an office block were built. The plan was to transfer all activity to Catterick from York but this was never completed owing to rearmament and mobilization.

Activity in Scottish Command led to reorganization and increase in the workshops at Stirling, and a sub-depot being opened on an aerodrome at Montrose, the most northerly ordnance site between the wars.

Improvements and additions to other depots included new workshops at Kinnegar, Northern Ireland, to replace the out-of-date site at Carrickfergus, enlargements at Bovington and Hilsea depot workshops and a new workshop near Chatham. New barrack accommodation and extensions to the workshops were made at Tidworth, and a new depot at Ashford, in Kent, was begun to relieve the pressure on storage space in that part of the Eastern Command.

To offset these, and because of a reduction in activity in the area, Pembroke Dock depot closed on April 1933 and the DADOS office was transferred to Shrewsbury. The workshop remained. The small Ordnance establishments in Jersey and Guernsey were closed down in April 1930 when Regular troops ceased to be stationed in the Channel Islands.

Aldershot continued to be the most active of all the Home Command Depots and a valuable centre for training, as Lieutenant-Colonel Verschoyle-Campbell found when he returned from the comparative peace and quiet of Gibraltar in 1934. "Basil Hill was ADOS and he had drawn up a most comprehensive plan of war exercises in which officers had to perform the duties of higher ranks and also were attached to brigade headquarters."

Workshop costs were also investigated by Colonel Hill, who arranged for a leading motor firm to send down their production planners to advise on the repair of tanks. As a result of this it was possible to reduce the cost of tank repairs by a large percentage.

The Colonel-in-Chief paid a visit to the Field Stores in June 1934 to see the Corps at work. He toured the mobilization stores and the workshops and watched a demonstration of tank recovery at Rushmoor. Of this visit, his equerry wrote to the DOS. "I am desired by His Royal Highness the Duke of York to tell you how very much indeed he enjoyed his visit to the Depot at Aldershot . . . and how very interested he was in all he saw. His Royal Highness was much impressed by the smartness and turnout of his Guard of Honour . . . and would like you to convey to all ranks his appreciation of everything he saw."

Like the rest of the Army, the Corps did everything it could to make up for lost time and get the most out of existing resources. "Work Planning" was discussed as a means of eliminating unnecessary operations.

In February 1936, General Hill wrote a study on the application of work planning to Ordnance duties in which he dealt with the need to modernize accounting and storehouse duties. "The limitation of extra numbers [of personnel] can only be brought about by introducing methods which will eliminate unnecessarily elaborate checks and redundant operations by establishing standard times for clerical operations and workers' jobs." He went on to cite the research of Lieutenant-Colonel Haigh on office work at Weedon and suggested that such storehouse activities as the overhaul of camp equipment and the care and preservation of reserves were also amenable to standard timings.

Mobilization schemes were beginning to assume growing importance in the depots by the mid-thirties. Rearmament made mobilization more complex and depot plans had to cover many more aspects. The general mobilization policies were reviewed in 1937 and units were now to be fully equipped at their mobilization stations before moving to the theatre of operations, as opposed to the former scheme of separate bulk shipments of vehicles. The arrangements for the impressment of civilian vehicles were also studied. Requirements for the MGO establishments were to be arranged through RAOC depots and for those of the QMG through Vehicle Collecting Centres set up in Commands, by the RASC.

THE RHINE 1928–29

In Germany the winter of 1928–29 was especially severe, and the Rhine was frozen over. In February 1929, a Rhineland Evacuation Committee was set up at the War Office with the DOS as a member. With the Committee, the DOS came to Wiesbaden and they all agreed to the local scheme on the basis of a 6 months' programme.

It was later decided that the evacuation would have to be done in 3 months and in September this was announced. As far as the Corps was concerned plans were well advanced. A visiting representative of the Army Contracts Branch of War Office found the programme complete even to the number of barges required to move the stores. Tenders had already been invited for surplus and obsolete MT vehicles. Some Ordnance stores were being despatched to Woolwich for sale there. Harness, saddlery and tools were being sent home as good prices were not obtainable locally. The RAOC had obtained estimates from all units for wooden packing cases, crates, packing materials and ropes. They had 3,000 cases in stock, 1,000 were purchased locally at below vocabulary rates and 1,000 special sizes for hospital equipment, typewriters, motor cycles, etc., had been manufactured in Ordnance workshops from stocks of wood and old racking.

On September 14th, the first barge of stores left for Rotterdam. There was some delay at Schierstein where the ammunition was being loaded because only one crane was available, but otherwise all was plain sailing. At Bingen, RAOC men supervised the transfer of other stores into barges for Rotterdam. At Rotterdam, transhipment of stores was supervised by an officer sent there for the purpose.

The Rhine had been a good station. Many friends had been made and the majority of the officers and men left with regret. Few then gave much thought to the future or what our relations would be with these same people in 10 years' time.

THE SAAR PLEBISCITE FORCE 1934–35

In 1934 the idea that an International Force should go to the Saar territory was proposed by Mr. Anthony Eden at the League of Nations, in order to assist in the task of maintaining order during the plebiscite to be held in accordance with the Treaty of Versailles. The whole force was commanded by a British officer, Major-General J. E. S. Brind, the British contingent consisting of the Headquarters 13 Infantry Brigade and two Battalions from Catterick, a detachment of the 12th Lancers (armoured cars) from Tidworth, with detachments of administrative services. The RAOC Detachment consisted of one officer, Lieutenant B. D. Jones, DADOS, SAAR force, and 12 other ranks from Catterick. A Light Aid Detachment under command of Lieutenant G. E. Butler accompanied the 12th Lancers from Tidworth.

The main body of the British contingent left on December 21st 1934 and was established in the SAAR by January 1st 1935. The despatch of the force was regarded as a peace-time move, although certain additional stores and MT were taken.

The stores for the force were all shipped over to Calais on the SS *Autocarrier,* one of the few occasions when men accompanied the stores. When the train arrived at Saarbrucken the DADOS had a number of hired lorries waiting, and the stores were quickly transferred to the Kaserne Artillerrie. The initial scaling for the force prescribed a somewhat austere mode of living which simplified Ordnance work, but when it was discovered that other contingents were living in style, complete scalings of mess equipment were sent out from home so that British prestige would not suffer by comparison. By working long hours for the first few days, all issues were made and maintenance items put to stock by Christmas Eve which allowed the little detachment to suspend work and join in the local *Weihnacht* celebrations.

The plebiscite was held on January 13th 1935. It passed off quietly. The task of the force was now over. Withdrawal began in February and was completed by the end of the month when the various units returned to their original locations. The detachment were given 10 days to pack up all the stores, send them home and close the account. Owing to the extra mess equipment sent out to the force there was the problem of packing delicate glass and crockery, a task outside the experience of the detachment, so the DADOS asked for the services of an expert from Didcot who came out and supervised the work. The participation by the

RAOC in the force was a limited exercise from which useful experience was gained by those who took part.

EGYPT

The presence of the British troops was an important factor in maintaining order in Egypt at this period and the official view at the beginning of the decade was that it was essential to retain Cairo Citadel and Kasr-el-Nil Barracks as key points, as well as the area of Abbassia. The depot at the latter place became the most important in the Middle East although economic pressure and Government policy kept manpower as low as possible.

The 1936 Treaty of Alliance between Britain and Egypt provided for withdrawal of all British from the Egyptian Army, limited the size of British forces to 10,000 and envisaged their eventual withdrawal from the Cairo area to the Canal Zone when suitable accommodation had been built by the Egyptian Government. In early 1937 a Treaty Building Committee was set up to begin planning and supervise the construction of a cantonment in the Geneifa area but as the actual building was in the hands of the Egyptians it was assumed, not unreasonably, that no early move from the Cairo area would take place.[1]

The Italo-Abyssinian dispute of 1935 caused the forces in the Mediterranean and Egypt to be reinforced in case the League of Nations imposed sanctions on Italy. Drafts which included RAOC Artificers, Armourers and Artisans, were hurriedly sent off from home to Malta, the Sudan and Aden to bring the anti-aircraft and coast defences up to higher establishment. Part of the 5th Division was sent from Catterick which together with the newly mechanized cavalry, artillery, RE and RTC were to form the Western Desert Force with an advanced base at Mersa Matruh.

The maintenance of this force led to the sudden despatch of stores from home. At the same time, drafts were taken at short notice from units in the United Kingdom. The arrival of these reinforcements was welcome in Egypt where the depot staffs were working a 12-hour day in the summer heat.

In September 1935, two small parties consisting of two Ordnance Officers, and 16 other ranks were sent out as the RAOC contingent of a Composite Air Defence Brigade of the Mediterranean Base Defences. The work of the RAOC of this force was greatly facilitated by the system of different coloured and numerical markings for each unit, devised by the War Office and faithfully followed by home issuing depots. All documents relating to the stores were handed to the RAOC detachment before

---

[1] One effect of this policy was to inhibit any more building in the Cairo area. This had a crippling effect on the storage of reserves when they began to arrive and the best that could be done was to take over old stables which became surplus after mechanization of the Cavalry (Polgon and Porton Sub-Depots).

48

departure from the United Kingdom which enabled the preliminary paper work to be done during the voyage.

PALESTINE

In Palestine there had been riots between Jews and Arabs in August 1929. There were no troops in the country so an advanced party of Infantry was flown in from Cairo followed by an Infantry Brigade, a Squadron of armoured cars and other supporting units by rail. The headquarters included SQMS Hewitt as BOWO, who established a small dump at Lydda Station. His office consisted of a railway truck which he had to share with some naval personnel who used it as a lecture room. Before he had time to ascertain the requirements of his units, the first load of stores arrived without demand from Cairo consisting of ammunition, general stores and clothing, calculated as possible requirements. This early example of automatic maintenance was appreciated by the units in the force. There then followed a period of comparative quiet and the force was reduced until 1936.

In 1936 the various Arab elements united and declared a general strike against the Government to further their cause. Clashes took place between Arabs, Jews and the police, and armed bands began to roam the countryside. At the end of June, Cavalry, RA, RE, Signals and RTC were sent from Egypt and in September the Government decided to send a Division out from home. The 1st Division was taken off manœuvres in August, certain reserves called up and the Division, less artillery and "A" vehicles, went to Palestine where it landed the following month. The force was wholly equipped with MT, over 700 vehicles being shipped with it. Ocean liners were requisitioned off passenger trips and pleasure cruises.

It was also decided by the Government to move the 5th Division in from Egypt. The plan was therefore for a corps of 2 Divisions, the 5th Division in the northern part of the country with HQ at Haifa, and the 1st Division in the southern part with Divisional and Corps HQ at Jerusalem. The ADOS 1st Corps was Lieutenant-Colonel G. W. Palmer; the COME was Lieutenant-Colonel D. White.

Advance parties were sent in from Egypt. A Forward Ordnance Depot with 20 other ranks and an Ordnance Mobile Workshop with 30 other ranks were opened at Sarafand. To serve the increased forces, it was decided to establish a depot and a vehicle reception park at Haifa and for these another party was sent over from Cairo in August. Lieutenant-Colonel W. W. Richards came up from Egypt and gave the operations a characteristic impetus and the depot was sited, roads and railways laid out and the first receipt of stores dealt with by this party in just over a fortnight, well before the United Kingdom contingent arrived.

An interesting account of the work in the Haifa Depot was written by Captain A. U. Mackenzie soon afterwards. In this he summarized the lessons learnt: "The original party which opened up the depot was relieved almost *in toto* by the United Kingdom contingent. It was difficult to take over and there was a loss of continuity. As a result, important details were overlooked which caused a waste of time afterwards. It would have been of great assistance if RAOC personnel had accompanied the stores on store ships."

"The depot dealt with almost the whole range of Ordnance stores on a peace-time accounting basis handicapped by a lack of essential stationery. It was the first experience of holding MT spares and the bulk and the range of these was not foreseen. Work was characterized by one continuous rush. No sooner were the original issues made to 1st Division when the withdrawal of the 5th Division was ordered and stores and vehicles began to flow in from that formation. The rush of work increased by a tendency on the part of units to retain everything until the day of embarkation and then expect it all to be settled on the spot. A further tiresome matter was a temporary loan account for furniture issued to units for the use of the NAAFI."

The motto of the ADOS was "Deliver the goods first and if necessary settle the paperwork afterwards", a very proper one in such circumstances but the result imposed a great deal of work in reconciliation. Mackenzie summed up his account by stressing the practical value of such emergency depot work to the Corps especially in the experience learned of the extra work brought about by mechanization.

Soon after the force took up positions in the country the Arab rulers used their influence, the strike was called off on October 12th and the tension eased. The withdrawal of reinforcements began at the end of October and by 1937 the force was down to 6 Battalions and supporting units. Then trouble began again in early 1938 and reinforcements were brought in again from Egypt and India.

Egypt and Palestine provided many lessons, particularly for workshop staff. The various crises brought about an acceleration of mechanization for the forces in these countries and at one time strained Ordnance resources very severely as the following table will show:

Increase of vehicles (RAOC responsibility) 1936–38 with corresponding workshop personnel strengths

Year	Vehicles		Personnel[1]	
1935	"A" 210 "B" 170	} 380	Mil 58 Civ 59	} 117
1936	"A" 710 "B" 1,190	} 1,900	Mil 240 Civ 187	} 427
1938	"A" 514 "B" 2,500	} 3,014	Mil 146 Civ 270	} 416

[1] The figures for personnel include all those with LADs and Recovery Sections so the low military strength in the main Abbassia workshops can be appreciated.

INDIA 1935–39

Although possessing a separate Ordnance Service of its own, the Indian Army traditionally looked to this country from time to time for the loan of officers to help with special problems arising from major changes in organization or equipment. This assistance has always been gladly given, and the services rendered by General Perry and other officers in the early 1920's have already been mentioned. After that period, India continued to rely on us for workshop assistance to a considerable extent.

In 1935 a further occasion arose with the spread of mechanization when it was realized by the Indian Army that a major task of Ordnance reorganization faced them. They therefore again asked for the services of an RAOC officer to fill the post of DOS India, and Brigadier W. McN. Verschoyle-Campbell was selected and sent out to that country where he arrived at the end of 1936.

Whilst this history is not intended to do more than make a passing reference to events outside Corps circles, the work done by Brigadier Verschoyle-Campbell and other RAOC officers in India was so valuable in preparing that country for war that some details must be given.

Some reorganization was necessary in the Arsenals.[1] Whilst the earlier system of supply of labour by contractor, as required, was no longer in operation, the standard of the artisan was comparatively low. The IAOC had set afoot a sound system of supply and demand for stores and the depots were well-run but they were still antiquated in many ways. Owing to severe financial control there was very little reserve stock and a great deal of the equipment was old and worn out. All activity and planning was directed to one area—the North-West Frontier.

After a careful tour of inspection, the new DOS felt he had to make some changes, especially in the workshops to bring them into line with those at home and enable them to bear the load imposed by mechanization. A COME known as ADOS (Technical) was installed in Simla to direct workshop policy and make the Indian Army conscious of the value of the OME. This appointment was filled by Colonel F. Morris, an outstanding Ordnance Mechanical Engineer who became POME India and was promoted to Brigadier in 1939.

Mechanization of the Indian Cavalry had just begun and the first efforts were hampered by the excessive secrecy surrounding the order by which units were selected. India presented a host of problems when mechanization began, one example being that of getting men for Arsenal workshops in what were predominantly agricultural areas. The OMEs did the only thing they could in such a situation, picked the most likely youths and trained them in the Arsenals. This was initiated at Rawalpindi.

---

[1] In India "Arsenal" is a term to describe an organization similar to a Central Depot in the United Kingdom.

The introduction of specialization resulted in a large increase of output and a high standard of repair to a wide range of items including electronic equipment and instruments. In the general workshops important work was also carried out on the ammunition feed and cooling systems of machine guns in tanks, and the repair of gun carriages.

Under Brigadier Morris the Indian Ordnance in conjunction with the RIASC undertook the training of MT drivers at Jubbulpore. The IAOC School of Instruction at Poona was moved and formed the nucleus of what grew to a vast establishment by the time war began, training thousands at a time. The whole organization was supervised by OMEs of the RAOC.

When he turned his attention to the matter of reserves, General Verschoyle-Campbell[1] found that these were part of a most complicated system including a massive document known as the Standing War Indent which was deposited in London for action when war broke out. Nothing happened until then, as no money could be spent in peace. With his knowledge of the situation in Britain, he realized that the chance of India obtaining anything like the requirement was remote. As Deputy MGO he also had some responsibility for Indian Ordnance Factories, and realizing that these would have to produce equipment to fill the bill he had a survey made of what was needed to modernize them. Here again, no progress could be made for financial reasons, but space does not permit us to tell how by persistence he achieved his aim, seeing many people in high places and making them understand what was needed to put India's Army and munitions organization on a war footing. India owes a great deal to the drive, initiative and dynamic personality of General Verschoyle-Campbell.

SINGAPORE

By the late twenties, the Government had decided to create a large naval base at Singapore but owing to the economic crisis progress was negligible until April 1933, when the decision was made to complete the defences by 1936–37 and bring the permanent garrison up to a strength of 2 Infantry Battalions with supporting arms and services at higher colonial establishment. In 1935 Lieutenant-Colonel E. R. Macpherson was appointed the first ADOS Malaya Command.

The site, on a separate island, of Pulau Brani Depot made it unsuitable in the changed circumstances and the accommodation was badly congested. A new depot was planned at Alexandra on Singapore island. It consisted initially of an office block and two large rail-served buildings with some ground for expansion. This, however, proved inadequate and by the end of 1937 Pulau Brani had to be used again as an overflow depot.

[1] He was appointed Deputy MGO, India, at the beginning of 1939, a post which carried promotion to Major-General.

Storage of anti-gas clothing proved particularly troublesome in the hot, damp climate, the garments sticking together despite all the measures taken to prevent this happening. A good deal of this clothing had to be written off, but the policy to send it to Singapore at all was ill-advised, as anyone wearing it at work for more than 10 minutes collapsed from heat exhaustion.

Reserves included a quantity of Vickers machine guns, some mobile searchlights, two 6-inch howitzers and one spare barrel for the 15-inch guns.

By late 1937 mechanization became a factor. Vehicles were received to replace unit horse-drawn transport and to provide maintenance and reserve stocks. The state of these vehicles was very good. Although they had been at sea for 6 weeks every vehicle started without trouble when its batteries were connected up. The workshop at Pulau Brani was inadequate and that at Changi was in use for weapons and instruments. A new workshop for MT was therefore built in Alexandra Depot.

Preparations for the defence of the island do not appear to have been very active. Captain Finney, the OC Depot, was one of a party of officers which was sent to reconnoitre the north-west side of the island, on which there were no fixed defences. They reported that there was no significant obstacle to the landing of troops in the many creeks on that side. Subsequent events seem to show that little action was taken on the report.

THE CLOSING OF PIMLICO

The making of clothing was the sole surviving manufacturing activity of the old Board of Ordnance still retained by the RAOC. This was carried on at Grosvenor Road, Pimlico, London, in premises, acquired in 1863, which also held the central reserves of clothing including quantities made by the trade. This site covered 7 acres, chiefly of two-storey brick buildings the floor area of which amounted to 450,000 sq. ft.

In 1925 consideration was first given to the action necessary when the War Department lost possession of the premises of which the lease was due to expire in 1937. It was found that the factory did not compare so favourably with factories in the trade as in 1881. The investigating committee reported in favour of the continuance of a clothing factory:

1. For full dress, as it was doubtful if the trade could produce the quality required by the Household Troops and also to avoid dependence on a "ring".
2. For service dress, so as to be able to increase output quickly in an emergency, to keep stocks low, as a check against trade prices, and to be able to train new firms in any future war. The Committee recommended that a new site when acquired should begin with accommodation for 500 workmen, allowing room for expansion up to 1,000.

In 1929 the then Finance Minister (Mr. Shinwell) attempted to put the factory in a position to compete with the trade by the introduction of the "Higher subdivision of labour" method already widely used in the clothing trade. This consisted of specializing operatives on a particular task instead of working on a whole garment, and the first experiment resulted in a saving of £5,500.

Other measures suggested to reduce costs further included one apparently serious proposal, that, in order to avoid having stocks of various sizes, only men of one standard size should be enlisted in the Army. The idea did not appeal to the Adjutant-General's department which had to find the men.

When the policy was reviewed again in 1931, this time by Mr. Duff Cooper, he found that trade prices were substantially lower than factory costs especially on service dress. It was estimated that to obtain all the requirement of service dress from the trade would result in a saving of £25,000 per year. It was therefore decided to do this and to obtain trials of full dress from the trade in 1932. The decision was therefore made to abolish the factory altogether, although for a time a proposal had been entertained to move it to Chilwell. This would have had the advantage of being nearer the mills. But on investigation it was found to be too large and its large central power and heating system would have been uneconomic to run when only partially used.

There was no question of considering a new lease for Pimlico as a Store Depot. A committee headed by the IAOS had found that the area did not allow for expansion, lacked railway sidings and was old-fashioned, with floors on different levels. Some of the upper floors could only take a limited weight and there was a serious fire risk.

The lease was prematurely surrendered, and on September 23rd 1933 the Royal Army Clothing Department ceased to exist. Stocks of clothing were distributed to Woolwich (full dress) and to Didcot (service dress and remaining items). The office of the DDOS, which had also been housed there, was moved to Woolwich Arsenal together with the warlike stores provision branch. The clothing and general stores provision branches were moved to Didcot. The Inspectorate of Clothing was also divided between the two depots, the section going to Woolwich being designated Inspectorate of Full Dress.

Leaving aside the question of whether or not the Corps should have gone on being responsible for clothing manufacture, the wisdom of abolishing the factory as a War Department activity is open to question. The 1925 investigation stated a number of very sound reasons for retaining a factory and Mr. Shinwell demonstrated that the introduction of modern methods corrected any difference in running costs. It is obvious that the Pimlico premises were expensive to run on account of their age and layout but this would not have applied to a new site with everything on the ground floor. With careful planning and installation of further modern methods it is probable that the factory would once again have borne comparison with the trade. It must also be borne in mind that the clothing trade at that time was notorious for its sweated labour which no doubt enabled them to undercut the factory costs.

Whether the retention of a WD clothing factory would have met mobilization requirements is a matter of opinion. It is, however, a matter not of opinion but of fact that the machinery for obtaining clothing from the trade for a rapidly expanding Army was quite inadequate. Lord Woolton was called in to advise and assist the Government early in 1939 on clothing production for the Army. His comments are illuminating.

". . . from these I made a calculation that we had reasonable hopes of having the Army clothed in four years!"

"At my wits end to know what to do, I had what must have been an inspiration—I asked what orders had been placed for trouser buttons. The answer 'none', trouser buttons were supplied by the contractors not the War Office. I inquired if the contractor had placed orders for trouser buttons. No one knew."

"I asked them what they had done about cap badges, which in my view came only second to trouser buttons in the building of morale. Of course, they had found Army badges generally difficult to come by. . . ."

"The operation demonstrated to the Contracts Department at the War Office that there was really something more to do than rely on the makers-up of Army clothing; obviously we had to place our own orders, not only for trouser buttons but for khaki and everything that was required, in order to ensure that supplies would be available. The job involved money running into millions of pounds. It was quite outside the capacity of the existing Army clothing contractors."

"The trouble was that the Contracts Department placed orders for the goods they were to receive—the finished product; it was the business of the contractors to obtain raw materials. But the clothing manufacturers were fully and profitably engaged on civilian work. . . ."

"I told Sir Warren Fisher that I was up against a machine, that I was completely convinced that the Army could not be clothed unless I was allowed to put aside all this peace-time system of contracting and given a completely free hand. I told him of the minute I had dictated, and read it to him. He listened very carefully and then quietly told me, 'You have complete authority. You must send your minute and put this note on it: "The Treasury concurs, I will give instructions in the Treasury in accordance with this interview" . . .'. . . ."

"It was, of course, essential that I should work in the closest harmony with the soldiers, some of whom I found seriously alarmed at the state of unpreparedness. I took it upon myself to tell the Secretary of State what I thought of the matter and the lack of liaison (as it seemed to me) between the civilian and military sides of the Department and the absence of any sense of urgency, though I praised the efforts that General Basil Hill was making. Personally I felt that I was walking in a fog of un-realism. . . ."

"Certainly the most difficult job I have ever done in my life, and the one that caused me the greatest anxiety, was this, the task of clothing and equipping the Army in four months."

REARMAMENT

The circumstances which led to the rearmament programme of the 1930's have been stated many times and with many degrees of emphasis and it would be wearisome to discuss them all again here. However, when they came, the various decisions to re-equip the Army had so many effects on the Corps that our story would not be complete without a brief reference to them.

For many years the Estimates had been framed on the "no major war for 10 years" hypothesis and between 1923 and 1933 the amount of money allotted annually for weapons and warlike stores averaged £2 millions. The doctrine of the period of a small professional mobile army was expressed in a number of highly trained units, mobile in the sense that they were grouped in 4 or 5 Divisions[1] and that mechanization was pursued as far as funds would permit. Except for MT vehicles and 160 tanks produced in the late twenties most of the equipment comprised out-of-date items which had survived the war in large quantities and which the economic conditions of the time compelled us to use.

Apart from the financial stringency there was also a strong national aversion to any form of war preparation which might repeat the horrors of 1914–18, and the general public pinned great hopes in various disarmament proposals and the ability of the League of Nations to keep the peace. In such an atmosphere, research, development and experiment had a thin time and members of the Army who took their profession seriously went through a long period of frustration.

Even when the 10-year rule was revoked in 1932 the Army continued to be the Cinderella of the three services and budgetary cuts necessitated a system of priorities. These were laid down in the following order:

1. The Air Defence of Great Britain (ADGB).
2. The protection of overseas trade routes.
3. A Regular expeditionary force of 5 Divisions for "a war of limited liability of a colonial type".

The new rearmament programme demanded a complete recalculation of maintenance stocks and reserves by the Ordnance branches at the War Office and provision branches at the depots.

The public announcement that new weapons and equipment "were to be provided" was evidence of parliamentary recognition that readiness for war was a condition of survival—a fact that had been obvious to most people long ago. But it was less rapidly understood that the period

---

[1] Even the Divisions were not self-supporting in that they consisted only of the fighting arms and did not include organic RAOC or other units.

between the announcement of the new policy and its fulfilment in terms of arms, equipment and ammunition in the hands of the troops was at best a very long one. Design had to be completed, trials carried out and industrial capacity converted from peace to war production.

Responsibility for production to remedy the acute shortage of all forms of war equipment did not rest with the RAOC, but the consequent inability to meet many unit demands at this stage was frequently attributed to inefficiency on the part of the Corps. The concept of a well-equipped peace-time Army as an insurance policy against war is not much favoured in Britain even in these days with the experience of two world wars in which a week's expenditure on the Army is equivalent to a year's expenditure in peace. The premium paid by successive governments in the years of peace has always been so small that, far from being a deterrent, it has given positive encouragement to potential aggressors by advertising the military weakness of the country and the apparent unwillingness of its people to defend their interests and liberty.

Rearmament created for the RAOC a corresponding need for additional manpower and accommodation to handle and store the new equipment. Existing workshops had to be modernized and new workshops built.

The role of the Territorial Army was changed from that of reinforcing the expeditionary force on the Continent to assisting in the anti-aircraft defences and duties in connection with maintenance of law and order and essential services in the country in time of war.

After the Munich agreement a war involving Continental participation was accepted as probable and, in the planning, equipment requirements for 10 Divisions became high priority as well as the completion of ADGB. At the same time a long-term plan was drawn up for equipping 36 Divisions based on 6 Regular Divisions at home, 4 in Egypt and the Far East and 13 TA Divisions which were brought up to war establishment in 1939 and then doubled. Twenty of these were to be ready by September 1940 and the remainder by September 1941.

The majority of warlike stores passed through Woolwich Arsenal and Dockyard and the increase in range and quantity imposed a strain on the resources there. Up to 1937, "A" vehicles were handled there and some hundreds of dragons, carriers and tanks were issued to units. Other aspects of the load on Woolwich were conversion programmes to fit pneumatic tyres on all field guns, the distribution of 6-pounder guns for coast defence, the new 3-inch mortar, the 2-pounder gun for both the tank and anti-tank roles, the despatch of heavy guns to Malaya and the distribution of the 18-pounder field gun in its converted 25/18-pounder gun-howitzer design. There was an increasing volume of wireless and signal stores including the No. 9 and No. 3 sets, new switchboards, telephone sets and charging sets. Other sub-depots in the London area were acquired between 1936 and 1939 to relieve pressure on Woolwich, but the DOS and DDOS both realized that the days of this historic centre of

Ordnance activities were numbered and a new site was necessary for war-like stores.

As early as September 1936 Brigadier Hoare had submitted a memorandum to General Hill on an alternative site for Woolwich which he said was "the most hopelessly inconvenient COD we have, terribly scattered and impossible to run efficiently. . . . Above all, there is an extremely grave war risk [of holding all our warlike stores there]. . . . I therefore propose that a new COD be built . . . and at the new depot we could train RAOC men for these important base duties in war *which we are not allowed to do at Woolwich*. The requirement for a modern layout is one million square feet of covered accommodation, but to allow for future expansion we should acquire an area of 500 acres, the surplus being left under agriculture with the WD as landlord."

Woolwich also came in for criticism from other Ordnance depots. At Singapore, "The out-of-date methods used by Woolwich over gun parts were a constant cause of muddle and irritation. It appeared to us that people in Woolwich knew everything by sight and as a result no proper cataloguing system was devised and parts were known by their full vocabulary description which in many cases occupied several lines on the voucher.[1] In mixed consignments one could not identify the stores as no means of identification was attached to them. We used to spread them out and compare them with items in stock that we knew. Those that could not be identified used to be held aside until a very knowledgeable Armament Artificer Warrant Officer came in off detachment for his pay. Washers were especially tiresome and had to be gauged with a micrometer to establish identification." (Captain Finney.)

ADGB

Top priority was given to the Air Defence of Great Britain. The programme involved the conversion of some 470 of the 3-inch guns on a lorry mounting and the receipt and distribution of over 1,200 40-mm. Bofors, 3·7-inch and 4·5-inch AA guns, a wide range of searchlights, locating equipment, predictors and many other associated items. To meet the operational requirements these stores were all eventually deployed in specially constructed depots which were placed under the control of Anti-Aircraft Command with a DDOS to supervise them.

The training of TA units newly converted to AA roles threw much work on the Corps in the form of Camp Depots from which equipment had to be repeatedly issued and received during the training season.

SMALL ARMS

At the small arms depot at Weedon a general overhaul of the reserves of stores took place, and on War Office orders a large quantity of the

---

[1] A typical example was "Ordnance QF 18-pounder breech mechanism lever retaining catch latch stop stud with check screw".

1914 pattern rifle which had been reported surplus for many years was put back into service. Holdings of pistols were turned over, the repeating action type of the ·38 inch replacing the earlier model and the heavier ·45 inch. The first dozen Bren light machine guns, designed to replace the Lewis, were received in October 1937 and thereafter arrived in ever-increasing numbers to be issued as fast as they came. In 1938 the Boys ·5 inch anti-tank rifle was brought into service through Weedon and a new short bayonet introduced for the SMLE Rifle.

AMMUNITION

A considerable part of the rearmament programme covered ammunition, and by the end of 1937 streamlined projectiles were coming into service together with new types of propellant. It was clear that Bramley alone would not be big enough and that other ammunition depots would be needed. Underground storage was studied at the War Office by Brigadier Verschoyle-Campbell and Colonel Stokes and among the places considered were the quarries near Bath. Initial surveys had shown this site to be a possibility but there was a delay in beginning work due to difficulties in preparing an estimate. Verschoyle-Campbell, however, was able to persuade the Finance Branch to allot a credit of one million pounds enabling the work to be started in 1936, and a party which included Major P. W. F. Brown as COO, Major A. T. Green and Lieutenant H. Cripps were there in that year. The works project was in the hands of a most capable RE officer—Lieutenant-Colonel Minnis, whose share in the making of Corsham was commemorated by the sports ground named after him located on soil taken from the quarries.

The development of Corsham as the first underground storage depot of the Corps was pressed on as fast as possible, Major Brown and his staff taking over every available piece of space as fast at the Royal Engineers completed it. There were many novel features to be dealt with for which there was no precedent. All internal movement was on conveyor belts, only one-way traffic was possible on these, and issues and receipts needed careful synchronizing to avoid losing time. At the Monkton-Farleigh Sub-Depot, ammunition was moved away from the surface loading platforms to the railway sidings by a ropeway which had been acquired from a colliery.

ANTI-GAS STORES

Because of the threat of gas warfare rearmament plans included enormous quantities of anti-gas stores. As well as the respirator a whole string of items was added to personal scales such as eyeshields, tins and pots of ointment, cotton waste, sleeve detectors and capes. Unit stores included anti-gas hoods, jackets, trousers and gloves for decontamination squads, "pathways" of impregnated paper, bleach powder and special paint which would change colour when gas came in contact with it and so give a warning of gas attack. Every unit had to have a gas defence and decontamination centre holding the above items and a large range of general stores. To meet this load a new Central Depot for anti-gas stores was opened at Leyland, Lancashire, which was near the centre of manufacture of many of the items.

In 1928 it was decided that the inspection and repair (component replacement beyond unit capacity) of anti-gas respirators was the responsibility of IOOs and Ammunition Examiners. This was a formidable addition to the work of the ammunition staff and involved an extra course at Winterbourne Gunner. The decision was not a very sound one as the work had nothing to do with ammunition and frequently men were taken away from ammunition duties for long periods on full-time respirator inspection and repair. The work did not cease to become a responsibility of the ammunition inspection staff until some time after the outbreak of war.

CLOTHING—OPENING OF BRANSTON

In 1936 a new blue serge uniform and blue forage cap were introduced for wear by troops taking part in the forthcoming Coronation. It was the first change in the soldiers' uniform since the withdrawal of full dress and aroused a lot of interest. Three of the smartest men stationed at Didcot were selected to "model" examples of this dress and were paraded before King Edward VIII. Worn with drab gloves and either the brown leather or web belt this dress was not very inspiring and was not popular with the troops to whom it was eventually offered at a reduced price.

Part of the programme to attract recruits to the Army was to make improvements to the clothing, not only in the scale of items issued and their style and quality, but also the rates of clothing and kit allowances issued to soldiers. In 1937 a War Office Committee recommended an increase in clothing allowance.

The fighting dress of the Army came under scrutiny in this period. With the increase of mechanized forces something more suitable than service dress was required. Service dress had been the fighting dress since the end of the South African War. The new pattern was based on the ski suit and the material was strongly woven cotton called denim. It was intended to be substituted for overalls on active service. After trials in 1938 it was decided to adopt this for all troops, but in the case of the Infantry to make a similar dress in serge to provide warmth. The winter of 1938–39 showed that the denim version was not warm enough so it was finally decided to issue the serge dress to all units and to adapt the denim garments for use as fatigue dress. It was also intended to issue a coloured field service cap with this battledress in peace but mobilization came before this could be done.

A further measure of war preparation was the provision of a reserve of materials to make 8,000 officers' uniforms on mobilization, by increasing the stocks of materials from which Class One Warrant Officers' uniforms and men's greatcoats were made.

The outcome of these and other changes in clothing scales was to make the storage at Didcot inadequate and it was decided to find a site for a central depot for clothing. A preserve and pickle factory with an area of 300,000 sq. ft. at Branston near Burton-on-Trent was selected, and obtained at a cost of half a million pounds. It opened in February 1938 when clothing stocks were transferred from Didcot.

EFFECT OF THE CZECHOSLOVAK CRISIS OF 1938

The emergency action during the Munich affair provided many useful lessons concerning the readiness for war of the Ordnance Services.

The Territorial Army was embodied and large quantities of mobilization equipment, including ammunition for AA units, and camp stores were issued. The processes of issue and return of equipment showed up certain defects in the system which were then rectified. The weather was bad and the effect of field storage on equipment was seen. The package of the new 3·7-inch AA round collected and held water, which was a bad design, particularly for a round with a time fuse. In general, more attention had been given to the design of ammunition than to its packaging, which was to prove a troublesome factor throughout the war.

It was revealed that no special reserve of clothing or equipment had been created to meet possible further increases in the strength of the TA (other than ADGB). As a result authority for additional equipment was granted. The need to hold considerable war reserves of accommodation stores was proved. Before the crisis the attempts by the DOS to establish these reserves had failed for lack of financial approval.

Before this crisis Passive Air Defence had been discussed in a rather abstract way but it now became extremely "active", and much energy was expended on air raid shelters and other PAD measures and training. Mobilization schemes were overhauled and rehearsed.

Revision of the *Ordnance Manual (War)* became urgent. Previously revised in 1931 it contained none of the latest ideas which had been developed as a result of study and experiment since then. Methods and procedures suitable for Base Ordnance Depots and also for Ordnance Field Parks had been devised and tried out at Chilwell. The OFP organization had been tried out on manœuvres in Eastern Command. The latest field workshops organization had to be included. The writing of the new edition was entrusted to Colonel R. F. Johnson, who tackled the task with great energy, the new version being published just before mobilization.

RAOC ORGANIZATION IN THE WAR OFFICE

The Ordnance Directorate remained a part of the department of the Master General of Ordnance up to the formation of the Ministry of

Supply just before the war. The MGO then disappeared and the Ordnance Directorate reverted to the control of the QMG, but before this occurred some important changes were made.

Personnel administration in the RAOC had been one of the responsibilities of QMG 8 (later MGO 8), a branch of the Ordnance Directorate. In 1929 it was decided to transfer these duties to a branch under the Adjutant-General thus bringing the Corps into line with other Arms of the Service. After a trial period of a year the arrangement was confirmed, and the branch named A.G.9. The branch still incorporated MGO 8 as a sub-branch to administer the civilians employed under the DOS. In the mid-thirties there were about 7,000 of them.

The provision organization was also changed in 1929 when the offices of Directing Ordnance Officer and ADOS (Provision) were amalgamated under a DDOS (Brigadier) who became responsible to the DOS for the supervision and administration of all central Ordnance depots and for the Central Provision Office.

In this latter capacity the DDOS served several masters. In addition to the DOS for Vote 7 (Clothing) and Vote 8 (General Stores), he served the Directors of Artillery and Mechanization for Vote 9 (Warlike and MT) provision and the Director of Movement and Quartering for Vote 5 stores. He prepared Contract Demands, submitted the annual certificate concerning War Reserves and dealt direct with the Army Contracts department and the Headquarters of Commands. In February 1938 the DDOS was renamed Principle Ordnance Officer and moved to the War Office with the rank of Major-General.

THE MINISTRY OF SUPPLY

In spite of the available evidence, particularly in the development of Chilwell, recognition of the RAOC as the main supply service of the Army was gradual and in some cases reluctant. The duties allocated to the Corps were unbalanced and followed no logical pattern of organization.

The creation of the Ministry of Supply had a considerable effect on the duties assumed by the RAOC during the war. In 1936 the Warrenden Committee considered the problem of the coordination of armament supply functions. The Directorates of Artillery and Mechanization, the Royal Ordnance factories and the Army Contracts Department were variously concerned with armament supply, but there was no coordinated planning of the use of the industrial resources of the country to provide the needs of the Army in a possible future war.

A number of schemes were considered and this led to the creation of the appointment of Director-General of Munitions Production as a member of the Army Council. The man selected for the post of DGMP was an Engineer Admiral. His duties were to act in a liaison capacity between the Army and the sources of supply and to accelerate the production of items specified by the MGO. The Directorate of Army Contracts and the Royal Ordnance factories were transferred from the MGO to the DGMP, who also created two new directorates to cover "industrial planning" and "progress". The scheme had dismembered the department of the MGO and inevitably, at the end of 1937, the appointment of MGO disappeared and his department was merged with that of DGMP. A DMGO remained to administer the Army Ordnance Services and their civilian staff.

The concept of the Ministry of Supply as an agency for the supply of equipment for all three Services did not long survive the objections of the Royal Navy and RAF in respect of warships and aircraft respectively. In the end, the Ministry of Supply became an agency for the Army with certain responsibilities for common user stores.

As the inter-service aspect had disappeared it is doubtful whether any advantage was gained by turning the agency into a separate ministry, independent of and equal to (some thought superior to) the War Office, who lost control over it. This is not a factor in war, when the needs of the fighting Services are paramount, but it is interesting to reflect on what would have happened if war had not broken out for several years after the creation of the Ministry of Supply in July 1939.

As the MGOs department had disappeared, Ordnance again became a "QMG Service". The Ministry of Supply took over design, production and inspection responsibility while the DOS assumed full responsibility for the provision, storage and issue of all Ordnance stores, including MT and ammunition. The Corps gained by this rationalization of its responsibilities. The increase in the size of the task was obvious and it was urgently necessary to reorganize and build up a Directorate which had hardly changed since 1920.

Some of these changes took place before and some after the creation of the Ministry of Supply but they all occurred during the summer of 1939. A Controller of Ordnance Services was appointed to deal with broad policy and planning. Under him were a DOS and a POME, both Major-Generals. Under the DOS two new Deputies (Brigadiers) were appointed, DDOS (A) for ammunition, warlike and technical stores, and DDOS (MT) for all "A" and "B" vehicles and their spares (except that the DST still retained responsibility for MT driven by RASC drivers—an obvious duplication owing to the degree of commonality which existed). The Directorate absorbed various branches previously under the Directors of Artillery and Mechanization.

Thus the old responsibility of the POO was split up into three branches each of which carried out all activities in connection with the range of stores allotted to it. General Hoare retired in June 1939 and his place was taken by Brigadier Grylls.

Some difficulty was encountered in obtaining financial approval for what were in the circumstances very modest increases in staff. Grudging approval, when eventually received, was "subject to review in 6 months to see what reductions could be made", not a very helpful attitude in an emergency with time running out.

The Ministry of Supply had the assistance of a number of Ordnance Officers, serving and retired, with experience in the work which had been transferred from the War Department. Among them was General Hoare who became Chief Superintendent of Production Progress and Inspection in the Directorate of Stores.

The revised organization of the Ordnance Directorate was as follows:

New Branch		Responsibility	Old Branch
DOS	OS 1	Mobilization equipments and war reserves	MGO 7 (A)
DDOS(A)	OS 2	Provision, distribution and storage of:	
	OS 2A	Ammunition	MGO 1, 2 and 3
	OS 2B	Anti-gas equipment	MGO 1(c)
	OS 3	Provision, distribution and storage of:	
	OS 3A	Engineer equipment	MGO 11
	OS 3B	Signal equipment	MGO 13
	OS 4	Provision, distribution and storage of:	
	OS 4A	Coast defence armaments	MGO 1
	OS 4B	Field armaments	MGO 2
	OS 4C	Small arms	MGO 3
	OS 4D	AA equipment	MGO 14
DDOS(MT)		Provision, distribution and storage of:	
	OS 5	"A" vehicles	MGO 5
	OS 6	"B" vehicles	MGO 6
POO	OS 7	Provision, distribution and storage of:	
		Clothing	MGO 9C
		Dress questions	MGO 7B
	OS 8A	Provision, distribution and storage of general stores and equipment	MGO 9A
	OS 8B	Design and research, etc.	MGO 9B
DOS	OS 9	Civilian employees	MGO 8
POME	OS 10	Provision of machinery for workshops and laundries, inspection and repair of equipment	MGO 10
	OS 11	Mobilization of Ordnance workshop units, etc.	MGO 15

THE OFFICER SITUATION IN THE THIRTIES

The traditional way of obtaining officers for the Corps became affected by the changes occurring in the Army, chiefly as a result of mechanization.

The Corps had relied on the better pay and prospects which were offered to attract sufficient of the best type of regimental officer with a flair for Ordnance work. But the previous "differential" in pay now disappeared at the rank of Lieutenant-Colonel, and in a period of rearmament officers are naturally reluctant to leave their regiments. It was evident that the Corps was likely to face a shortage of Ordnance Officers in addition to the existing shortage of OMEs. The problem was not only to maintain the flow but also to plan for future expansion.

In 1936 the DOS, Major-General B. A. Hill, made a number of proposals to the MGO. He particularly stressed the importance of improving the career prospects for OMEs. Mechanization and development of wireless communication in the field had indicated the need for many more qualified engineers to deal with the problems of repair and recovery. This commitment had grown and changed to such an extent that it bore no resemblance to the task of the Workshop Branch immediately after the 1914–1918 war. A new approach was necessary. Although some people thought that a separate Corps manned by qualified engineers was already justified, the DOS took the realistic view that an improvement on the existing organization stood more chance of acceptance than a revolutionary proposal which might be rejected out of hand. Although war was only three years away, this was not foreseen by the Government or the public. By no means every soldier realized how imminent the danger was. For financial and other reasons there is bound to be considerable opposition to the formation of a new Corps in peace-time.

Under the existing rules OMEs were unable to attain the higher administrative[1] posts in the Corps and few had the prospect of reaching the rank of Colonel. The DOS expressed the view, based on years of study and consultation with many officers of the Corps, that the best solution was to retain the administrative side, increase the pay in the higher ranks, increase the number of higher ranks of the mechanical engineering branch, and open up the higher administrative appointments to mechanical engineers of proved administrative ability.

He asked for charge pay for all Colonels and Lieutenant-Colonels, and proposed a radical change in that where there were two Colonels or Lieutenant-Colonels in a Command, one of them was to be appointed DDOS and OC RAOC whether he was in the administrative or engineering branch. He recommended a number of specialist appointments with appropriate pay for OMEs. He asked for a new Major-General's post, Principal Ordnance Mechanical Engineer, to be created and for an OME Colonel to become ADOS of a War Office branch. He also asked for the DDOS to be upgraded and moved from Woolwich to the War Office with additional responsibilities for provision in Command Depots.

These proposals were considered in committee at the War Office, and it was admitted that some adjustment in the conditions of service was necessary by reason of the considerable increase of work and responsibilities on account of the progress of mechanization.

It was noted that, in comparison with the RASC, the RAOC had a slight advantage in higher ranks, but this was offset by denial of the opportunities for outside appointments, occasioned by the non-combatant status of the Corps.

No change of status was recommended on the grounds that RAOC officers were not brought into touch with fighting troops to any great extent nor did they obtain the opportunities to acquire the necessary experience in the command of troops of all arms. As this state of affairs,

---

[1] In this context administrative officer is synonymous with Ordnance Officer and mechanical engineer with OME. A Quartermaster Class officer—Assistant Ordnance Mechanical Engineer—was introduced in 1927 to which Warrant Officer Armament Artificers were commissioned.

in so far as it was true, was caused by the non-combatant status, it was a remarkably unsound argument for not making a change. It also apparently escaped the authorities at the War Office that something must be wrong if the Corps which supplied the Army with most of its equipment was out of touch with the troops. It seemed to have been forgotten that Ordnance Officers were transferred to the Corps from what are now called "Teeth Arms". Much was made of the "user experience and outlook" which this arrangement was deemed to provide, a point of view markedly inconsistent with the isolationism of non-combatant status.

What was the real significance of experience in the command of troops of all arms? If it was essential for officers of the supply services, then it was equally important to the RAOC and the RASC, and the situation must be rectified by changing the RAOC status to combatant. If the officers of a supply service did not need to have the knowledge for the command of troops of all arms there was no case for discriminating between one Corps and the other. These vital and obvious questions were ignored or suppressed.

If the War Office showed signs of confusion of mind in this matter it is not surprising, for the whole question of non-combatant status was extremely confused and some of the anomalies still persist.

In the first place, the expression "non-combatant" was a misnomer. The question of fighting or not fighting was not a factor. Naturally, the RAOC were expected to fight when the circumstances required it, and weapon training was carried out. That this was not merely a gesture is evident from the Bisley records.

The real point at issue was whether the RAOC was to be considered as a specialist Corps. In such a case an officer never leaves the Corps and an RAOC officer would only be eligible for Ordnance appointments. A parallel case would be that of the RAMC whose officers specialize in medical work and are limited to medical appointments.

But this concept assumes that highly qualified officers are required and that they cannot be spared from their specialist work for which a special rate of pay is justified. The alternative is to make no "cap badge" distinction, and this was the position—in theory, at any rate—in which RASC officers were placed. It should have been obvious that the task of the RAOC placed the Corps in one category or the other. There was logically no half-way house. But at this stage logic never had a chance. It was a foregone conclusion that victory would go to the "status quo".

As a result of this futile compromise, the Corps was left with the worst of both worlds—all the commitments and responsibilities which accompanied combatant status, but the restrictions and lack of authority which were associated with non-combatant status. To take but one example; RAOC officers were not eligible to take the Staff College examination nor for nomination to Staff College courses, until an isolated exception was made shortly before the war.

It is a fair assumption that the supply of equipment was not given much thought at the Staff College. As the subject was neglected the Corps responsible for this aspect of logistics suffered equally. The lessons of the last war had been forgotten and we were back in the period after the Boer War when the Adjutant-General of the day stated that: "the place for an Ordnance Officer is at his depot with his stores", rather as if he were the curator of a museum. Old ideas die hard and comfortable old ideas refuse to die at all. There are still people today who think that the RAOC function is purely storekeeping, and deny the responsibility of the Corps for ensuring that the stores reach the troops in the quantity and at the time required, and in a condition fit for use.

The proposals of the DOS were considerably watered down and suffered a further set-back when the suggested improvements in the conditions for RAOC officers were rejected on the grounds of the repercussions on the equipment branch of the RAF, an example of the fashionable technique of setting one Service against another in accordance with a levelling-down policy. Such devices are to be deplored as they have a detrimental effect on inter-Service harmony and cooperation without which success in war cannot be achieved.

However, the DOS was a determined man and pursued his objective. By now the situation was critical. There was a deficiency of 36 administrative and 96 mechanical engineering officers, which would rise to 54 and 140 respectively when the proposed increase to establishments were authorized. In consequence the comparison with the RAF equipment branch was considered not to be a valid reason for refusing to deal with the RAOC problem on its merits.

Direct entry from the RMA Woolwich or RMC Sandhurst, as was the case with the RASC, was rejected on the grounds that the non-combatant status of the RAOC would be a deterrent to the right type of cadet. The obstinate refusal to consider changing the status of the Corps is incomprehensible having regard to the facts at the time and also in view of the events which followed.

It was agreed in principle that as administrative officers were comparable technically with RE and RASC officers their conditions of service should be slightly more favourable in order to induce the combatant officer to transfer and also to attract direct entrants.

On the engineering side a plan to obtain OME cadets from selected boys at school, and give them works training before going to a university for an engineering degree, would have taken 6 years to mature.

In 1939 OMEs 5th Class in the rank of 2nd Lieutenant were commissioned. These officers were academically qualified engineers. This scheme was followed in 1939 by the introduction of Short Service OMEs with apprenticeship training but no academic qualifications.

On rates of pay there was a measure of support for giving combatant pay plus "Ordnance pay" up to Lieutenant-Colonel, a special rate for that rank, and the normal rates for technical Corps in the case of Colonels and above.

If all these proposals and decisions carried the imprint of "too little and too late" it must not be supposed that the work put into them was wasted. It served to accelerate essential measures when the war came and many of the proposals affecting the RAOC in peace have been accepted since the war.

The RAOC, REME and the Army as a whole have good reason to be grateful to General Hill for the quiet determination, unshakeable common sense and amazing patience with which he pressed the case for creating a Corps adequate to the tremendous task which it was shortly to undertake.

As it was already too late for long-term plans to meet immediate needs a number of expedients were adopted. Retired officers from other Arms were re-employed in the Corps on regimental administrative work. An increase in the establishment of WOs Class I enabled some of them to be given duties which had previously been the responsibility of junior officers. A new grade of Workshop Executive Officer (in the Quartermaster class of commission) was created. These were commissioned from Artisan Sergeant-Majors, WO Class I, and brought these types of commission for the Workshop Branch up to three:

1. Assistant Inspectors of Armourers (AIAs) ex-Armourer Section.
2. Assistant Ordnance Mechanical Engineers (AOMEs) ex-Armament Artificers Section.
3. Workshop Executive Officers (WEOs) ex-Artisan Section.

EXPANSION FOR WAR

The peace-time measures which have been described could not in themselves suffice to cope with the RAOC task in a large-scale war. Considerable increases in the officer establishment would obviously be necessary early in the war and the problem was to find and earmark suitable material.

Constructive ideas from outside the Corps were not to be expected. In any event the creation and training of many new fighting units was given, quite properly, the highest priority. The Corps had to work out its own salvation.

Colonel Williams, when consulted on this matter, pointed out the value of the best of the young men in commerce and industry as potential RAOC officers. After the Munich crisis the War Office had opened a register called the Army Officers Emergency Reserve (AOER) and Colonel Williams, writing of this new organization in terms of the needs of the Corps, said, "There is no doubt that, with the vast expansion which will take place, the efficiency of the Ordnance Services will largely depend on the standard and experience of these new officers. One of the most complicated and difficult problems is the supply and maintenance of MT and it is desirable that as many officers as possible should have experience in these spheres. . . ."

"Discussions with some of the leaders of the motor industry have, however, produced a strong view that although we shall find a certain number of good executives in some of the larger garages and distributors, the most prolific source will be the vehicle and equipment makers and factors. Production staffs will of course be wanted for munitions but the general organizing, distributing and sales staffs will be largely redundant in war. . . . This is the material for the RAOC temporary officers—men with drive, imagination, initiative and a sound training in business organization with possibly a technical background."

"Officers drawn from this source would be suitable not only for MT but for other Ordnance activities as their training is broad enough to fit them for other posts. They would of course be supplemented in certain cases by business executives from other industries such as clothing and radio."

Colonel Williams found leaders of the motor industry ready to help. They suggested the formation of a strong committee representative of the trade which would request managements to submit the names and qualifications of suitable members of their staff as candidates for the RAOC (AOER). The President of the Society of Motor Manufacturers and Traders, Mr. W. E. Rootes (later Lord Rootes), agreed to head the committee, it was given War Office recognition and a War Office official was appointed as Secretary. Names were carefully screened and only men who would make good officers were recommended.

Thus the contacts which Colonel Williams established with industry at the time of the creation of Chilwell as an MT depot paid handsome dividends. Not only was Chilwell built up as a modern organization capable of taking the tremendous loads which were shortly to be imposed, but the source was found of large reinforcements of the right type for the management of an organization which would have to expand rapidly to cope with the new commitments.

In retrospect it is difficult to see how the RAOC could have weathered the storm but for the initiative and anticipation shown by General Hill, Colonel Williams and others at this critical stage.

OTHER RANKS

In 1930, the trade group organization was divided into two branches, the Store Branch (Clerks, Storemen and Ammunition Examiners) and the Workshop Branch (Armament Artificers, Armourers and Artisans). This was logical and corresponded with the officer structure. Previously, Artisans had been with the Store Branch.

Up to the mid-thirties the Corps managed to obtain a good proportion of the number of recruits wanted whilst maintaining a high standard. This was largely because unemployment was high and the RAOC establishment small.

Rearmament and mechanization, with a corresponding policy of expansion of the Corps, coincided with the recovery of the country from the slump and a reduction in unemployment. The type of man required by the Corps was also the type who would find better paid work in industry now that prospects of employment had improved. This is a situation with which the Army is familiar, and it is doubtful whether it can ever be satisfactorily solved in peace-time without the backing of some form of conscription.

In 1936 the RAOC possessed two slight advantages. The Corps contained a number of trades which were the passport to employment when service with the Colours was over, and during service the opportunities for promotion in relation to total establishment were better than in most regiments and corps.

Nevertheless, manpower shortages continued and the situation was aggravated by emergencies such as the Italo-Abyssinian war which resulted in large reinforcements being sent to the Mediterranean, Aden and Port Sudan.

The best investment was to recruit and train boys and the facilities for boys' training were considerably extended. At the end of 1936, 200 boys were enlisted for training as fitters, units being located at Hilsea and Bramley. When Brigadier Penn, the IAOWS, inspected the trainees in April 1939 he was greatly impressed by the standard reached both at trade tests and production work. The target set for the number of boys under training had not yet been reached by the time war broke out in September 1939.

Outside the United Kingdom efforts were being made to recruit and train tradesmen. In 1938 in Malta, Lieutenant-Colonel de Wolff sponsored a scheme for raising an Artisan Section of 100 for service in Egypt. Technical training was organized by Major Tyler, the SOME, and the Devonshire Regiment assisted with military training. The all-round standard was remarkably high. The president of the Command Trade Testing Board wrote: "I would like to say that in my experience I have never viewed such consistently excellent work as that put up by the Maltese Section on this occasion." They provided valuable reinforcements in Egypt early in 1939 and were eventually absorbed into the Malta Detachment RAOC on their return.

In India a similar section of 100 fitters was raised from the Anglo-Indian section of the population. They signed on for service in any part of the world—Egypt and Palestine being the most likely places at that time. The section was effective by the early summer of 1939.

In 1938 the Auxiliary Territorial Service was formed. This Service recruited women for such duties as driver, clerk and typist, thus providing a nucleus for large numbers of reinforcements for the Ordnance Services when war came.

THE MILITIA

In 1939 the Government introduced compulsory military training for men between the ages of 20 and 24. Those in the 20 and 21 age group were to receive 6 months' initial training with a period of annual training thereafter. Of the first 170,000 men to be called up, the RAOC quota was 3,900.

This was an emergency measure requiring quick action and inevitably a good deal of improvisation. On duty the men wore the new battle dress. They were the first troops to do so. As service dress was not available and battle dress was considered unsuitable when not on duty, it was decided that a walking-out dress would be issued to the first batches to be called up. A preposterous "uniform" was devised—black beret, blue serge jacket, grey flannel trousers, collar and tie. For some reason this sartorial atrocity proved unpopular. Perhaps it was intended to encourage the troops to remain in barracks. Full peace-time scales of accommodation stores were authorized, a heavy drain on the stocks of furniture and general stores in depots.

In addition to equipping the Militia, the RAOC had to train its own intake. Urgent arrangements for their reception and accommodation were made. New hutting had been approved but where it was not yet ready tentage was used or space found in existing barrack rooms. Special instructions were issued by the War Office on the duties of the Militia during training. They were not to do fatigues or other extraneous duties for the training must be intensive and concentrated. For this purpose officers and men must be specially selected as instructors. For non-technical subjects the RAOC had the assistance of reinforcements from other arms who did invaluable work.

The Militia man was only paid 1s. 6d. per day although he was excused certain charges which the Regular soldier had to pay. He also received a hot drink in the morning and a special supper at night. The men settled down quickly to Army life, and this proved beneficial both to them and the Service when mobilization took place before the training period was over. They were already part of the unit and able to do useful work, and they had a start over the numerous volunteers and conscripts who joined the Colours as soon as war broke out.

THE TERRITORIALS

As the need for Light Aid Detachments and Divisional Workshops became apparent Divisional Ordnance Companies were renamed Divisional RAOC on an establishment which covered the stores and the workshop element. The opportunities for useful, practical training were few. Until shortly before the war the Territorial Army was a very poor relation so far as the expenditure of money and the issue of equipment were concerned. However, workshops were sometimes able to do useful repair work during annual camp with units of their division.

In the 1938 manœuvres in Eastern Command, the Divisional Ordnance units of the 2nd Cavalry, 3rd London, 44th and 54th Divisions were in camp together, a total of 26 officers and 200 other ranks. There was considerable scope for both field training and actual repair work. Some idea was gained of the nature and size of the task which the Divisional RAOC would have to face in modern war. The DOS inspected the various units which included Ordnance Field Park Sections, LADs with each artillery brigade and a composite Mobile Workshop.

In the spring of 1939 it was announced that the Territorial Army would be doubled. Intensive recruiting followed without any falling off in the standard of recruit in the RAOC. Existing units were brought up to establishment and new ones were formed.

The motor trade found many of these reinforcements and formed a number of complete units. The OC 5 OFP was Lieutenant-Colonel K. C. Johnson-Davies, Secretary of the Motor Trades Association, and the officers of his unit attended a course at the School of Instruction shortly before mobilization.

The 2nd AA Divisional Workshop at Sheffield reported themselves up to strength in May "with a high class of Sheffield craftsmen".

Sixteen divisional Ordnance units were scheduled for training at camp that year. Some were mobilized while still at camp but for others mobilization occurred before the date when they were due for their annual training.

CEREMONIAL AND REGIMENTAL

In August 1935 General Baker, the DOS, raised the matter of increasing the number of Colonels Commandant from one to three, so as to give the RAOC the same proportion to officer strength as was customary with other Corps.

This was approved and the two new Colonels Commandant appointed were General Baker from December 12th 1935 and General Hill from January 17th 1936 after taking over the appointment of DOS from General Baker. The three Colonels Commandant were then Major-General C. D. R. Watts, Major-General J. Baker, Major-General B. A. Hill.

It was a proud moment for the RAOC when soon after his accession King George VI sent a message conveying his decision to remain as Colonel-in-Chief. General Hill said, "All ranks will be aware of this high honour which will be an inspiration to us all." This gave the coronation a particular significance for the RAOC, which provided a contingent under Captain T. H. Clarke to march in the return procession from Westminster Abbey.

In 1938 the RAOC Band which had struggled on for 20 years "recognized but unauthorized" was at last officially recognized "in view of the need to encourage recruiting" and became eligible for the annual band allowance of £100 from public funds.

CHAPTER THREE

FRANCE AND NORWAY 1939–40

Mobilization

Plans for mobilization had been drawn up by AG 9 (the War Office) and RAOC Records (Hilsea), and the schemes were kept up to date and rehearsed at the stations concerned. Many RAOC units were to mobilize at Hilsea.

Mobilization was ordered on September 1st 1939. Simultaneously AG 9 received a change of plan which increased the difficulties of that small and overworked branch. Hilsea was well organized to deal with the units which had to form there. Apart from taking over a number of schools and the local lido to accommodate men the activities such as documentation, medical inspection, drawing of kit and messing were centralized at Hilsea Barracks. This part of the scheme gave little trouble.

However, exceptional difficulties occurred with the flood of volunteers who having joined up immediately war was declared and having been recruited into the RAOC, poured into Hilsea by every bus from Portsmouth station. The staff to deal with recruits was the same as that which took over the additional accommodation and consisted of one Captain and a Staff Sergeant. This was sufficient for the numbers expected. The planned figure was given with rather misleading precision as 237.

Within a fortnight about 6,000 volunteers had passed through Hilsea which severely strained the resources and resourcefulness of those who had to handle the problem. Very few of these volunteers had any military experience, so there were no ready-made NCOs to enable a proper unit organization to be created. Mobilization appointments had taken away a high proportion of the permanent staff, and those that remained were entirely occupied with the administrative problems created by this large and unforeseen intake of recruits. Military training had perforce to wait.

It was necessary to take over nearly every school in the area of the northern part of Portsmouth and Cosham. Although this solved the problem of accommodation after a fashion, the troops still had to march to Hilsea for meals, documentation, inoculation and so on. The feeling that they were under the command of the "grand old Duke of York" must have been irresistible. The NAAFI was quite unable to cope with the requirement to establish canteens at all the schools which had been requisitioned. Luckily rationing had not started and local resources met the need quite well.

AG 9 and Records quickly arranged to post large numbers of these volunteers in drafts to various units where they could be trained and where their services were badly needed. The decision to divert so many volunteers into the RAOC proved very beneficial to the Corps in the long run. Nevertheless it was a testing time for them. A proportion of those who started their military life in such uncompromising circumstances were later commissioned, remained in the RAOC as Regular officers after the war and have qualified for the highest appointments.

Thus quite early in the war, the RAOC was made up of a number of elements which had to be blended into an effective team. These were:

(a) Regular officers and other ranks.
(b) Regular officer and other rank Reservists.
(c) AOER.
(d) Militia.
(e) Territorial Army.
(f) Supplementary Reserve.
(g) Volunteers coming in after the declaration of war.
(h) ATS allocated to RAOC units.

Regular officers and other ranks were needed in field force units, at the War Office and for technical training appointments. This left depots in the United Kingdom very short of people who "knew the answers".

Regular RAOC Reservists were also required to bring field force units up to establishment. Many of the officers, when they reported for duty, were found to be medically unfit. A regular medical inspection, or even a special inspection when war appeared imminent, was not considered necessary for officers of the Regular Army Reserve. Instead the numbers with a Reserve liability were kept above the requirement to fill establishments by a figure representing the percentage unfit, worked out by an actuary. This actuarial cover gave little satisfaction to Commanding Officers who were faced with an actual shortage of officers when several failed to pass the doctor. In this case the gap was partly filled from the AOER register which provided excellent material but with no military training.

The opportunities for Regular Warrant Officers and other ranks were great. They proved to be key men in the circumstances of war and expansion of the Corps. Many were commissioned and later attained high rank. It was fortunate that, during much of the period between the wars, the RAOC was able to recruit men of high quality. Indeed this is always essential as in war, however good the new intake, a significant period must elapse before they attain even a reasonable level of efficiency, unless of course they have previously served a term of national service in the RAOC.

The significance of the AOER has already been mentioned. As the war progressed their value increased but lack of military training and of knowledge of RAOC work prevented most of them from contributing much during mobilization. This was due to lack of time. The AOER had not progressed beyond the stage of being a register of names when war was upon us.

The Territorial Army RAOC consisted mainly of organic units of TA formations and they mobilized with those formations. A few did not, and these proved useful trained reinforcements, but the numbers were small.

The Supplementary Reserve was in various categories, some of which did no military training on the grounds that their work was the same in war as in peace. This argument might have had some validity in the case of individual tradesmen, such as shoemakers attached to Infantry Battalions, had there been any means of verifying the trade standard of the men. When on mobilization the standard proved to be too low, RAOC Records were involved in a good deal of cross-posting to put matters right. Fortunately, the RAOC was not burdened with complete units of Supplementary Reservists who were given no military training. While there may, for example, be a close technical resemblance between the handling of cargo in the London Docks and in a port abroad, the circumstances in peace and war are so different as to necessitate training for war. Military training and military discipline are essential for all Reservists, whatever arm of the Service.

ISSUE OF WAR EQUIPMENT

The issue of their war equipment to units on mobilization was mainly the task of Command Depots. They were under strength because many Regulars and Reservists had left to join field force units. Working in the blackout also made things difficult when issues had to be made at night. However, these difficulties were foreseeable and the programme did not fall behind schedule.

There were significant shortages for the lower priority units, but this was inevitable as there had not been time for production to catch up with the increase in the size of the Army, nor were war reserves planned to deal with the rapid rate of expansion. The hard fact was that the country was not ready for war on such a scale.

THE BEF—FRANCE, 1939–1940

The British Army which crossed to France in 1939 differed from other armies at that time in being fully mechanized. The Army was, however, better equipped on paper than in practice. The speed of rearmament had been too slow and the modern vehicles and equipment had, except in a few cases, hardly passed beyond the stage of initial issues. There was very little in reserve and the supply of spares had lagged far behind that of complete equipments. Production was not anything like up to war-time tempo and at this time the means hardly existed to maintain the few Divisions which could be immediately mobilized, still less to equip the large force which our allies considered we should be able to form at an early date.

The plan for maintaining the BEF was bedevilled by an excessive esti-mate of enemy resources for air attack, and by security measures which denied essential information to those who could not properly do their work without it.

The maintenance project and first key plan had not been shown to the DOS BEF designate nor to any of his senior officers before mobilization, so no action or planning could be undertaken in advance. Only the wes-tern ports were used initially which made an unnecessarily long L of C and caused a corresponding delay in meeting demands for stores held in the BOD. Movement was uncoordinated so that personnel disembarked at one port, vehicles at another and stores were shipped unaccompanied. Many of these mistakes would have been avoided if there had been RAOC representation at the planning stage, as occurred later in the war.

Although, to allow for expansion, the base was planned on a scale larger than was necessary for the initial force, the storage and workshops accommodation had been seriously underestimated. The BOD and BOW were located in Nantes. At that time the Vehicle Depot was part of the BOD. A separate organization emerged much later. The storage accom-modation, which had been selected as a result of a reconnaissance in September 1938, had not been earmarked and was found to be occupied by the French Army and by Civil Ministries transferred from north-east France. Billets were also a problem as the area was crowded with people who had moved from the potential war zone. Requests for accommoda-tion had to be submitted through the local French authorities who, though friendly, invariably gave priority to the French Army and local civilian requirements.

Examples of locations allotted were a disused part of a bottle factory strewn with broken glass, a tram depot which was later reclaimed as it was needed for the repair of trams, and a site which was the subject of a claim by the owner's lawyers concerning the RAOC "right to occupy". Depot equipment was scarce and some of it did not appear for a long time, having been shipped separately. Local purchase provided a partial solution to the difficulty.

The Base Workshop situation was no better. Satisfactory sites could not be obtained and by September 14th when the main body of 2 BOW arrived in Nantes only a garage of about 5,000 sq. ft. had been obtained. On September 17th the QMG was told: "It is not necessary for me to point out how much this completely mechanized force depends upon the efficiency of its repair organization, and my estimate of our immediate minimum requirement for the Base Ordnance Workshop is 135,000 sq. ft."

"Within 6 months in any event, and much earlier if operations begin, this figure will require to be increased three or four times. . . . In the meantime there is a grave risk of a breakdown in the Ordnance Repair Organization. . . . To overcome this risk I suggest the French authorities be requested to make available for 6 months two complete engineering works, to be approved by me, of a total area not less than half a million square feet."

This blunt statement had some effect and pressure was brought to bear with the result that by October 4th the French had made available 6 buildings with a total floor space of 250,000 sq. ft.

The initial plan for ammunition involved the establishment of 2 BADs, one in the Forêt de Gavre near Nantes and the other at Plouaret east of Brest. Both sites were faulty, the areas being damp and the roads insufficient and not capable of taking heavy traffic without breaking up.

The policy was to hold ammunition in wooded areas for concealment but, apart from the fire risk, this policy tended to override the factors of accessibility and the rapid movement of large tonnages which should be paramount considerations. As will be seen, useful lessons were learnt in France concerning the siting of ammunition depots both in the United Kingdom and theatres of operations. Plouaret was not a wooded area and it was intended to be temporary pending the construction of a depot in the Forêt de Rennes. However it remained throughout the campaign.

The Ordnance Directorate had its own problems. Of the 66 other ranks 44 were either Reservists or Militia. They did not at this stage know the basic administrative work such as documentation and reporting of arrivals, reinforcement demands, medical inspections, organization of billets, general duties and elementary welfare. The burden initially had to be borne by the Regulars to the detriment of their Ordnance duties.

At Le Mans, where the Directorate was first established, there was inadequate office accommodation, the unaccompanied stationery and office furniture failed to arrive and the billets and feeding arrangements were unsatisfactory.

Apart from these domestic difficulties the DOS was immediately faced with complaints about shortage of stores. At this stage accommodation stores caused most trouble, for which to a large extent local purchase provided the remedy. However, the urge to send units out as quickly as possible, so as to maintain or even improve on the promised rate of build-up of the BEF, caused many of them to arrive with serious deficiencies in their war equipment. They were allowed to think that stores would be available "on the other side", despite the fact that even modest levels of maintenance stocks had not yet been reached, let alone stocks adequate to fill gaps in unit equipments.

It is a common fallacy to suppose that units can be completely equipped or largely re-equipped from maintenance stocks. Such an idea is only valid when the unit is going to a theatre in which a large base has already been established, with massive stocks and reserves of equipment, a situation which never has applied and never will apply to a British Army at the beginning of any large-scale war.

THE WINTER PERIOD

The period between the beginning of October 1939[1] and May 10th 1940 has often been described as the "Phoney War". The reason for this is well summarized in the *Official History of the War in France and Flanders, 1939–40.* "The six months which followed are unique in the history of modern warfare. Germany had attacked Poland, and because of this Britain and France had declared war on Germany. It was a brave act, for neither country was equipped for such a fight, and other free nations applauded as the Allies mobilized their forces and arranged them for a battle on the French frontier. And then we waited. We waited while Germany conquered Poland and divided the spoils with Russia. We waited while Germany moved her armies to the west and disposed them to attack us. We waited, then, for Hitler to choose the time and place for his assault. And while we waited, the applause of a world which could not know how ill-prepared we were changed into wonder, as Germany was allowed to mass her armies without interference on the western frontiers while the Allies prepared to defend themselves."

A government dedicated to appeasement, which by its weakness had encouraged the warlike ambitions of the dictators, was still in office though not effectively in power. The Opposition, hypnotised by the Spanish Civil War and by ideological theories associated with but in fact irrelevant to that extremely parochial contest, would have no dealings with the Government.

To most people in the Army it seemed that effective political leadership was absent at this critical period, and without it the country could not be expected readily and immediately to make the sacrifices necessary for the radical change from a peace to a war economy. In relation to the emergency the production of equipment for the Army was far too sluggish.

The situation in the BEF was very different. From the Commander-in-Chief downwards it was realized that sustained and exceptional efforts were necessary if the BEF was to play as important a part in this war as the Old Contemptibles had in 1914. Training and work on the defences continued at high pressure. Each unit settled into an efficient smooth-

[1] By September 27th, the following had been shipped to France:

152,031 Army personnel	36,000 tons of ammunition
9,392 Air Force personnel	25,000 tons of motor spirit
21,424 Army vehicles	60,000 tons of frozen meat
2,470 Air Force vehicles	

working machine. Officers and men found to be below standard were replaced. Regrouping of units took place so as to give a balanced distribution of experience and up-to-date knowledge throughout the force.

The first contingent of the BEF, consisting of two Corps of two Divisions each, moved up to their positions on the Belgian frontier. The BEF was under French command and the position of our troops in a linear defence on the frontier was decided by GQG (Grand Quartier Générale).

The British Army was not on the left flank—nearest to the United Kingdom—but had French troops on either side. There was no Army Headquarters although it was planned to introduce one when the number of Divisions in France was sufficient to justify it. This plan had not been put into effect when the Germans attacked on May 10th 1940 and so for the whole campaign GHQ had to function in a dual role. It is impossible in modern war for one man effectively to command an Army in battle and at the same time deal with the complex political and logistic problems from which a GHQ cannot escape. For the same reason one headquarters cannot be located and organized to do both tasks effectively.

During the winter period GHQ was located in the Arras area, widely dispersed in various villages and tending to develop into a number of water-tight compartments, out of touch with each other. The Ordnance Directorate was in the small village of Barly not far from the village of Noyelle Vion, which housed the associated Staff branch (Q Maintenance). The "Q" branch dealing with Ordnance Stores and Ammunition was manned mainly by RAOC officers. This injected into the Staff branches some degree of experience of the problems of the supply and repair of equipment in war, and it repeated an arrangement adopted in France in 1917,[1] but it contained the seeds of duplication of work between the Staff and Services and inflation of the numbers in headquarter branches.

The RAOC representation at formation headquarters allowed for separation of the stores and workshop functions. At divisional headquarters there was a DADOS and a SOME. At Corps Headquarters an ADOS and a COME. At GHQ a DOS and a POME. At this time the senior of the two representatives in a division was a Lieutenant-Colonel and in a corps a Colonel. The arrangement was workable in peace but in war, when moves were frequent, it tended to cause confusion, misunderstanding and perhaps friction, and was soon discarded.

There were no divisional Ordnance field parks. OFPs were on a scale of 1 per corps, organized into 1 reserve section, 1 corps troops section, and 1 section for each division. The OFPs were fully mobile and the

---

[1] For an account of the arrangements in the First World War see Forbes, Vol 3, pages 59–60. By a coincidence one of the Q (Maint) staff in 1939/40 was the son of the first Ordnance holder of a similar appointment in the BEF 1914–19.

various sections could operate independently, though centralized control was clearly considered to be the normal arrangement.

Army Field workshops were on a scale of 1 per division. In addition there were GHQ workshops and 2 AA Brigade workshops. Formation workshops did not have a stores section but drew their stores from the associated ordnance field park.

None of these units existed in the Regular Army in peace. Some were Territorial Army units which had to be made up to war establishment on mobilization, others had to be created from Regulars, Reservists, Militia and volunteers who were recruited early in the war. The "phoney war" period was a godsend to these units as it gave them the opportunity to develop their military, administrative and technical efficiency in field conditions before the shooting war started. The opportunity was not wasted.

With the Base so far from the GHQ and Corps areas, and Advanced Depots not yet established, the Supply and Ammunition Railheads acquired great significance. These were staffed by detachments sent out from BODs and BADs, not a sound arrangement.

In the case of Ordnance Stores the official plan was that, after sorting at railhead, they would be loaded on the appropriate vehicles of the RASC Supply Company and would thus find their way with the rations to the troops. Needless to say stores went astray, and it was soon realized that the DADOS must have allocated to him a certain number of RASC lorries to ensure the prompt and correct issue of Ordnance stores to the units of his formation.

The problem was not a new one. Replenishment of Ordnance stores nearly broke down in 1914 because the recommendations of Ordnance Officers had been ignored, but these recommendations were then adopted "as a result of the experience of the war".[1] After the war the lesson was quickly forgotten and it took another war to learn it again.

This example is mentioned at some length because it illustrates the effect of the parochialism which was a feature of RAOC existence between the wars, and which the Corps had gradually come to accept. The non-combatant status, denial of entry to the Staff College, lack of representation or consultation in administrative planning for war, separation of training from the DMT—all these things led to a general neglect and ignorance in the Army as a whole of essential matters connected with the supply of equipment to an army in the field.

By contrast the RASC had introduced what they called "divisionalization", that is their organization was closely related to the current structure of field formations. By subordinating their training organization to the DMT they kept pace with the latest doctrines and could influence logistic concepts. Although they suffered, like everyone else, from financial stringency and manpower limitations, they had already obtained

[1] See Forbes, Vol. 3, pages 28–30.

agreement for the means necessary to achieve their task in the field. Therefore, when restrictions were lifted, they were able to move smoothly into an organization which was fully accepted and generally understood.

THE BASE AND LINES OF COMMUNICATION

The initial plan provided for the following installations.

One Base Ordnance Depot.
One Advanced Ordnance Depot.
Two Base Ammunition Depots.
One Base Ordnance Workshop.
One Advanced Ordnance Workshop.
Four Port Workshop Detachments.

Stores Depots. The early difficulties caused by inadequate accommodation, separately shipped and insufficient depot equipment, and security measures which bewildered our own troops without deceiving the enemy, have already been mentioned. If fighting had started at once it is probable that a breakdown in the supply of equipment would have occurred. As it was there was time to sort out some of the initial errors, but others persisted.

By the end of October the BOD at Nantes had acquired 566,000 sq. ft. of covered accommodation, but this was in 28 buildings and store tents which reduced the effective storage area. Many of the buildings were in a bad state and lacked proper facilities for transport. The congestion became so acute that for a time barges had to be used for storage purposes. Consignments from England had to be temporarily curtailed.

Apart from the initial requirement for accommodation not being met it proved to be an underestimate partly because it was not based on the indifferent, scattered accommodation which is often all that can be obtained in war, and partly because of recent increases in the commitment to hold bulky anti-gas reserves particularly of clothing, to replace that which might be contaminated. The war establishment of the depot was inadequate but the immediate solution was to absorb most of the AOD as it was decided not to establish one until later.

For some time the manpower of the unit was not fully effective because of the high proportion of untrained men on the strength. To maintain the force even though there was no fighting kept them at full stretch while the depot was being built up.

Even the Regulars and Regular Army Reservists were in many cases unfamiliar with the new depot procedure. This had been developed from the system adopted at Chilwell, but it was too recent an innovation to allow for a proper study of it to be made throughout the Corps by the time war broke out. Initially, it was something of a mystery to all except those in the MT sub-depot, who had been trained at Chilwell.

These "growing pains" contributed to delays in meeting unit demands,

4+   81

though there were other factors such as the time taken for an indent to reach the depot from the forward areas. Excessive security measures played their part. It was surprisingly difficult to make some Staff Officers realize that if units were to receive their Ordnance stores it was necessary for Ordnance depots to have a force order of battle, location lists and prompt notification of changes thereto. The system of serial numbers, code addresses and other markings was so complicated that to begin with Movement Control were daily refusing railway wagons labelled correctly according to the instructions held by the BOD. As late as mid-December 1939 the AOD, which had by then been established, could not issue some important signal stores because the depot was not allowed a location list.

Nevertheless the will and ability were not lacking progressively to overcome the various obstacles to technical efficiency. But the depot could not issue stores which did not exist and as war production lagged far behind the needs of the time critical deficiencies of equipment were revealed. For many items the level of 3 months' stock in the theatre could not be attained and, despite the absence of active operations, day-to-day requirements could not be met.

Right up to February 1939 the Cabinet was firm in its decision that no part even of the Regular Army should be equipped on the scale necessary for war against a first-class power.[1] A reversal of this decision was not likely to have any significant effect in peace-time in so short a period as 7 months.

Once war had begun it was naturally unwise to advertise to the enemy our critical shortage of equipment. But this also meant that most people in the United Kingdom and units in the BEF were in the dark. The rate of war production was not appropriate to the emergency because too few people, including those in industry, recognized that a real emergency existed. It was natural that units in the BEF unable to obtain stores to which they were entitled, and unaware of the general supply situation, should assume that they were victims of inefficiency or even deliberate obstruction on the part of the RAOC.

The most significant deficiencies were in warlike and technical stores. At the beginning of December 1939 there were only 70 infantry tanks out of a requirement of 204 and it was expected that by the end of February there would be only about 130 out of a requirement of 461. Other serious deficiencies were in anti-tank guns, light anti-aircraft guns, vehicles and signal stores. Many of these equipments were incomplete and as spares production lagged behind that of equipments it was sometimes necessary to resort to "cannibalization" of some equipments to make the remainder battle-worthy. Modern field and medium artillery (25 pounder, 4·5-inch gun and 5·5-inch howitzers) was also scarce and the

---

[1] See Mr. Hore Belisha's speech on the Army Estimates March 8th 1939. *House of Commons Debates*, Vol. 344, cols. 2161 ff.

Army had to go into battle with obsolete guns such as the 18 pounder, 4·5-inch howitzer (of 1914–18 vintage) and 6-inch howitzer.[1]

OPENING OF THE AOD AND 2 BOD

At the end of October it was decided to open an advanced ordnance depot. Its purpose was to hold forward reserves of selected stores of operational importance not included in the field park scalings. It was also to hold reserves of anti-gas stores, reserves to replace contaminated clothing and stores required by the advanced ordnance workshop. Except in its role as a sort of stores section for the AOW it was not planned as a link in the supply chain for normal maintenance which still operated from the BOD.

The sites selected were in the St Pol–Doullens–Arras area, and the depot consisted of scattered buildings in the towns and villages throughout that area. Control was very difficult and the 150,000 sq. ft. of this type of accommodation proved inadequate for the reserves which increased with the size of the force.

It was clear that a second BOD would be needed, and this was originally to be in the Rennes area. However, the Navy had effectively controlled the Channel and it was obviously sound to make more use of the Channel ports. It was therefore decided to locate 2 BOD in the Le Havre peninsula. The French authorities, true to form, offered an area spread over about 600 square miles, centred on Yvetot and consisting of isolated barns and similar unsuitable buildings.

Fortunately, the COO of 2 BOD (Colonel W. W. Richards) with characteristically swift initiative had by personal contact with the President of the Compagnie Générale Transatlantique (CGT) secured some of the finest storage accommodation in Le Havre, including the Gare Maritime of the CGT and other warehouses outside the dock area totalling more than one million square feet.

Thus the difficulties of 1 BOD were not repeated, and 2 BOD being much nearer the forward areas was in a better position to give good service to the fighting formations whose indents they received. The congestion at 1 BOD was eased by the construction of a new sub-depot at Savenay, 20 miles to the north-west.

The decision on the distribution of the load between 1 and 2 BODs was based on the action necessary to give the greatest immediate relief to the overworked unit at Nantes and not on an optimum long-term plan. It was also necessary, in view of the shortages of warlike and technical stores, to concentrate them in one depot, and as they were already at 1 BOD it was desirable that they should remain there despite the long haul from Nantes.

---

[1] The French were even worse off. Most of their field artillery units were armed with the 75-mm. (the famous Seventy-Five), which was the finest gun of its day, but that was the year 1898.

PROVISION

With the creation of two BODs the arrangements for provision had to be decided. If each BOD carried out its own provision independently there was neither coordination nor stock control. The acute shortages in a high proportion of the range of Ordance stores held in the BEF made some form of stock control essential. This could be done by concentrating each group of stores in one depot only or by setting up a central provision office. Central provision involves additional records and manpower and because of this the first of the alternatives was adopted. The campaign did not last long enough for the arrangement to be fully tested.

SIGNAL STORES

The supply of signal stores to the BEF caused trouble throughout the campaign. Production difficulties were the main cause of shortages, but the commitment created by the long L of C had been underestimated. The War Office was receiving uncoordinated demands from Royal Signals and RAOC.

In November 1939 the QMG War Office, during a visit to the BEF, ordered that all demands on the War Office for signal stores would be through Ordnance channels. It was also arranged that the SO in C would compile each quarter an estimate of the next quarter's requirements, notifying revisions monthly. In this way an up-to-date picture would be available to assist production progressing and priorities. At the same time, the storage and control of the SO in C's Reserve was changed. It had been held at the BOD, earmarked on the account but not physically. This did not give the SO in C the direct control he required and to meet his needs the Reserve was transferred to the AOD at Arras.

MT SPARES

The supply of MT spares became precarious at an early date. There was, of course, no previous experience of wastage rates for MT spares in a fully mechanized army in field conditions. Experienced Regular units who had been mechanized for some years had a high standard of driving, maintenance and road discipline, but most units in the BEF in the early months of the campaign had to learn these things the hard way. Wastage rates were astronomical. The position was aggravated by the existence of a high proportion of vehicles which were non-standard, impressed types comprising a very wide range of makes, for which it had been impossible on mobilization to prepare a census, a supply of spare parts lists or an initial maintenance stock of spare parts.

The force reserve of "B" vehicles was initially regarded as a repair pool, but it was insufficient for that purpose and the War Office intimated that the vehicle reserve in England would not be able to meet heavy wastage rates in the BEF.

Care and strict economy were necessary until the vehicle supply position should improve and also that of spares for the normal range of Army vehicles. Spares supply for impressed vehicles was not likely to improve and the large number of outstanding indents which had accumulated in 1 BOD by April 1940 was in the main for that class of vehicle.

The necessary steps were taken during the winter, while no fighting was taking place. A proportion of unit vehicles was withdrawn to form a local reserve. Gradually the position improved and by the end of April 1940 there were sufficient reserve vehicles to create a chain of vehicle parks at intervals of about 100 miles along the L of C, thus providing a system for the replacement of battle and other casualties. In the event the course of the campaign was such that the scheme was never tested.

FAULTY PRODUCTION

One of the effects of the attempts to speed up production was that technical equipment reached units in defective or unserviceable condition. The causes were faults in manufacture and inadequate inspection before acceptance into the Service. All cases were represented to the Ministry of Supply through the War Office but the additional precaution was taken of a 100% inspection of all stocks at the Base and of new receipts.

ESTABLISHMENTS

It was clear from the experience of BODs up to the end of 1939 that changes were required in the establishment and organization. A committee was formed which included the COOs and Senior Provision Officers of both BODs.

The main recommendations were that:

1. The various detachments included in the BOD establishment such as railhead, regulating station, port and HQ L of C area staff, be provided in separate war establishments independent of the BOD.

2. A separate war establishment be provided for each sub-depot which should be self-contained administratively, based on supplying a force of 6 Divisions with increments to allow for an increase in the force by stages. This was in fact a recommendation for the creation of specialist companies trained to deal with particular types of store according to the sub-depot holding.

The recommendations were accepted and proved of great value in future operations.

AMMUNITION

The original plan for the supply of ammunition required 45 days' stock in the BADs. The planned capacity of a BAD was 21,000 tons and initially two of these depots were required.

As the L of C was such a long one it would have been normal to form one or more advanced ammunition depots, but the French objected to these depots being located north of the River Somme and instead a mobile reserve was established consisting of standard trains called Ammunition Sections En Cas Mobile, or ASE for short. Each train held one day's supply for a Corps based on the weapon strength of the Corps and the authorized wastage rates.[1] Some of these trains were held near St. Pol within 12 hours of Ammunition Railhead, others in the Rennes–Vitre area within 36 hours of Ammunition Railhead. Each Corps had an ARH at which stocks of ammunition were dumped, these dumps being in the charge of an RAOC Railhead Detachment found from BAD Establishments.

The ARH for 1 Corps was at Ecoust, 10 miles south-east of Arras. That for 2 Corps was at Aubigny, 8 miles north-west of Arras.

On the assumption that the BEF would hold a prepared defensive position on the frontier, and allowing for the replenishment time from the Base, the plan was to hold 9 days' stock at ARH and on rail, made up as follows:

1 Corps	5 days at ARH	
	2 days on rail within 12 hours of ARH	
	2 days on rail within 36 hours of ARH	
2 Corps	7 days at ARH	
	2 days on rail within 36 hours of ARH	

In due course the plan was expanded and also modified.

The expansion followed the increase in the size of the BEF. When a third Corps was formed, shortly before the German attack, additional ASEs were formed to support it. In the same way the number of BADs was increased so as to hold the additional tonnage for the larger force.

Modification followed the change of plan whereby in certain circumstances the French and British Armies would advance into Belgium to meet a German invasion of that country. The advance to the River Dyle (the "D" plan) did in fact take place. The railhead stocks in France remained and ASEs were to be sent forward to stock up the new ARHs in Belgium. This modification amounted to the employment of the ARHs in France as small advanced ammunition depots.

The weakness of the plan was in its lack of flexibility. ASEs were loaded with balanced stocks of ammunition on the assumption that all natures would be expended at an even rate. In battle this never happens so that shortages of some natures quickly occur while others are not wanted. Replenishment by standard trains is no good in these circumstances. Replenishment of actual wastage is too slow when only stocks

---

[1] These were: 25 pr: 35 rpg a day; 60 pr: 30 rpg a day; 6-inch howitzer: 28 rpg a day; 3-inch (20 cwt): 50 rpg a day; 40-mm AA: 40 rpg a day; 2-pr anti-tank: 5 rpg a day; 3-inch mortar: 13 rpg a day; 2-inch mortar: 10 rpg a day; SAA: 6 million a Division each month; Anti-tank mines: 1,500 a Division each month.

in the Base can be used and the Base is at a great distance from the front. In fact, the ARHs in France were the means to create some degree of flexibility and served this purpose for a short time.

Another disadvantage of the ASE was that it was not really a standard train, because the armament of formations was not standard. A remarkable variety of weapons existed and the types and quantities held in each Corps changed constantly.[1] This meant that the composition of each ASE had to be changed continually, no easy matter when it was "stabled" many miles from the depot which had to issue the new ammunition and take back the surplus. Of course, an ASE for 1 Corps was of little use to 2 Corps and vice versa.

Towards the end of 1939 the War Office requested the BEF to increase the stock levels in BADs from 45 days to 6 months. This was a tall order in view of the fact that the BEF was being steadily built up. Although the reason for the requirement was congestion in the United Kingdom resulting from increased production without corresponding expenditure, the ammunition position was not good. Production was badly out of balance chiefly because many new natures of ammunition had not yet passed or had only recently passed the design stage. Among other things there was a serious shortage of light anti-aircraft ammunition, there was no 2-inch mortar HE, the 2 pounder anti-tank gun had only the unfilled HE armour-piercing shell instead of the more effective design of a solid AP shot which had superseded it in 1938 (some of this AP shot arrived at Dunkirk at the very end of the campaign). AP ammunition for field guns was very scarce.

The fact is that armament production and production capacity had been allowed to fall to a very low level, and factory capacity for ammunition cannot be created quickly. Had prolonged fighting followed the German invasion of Belgium in May 1940, it is more than likely that an ammunition crisis similar to that in 1915 would have occurred.

As early as October 1939 it was decided to increase the number of BADs to four and the capacity of each to 34,000 tons.

By May 1940 the ammunition storage in the Base was as follows:

1 BAD near Nantes (Forêt de Gavre).

A new BAD under construction and partly stocked up in the same area. The unit only arrived in April 1940 and was named 6 BAD.

2 BAD at Plouaret.

3 BAD at Saint Saens north of Rouen, the most forward of the depots.

---

[1] To take an example, the up-to-date weapon for the field artillery was the 25-pounder gun/howitzer. This replaced both the 18-pounder gun and the 4·5-inch howitzer. Unfortunately, production of the 25 pounder and its ammunition was still in the early stages and many units still had the older weapons. Some units had 25/18 pounder, i.e. a 25-pounder Ordnance on an 18-pounder carriage. Cross-posting of units, Brigades or Divisions between Corps was common at this stage, and each time this happened, the ammunition backing at ARHs and ASEs had to be adjusted.

4 BAD at Rennes.

22 BAD, a small rail-served depot near St. Malo to hold ammunition shipped through that port and increase the overall storage capacity in the theatre.

21 BAD near Fécamp to hold reserves of chemical ammunition in case the enemy resorted to chemical warfare. This was originally known as 5 BAD.

In January 1940 an ADOS (Ammunition) was appointed with his headquarters at Le Mans. His function was to supervise the development and operation of the ammunition depots, to exercise control over the stock levels in each and to control the issue of ammunition to meet the operational and training requirements of the Army and the RAF. Le Mans was a focal point on the L of C with good communications both to GHQ and to the various ammunition depots.

As the operational plan was based on the issue of standard trains (ASEs) it was important that the stocks in the large BADs should be kept in balance so that each depot could issue the largest possible number of standard trains. This would normally be done by ordering ammunition from the United Kingdom to adjust the stock levels of each nature. However, as time went on, there were serious deficiencies of some natures in the shipments to France and stock levels had to be adjusted by moving ammunition between BADs. This was strongly opposed by Q (Movements) at GHQ on the grounds that it was "against the principles of movement". It is hard to see what principle was at stake but it had to be sacrificed to operational necessity.

Additional commitments were the supply of ammunition to the Air Component of the BEF, the Advanced Air Striking Force (AASF) and the Brigade (later Division) on the Saar Front. The Air Component required small quantities of ammunition to be sent to their airfields, which were of course not as a rule conveniently placed for supply through the Corps ARHs. The ammunition was usually sent with a pack train to the nearest Supply Railhead. AASF requirements had to go to Mont Notre Dame near Rheims. A small ammunition depot was formed in the Forêt la Tracoue to store a forward reserve of Army and RAF ammunition. Neither side was active on the Saar front, so that ammunition supply presented no serious problems. When active operations started 51 Division was quickly moved to the River Somme and supply to the Saar front ceased.

The concept of a BAD as a rail-served depot derived from the experience of the 1914–1918 war, when road transport was limited, and from the construction of Central Ammunition Depots in the United Kingdom. Although the last BAD to be formed in the BEF was rail-served the experience of the campaign led to the concept of a road-served depot with a local railhead as the normal ammunition depot in the field and as a wartime expedient in the United Kingdom.

The difficulties of the RAOC, caused by massive dilution of experienced staff with those who initially had neither military nor technical knowledge, has already been mentioned. The problem was most acute in the case of RAOC ammunition units in the BEF.

The burden bore heavily on the handful of technical staff with the units. That the difficulties were overcome was due mainly to the work of the two officers who occupied the appointment of ADOS (Ammunition) at Le Mans.

Lieutenant-Colonel Temple Morris was, at the beginning of the campaign, a DAQMG dealing with ammunition at GHQ. His technical knowledge and his experience of ammunition were great (he had been in charge of the School at Bramley) and were only equalled by his drive and enthusiasm. His influence over the organization and operation of BADs in the first 4 months of the war enabled him to control their development effectively. He never spared himself and as a result of this, the severe winter and the effect of having been gassed in the First World War he became seriously ill and was invalided to the United Kingdom in March 1940.

His successor, Lieutenant-Colonel Lonsdale, was not in the same sense an ammunition specialist, but he had a degree of common sense amounting to genius. More than anyone else he was to guide the development of the RAOC ammunition organization for the rest of the war and his influence remains to this day.

WORKSHOP SERVICES

It was realized that workshop services would be needed immediately on arrival of the BEF in France. The headquarters and advanced section of the AOW were accordingly sent with the first RAOC contingent to act as the nucleus of a BOW until a complete BOW could be installed. Suitable accommodation in a large garage had already been allotted, and by September 19th the machinery was installed and working.

In order to operate fully this unit needed an ordnance workshop company, but as the allotted company did not embark until a fortnight later, a company was loaned from 2 BOW which had arrived but was not yet established. The difficulties of accommodation for the BOW have already been mentioned. When these had been overcome the AOW moved to the Arras area late in October 1939. At first the administrative planning at GHQ excluded the establishment of installations in the Arras area, but the POME continued to reconnoitre suitable sites and was able to make his point that, with such a long L of C, all possible repair must be undertaken in the forward areas.

Four army field workshops (AFWs) were sent to France at the beginning of the campaign. Others followed as further divisions arrived. It was fortunate that there were no active operations shortly after the force landed, as the units were incompletely organized, and untrained. A large number of the officers and at least 80 per cent of the other ranks belonged to the Supplementary Reserve, many of whom put on uniform for the first time when they mobilized. Willing though they were, they knew nothing of the Army and were entirely lacking in military training, including the use of their weapons.

No. 1 Army Field Workshop arrived in France ahead of the 1st Corps to organize a breakdown service on the roads from the ports to the assembly area. The location was at Chateaubriant on the St. Nazaire–Laval route. It was intended that this duty should be undertaken by an AFW from 2 Corps, when 1 Corps had reached the assembly area, but it was later allocated to the L of C recovery sections of the GHQ troops workshop.

Generally speaking it was found that these AFWs were too large for the conditions in North-West Europe. They took up a great deal of road space when on the march, and it was only with difficulty that accommodation could be found for their installations, especially the main shop. The consequence was that the main shops had either to be placed at inconvenient sites, or divided into two locations.

It was a moot point whether repair sections should be sent forward or retained with the main shop, and it was left to the OC to settle, in consultation with the staff of the Division which the workshop served. When the sections remained in the main shop, they were kept as separate entities, so that they could be despatched forward quickly.

Normally, the technical control of the recovery sections remained with the OC AFW, and the Senior Ordnance Mechanical Engineer (SOME) of the Division possessed no control over their work, save when they were specifically formed into a divisional workshop.

The organization of GHQ Troops Workshop RAOC consisted of a main workshop, whose function was to serve units in GHQ area; a main recovery section capable of acting as a workshop in addition to carrying out light recovery work primarily for the artillery units of GHQ troops, and 6 L of C recovery sections. These sections were equipped for heavy recovery work and had no workshop machinery. They were intended to work between AFWs, GHQ troops workshop and railhead.

The main shop and four recovery sections arrived in France at the end of September 1939. To meet the frequent demands for recovery work on the routes from the ports to the assembly area, Nos. 1, 2 and 3 L of C recovery sections were sent, as soon as they landed, to Domfront, Rennes and Craon (40 miles SE of Rennes), respectively. It was intended that these three sections should rejoin their parent workshop about 14 days later, but this they never did, as their retention indefinitely on recovery work in the L of C area proved to be necessary.

The main shop and 4 L of C recovery section were located at Saulty 11 miles WSW of Arras. Here they were joined in October by the main recovery section, and by 5 and 6 L of C recovery sections, on arrival

90

from England. No. 2 L of C recovery section moved to Poix, 14 miles SW of Amiens in October for recovery work in the rear of GHQ area.

GHQ troops were spread over a wide area which necessitated the placing of a detachment of the main recovery section at Lumbres in October for the maintenance of searchlights, to act as a workshop section for 2 AA Brigade Workshop and for local repairs.

The two AA Brigade workshops were efficient units equipped to do all second line repair to the equipment of an AA Brigade, but they suffered from the handicap that circumstances necessitated their dispersion in detachments over a wide area. The most noticeable instance was 2 AA Brigade Workshop, with HQ and one section near Doullens and one section at Epernay 105 miles distant.

The four port workshop detachments sent to France at the beginning gave invaluable service. Their primary duty was to assist in the speedy disembarkation of MT vehicles and to effect any repairs necessary to enable them to be cleared from the dock area. These units were stationed at Nantes, Brest, Cherbourg and St. Nazaire.

They found much needless damage caused by the neglect of units to carry out orders regarding the preparation of vehicles and the method of loading.

The principal points brought to notice were that:
1. Vehicles had not been properly stowed in the holds resulting in damage to mudguards, radiators, headlamps and track rods.
2. Vehicles had been manœuvred into holds by means of the engine starter motors. This caused delay and congestion in the docks, while the batteries were being recharged.
3. Ignition keys were not attached to the panel or steering column. In the case of Yale type locks, this necessitated modification to the wiring system before the engines could be started.
4. Petrol cans, marked for petrol, were filled with diesel fuel or water in England. These were poured into vehicle fuel tanks in error, and the complete fuel system had then to be dismantled.

ARMOURED FORMATIONS

One of the most significant, and as it proved decisive, differences between the Germany Army and the Allies was in respect of Armoured Formations. These were the basis of the *blitzkrieg* defeat of Poland, but both Britain and France were woefully deficient of the means to fight a war of this kind. From the British point of view the production of armoured fighting vehicles after the First World War can only be described as pathetic. There was no lack of ideas so far as design was concerned but all these ideas died at the production stage. In France some tanks had been produced but resources were dissipated and tactical ideas had not progressed after 1918 when the tank was only used in support of infantry.

The BEF was to include one Armoured Division and more were anxiously awaited. It was realized that Armoured Divisions posed a supply and repair problem of their own and plans were made accordingly. In February 1940, an Ordnance Officer was attached to GHQ AFV branch for liaison duty on matters affecting the supply of AFV stores and selected RAOC officers and other ranks were sent on courses of instruction in stores special to AFV. In the same month the French Government agreed to allot to the BEF a considerable area in the region of Pacy-sur-Eure, some 35 miles SSE of Rouen, for the formation of a tank-training area and for the construction of Base AFV installations comprising storehouses and workshops.

Both short-term and long-term plans were considered, and the main decisions reached by April 1940 were that a BOD and a BOW should be constructed in the AFV Base area, the BOW to comprise an area of 600,000 sq. ft., the BOD to be large enough to supply 10 Armoured Divisions and to expand to 12 Divisions. Detailed locations were settled and provided for the warlike stores (including MT) sub-depots of the BOD to be sited near the BOW. During the construction of these new installations, 1 BOD and 2 BOW at Nantes were to operate as the AFV Base installations assisted by a small Ordnance depot for AFV stores to be formed in available accommodation at Bonnieres-sur-Seine in the Pacy area.

LABOUR

From the very beginning it was difficult to find labour both for construction of new accommodation and for handling the stores required by a modern, mechanized force. French manpower resources had already been largely mobilized for their own needs. As a temporary measure Cavalry and Infantry Reservists were formed into labour units and did excellent work though there were too few of them.

Later the Auxiliary Military Pioneer Corps was formed. The Director of Labour, responsible both for the AMPC and for finding and employing all possible local resources was Major-General Amps. Even the possession of so appropriate a name did not suffice to solve this intractable problem, and it was decided in March 1940 to send 3 Divisions to France to undertake labour duties and at the same time to continue their training.

These Divisions, besides being incompletely trained, consisted of 8 Battalions only with divisional Engineers, but no Artillery and with Signals and administrative units in no more than skeleton form. Armament and transport were on a much reduced scale. It was repeatedly stated that the French fully understood that these Divisions were purely for labour duties and were not to be regarded as effective combat formations. No plans were made to bring them up to full strength or complete their war equipment at short notice.

THE ADVANCED AIR STRIKING FORCE

The AASF operated at some distance from the BEF area and the arrangements for the supply of Ordnance stores were not adequate. The maintenance project envisaged direct supply from Base installations to RAF and Army units 300 miles away.

Early in October 1939 a DADOS and an OME with an RAOC detachment were added to HQ AASF and later a small ammunition depot was formed, as has been mentioned. However, there was no pool of transport or labour to handle the stores at railhead and the difficulty caused by this persisted to the end of the campaign.

SITUATION AT THE BEGINNING OF MAY 1940

The early difficulties which the RAOC had to face have already been mentioned, and they were aggravated by an exceptionally severe winter, but by May 1940 they had largely been overcome and an efficient system for the supply of Ordnance stores, vehicles and ammunition had been created. The repair organization had also reached a high standard.

This development in the efficiency of the organization for the supply of equipment in the field was not matched by a corresponding improvement in the production of that equipment. Only 15 months had elapsed since the decision to equip the Army for a Continental war. The rate of production was steady rather than spectacular, and the last 8 months of war had not revealed any significant acceleration. The impressive tonnage of equipment and ammunition available for the support of the BEF hid the fact that in many important respects the cupboard was bare.

OPERATIONS NORTH OF THE RIVER SOMME MAY 1940

On May 10th the Germans invaded Holland and Belgium. Plan "D" was put into operation and the BEF moved up to the River Dyle position and occupied it without serious interference. 5 Division had sent a Brigade to Norway and was in the Amiens area, but it was quickly resupplied with its second line ammunition and moved forward into Belgium in reserve. There were 3 Corps (9 Divisions) occupying the British sector, on a 2 Corps front. The tenth Division (51st Division) was on the Saar front.

The organic units, OFPs and Field Workshops, had no serious problems at this stage.

The ammunition supply arrangements were that ASEs were sent forward to stock the new railheads in Belgium, the detachments at Ecoust and Aubigny moving forward to run these ARHs and being replaced by reinforcing detachments found from the BADs. Six 36-hour ammunition trains (ASEs) were ordered forward and replaced by 6 ASE's loaded and despatched from the BADs.

The process worked smoothly, the only variation from the original plan being that the QMG decided to slow up the rate of build-up of the new ARHs and hold more ASEs "stabled" and ready in northern France, an example of administrative wisdom and foresight which was to be vindicated by the events which followed in a few days.

THE GERMAN BREAK THROUGH

On May 14th the Germans broke through the weakly held portion of the French line near Sedan. A large force of armour passed through the gap and headed for the coast north of the River Somme. There was no mobile reserve adequate to deal with such a situation. The best equipped mobile French formations were already committed in Belgium and Holland, and although the Seventh Army on the left flank was quickly withdrawn it merely reinforced the forces to the south of the break through but without affecting the swift execution of the German plan.

The only British formations available to meet the threat were the 3 "labour" Divisions (12th, 23rd and 46th) and these were rapidly equipped, so far as this was possible, by issues from the reserves in the AOD. The deficiencies of these incompletely trained Divisions in staff, supporting arms, services and equipment placed them in a most unenviable position but they played a vital part in the fighting which followed.

By May 19th the AOD and AOW were ordered to withdraw south of the River Somme. The residual, widely dispersed stocks of the AOD could neither be moved nor entirely destroyed in the time available.

The AOW dismantled, packed and placed on rail for movement to the Base its valuable stocks of machine tools. The unit then withdrew with its vehicles and equipment for light repairs, setting up a light repair shop first at St. Pierre les Elbœufs and later at Alençon.

It was apparent by May 19th that communication with the Base south of the River Somme would soon be cut, supply trains having already been re-routed through Abbeville. Communications were completely, and as it proved finally, severed by the German occupation of Abbeville on May 21st and future supplies to the BEF could only be sent through the Channel ports—Boulogne, Calais, Dunkirk and Ostend.

The Ordnance Directorate was ordered back from Barly to Boulogne on May 17th and the "Q" staff at Rear GHQ at Noyelle Vion moved on May 19th to Hazebrouck (German troops occupying St. Omer to the west while they were there), and later some of the staff went to Boulogne and others to the Dunkirk area. The Boulogne contingent withdrew to the United Kingdom before German occupation of the town.

Meanwhile the railhead detachments at Ecoust and Aubigny found themselves in the path of the German advance. They were ordered to destroy their stocks of ammunition and withdraw if circumstances compelled them to do so. A surprising amount of time and equipment is necessary to destroy ammunition which is properly sited and dispersed. Ecoust was the first location to be overrun but destruction of the stocks was achieved in large measure. The same was not possible at Aubigny, the stocks being alongside a main road which carried essential military traffic apart from the innumerable refugees. Aubigny was again in our hands for a short time when the counter-attack at Arras took place, but it is not known whether an opportunity occurred to refill ammunition echelons from there. By then communications were inevitably chaotic.

The ARH detachments reported to Hazebrouck and were re-directed to Boulogne but had to withdraw before the German advance, arriving at Dunkirk on May 24th. Providentially they appeared at the same time as a ship loaded with ammunition, and their knowledge of ammunition enabled them to do invaluable work in identifying the various natures, sorting them as far as possible and supervising the loading of railway wagons for forward movement. Unfortunately rail movement through Dunkirk was soon halted by bombing of the town. It would have been better if road transport could have been found to clear the whole of this ammunition to the points in the perimeter defence where it was required. Some vehicles would not have got through but the majority would have reached their destination.

It was a serious error that the ship was not loaded operationally, that is with components making up complete rounds stowed together. It was impossible to match components on the quayside in the existing conditions. The ammunition had to be cleared quickly to a less vulnerable spot and the components matched there. Inevitably some components went astray *en route,* and this ammunition, being incomplete, was useless.

The OFPs and AFWs began to experience difficulties resulting from an over-centralized organization. A static situation always leads to an increase in the stocks of an OFP which soon ceases to be mobile. In the BEF this condition was aggravated by the fact that the static period had lasted for 8 months, the unit was a Corps and not an organic Divisional unit, there was no active depot to meet maintenance demands forward of the Base, and there were no stores sections to deal with the needs of field workshops.

The demands on OFPs were not as heavy as they might have been, partly because the campaign lasted for such a short time and partly because the withdrawal was in the general direction of stocks already established. It is true that the retirement was west rather than south but the original Corps areas on the French frontier were north of the axis of advance of the German armoured drive to the coast.

The rapid tactical moves of Divisions from one part of the line to another made it difficult to keep in touch with them and meet their needs. But on the whole units were not operationally hampered by lack of the stores normally held by Ordnance Field Parks.

Operations were too mobile and lasted too short a time for AFWs to be able to play a significant part. The organization of these units had

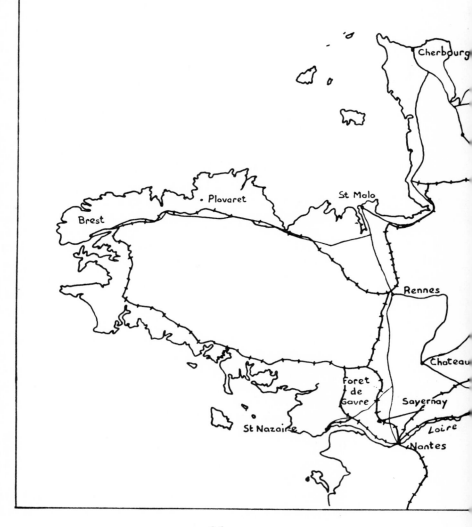

FRANCE

(NORTH OF R. LOIRE)

SCALE   I INCH = 16 MILES

ROADS

RAILWAYS

16   0   16   32   64

Cherbourg

Plovaret

St Malo

Brest

Rennes

Chateau

Foret
de
Gavre

Sayernay

St Nazaire

Loire

Nantes

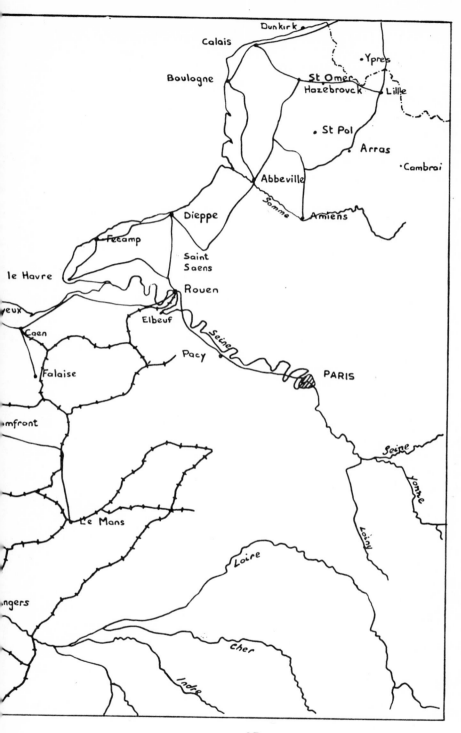

Dunkirk

Calais

Boulogne

•Ypres

St Omer

Hazebrouck

Lille

• St Pol

Arras

•Cambrai

Abbeville

Somme

Amiens

Dieppe

Fécamp

Saint
Saens

le Havre

Rouen

yeux

Elbeuf

Caen

Seine

Pacy

PARIS

Falaise

mfront

Seine

Yonne

Loing

Le Mans

Loire

ngers

Cher

Indre

97

already proved to be unduly cumbersome and the campaign in Belgium and Northern France served to underline the need for a change which had already been recognized. But the campaign was over before the recommendations could be put into effect. On the other hand the LADs proved admirable for these conditions, and by their magnificent work fully justified the concept on which their organization and employment was based.

The immediate ammunition situation was not critical in so far as the mobile echelons of gun and small arms ammunition were full, but replenishment was uncertain, and in anticipation of this ammunition was in some cases rationed. The "stabled" ASEs could have helped here, but no one had shut the stable door and the French railway authorities moved the trains frequently without asking or telling anyone who might need the ammunition. The consequent games of hide-and-seek did not always yield satisfactory results. The success of Operation Dynamo (the withdrawal of the BEF from Dunkirk) has tended to obscure the fact that before long lack of ammunition would have compelled the surrender of the BEF.

OPERATIONS SOUTH OF THE RIVER SOMME

With the capture of Abbeville on May 21st maintenance of the BEF from south of the River Somme ceased.

The immediate task was to maintain the 51st Division, which had moved right across France from the Saar to the left flank of the River Somme position, and such other *ad hoc* formations as could be built up from miscellaneous units, men from reinforcement depots and those elements of the 3 "labour" Divisions which had not been committed in the fighting north of the river. Of these improvised formations Beauman Division[1] was the most important. The 1st Armoured Division began to disembark on May 20th. In the circumstances it was bound to be committed to battle piecemeal and never operated effectively as a Division.

As soon as control from GHQ became impossible the Commander L of C Area assumed GHQ authority so far as concerned, *inter alia,* the control of the activities and stocks of Base installations. The L of C had been divided for administrative convenience into North and South Districts and, in the absence of GHQ coordination, they had authorized issues independently. The Commander L of C Area ordered the DDOS North District (Colonel Cansdale) to move to HQ, L of C Area at Le Mans as DOS, and he had to create the machinery for the control of the issue of important stores and the repair of vehicles and equipments.

On May 23rd Lieutenant-General Sir Henry Karslake arrived to take

---

[1] An improvised force under Brigadier (later Major-General) Beauman, who had commanded North District L of C. It comprised one brigade formed from AMPC, one brigade from Infantry base depots, one anti-tank regiment (improvised), one field battery (improvised), two army troops companies RE. They had no transport or signal equipment and were untrained in the use of weapons except rifles and Bren guns.

over operational command. By the end of May the Government was in a dilemma, which was reflected in the many contradictory orders received by the headquarters and units still in France. The British policy not to intervene in land warfare on the Continent had been consistently followed until about a year before the outbreak of war. There had been a significant, if belated, change of heart, but this was not a sufficient stimulant fully to convince the French whose morale was low. France, lacking the ferocious patriotism and leadership of a Clemenceau, was defeatist, and this affected a large part of the Army, though many units fought with great gallantry.

Now, at the beginning of June 1940, the burning question was whether or not French resistance was crumbling. If collapse was imminent, there was no time to lose in bringing all men and equipment back to the United Kingdom. But if collapse was only a probability, it could be made a certainty by the premature withdrawal of the rest of the British Army.

In addition to these general considerations the particular one affecting the RAOC was that the Base installations now contained numbers of men and quantities of material far in excess of the requirements for the maintenance of any fighting forces which could be deployed or sent from the United Kingdom for some time. Moreover, Le Havre as a base was now distinctly vulnerable.

Some stores were sent back to the United Kingdom and some to 1 BOD at Nantes. The work was carried out at high pressure and inevitably, owing to the factors mentioned, in an atmosphere of "order, counterorder and disorder". Initiative and powers of improvisation were at a premium. The equipment of new units and maintenance of those in the line, simultaneously with the transfer of depot stocks ensured that depot staffs had no rest for long periods. Both 2 BOD and 3 BAD were ordered to embark and then ordered back again to reopen their depots.

The staff of the AOD, which had withdrawn from the Arras area, undertook the work of collecting and sending back several thousand tons of accommodation stores which had been abandoned in reinforcement depots in the area north of Rouen.

Meanwhile receipt activity in the BODs was not negligible. Certain vehicles and urgent fighting stores which had not been in the theatre at the beginning of operations, or the stocks of which had been expended, were being received from the United Kingdom and were immediately issued. The same applied to certain natures of ammunition.

By May 29th, 1st Armoured Division had already suffered battle casualties to half its tanks, although it was hoped that many of them would be recovered and repaired. The mobile workshop and the field park were located at Lisieux but the static workshop and AFV sub-depot were at Nantes, too far back to influence the battle.

The need for the Armoured Division was so great that it had to be sent out deficient of a good proportion of essential spares backing. These stores, as they were produced, were sent out from England in urgent consignments. Some were sent by air, and demands went by teleprint to the War Office (OS 5). All these urgent consignments were collected by RAOC vehicles on arrival and delivered to the field park sections.

There were only 2 Scammell tank transporters with the BEF, both with the Armoured Division, which is a fair illustration of the scarcity of repair and recovery facilities and of essential spares. The RAOC units did everything possible with the means at their disposal, but the circumstances necessitated committing the Armoured Division to battle piecemeal and without proper logistic support. Early in June it ceased, for lack of fit tanks, to be capable of offensive operations, but recovery and repair continued, tanks requiring heavy repair being sent back to Nantes by rail.

In the second week in June the 51st Division, less one Brigade, was surrounded at St. Valery and forced to surrender. Despite weakening French resistance reinforcements in the shape of 52nd (Lowland) Division and 1st Canadian Division were sent out to France.

It was even planned to open up a new Base at La Rochelle in place of Le Havre, and a reconnaissance party was sent out on June 12th, landing at St. Malo and proceeding to Le Mans, Saumur and Niort. But events moved too fast and the party, together with a large contingent of the AASF, sailed from La Pallice on June 17th arriving at Newport 3 days later.

This scheme had its effect on 1 BOD, who were told to pack half their stocks for transfer to the new Base. The Commander L of C Area also had instructions to arrange to find the staff and war equipment of a BOD, BAD and BOW from existing resources, but the process of sending surplus RAOC men and Ordnance stores back to England, in accordance with earlier orders, had progressed too far.

Lieutenant-General Sir Alan Brooke had been sent out to take command of the forces which were being created to fight alongside the French and restore the situation. He soon saw the real state of affairs, obtained approval for the whole British Army to be embarked for England, and orders to that effect were issued on June 14th.

Colonel Palmer (COO 1 BOD) had sent considerable quantities of stores back to England, but his stocks were continually augmented by returned stores from 2 BOD, the AOD and various *ad hoc* organizations set up to recover and return equipment. In fact the feature of RAOC activity at this stage of the campaign was the initiative and perseverance devoted to the collection, recovery and return of all types of equipment. These efforts could have saved the situation if fighting had continued and wholesale re-equipment had been necessary, but in the event they were largely wasted as priority had to be given to the movement of troops at the end. Destruction of vehicles and stores which had to be left was carried out to the greatest possible extent in the time available.

Most RAOC units left from St. Nazaire on June 17th or 18th. Many were on board the *Lancastria,* which was bombed and sunk with the loss of about 2,000 lives of whom 50 were RAOC.

LESSONS OF THE CAMPAIGN

In his final despatch the C in C stressed "The paramount importance of equipment". After comparing the 10 Armoured Divisions of the enemy with the light tanks of 7 divisional Cavalry Regiments, which was all that he had at his disposal, he also commented on the inadequacy of anti-tank armament which did not extend further back than Division.

He went on to say: "The days are past when armies can be hurriedly raised, equipped and placed in the field, for modern war demands the ever-increasing use of complicated material. . . . Modern equipment requires time to design and produce, and once it is produced, further time is required to train troops in its technical and tactical uses. Improvised arrangements, made at short notice, can only lead to the shortage of essential equipment, the production of inferior articles, and the unskilful handling of weapons and vehicles on the battlefield."

This was a severe criticism of the policies of the various peace-time governments in relation to the equipment of the Army. The comment on "training troops in its technical uses" particularly applied to the RAOC, who must be familiar with equipment if they are to avoid mistakes in its supply, storage and repair.

The campaign provided tough and effective training for RAOC units. The conditions in which units had to operate at the beginning of the campaign could not have been more severe had they been deliberately contrived. These were not trained units or Regulars and Regular Reservists, formed and working together in peace, but a scratch collection of, at the outset, civilians in uniform with a tiny nucleus of Regular officers and other ranks to provide leadership and experience.

The surprising thing is that chaos was not complete. It probably would have been if operations had started in the first 2 months after the arrival of the BEF. The greatest credit is due to these units. They received little help but abundance of criticism. From such painful and unpromising beginnings emerged the qualities necessary for efficiency in the field— discipline, administrative ability, self-reliance and technical skill. The foundation had been laid for the massive structure of Ordnance Services which would be needed before the war was over.

The lesson of the 1939–1940 campaign in France is that readiness for war is the primary duty of the Army in peace. Failure to recognize this until war is imminent can be disastrous. For the rest of the war it was never necessary to send completely untrained RAOC units into a theatre of operations.

Other lessons of value later in the war were:

1. Improved organization of BODs.

2. Separate organizations for railhead and port units instead of details detached from larger units.
3. Roadside layout of BADs with established safety distances between storage locations.
4. Depot and unit war equipment to accompany units to the theatre of war.
5. RAOC representatives to know and contribute to key plans and maintenance projects.
6. The value of tactical loading of ships in certain circumstances and supply of ammunition by complete rounds at all times.

THE CAMPAIGN IN NORWAY, APRIL–JUNE 1940

"The real foundations of military knowledge are topography, movement and supply, not strategy and tactics as most people think" (General Sir Archibald Wavell on "Generals and Generalship", 1939).

"It has become the habit of the British Army in recent years to assume that what the General Staff consider to be politically or operationally desirable is administratively possible" (Major-General B. C. T. Paget. Report on the operations based on Aandalsnes).

The campaign in Norway, like that in Greece the following year, was doomed to failure from the start. In both cases, for political and ethical reasons, Britain was bound to be influenced by the attitude of the neutral countries concerned whilst Germany was not hampered by such considerations. Inevitably the British plans were tentative, half-hearted and subject to kaleidoscopic changes. Consequently the logistics can hardly be said to have been planned at all, and perforce took the form of a series of last-minute improvisations. There were serious deficiencies in administrative intelligence and in the planning based on the limited information available. The estimated port and storage capacities at Aandalsnes, Namsos and Harstad were not realistic and the effect of enemy air superiority was not taken into account.

The Government kept on varying the objective with little regard to the havoc wrought at lower levels down to the man on the quay grappling with arrivals of equipment, often under air attack, and sometimes the failure of vital equipment to appear at all. Thus the RAOC was given neither the opportunity nor the means to ensure that the troops were supplied with the equipment they needed to fight an enemy whose thoroughness and foresight in providing everything required for fighting were extraordinary.

There were two main areas of operations, Central Norway and Northern Norway.

The Central Norway operations were undertaken to reinforce the hard-pressed Norwegian Army, stem the German northward advance from Oslo and encircle and capture German-occupied Trondheim. A direct attack on Trondheim was contemplated but never materialized.

These were somewhat conflicting aims, and two separate forces were designated for the task under a Corps Headquarters that was never established in Norway but had to attempt control of the operations from the United Kingdom.

One force landed north of Trondheim at Namsos. The commander was Major-General Carton de Wiart. The other force landed south-west of Trondheim at Aandalsnes and was commanded by Major-General B. C. T. Paget.

Theoretically, these two forces would encircle and capture Trondheim but this takes no account of the topography of Norway, a mountainous country in which the valleys, and therefore roads and railways run mainly from north-west to south-east. A move "across the grain" of the land from Aandalsnes towards Trondheim would have been difficult and slow for troops neither trained nor equipped for mountain warfare. Moreover, the calls to reinforce the Norwegian Army were insistent and could be met fairly easily. In the end the force was never able to move on Trondheim.

One Brigade was drawn well to the south and heavily engaged without Artillery or air support. A second Brigade—15 Infantry Brigade from 5th Division then in France—landed at Aandalsnes and was moved by General Paget south-east down the Gudbrandsdal valley to reinforce the Norwegian Army and the badly mauled 148 Brigade.

But the Norwegian Army could do no more in that area, and the remnants of 148 Brigade withdrew through 15 Brigade, who carried out a series of skilful rearguard actions culminating in the successful evacuation of the force from Aandalsnes. The distance from Aandalsnes to the furthest point reached by British troops was about 140 miles. From the landing of the first troops of 148 Brigade to the embarkation of the last troops for the United Kingdom a period of only 14 days elapsed.

Lieutenant-Colonel W. T. Cobb was the ADOS at Aandalsnes. The provisional First Key Plan and Maintenance Project gave little to work upon and were no more than a basis for immediate reconnaissance on landing. He also received a list of Clothing and General Stores which it was intended to despatch but there were no shipping details.

The ADOS landed on April 25th and was joined later by Captain Downer, who was on the headquarters Base Sub-Area and 3 other ranks. This was the total RAOC strength for the operation, which can hardly be described as over-staffing, even allowing for the limited activity which was possible as the operation developed.

Only a very limited amount of MT was landed and it was all needed to take forward the fighting troops who were trying to hold off a numerically superior, well-equipped and trained enemy. Some of these troops went forward by rail and others by road, but they could take little more equipment and ammunition than the men could carry themselves.

There were considerable stocks of dumped war equipment and ammunition which units had been unable to take with them, and the task was to move this material to suitable depot sites clear of the dock area without labour or transport. A site was found but before the stores and ammunition could be moved away a heavy air raid with incendiary bombs set fire to the docks and adjacent buildings. Much equipment and two-thirds of the ammunition was lost.

Sufficient ammunition was saved to enable a demand from the forward area to be met by rail, and the Base Sub-Area staff produced a train of a few wagons to take the remainder to a better location near Romsdalshorn station.

After this only one store ship, the SS *Delius,* docked. There were urgent requirements for AA guns with their associated equipment and ammunition, load-carrying vehicles and barbed wire. But the ship had not been stowed with these priorities in mind, and in fact no stowage plan was available. Unloading facilities were poor and, owing to the short period of darkness, only about 4 hours were available for clearing the ship. Finding the stores was a sort of "lucky dip" and the ADOS had to identify the items and arrange their unloading himself. He was able to obtain a fair proportion of the requirement, some of which was sent forward by rail and the remainder moved to a safe place before daylight.

Even in good conditions the port capacity and facilities would have been inadequate but the Germans had complete air superiority and by a suitable mixture of high explosive and incendiary bombs they were able to destroy complete towns, all Norwegian houses in this area being made of wood. Further difficulties were caused by the fact that the thaw had started and the one road leading to the front became a quagmire. This would have strictly limited the use of MT even if the supply of vehicles had been all that was required. The life-line was the railway, and this was liable to interruption by frequent bombing.

The RAOC staff were tireless in locating and salvaging dumped unit war equipment and ammunition. In this way the needs of the force were met within the limits of the existing supply facilities. The limited amount of equipment which remained at the time of the final embarkation was either left for the Norwegians or destroyed.

The story of the Namsos expedition is similar to that of Aandalsnes. The force moved fairly rapidly southward and therefore towards Trondheim, but as it advanced the right flank was exposed to Trondheim Fiord which was controlled by the Germans. A vigorous attack by the Germans forced the Brigade to withdraw to the north, and even the arrival of French reinforcements did not suffice to enable the advance to be resumed. In the end the whole force had to retire and re-embark at Namsos.

The RAOC was given hardly any opportunity to play its part in this operation. Failure to load ships tactically was disastrous when Namsos was destroyed by bombing and the equipment which had not accompanied units never reached them.

The ADOS was Lieutenant-Colonel L. E. Cutforth. He landed at

Namsos with a bulky list of stores which were to maintain the force. In fact, they never reached Namsos and he could only deal with unit war equipment and ammunition which had been left at the port because the troops could not carry it when they advanced.

The force had been involved in heavy fighting before transport arrived and that consisted of a mere fifteen lorries. A light anti-aircraft battery also appeared but without predictors, and a 3·7-inch howitzer battery without ammunition.

The main effort was made at Narvik in the north and this operation lasted for 7 weeks. The Allied Force consisted of British, French and Polish troops, the British contingent being a Brigade with supporting arms.

The ADOS to the force was Lieutenant-Colonel T. H. Clarke and a composite depot was formed known as Detachment BOD under Lieutenant-Colonel St. J. C. Hooley. It comprised one sub-depot for clothing and general stores, one sub-depot for technical and warlike stores, and an ammunition section. There was no MT sub-depot as it was considered that vehicles could not operate in northern Norway. The unit was originally formed in case a force was sent to the aid of Finland and it was not disbanded after the peace treaty between Finland and Russia had been signed. The stores portion of the depot was scaled for about 30,000 items.

The Detachment BOD disembarked on April 15th 1940 at Harstad, situated on an island about 20 miles north-west of Narvik. The landing was unopposed and the people were friendly. The area allotted for Ordnance Stores consisted of barns normally used for salting fish. They were alongside small wharves and were full of rats, salt and fish oil. Clearance of the sheds and receipt of the stores had to be carried out at the utmost speed in deep snow and a temperature of 30° below zero. Clothing and general stores were in the northern part of Harstad, technical stores in the middle of the town and the ammunition at the far end of the fiord at Mercur.

The store ships containing depot stocks arrived on April 23rd during a blizzard and were off-loaded while the harbour was being bombed.

The packing and documentation were not suitable for issue to a depot forming in a theatre of operations. The contents of cases could not be identified until the cases had been opened. Many cases and crates were too bulky and heavy to be manhandled, which was a serious matter in view of the inadequacy of depot equipment and lack of transport. There was a lack of essential documents such as vouchers, and stencilling was inadequate. Many units, including the Ordnance Depot itself, had been separated from their war equipment and deficiencies had to be made up as far as possible from the maintenance stocks in the depot.

On April 29th there was a heavy thaw. Every road and track became a torrent up to 2 ft. deep, which flowed through the storage locations.

As a result of the sinking of 2 ships carrying unit equipment, 2 units had to be equipped from depot stocks most of which still had to be un-packed and binned. In some cases the stocks were insufficient and it was necessary to withdraw certain items such as web equipment, compasses, binoculars and revolvers from units at the Base.

Anti-aircraft units were not phased in soon enough and incessant bombing increased the difficulties of the units at Harstad.

Snow camouflage clothing had not been supplied, but local resources solved the problem, all available white sheeting being purchased and the clothing being manufactured by Norwegian women volunteers.

The system of demanding replenishment of Ordnance Stores was cum-bersome. Requirements had to be checked by the ADOS and the demand supported by the staff before a signal could be sent on to the United Kingdom. The signal had then to be coded. Apart from these unneces-sary delays, the production of the required statistics and information in justification of each demand imposed a much heavier burden than could be carried by the very small staff available to the ADOS.

Towards the end of May a Corps HQ staff, which included a DDOS, arrived but they only remained a few days before the order for the evacuation of Norway was received, and therefore they could not signi-ficantly influence events. It must have been difficult for them to appreciate the problems which faced the detachment BOD in having to establish a depot in deep snow and severe arctic conditions, and then continue to operate it in conditions of thaw and floods. The withdrawal from Nor-way was successfully completed by June 19th 1940.

LESSONS OF THE CAMPAIGN

The main lesson of the campaign is that there is no substitute for thorough training and preparation based on knowledge and study of the factors of topography and climate in the theatre. The campaign required the full combination of all three Services and illustrated the importance of Combined Operations and a unified system of command.

The RAOC lessons must be viewed against the background of the main lesson. They were:

1. Those that take part in the operation must also do the detailed planning.
2. Tactical loading of ships. Units must move with their war equip-ment. This applies not only to the fighting units but also to Base Depots. Without their depot equipment they cannot handle the stores.
3. Packing of stores. The design, size and weight of packages must be such as to enable stores to be manhandled wherever possible.
4. Marking, stencilling and documentation must facilitate quick identification and enable stores to be issued direct from the cases in the early stages while the depot is being established.

106

5. There must be sufficient RAOC staff from the beginning. The most acute problems always occur at the beginning of a campaign, when a firm base for the maintenance of the force is being created. It is exactly at this stage that the demands of our own troops are likely to be heavy and urgent. It would be an advantage if the enemy did not interfere too much at this critical stage and the plans for war, made in peace, usually include this convenient and comfortable assumption. But real war is different. Of course, in a combined operation shipping (and in modern war air transport) will always be limited and a nice balance must be struck on the "not too little, not too much but just right" principle.

6. RAOC units must be comprehensively trained. Unless the technical standard is high the small numbers will not be adequate to the heavy initial burden. Discipline, fitness and administrative efficiency are essential to cope with the field conditions in which the unit will have to operate from the beginning. An adequate weapon training standard is essential.

7. The bulky arctic clothing was useless. There was no transport for it and the surplus, which could not be carried on the man, was dumped and left for the Norwegians. The combat and administrative troops had no training in how to fight or even exist in arctic conditions. It is useless to expect troops to wage war in special conditions of climate and terrain such as arctic, jungle and desert, without appropriate preparation and training.

CHAPTER FOUR

THE MIDDLE EAST 1940–1941

The Western Desert, Greece, Crete, Iraq and Syria

So far as this history is concerned the Middle East is taken to cover activity in the following places:

Egypt, Cyrenaica, Tripolitania;
Palestine, Cyprus, Syria and Iraq;
Greece and Crete;
the Sudan, Eritrea, Somaliland, Abyssinia, East Africa.

When fighting started, which was not until after June 1940, military operations in all these areas were controlled by the Commander-in-Chief Middle East. He worked as one of a triumvirate with the Naval Commander-in-Chief, Mediterranean, and the Air Officer Commanding-in-Chief.

But this was not the situation before the war. The British spheres of influence, Egypt, Palestine, Iraq, Cyprus, the Sudan, British Somaliland and East Africa, were independent of each other and controlled from the United Kingdom, the last four coming under the Colonial Office. The forces in Cyprus were negligible whilst only local forces existed in the other colonial territories.

Sir Archibald Wavell was appointed GOC-in-C Middle East in July 1939. He was to command, in peace, all troops in Egypt, the Sudan, Palestine, Transjordan and Cyprus. In the event of war his command was to extend to include British Somaliland, Aden and Iraq.

He had no GHQ and his staff consisted of five officers with but one DAQMG for administrative duties. He could only exercise command through the various headquarters of existing Commands, and his staff could do little more than operational planning.

General Wavell strengthened his staff by transferring Brigadier B. O. Hutchinson from Palestine, so that movement and maintenance could be given full weight in the earliest stages of planning.

The administrative staffs and services in the various Commands, together with their material resources, remained at little more than peace-time level and continued to be directed from the War Office, but General Wavell was compelled to lean heavily on them for assistance in the preparation of plans.

When the war came Germany was at first the only enemy. Britain and France together dominated the Mediterranean and were in a position to isolate from Italian control the new and restive colony of Ethiopia. Even Mussolini could see that it was not to his advantage to go to war with us at this time. It was obviously sound policy to encourage this attitude in the Italians, but it is possible that eagerness to avoid provoking Mussolini was interpreted as weakness and so may have contributed to his decision to enter the war against us later on.

General Wavell started the process of converting his planning headquarters into an effective GHQ so that he could exercise command over the vast area which was now his responsibility. But owing to the other priorities and the shortage of trained staff officers progress was slow, particularly in the administrative field.[1]

Top priority for men and equipment was naturally accorded to our forces in France, and as the rate of production of equipment and ammunition was still slow both before the war and for some months after it had started, the material resources of the Middle East forces remained at a very low level.

It was generally recognized that Egypt, as a focal point of communications, was the ideal place for the creation of a base in which a central reserve could be located, and indeed a vital place if Italy, Greece or Turkey should become involved in the war. GHQ Middle East also pointed out that the immense amount of construction necessary for such a base would take time and therefore work should start now.

But Treasury approval for the various projects was reluctant and piecemeal. This was because they continued to apply the peace-time procedure which involved submitting a case, detailed examination of it at the War Office, approval in principle and so on, before work could proceed. Thus financial support failed to keep pace with the forward planning of GHQ Middle East.

ORDER OF BATTLE

When mobilization was ordered there was in the Middle East no proper Order of Battle in the sense of complete formations made up of units on war establishments. There were various miscellaneous units forming the garrisons of the various Commands with the Services on a minimum, peace-time basis.

In Egypt 7th Armoured Division had been formed from 2 Armoured Brigades each of 2 Regiments, 1 Armoured Car Regiment and a Motor Battalion with an incomplete proportion of supporting arms and ser-

[1] A fully operative GHQ was formed in February 1940. By October 1940, the establishment provided for 1,061 officers and men of whom 700 were for administrative duties.

vices. In addition to the units of 7th Armoured Division there were 8 Infantry Battalions.

The advanced elements of 4th Indian Division had begun to arrive.

In Palestine there was: HQ 6th Division with a few units, 8th Division (2 Brigades), 2 horsed Cavalry Regiments, 4 unbrigaded Infantry Battalions.

In the Sudan there were 3 Infantry Battalions and the Sudan Defence Force; in Cyprus 1 Infantry Company; in Kenya the King's African Rifles.

Very roughly this added up to a force of combat units amounting to 1 Armoured and 3 Infantry Divisions, but with serious deficiencies in supporting arms and organic service units and no effective Base organization with reserves of vehicles, equipment and ammunition held there.

DEPENDENCY CALCULATIONS

Provision was hampered by frequent changes in War Office policy on the forces to be maintained in the Middle East. In October 1939 the plan was for the Middle East to have a dependency of 15 Divisions with Corps and GHQ troops (roughly 297,000 men). Reserves to be calculated for 150 days. In January 1940 the dependency was changed to 9 Divisions and the reserves to 90 days. In June 1940 the figure went up again to 15 Divisions and absurdly complicated ways of calculating the reserves were ordered. In August 1940 the divisional "slice" figure was greatly increased and the manpower dependency approached 500,000. In November 1940 the War Office plan was to build up to 23 Divisions by March 1942.

Five changes of plan in little more than a year made all calculations worthless, and the situation was aggravated by the time taken between the submission of a demand and the receipt of stores in response to it, the slow rate of production and the low priority for equipment of the Middle East.

THE RAOC SITUATION

It has been shown in Chapter 2 that events in Egypt and Palestine before the war provided some useful experience, both organizational and operational, for RAOC units in field conditions. But it ended there. The low priority of the Middle East for manpower and resources meant that RAOC reinforcements were insufficient to create organic units for the formations likely to be deployed or even to build up the strength of the various peace-time Base installations to a level adequate to their increased commitments.

RAOC installations comprised a Command Ordnance Depot and Workshops at Abbassia, a clothing and mobilization sub-depot at Kasr-el-Nil and a small sub-depot at Alexandria. A small ammunition depot existed at Abbassia, and construction was beginning in Tura Caves. In

Palestine there were small depots at Haifa and Sarafand. Forward dumps for tentage, accommodation stores and ammunition had been created at El Daba and Mersa Matruh. The Abbassia Depot consisted of an inadequate collection of buildings in a congested area with no room for expansion. The only modern building was the MT storehouse.

This was a peace-time organization for two independent Commands and the manpower allotted was just about enough for those conditions. The resources bore no relation to war requirements.

The cumbersome manpower planning in peace, whereby more than a year elapsed between the submission of an establishment and the arrival of men to fill it, effectively guaranteed that the rapidly increasing RAOC commitments were not matched by any corresponding reinforcements.[1]

ACCOUNTING

That the Middle East was not being taken seriously as a theatre of war is shown by the nonsensical War Office ruling that peace-time accounting was to continue.

The troops already in the Middle East drew clothing allowance, paid for boot repairs and so on. They did not hand in the "second suit" on mobilization, which would normally be the case. Meanwhile reinforcements from India, Australia and the United Kingdom were on active service scales and did not draw clothing allowance.

These complications increased the difficulties of the RAOC and hampered preparations for war. The creation of boot repairing and of laundry facilities required in war should not have been complicated by elaborate procedures associated with the grant of clothing allowance to the soldier.

Similarly, Base Ordnance Depots, short of trained supervisors as always at the beginning of a war, should not have been forced to maintain unnecessary records simply because they formed part of elaborate checks demanded in peace.

UNIT EQUIPMENT

The stocks of Ordnance stores in Egypt and Palestine were inadequate to make up the deficiencies in unit equipment. General Wavell commented that the Egyptian Army was in some respects better equipped than most of the British forces. Naturally they were given priority because they paid, or at any rate owed, for the equipment whereas British

---

[1] The Establishment and Strength figures for this period are:

	Officers	*ORs*
(i) Approved Peace Establishment as from April 1939 (based on known tasks in June 1938)	53	837
(ii) Establishment submitted to War Office for approval September 1939	89	1,670
(iii) Establishment submitted to War Office based on that of September plus increased commitments since that date	100	1,827
(iv) Actual strength September 3rd 1939	40	804
(v) Actual strength December 31st 1939	69	920

troops were regarded as a financial liability. The fact that such a policy seriously hampered the readiness for war of the British forces in this area was not apparently, in peace-time, considered important.

SPARES

The policy in the United Kingdom was to stop production of spares for obsolescent vehicles and equipment before the new items had been produced in sufficient quantities. The Middle East, being very low on the priority list for new equipment, had to make do with obsolescent material and the lack of spares caused by the United Kingdom policy was a serious embarrassment. The shortages which troubled the BEF in France, and which were due to the lag in war production, also existed in an aggravated form in the Middle East.

RESERVES

The time taken to obtain stores from the United Kingdom, together with the possibility of the Mediterranean being closed, indicated the necessity for a War Reserve of stores to be established and by the middle of 1939 a 90-day reserve was held for approximately 20,000 troops. On paper this appeared to be an adequate safeguard but three factors reduced its value in practice. First, the number of troops to be equipped did not remain steady at 20,000 but was continually increased. Secondly, there was a significant proportion of vital stores (mainly warlike and technical) which did not exist in the Middle East and would not be available from the United Kingdom for some time. They were of course "Due In", but this gave no immediate satisfaction to anyone. As the DOS Middle East never failed to point out, "You can't fight a war on Dues In." The third point was that the wastage rates on which the reserve was based had been underestimated by the War Office. No one could be blamed for this as for many of the stores in the MT and technical range there was no previous experience to act as a guide. In peace something more than a bold guess is needed to obtain financial approval, and it is peace-time provision which produces the available stocks at the beginning of a war.

CONTROLLED STORES

The acute shortage of MT and technical stores made it necessary to ration issues on an operational basis. Such control was quite rightly exercised by the staff and in the Middle East the function was undertaken by G(SD). The system was that demands for controlled stores had to be approved by G(SD) or, more often, these stores were not to be demanded and G(SD) undertook to issue without demand in appropriate circumstances.

Although the system served its purpose, particularly in the early part of the war, it was too cumbersome and inflexible to be easily adjusted when the supply position improved. Issue without demand is all very well but it presupposes knowledge of unit deficiencies and of the supply position at all times and leads to the staff taking over work which is the province of the Services and for which the Services are qualified and trained. Later in the war the supply of stores which had been scarce became good, even lavish, yet by then the machinery of control had grown to such an extent that there was hardly a main item of equipment which was not controlled by some branch in GHQ. Scales of unit equipment had practically ceased to exist, and while "authorized scales" do not justify refusal to issue in excess of them in war, they do provide a useful "dependency" basis on which to take provision action. Without such information provision is apt to become sheer guesswork and over-provision gets out of hand.

One example will suffice. A certain unit in the Cairo area in mid-1944 was still using Lewis guns for military training although the storehouses in the BODs held so many Bren guns that they constituted a storage embarrassment. The unit was not operational—the war had moved away from Egypt to Italy by then—so G(SD) saw no need to issue without demand and the unit was forbidden to demand. Ultimately RAOC pressure led to the elimination of a system which had long outlived its usefulness.

It would have been better if G(SD), and the other staff branches which copied them, had refrained from the direct control of stores, and had contented themselves with keeping the RAOC informed of the units which had top priority and the reserves necessary to meet further demands from those units. When the supply position improved stocks would automatically become available in excess of priority needs and no special steps would be necessary to alter a system which already provided sufficient control and flexibility.

APPOINTMENT OF DOS

It has been seen that for various reasons it was not feasible before the end of 1939 to create a fully operative GHQ in the Middle East. However, this was done early in 1940, and Colonel W. W. Richards was transferred from his appointment in France to DOS with the rank of Brigadier. His initiative and powers of persuasion in finding excellent accommodation for 2 BOD in Havre have already been mentioned.

He had considerable experience of the Middle East, understood the people and made it his business to study local resources and sources of supply such as South Africa and India whereby demands on the United Kingdom could be reduced. Later in the war a large organization was established for developing these Eastern Group resources, but Brigadier Richards anticipated the process so far as Middle East requirements were concerned.

It was a stroke of genius on the part of General Hill to select Brigadier Richards for this appointment. Historically Egypt is a place where people are expected to make bricks without straw and it can also engender a paralysing apathy. These were not serious factors as long as the war was confined to north-west Europe but it could easily spread, and delay in anticipating such a situation could be fatal.

Brigadier Richards was a man of tremendous drive and initiative and a colourful personality. Orthodox methods held little attraction for him. He considered that too often they failed to get results or were slow, which to him was the same thing. His fertile imagination and the capacity to "think big" had not been impaired by years of financial stringency and the stultifying insistence on providing full justification for needs which were obvious from the beginning. He was later promoted to Major-General and became DQMG(AE), Middle East. For those who served under, or were associated with General Richards it can truly be said that there was never a dull moment.

After the war he became DOS at the War Office, and his qualities of initiative and originality had less scope there, but the primary duty of a soldier is to serve his country in war, and by that standard his reputation is deservedly very high indeed.

The most pressing task of the newly appointed DOS was to place Ordnance Services in the Middle East on a war footing.

This entailed

1. Increasing storage accommodation for stores, vehicles and ammunition by building new depots and enlarging existing ones.
2. Increasing workshops capacity.
3. Establishing manufacturing capacity for a large range of stores either by building workshops for this purpose or taking over existing resources. Clothing, MT parts and anti-tank mines are but a few examples.
4. Creating a provision organization which would be able fully to investigate future requirements and exploit local and accessible resources. For obvious reasons local purchase had to be used to the full, consistent with the needs of the economy of a country which was still, and continued to remain, officially neutral.
5. The creation of RAOC field force units appropriate to the needs of war in the Middle East. This often required modified establishments and sometimes special units.

It is an understatement to say that this was a formidable task, and time was not on our side, but remarkable progress was made in the rapid conversion of available money into tangible assets. The development of RAOC installations entailed the construction of a Base Ordnance Depot and a Base Ordnance Workshop near Tel-el-Kebir and of a Base Ammunition Depot at Abu Sultan on the Suez Canal south of Ismailia. The dump at El Daba was converted into an AOD.

These installations and others which were contemplated had not only to be built but to be manned in such a way as to give efficient service in all conditions. Unskilled and semi-skilled labour was available in considerable numbers, but supervising capacity hardly existed at all. A strong nucleus of trained and disciplined military staff was essential, not only to direct the enterprise but also to provide a stiffening for organizations which contained so many of the nationals of a country which was not even at war and whose loyalty could not be guaranteed in times of stress.

It was inevitable that the demands for administrative troops, even if kept to a minimum, would be heavy. As far as the RAOC was concerned there were three main reasons for this

1. The RAOC establishments were ridiculously low even for the modest commitments of the Middle East at the beginning of the war. Deficiencies had not been made up by the time the situation changed for the worse.
2. The number of troops to be maintained was continually increased and included Indian Army formations which were not equipped to British scales when they arrived. This was an additional burden casually imposed on an already overburdened Corps.
3. The collapse of France and the entry of Italy into the war created the need for a very large Middle East Base. The new installations had to be manned, but not at the expense of the RAOC field force units in support of the various forces logistically based on the Middle East.

Other administrative Corps had similar difficulties and the struggle between Teeth and Tail developed. Fortunately, General Wavell had an exceptional knowledge of logistic factors and strongly backed the case for adequate support of those formations which he committed to battle.

As early as March 16th 1940 an RAOC reinforcement demand for 113 officers and 2,267 other ranks was backed by the DQMG, who pointed out to the War Office that the enormous lag which then existed between the number of fighting units and formations and the number of Ordnance units to maintain them must be made up. Otherwise, there would be very serious deterioration of unit's war equipment during concentration and training, Ordnance personnel would not be available in formations for training, and there would be a major administrative crisis in any operation undertaken.

The relatively peaceful situation which prevailed in the Middle East for the first 10 months of the war was violently changed by the entry of Italy into the war and the collapse of France. Neither reinforcements nor equipment could be immediately sent out because of the danger of invasion of England and the heavy losses of equipment sustained by the BEF in France.

Thanks to the initiative of Brigadier Richards and others in GHQ, local resources had already been fully explored and extensively used, but

RAOC reinforcements did not arrive in significant numbers during the critical defensive period which lasted until December 1940, nor for the operations which followed.

The anxiety about the situation in the Middle East as a result of the French collapse led to a detailed report by General Wavell. Referring to the state of equipment of the Army he mentioned that 7th Armoured Division had 65 cruiser tanks instead of 220, while not even all these had their proper armament, and the lack of spare parts was very serious. The 4th Indian Division was short of a brigade and much of its artillery. The Australian and New Zealand troops were very short of equipment; in an emergency a system of pooling would make it possible to use about one-third of their numbers for something more than internal security duties. The Army had no adequate protection against low-flying attack, as the only Bofors guns in the country were twelve at Alexandria; the heavy anti-aircraft guns were mostly manned by Egyptians. There was a general shortage of anti-tank guns and of ammunition of all kinds.

It will be noted that he concentrated on the requirements of the fighting stores which could only be obtained from the United Kingdom. There was also an acute shortage of wheeled vehicles which proved a constant anxiety in the campaign shortly to be undertaken, but some sources of supply, other than the United Kingdom could be exploited.

Immediately Italy came into the war the DOS Middle East produced a scheme for the local purchase of lorries and the impressment of vehicles of all types. The next day he purchased 207 vehicles from General Motors and on June 16th a further 200 of various types.

He obtained a number of Marmon-Harrington tractors and their conversion to recovery vehicles was put in hand. American vehicles were obtained through their agents in the Middle East from places as far afield as Bombay and Baghdad. To keep these vehicles of American origin on the road he obtained GHQ Middle East authority to purchase locally spare parts to the value of £100,000.

A useful windfall came from the Italians, one of whose cargo ships was detained at Port Said. This produced many vehicles and some weapons and ammunition, and the RAF transferred a number of armoured cars with their assemblies and spares. The DOS also "borrowed" 14 light tanks from India and persuaded the Egyptian Army to part with 13 light tanks and 50 Vickers machine guns.

The frontiers of Egypt, the Sudan, Kenya and British Somaliland were threatened by vastly superior forces and the communications between the United Kingdom and the Middle East were long and uncertain.

During the dangerous period up to December 1940 we suffered the temporary loss of British Somaliland and a few unimportant frontier posts in the Sudan and Kenya. In the Western Desert a large Italian force had advanced ponderously to about 15 miles east of Sidi Barrani and there they remained in a number of defended camps with all round perimeters, obsessed by administrative difficulties and apparently not contemplating any further advance.

The cautious and unenterprising Italian attitude was fostered by the daring patrol activity of the small, mobile covering forces deployed against them. Led with great tactical skill they caused heavy casualties to the Italians at very small loss in men and equipment to themselves.

Thus General Wavell kept the initiative, husbanded his resources and acquired a good knowledge of the low state of leadership and morale of the opponent he planned to attack at the earliest opportunity.

DEFEAT OF THE ITALIAN ARMY IN THE WESTERN DESERT

By the end of November 1940 General Wavell felt that he was strong enough to attack the Italian forces which had invaded Egypt.

The enemy had not moved for 6 weeks and his defended localities were faulty in that they were not mutually supporting and lacked depth.

The troops taking part in the attack were: 7th Armoured Division, 4th Indian Infantry Division, 16th Infantry Brigade, 7th Battalion RTR (Infantry tanks—"Matildas"), Matruh Garrison Force (a Brigade Group under Brigadier Selby).

The total force comprised 31,000 men, 120 guns, 275 tanks of which 50 were Infantry tanks, and 60 armoured cars.

This was less than half the strength of the enemy, but our training, equipment and morale were expected to compensate for the numerical disadvantage. The equipment was superior in design and battle worthiness but reserves and spares were woefully short. Logistically there was sufficient punch but not much in reserve. Success depended on quick results. It was a military gamble but differed from the Norwegian campaign in being a gamble in which the risks (tactical, psychological and logistic) were carefully studied and skilfully calculated.

It was almost a one-man job on the part of General Wavell. Egypt was neutral and there were many Italian nationals at large. General Wavell had to take the additional risk of keeping all but a select few of his subordinates in the dark about his plans and the purpose of the preparations which he ordered.

The essential features of the plan for the Sidi Barrani operation were surprise, mobility and speed. Transport was limited and dumps of ammunition, water, supplies and petrol were established well forward. Several days supplies for the whole force were stored some 20–30 miles in advance of our fortified lines covered only by our advanced patrols.

The stocks for these Field Supply Depots had to be carried by all available MT and thereafter replenishment could not take place as the transport was needed for troop carrying. For administrative reasons the first phase of the operation was planned to last 5 days. On this short-term basis Ordnance stores need not be held in the Field Supply Depots, but in later operations they developed into the more elaborate Field Maintenance Centres, where stocks of all essential commodities, including Ordnance stores were held and authorized stock levels maintained. The concept remains to this day in the form of Maintenance Areas, and units are included in the Order of Battle to operate them.

The Sidi Barrani battle was strikingly successful, the enemy forces being driven into Libya having lost over 38,000 prisoners, 237 guns and 73 tanks. British casualties were only 624 killed, wounded and missing.

No time was lost in exploiting this success to the full. Although 4th Indian Division was withdrawn to strengthen the Sudan front, it was replaced by 6th Australian Division. A brilliant campaign followed. First Bardia and then Tobruk were captured. The Italians were driven westward along the coast road, and, when they attempted to withdraw from Cyrenaica, a force advanced across the desert, cut them off at Beda Fomm, and after heavy fighting forced their surrender.

In 10 weeks a British force of never more than 2 Divisions—one of them armoured—with a proportion of corps troops, had totally destroyed an army of 10 Divisions for a loss of 500 killed and 1,400 wounded and missing.

The campaign is a perfect example of the skilful adjustment of limited means to suit the end. The equipment available to the force was of good quality and stood up well to the severe test of a 500-mile advance in desert conditions. But shortages were acute and reserves hardly existed. The Infantry tank proved to be a battle winner in this campaign but the appalling scarcity of spares for it caused constant concern. Maintenance throughout was a hand-to-mouth affair.

The exploitation of local resources has already been mentioned and in addition, from the end of September, a steady flow of vehicles, armament and arms was received from the United Kingdom, a courageous decision in view of the threat of invasion and one which was fully justified by results. These preparatory efforts served to bring most units of the Western Desert force up to their full scale of war equipment, but reserves were still lacking.

The following examples illustrate the part which the RAOC was called upon to play in this campaign:

1. *Modification of Tanks.* In September 161 tanks were received from the United Kingdom. They had to be modified for desert warfare which included the provision of fittings for the carriage of extra water and rations, fitting of locally made air cleaners to some of them, and a very heavy modification to the suspension of 14 Infantry tanks. All these vehicles were completed in the Base Workshops in 12 days.

2. *Recovery.* It was obvious that recovery difficulties would increase in relation to the rapidity of the advance, and considerable ingenuity was necessary to meet this special need, particularly as there was a general shortage of recovery vehicles in the Middle East.

No vehicle capable of recovering an Infantry tank in the desert had been provided from the United Kingdom and it was necessary to arrange local purchase of suitable high-powered vehicles and modify them by fitting winches, cranes and desert equipment. Types used included Marmon–Harrington 6-wheel drive, and Chevrolet 4-wheel drive lorries, D6 and D7 caterpillar tractors, and AEC 4-wheel drive tractors. In addition light breakdown vehicles were created by fitting certain Morris 3-ton lorries with cranes. At the end of the operation the actual number of recovery vehicles held by the Armoured Division Workshops and GHQ Troops Workshops was 150 per cent above establishment.

3. *Water*. Lack of water both for men and vehicle radiators was a major problem. The War Establishment of 7th Armoured Division allowed twenty 15-cwt water trucks, which was roughly one per unit. This made no allowance for detached sub-units, and the Division already held 35 water trucks by September 1940. Later it was necessary to increase the scale to 64.

There was no reserve from which these additional issues could be made and the problem was solved by the production of a local pattern 160-gallon tank mounted on a 15-cwt GS Morris truck. No filtering apparatus was fitted, so that when only doubtful sources of supply were available the local pattern tanks had to be filled through a standard water tank which had a filter.

Local manufacture of distilled water and containers for it was undertaken at the Base, and during this campaign 5,000 gallons per week were issued from 4 BOD (Abbassia) for the batteries of vehicles and wireless sets, and for the radiators of tanks.

4. *Navigation*. Sun compasses were necessary for desert navigation and the RAOC arranged the local manufacture and issue to units of approximately 3,000 of them.

5. *Anti-tank mines*. These were arriving in insufficient numbers from the United Kingdom, so local types were designed and manufactured. The RAOC designed a mine containing $6\frac{1}{2}$ lb of explosive, the RE one containing 5 lb of explosive. All filling was done by the RAOC. Quantities produced were:

> Mine bodies manufactured by RAOC   38,000
> Mine bodies manufactured by RE   65,000
> Mines filled by RAOC   90,000

As, in the event, we advanced 500 miles at a considerable speed it may be assumed that the Italians were in greater need of anti-tank mines than ourselves, but our requirement was to come later.

6. *Base Repairs*. Although GHQ had ruled that no Base installations were to be located in Alexandria, special permission was given for a Base Ordnance Workshop to be opened there.

Suitable accommodation was found which had the enormous advantage of lifting gear capable of dealing with the heaviest types of tank.

This afforded relief to the hard pressed No. 4 Base Ordnance Workshop in Cairo, and also saved the extra haul between Alexandria and Cairo, a distance of about 150 miles. Thus the turn-round period for vehicles requiring base overhaul was substantially reduced.

SYSTEM OF SUPPLY AND LESSONS

An Advanced Ordnance Depot was located at El Daba and held 14 days maintenance of MT spares for the Western Desert Force, reserves of clothing and stocks of camp equipment and signal stores. Originally this depot held no more than 7,000 items, but during the operation the stocks of MT parts alone grew to 25,000 different items. No portion of these base stocks was held in advance of El Daba except that a 30-day reserve of Ordnance stores was held near the railhead at Mersa Matruh for the garrison of that place.

The rail capacity for the long distance from Cairo to Mersa Matruh was inadequate. The difficulties were aggravated by the shortage of rolling stock, particularly flats, and by the poor rail facilities at 4 BOD at Abbassia which during the whole of the operation functioned as the main depot for the supply of MT and warlike stores.

A daily pack train failed to meet requirements and it was necessary to introduce a road convoy service provided by reserve vehicles specially allotted for the purpose and by replacement vehicles going forward. The convoy service was operated by 1 Ordnance Field Park and 1st Cavalry Division OFP, which was a reserve unit.

The system started as a means to supplement supply by rail from Cairo to Mersa Matruh, but was later extended to deliver vehicles and urgent fighting stores to the Armoured Divisional Ordnance Field Park throughout the advance.

The shortage of stores and equipment resulted in much additional work to meet urgent issues, notably the search required at the docks to locate items in recently off-loaded cargo and arrange special despatch to the forward area of the base as appropriate.

The whole situation brought out a feature of the supply of Ordnance stores which is not always understood. These stores differ from rations, petrol and ammunition in consisting of a very large range of items for a relatively small tonnage. Apart from a small proportion of known fast moving items, the actual needs of the user at any one time cannot be predicted. It is obviously impracticable to place complete stocks of everything just behind the forward troops, who may be holding a wide front. Moreover, these stocks could not be moved in the event of a withdrawal. Therefore a fast service must be provided so as to supply urgent needs from the nearest large holding—in this case the BOD. This is a matter not of opinion but of hard fact. Yet surprise is often expressed when the RAOC ask for the fastest means to supply urgent fighting stores.

AMMUNITION SUPPLY

Railheads were established at Fuka, Sidi Heneish, Qassaba and Mersa Matruh, and an Advanced Ammunition Depot at El Daba holding a modest 1,600 tons. Stock levels were laid down for each FSD and these levels were maintained by automatic replenishment as issues were made to formations.

The supply system was rapidly switched as the operation progressed. There were three phases:

Phase A Before the capture of Bardia. Rail to ARH thence by road to FSD or Refilling Points.

Phase B As for Phase A or by sea to Sollum and thence by road.

Phase C By direct shipment from Alexandria to Tobruk and thence by road.

REPAIR AND RECOVERY

The campaign indicated the importance of sufficient recovery vehicles and transporters if the maximum number of AFVs was to be kept in action.

Rapid repair in the field was best achieved by assembly replacement which demanded a high scale of assemblies and a corresponding capacity for assembly repair in Base Workshops. Desert conditions were particularly hard on engines.

An organization for the rapid return of repairable equipment was essential. In this campaign priority was sometimes given to the return of enemy equipment. This should not have been done at the expense of our own.

LAUNDRY SERVICES

Under the peace-time system units had their own "Dhobies". They probably preferred this system and it continued after mobilization, supported by the ruling to retain peace accounting. Unfortunately the loyalty of the dhobies to their units did not extend to following them to battle in the Western Desert, and the "flight of the dhobies" threw the whole burden of laundry services for the force on to the laundry at Alexandria.

A laundry plant at Alexandria, previously owned by a steamship company was purchased at a cost of £6,000 and began work in July 1940 under RAOC control. During operations in the Western Desert the weekly output of this laundry was between 60,000 and 90,000 items.

Nevertheless the system was not satisfactory. Water was very scarce in nearly the whole theatre of operations, and had mobile laundries been available there were only a few places where they could have operated. The solution was an ample supply of replenishment clothing but as transport was scarce the clothing could not be carried in sufficient quantities.

The "exchange system" operative in peace was not workable in war, though attempts to make it do so were applied with a dogged persistence worthy of a better cause. This may have been due to the significance attached early in the war to decontamination on the assumption that sooner or later chemical warfare would break out.

Ultimately the correct balance was achieved. Base laundries were established on a large scale. Dirty and worn clothing was returned to the Base, cleaned and repaired there and put back to stock in the BOD. Mobile laundries were established in the theatre of operations wherever sufficient water existed. Troops who were unable to make use of this service washed their own clothes as best they could and obtained replacements when necessary by the normal supply system.

CONCLUSION

The operation was completed so successfully and quickly that there was a tendency to draw false conclusions about the logistic support necessary for future campaigns.

The defeat which followed when German reinforcements arrived has been attributed to the weakening of our own forces by the expedition to Greece. This was a factor, but even without that diversion there are logistic reasons for concluding that we should have had to withdraw from Cyrenaica or a large part of it. To obtain quick results General Wavell had expended all his resources of equipment in the Western Desert, the Sudan and Eritrea. A pause was necessary to build up sufficient resources for future campaigns, but he was not to be granted that respite.

Risks which were justified by results against the Italians could not be taken against the Germans. General Wavell knew this. He had gone near to achieving the impossible already but the odds against him were to become too great.

THE CAMPAIGN IN GREECE AND CRETE

On October 28th 1940 Italy invaded Greece. This was another reckless gamble by Mussolini. The step was taken without previous consultation with Hitler from whom it had a cold reception. Hitler had other plans which did not include the invasion of Greece. Normal diplomatic relations were maintained and German nationals remained in the country.

But the move did not fail to embarrass the British. We were at war with Italy and were bound to give what assistance we could to Greece, yet we had other pressing commitments. At home the Battle of Britain had been won in the previous month and the danger of invasion had passed, but this was not known at the time and the night bombing of London and other cities was at its worst.

In Egypt General Wavell's plans for defeating Marshal Graziani were maturing and it was vital that they should not be disrupted for, without a secure base in Egypt, Britain could not help Greece, Turkey or any other ally in the Mediterranean theatre.

Fortunately, the Greeks did not want a military force to land in the country for fear of provoking the Germans. Their immediate need was for air support and anti-aircraft weapons and ammunition to counter the Italian Air Force. Accordingly, despite the fact that our resources were as meagre in this field as elsewhere, it was decided on November 4th to send an air contingent to Greece under Air Commodore J. H. D'Albiac.

In addition to the RAF, he had under his command 2,000 men from over 40 different units of the Army, comprising anti-aircraft, engineer, signals and administrative elements, including RAOC. Detachments of an AOD and an AAD were established outside Athens and a Workshop in the town. These units were small, their responsibilities being confined to the supply of the needs of the British Army, common user items for the RAF, certain RAF ammunition and such requirements of the Greek Army as could be met from available resources. In addition, they formed a nucleus from which larger depots and workshops could be developed, should a British force be landed in Greece for operations later on.

No exceptional difficulties were experienced though there were certain problems in the loading of ships which appeared regularly in every operation in the first 2 years of the war. For example vehicles were arbitrarily shut out of shipments and several units arrived without their war equipment.

The Italian plan was dependent on their superiority in armour and in the air. They hoped to break through early to the plains after which a Greek collapse was confidently expected. In fact they met a sturdy resistance in the mountains. Not only were they checked but the Greeks counter-attacked and advanced some distance into Albania. British assistance was given by bombing the ports and concentrations of Italian troops, and the raid by the Fleet Air Arm on Taranto immobilized a large part of the Italian Fleet.

The Greek victory removed the danger of any invasion launched by the Italian forces alone, but the German threat remained. A quiet period followed, and during the next 3 months General Wavell won his spectacular victory in the Western Desert and was engaged in the early stages of an equally spectacular conquest of the Italian colonies in East Africa.

These events finally convinced Hitler that German intervention in the Mediterranean theatre was essential. The advanced elements of the Afrika Corps under General Rommel were sent out, and the preliminary steps were taken to obtain control of the Balkans, preferably without recourse to military operations. After a promising start these manœuvres failed and the invasion of Yugoslavia and Greece had to be undertaken.

Meanwhile, GHQ Middle East had seen the danger and formed a force to move into Greece as soon as the Greek Government asked for armed assistance.

This force, under the command of Lieutenant-General Sir Maitland Wilson, consisted of, HQ 1st Anzac Corps, Australian Corps troops, 6th Australian Division, 1st New Zealand Division, 1st Armoured Brigade Group, Force troops, Base and L of C units. The RAOC Order of Battle is at Appendix A to this chapter.

When German intentions were unmistakable, the Greeks asked for military support and the Army units started moving into Greece on March 5th. Between March 9th and 16th the Italians launched another strong offensive in Albania. This also failed but it left the Greek formations opposing it exhausted and unfit to resist a German attack. Although British reinforcements had been requested, and General Wilson arrived in Athens on March 4th, Germany and Greece were not yet at war and General Wilson was asked to remain incognito and in plain clothes which did not assist either reconnaissance or command.

Seven FSDs were formed in the forward areas and each held 7 days' stocks of essential commodities. The plan was to hold 90 days' supply of Ordnance stores and ammunition in the country and 70 days' supply of Ordnance stores had been received by April 6th. The scene is vividly described in the *Official History* of the campaign which states: "The unloading of all this and the disembarkation of the troops and their equipment was solemnly witnessed by the staff of the German Embassy, who were free to come and go as they liked. It is hard to picture a more ridiculous situation in war-time than that of the German Military Attaché standing on the quay and counting the British troops, whose own Commander was not allowed to show himself to them."

The Germans invaded Greece on April 6th. The British campaign was from start to finish a withdrawal. The forward position from the Yugoslav border to the mouth of the River Aliakmon was not fully manned by the time the Germans advanced. On the left flank the collapse of Yugoslav resistance opened up the Monastir Gap, and further to the west the Greek troops facing the Italians were exhausted. To the east, in spite of gallant resistance by the 3 Greek Divisions under General Bacopoulos, Salonika was captured and that part of the country was in enemy hands by April 10th.

The withdrawal took place by stages, first to the line Olympia–Servia between April 11th and 14th, then to Thermopylae between April 15th and 19th and finally through Athens to Corinth and embarkation from beaches at Nauplia, Myloi, Monemvasia and Kalamata, though small numbers were taken off at Raphina and Megara east of the Corinth Canal.

THE RAOC SITUATION

The DDOS Colonel C. Douglas White arrived in Athens early in February 1941. Force Headquarters was at the Acropole Hotel. There were some RAOC personnel attached to the British Military Mission on liaison duties in connection with the supply of equipment to the Greek Army, and the intention was that, after arranging the accommodation for the staff of the DDOS, they would be absorbed into his headquarters.

The staff of the DDOS brought with them a considerable amount of equipment and vehicles, which they were not destined to keep as they were transferred to the Greeks, leaving the DDOS with a completely static and lightly equipped headquarters.

In the early stages stores were arranged by sub-depots in the "go-downs" of the harbour at the Piraeus until staff and transport could be found to move them. After that the BOD (really an AOD in size) was organized as follows:

The headquarters and clothing sub-depot in a school at the northern end of Athens; MT sub-depot in open ground 8 miles north of Athens; General Stores in tents at Monidion just north of Athens; Technical and Warlike Stores sub-depot a mile or so from the Piraeus.

It was planned to establish an AOD in the Larissa area, and staff was sent forward for that purpose, but events moved too quickly for any real progress to be made.

In the ammunition field the small detachment of 2 officers and 30 ORs, which had been established in the Kukuvaunes area north of Athens since the previous November under Major W. P. Dixon, was reinforced so that it might develop as a BAD. However, large stocks of ammunition were not received and the depot strength never exceeded 5 officers and 60 ORs. An additional detachment arrived with the force and was sent to the Larissa area to form a forward ammunition depot there, but could only operate as a sort of railhead detachment for a few days before the withdrawal took place.

The COME was Colonel J. F. X. Miller. A small workshop had already been established in a garage at the north end of Athens, but base repair was not possible and all efforts were concentrated on getting the most out of formation workshops and LADs.

Colonel Douglas White did not consider that depot arrangements were satisfactory. He reconnoitred new sites, clear of Athens, which would allow room for expansion and development, and these would have been occupied had the force remained in Greece.

Depots were functioning normally by the time the Germans entered the war against Greece, but a disastrous explosion in the Piraeus Harbour destroyed all facilities for getting heavy equipment into the country, and considerably hampered the future maintenance of the force.

The explosion was caused by a German air raid on the port. Bombs hit an ammunition ship full of explosives for the Greek Army, and it blew up destroying the berthing facilities. Fifteen railway wagons which had not been pulled clear of the harbour area went up and also a lighter containing 100 tons of ammunition for the British Army. The timing of the raid and the accuracy with which the targets were located show that the many German agents in the neighbourhood had not been idle.

It was no easy matter to move stores and ammunition forward to meet the needs of the fighting units. Greece is a very rugged country with poor communications. There were no railways to the west of the Pindus Range. To the east a broad gauge line ran from Athens to Salonika, and there was a narrow gauge line from Athens over the Corinth Canal Bridge and on to Nauplia, Argos and Kalamata. A reasonable road ran from Athens to Salonika, but many roads were narrow, and, where they passed through mountains, vehicles were necessarily road-bound and extremely vulnerable to air attack. In these circumstances units were almost entirely dependent on their own resources with the assistance which could be given by the RAOC units with formations—Field Parks, Light Repair Sections and Recovery Sections. The LADs did invaluable work.

The enemy deployed formidable air forces operating from airfields well forward. The gallantry of our pilots could not make up for the small number of obsolescent aircraft with which they were provided. Thus the enemy enjoyed complete air superiority. The methods which had been so successful in France were repeated with improvements, but fortunately night attacks were rare. Nearly all movement was by night, a process which was sufficiently hazardous on these roads.

Signal communications were sketchy and ignorance of the situation was common. In a withdrawal this is liable to lead to units and individuals being left "in the air" and captured. No doubt this occurred in a number of cases, though the majority of prisoners were trapped at the beaches from which the Navy was unable to rescue them.

When the decision to withdraw from Greece was conveyed to the depots it was clear that there was only sufficient transport to carry men with their weapons and such technical equipment as could be carried by individuals. No kit-bags or anything of that sort could be taken and depot equipment had to be handed over to the Greeks or destroyed.

The difficulty of destroying well-sited stacks of ammunition has been mentioned elsewhere, but Major W. P. Dixon who commanded 4 AAD sent the greater part of his unit on to the embarkation point, and remained with a small party to destroy the depot stocks. He used a variety of devices and observed the results which appeared to be satisfactory. He also destroyed those vehicles which had to be left behind.

At about midnight on April 21st/22nd Colonel Douglas White received orders to collect as many RAOC units as possible and move to Anno Lissa station. He was able to collect about 700 officers and men from various units. It was daylight by the time the train arrived and enemy aircraft were active, also the engine had a mechanical defect. Luckily no attack took place and Lieutenant Farley of 1st Armoured Brigade LRS repaired the engine.

The party moved by stages to the Corinth Canal area where Brigadier

126

Parrington was in charge. Vehicles were being organized to take parties to Nauplia to await embarkation and Colonel Douglas White suggested that he should go there to take charge and particularly to ensure that vehicles which had taken troops to the beach area were sent back to collect further parties. This was agreed.

When he arrived at Nauplia he found a good deal of confusion. Vehicles were not being unloaded and returned. He was able to clear the roads and he set up a control point at the cross-roads at Nauplia at which he recorded details of all arrivals in the area.

On April 24th Colonel Douglas White was joined by a major of the Q (Movements) Staff and later that day he received orders from Brigadier Lee, then commanding in the Peloponnese, to assume command of the Nauplia area. The embarkation arrangements went well and during the night about 7,000 men were embarked. Discipline was good.

On April 25th about 6,000 men came into Nauplia and as this seemed likely to exceed considerably the capacity of the ships expected in the bay a convoy of 170 lorries was collected and the men were sent on to Kalamata. The naval officers at Nauplia were told of this so that ships could be diverted to Kalamata if necessary.

Early on April 26th two trains left Nauplia for Kalamata, so that by road and rail more than 6,000 men had been moved southward to what was considered a safer and better locality for embarkation. Unfortunately, in the end, about 7,000 men were captured at Kalamata, owing to the rapid cross-country move of a small German force and resultant misunderstandings as to whether the enemy was in occupation of the town.

During the night of April 26th/27th the caiques which had been expected did not turn up, except for two which had been chartered and were under Royal Navy command.

Just after midnight it was learnt that the *Glen Carn*, which carried all the landing craft for ferrying to the ships had been damaged.

It was decided that merchant ships must leave by 0300 hours and ships of the Royal Navy by 0400 hours. When the ships had sailed there were still about 700 men on the quay. An order to send them on by MT could not be carried out for lack of vehicles. The party was sent to a beach not far away from which the Royal Navy planned to take them the following night. They eventually sailed in the cruiser HMAS *Perth*.

When the beach was clear of troops a small number of officers and men, about 40 in all, remained with Colonel Douglas White. They boarded a caique—the *St. George*—commanded by Lieutenant-Commander Hook, RN, and proceeded to "creek-hop" southward.

They eventually arrived about 15 miles south of Monemvasia. A party, which included Captain Casdagli, RAOC, a Greek-speaking officer, landed to try to obtain a motor boat to visit Monemvasia. In this they succeeded and returned with a request to bring the caique there to assist

EASTERN MEDITERRANEAN & MIDDLE EAST
SCALE   1 INCH = 300 MILES

0   100 200 300   600   900

129

in the embarkation of troops. They moved to Monemvasia on the night of April 28th/29th and ferried New Zealanders from rowing boats to HMS *Isis*, finally embarking themselves and sailing to Crete. There they transferred to the *Thursland Castle* which was part of a convoy sailing to Egypt.

Altogether some 18,000 men were moved through Nauplia when Colonel Douglas White was in charge, 12,000 by sea and 6,000 by road and rail towards Kalamata. Not all these men reached Egypt. Some were captured at Kalamata, some were lost at sea and others were captured in Crete.

CRETE

Although the short campaign in Crete was an extension of the Greek operation, GHQ Middle East did not appear to have a coordinated plan for the two areas. Crete was treated as a separate commitment, very low on the priority list. In practice little could have been done as the meagre resources of the Middle East were stretched to the limit.

April 1941 was probably the worst period in the whole war for the Middle East Command as a glance at the many simultaneous activities will show:

Malta	Heavy air attacks. Two operations to reinforce.
Western Desert	British driven back to the Egyptian frontier. Tobruk besieged.
Greece	British forces driven from Greece.
Syria	Axis scheme to use Syria, with the acquiescence of the Vichy French, as a base for supporting the Iraq revolt.
Iraq	Siege of Habbaniya.
East Africa	Capture of Asmara, Addis Ababa and Massawa, but the campaign in Ethiopia not yet finished.

It is true that if Greece or part of it were held, Crete was in no danger, but the island would have been a convenient advanced base for small reserves of equipment and to commit everything to the mainland was to invite disaster in the event of the collapse of Greek resistance.

When Italy attacked, all Greek soldiers on the island were sent to the mainland to reinforce the Albanian front. The British Army replaced them with a weak Brigade Group (partly at the expense of Malta) and provided 8 heavy and 12 light anti-aircraft guns. A landing ground was made at Maleme from which fighters could defend the harbour at Suda Bay. This was considered sufficient to deal with any attacks which the Italians might make from the Dodecanese Islands, a view which was justified by events.

Reserves of transport, equipment and ammunition were not provided on a scale which could enable the defence of such a long coastline against

130

a powerful invasion to be undertaken effectively with the small force available, and the RAOC only provided a small camp depot at Canea.

The topography and backward state of the island added to the difficulty of defending it against attacks from the north. Crete is about 160 miles long from east to west and 40 miles across at its widest point. Barren mountains run the entire length with steep slopes to the southern coast, more gradual slopes to the north. The only ports fit for cargo vessels were on the north coast and of these Suda Bay was a good anchorage. To get there ships had to run the gauntlet of the Kithera Channel and as the bay was an obvious target it soon became a graveyard for ships. In the south there were only a few small fishing harbours, exposed to the full force of the weather and useless, without elaborate harbour construction, as ports of entry for significant quantities of equipment. Those which figured in the operation were Tymbaki (linked by a track to Heraklion) and Sphakia on the coast south of Suda Bay. There was no railway and the roads were mere mountain tracks except for the coast road linking Heraklion and Canea.

Outside the ports and fishing villages the population consisted of peasant farmers living in primitive conditions. The barren country could hardly support the normal population and could provide nothing for military units who must be maintained from outside sources. Water was very scarce in May, the level in the wells being low and the weather hot.

The 14th Infantry Brigade was already established at Heraklion, and large reinforcements of manpower resulted from British and Greek units and miscellaneous parties of troops which had been brought back from Greece.

The defence of the island was assigned to General Freyberg on May 1st, and he disposed his troops in four sectors as follows:

Heraklion:

HQ 14th Infantry Brigade.
2 British battalions.
3 Greek battalions.
300 Australian riflemen.
250 artillerymen armed as infantry.

Retimo:

HQ 19th Australian Infantry Brigade.
4 Australian battalions.
6 Greek battalions.

Suda Bay:

Mobile Naval Base Defence Organization (MNBDO).
2 Australian battalions (improvised).
1 RHA regiment armed as infantry.
2 Greek battalions.
1st Battalion Welch Regiment and riflemen from various regiments.

Maleme:

4th New Zealand Brigade, west of Canea.
5th New Zealand Brigade, in Maleme area.
10th (improvised) Infantry Brigade made up from New Zealand units and 2 Greek battalions.
1 Greek battalion.

Although this appears to be a perfectly adequate force for the defence of the island there were several factors which greatly diminished its fighting efficiency.

1. The Germans continued to have complete air superiority. Before the German attack began the RAF had ceased to be able to maintain aircraft on the island. Everything possible was done by means of sorties from Egypt but these could not influence the battle in face of the German superiority in aircraft.

2. Only the units of 14th Infantry Brigade were fully equipped for battle. The MNBDO was not fully operational even within the limits of the task for which it was formed owing to some elements still being at Haifa. But of the remaining troops in some cases complete or nearly complete units had come back; in other cases parties from units which had suffered heavy casualties were formed into improvised composite units, while the Greek battalions were units in name only. Only personal weapons, light machine guns and a few anti-tank rifles had been brought back. There was an acute shortage of small arms ammunition. Shortcomings in organization and fire power were very serious.

3. There was such a shortage of vehicles that mobile defence was impossible. The four sectors had to operate a static defence each in its own locality. Lack of mobility was, as much as anything else, the cause of our failure to defeat the enemy in Crete. Lack of vehicles also contributed to prevent equipment and ammunition from reaching the troops whose need was most urgent.

4. There were far too many men on the island. Considerable numbers of administrative troops had been landed from Greece, but they were indifferently armed, in some cases having unsuitable weapons such as revolvers, and in all cases having only a few rounds of ammunition. In this state they were of limited value as reinforcements to the fighting troops who were themselves extremely short of weapons and ammunition. They were not needed to run depots for the supply of war material because there was hardly any in Crete and during May it was only possible to send very small quantities from Egypt in face of enemy air attack. There was nothing that many of these troops could do, but they had to be fed and the same applied to the large influx of Greeks and to the considerable number of Italian prisoners held in the island before the emergency.

The 3 weeks' respite between the evacuation of Greece and the start of the German invasion of Crete was spent in organizing and equipping as far as possible the units of the defending force. This would have been a golden opportunity to transfer back to Egypt the men who could not be employed in Crete but were badly needed in Egypt.

The history *Australia in the War of 1939–1945*, Series One, Army, Volume II, states: "The problem of supply which was certain to become acute sooner or later could have been greatly lessened by removing from the island all except strong and fully-equipped or re-equipped units. The eventual removal of about 16,000 troops in four nights demonstrated that the embarkation of all ill-armed or inessential detachments could have been carried out much earlier by employing similar methods."

The story of the battle is well known and need only be summarized here. Enemy air attacks were unsuccessful at first and their paratroops failed to occupy any of the airfields. Then elements of a mountain division were brought in using transport planes and gliders which crash-landed at Maleme landing ground and captured it. They were never driven off, partly because transport was lacking to bring reinforcements quickly to the threatened point, and partly because the troops were disposed to deal with a landing from the sea as well as the air. The seaborne invasion was a real threat which was defeated by the Royal Navy, but not until after it had prevented concentration of our forces at the vital point of Maleme. The enemy could now bring in reinforcements of men, mountain guns and mortars which, combined with air bombardment, gave them a decisive superiority in fire power.

When the decision was made to withdraw from Crete, the troops at Heraklion left by sea on the night of May 28th/29th. When daylight came the ships were attacked and some were lost. Of the 4,000 troops embarked 800 were killed, wounded or captured after being picked up by Italian motor boats. The units manning the sector at Retimo were surrounded and eventually surrendered after running out of ammunition.

The troops to the west withdrew down the mountain track to Sphakia. The rearguard successfully held off the enemy at Stilos and Babali Hani. The marching troops were organized into small groups of about 50 men and the groups moved at wide intervals as dispersion against air attack. There was an appalling shortage of water and the heat and dust on that mountain road made the march exhausting in the extreme. Some straggling and disorder was bound to occur. A control point was established some distance along the track north of Sphakia. Parties were dispersed to concealed localities from which they were to be called forward for embarkation when night fell. Many of these parties—well disciplined and controlled by Warrant Officers and senior NCOs—were sent to Sphakia some days before the final date for evacuation, June 1st. They arrived at the control point, were given a location in the dispersion area and told to wait until called forward for embarkation. They never heard any more and were duly captured. Some took to the hills and escaped later. Others managed to escape from Greece, but the number was very small. A high proportion of RAOC casualties of the campaign consisted of men who had been brought out of Greece but landed in Crete instead of Egypt. They could do nothing in Crete and were eventually captured there.

RAOC UNITS IN CRETE

A small depot existed in Canea and an ammunition depot was established at Katisfariana about 2 miles south of Canea. The immediate task in early May was to provide clothing, necessaries, blankets and accommodation stores for several thousand troops, including Greek soldiers, who had been landed in the island from Greece.

This was the responsibility of Lieutenant-Colonel J. Hitchcock, ADOS Crete, who arrived there on April 24th, although in the second week in May he was recalled to Egypt for another appointment and handed over to Lieutenant-Colonel S. T. Rooke, who had returned from Greece.

Three camps were formed for the troops who had to be re-equipped. They were at:

Peribolia for 17,000 men;
Kalibes for 12,000 men of 6th Australian Division;
Platanias for 14,000 New Zealanders.

This total was eleven times the number for which supplies of clothing and equipment had originally been planned.

Transport was at a premium and the decision was made to pool all transport under the ADST. It was almost impossible to clear Ordnance stores from ports to depots or make issues direct to the troops unless units could collect. Transfer of stores from one port to another was done almost entirely by caique at night.

The supply of weapons was never satisfactorily solved. A trial of captured Italian guns, with no instruments, and ammunition sent from Egypt was not a great success. There were the usual difficulties in ensuring that weapons and their associated stores did not become separated during shipment. Nineteen Vickers machine guns arrived without tripods and other items. These guns were undoubtedly complete when they left the BOD in Egypt, but the important components had either been shut out at Alexandria, loaded into a different ship or stored in a different part of the same ship which returned with them, a fairly common operational situation. The link between Movements and Ordnance was not close enough to prevent such mistakes which might have serious consequences. It was more than a year before this situation was rectified.

The Ordnance Depot created an efficient salvage organization under Captain Casdagli. Equipment and weapons brought back from Greece and dumped at or near the transit camps were collected, sorted and made ready for re-issue.

Supply of ammunition was extremely difficult. The general plan was to hold it in fighting sectors of the front with only one fifth in the ammunition depot. Distribution was largely by caique and demands were conveyed by despatch rider while it was still possible to use that method. The RAOC staff at the ports did good work unloading stores and ammunition during air raids.

Major H. F. Stubbs was in charge of the workshops and he was assisted by technical staff who had returned from Greece. Heavy air attacks compelled the strictest attention to concealment and dispersion which hampered the efficiency and continuity of work. The workshop at Canea was bombed out and the small amount of vehicles and equipment which survived was transferred to Kalibes, about 10 miles away on the coast road. By this time it had become impossible to operate static workshops effectively and all efforts were concentrated on the maintenance of guns and other equipments *in situ*. Fortunately all the vehicles of the workshop were wisely excluded from the scheme for pooling transport, and it was possible to move maintenance teams quickly to those points where their services were most in demand.

The repair of Infantry tanks (a handful had been sent to the island for airfield defence) and of AA guns was of primary importance. Guns which were knocked out or beyond repair were cannibalized to keep others in action. When the order to leave Crete was received all equipment was destroyed or handed over to the local inhabitants who took to the mountains.

The LADs, having been compelled to leave their machinery, lorries and other equipment in Greece, were limited in the scope of first line repair they could undertake. They nevertheless continued to be an asset to their units. The LAD to the 102nd (Northumberland Hussars) Regiment RHA may be taken as an example. The Commanding Officer reported that during the retreat in Greece the LAD under Lieutenant A. L. Taylor, rendered most valuable service. Without the LAD the unit would never have got its vehicles (less those destroyed in action) to the beach. The LAD brought its Bren gun back to Crete where it was used with effect. Lieutenant Taylor commanded HQ Troop of the Regiment during the fighting in Crete until May 20th, when he was killed. Throughout the operations in both countries from April 6th to May 20th he set a fine example.

LESSONS OF GREECE AND CRETE

Weapon Training. RAOC units frequently had to operate as infantry or defend themselves and their equipment against air attack. Although most of the men were in possession of rifles and had received some training, few had handled anti-tank rifles or Bren guns. Perhaps this situation was caused by the shortage of these weapons at that stage of the war, but more training should have been given to men posted to units forming part of a force such as that which went to Greece.

Loading of Ships. The Movement and Transportation Staff were concerned with the application of certain principles in the stowage of freight ships which were related to loading the ship to maximum capacity and the importance of quick turn-round. These are, of course, important principles, paramount in peace, but affected by other factors in war.

From the RAOC point of view the issue of complete equipments and complete rounds of ammunition caused the greatest concern. It was easy enough to send the associated stores, such as dial sights, forward to the ship with the guns, and equally to send forward complete rounds but the association between the various elements was liable to be lost when the ship was loaded. We have seen the example of Vickers machine guns being loaded and the tripods apparently shut out.

It was not only necessary to ensure that the associated stores were loaded in the same ship. They must be in the same part of the ship. It was so common as to be almost normal for a ship to return to port with a significant part of the cargo still on board. If the ship was ever completely discharged later on, it was probably at a different port and the equipment was deficient of essential components for an indefinite period. This was a very serious matter when equipment was scarce.

It is easy to understand the reluctance of Movement and Transportation Staff to accept what must have seemed to them interference from another Service. There must must be one authority at the port if chaos is to be avoided. Possibly for this reason it was not until quite late in the war that the importance of tactical loading and of the stowage by complete equipments and complete rounds was fully appreciated. Port ordnance and ammunition detachments then took their proper place in the scheme of things.

Air Superiority. A decisive factor in the Germans' success was their complete superiority in the air and the skilful use which they made of it.

The majority of Ordnance Stores, vehicles and ammunition had been landed in Greece before the Germans attacked. The Piraeus, the port of Athens, was then so heavily bombed that it was put out of action. No further heavy equipment could be landed, and none could be taken away, which, as events developed, proved to be the more serious blow.

In Crete, by May 25th 1941, no merchant ship had any chance of survival within 50 miles of the island. No more guns or other heavy equipment could be sent after that. Previously half the field guns sent to strengthen the defences of the island had been lost at sea.

RAOC CASUALTIES IN GREECE AND CRETE

These were heavy in proportion to the number of RAOC men in the force and amounted to 38 officers and 750 other ranks killed, wounded and missing. A serious factor was the number of experienced Warrant Officers and NCOs and skilled tradesmen who were lost and could not be replaced. This could not but be detrimental to the standard of service which the Corps could give in the immediate future.

IRAQ AND SYRIA

Between the wars Iraq had become an independent nation. She had a Treaty of Alliance and Mutual Support with Great Britain by which in the event of war, she was bound to give us all possible aid including the use of railways, rivers, ports and airfields. The RAF retained bases at Shaiba near Basra and Habbaniya west of Baghdad. The protection of the oilfields and the pipelines to the Mediterranean was of obvious importance to us.

But the strength of such an alliance is largely the strength of the senior partner, and nations which have recently attained independence are understandably more concerned with being on the winning side than with moral obligations attached to a mere paper transaction.

At this stage of the war no one could say that Great Britain was doing particularly well, and the fate of our allies—Poland, for example—was not calculated to inspire confidence that an alliance with us would bring agreeable results. The prestige of the Axis powers was high, and they made full use of the excellent opportunities for anti-British propaganda which the situation provided.

It was agreed in March 1941 that if any troops had to be sent to Iraq, they would come from India, and operations would at first be under the control of India. On April 3rd 1941 Rashid Ali, the pro-Axis prime minister, seized power and proclaimed himself Chief of the National Defence Government. One Infantry Brigade Group was diverted by sea from India to Basra, the balance of the 10th Indian Division being due to follow as shipping should allow. On April 17th the first flight of 1st King's Own Royal Regiment was flown from Karachi to Shaiba. Rashid Ali, realizing that the British Government intended to establish troops in Iraq rather than move them through the country, decided to bring matters to a head by means of an armed demonstration against Habbaniya.

The Air Officer Commanding at Habbaniya, Air Vice-Marshal Smart, had at his disposal a miscellaneous collection of obsolescent training aircraft piloted by instructors and trainees of the Flying Training School located there. The garrison consisted of about 1,000 RAF personnel, a British Battalion flown in from Basra, an RAF Armoured Car Company of 18 cars and 1,200 Iraqi and Assyrian Levies. Reinforcement, except by air, was difficult as it was the flood season. An Iraqi force of about a Brigade occupied a plateau overlooking the airfield and their guns shelled the camp, but the garrison showed such initiative and activity that the enemy withdrew on May 6th leaving a quantity of arms and equipment for which good use was soon found.

Meanwhile, control of operations in Iraq had been transferred from India to the Middle East Command, which was an embarrassment to General Wavell, whose resources were already stretched to the limit.

A scratch force, called Habforce, was formed to advance on Habbaniya and Baghdad along the desert pipe-line route from Transjordan via Rutba. The force was based on the 1st Cavalry Division, an under-strength and only partly mechanized formation with very few vehicles and hardly any of these desert-worthy. There were no armoured cars or tanks and very few anti-aircraft or anti-tank weapons. Needless to say, administrative services were improvised, the RAOC contingent consisting of one L of C Recovery Section, two Brigade Group sections of a divisional workshops and a divisional section of an Ordnance Field Park. Small stocks of essential stores were established at H4, a pumping station on the pipe-lines on the Transjordan side of the Iraqi frontier.

Vigorous action on the part of Habforce and the garrison of Habbaniya, combined with a good deal of bluff led to the defeat of Rashid Ali and the signing of armistice terms with a friendly government in Baghdad on May 31st.

It was fortunate that this brief campaign had a happy ending, for trouble was brewing in Syria. From early May, Germany had been using Syria as a base, and no resistance to German demands could be expected from the Vichy-nominated High Commissioner, General Dentz. Obviously German occupation of Syria could not be tolerated and a force was formed under General Wilson to move in and forestall the Germans and Vichy French. The advance began on June 8th.

The force available to General Wilson consisted initially of:

1 Australian Corps HQ;
7th Australian Division;
5th Indian Infantry Brigade Group;
Free French Division (at Brigade Group strength only).

Later in the campaign reinforcements were sent. They included HQ 6th Division and 16th and 23rd Infantry Brigade Groups. Organic Ordnance units (which included Australian and IAOC units) were provided for all formations in the Order of Battle except the Free French.

General Wilson's force was not considered to be sufficient to conquer the whole of Syria against an allied army of Germans and Vichy French with strong German air support, but the gamble was a calculated risk which had to be taken.

As it happened the invasion of Russia was imminent and from the German point of view further adventures in Cyprus, Syria or Iraq were now of minor importance. They decided to withdraw from Syria so as to give the British no pretext for moving in, but it was rather late in the day for such diplomatic niceties to influence a decision which had already been made.

Unfortunately, any idea that there would be little more than token resistance was quickly dispelled. The Vichy French fought well and were very bitter at the use of Free French units against them. They had a compact organization, suitable equipment including superiority in armour, knowledge of the ground which was particularly suited to defence, and ample time to prepare defences.

Thus the campaign dragged on for 5 weeks from the first move on June 8th, and it fell into three phases. The first lasted until June 13th when the advance was held up after early successes. In the second phase, the Vichy forces counter-attacked, re-capturing some points and taking prisoners, but they lost Damascus. In the third phase General Wilson, now helped by reinforcements, advanced all along the line and the enemy were outflanked by the advance of Habforce from Iraq on Palmyra and Homs, and by the move of the 10th Indian Division on Aleppo. A Convention was signed on July 14th. The danger of a German or Italian invasion through Syria had now passed but the Syrians were merely exchanging one unpopular French government for another and political unrest was certain to continue. Bases must be maintained in Palestine and Syria, and this situation continued until the end of the war in Europe.

Apart from the organic units of formations, the RAOC support for the campaigns in Iraq and Syria was as follows:

Base installations comprised a BOD and BOW at Rafa near the Sinai–Palestine border.

In Palestine 3 AOD was established partly at Sarafand and partly at Haifa, and there was also an Australian AOD south-east of Gaza.

On the workshops side 3 AOW was dispersed at Haifa, Tel Aviv and Sarafand with an Australian AOW near Gaza.

Ammunition stocks were held at Wadi Sarar, 30 miles west of Jerusalem.

There were three lines of advance, each of which required its own line of supply. These were the coastal route towards Beirut, the valley route north from Lake Tiberias and flanked by the Lebanon and Anti-Lebanon ranges, and the eastern route via Deraa, Damascus and Homs with the right flank on the desert.

Forward Ordnance Depots were set up as follows:

For the coastal route at Tyre.

For the valley route at Rosh Pina north of Lake Tiberias.

For the eastern route at Damascus as soon as it was captured.

As soon as Habforce reached the area of Palamyra it was maintained from the FOD at Damascus and the stocks of H4 were run down.

Ammunition was supplied to railheads at Kiryat Motskin (north of Haifa), Jisr-el-Majamie (south of Lake Tiberias), Damascus and Mafraq (on the line between Amman and Deraa). The last of these was the original Habforce railhead and was no longer needed after the end of the operations in Iraq.

The arrangement was that the RASC force transport would deliver ammunition from railheads to units, and no stocks were established under RAOC control forward of railheads. This had unfortunate repercussions at the end of the campaign. The chronic shortage of vehicles was bound to lead to ammunition being dumped all over the place. No scheme existed for notifying quickly to Ordnance the position of dumps of ammunition which had been left as the operations progressed. Consequently, the safe clearance of such ammunition tended to be neglected and it became not an asset but a dangerous liability. Some months later a shipload of ammunition arrived in Port Said from Syria. The ammunition was in a dangerous state and dangerously stowed. An explosion occurred and there was considerable loss of life.

APPENDIX A

ORDER OF BATTLE—RAOC GREECE

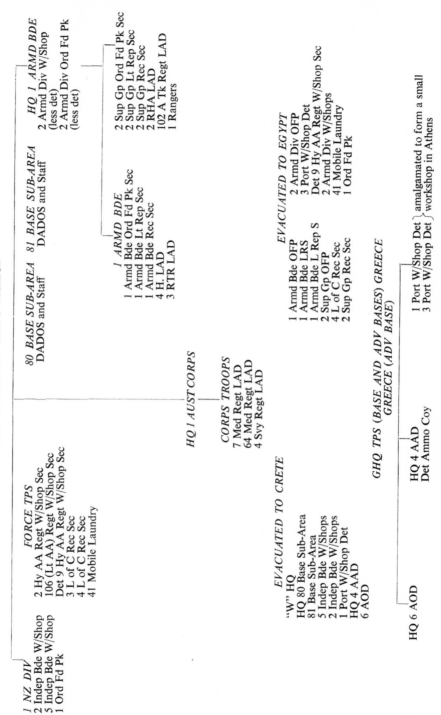

1 NZ DIV
2 Indep Bde W/Shop
5 Indep Bde W/Shop
1 Ord Fd Pk

FORCE TPS
2 Hy AA Regt W/Shop Sec
106 (Lt AA) Regt W/Shop Sec
Det 9 Hy AA Regt W/Shop Sec
3 L of C Rec Sec
4 L of C Rec Sec
41 Mobile Laundry

80 BASE SUB-AREA
DADOS and Staff

81 BASE SUB-AREA
DADOS and Staff

HQ 1 ARMD BDE
2 Armd Div W/Shop (less det)
2 Armd Div Ord Fd Pk (less det)

2 Sup Gp Ord Fd Pk Sec
2 Sup Gp Lt Rep Sec
2 Sup Gp Rec Sec
2 RHA LAD
102 A Tk Regt LAD
1 Rangers

1 ARMD BDE
1 Armd Bde Ord Fd Pk Sec
1 Armd Bde Lt Rep Sec
1 Armd Bde Rec Sec
4 H. LAD
3 RTR LAD

HQ 1 AUST CORPS

CORPS TROOPS
7 Med Regt LAD
64 Med Regt LAD
4 Svy Regt LAD

EVACUATED TO EGYPT
1 Armd Bde OFP
1 Armd Bde LRS
1 Armd Bde L Rep S
2 Sup Gp OFP
4 L of C Rec Sec
2 Sup Gp Rec Sec

2 Armd Div OFP
3 Port W/Shop Det
Det 9 Hy AA Regt W/Shop Sec
2 Armd Div W/Shops
41 Mobile Laundry
1 Ord Fd Pk

EVACUATED TO CRETE
"W" HQ
HQ 80 Base Sub-Area
81 Base Sub-Area
5 Indep Bde W/Shops
2 Indep Bde W/Shops
1 Port W/Shop Det
HQ 4 AAD
6 AOD

GHQ TPS (BASE AND ADV BASES) GREECE
GREECE (ADV BASE)

HQ 4 AAD
Det Ammo Coy

HQ 6 AOD

1 Port W/Shop Det ⎱ amalgamated to form a small
3 Port W/Shop Det ⎰ workshop in Athens

CHAPTER FIVE

THE MIDDLE EAST—
THE WESTERN DESERT
MARCH 1941 TO MARCH 1943

This 2 year period falls into well-defined phases as follows:

1. The arrival of General Rommel with the Afrika Corps, which coincided with the weakening of our forces in order to aid the Greeks. The consequent loss of Cyrenaica.
2. The build-up of British forces in the Western Desert, and the failure of the Battleaxe operation.
3. The formation of Eighth Army, the partially successful Crusader operation, occupation of Cyrenaica and withdrawal to the Gazala line.
4. Gazala battle, defeat and withdrawal to the Alamein line.
5. Battle of Alamein and advance into Tunisia.

GENERAL ROMMEL APPEARS

We have seen that by March 1941 the Italian Army in the Western Desert had been utterly defeated with the loss of many prisoners and much equipment. Cyrenaica was occupied and only German intervention could restore the situation for the Axis powers.

But the units which had beaten the Italian Army were badly needed elsewhere. Quite early in the campaign 4th Indian Division had been moved to the Eritrean front and other troops were wanted to build up the force which was going to the aid of the Greeks. The 7th Armoured Division had to be withdrawn to Egypt for a complete refit before it could again be ready for battle, and this involved the repair of all tanks which had been recovered, as replacements did not exist in the theatre. The result was that only a token force was left in Cyrenaica—adequate to occupy the country but lacking the means successfully to resist an attack by any but the most poorly trained and equipped troops. Thus General Wavell had to take the risk that there would be no German attack, even on a small scale, until reinforcements of men and material could be sent to the Western Desert.

Our troops came under Cyrenaica Command which was organized as a static rather than an operational headquarters. The commander, General Neame, lacked the trained staff and signal equipment to control mobile operations over such a large area. The formations available to General Neame were 9th Australian Division and 2nd Armoured Division.

The 9th Australian Division had exchanged two of its brigades for two less well-equipped brigades from 7th Australian Division. The headquarters staff was below strength and not fully trained and the Division was very short of machine guns, anti-tank weapons and signal equipment. But the most serious limitation to operational efficiency and maintenance was the lack of transport.

The 2nd Armoured Division was a Division only in name. A great deal of work had to be done on the tanks on their arrival from England to make them fit for desert warfare. The formation had been milked to reinforce 7th Armoured Division in its battle in Cyrenaica and had suffered the same wear and tear on its vehicles. A Brigade Group had been detached for the operations in Greece taking with it a number of units from the Support Group. Therefore 2nd Armoured Division was in effect a weak, improvised Brigade Group with worn out and mechanically defective British tanks supplemented by Italian M13 tanks which were so unsatisfactory that they earned the nickname of "self-propelled coffins". Like the rest of the force, the Division was very short of transport, its Ordnance Workshop was short of men and its Ordnance Field Park was short of essential spare parts and assemblies. This state of affairs reflected the general shortage of manpower and equipment in the Middle East and the higher priority given to other operations such as those in Greece. At that time also many ships were being sunk.

German intervention was first felt when their Air Force took part in attacks on Tobruk and Benghazi and on ships moving between those ports. The ultimate effect was to deny the use of Benghazi as a port and so to place a further strain on road transport. It became necessary to establish a series of Field Supply Depots at Mechili and Msus on the inland route and Tecnis (north-east of Benghazi) and El Magrun (south of Benghazi) on the coast road. This was making the best of a bad job as it hampered mobility and in a withdrawal the stocks had to be destroyed or abandoned.

The ADOS Cyrenaica Command was Lieutenant-Colonel C. H. Cooper, who had previously been with 7th Armoured Division and Western Desert Force. His first task was the usual RAOC one of tidying up. The large stocks of Italian stores and ammunition were required in the Middle East, but shipping and transport did not exist to backload the stores, which were nevertheless of some value in making up the deficiencies of 9th Australian Division. Units helped themselves to Italian weapons and then drew ammunition from the dump, taken over by the RAOC, by the simple process of producing samples for identification.

The Italian Ordnance Depot at Benghazi contained stocks of MT Spares which would have been invaluable to maintain the many vehicles captured during the advance. But as they could not be moved back to Egypt, the ADOS did the next best thing and formed a sort of static Ordnance Field Park south of Benghazi from which he met the needs of the forward troops.

The special road delivery service, which had been so successful in meeting unit needs for Ordnance Stores during the occupation of Cyrenaica, was withdrawn and "normal" methods were resumed. By this system the time taken to get demands back to the Base and the stores delivered to the unit was from 21 to 28 days.

If stores were available in Tobruk the round trip was 500 miles. Although the ADOS asked for two lorries daily to draw his requirements from Tobruk, priority was given to relatively luxury items not of RAOC supply and he was not told. Constant vigilance was necessary to ensure that transport was allotted to meet unit requirements of Ordnance Stores.

The many small dumps of ammunition formed during the advance were located and inspected by an IOO and arrangements were made to move them. A mobile laboratory was formed to inspect and where possible, repair ammunition *in situ*. There was insufficient time or transport to move many of these dumps. In some cases the stocks proved useful during the withdrawal from Cyrenaica which took place soon afterwards.

In April 1941, General Rommel moved into Cyrenaica with the advanced elements of the Afrika Corps. This consisted of the 5th Light Division with the 15th Panzer Division due to arrive in May. Although the German troops were few in number and the logistic support for an advance of many miles in the desert had not yet been built up, they had certain important advantages. The men were extremely well trained and had practical experience of mechanized warfare though not in desert conditions. Their battle drill was well established to a uniform doctrine which made it possible for units to settle down to new grouping under new commanders without confusion.

There was a good balance of units in the formation with a reasonable amount of armour. The tanks were of a sound and well-tested design with greater hitting power than ours. But they also had "tank-hunting" units with weapons which included a few of the dual purpose 88-mm anti-aircraft/anti-tank guns. The necessary supply units and mobile workshops were not forgotten.

Nevertheless, there were enough difficulties to justify caution, a policy which the German High Command repeatedly urged at this stage. But they happened to have selected a commander whose tactical skill and ferocious drive were not amenable to control by those who were ready to take counsel of their fears.

The result was that the British were driven out of Cyrenaica in less than a month, though they held Tobruk thus denying General Rommel the use of a good port which he would have to capture before undertaking an advance of any distance into Egypt. Our losses of equipment were not serious, partly because 2nd Armoured Division was so badly equipped from the beginning and partly because 9th Australian Division fell back in good order to the base at Tobruk and then held it, with all the stores there, against a series of attacks.

With the forward troops once more on the frontier, Western Desert Force was reconstituted with its headquarters about 30 miles east of Mersa Matruh. The 4th Indian Division, back from Eritrea, occupied that part of the line near the coast and 7th Armoured Division, now largely re-equipped, was on the left flank.

OPERATION BATTLEAXE

However, 7th Armoured Division would not be fully up to strength until a special convoy, known as "Tiger" convoy, carrying tank reinforcements, had been escorted through the Mediterranean by the Royal Navy.

Before this happened a small force under Brigadier Gott attempted to capture Halfaya Pass, Capuzzo and Sollum as a prelude to a further advance into Cyrenaica and the relief of Tobruk. This operation failed and although Halfaya Pass was captured, it was later lost to a strong and well-planned German attack. The "Tiger" convoy was successful and delivered 238 tanks to Egypt on May 12th. Numerically the Western Desert Force was now well off for tanks but the types were not well balanced, the reinforcements consisting of 82 cruiser, 135 infantry and 21 light tanks.

The tanks required considerable modification in workshops before they could be issued to units in a condition fit for a desert battle. This delay, though unavoidable, was particularly irksome as there were strong strategic reasons for taking the offensive at an early stage. The enemy was still in administrative difficulties and the golden opportunity to re-occupy a large part of Cyrenaica and destroy the enemy forces there might not recur.

The 7th Armoured Division had not operated as a formation since the previous February and many who had fought in the Division then had been transferred to other duties. This was virtually a new Division and many of the crews were unfamiliar with the tanks which they had to take into battle. To give them a chance against experienced Germans, some training was necessary and General Wavell was not given what he considered to be the necessary time for this.

Operation "Battleaxe" started on June 15th and was given strong and effective protection by the RAF. After some early successes in which our troops in the centre occupied Capuzzo and Sollum, the Germans developed a wide outflanking movement which threatened to surround our forward troops by linking up with the Halfaya position which still held out. Our losses in tanks had been too heavy to give a reasonable certainty of countering this threat and our troops were withdrawn to their original positions.

Many factors contributed to the failure of "Battleaxe" and not the least of these was the fact that the battle of Crete coincided with the preparatory period and the operation itself took place at the same time as the Syrian campaign.

The decision was made to replace General Wavell by General Auchinleck. General Wavell retained the confidence and respect of his officers and men during the bad as well as the good periods of an appallingly hectic year of almost continuous fighting on many fronts. No man could have done more with such meagre resources, and this was largely due to his exceptional knowledge of logistic problems—of what was or was not administratively possible.

It was indeed fortunate for the administrative services, and particularly the RAOC, that General Wavell was in command at this critical period. He was under constant pressure to accept new combat units when he had insufficient administrative backing to maintain those already in the field. These factors never seemed to be understood in Whitehall and there was also a notable reluctance to trust the judgement of the man on the spot. Luckily, General Wavell was not lacking in moral courage but even he was beginning to feel the strain by June 1941.

"Battleaxe" was the first of a series of operations in the Western Desert in which the British and German armour fought on roughly equal terms, not always with results satisfactory to the British. Our failures were attributed to a number of causes including inferior equipment and inferiority in the processes of recovery and repair.

To get a true picture it is necessary to go back as far as 1923. In that year a medium tank was produced and issued to Regular units of the Royal Tank Corps. It was not heavily armoured but was fast and manœuvrable, for the period, and equivalent in role to the cruiser tank of a later date. In 1926 a self-propelled field gun was fully tested by a mechanized RA unit. It had a fast all-round traverse and besides being a good field gun was admirably suited to the anti-tank role and the close support of tanks.

The tactics of armoured forces using these weapons were tried out by the Experimental Armoured Force on Salisbury Plain in the late 1920's, but by the end of that decade the world depression was having its effect on the Army. Financial stringency practically put an end to further progress, and to exercises involving the cooperation of all arms. The potentially excellent tank-hunting weapon—the self-propelled gun—was discarded. The anti-aircraft gun of the time, the 3-inch 20 cwt, was designed to have a secondary role as an anti-tank weapon, and the same military characteristic was incorporated into the new 3.7-inch AA gun when that was introduced into the service. But the anti-tank role was very secondary and there seems to have been no serious consideration of the use of these technically excellent weapons in support of tanks in the armoured battle, and a suitable sight was not produced.

Tank design continued but not production so that the troops continued to use the old medium tank until shortly before the war. By then, policy had switched over to the Infantry tank. Some of these were armed only with machine guns, though the best of them (the "Matilda") had a 2-pounder gun.

The Army was so small that the opportunity of practising the handling of formations of all arms, including armour, did not exist. Higher training was largely a matter of make-believe. In battle this led to inability to concentrate strength at the decisive point resulting in defeat in detail.

British tactical doctrine seemed to be dominated by the "tank versus tank" concept, as if the Royal Armoured Corps was an independent army within an army which could operate without reference to other arms of the service. In the open desert the British armour tended to "mix it" with the German armour and supporting artillery in a series of disconnected "dog fights" which played into their hands. British tank strength kept melting away.

Complaints were beginning to be made of the inadequacy of the British 2-pounder tank gun. There was, however, little to choose between it and the German 50-mm tank gun so that in fire power the two sides were fairly evenly matched in a purely tank versus tank battle.

The difference was that the Germans used their anti-tank weapons aggressively moving them well forward with the armour. The 88-mm gun could knock out the British tanks at long range while the new 50-mm anti-tank gun was superior to the 2-pounder. In this respect the balance would be restored as the new 6-pounder replaced the 2-pounder.

Failure to use the 3.7-inch gun in the same way as the Germans used their 88-mm gun does not seem to have been satisfactorily explained. This gun was given a high priority for production before the war and it is reasonable to assume that supply of the gun, as distinct from the AA fire control instruments, was good.

As far as recovery and repair were concerned, the Germans had the advantage of good quantities of well-tested mobile equipment whereas the British had to resort to improvisation from the beginning. It has been seen that there was no lack of energy or ingenuity in the efforts which were made to close the gap between the enemy and ourselves in this respect. Repair difficulties were increased by the unreliability of certain British tanks so that when the tide of battle turned many repairable tanks had to be abandoned.

"CRUSADER"

General Auchinleck was given the task of defeating the enemy in the Western Desert and reoccupying Cyrenaica as a prelude to the capture of Tripoli. For this he was given considerable reinforcements in men and equipment and was under strong pressure to commit these reinforcements to battle almost as they arrived. The Royal Navy was playing havoc with the supplies across the Mediterranean to the Axis forces and the RAF was greatly strengthened but this advantage over the enemy could not be expected to last indefinitely.

On the other hand the British forces must be equipped and trained to a high standard if they were to have a reasonable chance not only of defeating but destroying the enemy armoured formations as this was the key to victory in the desert. After a period of four months' intensive preparation Operation "Crusader" was launched on November 18th 1941.

There was a good deal less of the hasty improvisation which had been an unavoidable characteristic of earlier operations in the Middle East. Administrative planning was thorough and the resources were by now considerable, which gave the Eighth Army, as the Western Desert Force had now become, an advantage over the enemy in a prolonged period of fighting.

The Eighth Army (Lieutenant-General Sir Alan Cunningham) consisted of two Corps.

13 Corps (Lieutenant-General A. R. Godwin-Austen) comprised:
New Zealand Division (4th, 5th and 6th NZ Infantry Brigades).
4th Indian Infantry Division (5th, 7th and 11th Indian Infantry Brigades).
1st Army Tank Brigade.

30 Corps (Lieutenant-General C. W. M. Norrie) comprised:
7th Armoured Division (7th and 22nd Armoured Brigades).
4th Armoured Brigade Group.
1st South African Division (1st and 5th South African Infantry Brigades).
22nd Guards Brigade.

Other formations under Eighth Army Command were:
Oases Force
29th Indian Infantry Brigade Group.
6th SA Armoured Car Regiment.
Tobruk Garrison
70th Division (14th, 16th and 23rd Infantry Brigades).
Polish Carpathian Infantry Brigade Group.
32nd Army Tank Brigade.
Army Reserve
2nd SA Division (3rd, 4th and 6th SA Infantry Brigades).

Broadly speaking the plan was for 30 Corps to make a wide sweep round the southern flank of the enemy occupied area and advance to the vital ridges of Sidi Rezegh and El Duda. Tobruk Garrison would, at a time to be decided by GOC in C Eighth Army, break out to the south-east and link up with 30 Corps at El Duda. It was considered that these

148

moves could not fail to produce a reaction from the Afrika Corps and our superiority in armour would enable us to destroy 15th and 21st Panzer Divisions which were the backbone of the enemy forces.

Meanwhile, 13 Corps would bottle up the enemy in the frontier posts of Bardia, Sollum and Halfaya or attack and destroy them if they attempted to withdraw to the west.

The Oases Force was to secure Jarabub and Jalo oases well to the south of the main battlefield and be available to exploit towards Agedabia to cut off the withdrawal of enemy troops from Cyrenaica.

Actual events differed very much from the plan. The 30 Corps did not succeed in taking a firm hold of the vital Sidi Rezegh area nor did they manage to concentrate a superior force against the enemy armour, which reacted as expected.

The first 3 weeks of the campaign brought heavy and confused fighting with great losses of men and equipment on both sides.

A brief summary of the main events is as follows:

1. The 7th Armoured Brigade and 7th Armoured Division Support Group occupied Sidi Rezegh airfield.
2. The Afrika Corps moved east and then south and severely mauled 4th Armoured Brigade Group which was unsupported.
3. 70th Division broke out towards El Duda and formed a salient short of that point. Heavy fighting at Sidi Rezegh.
4. 15th and 21st Panzer Divisions moved north-west on Sidi Rezegh pursued by 22nd Armoured Brigade and 4th Armoured Brigade Group, while the New Zealand Division of 13 Corps moved north to Sidi Azeiz and then advanced on Sidi Rezegh from the east.
5. The armoured brigades and 5th South African Brigade from the south failed to prevent 7th Armoured Division from being driven from Sidi Rezegh, and then 15th Panzer Division over-ran and virtually destroyed 5th South African Brigade.
6. Rommel took his armoured divisions south-east and then east in what became known as the "dash for the frontier", while the New Zealand Division advanced nearer to Sidi Rezegh.
7. The confusion caused by Rommel's move was only temporary. 13 Corps held fast and his Divisions were harassed by the surviving elements of 7th Armoured Division so that he gained little advantage and lost many tanks.
8. Meanwhile, 70th Division had occupied El Duda and linked up with the New Zealand Division in the Sidi Rezegh area. Rommel had to turn back.
9. He managed, with the help of two Italian Divisions, to recapture Sidi Rezegh, and the New Zealand Division was withdrawn to the east except for some units which moved into the El Duda salient of the Tobruk defences.

10. But by now the British were able to introduce reinforcements of men and equipment and the enemy was not. He was out-flanked and withdrew to the west, Tobruk being relieved on December 11th.

11. Attempts to trap Rommel on the Gazala line failed because administrative limitations made it impossible to maintain strong enough armoured forces behind his defensive position. He brushed them aside and withdrew in good order from Cyrenaica to El Agheila; leaving the vital Gebel Akhdar area, with its airfields, in our hands.

By now the situation at sea and in the air had changed. Malta was virtually neutralized and supplies for the Axis forces in Tripolitania were subject to far less interruption. In occupying Cyrenaica the Eighth Army had overreached itself and was vulnerable to the counter-attacks which occurred only 3 weeks later, but the enemy garrisons of Bardia, Sollum and Halfaya were captured during this period.

Tactically it might have been better to halt on the Gazala line and consolidate there, but this is, of course, wisdom after the event and ignores political factors.

THE RAOC PROBLEM

"Crusader" provided many new problems for the RAOC but also far better resources than had ever been available before. Home Defence requirements were cut to a minimum in order to strengthen the Eighth Army. Considerable reinforcements of the latest cruiser tanks and of infantry tanks arrived from the United Kingdom. Thanks to Lease-Lend the United States supplied large numbers of their "Stuart" Light M3 tank, used by us as a cruiser tank.

At the beginning of the battle, approximate tank strengths were:

With units under command	340 cruisers
Eighth Army, including	173 Stuarts
Tobruk fortress:	200 infantry tanks
In reserve or in	90 cruisers
workshops at the Base:	90 Stuarts
	77 infantry tanks
At sea *en route*	124 cruisers
for Egypt:	60 Stuarts
	52 infantry tanks

The enemy had no reserves, and no reinforcements until after the battle. His approximate tank strength was:

250 German tanks
150 Italian tanks

Numerically the British advantage appears to be overwhelming, and the reserve tank strength was the ultimate deciding factor in this battle, but numbers alone can be most misleading. Apart from the tactical factors which have been mentioned, the German tank was more reliable and a better weapon in every way than any of ours. The Crusader tank was mechanically unreliable, only had the 2-pounder gun with uncapped ammunition and was lightly armoured. It was much too easily set on fire. The Stuart was most reliable and fast and had an excellent cross-country performance, but a very short radius of action and poor hitting power with its 37-mm gun. The infantry tank could not be used in a fast moving armoured battle and was confined to the Army Tank Brigades working with Infantry formations. Its usefulness was limited by its 2-pounder gun.

So great were the disadvantages of the Crusaders and Stuarts compared with the German tanks that it was eventually estimated that parity in armour could only be achieved by means of a two to one numerical advantage in favour of the British. Nothing could exceed the dash and courage of the crews of these inferior tanks who repeatedly took them into action against the massive fire power which the Germans were able to deploy.

In "B" vehicles the Middle East situation had improved enormously by the shipment of large numbers of lorries of robust design and excellent performance from North America. The improved vehicle supply position made it possible to adopt a plan which did not depend on the early capture of Halfaya, Sollum and Bardia. It was hoped that the siege of Tobruk would be raised within the first week. But the actual date proved to be 24 days from the start of the battle.

However, the rail head had been pushed forward to Misheifa, 80 miles to the west of Mersa Matruh. Forward bases were established at Sidi Barrani for the troops in the coastal sector, at Thalata, near Misheifa, for 30 Corps and part of 13 Corps and at Jarabab for the Oases Force. The forward bases supplied Field Maintenance Centres which were formed at suitable locations according to the way the battle developed.

These Field Maintenance Centres were a great improvement on the earlier Field Supply Depots. They were on a much larger scale and, in addition to petrol, water, rations and ammunition, included stocks of essential Ordnance Stores. An FMC commander was appointed. He had a small staff and was responsible for the allocation of areas within the centre to the various services and also for local administration, including movement orders. RAOC units were formed to handle and store the Ordnance Stores and ammunition in the FMC. In the fluid desert battle the protection of these FMCs presented quite a problem. In the "dash to the frontier" No. 50 FMC which served 13 Corps, was overrun by a hostile column, which eventually moved on after doing very little damage, even failing to locate the petrol stocks or release the 900 prisoners held there. No. 62 FMC, which served 30 Corps, was so "out on a limb" that the Corps Commander moved 22nd Guards Brigade there for a time to protect the valuable stocks.

The DDOS Eighth Army was Brigadier H. F. S. King. Colonel C. H. Cooper was DDOS 13 Corps and Colonel L. H. Howard Jones, an OME, was DDOS 30 Corps. The RAOC Order of Battle included the organic units of formations on the following basis:

Each Armoured Brigade, Army Tank Brigade and Support Group had an Ordnance Field Park, Light Repair Section and Recovery Section. The Headquarters and Divisional Section of the OFP was with the Armoured Division, which also had divisional workshops.

Infantry Divisions each had an OFP and workshops, which could be dispersed on a Brigade basis in appropriate conditions.

Brigade and regimental workshops were provided for AA units.

Corps and Army Troops needs were met by the allocation of GHQ Troops Workshops and L of C Recovery Sections, but no Corps Troops OFP had yet been created.

Other units included Forward Ammunition Depots, Mobile W/T Repair Sections, Mobile Ammunition Laboratory, Vehicle and Stores Convoy Unit, the RAOC element of the Tank Delivery Squadron, Railhead and Port Ordnance Staff.

URGENT FIGHTING STORES

Earlier operations had shown the need for having a system for the rapid supply of urgently required Ordnance Stores. Previously an Ordnance Field Park had been used to provide an improvised road delivery service, but this was later replaced by 510 Vehicle and Stores Convoy Unit on an approved establishment. This supplemented the normal system of supply. In addition an air delivery service was used for urgent fighting stores and proved invaluable while aircraft could be made available. The vehicle and stores convoy unit provided landing ground detachments which lived on the airfield.

STOCKS OF ORDNANCE STORES

Advanced Ordnance Depots in Egypt were stocked with a range of controlled stores placed at the disposal of Eighth Army. The forward bases held fast moving Ordnance Stores. The depot at Tobruk had been allowed to dwindle during the siege and was below establishment. In anticipation of the siege being raised and Tobruk being required as an advanced base for operations to the west, reinforcements were sent forward in small numbers. Stores were selected and packed so that they could be despatched as soon as the port could receive them.

MT STORES

Indents for these, and for armament and wireless spares and assemblies were passed direct to the OFP and not to the DADOS or Brigade Ordnance Warrant Officer of the formation. A great deal of trouble was taken to ensure that the initial scaling of OFPs included all the vital items, that is those which were fast moving or essential to the operation of the equipment.

AMMUNITION

Stocks were established at 508 Depot, El Daba, at ammunition railheads and at the forward bases. 501 AAD at Tobruk held ammunition for the fortress only. Third line ammunition was not held on wheels but in dumps in the FMC run by RAOC Forward Ammunition Sections. Unit requirements were drawn from these dumps by formation RASC transport.

Stock levels at ARHs were wired daily to GHQ by Eighth Army and replenishment to predetermined levels was made automatically from the Base. Once the forward railhead at Misheifa was working smoothly it became the only issuing railhead, the others holding reserves.

The forward bases were not much used in the supply of ammunition, except that the base at Sidi Barrani supplied troops in the Halfaya area. In the main these bases served as dispersed reserves of ammunition. Tobruk was replenished as shipping became available. Requirements were known from stock wires and urgent demands from the fortress. Some SAA was packed in specially designed padded moulds and dropped from aircraft without the use of parachutes. This method, though workable, was not much used in the "Crusader" operation.

VEHICLE REPAIRS

Field repair involved the exchange of major assemblies. These were scarce and special steps were taken to ensure that repairable assemblies were returned intact to the correct Base Workshop for repair. Detailed instructions were issued to DADsOS and officers in charge of OFPs and LADs indicating the code marks to be used for ease of identification of the contents, and stressing the importance of returning major assemblies in their correct cases.

In addition to these arrangements within the RAOC, General Orders and circular letters were issued by GHQ Middle East warning all units of the effect on future supply of major assemblies caused by indiscriminate cannibalization of repairable assemblies. Despite these instructions and warnings, the practice persisted throughout the operations which followed, and field repair suffered accordingly.

6*

TANK DELIVERY

There was no Armoured Corps Ordnance Field Park and a Squadron of 7th RTR was detailed to act as Tank Delivery Squadron working in conjunction with the RAOC Vehicle Parks. This improvisation worked quite well. It was the forerunner of the Armoured Replacement Group which developed later in the war.

CAPTURED MATERIAL

The importance of special arrangements to recover captured enemy equipment and ammunition had been learnt in the previous campaign in Cyrenaica. A GHQ Recovery Section was formed to deal with this problem and a list was drawn up giving the priority of requirements for the various equipments which might be captured. All captured weapons were returned to 6 AOD Alexandria, and by the end of January 1942 nearly 500 miscellaneous guns and small arms had been received there.

NARRATIVE OF THE OPERATION

When 30 Corps carried out their wide turning movement round the southern flank, Light Repair Sections, Recovery Units and Armoured Divisional Workshops moved well forward.

In the "dash for the frontier", 30 Corps Rear HQ was overrun. Colonel Howard Jones found sanctuary for a short time with DDOS 13 Corps but rejoined 30 Corps immediately the "flap" was over. Lieutenant-Colonel McEwan was less fortunate. His vehicle broke down and he was captured on November 24th. The prisoners remained in the same locality for about 24 hours. Although there were Italian officers present the party seemed to be controlled by a German NCO. In conversation with the Italian officers, McEwan gathered that they loathed the Germans and hoped for a quick end to the war. The party then moved on to the neighbourhood of Halfaya Pass. McEwan took careful note of the composition of the enemy force. The total number of prisoners at this place was 14 officers and about 280 ORs. Next morning, November 26th, he noticed that a considerable number of the enemy had left and, as senior officer present, he planned an escape. Organized in 8 groups of about 35, they moved out that night, the groups keeping in touch with each other. After a long march they found their way to railhead where McEwan handed over two Germans they had brought with them. He then returned to 30 Corps HQ.

This event was typical of the somewhat chancy existence of the administrative echelons in desert warfare. Swarms of vehicles, widely separated but keeping in touch moved in all directions on their various tasks. They had to keep alert for enemy air attack or the sudden appearance of hostile armour. At night they closed in to a compact formation or leaguer for better control and defence. This was the time for rest, maintenance or replenishment.

With movement and fighting taking place over such a large area, it became essential to locate quickly the various dumps of tank crocks so that repair and recovery should proceed without delay. For this purpose HQ Eighth Army organized a forward information station. For the first week or so of the operation, DDOS and DADOS(E) 30 Corps devoted most of their time to the organization of recovery.

By December 12th, 30 Corps had suffered approximately 530 vehicle casualties. Initial recoveries amounted to 456. Repairs to 230 tanks had been completed and a further 50 were under repair. In the armoured battle the importance of repair and recovery was paramount. Colonel Howard Jones was right to adopt a forward policy and to give repair and recovery his direct supervision. He could justly claim that he made the best use of the available resources. He left the complicated process of supply of vehicles, stores and ammunition to this highly mobile Corps in the able hands of his ADOS, Lieutenant-Colonel McEwan.

Tanks which could not be repaired on the spot were brought back to Collecting Points by RAOC 2nd Line Recovery Units. L of C Recovery from these points was undertaken by RAOC L of C Recovery Sections, supplemented by RASC 3rd Line Transporters which were not under the control of RAC or RAOC.

DDOS 13 Corps also had his problems. The "dash to the frontier" separated Rear HQ 13 Corps from the Advanced Headquarters and also from the New Zealand Division and 1st Army Tank Brigade. As a result the supply system was switched to the 30 Corps axis based on No. 62 FMC, and 4th Indian Division passed to Army command. This put an additional strain on RASC transport with the result that Ordnance Stores were shut out altogether, including controlled stores which had been released some days before the operation started.

510 Vehicle and Stores Convoy Unit worked under difficulties because of the frequent changes of location of units. Colonel Cooper advocated control of delivery as far forward as possible. He also recommended that the Vehicle and Stores Convoy Unit should "hook on" to the OFPs and not operate a separate service. This unit had only arrived on the scene just before the campaign started and was not fully trained in desert warfare.

One problem had not been anticipated. Several thousand stragglers found their way to railhead and had to be re-equipped before being returned to their units. Insufficient stocks were held for this sort of situation and reinforcements for the railhead staff were also needed.

Headquarters 13 Corps moved to Tobruk on December 8th and the recovery of infantry tanks was placed in the hands of the OME of 1st Army Tank Brigade, Captain F. E. Norris. This officer and the RAOC units in support of 1st Army Tank Brigade (Light Repair Section, Recovery Section and Ordnance Field Park) had some interesting experiences which are worth recording as they are typical of the impact of operations in the Western Desert on administrative units of the Eighth Army.

From November 21st to 24th the Recovery Section was engaged on the recovery of infantry tanks which had been mined in the attack on Omar Nuovo and Sidi Omar. Tank casualties were high, amounting to 46 infantry tanks, but it was expected that 7 would be repaired locally by November 25th. During this recovery activity Captain Norris and his vehicle were blown up by a mine in an area supposed to have been cleared but, though somewhat shaken, he was fortunately none the worse.

On the afternoon of November 25th, an enemy mobile column attacked the area in which the Light Repair Section was working. Men from the Royal Tank Regiment manned the tanks and the RAOC units used anti-tank rifles and other small arms. After about $1\frac{1}{2}$ hours' fighting, in which two German Mk III tanks and an ammunition lorry were knocked out and seven RTR men were killed, the Germans occupied the area and our units were dispersed, re-forming later. Tank recovery was resumed in this area on November 30th.

On November 27th Rear HQ, 1st Army Tank Brigade was heavily bombed by British aircraft. Some 20 vehicles were destroyed and there were 20 casualties of which the RAOC had one officer wounded and four men killed. As there were considerable enemy forces in the area this type of hazard was inevitable, and both sides occasionally suffered casualties from their own aircraft owing to the difficulty of identification.

Up to December 2nd, recovery was considerably hampered by enemy forces which suddenly appeared on the scene and fired on our transporters. Sometimes recovery units were turned back by our own armoured forces who were in contact with the enemy. By December 2nd the situation had become less confused. Systematic repair and recovery was possible. Tanks which could not be repaired in the forward area were taken over by 5 L of C Recovery Section at Conference Cairn not far from Sidi Omar. The balance of 1st Army Tank Brigade Light Repair Section and that of 32nd Army Tank Brigade undertook repairs in the forward area.

When the siege of Tobruk was finally raised on December 11th and the enemy withdrew to the Gazala position, it was only possible to maintain one Corps in the field for operations in western Cyrenaica although 30 Corps controlled the operations to capture the isolated garrisons of Bardia, Sollum and Halfaya.

From December 13th control of 3rd line transport was transferred from Corps to Army and a definite allotment was given to Ordnance Stores. As an allotment of railway wagons was also made there was a big improvement in supply. Colonel Cooper had repeatedly stressed the importance of a "daily dose" of Ordnance Stores but so far without effect. He pointed out that after a long period during which essential Ordnance Stores failed to appear there was a delivery of all the quantities which had accumulated. This was more than formation and unit transport could cope with and so uncontrolled dumps of stores developed in the forward areas. In despair he advocated the supply of all Ordnance Stores by

RAOC transport through Ordnance Field Parks, but this now proved unnecessary.

Nevertheless, transport difficulties were acute while supply through the port of Tobruk was being built up. So serious was the shortage of petrol that the DDOS Eighth Army was hard put to it to obtain an allotment for the vehicles engaged on the delivery of urgent fighting stores sent by air from the bases to forward airfields. Stores continued to pour into 500 AOD Tobruk at a tremendous rate. This small unit was under extreme pressure, simultaneously receiving large shipments of stores, issuing to maintain 13 Corps and backloading much needed equipment to Egypt. 503 AOW, Tobruk, was given the vital task of repairing Crusader and Stuart tanks and experts in these types of vehicles were sent from Egypt to assist.

On January 14th all demands from units forward of Rear HQ Eighth Army were switched to 500 AOD. Up to this date the air delivery service of Ordnance Stores to the forward landing ground at Msus worked well. Now was the time to make special efforts to return repairable assemblies and other equipment to the Base. In addition to the use of shipping, 32 full lorries were sent to railhead for despatch and it was planned to send an average of 6 lorry loads daily. There was a shortage of cases for assemblies largely because of their use for firewood by units in the bitterly cold conditions in the desert at this time of the year. It was evidently considered that neither persuasion nor disciplinary action would stop this practice, for a trial fireproofing was undertaken at the Base and the cases marked accordingly.

Headquarters 13 Corps was established at Msus. A situation developed which was almost identical to that which had occurred a year previously. In this case, 1st Armoured Division took over from 7th Armoured Division. The formation was sent into action incompletely trained for desert warfare. A number of part-worn tanks were taken over from 7th Armoured Division but the Division's own tanks had run some 700 miles on their tracks and were developing the mechanical troubles which were all too common with the Crusader.

The OFP and Workshops had not trained with the Division in England. The stores for the OFP did not travel with the unit, which had to be hurriedly scaled at the Base and was moved forward with the stores still in packing cases. Sorting and binning of the stores had to be done in the forward area simultaneously with the receipt of urgent demands from units, which was detrimental to efficient service.

The changes in command and regrouping of units after the relief of Tobruk, though an operational necessity, caused difficulties in the supply of Ordnance Stores. Both the Q Staff and the Services lacked up-to-date information of the moves of units, including those which had been withdrawn to refit. It was not easy to find out details of unit deficiencies of vehicles and stores, and when stores arrived delivery was held up by ignorance of the location of the unit. Significant quantities of stores arrived when they were no longer wanted owing to the unit having left the forward area. Obviously improved administrative wireless communications were necessary and this was not possible with the resources available at the time.

In other ways the RAOC situation had improved. Although there was no Corps Troops Ordnance Field Park, a small Vehicle Park was situated near Corps Headquarters at Msus. There was also an airfield at Msus where a small FMC was established. An officer with an RAOC detachment was established there and took delivery of all Army Stores, including those of Ordnance Supply, so that quick distribution was effected. In reverse the same system ensured that indents for urgent stores were passed quickly to the Base.

Wheeled vehicles went by road from Egypt to the Army Vehicle Park, from which reinforcement drivers took them to the Corps Vehicle Park at Msus. This was a small organization and could not normally deliver to units which had to send drivers to collect vehicles.

A few armoured cars but very few tanks were delivered. In fact, the Armoured Division had a surplus of tanks, but most of them were in poor condition and some degree of cannibalization of unserviceable tanks was necessary to make others battle-worthy. Tanks which could be recovered were sent back to Tobruk.

When 13 Corps was driven back to the Gazala line, the following RAOC units were in the Msus area :

> 4 GHQ Troops Workshops;
> 7th Armoured Division Workshops;
> 5th Indian Division OFP;
> 7th Armoured Division OFP.

These units retired to the Tobruk–El Adem area with small loss of stores. 1st Armoured Division OFP and Workshops were less fortunate and were overrun, but a certain number of men and vehicles made their way back to Tmimi and Tobruk.

The "Crusader" battles had exhausted both sides and for about 3 months the front stabilized on the Gazala line until the next trial of strength towards the end of May 1942.

RAOC LESSONS FROM "CRUSADER"

Supply of Ordnance Stores. The necessity for special arrangements to deal with urgent demands had been recognized and was reflected in the creation before the campaign of 510 Vehicle and Stores Convoy Unit and of the Air Delivery Service. These were new devices and without them the supply of urgent fighting stores would almost certainly have failed when the need was greatest.

But these arrangements were intended to supplement not replace the normal system and this important aspect was sometimes forgotten. Rather late in the day it was realized that a regular daily allocation of rail and road transport capacity for Ordnance Stores was essential.

Cannibalization. The steps taken to prevent indiscriminate cannibalization of vehicles and repairable assemblies did not suffice to control the process. The most popular items were carburettors, fuel pumps, fan assemblies, distributors, tools and mirrors. Units had to realize the effect of cannibalization on the future supply of the items taken, and a programme of education in this matter, supplemented where appropriate by disciplinary action, finally cured the trouble.

Tyres. Desert conditions were very hard on tyres, the supply of which was not unlimited. A comprehensive programme of salvage was undertaken, these tyres being sent to Returned Stores Depots for examination by experts. After repair worn tyres with 1,000–2,000 miles of remaining life were issued to L of C units in Egypt and Palestine. Retreadable tyres were sent to BODs and facilities for retreading in Egypt, Palestine and Eritrea were used to the utmost. Plant was ordered from Australia and the United Kingdom.

Tank Design. The inaccessibility of major and minor assemblies on British tanks hampered and delayed field repair. American Stuart tanks did not suffer from this defect.

Tank Delivery and Recovery. In the delivery of replacement tanks there does not seem to have been a simple, clearly defined division of responsibility between RAC, RAOC and RASC and, in the case of the staff branches, between G(SD) and Q. It is probable that this led to an unnecessary amount of track mileage, but the main trouble was shortage of transporters in relation to the vast distances which tanks had to travel.

There was a good deal of criticism of our recovery and repair. Much of this criticism was ill-informed and unjustified but our heavy tank casualties naturally led to investigation of the cause and comparison with the Germans. Good came of this as it led to the creation of a first class system and greatly increased facilities by the time the Gazala battle took place.

As the advance continued recovery had to take place well forward. More units had to be found to fill the gaps in the chain of recovery on the lengthening L of C, and although everything possible was done there were not enough recovery units to meet this need in every case.

Second line recovery was good but it was suggested that units should be given vehicles to enable more First Line recovery to be undertaken. This was probably sound in principle but for it to be effective more recovery vehicles would be needed than were available at the time.

RASC Transporter Companies were not used to full effect for recovery. This was because they were placed under the control neither of the RAC nor the RAOC, with the result that after delivering tanks they sometimes returned with loads other than AFVs. This organizational fault was rectified in later operations and the assistance given by the RASC was invaluable. It was gratefully acknowledged by the DDsOS of 13 and 30 Corps.

The reluctance in the Middle East to give direct responsibility to the Services which had to do the work was revealed in the proceedings of a conference held at Rear HQ Eighth Army to deal with the delivery and recovery of "A" and "B" vehicles. Among the "principles" laid down were:

(a) Responsibility for the organization of delivery rests with "Q" through Ord.

(b) "Q" through Ord will arrange for a workshop and OFP to be located near the Tank Reorganization Centre to carry out minor repairs and re-equipment, if required, of tanks.

(c) If it is required to use tank transporters for delivery from railhead to the forward areas, G(SD) will inform "Q" who will arrange to allot the transporters through ST.

(d) Responsibility for the organization of recovery to the Base rests with "Q" through Ord.

(e) The allocation of Transporter Companies will be by "Q" through ST as requested by G(SD) and Ord.

On the face of it the system appears to be based on the principle that responsibility should never be given to one branch when four would do. In practice there was less confusion than one would expect, because there was no shortage of officers who had worked together on these problems in operational conditions.

Administrative Communications. The lack of wireless communications between headquarters and administrative units caused great maintenance difficulties in mobile operations such as "Crusader". Control of railheads, dumps, field maintenance centres and forward bases could not be effective when up-to-date information was lacking. When extensive regrouping took place stores could not be sent to units because their correct location was not known, or more often stores were sent to the last known location which had changed. Recovery to be effective must be based on up-to-date information of the location of "crocks".

Of course these factors were well known and understood but the design and production of wireless sets had been sadly neglected in the years before the war and the scarcity persisted for a long time.

There was no substitute for wireless communication in this type of warfare and when the supply of sets improved, administrative communication and the maintenance of the force improved with it.

Training of RAOC Units. The RAOC units of some of the reinforcing formations sent out from the United Kingdom had not trained with their formations and in some cases had only been formed shortly before the formation sailed. It was difficult for them to do themselves justice when they had to settle down as units during operations. This was probably a

160

reflection of the general situation at a time when fighting units were sent into battle with insufficient training.

GAZALA

The period from February 2nd to May 26th 1942 marked a lull in operations with intense administrative activity on both sides in preparation for a resumption of the offensive. In the end it was the Germans who attacked, and this should have been to the advantage of the British, who were not yet completely organized or trained for further offensive action but were better placed to fight defensively. Moreover, administratively they had never been better off.

This is not to say that the situation was easy. The Middle East was no longer the only British theatre of land warfare, and the disastrous events in the Far East which followed the Japanese entry into the war—the fall of Hong Kong and Singapore and the loss of Burma—inevitably led to the diversion of some resources away from the Middle East.

The Gazala line had no important tactical features but it was artificially strengthened and mined to an extent never before attempted, with the object of preserving Tobruk as the base for a new offensive. The railway had been extended as far as Belhamed, about 15 miles south-east of Tobruk and a large forward base had been established there. The railhead at Belhamed was due to open on June 12th. Large stocks were built up at Tobruk and Belhamed in order to provide the backing for an advance into Tripolitania.

The Gazala Line was extended as far south as Bir Hacheim largely with the object of holding off from the forward base any outflanking movement which the enemy might undertake. Unfortunately this extension was excessive for the 3 Divisions holding the line (from north to south 1st South African, 50th and Free French) so that considerable portions of the minefields were not covered by fire and given time could be breached.

The whole plan was a compromise in which defensive risks were taken on the assumption that we could still defeat the enemy if he attacked, and then move over rapidly to the offensive with our administrative backing established well forward. There was no thought of repeating the role of Tobruk as a fortress, though it was strong enough to withstand raids. These were risks which had to be taken if we were to fight at all, and it was hardly to be expected that anyone either in the Middle East or at home would contemplate the disastrous results which would follow defeat in the armoured battle. Grant tanks, with their 75-mm gun, and 6-pounder anti-tank guns had been received in sufficient quantities largely to redress the balance of fire power.

But the British commanders had not learnt the tactical lessons of "Crusader". Undue dispersion led to defeat in detail at the outset. Later, when Rommel's over ambitious plan placed his armour in the precarious position of being trapped to the east of the minefields, the British reactions were too slow and the Afrika Corps formed a defensive stronghold which held off all attacks until the minefields had been breached and supplies could be received direct.

The Eighth Army was unable to prevent 150th Brigade of 50th Division from being surrounded and overwhelmed nor the more gradual reduction of the strong point at Bir Hacheim held by the Free French. By June 12th the British armour had lost the battle with the Afrika Corps, and its tank strength was reduced to 50 cruiser and 20 infantry tanks. The Gazala position was abandoned. Tobruk was exposed to the full force of Rommel's attack without interference from Eighth Army and fell on June 21st. The Eighth Army withdrew to the El Alamein line, defeating Rommel's attempt to break through on July 1st to 5th.

RAOC PROBLEMS

The 4-month lull in the fighting gave the RAOC as an administrative service the opportunity to restore and improve the arrangements for the supply and repair of the equipment of the Army. Full use was made of Tobruk as an advanced base and this involved the development and increased activity of 500 AOD, 503 AOW and 501 AAD.

500 AOD

As early as January 1942, 5 officers and 100 ORs had been sent to reinforce 500 AOD. Progressively the establishment was built up so that by May it was practically at the approved level of about 400 all ranks.

The storage accommodation may have sufficed for the original use of Tobruk as a fortress which must be denied to the enemy. Stores and ammunition were limited to the needs of the Garrison. But an advanced base is a very different matter and improved storage facilities assumed great importance. The limited covered accommodation consisted of buildings which had been so damaged by bombing and shell fire that very poor protection against the elements remained.

The depot was therefore dispersed and effective use was made of some caves which existed outside the town. No. 3 Sub-Depot with its warlike and technical stores—many of which were delicate and needed good storage—was housed in these caves.

The MT Sub-Depot was hard pressed by heavy receipts of stores both by sea and land. Luckily they had time to absorb these stores during the lull in operations. They were well supplied with portable bins of a Middle East design which made it possible to move their binned stores into a new location, such as the caves if the situation should demand it.

The decision, reached after some argument, that the workshops at Tobruk would be limited to repair by assembly exchange, or work taking the same time to complete, increased the stocks of assemblies in the MT Sub-Depot. It also enabled a considerable range of stores to be returned to the Base. Facilities in Tobruk for handling heavy assemblies were poor, and when movement was by sea the number of handlings, sometimes using unskilled labour was considerable which increased the risk of serious damage to these valuable stores. However, these difficulties were overcome and by the end of May the depot was well organized and ready to play its part in any future operations.

In April, General Richards made a change of command, replacing Lieutenant-Colonel A. F. Harding by Colonel T. G. Gore. Harding was an experienced and competent officer who had served in Greece and the Western Desert. He had done excellent work in sorting out the problems of 500 AOD, and building it up for its new and extended role. He may possibly have felt that he had borne the burden and heat of the day only for someone else to step in and get the credit for his work. But this is, and always has been, a common enough experience, and in the process he avoided the much greater misfortune of being captured when Tobruk fell.

Colonel Gore was selected because he had qualities which were much needed in Tobruk at that time. Tobruk was a dreary, squalid and un-healthy place. It had few amenities, was frequently overcrowded, and was an obvious target for attack by enemy aircraft. These were testing conditions for administrative units which had to work in them for long periods. People tended to become stale and the tempo of work was liable to fall off just at the time—a lull in operations—when the greatest effort was required from RAOC units.

Colonel Gore provided the inspiration which was needed. He was well aware that in desert warfare administrative units are frequently left unprotected. If they cannot defend themselves no one else is going to do the job for them. He adopted an aggressive policy, forming and training a light anti-aircraft platoon and a mortar platoon of twelve 3-inch mortars. Even if Tobruk had not been attacked and the fortunes of the Eighth Army had taken a more favourable turn in the Gazala battle, this policy would have been justified by the effect on morale and the added confidence which it gave to the unit.

As it happened, when the decision was made to withdraw from the Gazala line, a reduction was made in the staff and stocks of 500 AOD. A quantity of controlled stores and other important items was moved back progressively to Mersa Matruh. The temporary depot so formed was operated by the staff withdrawn from Tobruk.

This left Colonel Gore with 5 officers and 120 ORs to look after the stores which remained. As Tobruk fell within a few days there was a good deal of equipment to be destroyed or made unfit for use by the enemy and this process was carried out under cover provided by the depot defence unit. fighting continuing even after most of the garrison had been overrun.

Colonel Gore himself escaped from an Italian prisoner-of-war camp in 1943 and with the help of some friendly Italians managed to acquire a boat in which he sailed to Corsica from where he flew in a French aircraft to Algiers.

503 AOW

This workshop was under the command of Lieutenant-Colonel Beahan early in 1942 but was later taken over by Lieutenant-Colonel Ralphs. For some time it did not carry the complete repair load in Tobruk but worked in conjunction with other units located there such as 70th Divisional Ordnance Workshops and 2nd Armoured Divisional Workshops.

By the middle of February 1942 the plan was to limit the size of the workshops and its activity. The number of vehicles immobilized for repair was not to exceed a certain figure. Vehicles on wheels and tanks on their tracks could be held awaiting repair but only in sufficient numbers to maintain an economic flow of work. Speedy evacuation of all vehicles in excess of these figures was to be undertaken. Ambitious repair programmes were to be avoided and assembly exchange to be used to the full.

As the front stabilized on the Gazala position and the plans for a further offensive matured the desire to extend the scope of repairs, particularly of tanks, developed. This was, however, a slow process, for even in March the staff at Eighth Army laid down a 48-hour limit for repairs and limited the number of vehicles to be held to 50 per cent of the total capacity of the workshop. In practice this meant that very little work could be done.

The pendulum soon swung the other way. The policy of the DOS was to send reinforcements to 503 AOW, and to increase its capacity to carry out field repair (for example assembly exchange) but not to increase the scope in the direction of base repair.

On the other hand Eighth Army wanted to do as much repair forward as possible. They may have been influenced by receiving tanks from the Base which in their view required too much attention in field workshops before they were battle-worthy.

The DOS wrote to the Army Commander explaining the reason for his policy and followed this up with a visit to the Army. His views prevailed. The objections to undertaking ambitious repairs in the field were as follows:

Factor	*Effect*
1. Personnel must all be military.	Impossible to dilute, so that one Armament Artificer instead of being a supervisor of several dilutees is only one digit in the workshop on the field.

Factor	*Effect*
2. Lack of handling and repair facilities in the field compared with the base.	Capacity is strictly limited.
3. Working hours are interrupted by enemy action and by sandstorms.	Skilled staff cannot be employed so effectively in the field as in Base Workshops.
4. Extensive repair requires large stocks of spares on the spot if delays are to be avoided.	There would never be sufficient stocks of tank spares to permit wide dispersion in the forward areas. Held centrally at the Base they could be diverted to any point where the need was greatest.
5. The vulnerability of a forward workshop imposed considerable dispersion.	Output would be slowed down by an industrially uneconomic lay-out with considerable "walking time" and delays while an item was moved from one operation to another.

The answer was of course not to do the work in the wrong place but to improve the liaison between the Base Workshops and the forward units. The steps taken to this end undoubtedly increased confidence in the efficiency of the Base Workshops.

Steps were taken to increase the capacity of 503 AOW by making it more mobile, and self-supporting as regards power. Also a sufficient number of field shelters was provided to improve working conditions. The unit was brought up to 8 officers and 218 ORs.

When the battle started 503 AOW acted for a time as a second line workshop for 1st Armoured Division when it was separated by an enemy thrust from its administrative units. This was of course additional to the advanced workshop task and it was impossible to apply the limit laid down for the number of tanks in the shops at any one time. By June 1st 503 AOW had repaired and re-issued 20 tanks.

By June 18th men and equipment had been withdrawn from Tobruk, reducing 503 AOW to the size of Independent Brigade Workshops. Its trailer machinery was brought down to Mersa Matruh with the surplus men. This part of the unit operated later at El Deba and moved to the Delta after the El Alamein line was occupied. The main body of the unit remained at Tobruk and was captured when that place fell.

501 AAD

This unit was at first commanded by Major Walker and later by Major Bromley. The ammunition was laid out on both sides of the Tobruk–

Derna Road. The losses of ammunition were small owing to the excellent dispersal arrangements and camouflage.

Unlike the other two installations 501 AAD was not drastically reduced on June 18th and nearly the whole unit was captured when Tobruk fell.

STRAGGLERS

It has been seen that one of the features of desert warfare was the liability of administrative units to be overrun by enemy armour. Sometimes individuals were cut off from their units or headquarters. In "Crusader" this led to an astonishing number of stragglers appearing in the railhead area.

Before the Gazala battle this situation was anticipated by the establishment of Road Report Centres on the main axis of advance and withdrawal. The scheme proved to be most effective and, from the RAOC point of view at any rate, eliminated stragglers. To take but one example, 4 L of C Recovery Section was shelled out of its position and scattered. The various elements of the unit went to No. 3 Report Centre and within an hour the unit was complete and ready for further recovery work.

AIR DELIVERY SERVICE

The value of this service had been demonstrated in "Crusader". However, early in the Gazala battle it was described by DDOS Eighth Army as "grudging". He was only receiving a maximum of 2,000 lb of Ordnance stores a day. He quoted an Army Intelligence Summary which showed that the enemy sent once or twice daily flights of 30 three-engined planes to Derna. They carried petrol, rations and urgent spares which were taken on to the forward area by road.

It was hoped that this information would stir up those people at GHQ who were lukewarm about air delivery of stores. It is more likely that the disappointing service was due to a temporary shortage of aircraft, for the advance from Alamein to Tunisia was aided by air delivery of stores on a much larger scale.

THE BATTLE OF ALAMEIN AND ADVANCE TO TUNISIA

Although the defeat of the Eighth Army at Gazala was very serious it could not be decisive as long as the Army remained in being and the Alamein line held. Reinforcements of men and material were moving into the Middle East where a very large base had been established. On the other hand Rommel faced increasing difficulties of supply. His failure to break through the Alamein line at the beginning of July 1942 proved to be the turn of the tide.

The RAOC task of supplying the Eighth Army while it was so near the Delta was relatively easy. The real problem was to equip reinforcements and to create the means not only to defeat Rommel at Alamein but to drive him out of Africa altogether.

FORMATION OF REME

The four months before the decisive battle of Alamein was a hectic enough preparatory period and was further complicated by a major event affecting the Corps, namely the formation of a Corps of Electrical and Mechanical Engineers (REME). This is covered in greater detail in Chapter 11, but the main effects were that responsibility for repair of equipment and vehicles and for recovery was transferred to the new Corps leaving provision, storage and supply of Ordnance stores, vehicles and ammunition and the repair of ammunition, clothing and general stores with the RAOC. The duplication of function, whereby the RASC supplied and repaired their own vehicles, ceased. The vehicle and MT Stores holding units were transferred to the RAOC.

SUPPLY OF VEHICLES

At the beginning of August the Eighth Army was about 25 per cent below vehicle establishment and many of the existing vehicles were almost worn out. Large reinforcements were needed if mobility was to be maintained right through to Tunisia. Enemy submarines were very active in the Atlantic and shipping losses were at a dangerous level. It was many months before the Battle of the Atlantic was finally won. Shipping space must be saved and nearly all wheeled vehicles were sent "knocked down" and assembled in the Middle East on arrival. This method was standard practice in the case of vehicles exported from North America to their agents overseas and all that was required was to obtain plant and set it up in the Middle East. The first assembly plant was in operation in June 1941 at Ataka, west of Suez. By August 1942 three other assembly units had been established, at El Shatt on the east bank of the canal opposite Suez, at Port Said and at Alexandria. The combined average daily output of the four units was 180 vehicles.

URGENT FIGHTING STORES

The importance of a rapid delivery service from the Base was fully appreciated as a result of experience in earlier campaigns in the Western Desert. Stocks of specially selected stores such as AFV spares, signal stores, small arms, gun barrels, etc, were held at 6 AOD, Alexandria at immediate call of the Eighth Army with whom the range and quantity of items was worked out. The road delivery service was extended and now comprised 510 L of C Vehicle and Stores Convoy Unit, 10 Corps Stores Convoy Unit and 30 Corps Stores Convoy Unit. The Vehicle and Stores Convoy Unit provided staff on both rear and forward landing grounds so that air delivery was tied in with the stores convoy system and demands could be conveyed rapidly to base by returning aircraft. The system worked admirably. From the earliest days of Western Desert campaigning it had been advocated by General Richards and its full adoption in the final advance to Tunis is a tribute to his foresight and powers of persuasion.

The turn-round for convoying vehicles was 20 days from the Delta to Benghazi (740 miles) and 15 days from Benghazi to Tripoli (675 miles). In the 4 months from November 1942 to February 1943 the unit delivered nearly 8,000 vehicles and 2,350 tons of stores.

ROADHEADS

Although full use was made of ports as they were captured, and the railway was pushed as far west as possible the Eighth Army was mainly supplied by mechanical transport and operated a roadhead system.

The roadhead really replaced a railhead and the same RAOC units were required for both. When a new roadhead was opened the load did not immediately decrease at the old one and staff was necessary to operate the two simultaneously. Stocks were established at roadheads but it was only possible to predict the requirements of a limited range of items, notably clothing and accommodation stores. These were also bulky items and standard packs were made up at the Base and sent to arrive at the railhead by the time it was ready to receive them. Other items were demanded as soon as the requirement became clear.

As an experiment a forward trailer unit was formed and sent to Army roadhead to be deployed as required. The object was to supplement the forward holdings of vital items such as tank and gun spares for which the field park stocks might not be adequate. In this form the scheme did not prove a success. Stores held with formations, backed by the "urgent fighting stores" supply system were quite adequate to meet the needs of the Army, and the trailer unit only served to cause an undesirable dispersion of advanced ordnance depot stocks.

ADVANCED ORDNANCE DEPOTS

It was decided that these would be established at Benghazi as well as Tripoli. The former would only be operative for a limited time and the damage done to Benghazi harbour also reduced the amount of shipping which could be cleared. Nevertheless the circumstances justified the placing of stocks at both ports and the additional work. The early opening of the port at Tripoli could not be guaranteed and the AOD there was able to function more efficiently because the load did not have to be transferred from Benghazi until all was ready. The Benghazi AOD refitted 10 Corps, which had to be grounded there for a time while its vehicles were used to keep 30 Corps mobile for the advance to Tripoli.

The stocks also sufficed to replenish the various OFPs in the Army and thus reduce the demands on the BODs. The L of C was so long that an intermediate depot was useful to serve units on the L of C in Cyrenaica. By now there was ample experience to enable the AODs to be limited to items known to be essential. By the time the Army was concentrated before the Mareth Line in Tunisia its state of equipment was as good as it had been at the Battle of Alamein, fought almost on top of the main base in the Delta.

SEASONAL CHANGE OF CLOTHING

Bulk issues of this sort cannot be made at the last minute or when operations are imminent. Experience showed that stocks had to be established in AODs or other forward locations a long time, amounting to months, before the change was due to take place. This gave the maximum time for final distribution. The lesson was apparently forgotten, or RAOC representations were ignored at the time of the landings in Italy only a year later.

ANTI-TANK MINES

The demands for the Alamein defences at the end of June were very heavy and even the monthly local production figure of 270,000 was well below the requirement. By remarkable efforts this monthly figure had been doubled before the end of August, and although shortage of explosives reduced the quantity in September the danger had passed and we were more concerned with breaching the enemy mine-fields.

MINE DETECTORS

This equipment was of great and increasing importance. It was also very scarce. Sources of supply were United Kingdom, U.S.A. and South Africa, supplemented by local manufacture using components sent from the United Kingdom and U.S.A. More than 400 were issued in the 3 months before the Battle of Alamein.

SUPPLY DROPPING

This method of supply was given considerable thought and thorough preparation. 25,000 sets of parachutes and harness were manufactured locally, and a stock of filled and labelled containers was held, ready harnessed at Khanka airfield 25 miles east of Cairo. Additional stocks of supply dropping equipment were held at 8 BAD for ammunition and 4 BOD for AFV spares and vital items so that they could be packed on demand and sent direct to the airfield ready for loading. Just before the offensive began 34 tons of packed and harnessed ammunition, with spare parachutes, harness and containers, was sent to Amiriya for use if required by Eighth Army. Trained RAOC packers accompanied the consignment. All this effort was wasted in the end as for the rest of the campaign in Africa the need for this method of supply did not arise. But it was a wise precaution and could have been decisive had events taken a different course.

After the successful landing in French North Africa it was obvious that the Axis forces would have to withdraw into Tunisia and only a series of rearguard actions were likely in Libya. In the advance after Alamein the Eighth Army was not able to cut off and destroy any significant numbers of the enemy forces, but this only postponed the day of reckoning for the whole of the Axis army was later captured when Tunis fell.

It is evident that the DA and QMG Eighth Army (speaking shortly after the fall of Tripoli on administration of the Army in the field) had in mind only the local situation when he described maintenance of armies by the use of air transport as picturesque nonsense and the resort of the destitute. Certainly the value of supply by air was never underestimated in the RAOC. The difficulty always was to get the requirements of Ordnance stores given sufficient priority.

CONCLUSION

Fighting was almost continuous in the Western Desert from the Italian advance in 1940 to the final occupation of Tripolitania early in 1943. Logistic problems were varied and complex, testing to the utmost the ingenuity and judgement of those responsible for solving them. The RAOC story in these operations is one of "rags to riches", of extreme scarcity of all types of equipment and of manpower to lavish supplies of equipment of high quality and sufficient, though by no means excessive, manpower.

The organization finally evolved from all this experience was excellent for desert warfare and in many respects ideal for all conditions. The original, over-centralized, Ordnance Field Park organization was broken down on a formation basis to an Army Troops OFP, Corps Troops OFPs and Divisional OFPs. The Army and Corps Troops units held reserve vehicles as well as stores. The OFPs also supplied spares to formation workshops but with the creation of REME as a separate Corps the policy of giving each workshop its own RAOC Stores Section ultimately emerged. It was a sound scheme, for workshops in operations were often in isolated locations and their requirements were for stores in one specialized range only.

The Vehicle and Stores Convoy Unit was the most effective means of ensuring the supply of "urgent fighting stores", and proved its worth in later campaigns. It infringed the principle, if indeed it is a principle, that all transport must be pooled and allocated by the staff according to priorities. The application of this principle invariably led to failure to supply urgently required Ordnance stores. This consistent failure was due to insufficient training of staff officers in the problems of the supply of Ordnance stores, a contributory factor being the denial to RAOC officers before the war of Staff College training and staff appointments. The creation of the Vehicle and Stores Convoy Unit on an approved establishment was an acknowledgement that there was a minimum perpetual need for this service.

The creation of units on separate approved establishments to deal with stores and ammunition at railheads, roadheads and in field maintenance centres was a Middle East organization which became accepted as normal administrative practice in the field. The FMCs became Maintenance Areas and the detachments Ordnance Maintenance Companies. Vehicle units continued in the main to be adjuncts of stores units such as BODs or Field Parks, but at the time REME was created the dual supply system (RAOC and RASC) for vehicles ceased and full responsibility was taken over by the RAOC. Gradually the concept of a separate vehicle organization developed.

A less satisfactory feature of the Eighth Army system was the control of stores. No one would deny the necessity for operational control of certain items, particularly in times of scarcity, but when stores were plentiful there remained an excessive number of staff officers doing what was really Ordnance work and inadvertently making the task of RAOC officers unnecessarily difficult.

At the time that REME was formed a new staff branch, Q (Army Equipment) was created at GHQ Middle East under a Major-General. The task of this branch was to do the staff work and co-ordination affecting the RAOC, REME and Salvage, which was organized as a separate Service. General Richards was transferred to this appointment, and as he had been responsible for REME services while they were still part of the RAOC task the arrangement ensured continuity of control and assisted REME in its early days as a separate Corps. After a time General Richards was required at the War Office as Director of Clothing and Stores, and Major-General C. H. Geake took over DOS Middle East.

General Richards inspired the RAOC officers and men in the Middle East with much of his own relentless drive and initiative and to him must go the credit for the great achievements of the Corps in that theatre.

General Geake had considerable knowledge of the equipment supply situation, gained from his previous War Office appointment which was a great asset. He had a flair for cooperation with other branches of the Staff and Services and received cooperation from them. He had an equable temperament and a saving sense of humour. Under his leadership, both in the Middle East and later in AFHQ, Ordnance Services worked at a consistently high level of efficiency but without tension.

CHAPTER SIX

THE MIDDLE EAST BASE

General Wavell had served in Egypt and Palestine in the First World War. He therefore had practical experience of the strategic importance of the Middle East as a Base, and he well realized that its significance had become greater in the interval between wars, owing to mechanization and the increased material requirements of the fighting services.

Before the war, preparation was limited to planning on a small scale, but once war was declared it would have been an elementary precaution to build up the Middle East Base, thus placing the British and French forces in the Mediterranean theatre in a position of overwhelming strength and discouraging Italy from repeating those acts of aggression which had been too successful in the recent past.

Unfortunately the mentality which characterized the "phoney war" period had its effect also in the Middle East. The Middle East was not yet a theatre of operations and it was thought that any work to improve the Base would be regarded by Mussolini as an act of provocation. Moreover, such work would cost money and the delusion still prevailed that victory in a world war comes automatically to those who, having made no preparations, try to conduct a war on the cheap.

All this was swept aside when Mr. Churchill became Prime Minister in May 1940, but it could easily have been too late as by then the United Kingdom was in danger. A great opportunity had passed. Soon France was out of the war and Italy had come in against us. The Middle East was now very much a theatre of war and our situation was extremely precarious.

Luckily the new Prime Minister had all the strategic courage and imagination which had previously been lacking. He saw the Middle East as a springboard from which attacks could be launched on the Axis powers, and he actively supported every scheme for strengthening our position there. He took great, but justifiable, risks by transferring troops and tanks from the United Kingdom even before the Battle of Britain was won.

From that moment the energy and ingenuity of those who directed the war effort in the Middle East had full scope, and although there was now no time to develop the resources which might have prevented our early failures in the Western Desert, Greece and Crete, an effective base had been formed by the time of the "Crusader" operation. Eventually the means were created to sustain the campaigns to clear North Africa and the Mediterranean, capture Sicily and Italy and invade the south of France, a formidable contribution to final victory. There is also no doubt that the Middle East Base would have formed a most useful entrepôt in the chain of supply to South-East Asia had the fighting there not been ended by the sudden collapse of Japanese resistance in the face of atomic attack.

THE NATURE AND EXTENT OF THE TASK

The first essential in the development of any base is to improve communications and transportation facilities. As the Mediterranean was soon closed nearly all material had to be brought in at the southern end of the Suez Canal. The port facilities in that locality were greatly extended. Inland Water Transport linking the Nile Delta with the Suez Canal was developed. Additional railway lines and many miles of road were constructed. Depots and workshops were built but the majority of men crowded into this relatively small area were housed in tents.

This achievement in the field of transportation was remarkable and it was matched by the full and rapid development of all aspects of Ordnance Services under the tireless and ubiquitous direction of General Richards. The scope of the work was immense and covered the following activities:

1. Engineering. Repair and manufacture of electrical and mechanical equipment. Supervision of local resources in this field. This work was transferred to REME on the formation of that Corps.
2. Provision. The creation of a Central Provision Office coordinating provision and stock control of Ordnance Stores throughout the Middle East which ultimately included North Africa, Italy, Syria, Palestine, Persia, Iraq, the Sudan, Eritrea and East Africa as well as Egypt.
3. Storage and Supply of Ordnance Stores and Vehicles. Inspection and repair in Returned Stores Groups.
4. Ammunition storage, supply, inspection, repair and manufacture.
5. Miscellaneous. Clothing factory, clothing repair factory, paint factory, officer's shops and other means for the exploitation of local resources.

It is interesting to note that, although fighting in Africa and the Middle East ended with the capture of Tunisia in May 1943, activity in the Middle East Base, particularly in Egypt, continued to increase and did not reach a peak until 1944. The main reason for this was the importance of sustaining the campaign in Italy and reducing the logistic strain on the United Kingdom and North America. Priority of supply from those

173

sources had to be given to the campaign in North-West Europe on the success of which early victory in Europe chiefly depended.

Thus the story of the Middle East Base continues until the end of the war and, although it is encroaching somewhat on REME history to describe events which occurred after the formation of that Corps in late 1942, this is done to some extent in order to complete the picture.

ENGINEERING ACTIVITIES

RAOC Base Workshops in the Middle East hardly existed at the beginning of the war, consisting of a small workshop in Abbassia, an anti-aircraft workshop section in Alexandria, and in Palestine small installations at Sarafand, Haifa and Tel Aviv.

Local resources were not great. There was, however, ample unskilled and some semi-skilled labour. By systematic recruiting, selection and training of this labour the means was created not only to increase the capacity for repair of equipment, but also to build up local manufacture to an astonishing degree by 1944. It is only fair to say that many of the local employees showed considerable intelligence and aptitude, responding well to the training schemes which were put into operation at the beginning.

Additional facilities were needed, and several established engineering concerns—the property of enemy aliens—were taken over by the Custodian of Enemy Property. The Base Ordnance Workshop organization, by July 1942, was as follows:

No. 4 in various sites in Cairo;
No. 2 at Tel el Kebir;
No. 7 at Alexandria;
No. 3 at Haifa.

In addition there was No. 1 in Iraq, which cannot strictly be included in the complex of installations forming the Middle East Base.

On the formation of REME the maintenance workshops of No. 4 BOW were combined with the Heavy Repair Shop RASC at Abbassia to form No. 533 Base Workshop REME.

NO. 4 BASE ORDNANCE WORKSHOP

This was the nucleus of the vast workshop organization which finally developed. In the beginning it was a very small unit in Abbassia forming part of 12 Section RAOC. It bore the brunt of the acute shortages in the early part of the war—shortages of men, technical equipment, accommodation and spares. Ingenuity and improvisation were at a premium and local resources had to be exploited to the full. This workshop became the centre for local manufacture, but it also carried a considerable load of maintenance and repair until 533 Base Workshop REME was formed.

Some idea of the expansion of 4 BOW is given by the strength of the unit in January 1941 and September 1942.

	Military	*Civilian*	*Total*	*Dilution*
January 1941	1,300	2,600	3,900	2 to 1
September 1942	2,300	11,500	13,800	5 to 1

By September 1942 dilution had just about reached the limit consistent with an acceptable level of efficiency. The proportion of skilled and semi-skilled to unskilled labour remained at roughly 2 to 1 throughout.

4 BOW was commanded by Colonel A. J. Wright, and was progressively built up from 13, 14 and 20 Ordnance Workshop Companies. By mid-1941 there were 11 sub-workshops under the headquarters in Abbassia. The grouping was as follows:

Abbassia	3 sub-workshops	"A" vehicles.
		Guns and "B" vehicles.
		Armourers.
Choubra	2 sub-workshops	Machinery.
		Sheet metal work, manufacture.
		Casting and "B" vehicles.
Ghamrah	1 sub-workshop	"B" vehicles.
Morris	1 sub-workshop	"B" vehicles.
Bertolisse	1 sub-workshop	Wood machining.
Testa's	1 sub-workshop	Aluminium casting and machining.
Boba's	1 sub-workshop	Machining.
Zeitoun	1 sub-workshop	Motor cycles and light cars.

Some repair was carried out by contract with local firms. In this way some 30 Ford vehicles per week were repaired.

The field of design and development was an important one, covering the design and production of many items to meet military requirements as they arose, the re-design of approved patterns to facilitate production with the materials available, and modification of existing equipments.

Before the battle of Alamein, deceptive devices were produced by 4 Base Workshop on a large scale. These included "sunshields" for tanks, which gave the tank the appearance from the air of an ordinary lorry, and dummy aircraft.

In addition to design a considerable amount of experimental work was carried out in connection with the testing of equipment and the investigation of failures. Laboratory work was undertaken in conjunction with Giza University and the Cairo Physical Laboratory.

Many thousands of spares and components were produced. A few examples will suffice to illustrate the versatility of 4 Base Workshop:

1. Manufacture of moulds and the production of rubber and bakelite items such as tank tyres.
2. Manufacture of grinders and mixers for the paint factory.

3. Manufacture of pistons, piston rings, gudgeons and circlips.
4. Production of soyer stoves, kit boxes, first aid boxes and other equipment involving sheet metal work.
5. Production of tables, special cases and all types of accommodation stores.
6. Manufacture of spur and spiral gears, gun sights, breech mechanism parts, tank power traverse components.
7. Production of special castings, gauges, tools and dies, modification parts.
8. Manufacture of bivouac shelters, canvas covers, field ambulance stretchers.

NO. 2 BASE ORDNANCE WORKSHOP

2 BOW was one of the group of installations built in the Tel-el-Kebir area on the Sweet Water Canal between Cairo and Ismailia. From the strategic and administrative point of view this was a good position. Difficulties occurred during the building stage, but when completed these installations had obvious advantages over the scattered collection of miscellaneous requisitioned premises with which 4 BOW had to be content.

Four workshop companies arrived at Tel-el-Kebir in the summer of 1941 but only one building of 5,000 sq ft had then been finished. 2 BOW ultimately grew to 46 workshops, the total covered accommodation amounting to one and a quarter million square feet with good roads and railway sidings.

Power was supplied from a central power station run by the Royal Engineers. A good water supply system was installed with a head of approximately 50 ft. Some of the water came from wells, but most of it from the Nile via the artificial ditch known with unconscious humour as the Sweet Water Canal. The charming picture of a pellucid stream, which its name evoked, was somewhat marred by the dead camels and other foreign bodies which it carried towards Ismailia. Nevertheless it served its purpose.

2 BOW was commanded by Colonel C. F. D. Suggate. A comparison of the manpower in June 1941 and December 1942 is interesting:

	Military	*Civilian*	*Total*	*Approx. Proportion Mil/Civilian*
June 1941	1,250	350	1,600	4 to 1
December 1942	3,050	5,650	8,700	1 to 2

The proportion of skilled to unskilled labour was 5 to 2 in June 1941 and 5 to 4 in December 1942.

Most of the equipment returned to the base required complete overhaul, and with the class of labour available this work could only be done efficiently by adopting a "line system" of overhaul. Such a system depends on a continuous flow of vehicles of the same type requiring overhaul, and also a good supply of the considerable range of base repair spares and components. These conditions could be fulfilled for a limited number of vehicle makes and types only, but successful line overhaul was introduced for the common makes of trucks and lorries, for American tanks and for the engines of many vehicles.

Modifications to vehicles absorbed about 50 per cent of the capacity of the workshop. This was chiefly due to the requirements of desert warfare. Additional stowage facilities had to be made for carrying extra water, blankets and items of personal equipment. Petrol tanks which could be jettisoned were introduced to increase the radius of action of certain vehicles. Sand shields were fitted to minimize the effect of dust and sand. New air cleaners were necessary to prolong engine life. Other modifications arose from the failure of vehicles or equipment to stand up to field conditions or from new operational requirements.

Between May 1941 and March 1944 the workshop output included:

> Complete overhaul of 4,300 "A" vehicles.
> 19,750 "B" vehicles.
> 33,500 engines.
> 2,300 guns.

> Modification of 17,500 armoured fighting vehicles.

> Modification and repair of 10,000 guns.
> 144,000 small arms.
> 52,000 wireless sets.
> 60,000 instruments.

NO. 7 BASE ORDNANCE WORKSHOPS

At the beginning of the war Alexandria could boast only a workshop section RAOC, engaged in the installation of anti-aircraft defences. It also undertook all work required by the Port Said area and recovery on the L of C between Wadi Natrun and El Daba.

In the autumn of 1940 the Stagni works at Wardian and the General Motors premises at Minet El Bassal were taken over. The unit became an Advanced Ordnance Workshop and later on was developed into a Base Workshop. It was commanded by Colonel A. O. Samson. It ultimately consisted of 2 main workshops and 12 sub-workshops. The engineering resources of the district were fully exploited.

The activities of the various elements were as follows:

Main Workshop "A"	Tank overhauls.
Main Workshop "B"	"B" vehicle overhauls.
1 Sub-workshop	Instruments and plastics.
2 Sub-workshop	Tyre repairs.

3 Sub-workshop	Cased vehicle assembly. Gun workshop, including captured equipments. Wireless workshop.
4 Sub-workshop	High precision work for manufacture of gun parts.
5 Sub-workshop	Machinery maintenance.
6 Sub-workshop	"B" vehicle engines. Battery and gasket manufacture.
7 Sub-workshop	"B" vehicle overhaul. Special types.
8 Sub-workshop	Repairs for "B" vehicle park.
9 Sub-workshop	Crankshaft grinding.
10 Sub-workshop	Woodwork.
11 Sub-workshop	Cased vehicle assembly.
12 Sub-workshop	Small arms.

The unit reached its manpower peak in November 1942. Comparative figures are as follows:

	Military	Civilian	Total	Approx. Mil/Civ proportion
February 1941	350	100	450	3·5 to 1
November 1942	1,700	3,600	5,300	1 to 2

The ultimate proportion of skilled to unskilled civilian labour was 3 to 2.

This was one of the most versatile workshops. A systematic analysis was made of all local engineering firms and many items were put out to contract for local manufacture. At the peak period some 8,300 different items were made per annum, either by sub-workshops or by contract controlled by 7 Base Workshops.

Battery repair was of great importance for a force with 150,000 vehicle batteries in use, in addition to those required for wireless sets and predictors. Had all batteries been replaced from the United Kingdom or North America the problem of shipping space as well as deterioration and damage in transit would have been formidable. The number of batteries repaired per month reached a figure of 5,000. The work was transferred to 4 Base Workshops in 1943.

Wireless repairs were a vital necessity. The modern technique of designing sets so that repair could easily be effected by replacement of components and sub-assemblies had not been perfected, and to a large extent the rebuilding of sets was necessary. This was no easy task with a handful of skilled mechanics and very little test apparatus or spares. The difficulty was overcome by organizing intensive training of mechanics to create a nucleus of highly trained staff. Not only was workshop capacity increased, but also a pool was provided for field workshops in exchange for less skilled mechanics who could obtain further training.

NO. 3 BASE ORDNANCE WORKSHOP

At the beginning of the war the workshop facilities in Palestine were limited to small installations at Sarafand, Haifa and Tel Aviv with a service station at Jerusalem. These installations were grouped to form 3 Advanced Ordnance Workshop, which developed into 3 Base Ordnance Workshop in September 1941. Civilian artisans were difficult to recruit owing to the location of the workshops but this problem was later solved by forming Palestinian (Jewish) Workshop Companies from personnel in the Middle East and posting them to 3 BOW.

Ultimately minor installations were transferred to the L of C and 3 BOW was concentrated in Kiryat Motzkin, 14 miles north of Haifa, Neuhardof south of Haifa and Tel Aviv. The largest of these locations was Kiryat Motzkin with 500,000 sq ft of covered accommodation, but it had serious drawbacks. Buildings were widely dispersed and design and construction were quite inadequate to stand the climate in Palestine. The area was highly malarial.

The unit was a useful subsidiary to the workshops in Egypt but was never developed to comparable capacity and output.

Examples of maximum annual output:

    1,260 "A" vehicle engines.
    2,250 "B" vehicles.
      250 "A" vehicles.
    1,670 Guns.
   63,630 Small arms.
   20,730 Wireless sets.

A complete battery reconditioning plant was installed at Kiryat Motzkin with a capacity of 2,000 secondary batteries a month.

The peak figure of manpower was 2,200 military, 2,100 skilled civilians and 2,000 unskilled civilians. This was in September 1942.

NO. 533 BASE WORKSHOP

This was never an RAOC unit but the majority of sub-workshops were originally the maintenance sub-workshops of 4 BOW. There were 13 of these and the main task was repair of "A" and "B" vehicles and assemblies. Repair of weapons, wireless sets and radar was also undertaken. 533 Base Workshop became a large unit with very impressive figures of production, but as this occurred after the formation of REME and the absorbtion of RASC Heavy Repair units, the events are not relevant to this history.

CENTRAL PROVISION

Like many other RAOC activities in the Middle East, provision developed from small beginnings into a most important organization at this focal point in the supply system.

179

At the outbreak of war the provision office was part of the Ordnance Depot at Abbassia and consisted of 2 officers and 25 clerks of whom about two-thirds were locally engaged Egyptians. The dependency was a force of 70,000 troops dispersed over Egypt, Palestine and the Sudan, and the number of item headings was of the order of 60,000.

As the Abbassia depot grew into a full-scale BOD, its three sub-depots for MT, Clothing and General Stores and Technical Stores maintained separate provision branches, but an ADOS (Provision) was appointed at the headquarters of 4 BOD.

The provision branch grew with the task and full use was made of locally engaged employees who were specially selected and trained. They did very good work.

The general shortage of stores and the long and dangerous L of C combined to stimulate local purchase and production, and in August 1940 a branch under an ADOS was formed to exploit local resources to the full. The headquarters was in Cairo with branches in Jerusalem and Alexandria. Initially the organization came directly under the orders of the DOS, but later on it became part of the Central Provision Organization.

Towards the end of 1940 5 BOD began to arrive and was formed at Tel-el-Kebir. The initial stocking was carried out by the provision branch at 4 BOD, but by March 1941 5 BOD had its own provision branch and ADOS. As the two depots were given different areas of supply their independent operation was theoretically feasible, but in practice an impossible situation quickly developed. More often than not, advice copies of vouchers or those which should have accompanied the stores, did not arrive. Frequently stores were addressed to the Middle East instead of to a specific BOD. Stores which were accompanied by the correct documents sometimes became separated from them in the process of transit from port to depot. Transportation difficulties sometimes compelled diversion of stores to a depot other than that to which they were consigned.

These circumstances, though normal in war, made it almost impossible to relate receipts to the original demands, and although the provision officers of the two depots kept in constant touch the utmost confusion prevailed. With the creation of 2 BOD in Palestine in September 1941 confusion was worse confounded. The problem was resolved in the only possible way by the formation of a Central Provision Office in November 1941. The provision elements of the BODs were concentrated in one organization and housed at Mena, some 8 miles west of Cairo.

The theoretical manpower requirement was 48 officers and 380 RAOC clerks, but the actual numbers were rather less than this figure. Some 500 Egyptian clerks had to be recruited. This was the first occasion on which a move of the unit compelled the discharge of locally employed staff and their replacement by others who had to be trained.

Additional work was involved in the posting of accounting documents in the Central Stock Record, which duplicated the BOD accounts. Provision Review Forms for the same items in all three BODs were married up to provide one record for the whole Middle East and enable one maintenance figure to be assessed for each item. Special express letter arrangements were made for the despatch of provision documents from Haifa to Mena.

The system worked well and the newly recruited staff settled down to business. But not for long. In June 1942 the Eighth Army withdrew to Alamein and the DDOS(P) found himself one morning in advance of Rear Headquarters of the Army.

GHQ decided to move the Central Provision Office to Haifa. This was a bad decision. There was no intention to withdraw from the Alamein position, and even if the worst happened, the unit could have moved at short notice. It might have been necessary to destroy all the records, but with the enemy in occupation of the Nile Delta these records would have related mainly to captured or destroyed stores. Even 7 Base Workshops at Alexandria, and therefore much nearer the front line, was kept in operation.

The trained Egyptian staff, half the strength of the unit, had to be left behind and the office records and equipment did not turn up in Haifa until a week after the unit had arrived. A Company of Palestinian ATS, by which the organization had been reinforced in the spring of 1942, had to be sent to Tel-el-Kebir for several weeks until accommodation was ready for them in Haifa.

Immediate action was taken to recruit and train new staff. Fortunately the Palestinian civilians were first class material, but even then the process took time. The effect of this dislocation was to produce an enormous build-up of unposted documents, which was, however, somewhat reduced in the next two months.

In Mid-August 1942 an order was received to move the branch to Tel Aviv, 75 miles south of Haifa and the dislocation was repeated. Hardly had the unit finished recruiting staff at Haifa when those who could not move to the new location had to be discharged.

Once again the pile of unposted documents mounted alarmingly and the records became increasingly suspect as a basis for provision. More than ever, at this stage, provision officers had to rely on instinct developed from experience, or imagination and foresight as the inspiration for their provision action.

In spite of all these difficulties liabilities seldom failed to be covered by stock or orders although the lack of reliable information undoubtedly led to over provision in some cases. By dint of drive, and the employment of night shifts on posting, the records were progressively brought up to date.

After the Alamein battle it was decided that the Central Provision Office should move back to Cairo. Close touch with operational policy was essential to ensure that the supply of equipment corresponded with the latest operational plans. This meant that the Central Provision Office must be reasonably close to GHQ and Tel Aviv was 400 miles away.

Early in January 1943 the move back to Mena was ordered. In this case it was done in phases so that the necessary recruitment and training of civilian staff could precede the actual move. Thus the inevitable dislocation was reduced to a minimum.

But further problems now arose. Cairo was overcrowded and its somewhat ramshackle transport system was not really up to the increased load. Five hundred clerical staff were transported in special trams from the centre of Cairo to the terminus at the Pyramids, a distance of about 7 miles. The men had to walk a further $2\frac{1}{2}$ miles to the office where they were expected to arrive at 8 o'clock each morning. Lorries were supplied to take the female staff on this last part of the journey. When work finished—at 6 pm—the reverse process took place, in pitch darkness. This had a bad effect on the efficiency of the staff. Absenteeism and resignations increased.

After a time it became clear that Mena was an impossible location, and excellent accommodation was found in the old infantry barracks in the Citadel in Cairo. The move was accelerated by an abnormally heavy rainstorm which practically washed out the offices and camp and stopped work altogether for 48 hours.

The move occurred so soon after the decision to bring the unit back to Cairo that the MT provision branch had not yet been transferred from Tel Aviv on the phased programme. However, the complete unit was in position by March 1943 and remained in the Citadel until the end of the war.

NEW PROBLEMS

From the time that the landings in North Africa took place it became clear that the supply arrangements for the armies in the Middle East and Mediterranean theatres must be closely linked.

The provision branches of the depots supporting the First Army had already been merged into a Central Provision Office and it was now decided that DDOS(P) Middle East would operate for the whole Mediterranean theatre. The stocks in the Middle East and North Africa were pooled.

With the invasion of Sicily and Italy the depots in these zones of operation submitted periodical stock states to DDOS(P) in the Citadel and the stocks in North Africa were eaten down, progressively reducing the size of these depots, which were then dropped out of the Central Provision organization. Later still PAIC (Persia and Iraq Command) and East Africa Command were brought into the same network.

The organization now included a Scales Branch and had increased in size to match the new commitments. The establishment consisted of:

Officers	79
RAOC ORs	457
Attached ORs (mostly REME)	91
Palestinian ATS	268
Civilians	369
Total	1,264

Add to these up to 400 civilian clerks and 100 casual labour which were engaged as required.

The number of item headings at this time was 402,000 and the average number of daily transactions recorded on the Central Stock Records between January and November 1944 was 38,000. The name of the unit was changed from DDOS (P) Middle East to Central Ordnance Provision Office or COPO (ME).

MACHINE ACCOUNTING

It had been realized, even before the "flight from Egypt" in July 1942, that the hand posting of stock records using local low grade civilian staff led to inaccuracies which could have unfortunate repercussions on provision. To overcome these difficulties it was decided to introduce the Power Samas Accounting Machine system.

The scheme could not be put into operation until late 1943 because of the shortage of certain essential equipment and the need for a complete check of stocks before the stock balances could be transferred to the new record. The system was basically a punched card process and stock states were produced as required. It closely resembled the Hollerith system, tried out at Didcot in the 1930's and eventually discarded in favour of the Visidex system adopted by Chilwell.

There were certain advantages in the system. Legible stock states were quickly produced for the cycle review and when stocks had fallen to a pre-determined level.

The key to the system was the Part Number, and owing to the variety of cataloguing systems in operation in the United Kingdom and U.S.A. it was necessary to code complicated Part Numbers so that the machine could take them. This introduced a new possibility of error.

A punched card was prepared for each accounting transaction and this could only be done correctly if the vouchers were well written and clear to the punched card operators. But most of the vouchers prepared by the clerical staff depots had to employ were in very poor shape and badly written. Under the hand posting system they could be interpreted, but this would not do for the machine and every voucher had to be screened. At one time as many as 400 clerks had to be employed on checking, amending and re-writing vouchers. This made nonsense of the savings in manpower claimed by the advocates of the introduction of the machine.

Stock states made out by hand continued to come in from Italy and other locations and these had to be studied in conjunction with the states produced by the machine which collated the information from Nos. 2, 4 and 5 BODs.

In spite of the difficulties encountered there is no doubt that great benefit was derived from the accuracy and clear presentation of provision states produced by the Power Samas system.

SCALES

From small beginnings the Scales Branch developed into a very important feature of the Central Provision Organization. It did most valuable work in preparing schedules of spares where none existed, collating wastage experience for the amendment of War Office and North American scales, and also preparing standard "Middle East" scales for:

LADs and Field Parks;
Advanced Ordnance Depots;
Landing Reserves and Beach Maintenance Packs;
Workshop Overhaul Programmes;
Special Projects.

In conjunction with the Special Issues Branch they were constantly engaged in scaling requirements of units and arranging issues, frequently at very short notice.

Owing to the unsatisfactory state of the U.S.A. spares schedules of automatic maintenance and documentation generally, a Scales Mission headed by the OC Scales Branch and ADOS(MT) went to America in 1943 to try to straighten things out. The visit resulted in considerable improvements in the system and was well worth while.

LOCAL PURCHASE AND PRODUCTION

The significance of making full use of local resources and manufacturing capacity has already been mentioned. Although GHQ exercised direct control over this activity initially, it was soon realized that local production and normal provision must be closely coordinated and the branch came under the control of the Central Provision organization.

The three main sources of supply outside the Middle East were the United Kingdom, North America and Eastern Group (which coordinated the sources bordering on the Indian Ocean). The Central Provision organization was able to see the state of supply of stores from these sources and so assess priorities for local production and also the requirements of raw materials.

Frequent meetings were necessary to allocate available material between the various workshops, to ensure that there was no overlapping of effort and that all spare capacity was fully used. Timber was always scarce in the Middle East and special arrangements were necessary for its recovery.

Long-term planning for the provision of raw material was extremely important. There was always considerable competition for these items and no certainty that the Middle East would be given priority. Yet the shortage of one item could hold up production altogether. Even indigenous items were not available in unlimited quantities as they were usually essential to the local economy.

The whole process required great foresight, ingenuity in the use of alternative materials and judgement in obtaining and distributing what was available locally. These qualities were abundant in the Middle East and account for the outstanding success of the policy in that theatre for making full use of local resources.

AUTOMATIC MAINTENANCE

It was decided quite early in the war that vehicles and equipments would be accompanied by spares to a pre-determined scale followed by automatic shipment of spares at regular intervals.

The system certainly produced an automatic supply of spares earlier than would have been the case if supply had been by demand. On the other hand great difficulties were experienced, especially with American equipments. There was no information on what was coming out. The U.S.A. automatic maintenance schedules were frequently altered without notice and for a long time there were important deficiencies in the shipments.

The scales were unbalanced, containing far too high a proportion of non-wearing parts such as cabs and wings. Moreover the proportions of over-size pistons, bearings and the like were quite out of line with REME overhaul schemes.

The system of documentation and demanding changed with bewildering frequency and the supply of spare parts from America was an absolute nightmare to all Ordnance Officers. However, as we were dependent on the goodwill and generosity of our ally for vehicles, equipment and spares we had to accept his scale of spares and adopt his method of demanding and documentation.

One particularly unsatisfactory feature of American automatic maintenance was the "lot" system of issue. Under this a set of spares for 100 vehicles was called a "lot", and a numbered case in each "lot" contained the same items. So with maintenance for 1,000 vehicles there were 10 lots and if, for example, all the pistons were required it was necessary to select 10 cases of a particular number and take out all the pistons. All this sorting resulted in the desert being littered with "lots" in various stages of completeness. Tidying up and putting to stock the residue was a monumental task.

LESSONS

Some interesting lessons were learnt from the experience of central provision in the Middle East.

It was found that text books would not cover all eventualities. Principles do not change but procedures and methods had to be adapted to unusual situations. In the words of Sherlock Holmes, "When you meet a variation from the normal you must deal with it, my dear Watson, in an abnormal manner".

There was immense scope for initiative and foresight and for the exploitation of local resources.

It was necessary to obtain from the staff information on dependency (manpower, vehicles and equipment) a very long way ahead, owing to the long lines of communication and the time which elapsed between the submission of a demand and the arrival of stores against that demand. It was necessary to stress persistently the importance of this advance estimating.

If stock records were in bad shape, a normal situation in war, provision officers had to learn to interpret this imprecise information and to provide the stores required without being wildly extravagant.

Efficient results were not obtained by becoming office-bound. Visits to units to discuss problems on the spot were essential and often produced a different picture from that which had filtered down to the base. Visits to suppliers were also essential, and on occasions officers went to America and were able to explain their difficulties over scales of spares, advice and documentation, and so on.

COMMAND

In the early days Colonel R. A. Weir was in charge of provision. Then Colonel R. R. M. Mayhew was in charge at 4 BOD and Colonel (later Brigadier) H. C. Whitaker at 5 BOD. Brigadier Whitaker took over DDOS(P) when the organization was centralized and remained in command for the greater part of the war. He combined a flair for provision work with a degree of human understanding which ensured harmony and cooperation in the diverse elements of which the unit was composed. As a result of his influence the efficiency of the unit came to be taken for granted.

Base Ordnance Depots

4 BOD

At the beginning of the war there was only a small Command Depot in Cairo, at Abbassia. The area was limited and there was no scope for expansion. There was a variety of buildings which, however, were uniform in their inadequacy for the task and the poor working conditions which they provided.

A camp equipment depot was established in the garrison area of Abbassia, about 1 mile from the main depot, and two sub-depots, known as Polygon and Porton were taken over from veterinary units and used for general stores and anti-gas stores respectively.

A clothing and mobilization depot was at Kasr-el-Nil in the centre of Cairo and about 4 miles from Abbassia. This depot was rail served.

One reason for these unsatisfactory facilities was that, under the Anglo-Egyptian treaty of 1936, the British troops in Egypt were to move to the Canal Zone. The actual move depended on the building of accommodation, which had not even started, but the decision was enough to stop any significant construction in the Cairo area until the war came.

Stores accommodation amounted to 458,000 sq ft, covered, and 72,000 sq ft, open. The covered accommodation was in seven separate locations. This was the nucleus of 4 BOD which developed piecemeal by the acquisition or construction of additional accommodation notably at Geneifa, near Suez, and in the Tura caves.

The depot was commanded by Colonel Wotherspoon and his immediate difficulty was to find staff to deal with the increased activity. Large numbers of civilians of varying quality were obtainable but they required training and supervision. The handful of RAOC men in Egypt at the time could not meet all commitments and inevitably priority was given to the Western Desert Force. Reinforcements did not arrive for some time and the staff had to work a seven-day week in the hot weather of 1940 and right through to the campaign which led to the occupation of Cyrenaica early in 1941. As a result the sickness rate increased.

However, reinforcements eventually arrived and the situation improved. In November 1940 Colonel Wotherspoon's health broke down and he was replaced by Colonel R. A. Weir from whom Colonel (later Brigadier) E. Tankard took over in February 1941.

The Middle East policy of self-sufficiency is reflected in the development of the Returned Stores Depot of 4 BOD as an organization for the repair and manufacture of general stores on a large scale. Tent manufacture was started as early as April 1940. In less than a year over 4,000 tents were produced. Boot and clothing repairs were also undertaken as the war requirement could not be met by the peace-time arrangement of putting this work out to contract.

The sub-depot at Geneifa, between Suez and the Bitter Lakes and 80 miles from Cairo, was started in the summer of 1941 and became 2 Sub-depot holding clothing and general stores. Transfer of stores from Abbassia to Geneifa began in August 1941. The process was slow because all accommodation had to be built on a desert location with no facilities and no local labour. On the other hand Geneifa was ideally placed for receiving stores from Suez which was for some time the only significant point of entry of supplies to the Middle East. One of the first officers to be posted there was Major (later Lieutenant-Colonel) E. A. Clutten, who commanded the sub-depot until the end of 1944.

By October 1941 the local labour force had been built up to a strength of about 800 but they were not much help and gave a good deal of trouble, a situation which was aggravated by administrative difficulties. No water supply and no lighting had yet been laid on and the field conditions at this time hampered the efforts to increase the capacity of the sub-depot by dilution with local employees. Cases of stores were broken open and the contents stolen. The provision of Libyan and Sudanese "ghaffirs" as security guards only served to stimulate the competitive spirit. There was no perimeter fence.

The "Crusader" operation took place at the end of 1941 and its fluctuating fortunes produced repercussions in the plans for Geneifa. At Abbassia, 2 Sub-depot continued to hold stores at what was known as Range Depot, Porton and Polygon sub-depots and Kasr-el-Nil, with small stocks at the Citadel and in one of the caves at Tura. When operations prospered there was a tendency for the overflow of stocks in the Abbassia area to be absorbed in forward holdings at Tobruk and elsewhere. During this time Geneifa combined the functions of transit depot, a depot to take the load off 5 BOD while it was developing and an Indian Army Ordnance Corps depot.

When our forces withdrew from the western part of Cyrenaica, Geneifa took the overflow from Abbassia and an increasing proportion of receipts. It gradually developed as the 2 Sub-depot of 4 BOD while most other locations closed down.

The climatic conditions and lack of amenities were probably worse at Geneifa than in any other installation in Egypt, but in spite of this morale and efficiency attained a high level.

In 1943 it was decided that more use could be made of the Tura caves. The danger of attack from the air had passed but the storage conditions were ideal for certain stores and the limited numbers of entrances facilitated security. Large stocks of tyres were held in the caves as they deteriorated in high temperatures and from the effects of the sun when in open storage. Electronic stores also benefited from the conditions in the caves and eventually 3 Sub-depot moved there from Abbassia.

The final situation in 4 BOD was that the headquarters, MT Sub-depot and a very extensive returned stores depot with considerable manufacturing capacity were located at Abbassia. Geneifa housed 2 Sub-depot and Tura 3 Sub-depot.

Vehicles were all important in the Middle East campaigns and considerable reorganization was necessary. The original command depot at Abbassia was a composite affair holding stores, vehicles and ammunition. Quite early in the war ammunition was formed into a separate organization and ceased to be the responsibility of the commandant of the BOD, but vehicles remained under his control.

There was no room to take all receipts into Abbassia which was turned into a returned vehicle park and depot for receipt of new "A" vehicles.

This decision was dictated by the presence of 4 Base Workshops at Abbassia and the availability of good railway sidings there.

Other vehicles went into the new depot at Mena, which provided 100,000 sq ft of covered accommodation and unlimited open storage. This depot was well placed for the supply of vehicles to units in the Western Desert. A depot was also established at Geneifa. This was in essence a transit depot to facilitate clearance of the port at Suez.

The story of 4 BOD falls into four stages:

1. The creation of an effective depot from nothing, involving recruitment and training of local employees, construction of accommodation, development of local resources. This was a period of improvisation and acute shortages requiring ingenuity in dealing with unexpected problems. These difficulties coincided with the commitments to support the first Western Desert campaign, the Abyssinian campaign and the operations in Greece and Crete.

2. A slightly less hectic period in which resources improved, other depots took a share of the load and the BOD developed to cope with the larger scale "Crusader" and Gazala operations.

3. Preparation for the battle of Alamein. Massive receipts of new equipment had to be cleared and issued urgently. New devices, mainly connected with camouflage and mine clearance, had to be produced and issued urgently. The capacity of 4 BOD, with other depots, must be such as to maintain the Eighth Army right through to Tunisia. By this time the staff of the depot had become highly trained and experienced. Resources were now excellent.

4. The support of British and Commonwealth forces in the Sicily and Italy campaigns. This involved new techniques of issuing stores for beach maintenance. It also increased the total work load for a time. The BODs in Algeria were really in fact only temporary depots, AODs, created solely to support the campaign in North Africa for which they proved adequate. They also provided a bonus in the support of the short campaign in Sicily, but the firm base for all operations in the Mediterranean area, once North Africa was clear of the enemy, was obviously the long-established Middle East base. Thus 4 BOD continued to carry a heavy load up to the time that 557 BOD near Naples was functioning to full effect.

At full strength 4 BOD consisted of about 2,000 military and 10,400 civilians.

5 BOD

Quite early in the war plans were made for the construction of a new depot in Egypt. It was the policy of General Richards to confine new construction of base installations to the area east of the River Nile. There were sound reasons for this as the depots were conveniently placed in relation to the port at Suez and the Canal. When the Eighth Army fell back to the Alamein line the base installations were able to continue operating at full pressure and without interruptions. The logistic plan was to hold in the forward area stocks of certain bulky items such as clothing and have a fast delivery service from base of urgent fighting stores for which the demand varied. Field Parks held fast-moving spares. The soundness of this scheme was proved in four years of war.

The site chosen for the new stores depot, which became 5 BOD was Tel-el-Kebir on the Sweet Water Canal between Cairo and Ismailia. It is east of the true Nile Delta and is in fact a small village in the desert.

The first shed was built in September 1940. Clothing, tentage and accommodation stores began to come in during October and November. A small quantity of technical stores arrived in November and MT stores were received in January 1941. By then some vehicles were being received and issued.

The main body of the depot arrived in March 1941 and a fourth stores company was added in September that year. The first commanding officer was Lieutenant-Colonel S. F. Clark and he was succeeded by Colonel (later Brigadier) G. C. H. Heron in March 1941. In July 1941 Colonel (later Brigadier) B. G. Cox was appointed Commandant. He retained the appointment until 1943. He was succeeded, after a number of temporary appointments, by Brigadier G. A. N. Swiney who later became DOS, Middle East.

Meanwhile progress in building the depot was slow. Many other large installations were under construction in the area and there was a shortage of material.

5 BOD was suffering from the occupational disease of all newly established depots in war. Shortage of staff was combined with lack of storage accommodation, receipts in excess of the capacity of the depot and constant pressure to make urgent issues. As a result receipts had to be dumped in any suitable or unsuitable outside location which could be found. Location records became inaccurate for lack of the means and manpower to keep them up to date and stock records followed suit.

The military staff, upon whom all supervision depended, were grossly overworked and in consequence their numbers were depleted by sickness.

In spite of all these difficulties the depot developed rapidly. By the end of March 1941 all sub-depots, the vehicle depot and a returned stores depot were fully active and there was a big increase in the stores received, both by rail and inland water transport, which carried a high proportion of the clothing and general stores.

A Middle East RAOC School of Instruction was set up in the depot for training both military and civilian staff.

The original plan was to allocate areas to be supplied by 4 and 5 BODs respectively but this was modified, particularly in the case of MT and technical stores, which were scarce and could not be dispersed. The arrangement also achieved a degree of specialization in the handling of these stores which was beneficial. A separate group was created for handling American AFVs and their associated equipment.

In course of time certain additional branches were formed. Special advisory staff dealt with the problems of American tanks. A mobilization branch received, assembled and issued unit war equipments as required. Detachments from the Royal Signals and Royal Engineers gave technical advice and assistance on stores of their concern. Most of their work related to returned stores, the identification, selection and conditioning of these stores so that they could be returned to stock and so increase the serviceable assets.

Prisoner of war tradesmen were of great assistance in the RSD. They were used for the repair and manufacture of boots, tentage and accommodation stores. They were of course equally useful in 4 BOD.

The RAOC personnel base depot, capable of accommodating 1,000 men was also set up at Tel-el-Kebir.

The commandant was also garrison commander and a number of units other than RAOC formed part of the garrison. The largest were 2 Base Workshops REME (originally of course RAOC), and 27 General Hospital.

This concentration of units in one location posed a security problem. The perimeter was several miles in circumference and the area was surrounded by a high wire fence outside which was a minefield. At first sight this might appear to be a rather excessive precaution, but in Egypt theft was a respected profession and the standard of living of the fellahin was so low that small rewards were deemed to justify considerable risks. The most attractive items were tentage and tyres, which attracted high prices in the black market.

Patrolling of the wire was of course undertaken but could not be continuous and the many races and nationalities to be found in the depot made it impossible to guarantee that any attempted theft was not an "inside job". The sails of craft seen on the Sweet Water Canal frequently displayed identification marks which supplied unmistakable evidence of War Department origin, and a village near Tel-el-Kebir was named by the local wags 6 BOD.

By the end of the war a swimming bath and other amenities had been provided for the garrison which became quite a popular station.

The ultimate total covered accommodation in the depot was 1,060,000 sq ft. The strength at the beginning of 1943 was 2,400 military and 9,000 civilians, Basuto pioneers and prisoners of war.

2 BOD

This depot was formed in Palestine. The frequent changes in the strategic situation and the state of supply of Ordnance stores caused corresponding changes in the role of 2 BOD, but as a base installation it

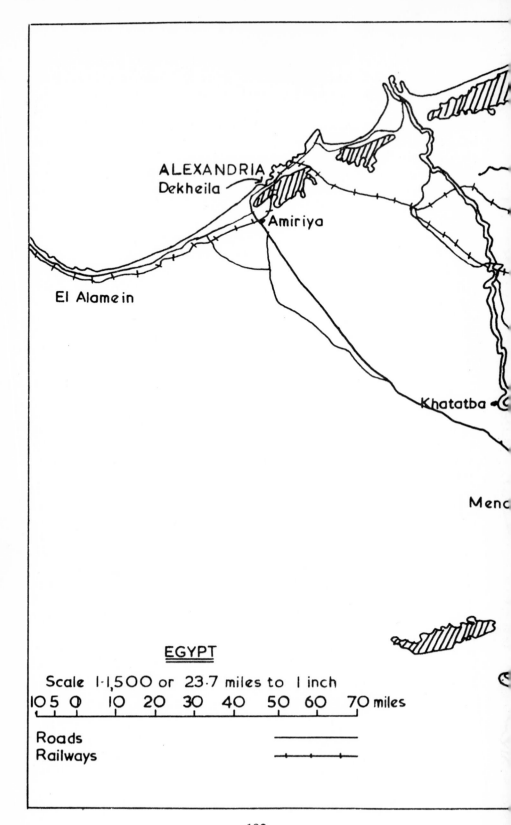

ALEXANDRIA

Dekheila

Amiriya

El Alamein

Khatatba

Menc

EGYPT

Scale 1·1,500 or 23·7 miles to 1 inch

10 5 0   10   20   30   40   50   60   70 miles

Roads
Railways

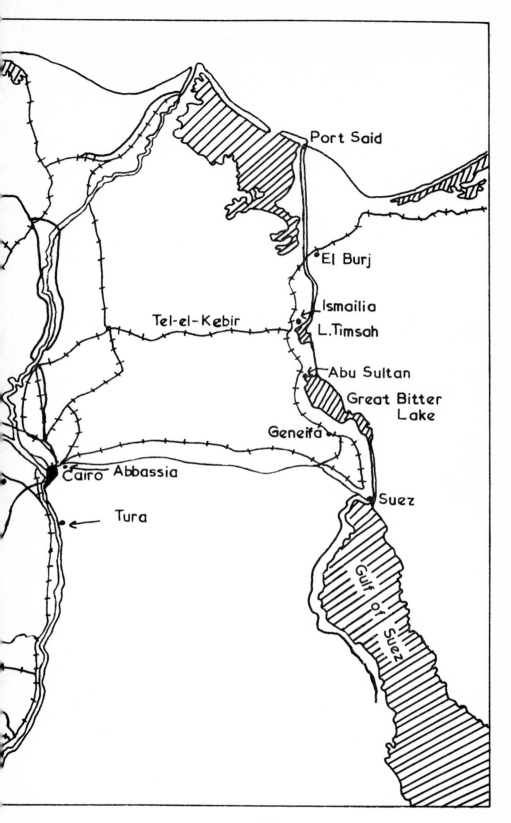

Port Said

El Burj

Ismailia
L. Timsah

Tel-el-Kebir

Abu Sultan

Great Bitter
Lake

Geneifa

Cairo Abbassia

Suez

Tura

Gulf of Suez

never attained the significance which their central position and proximity to Suez gave to 4 and 5 BOD.

Initially 2 BOD was formed at Rafa, near the Sinai border. It was only a small depot, holding mainly clothing and general stores and, in conjuction with 3 AOD at Haifa and Sarafand it provided support for the campaigns in Iraq and Syria in the summer of 1941.

Reinforcements were sent out and Colonel F. K. Lambert took over command in September 1941. He was replaced by Colonel (later Brigadier) B. C. Lester in November and in December Colonel (later Brigadier) J. F. H. Hitchcock became commandant remaining in the appointment for the next 3 years.

The threat from the north and the possibility of having to support Turkey if she could be persuaded to join the Allies kept the structure of 2 BOD and 3 AOD in being, but stocks of MT and technical spares remained at a low level because of the priority of requirements in the Western Desert.

In March 1942 staff from 3 AOD was sent to the Persian Gulf area, which had become a base for the supply of stores to Russia, and the depots at Haifa and Sarafand were absorbed into 2 BOD.

The depot was very dispersed. The headquarters was at Neuhardoff just south of Haifa with the majority of MT and technical stores there also. Some stocks were at Kiryat-Mutzkin near Haifa and the returned stores depot for these items was in Haifa itself. 2 Sub-depot was at Rafa, 130 miles south of Haifa with its returned stores depot at Sarafand.

In the crisis following the Gazala battle 2 BOD became more significant. It was a reasonable precaution to disperse some stocks to an area at a greater distance from the front than 4 and 5 BOD, and when the initiative passed to us there was the problem of holding the vast quantity of Ordnance stores which were moved in to the Middle East before and after the battle of Alamein. All available space was required.

The staff of the depot was built up to about 7,000. About 1,000 of these were military.

The depot played a useful part in the support of the Eighth Army advance to Tunisia, the campaign in Sicily and the early part of the Italian campaign. After this the load rapidly dropped. Three BODs were no longer needed and the stocks were progressively reduced.

Ammunition

8 BAD

The stocks of ammunition in Egypt at the beginning of the war were not sufficient to support any serious campaign even on the smallest scale. There was no proper ammunition depot and the small stocks in RAOC hands were held by a sub-depot of the Ordnance depot at Abbassia.

The idea, prevalent in peace-time, that a war in its early stages can be fought with very little ammunition, cannot be sustained once a war has started, and active steps as distinct from mere paper planning were taken to create suitable storage for the large stocks which would have to be held sooner or later.

The site chosen for the first depot was the area of the Tura caves in the Moqhattam hills on the east bank of the Nile opposite the great Pyramids. The caves had two obvious advantages as storage locations. They provided protection against air attack (a factor which was accorded undue significance at that stage of the war), and the temperature within the caves was steady and not too high, varying between 68°F and 78°F. The natural ventilation arranged by the ancient Egyptians proved excellent, and no artificial ventilation was necessary.

The earliest recorded use of these caves was to provide limestone blocks for the construction of the Giza pyramids, the first of which was finished in 3733 B.C. When this type of construction ceased to be fashionable there was a corresponding decline in quarrying and many of the caves gradually filled with rubble and sand.

When this was cleared some interesting relics were discovered, including a large stone slab nearly at the last stage of readiness for transporting across the Nile. The wooden wedges driven into the stone had petrified in course of time. Many oil lamps were found, and even a length of rope in excellent condition. These relics were presented to the Cairo museum.

The unit responsible for ammunition in the Tura caves was 8 BAD and it was formed in July 1940 under the command of Lieutenant-Colonel W. T. Cobb, whose experiences in Norway earlier in the year have already been recorded. He remained with the unit for a year.

By May 1941 the strength of the BAD was 17 officers and 271 men, but it was subject to considerable fluctuations through having to find drafts for various campaigns and for other ammunition depots which were being formed.

The Abbassia Depot was closed down as the stocks were issued or transferred to Tura but the repair and filling task remained. No. 1 Ammunition Repair and Filling Factory was created in Abbassia in July 1940, its main task being the production of Mines Contact Anti-Tank, Egyptian Pattern starting in August 1940. This unit was part of 8 BAD, but tasks other than mine production were progressively transferred until, at the end of October 1941, it became a separate entity and ceased to be the responsibility of the BAD. Thereafter the buildings at Abbassia were devoted to manufacture of locally designed booby traps and mine training sets. Some 30,000 Italian (Red Devil) hand grenades were converted to anti-personnel mines, and many thousand German Teller mines were emptied for training purposes.

Certain rules for the safe storage of ammunition had been formulated and were recorded in *Magazine Regulations*, between the wars. These rules derived largely from experience in the First World War and related to the risk of propagation or transmission of an explosion, which had been started in one building or stack by accident or enemy action, to other locations in the depot. The storage regulations sought to prevent this propagation of an explosion by imposing certain safety distances and explosive limits on surface depots.

However, there was no experience, nor had trials been carried out, to arrive at comparable safety rules for underground depots. Such a depot existed in the United Kingdom at Corsham, but it had been opened only just before the war started.

It was considered safe to accept a greater degree of concentration in an underground depot owing to the protection from air attack and the traversing effect provided by the walls separating the different galleries. But certain natures of ammunition were considered to have characteristics unsuitable for underground storage, and ammunition in repairable or doubtful condition was also excluded.

The standard surface BAD in those days held 21,000 tons of ammunition dispersed in three sub-depots each holding 7,000 tons. The plan for Tura was to have two sub-depots each holding 15,000 tons, although the ultimate peak holding exceeded this figure, reaching about 40,000 tons.

Movement of ammunition in the caves was effected by means of decauville railways laid along the side of the galleries to the entrance. Sometimes gravity runway had to be used but this was less effective than decauville. Heavy natures were stored nearer to the mouth of the cave than the lighter natures in order to reduce the burden of handling ammunition in receipt and issue.

Rail sidings were built about half a mile from the sub-depots. Between these sidings and the entrance to the caves ammunition had to be moved by road. This double handling was unavoidable and reduced the rate of movement. Inevitably there was also a bottleneck at the entrance to the caves.

Fire precautions posed a problem owing to the shortage of water. Chemical extinguishers were provided on a special scale. A serious explosion occurred in the Repair Factory at 8 BAD one morning in 1942, and for some hours exploding ammunition threatened the main storage depot. Due to determined fire fighting lasting for several hours the fire was eventually brought under control. The whole area by this time was covered with shell in a dangerous condition. Work on clearing the area started immediately but was stopped by the DOS in the late afternoon on the grounds of danger and the area was abandoned. A new factory on modern lines was built about a mile from the old site.

9 BAD

Late in 1940 a second BAD was formed at Abu Sultan on the Suez Canal south of Ismailia. This was a surface depot of the conventional type with rail-served storehouses. Its location on the main artery of sea, rail and road transport was ideal from the supply point of view, and the area of flat desert to the west provided ample scope for expansion.

The rules for ammunition depot lay-out formulated in the *Ordnance Manual (War)* were taken as a guide. In one respect they were taken too literally. The manual contained a plan showing a depot lay-out with the lines of storehouses radiating from a central point like the outstretched fingers of a hand. The plan purported to illustrate the use of natural features in ammunition storage and was meant to show the lines of store-houses running down valleys with intervening spurs acting as natural traverses. This plan was faithfully copied in the lay-out of 9 BAD, although the flat desert contained no features which could be used as traverses. Moreover, no arrangements were made to link up the ends of the lines and the more distant storehouses were often isolated by the formation of sand dunes across the railway when there was a wind.

The storehouse construction was adequate for war conditions and provided some degree of protection from the heat and direct rays of the sun. The design was not adequate to prevent propagation of an explosion whereby burning debris from one storehouse penetrated the roof of the next, starting fires and explosions. This misfortune occurred some years after the depot was built.

In spite of these disadvantages, 9 BAD proved to be the most effective ammunition depot in the Middle East with a peak capacity of 90,000 tons.

2 BAD

Storage of ammunition east of the Suez Canal and in Palestine developed piecemeal. A depot was constructed at Wadi Sarar between Jerusalem and Sarafand in 1941 and was then known as 3 Advanced Ammunition Depot. Further developments were influenced by the campaign in Syria, and the threat from the north which continued to be serious even after the occupation of Syria.

Another depot was constructed at El Burg near Kantara on the Suez Canal in October 1941. The planned capacity was 35,000 tons. No. 2 BAD was formed on that date from Wadi Sarar (1 Sub-depot) and El Burg (2 Sub-depot) with a further holding of 15,000 tons at Acre.

Stock levels fluctuated considerably, but at the peak period in December 1942, when all ammunition storage capacity in the Middle East Base had to be used to the full, Wadi Sarar held 18,000 tons, El Burg 37,000 tons and Acre 13,000 tons.

3 AAD

Ammunition depots established in the Syrian campaign remained, and were designated 3 AAD after the formation of 2 BAD. The depot was at Taalia with sub-depots at Tripoli and Aleppo. Early in 1942 the tonnage

197

held in 3 AAD was 27,000, but the significance of this unit declined as the threat from the north receded and the Eighth Army advanced towards Tunis.

4 AAD

This depot was established at Dekheila south-west of Alexandria as a forward holding for the Western Desert force, and it was later manned by staff from Greece and Crete, when it was renamed 4 AAD. Its position gave it importance at the time of the Alamein battle when the stock levels reached 18,000 tons, and it later became 4 BAD under the command of a Lieutenant-Colonel.

The depot occupied the site of a World War I Cavalry barracks. The storehouses were very close together and lateral stone traverses were built between them. Unfortunately these traverses did not cover the ends of the buildings. This omission proved disastrous when, early in 1944, an explosion took place in a 400-ton stack of grenades No. 75 (Hawkins) which had been segregated on salt flats some distance from the main storehouses. The lack of end protection led to the collapse of several storehouses and there was considerable loss of life.

MANPOWER

The manning of RAOC ammunition units in the Middle East Base provides an excellent example of increased productivity—particularly in activities such as manufacture, repair and salvage—without increasing military manpower. This was done by dilution of labour using mainly local civilian resources, by systematic training and by scientific planning and organization on the lines of what is now known as work study.

Taking the year 1942 as an example, the military manpower in base installations remained steady at about 1,300, but the civilian manpower rose from 2,400 to 6,500 at the peak period.

A school was organized in 9 BAD and here selected men were trained as ammunition examiners. The standard was high and the demand for trained technicians from the United Kingdom was kept to a minimum.

PORT AMMUNITION DETACHMENTS

It began to be realized that technical supervision of the handling of ammunition at ports was an essential safety measure. The serious explosion at Port Said (mentioned in an earlier chapter) would probably not have occurred had there been a technical expert on the spot to prevent the great and unnecessary risks which were being taken in the stowage and handling of ammunition and explosives. RAOC Port Ammunition Detachments became a normal element of port organizations in the Middle East, and indeed all theatres.

REPAIR, MANUFACTURE AND INSPECTION

These activities played a big part in ammunition supply in the Middle East campaigns. Many natures of ammunition were scarce and some were inferior in design and performance. Captured ammunition was examined and could sometimes be used. Captured enemy anti-tank and anti-personnel mines provided useful information to assist in the considerable local production of these items. The RAOC technical ammunition staff worked in close cooperation with the General Staff Technical Branch, which was originally SD 5 but was later replaced by a branch of the Weapons Technical Staff Field Force (known colloquially as "Wheat-sheaf") established in all operational theatres.

One example will serve to illustrate the significance of the work done on enemy ammunition and also the ingenuity of the technical staff engaged in the task.

75 MM (COMPOSITE)

It has been seen that the Gazala battle was a very close affair in which Rommel could have been defeated had events taken a different course. Many factors contributed to his victory in that battle and the relative significance of these factors will always be a matter of controversy.

Equipment played an important part in the armoured battle, and it did seem that with the arrival on the scene of American General Grant tanks, with their 75-mm gun, something approaching equality of fire power had been achieved.

Unfortunately the American ammunition, known in British nomenclature as "75-mm Shot AP M72", was useless against the hardened steel armour of a German tank. The steel used for the projectile was inferior, the hardness varied considerably over its surface, and it tended to break up on impact with armour plate.

The German tanks on the other hand had a 75-mm weapon which fired an armour-piercing shell with a charge of high explosive, a delayed action base fuse, and a tracer. It was capable of penetrating armour plate and of detonating inside the tank. A single direct hit could put a tank out of action, and the ammunition gave the Germans, gun for gun, tank for tank, a decisive element of superiority in a tank *v.* tank engagement.

For the same weapon the Germans had an HE/Smoke round which gave instantaneous screening and was far superior to anything we possessed at the time. Our shell relied upon white phosphorus or base emission fillings which tended to "pillar" in certain conditions and took time to develop adequate screening. The German round contained oleum-impregnated pumice, with a bursting charge of pentolite.

We had captured some of the German ammunition and were thus able to study it and assess its performance. The Chief Inspecting Ordnance Officer at GHQ Middle East at that time was an Australian, Major Northey, a man of forceful personality and lively intelligence.

The idea of using the German ammunition in our weapons was impracticable because the brass cartridge cases of the German and American rounds proved to be of different dimensions. The CIOO then suggested removing the shell from the German round and fitting it into the American cartridge case.

A further difficulty occurred because the diameter of the German shell at the driving band was slightly greater than that of the American shell. If this were not altered it would cause difficulty in loading and in the danger of "set up" of the shell whilst travelling up the bore of the gun, with a risk of premature detonation. The driving band had to be turned down a few millimetres on a lathe until the dimensions were correct.

A number of rounds were converted in this way at 9 BAD. The base fuses were removed for safety during the driving band modification and then replaced. Cartridge cases were removed from a corresponding number of American rounds. The brass case had to be coned and indented to make a rigid fit to the shell and fortunately an existing machine was found capable of doing this work.

An extra increment of propellant was placed in the American cartridge case to give the shell a muzzle velocity equal to that when fired from the German weapon. This was necessary to give the shell sufficient acceleration up the bore to overcome safety devices and arm the fuse. It also improved the penetration of the shell on impact. The trials of the Armour Piercing and Smoke Shell, modified in this way, proved highly successful in all respects.

The next step was to trace all captured stocks of this highly desirable 75-mm ammunition. Dumps in the desert were found, recorded and the stocks immediately reported to GHQ. The RAOC Mobile Ammunition Laboratories proved invaluable for this work. Eventually some 15,000 rounds of HE/AP and 2,000 rounds of HE/Smoke were found and transferred with all speed to 9 BAD. To ensure that the turning down of the driving bands should not prove a bottleneck in the process of modification, three mobile machinery lorries equipped with lathes were sent to the depot.

As planning for the battle had reached an advanced stage the conversion was given the highest priority and, by working day and night, the task was completed in 2 to 3 months. Every round on completion was carefully inspected, and chamber-gauged in a cut-down 75-mm barrel to make sure that it was perfect. This work was done by RAOC technically trained ammunition staff.

It was decided to conceal the true identity of this ammunition behind the desigation "75 mm (Composite)". The object of this decision was to prevent the Germans from making political capital out of the conversion of their ammunition and in the process exposing the inferiority of existing British and American anti-tank projectiles.

Unfortunately, as so often happens when security is involved, full information was not passed to the units who had to use the ammunition nor to the formation commanders. On this vital point communications between GHQ and the fighting formations was inadequate.

It appears that at an early stage in the battle, during a lull, a tank still had its gun loaded and instead of firing the round an attempt was made to unload it. As the driving hand had engaged this led to a separated cartridge case, the shell remaining in the bore. The round happened to be 75 mm (Composite).

A separated case is not uncommon with fixed ammunition, and later on it became such a frequent occurrence with American ammunition that shortened cartridge cases were manufactured locally and supplied to units so that rounds lodged in the bore could be cleared by firing.

At this stage, however, the removal of a high explosive shell, as distinct from the normal solid shot used against tanks, posed a problem which the unit could not solve, though had a technical expert, conversant with the ammunition and the modification, been present he could have dealt quickly with the situation.

As it was, the report that a tank was out of action with a "composite" shell stuck in the bore led to lack of confidence in the ammunition and the impression that many tanks were out of action as a result of its use.

The decision was made on the spot to ban the use of all 75 mm (Composite) and replace it by taking on stocks of the normal American rounds—the useless M72. This took place during the Gazala battle and by June 12th we lost 230 tanks and the long withdrawal to the Alamein position followed.

The order to replace the "composite" ammunition cannot be criticized. In battle immediate decisions have to be made on available information which is often incomplete and inaccurate. It is, however, a matter for regret that commanders and units were not fully "put in the picture" about the superior performance of this special ammunition. Also in retrospect it seems surprising that an IOO, conversant with the modification which had been carried out, was not sent forward to report on its performance in battle and assist if required.

That the "composite" rounds were technically perfect is not in doubt. 15,000 rounds were inspected and chamber-gauged at Fort Capuzzo by an IOO at the request of the Weapons Technical Staff Field Force. No defect of any kind was discovered but by this time it was too late. The entire stocks were captured by the Germans in their advance. Most of these stocks curiously enough, were recaptured by the Eighth Army in their final advance, but by then the quality of our own equipment had greatly improved.

It was heartbreaking that the ingenuity and industry which had produced a battle-winning missile were wasted in the end. No one will know whether the use of this ammunition would have been decisive in turning the tide of battle in our favour, but it can be reasonably claimed that it would have increased enemy tank casualties, reduced our own and saved many valuable lives.

ANTI-TANK MINES

It was decided early in the war to supplement the limited supply of anti-tank mines from the United Kingdom by local manufacture. Armour dominated the battlefield in the Western Desert, and from the beginning mine fields were an important feature of all defensive positions.

No. 1 Ammunition Repair and Filling Factory was opened in July 1940 at Abbassia, on the site of the old ammunition storage area. Two mines were designed, the Egyptian Pattern (EP) Mark I and the EP Mark II, both filled gelignite. Production of the mine bodies was a Royal Engineer responsibility but filling, assembly and inspection of the finished article was an RAOC task.

With a staff of twenty and limited accommodation a target was set of 1,000 mines filled daily and this target was reached by August 16th 1940. By increasing the staff and the employment of a night shift this figure was doubled during September.

During the summer of 1941 production of a Mark III mine filled TNT was started. This was a more satisfactory filling than gelignite, and eventually the majority of mines produced in Egypt were filled TNT; but for a time supplies were difficult and several ships carrying TNT were sunk by U-boats.

By September 1942 the output of this factory was 12,000 mines daily. The staff then consisted of 3 officers, 82 rank and file and 80 labourers. Similar filling factories were established at Mitoqba and in Wadi Sarar. The total Middle East production was 270,000 per month in June 1942, but was actually stepped up to 530,000 during the month of August to meet the needs of the Alamein defences. Production methods had by then reached a very high level of efficiency, but the supply of raw materials and components could not be maintained at this level indefinitely and the total production figures fell. However, all the needs of the Eighth Army were met. Regular production meetings were held and at these all supply difficulties were ironed out.

AMMUNITION EMPTIES AND SALVAGE

The recovery of material from expended ammunition increased in importance as the war continued. Metal packages were a valuable source of raw material for industry and in the Middle East an organization was developed for receiving these "empties", sorting them and despatching them to South Africa.

The main problem was to ensure freedom from explosive and the system must guarantee this whilst at the same time maintaining the supply of empties and employing small numbers of technical staff.

The system worked extremely well and there is no evidence that explosives found their way back from the enormous quantities of empties which passed through the sorting organization in Egypt.

Equally important were the valuable metals obtained from returned ammunition which was no longer required. The simplest, safest and quickest way of disposing of such ammunition was to dump it in deep water, and this is economically sound when supply of the raw materials is good. The arrangements made by the RAOC for the removal of explosive from surplus ammunition, and the recovery of brass and other metals, reached a high level of efficiency in the Middle East and contributed significantly to the war effort and to the needs of industry in the period of scarcity which immediately followed the war.

AMERICAN AMMUNITION

Some difficulty was encountered over an anti-tank mine, made in U.S.A. but called a "Dutch Anti-Tank Mine". A signal was received that if the packages, which contained both mines and fuzes, were dropped 18 inches they would detonate. It was thought that a ship had been lost off the coast of America from this cause.

A ship containing these mines was *en route* to the Middle East and had run aground somewhere in the Red Sea. Captain (later Brigadier) Eastman, who had already had bomb disposal experience in Malta for which he was awarded the George Cross, was sent out to the ship, removed all the fuzes and dumped them at sea, a rather gruesome task but the sort of thing which IOOs and AEs were expected to take in their stride.

Another problem, which affected all theatres of war, was the packaging of American 75-mm and 105-mm ammunition. The "clover leaf" pack did not properly protect the ammunition from damage. Dented cartridge cases were common. Every single round had to be gauged and the damaged ones broken down, repaired and reformed. The importance of packaging was a lesson which both we and the Americans learnt the hard way.

CENTRALIZED CONTROL

The ammunition branch of the Ordnance Directorate at GHQ (OS4) grew into a separate headquarters under the DOS and commanded by a DDOS (Ammunition). The headquarters was first located at Tura and then moved back into Cairo but outside the area occupied by GHQ.

The reason for this centralized control was mainly technical. There would never be enough technically trained officers or other ranks to meet all needs, and the requirements for technical staff changed so often that their deployment had to be controlled from some central point where the up-to-date situation and future trends were known.

Equally centralized control over manufacture, repair, inspection, recovery of ammunition and empties and the handling of captured enemy ammunition, was essential if urgent needs were to be met in time and waste of effort was to be avoided. For example, up to and including the defensive period of the Alamein battle anti-tank mines were of paramount importance. Thereafter we were advancing steadily and our concern was for dealing with enemy minefields rather than creating our own. The requirement for anti-tank mines still existed but on a much smaller scale and there was never again a general acute shortage.

The Chief Inspecting Ordnance Officer and DADOS (Production) were also at this headquarters.

Technical training of ammunition examiners was a most important factor, and DDOS (Ammunition) controlled the syllabus of the ammunition school at 9 BAD and the number of ammunition examiners it was necessary to select and train.

An attempt was made in 1943 to relate the appointment of AEs to specific unit establishments and to assess the number of AEs in accordance with the tonnage of ammunition held by each unit. This was a nonsensical yardstick in relation to technical activity and varying priorities. As a device for putting the right number of people in the right place at the right time it was archaic, cumbersome and wasteful. Up to the end of the war DDOS (Ammunition) had the greatest difficulty in maintaining the system of pooled AEs, which was the only guarantee of the efficient and economical employment of technical staff.

During most of the critical period of the war—that is until after the battle of Alamein—the DDOS (Ammunition) was Colonel C. Arnold Edwards.

Miscellaneous Services

CLOTHING FACTORY

In April 1941 a clothing factory was established at Gamrah in Cairo, for the manufacture of clothing for officers and articles for Officers' Shops. Manufacture extended to the production of other items for which local materials, such as cotton, could be used and in this way capacity in the United Kingdom was saved and also shipping space.

It could hardly be said that the Eighth Army, either in the desert or in Italy, wore uniform, and their sartorial fashions have been admirably portrayed by the cartoonist "Jon" in his "Two Types", but there were ceremonial and other occasions for which uniform was necessary, and the clothing factory produced well-tailored suits at a very reasonable price.

The unit was commanded by Lieutenant-Colonel E. Doffman with two other officers and a small number of other ranks who had been in the clothing trade in civilian life. The factory employed about 1,800 locally engaged workers in the end. Sewing machines were obtained from stocks held by Messrs. Singers in Egypt.

The factory acquired a world-wide reputation and many VIPs visiting the Middle East, or staging there, had occasion to obtain clothing made for them at short notice.

Towards the end of the war there was a scarcity of battle dress as production had ceased in some factories in the United Kingdom. Material was sent out to the clothing factory at Gamrah which produced 60,000 greatcoats and 80,000 suits of battle dress.

OFFICERS' SHOPS

These were formed to enable officers of the Services to buy authorized items of kit at reasonable rates.

The organization which developed in the Middle East became large, extensive and very popular. It consisted of a headquarters shop, and bulk store at Kasr-el-Nil, Cairo, Grade I Shops with monthly takings of over £3,000 at Alexandria and Haifa, Grade II Shops (monthly takings between £1,000 and £3,000) at Ismailia, Amiriya and Beirut, and Grade III Shops (monthly takings below £1,000) at Suez, Sarafand and Cyprus. In addition to these, Mobile Officers' Shops, stocked from the bulk shops, were formed and sent out as required.

Provision was controlled by the Central Provision Office and extensive use was made of local purchase. Clothing, camp kit, travel bags, leather jerkins and shoes were among the items provided.

CLOTHING REPAIR FACTORY

This was a large organization in Alexandria which worked in conjunction with the Base Laundry. Very large quantities of returned clothing were sorted, repaired, cleaned and put back to stock. Like the clothing factory this organization was entirely manned by locally employed civilians supervised by a few RAOC officers and other ranks.

AFRICAN RUBBER COMPANY

In 1941 the DOS appointed Major F. C. Johnson (a technical expert from Dunlops' in civilian life) as technical adviser on the production of rubber, ebonite, etc., stores and supervisor of work put out to contract with the African Rubber Company, Cairo.

Many MT spare parts and components of weapons and technical equipments were made of rubber. They were often vital items without which the equipment would not work, and they were difficult to obtain. Packing rings for 25-pounder recuperator systems and shock absorbers are but two examples.

In addition sheet rubber of various sizes, rubber and wired rubber hose, tubing, gaskets, pads, ebonite rods and sheets and rubber impregnated canvas items were required. Considerable quantities of more than 300 items were produced.

SIGNIFICANT STATISTICS

The following statistics may serve to illustrate the size of the load carried by the Middle East Base. They apply to October, the month of the battle of Alamein, and are peak figures so far as the support of the Eighth Army is concerned. It must, however, be remembered that the area dependent on the Middle East Base continued to grow until the end of the war.

RECEIPTS INTO BODS

40,000 tons, of which 4,000 tons were from local resources and stores recovered through Returned Stores Depots.

Issues from BODs
> 29,000 tons
> 595,000 items
> Boot repairs, 94,000 pairs

Ammunition

Received	73,000 tons
Issued	68,000 tons

Vehicles

New vehicles received	"A" vehicles	1,368
	"B" vehicles	10,600
From workshops	"A" vehicles	809
	"B" vehicles	5,200

Civilian Manpower

Clerks (exclusive of those in Central Provision Office)	1,600
Storemen	1,500
Unskilled (casual) labour	18,700
Tradesmen	8,700

CHAPTER SEVEN

FRENCH NORTH AFRICA— NOVEMBER 1942 to MAY 1943

Operation TORCH

Operation TORCH—the name given to the campaign which began with the landings in French North Africa—is of special interest for several reasons. Together with Alamein, which just preceded it, and Stalingrad, which followed soon afterwards, it marked the turn of the tide in the war against Germany and Italy. From that time events moved relentlessly, and almost without interruption to the day of final victory in Europe $2\frac{1}{2}$ years later.

It was the first large-scale combined operation, anticipating an opposed landing, at a place many miles from the main bases in North America and the United Kingdom. It was also the first Anglo-American project in which the concept of a Supreme Allied Commander was adopted. General Eisenhower commanded the Armies, Navies and Air Forces of both nations engaged in the operation, and exercised command through an integrated Allied Forces Headquarters (AFHQ).

Strategically the timing of the operation was perfect. It was no secret that the British Army was going to attack at Alamein, although great and largely successful efforts were made to achieve tactical surprise. But the German High Command was certain to be preoccupied with the fate of the Afrika Korps, and this provided the opportunity to land a force in French North Africa, advance on Tunis and, in conjunction with the advance of the Eighth Army, drive the enemy from Africa.

A beautifully simple plan in conception and also, because of its success, in retrospect. This has led some historians, with the sublime wisdom after the event which it is their privilege to possess, into the error of assuming that there was no need for the hard fighting and heavy losses which were the price of victory at Alamein. The argument is that the landing of troops in French North Africa would have forced the enemy to withdraw from the strong but distant Alamein position in any case, and without fighting.

Since such views are held it is perhaps not out of place to mention certain other factors which will serve to bring into perspective the events of the period, and assist in a proper understanding of the achievements and the mistakes which occurred.

For the Allies the first half of 1942 was a period of almost unrelieved disaster. Pearl Harbour had been followed by the fall of Hong Kong, Malaya, Singapore, the Philippines, the Dutch East Indies and Burma. The Eighth Army had been driven back to its Alamein line with heavy losses in men, vehicles and equipment. The Germans were advancing in Russia at apparently irresistible speed to the Caucasus. In Europe the Dieppe raid had proved to be a costly failure in its immediate effects, though valuable lessons were learnt. Losses at sea were enormous and the German submarine campaign seemed to be on the verge of success.

The Axis powers could hardly be blamed for assuming that the Allies had had enough of risky enterprises for the time being. It was obvious that the invasion of France was an ultimate objective, but if the Dieppe raid had shown that it was too early to land in France in 1942, an advance from Egypt with the object of clearing Cyrenaica and Tripolitania, raising the siege of Malta and thus opening up the Mediterranean was the most likely course of action. The success of TORCH depended on surprise, and surprise depended on creating in the minds of the Germans and Italians a certainty that Alamein, and Alamein alone, was the point of danger.

In fact complete surprise was achieved, and this may have been partly due to the fact that the TORCH decision was remarkably late in the day. The tremendous combined operation for the landing in Normandy was the result of at least two years' planning, war production and training. The equivalent period for TORCH was nearer two months. The alleged British genius for improvisation was to be worked to death yet again.

The explanation lies in the field of politics. The Americans, while not neglecting that scene of future triumphs, the Pacific Ocean, fully supported the idea that the defeat of Germany was to take first priority. They considered that to land in France and from there invade Germany was the only road to success. All other operations were side-shows, diverting effort from the main task and contributing little of real value. The view was not shared by British strategists, who considered that in Africa lay the best opportunity to contain and defeat the greatest possible number of Germans thus taking pressure off the Russians at a critical time and keeping them in the fight. Moreover, the advantages of re-opening the Mediterranean route were obvious and this could lead to the collapse of Italy. Malta was in danger of being starved out. The British naturally felt that this must be avoided at all costs, while the Americans were inclined to doubt whether the loss of Malta would affect the course of the war.

The British view prevailed in the end, but the delay led to hasty planning and preparation. The rule that those who take part in an operation must also be involved in the preparatory work was not invariably followed.

Task forces were to land at Casablanca, Oran and Algiers. Two of these task forces were American but the Algiers force was mainly British. Subsidiary landings were to take place east of Algiers, at Bougie and Bone and airborne troops were to occupy key points and pave the way for the rapid occupation of Tunis.

A critical factor was the attitude of the French, and if in retrospect the initial deployment appears to have been too heavily weighted in the direction of Casablanca and Oran, the explanation lies in an understandable reluctance to take risks in this matter.

If the French attitude proved favourable, it would be possible to concentrate entirely on defeating the Germans and Italians and all the early fighting would then fall to the mainly British forces, known as the First Army.

By the autumn of 1942, as a result of 2 years' experiment and training, the technique of combined operations had reached a high standard in the United Kingdom. Force 110, which consisted of units trained in combined operations, formed the nucleus of the assault and first follow-up units of First Army, and the spearhead was 78th Division, whose war record and reputation for all-round efficiency were to prove second to none. Commanders and staffs in the First Army had trained together and the whole formation was fully adequate to such an operation as TORCH.

Unfortunately, no corresponding GHQ organization had been created. Although Armies in a distant theatre of operations like to feel that they can campaign successfully without a Base and GHQ organization behind them, this is not so. A GHQ has to act as a link with the main base in the United Kingdom and deal with strategic, political and logistic problems so that the Army (or Army Group) Commander may concentrate his whole attention on winning the battle.

AFHQ did not begin to take shape as an effective organization until about September 1942, only 2 months before the landings were due to take place. Nor were AFHQ and First Army Headquarters in very close touch at this time, a situation which suited First Army, who cherished the hope they would be able to polish off the enemy in North Africa before AFHQ arrived.

AFHQ had enough troubles of their own. They were still in the design stage and a working model had not yet emerged. Indeed the organization continued to be somewhat experimental even after the campaign had started, but only the most prejudiced observer would deny that the final product (AFHQ in Italy and SHAEF in France) was a satisfactory organization for controlling Allied forces under a Supreme Commander.

An early mistake was that of over-integration. Every branch was to be a combined American/British branch based on the American organization. This placed the RAOC in an impossible position. Clothing and General Stores linked with the American Quartermaster Corps. Signal Stores were a matter for the American Signal Corps, and Engineer Stores

8+

of RAOC origin in the British Service were handled by the Engineer Corps in the American Army. With us REME had recently emerged as a separate corps, but in the American Army they were part of the Ordnance Corps.

Unless the whole British Army was to be reorganized on American lines, it was a short cut to chaos to reshuffle one headquarters. But the secret of General Eisenhower's success as Supreme Commander was that he was an extremist on the subject of avoiding criticism of one Ally by the other. To suggest that we should not adopt the American organization but retain our own, that is to advocate parallelism rather than integration, was to risk being branded as a non-cooperator or even a Quisling. Experience showed that full integration was only workable in certain fields such as Operational Planning and Intelligence.

The delay in forming a separate Ordnance (British) Branch of AFHQ was doubtless inevitable but caused difficulties which handicapped the work of the RAOC throughout the campaign. For example, the DOS (Brigadier W. E. C. Pickthall) was not appointed until a few days before First Army was due to sail. The one man who should have been in the picture from the beginning was forced to accept a plan and organization which he would probably have changed considerably had he been given the opportunity. There was not even time for him to select men of his own choice for key appointments.

Brigadier Pickthall was not the man to shirk this task even though he was shrewd enough to know that it was likely to get him more criticism than credit. He had all the knowledge and experience of Ordnance work necessary for the appointment, but his chief qualification was that he had the qualities of personality and character most needed at that time. His transparent honesty, integrity, friendliness and sense of humour ensured the maximum cooperation. The Americans liked and trusted him. Even those who prided themselves on being hard-bitten, "Vinegar Joe" types found difficulty in keeping up the act. His loyalty to his own staff evoked from them respect, admiration and a determination not to let him down. He lacked that element of ruthlessness which must be available in such a ruthless business as war. Later in the war he came under severe and unfair criticism, though not from his own Corps, where his qualities were appreciated. He felt this very deeply and his health suffered.

The Ordnance plan for the support of First Army was extremely good as far as it went. The most interesting feature was the scheme for beach maintenance on the assumption that the landing would be opposed. For this purpose the Ordnance Beach Detachment was created—there were five in this operation. Each detachment consisted of 6 officers and 110 other ranks and was organized to supply stores and ammunition over the beach. The men were specially picked and brought to a high standard of physical fitness and weapon training.

Stores were held in Landing Reserves, which were carefully scaled to exclude all but operationally essential items so as to keep the tonnage down to a minimum. Packing was done in such a way as to ensure that stores could be man-handled to the maximum extent. Cases were fitted with rope handles. Landing Reserve Schedules and Case Contents Lists were so arranged as to assist location and identification of items and simplify rapid issues under conditions of beach maintenance.

Landing Reserves were created on a Brigade basis and purported to supply a Brigade with the scaled items for 1 month. If beach maintenance had to continue after that period Beach Maintenance Packs, packed in the same way but scaled on a Divisional basis would be sent in.

In fact the system of beach maintenance by Landing Reserves was designed for and suited to a short period of beach maintenance pending the creation of a BOD. Perpetual beach maintenance under this system would break down. A month was about the limit of the system and by then a BOD must be established, even though it might be a small depot in a temporary location. For this reason Beach Maintenance Packs were never a success.

No improvement was necessary in the organization of OBDs nor in the system of Landing Reserves. In their first campaign they proved to be excellent units. If they failed in any respect at any time later in the war, it was due to a failure to observe the basic principles which had been applied before Operation TORCH. These principles were selection and intensive training of personnel, skilful and efficient scaling of Landing Reserves, correct packing of Landing Reserves and avoidance of straining the beach maintenance system by continuing it for too long. Similar difficulties were not encountered in the supply of ammunition. In this case the danger of perpetuating beach maintenance lies in the accumulation of excessive quantities of ammunition in a crowded beach area.

Other RAOC units in the Order of Battle were: 2 BODs, 2 BADs, 8 Ordnance Field Parks, 1 Ordnance Railhead Company, 9 Mobile Laundries, 1 Base Hospital Laundry, 2 Officers' Shops.

The plan for the BODs was that they should be based on Algiers (1 BOD) and Bone (3 BOD) with subsidiary depots at Bougie (satellite to 1 BOD) and Phillipeville (satellite to 3 BOD). The scheme reflected the intention to make use of all available port capacity initially with the future probability that the small ports at Bougie and Phillipeville with the adjacent depots would be convenient for supplying the L of C troops located near to them. The BODs were also responsible for the storage and supply of vehicles. The BODs were equal and independent. The establishment and stores scaling was the same for both and there was no coordination. Although this would not matter in the early days it was bound to cause trouble later on.

From west to east the four ports, Algiers, Bougie, Phillipeville and Bone, and their associated depots, were on a line which ran parallel to the axis of advance. It would have been better to establish Algiers as a BOD. Bone as an AOD and Bougie and Phillipeville as Command Depots with transit duties in the early stages.

This is not wisdom after the event. It merely indicates the effect of having no GHQ staff to plan and prepare their side of the business. An Army headquarters is concerned solely with operations and it is pointless to plan in detail too far ahead because a point is reached at which events, on which the operational plan depends, become unpredictable.

But logistics depend largely on geographical factors which do not change and therefore long-term plans are worthwhile. GHQ staff would be bound to plan and prepare for maintenance of the Army for an indefinite period. The Army might say (as the First Army staff did) that the campaign would be over one way or the other in 1 month. But this was merely another way of stating the limit of practicable operational planning. The Army would be justifiably incensed if, for lack of forward planning, maintenance broke down when a month had elapsed and they were still fighting.

The planning and execution of the landing in North Africa of the First Army and the operations which followed were extremely good, and from the RAOC point of view the main credit is due to three officers, Brigadier T. H. Clarke, DDOS First Army; Colonel A. N. C. Varley and Lieutenant-Colonel W. A. Kenney, ADOS 78th Division.

Brigadier Clarke had been an ADOS in Norway, which had given him the opportunity of seeing what can go wrong in a combined operation. He had a flair for Ordnance work in a formation, a sound instinct for essential matters, and he was completely imperturbable. He gave commanders and staff absolute confidence in the Ordnance Services in the Army and was later to become DDOS Second Army in the campaign in north-west Europe.

Colonel Varley—a civilian turned soldier—had a brilliant brain and unlimited restless energy. His speed of thought left lesser mortals standing, but there was nothing slap-dash in his planning and organization. Those who took over from him found very few loose ends. He was appointed DDOS L of C, and although he did excellent work there it would perhaps have been better for him to have been selected for DDOS AFHQ, thereby providing continuity with all the earlier planning of the operation. He also moved to France later in the war.

Lieutenant-Colonel Kenney, as ADOS of the "spearhead" division of the campaign, had to have a complete knowledge of combined operations and of the technique of keeping a Division supplied with its essential equipment at the difficult early period of an operation. He showed uncanny skill in anticipating requirements which gave time for them to be met, when other formations were making "flap" demands and were occasionally disappointed.

There were three stages in the 6-month campaign.

1. The race for Tunis, November 8th to 28th, followed by a withdrawal under heavy counter-attack to positions short of the objective and roughly on a line running north and south from Cape

Serrat–Sidi Nsir–Medjez-el-Bab–Bou Arada–Gafsa (November 28th to December 28th).

2. A mainly defensive period (December 29th 1942 to March 31st 1943) during which both sides were building up their forces. To begin with the German/Italian forces could be reinforced more easily than our own. The withdrawal from Egypt shortened their L of C and increased that of the Eighth Army, while the indifferent communications in North Africa limited the number of troops which could be deployed by the Allies west of Tunis. Our positions must be held so as to facilitate the final breakthrough into the plain west of Tunis. The weather, which had been fine up to the end of November and so had favoured the attempt to capture Tunis, broke early in December. This made any further attempt to capture Tunis in 1942 impossible, but it also hampered efforts by the enemy to drive our forces further back into the hills and contributed to the stabilization of this front, which was to our advantage.

During the last month of this phase the enemy made a series of violent attacks, first on the Americans at Kasserine and then on key positions held by the First Army further north. Their success was limited and temporary, all important positions being retaken by the end of March.

3. The final offensive (April 1st 1943 to May 12th 1943). In the month of April heavy fighting took place to secure positions necessary for the final assault. At the same time the formidable forces which had been built up were regrouped. Early in May the final assault on Tunis was staged in true *blitzkreig* style. It was decisive. The enemy lost 250,000 prisoners and vast quantities of equipment.

To complete the picture it is necessary to follow the progress during this period of the other forces which, together with First Army, made up General Alexander's victorious 18th Army Group. These forces consisted of American units, French units and the Eighth Army.

The American landings at Casablanca and Oran, and the occupation by them of that part of French North Africa, coincided with the race for Tunis by the Eastern Task Force. Apart from Combat Command "B" there were very few American troops with First Army at this stage.

In the second phase American units were moved forward as fast as the logistic situation permitted. But this meant that they arrived piecemeal and had perforce to be employed under British formation commanders until the opportunity occurred to regroup them into United States formations under their own commanders.

The "front" was so wide that it could only be held by covering the main passes through the mountains and dealing with the gaps between these defended areas by means of patrols. These gaps were from 10 to 18 miles wide as the crow flies. The urgent need was for Infantry and after that for Artillery.

It was only towards the end of February, when 18th Army Group was formed, that the United States 2 Corps could be concentrated under the direct control of General Alexander. The units had little opportunity to settle into an effective fighting formation before they were violently attacked at the Kasserine Pass and suffered a serious reverse. They recovered brilliantly and in a few weeks became a formidable fighting organization, advancing over difficult country in the north and capturing Bizerta.

French units were at first few and ill-armed but their contribution was of great value when Infantry were scarce, and they included the Goums, extremely tough Moroccan troops, experts in mountain warfare. As soon as possible the French troops were concentrated into 19 Corps under the command first of General Barre and then of General Juin. They operated in the hilly country of Le Kef–Teboursouk–Testour, and were assisted by placing under their command British Artillery units and other supporting arms, and also by the issue of a certain amount of British and American equipment.

Although the Eighth Army was the last of these forces to appear on the Tunisian scene, its battles and movements continuously and decisively influenced the progress of the campaign. In the first phase the Eighth Army advanced all the way to Tripoli. In the second phase, after the occupation of Tripoli, the capture of the Mareth Line took the pressure off the hard-pressed American Corps and forced the German and Italian formations finally onto the defensive. In the third phase the Eighth Army was held up at Enfidaville but, in the regrouping which followed, provided certain formations to reinforce First Army in the final battle.

From the RAOC aspect the first phase was one in which the Army lived on Landing Reserves. These were wisely provided on a lavish scale, 18 for the landing and 10 in follow-up shipments. As the landings were virtually unopposed and beach maintenance was therefore unnecessary, DDOS First Army was able to move his OBDs to suitable locations for the maintenance of the units which had arrived in the theatre pending the development of a normal system of supply.

So far as ammunition was concerned the arrangement worked admirably with the possible exception of AA ammunition, for the enemy had air superiority for some time. The first phase was highly mobile with small forces covering a very large area—not a situation which leads to heavy expenditure of ammunition.

The stores situation was less satisfactory. There was a very good supply of those items which were in the Landing Reserve scales, but these had been cut to the minimum for beach maintenance, and with units ranging all over North Africa other urgent requirements emerged. Nevertheless, there were no critical deficiencies in the early days and the Landing Reserves stood up to the extension of their role.

Inevitably the main problem was shortage of vehicles. Units landed with assault scales only and moved forward rapidly from the port where they landed, which was in most cases Algiers. Bone was heavily bombed and neither AA nor fighter protection was yet strong enough. The railway ran from Algiers inland to Setif, Constantine and on towards Tunis, but it had limited capacity and was very slow. The main road followed roughly the same route as the railway. It was a good road but could be treacherous in wet weather. A secondary coast road had its uses when traffic became heavier.

East of Constantine the L of C ran to Souk Ahras, Ghardimaou, where it entered a flat unsheltered plain, and Souk-el-Arba which was the railhead. The enemy had good, all-weather airfields near Tunis, while our forward airfields were liable to become unfit for use in wet weather. Thus the initial shortage of vehicles was aggravated by wear and tear, accidents and enemy action. The early shipments only carried the balance of vehicles to bring units up to full war establishment and it was some time before any began to arrive for the replacement of wastage.

The Ordnance Field Parks with formations were scaled for the vehicles with which the formations started the campaign, and a reasonable degree of standardization had been achieved in the case of the vehicles of 78th and 6th Armoured Divisions. However, in war such standardization does not last when vehicle casualties are heavy and replacement has to come from those vehicles which happen to be available.

The Order of Battle contained non-divisional OFPs whose function was to provide spares, mainly MT, for units on or moving up the L of C. Clearly accurate scaling of these field parks was not possible, and they tended to become static and build up considerable stocks to supply a variety of units and also serve adjacent workshops, but they did useful work.

REME was in its infancy. The importance of giving each field workshop a stores section to meet its needs was one of the lessons of the campaign. Ordnance Field Parks and other RAOC stores supply units could not be in several places at once. In the First Army the role of stores section had to be undertaken by a variety of units from non-divisional OFPs to Ordnance Beach Detachments. The DDOS First Army made the best use of the units available to him but this led to many units being employed on tasks very different from those for which their establishments and preliminary training had been devised.

An Ordnance Railhead Company had been included in the Order of Battle. The unit was established at the railhead at Souk-el-Arba and soon held considerable stocks of stores and ammunition. In fact Souk-el-Arba became a large Maintenance Area and played a very important part in the supply system to the Tunisian front. The roads converging on this vital point ran for some distance in a straight line over a flat, treeless plain. Stores and ammunition stacked alongside these roads provided a most inviting target for low flying aircraft, but there was no alternative location in the wet weather. Losses were surprisingly small and this is partly explained by the fact that the Allied Air Forces quickly overcame their early difficulties and gained air superiority.

In addition to Souk-el-Arba there was a small sea/road/railhead at the fishing port of La Calle. This was to maintain the Brigade advancing towards Bizerta along the coast road. The RAOC unit at La Calle was 5 OBD under Captain P. R. Butlin.

Ammunition was normally sent there by sea using an LCT or suitable ship. Stores were sent by road, normally from Bone. But there was also a narrow gauge railway, the line running partly across country and partly along the edge of the road. The engine was of that peculiar surrealistic design associated with French railway engines of the period. It was apparently trained to operate on indigenous fuel such as cork and esparto grass. The whole thing was an offence to the minds of the British transportation experts, who had ambitions to improve the capacity of the Bone–La-Calle line, took it over and fed the engine with high grade imported Welsh coal. The effect was that of giving an excessive quantity of oats to a high-spirited horse which has been out to grass for a year. The engine, emitting clouds of black smoke, bounced along the line, knocking down any vehicle which it met and frightening the remainder into the opposite ditch, whence their drivers emerged white, shaking and praying for the return of some lesser evil such as the dive bomber. Some compromise was necessary, and to a large extent the railway reverted to its normal state of apparently ramshackle inefficiency, which nevertheless concealed many virtues.

Headquarters L of C was established at Setif and exercised administrative control over the various Base Sub-Areas. For a time Bone was included in the First Army area, which was natural in view of its geographical position and importance to the Army. But in the planning it did not appear to have been given any special significance, being treated as a normal Base Sub-Area. In the Middle East they had learnt the lesson that an organization must be created which will advance behind the Army and open up ports as they are captured. The organization does not remain in the ports but hands over to a normal Base Sub-Area and moves on with the Army to the next port which is captured.

In fact Bone contained base installations like the other ports. After a time stores could be shipped from the United Kingdom direct to Bone and the coordination of these arrangements was a GHQ not an Army function. The Army rear boundary was later moved to the east of Bone, which was thereafter administered by HQ L of C, the installations being controlled by AFHQ.

We must now pick up the threads of the story so far as it concerns the British Ordnance Branch of AFHQ and the Base installations on which the continued maintenance of the Army depended. It has been seen that the British Ordnance Branch of AFHQ did not suddenly spring to life on a previously planned establishment but grew up slowly and painfully, almost as an afterthought.

The DDOS was appointed in September 1942, but instead of being allowed to get down to urgent planning activity with First Army Headquarters, he was sent to the American Headquarters at Cheltenham to assist them. They were not in need of assistance which, not knowing their stores, he was in any case not qualified to give. When eventually he was able to get in touch with the DDOS First Army he found that there would be no one in direct control of the GHQ Increment which had been formed, as the DDOS First Army would have operational responsibilities once he arrived in North Africa, and Colonel Varley was appointed DDOS HQ L of C. The GHQ Increment was also understaffed in clerks. The DDOS took over the GHQ Increment, obtained high class men as reinforcements, and followed up with War Office Branches the details of automatic maintenance shipments planned by First Army.

AFHQ was established in the Hotel St. George in the centre of Algiers, but certain branches including British Ordnance were located several miles away in the suburb of Maison Carree on the way to the airfield at Maison Blanche. The accommodation was good but the distance from main headquarters was inconveniently great and transport was almost non-existent. The DDOS had a two-seater requisitioned Hotchkiss car which was admirable for local transport but could not be used for long journeys owing to lack of spares.

1 BOD

No. 1 BOD had landed in the earlier convoys and had encountered great difficulties in obtaining suitable accommodation. These difficulties arose in the main from political considerations and the need to conciliate the French Command. The political situation was tricky and it is a measure of the diplomatic skill of General Eisenhower and his staff that the problems were solved so quickly and amicably, but no chances could be taken in the early days. This meant that reconnaissance parties could not just take the accommodation they wanted but had to engage in prolonged and tiresome bargaining when time was pressing.

Eventually the BOD acquired reasonable accommodation but it was dispersed about the town and there was no room for expansion. The transit facilities in the buildings were poor and it was essential to obtain a railway siding for receipts and issues, and also a sorting area for stores which had to be cleared quickly from the docks. This was done.

The main problems of the BOD were shortage of clerical staff, the clearance of receipts and confusion at the docks. The heaviest load of posting of receipts and issues always falls on a depot in the difficult early days of a campaign. Local clerical labour can never be obtained in large numbers at that time and those who are recruited must then be trained. BOD establishments had insufficient clerks and if it was essential to keep the total numbers down, it would have been better to increase the number of clerks at the expense of storemen. Local storehouse labour is easier to obtain and can work under a small number of supervisors. The BOD postings did not keep pace with the transactions and the account became inaccurate, making a really efficient service to the troops impossible. This problem was not confined to 1 BOD. It occurred in 3 BOD and also, later on, in Italy.

Clearance of receipts was made more difficult by the existence of a large number of multi-item packs (MT and technical stores in the main). Individual items could not easily be identified because the labels had come off and documentation could not always be associated with the stores which had arrived.

There were several causes. One was what might be called "chickenfeed scaling". Many fast moving items were badly under scaled. Had the scales of these been adequate there would have been a reduction in the number of multi-item packs and identification would have been facilitated. Another cause was over dispersion in shipping consignments. There is, of course, a risk of losing the complete stocks of a particular item if it is in only one ship of a convoy, but over dispersion so complicates the task of receiving, identifying and putting to stock the stores that many may be virtually lost in the process, that is they cannot be found when required for issue. Identification of individual items was later solved by the use of labelled cartons. This protected the store as well as ensuring that it could not escape from the means of identification which was the printed carton label. This excellent system was introduced as a direct result of the tribulations of 1 BOD in Algiers.

The organization at the docks did not go at all smoothly to begin with. Movement staffs seemed to be obsessed with the need to clear the docks at all costs. The result—owing to acute shortage of transport—was greater congestion. Instead of allocating to each vehicle the commodities for one Service, everything to hand was loaded into the vehicle and the driver told to get going, deliver the goods and return immediately. He might have a mixed load of supplies, NAAFI stores, Ordnance Stores of all groups and perhaps some ammunition. He had therefore to visit a bewildering number of scattered destinations in a large, strange, foreign town. Not surprisingly, vehicles were lost for long periods. Strong pressure from Ordnance AFHQ, the depots concerned, and no doubt also the representatives of other arms of the Service, led to a reasonable degree of sorting at the docks and to each vehicle being loaded with only one category of store and therefore having only one destination for its load. The Port Ordnance staff was thereafter correctly employed.

There was insufficient stores handling equipment in the depot establishment which delayed the turn-round of vehicles sent from the docks. This was another useful lesson of the campaign. The fault was probably due to a lack of appreciation of the fact that in war conditions it is rare to find storehouses which are rail-served when existing accommodation has to be converted for depot use. The normal situation is that there is a railhead for the depot, the storehouses themselves being road served.

Early in 1943 it was decided that the Crusaders of 6th Armoured Division would be replaced by Sherman tanks supplied by the Americans. Owing to the wide front on which the First Army was deployed and the lack of reserves at this stage of the build-up, it was not possible to withdraw units to the Base for re-equipment and all the preliminary work had to be done by RAOC and REME staff in conjunction with the Americans at Oran. The 241 Shermans were then delivered to First Army so that units had to be taken out of the line only for the training necessary to familiarize them with the new equipment.

A REME examination of the Sherman vehicle kits being supplied by the Americans led to a re-scaling and reduction, the balance of stores being sent to 1 BOD. The depot opened a special group to hold Sherman spares and very soon more than 3,000 item headings were held. The stores were all well packed and identified so as to facilitate binning, but multi-item packs were normal and there was no escape from having to bin all binnable items. There were many deficiencies at first but the "to-follow" service from Oran was good. This additional task is mentioned because it is the sort of thing which normally falls to the lot of a BOD in war, but tends to be overlooked when the manpower requirement is worked out at the planning stage.

It may be assumed that any BOD at the beginning of a campaign will be working at full stretch with no rest for some time. In the case of 1 BOD 2 months elapsed before any rest could be arranged.

Good qualities of command and administrative ability are required of the Commander if he is to ensure a consistently high standard of service from his unit in these conditions. Lieutenant-Colonel H. F. Friday, COO 1 BOD, had all the requisite qualities in full measure—determination, self-confidence and sound administrative instinct.

The War Office responded promptly to the observation from North Africa on the difficulties in dealing with maintenance shipments. Lieutenant-Colonels L. H. McCausland and D. H. Warren were sent out from Chilwell to assist the BODs and, more important still, to obtain first-hand information which would be of value in the maintenance of future operations. Lieutenant-Colonel Warren dealt with the provision and scaling side of the work. They quickly realized that the early shipments were inadequate and arranged changes in the scaling, packing and documentation of future consignments which enabled the Army to be satisfactorily supplied.

3 BOD

This unit was commanded by Lieutenant Colonel L. A. Burden. A party of 10 officers and 160 ORs landed in Algiers on November 22nd. Major C. Hopkins, who was in charge of the party, took 5 officers and 76 ORs on to Bone, arriving there on November 27th.

Stores were already being unloaded and the accommodation allotted to the BOD was quite inadequate, totalling only 30,000 sq ft in four separate locations. Nevertheless, they had to get the stores out to the locations quickly as the docks were under frequent and heavy air attack. This uncomfortable situation continued throughout the week that followed.

An attempt was made to use the largest site—the Centre du Sante, 15,000 sq ft—as a transit and sorting centre, but this was frustrated by the despatch of mixed categories of all stores to every location, action which was justified at Bone by the bombing of the docks, but for which there had been no such excuse at Algiers. Bone was a very small town compared with Algiers and the number of installations to be established there was also small. On the other hand, suitable storage accommodation for a BOD was extremely difficult to come by.

On November 28th DDOS L of C (Colonel Varley) appeared and said that he had found good storage accommodation at a "Tabacoop" (tobacco storage building) about 15 miles inland at Mondovi. This was excellent accommodation, but it was several weeks before it could be used. Tobacco had to be cleared from the site and 4 Base Sub-Area were very slow in giving approval for 3 BOD to take it over. On December 7th Lieutenant-Colonel Burden with 15 officers and 145 ORs disembarked at Bone, and the unit was up to strength by the end of the month.

The main problem was still storage accommodation with nearly 3,000 tons of stores awaiting clearance from the docks. It did not appear that the Base Sub-Area had been given the responsibility for obtaining suitable and sufficient storage accommodation and the desire to avoid doing anything which could possibly upset the French induced a spirit of procrastination when the need for action was urgent. The COO and his officers had to search for buildings and then engage in prolonged argument with the staff of 4 Base Sub-Area to obtain approval to use what they had found. This situation was the more unfortunate because Bone was ideally situated to supply First Army and it was important that the depot should be operating efficiently at the earliest possible date.

It was perhaps fortunate that the inability to protect Bone from air attack in November and December 1942 resulted in many store ships destined for that place being diverted to Algiers. The Ordnance Stores were taken into 1 BOD. The effect was to give 3 BOD a difficult task instead of an impossible one, and the unit overcame its difficulties in time to give all possible support for the battles in March, April and May.

A site (28,000 sq ft) for part of 2 Sub-Depot had been found at a cork factory and further space (50,000 sq ft) for General Stores in an abandoned prisoner-of-war camp which had been constructed on the orders of the Axis Powers. An abbattoir near the docks was taken over as a Traffic Centre, and a site for a vehicle park was found and occupied, despite the fact that it was not in the Ordnance area. There was no alternative. Periodical bombing continued and on January 2nd a severe raid wrecked the Traffic Centre, killing one man, wounding another and destroying six vehicles. A tanker in the harbour was set on fire and burnt for two days. Personnel accommodation was also a problem at first but was satisfactorily settled during January 1943.

The centre of gravity of the depot moved progressively towards Mondovi, which was an excellent site. Considerable RE construction was undertaken, using Romney huts for storage. The work was done efficiently and expeditiously so that an excellent depot was developed there by the end of the campaign, and it formed a suitable entrepôt for replenishment of the stocks of the AODs which were successively established in Sicily and Italy.

After the North Africa campaign all operational stocks were concentrated there, and staff, in proportion to the load, was transferred from 1 and 3 BODs. The unit was placed under command of Colonel Friday and was known as 32 BOD. Its problems and activities will be described later. At this point it will suffice to mention that Mondovi proved to be a bad spot for malaria and there was a good deal of sickness both in the BOD and the units attached to assist them in their work.

STORES SUPPLY AND PROVISION

The concept of two equal and independent BODs broke down almost at once. The first thing to happen was the diversion of convoys of store ships from Bone to Algiers, and the consequent unplanned build-up of 1 BOD stocks. Theoretically, these consignments should have been sent on to 3 BOD by coaster, rail or road, but this would have been a futile thing to do. Owing to the situation which has been described Bone was as yet unable to absorb all these stores and simultaneously meet heavy demands from First Army.

It was therefore decided to maintain the Army from Algiers via the railhead at Souk-el-Arba, leaving 3 BOD to meet such urgent demands as they could from the stocks already in their possession. This protection of 3 BOD was necessary so that the depot might, as soon as possible, be ready to take the main load of demands from the Tunis front. The winter period of heavy rains had completely bogged down operations, but the build up of forces would continue and those forces could only be effectively supplied with Ordnance stores, when the offensive was renewed, if 3 BOD were operating at full efficiency.

The plan was put into effect. Large stocks of MT and Technical Stores were taken on charge at Mondovi. Clothing and General Stores were of course more evenly spread in the theatre and the two subsidiary depots at Bougie and Phillipeville reverted to an essentially Command Depot function, holding only the needs of the troops in the areas which they served. Demands from the First Army were switched to 3 BOD in good time, and by then the Allies had command of the air so that stores could be shipped from the United Kingdom direct to Bone with impunity.

The defective provision organization could not be put right so easily, and the effect was felt throughout the campaign. Obviously depots could not do their provision and demanding on the United Kingdom separately and independently. It was essential to present the theatre requirements as a whole.

This meant central provision and stock control and arrangements were made as soon as possible to organize the existing staff accordingly. The manpower for the task was concentrated in Algiers and some of the clerical staff were transferred there from Bone. It has been seen that depots were under-established in clerical staff already and central provision and stock control, although essential, increased the clerical work. Reinforcements were required and a new establishment must be produced. This was done, with the active assistance of Lieutenant-Colonel Warren, but the campaign was over before the unit could be fully effective.

The provision of MT spares for base repair posed a further problem. Scales had been worked out and were reflected in maintenance shipments, but there are many items which appear in Unit, Field and Base repair scales. Quite properly, while the campaign lasted, priority was given to the demands of First Army, but as those demands sometimes absorbed the complete stocks of certain items, deficiencies occurred in Base Repair Scales and repair was liable to be held up.

Immediately fighting ceased priority switched to base repair programmes, but this was not a complete solution to the problem. The need was for realistic scaling for base repairs and the segregation of the stores from normal maintenance consignments. A trial was carried out on Bedford and Austin engines. The result was that a very good scale was produced. This was the start of a series of scales in which the CE scales dealt with engine assemblies. Parallel research took place in Egypt, sponsored by the REME scales branch there. When these scales were ordered they were always packed and shipped separately.

AMMUNITION

In the early days the OBDs played an invaluable part in the supply of ammunition, clearing the docks, holding stocks and making issues until the BADs and subsidiary depots were able to take over. They then moved on to operate small depots in the forward area under Army control.

The BADs were handicapped in a number of ways. The establishment was based on a holding of 21,000 tons, but in practice this figure was greatly exceeded, reaching 75,000 tons in the case of 1 BAD. Handling equipment was inadequate or arrived late. The COO had no control over the allocation of Royal Pioneer Corps staff, parties being taken away without warning and later replaced by men new to the work. Ammunition was not sorted at the docks and did not arrive by complete rounds, which meant that sorting was necessary in the depot, with consequent additional work, delay and double handling.

1 BAD

This depot, commanded by Lieutenant-Colonel W. B. Shine, was based on Algiers. An excellent site was found with ample road mileage and a railhead at Birkadem outside Maison Carree. Good personnel accommodation was obtained in the French equivalent of an approved school in the area.

The urge to clear the docks led to unsorted ammunition being sent to the depot both by road and rail. Transport available to the depot for internal work was insufficient. It was also necessary to take in such American ammunition as was landed at Algiers for there was no American unit at first to look after it. This ammunition included aircraft bombs for which the depot had no suitable handling equipment. But there were compensations when later on an American unit was sent to assist the BAD. Its transport, being on a lavish scale by British standards, was extremely welcome.

The subsidiary depot at Bougie was also under the wing of 1 BAD. This unit had the usual troubles of insufficient staff and inadequate equipment for the tonnage handled but managed reasonably well and in any case had no real long-term function in the chain of ammunition supply to First Army.

3 BAD

This depot, commanded by Lieutenant-Colonel J. A. Gibbons, had a start similar to that of 3 BOD in that the advanced party landed at Algiers and only a portion of it was sent on to Bone arriving on November 27th. The first consignment of ammunition was received 2 days later. The balance of the unit arrived early in December, but by then arrears of work had accumulated. It was an exhausting business trying to catch up. Difficulties over port clearance and labour were similar to those experienced by 1 BAD.

In January a detachment was sent to St. Charles outside Phillipeville to take over the ammunition there from 5 OBD, which had been doing the job from the early days of the campaign. This enabled 5 OBD to concentrate at La Calle.

The site of 3 BAD at Randon was quite a good one though flooding was a serious problem. During the wretched weather which prevails in North Africa in December, January and February these conditions are normal in the low-lying area outside Bone and they had to be accepted.

As at 1 BAD, American ammunition was sent to Bone, followed by a detachment which grew into a Company. Eventually the sub-depot became a separately operated American ammunition depot supporting the Corps which moved to the coastal region for the advance on Bizerta. Cooperation between 3 BAD and the American ammunition units was excellent throughout.

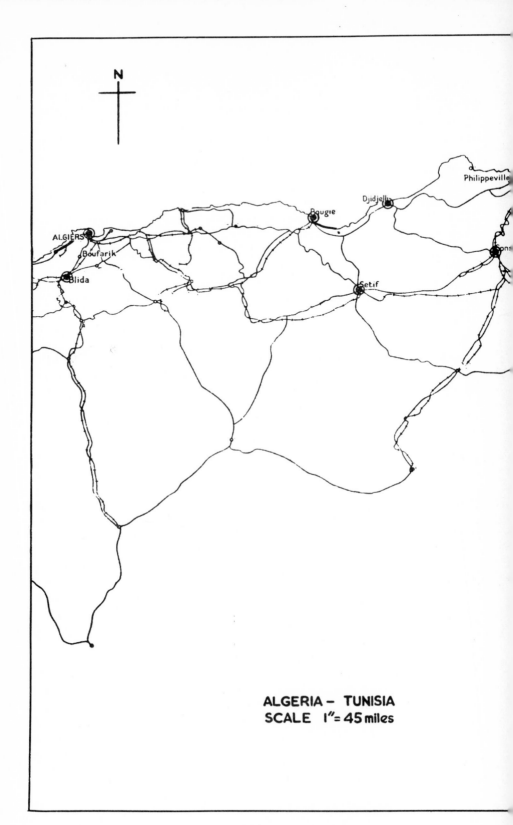

ALGERIA – TUNISIA
SCALE 1"= 45 miles

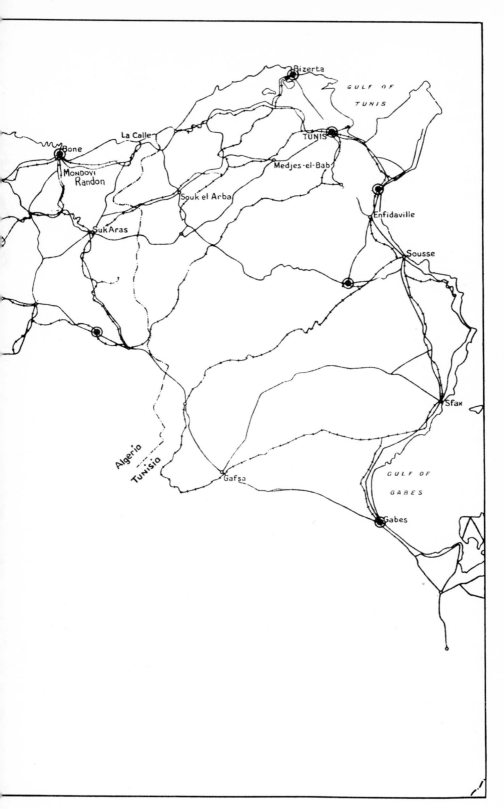

225

VEHICLES

Vehicle units were not independent but formed part of the BOD. It has been seen that the earlier shipments of vehicles represented the balance of unit entitlements. Reserves did not arrive for some time. By then vehicle casualties had been heavy. Everything was wanted in the Army area or to operate the long line of road communications. It was an advantage that the majority of vehicles which did arrive landed in Algiers. They were filled with badly needed stores for the Army before being sent forward.

Reserve vehicles did not come on wheels. The state of the submarine campaign made it essential to save shipping space. Vehicles were shipped "knocked down" and assembled by a REME vehicle assembly unit in the theatre. There was nothing revolutionary in this concept. The American motor industry had been doing it for years. But there is a big difference between assembling the bits and pieces of a vehicle for the first time, and breaking down a vehicle which has been in use and then re-assembling it. Nuts and bolts have been bedded in or even rusted in. For many reasons the jig-saw puzzle is much more difficult to do the second time.

It would have been an advantage if new components and assemblies could have been sent out, but vehicle production in the United Kingdom was not such as to permit this to be done in all cases. In this matter Middle East experience did not help greatly, because for some time they had been receiving most of their load and personnel carrying vehicles from North America.

Incidentally, the American vehicles were far superior to the British in design. On most British vehicles only one axle was driven whereas four- or six-wheel drive American vehicles were normal, which gave them an excellent cross-country performance in bad weather.

So great were the needs of the Army and L of C that for some time British Base Units and Headquarters had to exist on a curious collection of miscellaneous requisitioned vehicles. Pooling of vehicles between the British and American elements of AFHQ was not the policy. In general American units were supplied from the United States and British units from the United Kingdom, the basis being the allocations by the Munitions Assignment Boards. Allocation of American equipment in North Africa to British units could only be made on a high level in AFHQ. There were not wanting people who suggested that this was too rigid, that the Americans were very well off compared with ourselves and that "after all we are fighting the same war". But such criticism was unfair. The system of supply of Lend Lease stores was generous to us and in North Africa the Americans had a considerable commitment in equipping the French units which were being created. Moreover, there is no known case of a genuine requirement, raised to the proper level in AFHQ, not meeting with a ready response.

CONCLUSION

General Sir Kenneth Anderson, commander of First Army, in the final paragraph of his despatch on the campaign stated:

"When all have done so much, it is perhaps invidious to select particular services for mention, but I want to pay tribute to all ranks of the Royal Army Service Corps and the Royal Army Ordnance Corps, who, despite every difficulty of climate, terrain and enemy action, understaffed and overworked, nevertheless never failed to deliver the goods."

LESSONS

This short campaign provided many lessons which were helpful to future operations both in Italy and North-West Europe. Those which particularly concerned the RAOC were:

1. *The soundness of the system of Ordnance Beach Detachments and Landing Reserves*. However, the importance of special selection and training of the officers and men of these units, and the limitations of beach maintenance by landing reserves, were inclined to be overlooked by those who were not conversant with the work which preceded Operation TORCH.

2. *There must be only one BOD in a theatre*. It is true that there were in the end as many as three BODs in the vast Middle East Base. But they were organized so that the main holding of any one item was in one place only. It is chaotic to have two or more equal and independent BODs on the same line of communication.

3. *Central Provision and Stock Control* is essential so that requirements can be formulated on a theatre basis.

4. *The BODs, BADs and Railhead Company were understaffed*. It is a great temptation for the planners of an operation to cut the Services below the minimum necessary to do the job—the old "teeth and tail" battle. Of course the RAOC units expect to be worked to exhaustion, particularly in the early stages, but if the work gets out of hand stores get lost (location and stock records being inaccurate) and supply breaks down. This lesson has not been learnt—there was a notable failure in Korea—and it appears to be due to lack of knowledge of Ordnance problems on the part of the staff, combined with a reluctance to accept the RAOC assessment of the size of the commitment.

5. *Scaling and Packing of Stores*. It was learnt that the initial scales of automatic maintenance must be apparently lavish in quantity though not in range. This will increase the number of single item packs, reduce the amount of binning and simplify depot work at the most difficult time. Carton packing of small items is essential for their protection and identification. Base Repair Scales must be packed separately.

6. *Port Operation.* The importance of the work of the Port Ordnance and Port Ammunition Detachments emerged during this campaign and Movement Staffs learnt the necessity for identification and some degree of sorting of stores and ammunition at the docks—the reason why these RAOC units had been created.

7. *Ammunition Supply.* The new concept for the siting and layout of ammunition depots on a basis of roadside storage proved very satisfactory in North Africa.

Less efficient was the system forward of the BADs. As much as 43,000 tons were held at the railhead at Souk-el-Arba. This can be explained by the precarious L of C although large stocks were held well forward at Bone. But in addition to this the Army formed large dumps under the control of RASC units—far more than they could carry—and every battery seemed to have its own dump, in addition to the 1st and 2nd line holdings, which was left behind when the unit moved.

Worst of all these vast dumped quantities were not recorded and reflected in the information of stocks in the theatre held by AFHQ. This led to a slight panic that there was insufficient 25-pounder ammunition for the final battle and exceptional efforts were made to bring in more from the Middle East. After the capture of Tunis nearly a quarter of a million rounds of 25-pounder, much of it in unserviceable condition, were recovered by the RAOC. There was a similar situation with other natures.

The lesson was that proper control of dumping must be exercised by the staff of a formation. Casual dumping of large quantities does not improve the supply position as the units in charge of the dumps have neither the capacity nor the knowledge to maintain the ammunition which soon becomes unserviceable. When heavy dumping is unavoidable the dumps must be controlled by RAOC staff who will also submit the necessary returns so as to keep the theatre stock records in GHQ or Force Headquarters up-to-date.

8. *REME Workshops.* Owing to the recent formation of REME the organization was inevitably somewhat experimental. From the RAOC point of view it was clear that we must provide stores sections for field workshops and indeed any workshop not adjacent to a large depot.

CHAPTER EIGHT

SICILY AND ITALY

Sicily

The operations from the battle of Alamein to the victory at Tunis, resulting in the clearance of North Africa, relief of Malta and re-opening of the Mediterranean, represent a clear-cut phase in the course of the war. This period of little more than 6 months marked a dramatic change in the fortunes of the Allies following the disasters in the first half of 1942.

The eventual outcome of these operations was obvious to everyone except Hitler, and his obstinacy in reinforcing failure only served to magnify the extent of the Allied success. But this success was only one step on the road to final victory. The momentum must be maintained. Mr. Churchill realized only too well the danger of a slackening of effort after the capture of Tunis and did not fail to point out that North Africa was intended to be a springboard not a sofa.

Moreover, the possibility of an invasion of North-West Europe in the spring of 1943 was waning, and the only way to keep pressure on the Axis powers and assist the Russians was to strike at the "soft underbelly" of Europe. Late in January 1943 orders were received in North Africa to plan and mount operation "HUSKY" for the invasion and occupation of Sicily as a prelude to a move into Italy. A planning headquarters designated Force 141, was formed in Algiers for this purpose.

There were to be two task forces, a Western (American) and Eastern (British). The Army components were to be the American Seventh Army under General Patton and the British Eighth Army under General Montgomery with General Alexander as Army Group Commander for the whole operation.

However, the Tunisian campaign was at that time in its most "sticky" stage and all three commanders were necessarily occupied with existing operations. Planning in the absence of a guiding hand was tentative and slow.

Even the operational plan was changed late in the day. Originally the Western Task Force was to land near Palermo and occupy that port while the Eastern Task Force landed on the beaches at the south-eastern end of the island. When General Montgomery had the opportunity to study this plan he pointed out the dangers of such initial dispersion of the Army Group and it was decided to concentrate the landing of both task forces in the south-east.

The effect of such last minute changes on the administrative arrangements caused considerable difficulties owing to changes in the order of battle. It would not be known until the end of the North African campaign which troops would emerge in good enough shape for the operations in Sicily. The final order of battle consisted of formations based in localities so far apart that logistic difficulties were aggravated and misunderstandings were bound to occur.

A Canadian division was in England, Algeria was the base for 51st and 78th Divisions, the Middle East for 5th and 50th Divisions and 231 Brigade. There were two Corps, 13 Corps comprising 5th and 50th Divisions on the right, 30 Corps on the left comprising 231 Brigade, 51st and 1st Canadian Divisions. The follow-up formation was 78th Division.

The Eastern Task Force was to be mounted and maintained from the Middle East and the detailed Ordnance planning for this task fell to the lot of the DDOS 13 Corps, Colonel W. Grimsdale, who worked in close conjunction with the Planning Branch of DOS MEF.

He faced the immensely difficult problem of obtaining in good time sufficient basic information on formation holdings to enable the Central Provision Office to scale landing reserves and maintenance requirements. Landing reserves then had to be packed and the schedules for them printed—considerable work against time for the BODs.

Ordnance Beach Detachments had to be trained and everything done under a cloak of secrecy. An opposed landing and beach maintenance were new experiences in the Middle East—new also to the formations taking part except 78th Division whose comprehensive training in this field was thrown away by their employment in the follow-up role.

The RAOC staff and units in the Middle East Base showed that they could do this preparatory work and still maintain the Eighth Army in its advance to Tunis. The DDOS Eighth Army for this operation, and also in the campaign in Italy which followed was Brigadier C. H. Cooper, whose previous experience as DDOS 13 Corps and also in provision in the Middle East Base fully qualified him to anticipate the equipment problems which the Army would face.

There was some conflict of opinion concerning the stores units to be established in Sicily. One school of thought was that Sicily would be occupied in a few weeks (as indeed proved to be the case) and having acted as a stepping stone to Italy would be used no more. Therefore it would be a mistake to lock up large stocks there and the campaign could be sustained through Ordnance Beach Detachments and stocks established at Algiers, Bone, Tripoli and perhaps Malta.

This view may have been implicitly supported by Headquarters 15th Army Group, who soon discarded their Service representatives and acted in the same way as 18th Army Group in North Africa, namely as an operational headquarters with a small administrative staff in an advisory and liaison capacity.

The reluctance on the part of Headquarters 15th Army Group to be involved in executive administrative duties, though understandable in the limited context of the Sicilian campaign, was to cause difficulties in Italy as we shall see.

DOS MEF was determined in consultation with Brigadier Cooper to have a small AOD in Sicily. They considered that there was no substitute for stores on the ground and that failure to provide them constituted an unjustifiable risk. This view prevailed and events proved that it was right.

Beach Groups were formed on the same lines as those planned for the TORCH operation, the supply of Ordnance stores and ammunition being effected by means of Ordnance Beach Detachments. It was thought at that time that the early capture of a port was essential, but events were to show that large forces could be maintained over the beach assisted by very limited port capacity.

The early stores convoys contained a high proportion of ammunition, and also landing reserves and the initial stocks for the AOD. Ships were of course pre-stowed well in advance of the sailing date, and anything which had not been foreseen could not be obtained quickly by convoy. There was, however, a ferry service of small ships and tank landing craft which could bring urgently required stores to Sicily from Bone, Tunis, Sousse, Sfax and Tripoli. This gave some degree of flexibility to the maintenance arrangements.

The organization of beach groups reflected the complexity of the order of battle. Two were formed in the United Kingdom and accompanied the Canadians, one was formed in North Africa to support 51st Division and the remaining four were formed in the Middle East.

Another problem which was aggravated by the complex order of battle was the re-equipment of formations which had been fighting in Tunisia. The situation was relatively simple in the case of 50th and 78th Divisions because each operated a well-established drill with its original base of supply—Middle East and Algiers respectively. But 5th Division had moved all the way from Persia and Iraq Command in April and many of its vehicles were worn out, while 51st Division turned up somewhat unexpectedly in Djidjelli, between Bougie and Phillipeville. This was an ideal place for recuperation but not for re-equipment. It was out of reach of the Middle East Base and the task fell upon AFHQ whose resources were meagre. The stocks in 1 and 3 BODs had been drained to meet the requirements of the final battle in Tunisia and reserves of vehicles were at a low ebb. Most vehicles were received cased and time was so short that these new vehicles were not available for immediate issue to formations although they helped to build up reserves.

It was necessary to strip other formations of their vehicles, a process which, unless handled with diplomacy, can cause friction and recrimination. Most of the First Army vehicles came from the United Kingdom and in many respects they were inferior in design to those from North America with which the units in the Middle East had been supplied. For example in most vehicles from North America all wheels were driven but many British vehicles were 2-wheel drive.

It was difficult for 51st Division to see why they should not immediately receive from Ordnance at AFHQ, any vehicles they wanted from American sources. But these vehicles were not in the gift of the DOS at AFHQ, and the Americans had their own Army to equip as well as the new French forces which were being created. It was explained that if a request were submitted at a high enough level the Americans would find the vehicles from somewhere (as they did on a later occasion) but this suggestion did not go down very well. In spite of these misunderstandings and the consequent delays the Division was equipped on time and it was even possible to build up a small reserve of 400 vehicles.

The invasion began on July 9th 1943 and the whole of Sicily was in Allied occupation by August 17th. Initial enemy opposition was slight. Syracuse, Augusta and Licata (in the American sector) were soon taken. South of Catania resistance to the Eighth Army hardened. The country favoured defence and most of the German troops were in this area.

Meanwhile the Americans broke through to the north and west, occupied Palermo and then turned eastward, linking up with the British to encircle the Catania–Mount Etna–Messina bridgehead. The Americans were the first to enter Messina, from the north, but the German forces made their escape over the narrow straits to the Italian mainland, leaving behind a good deal of equipment.

The beaches were able to link up with each other on the first day and 5, 6, 32, 33 and 34 OBDs were quickly in operation. Syracuse was captured on the second day, and as ships were diverted there as soon as possible there was a general tendency to switch all other incoming consignments to the beaches immediately south of the port. These alterations led to the diversion of landing reserves and other maintenance requirements which had been consigned on a formation basis.

At about this time the DDOS and his DADOS (Ammunition) with other staff and services representatives from Headquarters Eighth Army were landed, and took stock of the situation.

An Army Roadhead was set up a few miles north of Syracuse to which all freshly landed consignments were sent direct. The roadhead was manned by detachments drawn from the OBDs.

Landing Reserves were ferried forward to the roadhead as transport could be made available and the stocks were thus centralized for ease of control and availability. Landing Reserves had of course been packed on a Brigade basis in small cases to assist manhandling. This complicated the process of holding stocks centrally, as individual items had to be found by searching through a number of landing reserve booklets (location index and stock record). This process had perforce to continue until 557 AOD was established and took over the normal system of supply. Ammunition expenditure was less than expected and the accumulation at the roadhead necessitated the opening up of a new site to the south which was manned by 25 AAD.

Colonel G. C. H. Wortham, the COO of 557 AOD landed on D plus 1 with a small reconnaissance party to find a site for his depot. Nothing suitable could be found in either Syracuse or Augusta and he was forced to establish a tented depot as a temporary measure. This in fact sufficed for the short period during which the campaign lasted. The depot staff prepared the site and roads and also gave assistance at the Army Roadhead pending the arrival of the full scale of initial stocks and a corresponding increase in issue activity.

The excellent Eighth Army system of having an "administrative spearhead", an advanced base headquarters which moved forward with the Army and opened up new ports as they were captured, was followed in Sicily. The team which had opened up Tripoli was moved to Sicily. This headquarters was designated FORTBASE and took over in the Syracuse area on July 22nd, moving on to Catania after its capture on August 5th. FORTBASE was under the command of 15th Army Group, but 103 Sub-Area, which had been sent from the United Kingdom to control the 30 Corps beach area, and 86 Area, which took over in turn Syracuse, the railhead at Scordia, Catania and Messina, remained throughout under Eighth Army command.

A good deal of ammunition had accumulated under Corps control for the heavy fighting to the south and south-west of Catania. On the capture of that town all stocks were brought in to a suitable location in the neighbourhood and central control resumed in anticipation of future operations.

ITALY

Although it was intended that the capture of Sicily would be followed by a move into Italy, the form which that operation would take depended on a number of factors, the evaluation of which was far from easy.

Answers had to be given to the following questions:

Would Italian resistance to the invasion of their country be strong or feeble?

Would the Italians surrender, and if so, would they be merely apathetic or turn against the Germans?

Would the Germans withdraw from Italy if the Italians surrendered or would they continue to fight there?

To what extent should we be involved in view of the priority to be given to the projected campaign in North West Europe?

These strategic imponderables led to a proliferation of plans, tentative in nature and lacking in substance.

The plans were:

"BUTTRESS." 10 Corps to seize Reggio and San Giovanni in the "toe" of Italy and advance to Crotone.

"GOBLET." A supplementary operation to BUTTRESS in which 5 Corps would carry out a direct amphibious assault on Crotone.

"BAYTOWN." A direct assault by Eighth Army, after capturing Sicily, from Messina across the straits. BAYTOWN and BUTTRESS might both be launched and coordinated by Eighth Army.

"BRIMSTONE." Fifth U.S. Army to capture Sardinia. This plan started as an alternative to the occupation of Sicily. It remained as an alternative to the invasion of the Italian mainland, but was finally dropped on July 20th.

"AVALANCHE." An assault on the Gulf of Salerno with a view to the capture of Naples.

While these projects were being studied secret negotiations were taking place with the Italians for their withdrawal from the war. It was vital that the Germans should be kept in ignorance of what was afoot and only a very few people were in the secret.

The planners at AFHQ studied the logistics of a campaign on the mainland of Italy and the formation of a base there. Naturally port capacity was an important factor in the initial stages and the small ports and fishing villages round the coast between Naples and Bari could not be ignored. But there was a school of thought which assumed that every point of entry would have its Ordnance depot and it was necessary to explain the effect of such dispersion on the availability of stores, especially MT and technical stores, the full range of which could not be held everywhere. Also the manpower required for operating so many depots would be excessive, and it was most unlikely that suitable storage accommodation would be found in these small ports.

The plan finally agreed was to establish one AOD in the Bari area and one in the Naples area, as there were two Lines of Communication separated by the Apennines, which ran down the centre of the country. The AOD in the Naples area would be ideally located at Capua as the railway from the east coast joined that from Naples south of Capua. This AOD would be developed into a BOD while the Bari depot would gradually be reduced in size and scope.

Gradually the AVALANCHE plan came to be adopted, Salerno was chosen because it was just within the fighter "umbrella" from the airfields in Sicily and the force nominated for the task consisted of the Fifth U.S. Army under General Mark Clark with 10 British Corps (46th and 56th Divisions) and 6 U.S. Corps under command. The Italian armistice was to be announced so as to coincide with the Salerno landings. The date was fixed at September 9th and meanwhile "BAYTOWN" was to be undertaken as soon as possible after the fall of Messina.

BAYTOWN depended on the availability of landing craft. This and the terrain in the "toe" of Italy limited the size of the force which could be employed, and 13 Corps with 5th and 1st Canadian Divisions and 231 Brigade crossed the straits and landed unopposed on September 4th.

HQ 30 Corps with 50th and 51st Divisions was shortly to return to the United Kingdom and it was decided that their equipment, other than personal weapons, would be used for other formations who would equip themselves in Sicily.

The unfit vehicles of 13 Corps were to be exchanged with fit vehicles from 30 Corps. Brigadier Cooper tried to get this done by a direct interchange between units but the staff insisted on placing the whole burden on the very depleted vehicle unit which remained.

All this reshuffling was a big headache to the small RAOC contingent in Sicily, and it was providential that 557 AOD was there to help. All landing reserves and beach maintenance packs other than those required for the maintenance of 13 Corps were taken into the depot, releasing the staff of the OBDs for other tasks. 557 AOD was nominated for duty in the Naples area, as soon as a base could be established there and was replaced by an improvised unit which cleared up the stocks in Sicily.

As the BAYTOWN landing was over what was in effect one long beach, Brigadier Cooper centralized all beach maintenance packs into one holding, an *ad hoc* depot made up of the stores elements of the OBDs and designated "Eighth Army Ordnance Field Stores".

The vehicle problem was less easy to solve. Sicily had become an entrepôt for the supply of vehicles to 13 Corps and later 10 Corps, receiving for that purpose the vehicles left by 50th and 51st Divisions and an increased flow from North Africa. The existing vehicle unit was well below strength and was very hard pressed even when reinforced by 13 Corps Vehicle Company for which the vehicle sub-park of 1st Canadian Division did duty with the Corps.

It was necessary to concentrate to the greatest possible extent the small resources of manpower available to Brigadier Cooper. Thanks to this, and the almost superhuman efforts of all concerned the various tasks were completed on time. Very soon the fragmentation of RAOC resources of manpower into numerous detachments was to be repeated, owing to the administrative complexities of the early stages of the Italian campaign.

The advance of 13 Corps in Calabria was delayed as much by the natural features of the country, assisted by demolitions, as anything else. The people were friendly and the enemy reduced his forces in the area to small rearguards in order to concentrate his available strength against the new threat in the Gulf of Salerno.

The Germans reacted very quickly to the Salerno landings and the Italian surrender. They took over the country against negligible resistance and disposed their forces skilfully to meet the new threat. After a few critical days, and heavy fighting the beachhead was firmly established at Salerno. The Eighth Army was also advancing from the south and the small port of Crotone was taken on September 11th.

On September 9th a new operation, called SLAPSTICK, was undertaken. The Royal Navy landed 1st Airborne Division at Taranto. The port was thus occupied but the Division had little transport and no administrative "tail". Nevertheless the occupation of Brindisi soon followed. By the middle of September Eighth Army forces occupied Sapri on the west coast. The Germans now started to withdraw from the Salerno position and it was also possible to use Sapri for supplies and stores thus saving transport.

Brigadier Cooper sent to Crotone a port ordnance detachment and the stores section of one of the Eighth Army Ordnance Field Stores OBDs also a port ammunition detachment and the ammunition section of an OBD. To Sapri he sent a port ordnance detachment and a port ammunition detachment together with the stores section of an OBD.

On September 18th it was decided that 231 Brigade which was north of Sapri would be withdrawn by sea to Sicily, handing in its vehicles and equipment. This was another task for the ubiquitous Eighth Army Ordnance Field Stores. The vehicles were taken over by the vehicle section of 13 Corps Troops OFP.

The administrative situation was by now showing signs of getting out of hand. General Montgomery had taken a necessary administrative risk by advancing in the "heel" of Italy so as to catch the Germans while they were off balance and take the pressure off the Fifth Army. As a result of this bold action, Bari and the important Foggia airfield were occupied, but Eighth Army outran its supplies at the same time as the axis of supply was being switched from the "toe" to the "heel" and east coast ports. A skilful amphibious operation at Termoli enabled 78th Division to force the line of the River Biferno, and the enemy was steadily driven back to the River Sangro where he was faced by 78th, 5th, 8th Indian, 1st Canadian and the New Zealand Divisions. But this gradual build-up still further stretched the already attenuated lines of communication.

The switch of the axis of supply was skilfully carried out by Eighth Army whose headquarters moved to the Taranto area. The DDOS also went there and transferred the Eighth Army Ordnance Field Stores by road, the move being completed by September 27th. The unit took over the Ordnance Stores which were beginning to be received into the port. By this time Brindisi, Monopoli, 35 miles to the north, and Bari, 30 miles beyond Monopoli, were all in use.

At this stage the lack of direction and coordination of the supply arrangements began to be felt. This lack of direction derived from the nature of the operations and the remoteness of the base. Firm decisions on the various operational plans were made relatively late, owing to the fluid strategic situation in the Mediterranean theatre at that time. As a result an overall administrative plan could not be prepared well in advance and arrangements had to be hastily made, taking the form of a series of improvisations.

The overall responsibility rested with AFHQ, located at Algiers, Anglo-American in composition and meeting requirements from its own resources in North Africa and by demands on Washington and London. All operations in Sicily and Italy were Anglo-American, that is to say some formations were supplied by the British on the British system and others by the Americans on a totally different American system. In the case of British supplies there were very important resources in the Middle East Base and GHQ Middle East was responsible for giving all possible assistance to AFHQ. But Algiers and Cairo are 2,300 miles apart and communication between AFHQ and GHQ Middle East was never easy. Sicily was never established as a base and the nearest large installations were those in the Middle East. British forces were divided between Eighth Army on the east coast of Italy and 10 Corps on the west. Headquarters 15th Army Group had, as we have seen, discarded its Service elements, relying on FORTBASE to cope with the detailed problems of supply to Eighth Army and leaving the American Seventh Army to work out its own salvation, dealing direct with its Services of Supply in North Africa. This arrangement, good enough for the short campaign in Sicily, seemed to induce a reluctance to assume full responsibility for control and coordination in the much more complex situation which inevitably developed in Italy. Moreover, it was now necessary to recruit staff and service officers to replace those who had been discarded. The newcomers would not immediately be effective because they were not "in the picture".

AFHQ was too far from the zone of operations to be in close touch with events which changed with bewildering speed, and therefore was not in a good position to meet the needs simultaneously of three separate "customers"—Eighth Army, 10 Corps and FORTBASE. A strong administrative staff and Service component of Headquarters 15th Army Group would have provided one point of contact with AFHQ, controlled and coordinated the requirements of Fifth and Eighth Army, stating priorities where appropriate, and acted as a catalyst between the various elements which had no previous experience of each others methods of doing business.

Naples had been captured on October 1st and although extensively damaged began to take stores on October 15th. Clearance and repairs were speedily undertaken and until the port was working to full capacity Salerno and Torre Annunciata were also used. Within 1 month, the port capacity of Naples had been fully developed.

General Alexander was given the task of containing the greatest possible number of German troops so as to divert attention from North-West Europe and assist the Russians on the Eastern Front. It was thought that the Germans would make a fighting withdrawal to the Pisa–Rimini line and the country south of this line favoured defence. The operation could have been successfully undertaken with relatively few troops.

When the Italian capitulation did not lead to any resistance to German control of the occupied areas the policy was changed and Field-Marshal Kesselring was ordered to hold a line as far south as possible. He was sent reinforcements for that purpose.

The line chosen was the Winter Line, a series of strong defended localities on natural features running along the River Garigliano to Cassino and across the country to the River Sangro to the east. On the west coast a fighting withdrawal was made from the Volturno Line to the Winter Line.

So far as containing large forces was concerned the enemy had played into General Alexander's hands, and by the end of 1943, 15th Army Group was halted in front of the Winter Line by an enemy of roughly equal strength to the Allies with considerable reinforcements readily available.

The administrative situation now had to be taken in hand. In October steps were taken to tidy up the arrangements already existing and build up stocks of the more urgently needed items. Then a fully stocked base with adequate storage and workshop facilities must be developed. Finally AFHQ must be moved from Algiers to Italy.

Both AFHQ and 15th Army Group produced appreciations and proposals on the future administrative problems in Italy and the arrangements necessary to deal with them. There were significant differences of opinion which had to be resolved urgently. A conference was held at Headquarters 15th Army Group on October 12th 1943 and the decision was made to form an advanced administrative echelon of AFHQ at Naples under the officer who had previously commanded FORTBASE, Major-General Sir Brian Robertson. He was appointed Deputy Chief Administrative Officer AFHQ and his headquarters was given the code name FLAMBO.

Action followed quickly. FLAMBO was set up on October 24th and took over control of all administrative and supply activities in Italy for both British and United States based forces. The DCAO was adviser to General Alexander on administrative matters and was responsible for providing immediate administrative support for the operations of 15th Army Group. Brigadier G. O. Crawford was appointed DDOS FLAMBO.

At last a sound organization had been produced which paved the way for the eventual move of AFHQ when the time was ripe for that large organization to be transferred from Algiers to Italy. But "if the trumpet give an uncertain sound who shall prepare himself to battle", and the earlier confusion had repercussions which caused embarrassment to the supply services and irritation to the troops who had to put up with shortages.

Administrative risks had to be taken (they cannot be truly described as calculated risks in the prevailing atmosphere of improvisation), and it has since been stated on the highest authority that the temporary administrative inadequacies did not reflect discredit on anyone. Nevertheless troops who are halted for lack of petrol, cannot call on Artillery support because gun ammunition is rationed or shiver in the hills because the sudden change in weather has not been accompanied by a supply of winter clothing, do not see these matters in the same perspective. Who shall blame them?

After the end of August 1943 supply convoys which had hitherto come from North Africa or the Middle East began to arrive direct from the United Kingdom and United States. This shifting of the base back to the producer countries meant that ships had been loaded in accordance with long-term forecasts made many weeks before their arrival. The effect was a loss of flexibility with a consequent waste of shipping and congestion of ports, due to convoys arriving with stores which were not immediately needed or in excess of current requirements. The effect of the Italian capitulation was to give priority to the movement of troops over that of stores. The two were not balanced because it was obviously necessary to take possession of the southern part of Italy before the Germans reacted to the Italian surrender.

Supply ships were not, and could not be tactically loaded so that although these convoys contained many items which were urgently required these items were inaccessible until the ships were discharged and the stores sorted. This could not be done in Italy until ports and depots were operating to sufficient capacity. Sicily was used to the full as an entrepôt but had obvious limitations and the stores still had to be moved on from there. The North African ports were congested and the movement of stores from the Algiers and Bone depots was difficult even when supply ships had been unloaded there. Urgent requirements were sent by air from Bone to 557 AOD when that depot was opened in Italy. This was a regular daily service run by the RAF and was invaluable. The service was later transferred to the Mediterranean Air Transport Service, an American organization, and was discontinued before 557 AOD was really in a position to dispense with it. This was in the early days of FLAMBO when the organization had not yet found its feet.

The Eighth Army, supplied through ports on the east coast of Italy, had a life line to the stocks in the Middle East which restored a degree of flexibility to the supply arrangements and enabled the difficult period of October and November 1943 to be overcome without critical shortages though not without anxiety.

Ammunition caused some concern but the situation was not really serious though it was to become so later on. Until fighting stabilized on the Winter Line this had been a "petrol" rather than an "ammunition" war. Consumption of ammunition was not high and Eighth Army held ammunition as far forward as possible. There was no shortage at the guns but stocks in RAOC hands were for a time very low. In some natures, such as 25-pounder, there were no stocks in RAOC depots in Italy in the middle of November but the pipeline was filling steadily.

The petrol difficulty has been mentioned and this was matched by a shortage of replacement vehicles during the months of September and October 1943. It was mainly an Eighth Army problem as 10 Corps had relatively short distances to cover from Salerno, Naples and the intervening ports.

By now the Eighth Army vehicle fleet was decrepit in the extreme. Many vehicles, particularly load carriers, had covered vast distances. The fleet had largely been kept moving by a system of engine assembly exchange which depended on the rapid backloading of repairable assemblies and the capacity of the Middle East Base Workshops to overhaul engines. But the Middle East Base was now a long way off and separated from the zone of operations by a considerable stretch of water. Although priority was given to the movement of engine and other assemblies the supply could not keep pace with the demand. Early in October FORT-BASE bid for 12,000 engines to be sent immediately from the United Kingdom and the United States of America.

Fortunately the Royal Navy had, by the summer of 1943, won the Battle of the Atlantic. The DCIGS visited the theatre in September and saw the problem for himself. The ban on shipping uncased vehicles was lifted for load carriers and gun towers in which the shortage was most acute. The situation gradually eased and was under control by the time that operations stabilized on the Winter Line.

The establishment of the Naples Base was hampered by the earlier lack of coordination between the American and British supply organizations. Events had caused an attitude of mind to develop which separated individuals into the Eighth Army "camp" and the AFHQ "camp". With the Eighth Army initially to the east of the Apennines and served by the Bari group of ports, and the Fifth Army to the west based on the Naples group of ports, coordination tended to be further postponed. Unfortunately this apparently tidy division was complicated by the presence of a British Corps in the Fifth Army, and the fact that the greater part of the Army Group must be moved to the west for any advance towards Rome.

These circumstances had an unfortunate effect on the siting of 557 AOD. The DOS had always realized that 557 AOD must become the BOD for Italy and he did everything possible, with the assistance of Brigadier Crawford at FLAMBO, to accelerate the process by increasing the resources of manpower and accommodation. But progress was delayed in the early days by many factors outside the control of the DOS. Probably the most important of these were the fighting withdrawal of the Germans to the Winter Line, which hampered reconnaissance and occupation of good sites to the north of Naples, and the fact that we were in competition with the Americans for the port and base area facilities.

Soon after this date the depot became known in the theatre as 557 BOD, which was an indication of its future role and the load it already carried, but the official status had not been changed. For example the COO was still a Colonel, not a Brigadier. The Americans were given priority of choice of sites for their installations in the Naples area, and the original, coordinated AFHQ plan, which allotted the Capua area to 557 BOD, was either ignored or not even seen by FLAMBO. Consequently Pontecagnano, near Salerno, was allotted to the Headquarters, MT and Technical Stores sub-depots, while Clothing and General Stores were located in Portici, a particularly sordid suburb at the southern end of Naples, with the RSD close by at Poggeriali.

Had these sites been regarded as a temporary arrangement, pending the establishment of permanent accommodation in the Capua area, no harm would have been done, but the decision was firm.

Pontecagnano was 40 miles the wrong side, that is to the south, of Naples. Stores landed at Naples had to be sent by road or rail back to Pontecagnano before being taken into the depot. Issues from the depot to the forward troops moved past Naples again. Thus the lines of communication were lengthened by 80 miles and significant delays occurred.

The selection of the Portici area for clothing and general stores, and for the RSD was equally unfortunate. Many of these items were very attractive to the poverty stricken people of that part of Naples. The problem of theft was not a new one, and we have seen that even the most thorough security measures in 5 BOD at Tel-el-Kebir were only partially successful in defeating the Egyptian thief. But the Neopolitan thief was in a class by himself. Years of adversity had sharpened his wits and he was playing the game on his home ground. He had a comprehensive knowledge of the exceptional facilities provided by the urban area which had been so conveniently selected for stores which attracted good prices in the black market. Vigorous and aggressive security measures only acted as an incentive to devise more ingenious methods for removing the stores, including the use of the sewers which ran under the depot. It was said that Al Capone used to come back to his home town every so often for a refresher course in the gentle art. Although losses were considerable they were low in relation to the total tonnage of stores handled, and the greatest misfortune was the diversion of manpower from the main task of supplying the troops to the secondary duty of protecting stores in the depot.

The RSD under Major S. W. Owen was sited at Poggeriali. The area was below sea level and one of the first tasks was the clearance of about 2 ft of Neopolitan sewage, the result of the Germans destroying the sewage works before they left. In addition there were some unsafe, damaged buildings to be demolished and booby traps to be made safe.

A damaged railway siding at Lanza was taken into use and restored. This siding proved of great value as the campaign progressed. Thousands of tons of stores were handled there by the RSD, including vehicle engine assemblies of which at one time there were 10,000 awaiting base over-haul. A damaged railway engine was patched up by the RSD and was used for all the shunting, driven by L/Cpl Jones, an Ordnance shoe-maker. So important did the Lanza sidings become that Q (Movements) took over control jointly with the RSD.

In 557 AOD one of the difficulties experienced by all newly formed depots until the Normandy campaign was the inadequacy in quantity and quality of cranes and other depot equipment for handling receipts. Nor was there enough racking.

Sorting of receipts and stocks was of paramount importance to 557 AOD, particularly in the MT and Technical Store range, as the receipts were either automatic maintenance packs issued many months before, or the residue of BMPs and other stocks from 32 BOD.

Inevitably these problems coincided with a peak period of urgent demands, and for a time problems accumulated more quickly than they could be overcome. Many loose ends remained and Colonel Wortham had to accept the position and concentrate on priority tasks. The shortage of racking was largely solved by local manufacture in Naples.

Reinforcements of labour were obtained from every source and varied in quality. Continuity of employment of military could not be guaranteed and the most promising source was the local civilian population from which selected staff could be trained. A training establishment was set up in the depot for this purpose.

On March 18th 1944 Vesuvius erupted and plans had to be made for the evacuation of 2 Sub-Depot at Portici, although in the end this proved to be unnecessary. Everything was covered with a layer of volcanic ash which blocked roads and railways, choked drains, started fires and caused the roofs of buildings to collapse under its weight. There were also accompanying earth tremors. Movement in the affected area was restricted. All water had to be chlorinated. Stores in the open could not be identified until the layer of dust had been removed, which was a con-siderable additional task.

The AOD was called upon to supply tentage and erect a camp for refugees from the surrounding villages. Blankets and other stores were supplied from repairable stocks in the RSD. It is an indication of the state of Italian morale that these stores were liable to be stolen by the local Italians as fast as they were provided for their homeless fellow countrymen.

The RSD achieved a greater degree of reclamation of stores than its opposite numbers in the American Army, whose policy was to scrap and replace with new items. By the end of the campaign the RSD had repaired one and a half million pairs of boots and 11 million garments.

The RAOC strength of the BOD in June 1944 was 64 officers and 1,209 other ranks.

The prelude to the establishment of 557 AOD had been as follows. At Salerno 2 and 4 OBDs supported the landing with stores and ammunition.

After the capture of Naples a small temporary depot, 511 AOD, was set up there. The OBDs were withdrawn for future amphibious operations. When 557 AOD was ready to function early in 1944 it absorbed 511 AOD and the residual OBD stocks.

Ammunition supply in the Naples area started with the OBDs at Salerno. The next phase was for 501 AAD to establish a depot at Nola, near Naples, and by the end of December 1943 16 BAD took over the Nola Depot and the residual stocks of the OBDs. This enabled 501 AAD to establish forward holdings at Teano in support of 10 Corps in January 1944. In the Naples area 574 Vehicle Company established parks at Pontecagnano and Portici.

THE ADRIATIC PORTS

Owing to the rapid advance of the Eighth Army and unopposed landings on the east coast, depots were established there with less difficulty initially than in the Salerno and Naples area. We were not in competition with the Americans for sites in this area.

500 AOD moved to Bari in October 1943. The depot was planned to operate on a limited range of items until it was properly established and could take the full load. But Colonel R. H. Ferguson realized that no time must be lost as the Eighth Army was already outrunning its supplies and the distance to the Middle East Base was 1,500 miles.

The depot opened for the issue of clothing and general stores in October, and to prevent overloading of this sub-depot in the early days Colonel Ferguson arranged with Brigadier Cooper to divert some items direct from the docks to the Army railhead and also to postpone the backloading of "returned" stores from the Army.

The depot started to make issues of MT stores in December, but although demands for items not held were sent by air to the Middle East the stores could not be expected for 6 weeks and an increase in the range and activity in Italy was urgently needed. As many as 3,600 engine assemblies were held but, as we have seen, this was not enough to keep the vehicle fleet on the road. The "Stores Convoy Unit" system was soon extended to the lighter engine assemblies.

An indirect effect on the build-up of the depot was caused by a successful German raid on the port of Bari. For once our anti-aircraft defences were taken by surprise and some 30 aircraft got through. Seventeen ships and 30,000 tons of cargo were lost. Fires were caused by the explosion of two ammunition ships and there were about 1,000 casualties. This raid occurred on the night of December 2nd/3rd 1943, and there was a second similar disaster a few weeks later. At last the lesson—so often taught in pre-war days—was learnt, and a separate ammunition port was opened at Barletta.

The supply of MT spares, engine assemblies and other urgent stores continued to cause concern and about this time, the DOS Middle East was asked to send Colonel C. G. Reynolds and Lieutenant-Colonel T. A. Band to investigate on the spot, and find a way of overcoming the more serious shortages. Experience had made the Eighth Army somewhat suspicious of visitors who were only "swanning" or joy riding and all liaison visits had to be approved by them. The process soon became little more than a formality and the signal received by Eighth Army merely requested "agreement to the visit of Reynolds and Band". Some dismay was caused in the Middle East on receipt of a reply which made agreement conditional on advising "number of players, weight of instruments and proposed programme". Protests that Colonel Reynolds was not the man to "blow his own trumpet" were treated with polite incredulity! But the result of this musical visit was that the Stores Convoy Unit system was considerably extended and supplemented by the setting up of a direct road service from Base Depots to Army and Corps Roadheads.

Ammunition stocks were built up gradually owing to the policy of holding ammunition well forward in the Corps and Army areas. The first unit to arrive was 3 AAD which, after leaving Sicily, was moved to successive locations in the "toe" and "heel" before establishing a more permanent depot at Bitonto north-west of Bari. This site was handed over to 14 BAD on the arrival of that unit at the end of December 1943, and 3 AAD again came under Eighth Army command, moving to San Salvo to take over railhead stocks there with a sub-depot at Capello.

The first vehicle unit on the Adriatic side was 10 Vehicle Company under Colonel Sellars. Improvised vehicle transit units were formed at Taranto, Brindisi and Bari to handle vehicles coming through those ports and a vehicle depot was established at Monopoli. Covered accommodation was good and suitable parking areas were found. The unit was reinforced by engaging local employees, with particular emphasis on the need for drivers. Vehicle units, like most other RAOC units, were under strength and there were not enough drivers even at full strength.

Port Ordnance Detachments and Port Ammunition Detachments did invaluable work in sorting, identifying and directing the consignments of stores and ammunition which arrived at the many ports which were simultaneously in use at this time. The necessity for these little units had been proved time and again in the Middle East and North Africa. The junior officers who commanded these detachments required knowledge, tact and strength of character. They had to deal with authorities at the port who frequently regarded any sorting of stores as an unnecessary device for delaying port clearance, and did not realize that without it Ordnance Stores would be lost or misdirected and ammunition would fail to be moved and stored in complete rounds.

Until an adequate base organization had been created Eighth Army was dependent on its own organic units and those which manned railheads, roadheads and FMCs. The policy was to hold maximum stocks as far forward as possible, which was essential until railways and roads had been repaired and sufficient transport was operating between ports and the forward troops. The Railhead Company, Forward Ammunition Sections and OFPs held much larger stocks than they were established to handle, and as the rain and snow of an Italian winter had now set in, storage under field conditions was not facilitated.

Industrial gas cylinders were in great demand, not only by REME workshops but also by RE units engaged in the repair of the railway and bridges.

The demand for engine assemblies has already been mentioned and the average stocks at Army rail and roadhead amounted to 400.

Foggia airfield was captured relatively early in the campaign and would have made a first-class maintenance area for the supply to Eighth Army of urgent stores by air. Unfortunately the current strategic policy gave priority to other tasks. The purely defensive situation of Great Britain from 1940 to 1942 led to a concentration on the development of long-range bombing of targets in enemy territory. This was certainly a sound decision at the time but it remained as something of an obsession even after the initiative had passed to the Allies. In some quarters Italy was not considered to be a theatre for land warfare but only an area from which long-range bombing attacks could be launched on otherwise inaccessible targets. Foggia was in fact developed as a base for the Strategic Air Force, greatly to the detriment of the needs of the Army though never to the extent originally planned.

Brigadier Cooper had continually stressed the need for a regular air delivery of urgent fighting stores, at least until comprehensive stocks had been built up in Italy. He asked for 5,000 lb per Corps daily, but the response in terms of actual items supplied by air was unpredictable, erratic and inadequate. While this situation was largely due to the excessive logistic capacity allotted to the Strategic Air Force, it was unfortunate that the persuasive powers of the FLAMBO authorities were inadequate to obtain such a modest requirement for the Army in its hour of greatest need. Perhaps FLAMBO had some difficulty in persuading themselves of the real importance of supply of urgent Ordnance Stores by air. It may have been true that the advance of the Eighth Army into Tunisia could have been sustained by road and sea alone. But this argument did not apply to the early stages of the Italian campaign, and although operations were not halted by difficulties of supply, the troops did suffer shortages of equipment which would have been avoided had more attention been paid to the demands made by Brigadier Cooper and others.

As soon as operations stabilized on the Winter Line early in 1944 steps were taken to concentrate RAOC units on the two lines of communication, east and west of the Apennines. Stocks were progressively built up behind the Armies and preparations were made for a further advance. In numbers of fighting formations the Axis had parity with or even slight superiority over the Allies, but we had the advantage of sea and air superiority. This gave us the initiative. In quality of equipment the advantage now lay with the Allies. Gone were the days when enemy armour had to be countered by a 2-pounder gun with the penetrating power of a pea shooter.

PROVISION AND BASE REPAIR

The logistic plan for the campaign in Italy was naturally influenced by the existence of a vast and highly organized base in the Middle East.

The decision was made to coordinate provision by means of the Central Ordnance Provision Office in Cairo to which demands and stock returns were sent. The advantages of this arrangement were that it simplified the work of the provision branches in Italy and enabled full use to be made of the resources in the Mediterranean, thus easing the burden on the main sources in Great Britain and America.

On the whole this arrangement worked well. Frequent visits by provision officers from the Middle East ensured that the requirements of the Italian theatre of operations were known and given priority. Some difficulty occurred over continued shipments of automatic maintenance from the United Kingdom and North America. These shipments were not controlled by the Central Provision Office in the Middle East and after a time this led to the direct supply of many items which were not required or were already held in the Mediterranean theatre. The load on 557 AOD was greatly increased at a time when that depot was already sufficiently hard pressed. The reluctance to "turn off the tap" was understandable even inevitable, and the means did not exist to screen automatic maintenance scales against existing Middle East stocks.

The same plan to make maximum use of the Middle East Base was adopted by the DME. It was decided not to undertake base repairs in Italy but to send vehicles and major assemblies back to Egypt for overhaul, the latter under the "green arrow" priority system.

Unfortunately it was never possible to overcome the difficulty of the time taken to return repairable equipment and issue replacements. This was now a "long sea voyage" and the system demanded repair pools on a scale which could not be met.

Soon after the capture of Naples the DME, Major-General W. S. Tope, went over to Italy and investigated the possibility of establishing base workshops there. He decided that a start could be made at once and the base repair load progressively transferred from the Middle East.

This was undoubtedly a correct decision but the abrupt change of policy posed an awkward problem in the supply of spares. It enormously increased the range of spares to be held by 557 AOD, which had not been given the manpower and material resources to deal with the extra commitment.

The original scales for engine overhauls, worked out by the Scales Branch at Chilwell, had proved inadequate for war conditions, and although in some cases trials had been carried out and more realistic scales evolved in the Middle East and North Africa, these were not accepted for all future issues, probably owing to the impossibility of stepping up production at the rate required.

However, all these difficulties were eventually overcome and new accommodation was found in Capua and elsewhere for the increased stocks of assemblies and special base overhaul scales.

ANZIO

The advance of the Eighth and Fifth Armies had eventually been halted at the Winter Line and attempts to capture the bastion of Cassino monastery had failed. It was vital to maintain the pressure on the German forces in Italy, and as the Allies now had command of the sea the best prospect of success seemed to lie in a landing at a suitable point north of the Winter Line.

The point selected was the locality of the small port of Anzio from which it was hoped that an advance would be made to secure a strong position in the Alban Hills astride the German lines of communication on the road to Rome. The name given to this operation was SHINGLE.

The landing of a combined British/American force in January 1944 was unopposed, but the Allied advance was somewhat sluggish and the German reaction was quick. Kesselring's regrouping of his troops to meet the new threat was masterly.

The beachhead was not enlarged but neither were our troops driven into the sea. Heavy fighting continued for 4 months. Then a well-planned attack on the Winter Line from Cassino to the sea was successful. The monastery fell to the Polish Corps and the Army advanced, linking up with the troops who broke out from the Anzio beachhead.

Administratively the Anzio plan was most unsatisfactory. General Robertson wrote to Headquarters 15th Army Group and pointed out the administrative difficulties, chief of which were the problems of maintenance over the beaches for an indefinite period, the mixed nature of the force with separate supply systems for the American and British elements which precluded unified control and the pooling of resources and the probability that a prolonged operation would prejudice the projected landings in the south of France (ANVIL) the build-up of the air forces and the accumulation of reserves for the ground forces.

All these risks were accepted and Fifth U.S. Army was made responsible for coordinating all administrative planning. There was inadequate British representation on this headquarters to deal with supply questions and indeed no Ordnance representative was appointed until January 26th, four days after the landing.

Ordnance representation was also inadequate on the Task Force Headquarters (American 6 Corps) and consisted of a DADOS but no clerks or transport.

AFHQ was still at Algiers and remained there until July 1944. At that distance it was impossible to influence plans for an operation which remained uncertain almost up to the last minute.

General Robertson may have considered that the Ordnance representation was adequate and perhaps consoled himself with the thought that any necessary reinforcements could be sent later. But even if he felt that more staff were needed, it would have been difficult to insist on an increase in numbers without appearing to interfere in the business of the two American headquarters which were responsible for the conduct of the operation.

Thus the politics of Anglo/American cooperation at Army and Corps level prevented the RAOC from being in the operational picture from the beginning and the familiar pattern of hasty improvisation was repeated.

Landing Reserves were hurriedly scaled and did not reflect the experience of earlier amphibious operations in North Africa and Sicily and at Salerno. There were insufficient blankets and stretchers.

The ammunition section of the first OBD was shut out and did not land until some time after the ammunition which it was to handle. Reconnaissance parties were not phased in early and therefore the proper selection of sites for the stocks of stores and ammunition was not possible.

The British element of the force (1st Division) arrived without its OFP. It is not known whether this was a deliberate decision or a mistake on the part of the staff of the Division, but the shortage of spares and assemblies was felt until the unit arrived a few days later. Some people suggested that the OBD should have been scaled to cover such a situation, but the two units have separate and distinct roles. The beachhead was very congested and there was no room to arrange stacks of ammunition at the proper safety distances.

Reports on the Ordnance aspect of SHINGLE forwarded to the War Office by the DOS, AFHQ, brought some criticism from the staff officer to the DCS. The criticism compared Anzio improvisation unfavourably with the very thorough preparation for OVERLORD.

It was overlooked that SHINGLE had to take place quickly or not at all. It must precede OVERLORD so as to attract enemy forces away from northern France, and the decision was further delayed by arguments over the availability of landing craft which had been earmarked for operations in the Far East.

The administrative risk of improvisation was not great as a firm base had been established at Naples not far to the south and the Allies had command of the sea and air.

Although the force was penned in the beachhead for 3 months considerable German reinforcements were drawn into Italy and the operation may fairly be described as a tactical failure but a strategic success.

Granted that hasty improvisation was unavoidable in the circumstances and that the chain of command limited British influence both operationally and administratively, the RAOC made the best use of available opportunities and resources.

Although the Task Force Commander lacked the personality and readiness to gamble which such a risky operation as SHINGLE demanded, he was a competent logistician. This helped the supply services and ensured that the fighting troops received full support.

One interesting and novel method of supply was adopted. Stores in response to unit indents were loaded at 557 BOD into lorries and these lorries were driven from the depot each afternoon on to LSTs. The landing ships sailed round to Anzio every night and on arrival the same lorries were driven off and delivered their loads at the beach dump, temporary depot or OFP. Indents were sent back by returning lorries in the LST.

RAOC men were sent as "escorts" in the LSTs which was a guarantee that the stores reached their destination. A liaison officer was appointed on the staff of the DDOS AAI. He coordinated requirements, checked availability of stores at 557 BOD, obtained tonnage figures and arranged for the provision of vehicles for the service. The scheme was particularly suited to the circumstances of the Anzio operation.

THE SPRING OFFENSIVE, CAPTURE OF ROME AND THE ADVANCE TO THE GOTHIC LINE

During the Anzio operations 15th Army Group undertook extensive regrouping of the formations of the Fifth and Eighth Armies for the break through the Winter Line and the capture of Rome.

The whole of the Eighth Army (except 5 Corps which remained to the east of the Apennines directly under 15th Army Group) was transferred to the west of the mountains and absorbed all British and Commonwealth formations except those in the Anzio beachhead. The Polish Corps was also under Eighth Army Command. Fifth Army controlled the American and French formations in that part of the line nearest to the coast, and also the force at Anzio.

This represented a considerable concentration of troops on a narrow front. In the Eighth Army the diversity of origin of the various formations added to the difficulties of administration and supply. In addition to the British units there were headquarters and formations from Canada, New Zealand, South Africa, India and Poland. Each had its own methods and establishments. Even among British units establishments varied according to whether they came from the United Kingdom or the Middle East.

The opportunity was taken before the spring offensive to reorganize and rationalize the RAOC field force units. The frequent regrouping of units made it necessary to adopt a flexible OFP organization similar to that used in the Western Desert.

Divisional OFPs were scaled only for divisional troops. Behind them were Corps Troops OFPs and an Army Troops OFP. The latter unit had the additional task of holding the army reserves of controlled stores released by AFHQ. REME workshops now had their own RAOC stores sections.

The Ordnance Maintenance Company establishment had now been approved and adopted and this essential link in the chain of supply replaced the somewhat improvised earlier arrangements. The unit had to hold and handle stores and ammunition at railheads, roadheads and in maintenance areas. In static periods the DDOS Army accumulated considerable reserves at roadhead, items such as clothing, boots, tentage, engines, tyres, tank tracks and gas cylinders. When the advance was resumed RASC transport to move all these stores to the new roadhead was not available. The old site had to be cleared by backloading to the AOD and the whole process started again at the new roadhead after the advance had been halted.

Ordnance Stores Convoy Units proved to be as essential in Italy as they had been in the Western Desert. Without a system under RAOC control for guaranteeing the rapid delivery of urgent fighting stores from the base to OFPs, excessive stocks would have built up in the forward areas to meet urgent but unpredictable demands.

The L of C Stores Convoy Unit consisted of a small headquarters at the base, air stores sections at base airfields and forward landing grounds and road sections *with their own transport*. The BOD had a separate area in the transit shed for urgent demands and the stores were collected by stores convoy unit vehicles and delivered by air, road or fast rail service as appropriate. Corps stores convoy units collected at the forward terminal and delivered to formations. The same organization was used for passing urgent demands back to the base.

In this way it was possible to keep the field park scalings down to items in frequent demand, and the result of the reorganization was to achieve a better service with a reduction in RAOC manpower in the Army, thus enabling the hard pressed base units to be reinforced.

The concentration of the Eighth Army to the west of the Apennines for the Spring Offensive posed a special problem in the supply of ammunition. Requirements for a break through on such a narrow front and for the capture of the Cassino position were obviously very great. It was therefore decided to establish 501 AAD well forward at Mignano with its own railhead. A target holding of 19,000 tons was set but the actual stocks were constantly diminished by heavy issues during the build-up period. In spite of this the stocks reached a level of 25,000 tons by May 11th 1944 when the offensive started.

The depot was in advance of some of the Ammunition Points and within range of enemy artillery fire, but, by reducing the size of stacks and skilful layout of the ammunition, casualties and losses of ammunition were kept to a minimum. The lesson was a valuable one—that AADs can be located well forward with reasonable safety, provided adequate dispersion of stacks is arranged. In this instance the forward holding proved to be useful when the advance to the Pisa–Rimini line began.

Ammunition repair in the depot was extensive and two Mobile Ammunition Repair Units were attached. Among other tasks the following work was undertaken:

> Re-fuzing of 50,000 rounds of PIAT (anti-tank projector).
>
> Re-fuzing, with Fuze 208, 40,000 rounds of 3.7-inch AA.
>
> Converting 100,000 rounds of 3-inch mortar from normal to high velocity.

The Commanding Officer, Major E. E. Walker, showed drive and initiative in the best tradition of RAOC ammunition officers.

MOVE OF AFHQ

AFHQ finally moved to Italy in July 1944. It was housed in the vast palace of Caserta south-east of Capua. This status symbol of King Ferdinand of Naples may have been inconveniently large for the royal family, but it was ideal for AFHQ and enabled the headquarters to be concentrated.

The operational duties of HQ, AAI had been somewhat hampered by the additional responsibility for the administration of southern Italy. It was now possible for AFHQ to take over full control including administration of the Base and L of C. The name of the headquarters was now changed to GHQ, CMF.

About this time General Alexander became Supreme Allied Commander and General Robertson moved from HQ, AAI to become Chief Administrative Officer CMF. HQ, AAI, as a separate headquarters disappeared, and 15th Army Group became an operational headquarters with associated administrative functions.

From the RAOC point of view the DOS, General Geake, was able to exercise that direct control over Ordnance Services which the situation had so long required. One of his most urgent tasks was the reorganization of the Stores depots. The transfer of the Eighth Army to the west of the Apennines together with the support of the Anzio operation had placed an immense burden on 557 BOD while 500 AOD only had 5 Corps on their side of the country.

The advance from the Winter Line eventually came to a halt in the Apennines roughly on the Pisa–Rimini line. Leghorn, Florence and Rimini were captured but the break through into the Po valley was not achieved. However, Ancona was captured and 35 AOD, under the command of Lieutenant-Colonel Walker from 501 AAD, moved in on the heels of the retreating Germans.

The first thing was to give 557 BOD the manpower, accommodation and capacity which was needed for its heavy task. We have seen that in 1943 the need to form a BOD in the Naples area had been realized at AFHQ. But HQ, AAI, absorbed by pressing problems of Army Group administration in the battles on the Winter Line and at Anzio, could not devote much time to the development of base installations which had to struggle along as best they could.

The Inspector, RAOC, had been sent out to Italy from the United Kingdom and his report was critical of some aspects of the working of 557 BOD. There were no errors of fact in his report, but a somewhat misleading picture was given of the circumstances in which the depot had to work and the resources available to cope with the many urgent problems which had to be faced.

As a result of this report and that of his planning officer on the Anzio operation General Richards came out at the end of June 1944. He visited General Robertson, who stated that the Armies in Italy had never been better supported in the supply of Ordnance Stores. He then visited 557 BOD with General Geake and soon saw that this was a BOD in all but name as it carried the load for the equivalent of 17 Divisions. In fact the COO, Colonel Wortham, had been given a load for which the manpower available to him was quite inadequate and, moreover, the location chosen for his depot was, as we have seen, unsuitable. He therefore had to concentrate on the right priorities, no easy matter in the face of conflicting criticism from all directions, but his judgement and common sense overcame all difficulties.

Nevertheless there was a great deal of work outstanding, notably in the sorting and clearance of receipts, and it was a relief for Colonel Wortham to have General Geake on the spot to support him instead of the unsatisfactory remote control from Algiers.

The need for reinforcements was now realized at the highest level and in August, 11 officers and 319 other ranks arrived. In September 1944 the depot was officially recognized at the War Office as a BOD and Brigadier G. T. W. Horne came out from the United Kingdom to command the unit.

In Ancona 35 AOD was rapidly developed as a forward holding of fast moving items and stores required for the winter campaign in the mountains.

At Bari 500 AOD was confined to local issues but also prepared for a move forward when the armies should break through into northern Italy.

DEVELOPMENT OF BASE INSTALLATIONS

The Ordnance Services in 15th Army Group had now been developed on sound lines and were working smoothly. The main task which faced General Geake was to create a firm base in Italy from which the Armies could be supported.

557 BOD

By the end of 1944, 557 BOD had expanded to 26 different locations from Rome to Picciola, 150 miles apart, and held 176,000 tons of stores. The dispersion was expensive in manpower and administrative overheads so that supervision of technical work tended to suffer. This RAOC supervision was particularly important owing to the dilution of English-speaking military staff by large numbers of employees of different nationalities speaking various languages, the only common factor being an inability to read or speak English.

The commitment continued to increase at a greater speed than the means to deal with it, and now equated to over 20 Divisions. Brigadier Horne asked for reinforcements of 8 officers, 393 RAOC other ranks and 430 British personnel other than RAOC (ATS, RPC, etc.).

Early in 1945 covered storage again became a problem. In spite of using Capua as a transit depot for the receipt of MT stores, the store-houses were full and 400,000 cases had to be stacked in the open. Apart from the obvious danger of deterioration of these stores in the Italian winter, it was extremely difficult to operate an efficient location system and items tended to get "lost".

In 2 Sub-Depot clothing and other items which should be under cover were in the open. There was not even enough open storage and the roads in the depot had to be used where possible for stores.

Additional covered accommodation was found in San Lucia for the valuable technical stores of 3 Sub-Depot, which was, however, hampered by having to operate in 10 different locations.

Transit facilities were also limited and an application for a large transit shed was rejected by Q (Maint), although large scalings were expected for 500 AOD when it opened in its new forward location.

In March 1945 the BOD was reinforced by an increment of the Italian Ordnance Corps consisting of 17 officers and 354 other ranks. They proved to be more of a liability than an asset, which was perhaps to be expected at that stage of the war.

In the RSD a trial was given to a bonus scheme for improving the output of work of the civilians. It was based on competition between teams, the team with the highest output receiving 6 hours' overtime pay and the runners up half that amount. The scheme was instantly successful. Before its introduction the average weekly output was 72 tons but under the scheme the output quickly rose to 125 tons.

The cost of this scheme in bonus payments was 3,627 lire. Without it the additional output would have required 15 additional employees at a cost over the period of 54,000 lire. But this deplorable example of initiative was too good to last. The scheme had not been officially recognised, and, on the advice of the "Labour" authorities, was dropped. The production figures also fell to "normal".

In April 1945 Major H. L. Lambert visited Central Ordnance Depots in the United Kingdom to obtain the latest information on packing and preservation techniques. On his return a preservation plant was established, using local resources. This plant was needed so that tropically-packed stores could be sent from Italy for the campaigns still to be fought in the Far East. At that time the early collapse of Japan was not anticipated.

An important factor in such a large and dispersed installation was depot transport. The problem was solved by allocating two Transport Companies RASC under command of the COO of the depot. Each unit operated 132 vehicles manned by Italian civilians or German prisoners-of-war.

The ultimate size and activity of the depot may be judged from these figures:

Covered accommodation more than 3,000,000 sq ft.

Tonnage handled between ⎫ Receipts 658,300 tons.
January 1944 and June 1945 ⎭ Issues 378,100 tons.

Depot strength by the end of the war in Europe:

79 officers, 1,750 other ranks, 18,000 civilians.

VEHICLES

The supply of vehicles proved to be one of the most intractable problems in the Italian theatre of operations.

For a long time, in the Middle East Base, vehicle units remained on the establishments of BODs, though they were largely independent in operation. A change came at the time of the formation of REME when the opportunity was taken to dispense with the dual system of supply by absorbing RASC Vehicle Reserve Depots into the RAOC.

The regrouping of units resulted in the formation of 10 Vehicle Company at Tel-el-Kebir under Lieutenant-Colonel C. Sellars, and this unit moved up in support of Eighth Army, finally being located at Tripoli. We have seen its appearance at Monopoli in the early days of the Italian campaign.

The remaining vehicle units in the Middle East Base were formed into another Vehicle Company. Colonel Hayne took over Tripoli as a staging and servicing establishment in support of the campaigns in Sicily and Italy, and 574 Vehicle Company was formed to operate in Italy to the west of the Apennines. This company, commanded by Lieutenant-Colonel A. Duncan, sent a vehicle park in to support the Salerno landings and was then located near Naples.

Thus we have two companies, No. 10 to the east and No. 574 to the west of the Apennines. The organizational structure is interesting and also rather misleading as the various designations are now used in a different sense.

The Vehicle Company was a large organization, not to be compared with Infantry Companies in size. It was divided into a number of groups, each group headquarters controlling a number of vehicle parks for stock vehicles. The number of groups and parks varied, depending on logistic and topographical factors. The vehicle group headquarters compiled vehicle states and other data from the parks under its command, and submitted them to Vehicle Company headquarters. In addition to stock vehicle parks, transit vehicle parks were formed as required. They did not come under group headquarters but answered directly to head-quarters Vehicle Company.

This organization was flexible, and well suited to operational conditions, except that there was no overall control and coordination of vehicle units in the theatre. In March 1944 General Geake established this control by the formation of a headquarters under Colonel Sellars (promoted for the purpose) and this was designated first "E" Vehicle Company and then 38 Vehicle Company.

At this time RAOC vehicle holdings in Italy amounted to 20,000 on wheels and 7,000 in crates. By the end of June 1944 vehicle park stocks amounted to 24,000 fit and 16,000 unfit (returned) vehicles.

Vehicle companies were seriously under-established in drivers and also for a time the Army had to exist on a fleet of worn-out vehicles. Many formations and units were moved from the Mediterranean to 21st Army Group and exchanges of vehicles between units were almost invariably undertaken via RAOC vehicle parks, which enormously added to their burden. Experience had shown that an efficient unit can keep a vehicle on the road long after it is theoretically unfit for use, but when the decision is made to transfer such a vehicle the receiving unit refuses to accept it. The inspection, repair and re-kitting of returned vehicles, so that they could be re-issued, was a task the size of which had not been foreseen.

Full use was made of Italian civilian drivers for the movement of "B" vehicles, but the shortage of trained RAOC "A" vehicle drivers persisted for some time and RAC drivers had to be called in to help. It was found necessary in the autumn of 1944 to form a unit, designated the AFHQ Driving Increment, consisting of seven officers and 400 other ranks to deal with the problem of delivering vehicles, movement between parks, and so on. This unit was a component of Headquarters 38 Vehicle Company and was located with it in Rome.

In 1944 a Base AFV Kit Store was formed to supply all items of AFV kit in the theatre, and support the Armoured Replacement Group. This unit was moved to Pesaro in November 1944 and renamed 38 "A" Vehicle Kitting Increment. Later on detachments were established at Ancona, Rome, Naples and Bisceglie.

During the early months of 1945, before the final advance into the Lombardy Plain, the vehicle organization was split into two zones, north and south of Rome.

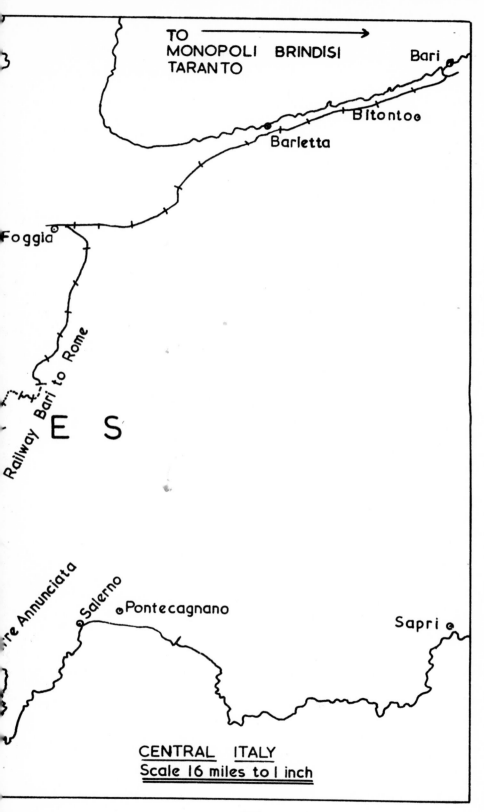

TO MONOPOLI BRINDISI TARANTO

Bari

Bitonto

Barletta

Foggia

Railway Bari to Rome

E S

re Annunciata

Salerno

Pontecagnano

Sapri

CENTRAL ITALY
Scale 16 miles to 1 inch

During February and March 1945 considerable reinforcements were sent through ports in the south of France to reinforce 21st Army Group for its crossing of the Rhine and final advance into Germany. This operation was known as GOLDFLAKE. The RAOC was affected in two ways. Large quantities of returned equipment had to be dealt with. For example 5th British and 1st Canadian Division returned 3,000 vehicles to 13 Vehicle Park at Foligno, and by the end of March, 38 Vehicle Company stocks had risen to 70,000. But, in addition to this, the RAOC had to transfer its quota of units under the GOLDFLAKE plan. The original planning figure, particularly of vehicle units, was lavish as no risk could be taken of failure in the Rhine crossing, but a rational decision was finally reached by agreement between DOS CMF and DOS 21st Army Group.

AMMUNITION

The two BADs which arrived in December 1943, 14 BAD at Bitonto near Bari and 16 BAD at Nola near Naples, formed a satisfactory base for ammunition supply up to the end of the war.

The depots were road served and located within a few miles of the docks. Ten-ton lorries were normally used for clearance from port to depot, and they proved ideal for the purpose. Both depots had trouble from the lack of sufficient depot transport and this was partly due to the units holding a good deal more ammunition than the planned figure on which the depot establishment was based. With roadside stacks and normal field storage safety distances the road mileage increased enormously, and a generous transport increment for extra tonnages should have been allowed on the establishment.

The night of the big eruption of Vesuvius in 1944 was an anxious one for 16 BAD. The river of lava flowed inexorably down towards the depot stocks, and a series of explosions would certainly have occurred if, almost at the last moment, the stream had not taken another course.

Perhaps the greatest problem which faced ammunition depots in Italy was the type of labour they were forced to employ. When each depot held as much as 90,000 tons and the daily issue and receipt tonnage averaged 2,000, exclusive of the handling of returned empties, it will be seen that the requirement of labour was considerable.

The importance of ammunition and the security risk would seem to indicate the need for military labour, but at this time the requirements of 21st Army Group and the situation generally caused an acute shortage of military manpower and local civilians had perforce to be employed.

They were on the whole extremely temperamental and unreliable. Their administration added enormously to the work of both commanding officers. Each depot employed about 4,000 of these civilians.

As always in that part of the world at that time the biggest problem was pilfering. It was impossible to ensure security over such a vast area and many of the ammunition components were attractive. Examples of such attractive items are:

> Primary cartridges for 3-inch mortar bombs (for conversion into shot-gun cartridges).
>
> The cloth bags from BL cartridges, cloth being almost unobtainable on the local market.
>
> Fabric belts for machine gun ammunition (for the material from which they were made).
>
> Brass cartridge cases.
>
> Copper driving bands.

Needless to say the removal of these components made the rest of the ammunition unserviceable. Hundreds of tons of ammunition must have been lost to the Armies in this way at a time when there was a general shortage of certain natures.

Pilferage sometimes made the ammunition dangerous. The packing design for the fuze of the Anti-tank Mine No. 3 included a protective cork disc, placed at the bottom of each metal cylinder containing five fuzes. The local inhabitants used to break open the wooden packages, unseal the metal cylinders and empty out the contents to expose the cork disc which was then removed.

On one occasion an Ammunition Examiner assisted by an RAOC storeman and a working party of local labour was given the task of clearing one of these pilfered sites. The loose fuzes had to be inspected, repacked and brought back for repair or disposal by sea dumping. A 10-ton vehicle was loaded with these fuzes when the load detonated, killing the whole working party.

AMMUNITION, INSPECTION AND REPAIR

The accumulation from these various sources of repairable ammunition in the BADs led to a proposal being submitted to the War Office in 1944 for the construction of an Ammunition Repair Factory. Other priorities delayed the project and the factory did not open until the campaign was over. It was then handed over to the Ministry of Supply. It has been suggested that a less ambitious scheme for building two smaller factories, one at each BAD, could have produced results earlier and reduced the amount of new ammunition sent out from home, but there were many factors, including the manning of the factories which might have halted any scheme.

Technical ammunition staff were in great demand and there were not enough of them. Priorities had to be carefully watched. The employment of Mobile Ammunition Repair Units in the Army area was an effective use of these experts. Ammunition which had been dumped by units could be dealt with on the spot and put back into circulation. These units also dealt with repairable stocks in the AADs but as a rule they worked independently. The Warrant Officer Ammunition Examiner in charge was empowered to employ local labour, and one of these small units took on as many as 80 of them for a particular battlefield clearance task.

One interesting special task undertaken by a MARU was the conversion of 25-pounder Base Ejection Smoke Shell into propaganda shell. Leaflets were supplied by the Psychological Warfare Branch at Eighth Army Headquarters and were usually rolled in bundles to the correct size for insertion into the shell. The base plate of the shell was removed (not always an easy task) and then the smoke canisters. The leaflets were inserted into the shell and the base plate replaced. The preparation of propaganda shell was usually urgent as it was useless to provide the enemy with stale news.

In quiet periods and at the end of the campaign there was a heavy programme of battlefield clearance and the disposal, sometimes by sea dumping, of unserviceable ammunition.

LAUNDRY SERVICES

The laundry units in the theatre in 1945 consisted of 2 Base Laundries, 2 Base Hospital Laundries and 21 Mobile Laundry and Bath Units. In addition there were 13 Mobile Bath Units which did not have laundry facilities.

Each base laundry had six sets of mobile laundry equipment and was capable of handling the equivalent laundry requirements of 90,000 men weekly. Each Base Hospital Laundry could cope with the needs of a 25,000-bed hospital.

The MLBUs were allotted on a scale of 1 per Division and 1 for Corps troops. They operated very efficiently and were much in demand. In addition to replacing clothing they undertook minor repairs to clothing, towels, blankets, mosquito nets, etc., and so reduced demands on the base. They employed Italian women for this repair work. Where possible these women brought and used their own sewing machines.

Mobility was somewhat hampered by the lack of a suitable vehicle to tow the heavy laundry trailer on the mountain roads in bad weather. The standard 3-ton four-wheel-drive vehicle was only suitable on good and reasonably level roads.

MOBILE STORES REPAIR UNITS

These units, allotted on a scale of 1 per Army, were established in the Army area to carry out minor repairs on general stores such as tentage, waterproof covers and canopies, chairs, tables, boots, pressure lamps and portable cookers.

They had a small military supervisory staff and employed local tradesmen. They thus reduced demands on the base for new items and reduced the load on Returned Stores Depots of base installations where similar work was done on a larger scale.

INDUSTRIAL GAS

Mobile Industrial Gas Units were provided on a scale of 1 per Army, but they could only turn out a fraction of the requirements of REME and RE workshops. In the main these requirements were met by repairing and putting into production existing facilities at the base, from which a very big output was developed. The return of empty cylinders for re-filling was always a bottle-neck.

MOBILE OFFICERS SHOPS

The organization was similar to that in the Middle East, but the shops were seldom well stocked owing to restrictions imposed at the source of supply where the full rigour of war-time austerity was in force. There was, however, quite a range of locally obtained items.

CLOTHING FACTORY

The main function of this unit was manufacture rather than repair. A nucleus of military supervisors controlled a staff of over 1,000 Italian civilians. Towards the end of the war there was a chronic shortage of many items of clothing and local manufacture was a great help in such cases or where shortages occurred owing to unexpectedly heavy demands of particular outsizes, etc.

PAINT FACTORY

This unit was formed in Naples in 1944. The majority of raw materials and equipment could be obtained locally. The factory achieved a weekly output of 500 tons and supplied the Royal Navy and Allied Control Commission as well as the Army.

CENTRAL PURCHASE AND PRODUCTION UNIT

General Geake was well aware of the importance of exploiting local resources so as to reduce the strain on the British economy, enable priority to be given to 21st Army Group and reduce the effort and cost of transporting stores from the United Kingdom and other sources to Italy.

The same sort of situation had existed in the Middle East and an organization existed there, working in conjunction with the Central Ordnance Provision Office. But the situation in Italy differed in many important respects from the Middle East. Southern Italy was ex-enemy-

261

occupied territory. The country had suffered the ravages of modern warfare. We had certain responsibilities for the inhabitants, and these responsibilities were exercised through the Allied Control Commission. The main industrial centres were in the north of the country, still occupied by the enemy. There were other competitors for the available resources, notably the American and French forces.

These considerations might well have deterred General Geake from venturing into such an apparently unprofitable field, but he had a shrewd suspicion that the resources were greater than appeared on the surface and he used his influence to create a branch which would produce effective results.

A unit was formed early in 1944 and was located at Naples, the main industrial centre of the occupied territory, close to Headquarters AAI and to 557 BOD.

The work was of a commercial rather than a military nature and officers were selected for their knowledge and experience of this type of work. Not surprisingly they also proved to be efficient and methodical in dealing with those other aspects of military administration which came their way.

The commanding officer was Lieutenant-Colonel W. Elborne and he investigated the resources at Naples and Bari. He discovered and requisitioned factories in Naples, but in Bari which is more of a fishing port than an industrial centre, he put work out to contract.

The main difficulties which suppliers faced were lack of raw materials, absence of transport and lack of communication by telephone. In some cases items were a normal supply from the AODs. Timber was obtainable from the packing cases of crated vehicles and other equipment imported into the country.

When Rome fell a branch was established there as the potential was good. Florence proved to be a useful source of raw materials which was backloaded, but there was no industrial potential. Even the prisons were not neglected and, with the cooperation of the local authorities, the skilled and semi-skilled prisoners were set to work with good results.

As the suppliers lacked transport and communications it was necessary for the various branches of the Central Purchase and Production Unit to be mobile and have the means to deliver and collect material as required. A new establishment was approved which provided the necessary facilities.

One factory was organized to cope with "flap" demands (unexpected, unusual and urgent requirements) for general stores. Samples were made of many items which could be made locally and these formed the basis for urgent contract action when a "flap" demand was received.

Plans were made in conjunction with the provision branches of 557 BOD, the Allied Control Commission, DME (for Base Workshop manufacturing capacity) and the Local Resources Board HQ CMF. The unit worked under the direction and authority of DOS, CMF and was given considerable financial powers for local purchase and production with the agreement of the Financial Adviser. At the end of the campaign another branch was set up in Milan.

The Central Purchase and Production Unit was a model of efficient organization and the economic employment of means to achieve the object. It introduced the required flexibility into the supply of Ordnance Stores in operational conditions and eased the burden on the United Kingdom economy. As an indication of its scope, the sum of over two million pounds sterling was expended in various central purchase activities in a single year.

SUBSIDIARY OPERATIONS

Italy was a base for the support of the partisans in Yugoslavia but the burden on Ordnance resources was not significant. But when the Germans withdrew from Greece a British force was sent into the country. This was in the autumn of 1944 and it was a matter of real difficulty to find RAOC units for the force from among the already overburdened resources in Italy. It was the old story of "robbing Peter to pay Paul".

140 Ordnance Depot was established in Athens, staffed from 3 and 8 OBDs. It was designed to handle only clothing and general stores, the replenishment of MT and technical stores being undertaken by the Middle East. 140 Ordnance Depot acted as a composite unit dealing also with the limited requirements of ammunition and vehicles.

In December 1944 the force found itself in the middle of a civil war— the ELAS rebellion—and the depot was withdrawn to a protected area near the Piraeus. It maintained the force from there throughout the occupation. At the time this was a unique type of operation although since the war it has become commonplace.

END OF THE CAMPAIGN

In March 1945 the advance was resumed and, despite the withdrawal of many units to France, 15th Army Group occupied the rest of Italy and the enemy capitulated on May 2nd, shortly before the surrender in Germany.

An occupation force was sent into Austria and this included 500 AOD which had been packed up and ready to go some months beforehand.

Having beaten the Germans, 15th Army Group became engaged in a wrangle with our Yugoslav allies in Trieste and our Russian allies who were reluctant to leave the British sector in Austria.

The main task of the RAOC was to tidy up the great residue of stores, vehicles and ammunition left in Italy, and this had to be done with a handful of men as the experienced staff immediately left on demobilization, posting home after long war service overseas, or transfer to the Far East for the continuation of the war against Japan. German prisoners were used very extensively for the work of clearance.

CONCLUSION

The campaign in Sicily and Italy must be seen against the background of the war as a whole.

Plans and operations were constantly affected by the preparations for and execution of the great invasion of North-West Europe which took priority. But to the Americans the war in the Pacific came a good second to North-West Europe and Italy was a bad third, while in England the reconquest of Burma was a most important factor even though the Fourteenth Army might be "forgotten" by press and public.

Field-Marshal Alexander loyally accepted the role of containing the greatest possible number of enemy troops and at the same time continually having to give up manpower and resources to other theatres. Moreover, his Armies fought in country and conditions which greatly favoured defence. Yet, in the end, he utterly defeated the enemy.

From the RAOC point of view the campaign started in most unfavourable circumstances. Strategic uncertainty and confusion, combined with important changes in the command structure led inevitably to hasty operational planning. As a result logistic planning was replaced by improvisation because there was no time for anything else. In the supply of equipment and ammunition advance action often has to be taken on insufficient information. This is another way of saying that the logistician is forced to guess and in the nature of things he is certain, occasionally to guess wrong. For this he will be blamed regardless of circumstances.

General Geake usually guessed right, but even when things did not go according to plan prompt remedial action was always taken. Under his leadership the RAOC in Italy, once the early difficulties were overcome, became an efficient and justifiably self-confident team.

CHAPTER NINE

THE INVASION OF NORTH-WEST EUROPE

OVERLORD

From June 1940 onwards the British Government and people had realized that the defeat of Germany could best be achieved by an invasion across the English Channel. This became the basis of the training and equipment of the British Army, and the policy was reinforced by the entry first of Russia and then of the United States into the war on the side of Great Britain. Although it was obvious that some time would elapse before a successful invasion would be possible, plans started as early as 1941 under the direction of the British Chiefs of Staff.

When America entered the war it was soon agreed that the cross-Channel invasion would be a top priority Anglo-American operation and the only controversial point was the timing of the invasion. In the end hard facts imposed a delay until the early summer of 1944, but as the objective remained unchanged the campaign had the benefit of very thorough preparation.

An Anglo-American planning headquarters known as COSSAC (Chief of Staff to the Supreme Allied Commander) was set up under Lieutenant-General Sir Frederick Morgan at the end of March 1943. Although General Morgan had for some time to plan without knowing who was going to be the Supreme Commander the main features of the plan remained firm, including the decision to land over the beaches in Normandy.

The machinery of an Anglo-American Supreme Headquarters had already been well run-in under General Eisenhower in North Africa, but there were important differences in the case of OVERLORD.

AFHQ exercised administrative as well as operational control. The new headquarters (SHAEF) did not. Its administrative role, so far as British and Canadian formations were concerned, was merely one of coordination and 21st Army Group was administered direct by the War Office.

RAOC planning and preparation were greatly facilitated by the fact

265

that the COS (General L. H. Williams) was in all essential matters kept fully informed from the beginning. But the COSSAC plan, good as it was, remained lifeless until the appointment of the various commanders. As soon as General Montgomery arrived to take over command of 21st Army Group things really began to move. With the knowledge that the oft-postponed invasion of France was really going to take place a tremendous wave of optimism and enthusiasm swept the country.

It was natural that morale should be at its highest in 21st Army Group, where every man felt that he had been chosen to take part in the greatest combined operation of all time, which would finish the war in Europe. In this atmosphere friction was reduced to a minimum. Commanders, units, staff and services in 21st Army Group were all out to help each other, while the War Office branches and Central Ordnance Depots, knowing the importance of the enterprise, gave it top priority and maximum support.

The DOS 21st Army Group had almost a free hand to select good people for his team and discard those who were not up to standard. Any equipment asked for was provided without question, subject only to availability (which was very good at that stage of the war) and limitations of shipping space. This was of particular significance in the case of depot equipment, the inadequacy of which had seriously hampered the operation of nearly every depot in all other theatres of war.

Although the experience and mistakes of other campaigns and combined operations proved beneficial, OVERLORD was unique in many respects.

The main features were:

1. The landing was certain to meet heavy opposition.
2. The sea voyage was a short one and full use could be made of the highly organized and well-stocked base which had now been created in the United Kingdom.
3. The Allies had absolute air and sea supremacy and vast transportation resources.

These factors considerably influenced the method adopted for the supply of Ordnance Stores, and to a lesser degree of vehicles and ammunition.

The essence of a successful combined operation is the early establishment of an adequate beachhead, its rapid reinforcement and enlargement and finally a break out. The build-up of units must be accompanied by a corresponding build-up of essential stores, equipment and ammunition, with a suitable margin to allow for interruption of supply caused by bad weather or enemy action.

Experience had shown the extreme difficulty of establishing a BOD in a zone of operations. First a site had to be found, and even the best available site was often quite unsuitable. Then the large tonnages and wide range of stores had to be received, located, put to stock and recorded on the account and this occurred under constant pressure to meet urgent operational demands.

In these circumstances some degree of confusion was inevitable, and although BODs managed, by superhuman efforts, to cope with the situation and meet essential requirements there was a great deal of sorting to be done later on. Until then many items were temporarily lost.

It was highly improbable that the 21st Army Group depots would find suitable accommodation for some time and a method was devised which would take much of the load off these depots until they were established and working smoothly.

The policy was to limit the range of stores to be held in France by concentrating on fast moving or vital items and eliminating certain activities such as Base Repair for which the vehicles and equipment could, if necessary, be returned to the United Kingdom.

It was, however, recognized from the beginning that, in spite of these measures, usage would often prove to be less than the rate reflected in the scales. Many factors contributed to this situation. The RAOC was kept informed of changes in the Order of Battle and of equipment, but sometimes these occurred too late for the re-packing of stores which had already been issued and surpluses could not be withdrawn. Many items such as project Signal Stores were issued on the assumption that civilian communications and other resources would have to be completely replaced. No risks could be taken as the lack of these stores might decisively affect the battle or pursuit. In 21st Army Group the Ordnance estimate was that about a quarter to a fifth of the stocks of stores landed over the beaches would be used, and this figure proved in the end to be substantially correct.

The system of supply of Ordnance Stores was given the name of Close Theatre Maintenance. Indents were sent by air in special bags to Northolt where motor cycle despatch riders took them to the Indent Clearing Centre which had been established at the neighbouring depot at Greenford. There the indents were sorted and despatched by motor cycle to the appropriate CODs.

The CODs then sent the stores to the Main Base Stores Transit Depot. The function of this unit was to collate all stores into formation packs, for which appropriate code numbers were provided, and send the consignments to the port for despatch by the Ordnance Ship to the Normandy beaches. The Ordnance Ship was a small coaster reserved entirely for Ordnance stores and RAOC staff controlled the priority of loading so that the most urgent items would be discharged first and important requirements would not be shut out. A secondary task of the unit was to receive repairable assemblies from 21st Army Group and pass them on to the repairer, normally REME or the Ministry of Supply.

The MBSTD was first established at Micheldever on the London–

Winchester–Southampton line and suitable sidings and other transportation facilities were created there, as well as accommodation for the men at the adjacent Popham Camp. Returned assemblies were received through Eastleigh.

The unit was organized to give a 24-hour service throughout the week by means of 8-hour shifts, and arrangements were also made to maintain liaison with the advanced base by sending officers to accompany the stores.

To complete the story of the MBSTD it should be mentioned that in September 1944, when 21st Army Group advanced into Belgium, there was a switch in the axis of supply and the Port of London replaced Southampton as the main issuing port. The unit then moved to accommodation which had been created at Stratford, although the troops were housed in the John Benn Institute at Stepney up to February 8th 1945. The accommodation was in the V1 and V2 target area and although unit casualties were few, assistance was given to the less fortunate civilian population, but with no falling off in the service to 21st Army Group. The commander was Lieutenant-Colonel S. Barrett and the regimental officer Captain M. Nicol. The unit remained throughout the operation at a strength of something over 700.

There was also an air lift to Normandy for urgent stores, but these were sent by CODs to nominated airfields and did not pass through the MBSTD.

When the stores from the MBSTD arrived at the beachhead they were sent to a special sub-unit of the AOD, known as the Stores Transit Sub-Depot. There the stores were assembled in formation consignments and despatched to or collected by the unit.

Special attention was given to the important matter of communications. A land line was established from Normandy to the War Office and the various "customers", including the RAOC, were given fixed times for its use. When the Ordnance time came up a team was assembled at the War Office end of the line so as to deal with any questions which were raised.

These arrangements were on the grand scale and unique both in the ingenuity and thoroughness of the plans and the wholehearted support which their execution attracted. If the enterprise should fail, it would be from some cause other than lack of preparation.

There was nothing unusual in the system of ammunition supply, and sound methods of field storage had been evolved as a result of experience in many campaigns.

Vehicle units were initially elements of the AODs, one vehicle company to each depot, but the DOS 21st Army Group planned to form a separate vehicle organization as soon as the situation required it, which would probably be when the breakout occurred. The main features of vehicle supply in the initial stages were the early phasing in of replacement stocks and the need to waterproof every vehicle until a suitable port could be brought into use.

THE PLAN

The plan finally approved was for the assault to be made over the Normandy beaches from the southern end of the Cherbourg peninsula on the west to the River Orne on the east.

The Americans were in the western sector and assault formations of 21st Army Group were to land over beaches roughly between Arromanches and the River Orne.

21st Army Group consisted of the Second British and First Canadian Armies with airborne troops, commandos, supporting troops and service units. In the 21st Army Group area there were, from west to east, three beach areas named GOLD, JUNO and SWORD, the first of these being allotted to 30 Corps and the other two to 1 Corps. Assault Divisions were 50th Division and 56 Brigade at GOLD, 3rd Canadian Division at JUNO and 3rd Division at SWORD. Beach Sub-Areas were Nos. 104, 102 and 101 respectively, 6th Airborne Division was to land in the area of the River Orne and secure essential bridges in advance of the assault landings. Small ports which might prove useful were Courseilles in the JUNO area and Port-en-Bessin to the west of the GOLD area. It was also planned to form an artificial harbour (MULBERRY) off Arromanches.

RAOC support in the early days, in addition to the organic units of formations, consisted of 7, 10 and 36 OBDs and 43 Ordnance Ammunition Company at GOLD, 9, 14 and 15 OBDs and 45 Ordnance Ammunition Company at JUNO and 11 and 12 OBDs and 44 Ordnance Ammunition Company at SWORD.

The DOS 21st Army Group was Brigadier J. G. Denniston with Colonel L. E. Cutforth as DDOS. The DDOS Second Army was Brigadier T. H. Clarke and Brigadier J. A. W. Bennett was DDOS First Canadian Army.

Important aspects of planning were kept under very strict security control by 21st Army Group. The need for this was obvious for in a crowded island with everyone speculating on the opening of a second front (which could not itself be kept secret) there was a real possibility that a "leak" of vital information would occur. It is a tribute to the skill with which this difficult security problem was handled that the Germans were completely deceived by the cover plan of a landing in the Pas de Calais and Rommel was away on leave when the landings took place in Normandy.

Nevertheless there were some awkward moments. On one occasion an exercise was held at the RAOC School at Leicester to study Ordnance problems in combined operations and methods of beach maintenance. The School had been told to produce a map of a coastline which could be used for exercise purposes. When, shortly before the exercise, Colonel Cutforth visited the School he was considerably shaken to find that an excellent map had been produced of the exact area selected for the landing. His abrupt rejection of the map for reasons which could only have seemed unconvincing must have been a great disappointment at the time to those who had taken so much trouble to produce a map which was obviously much better than the one eventually used.

On the other hand briefing for those actually engaged in the operation was very thorough. Everyone, down to the private soldier, knew exactly what he had to do and why. The more senior people were fully briefed on what others were doing also. In no other operation, with the possible exception of the preparation for the battle of Alamein, had this policy of "putting people in the picture" been carried out so extensively. The value of this process in reducing confusion and increasing confidence in the early days of a complicated combined operation was very great. It could not last for more than a month or two after the landing owing to casualties and unforeseen developments as the campaign progressed.

An important principle in the planning was that no stores were landed unless the men were already there to receive and handle them. Thus the build-up of stores, vehicles and ammunition was worked out. From this the phasing in of RAOC units, ahead of the stores, was calculated. If, owing to lack of shipping space or for other reasons, the rate of build-up of units had to be reduced, a corresponding reduction in the stores build-up was made.

Royal Pioneer Corps personnel were allotted to RAOC units and placed under command. This was mutually beneficial. The Pioneers became expert in handling the types of stores or ammunition for which the RAOC unit was responsible. They became known and valued as individuals instead of being "pool labour", changing in quantity and quality from day to day and therefore an unpredictable asset.

Port detachments trained with the Movements staff and precise responsibilities were mutually agreed. Identical instructions were issued by both. This was an ideal arrangement and should have been established for all time as the method for dealing with port and beach operation.

STORES

It was considered that the Stores Sections of OBDs would be able to maintain the force for 15 days from Landing Reserves. This was a safe estimate as Landing Reserves had been found reasonably effective for nearly 1 month.

Thereafter the AODs came into action. The first of these, 17 AOD, was to act as a temporary depot issuing from Landing Reserves and Beach Maintenance Packs, the latter being initially scaled and packed on a divisional instead of a brigade group basis.

The decision was made to reinforce 17 AOD with three store companies from 16 AOD, so as to match the planned phasing-in of stores.

As soon as possible 14 AOD was to reconnoitre and occupy suitable accommodation in Caen and progressively take over the load from 17

AOD. If suitable accommodation could not be found, building, using Romney and Nissen huts, was planned.

15 AOD, the last of the four in the Order of Battle, was held in reserve for future eventualities. While maintenance continued from a crowded beachhead three AODs would provide all the manpower which could be used, and, if the fourth were committed it might prove difficult to disengage and re-establish the unit in a forward area when the break out occurred. In the event this proved to be a very wise decision.

ANTI-GAS

The problem of chemical warfare nagged at commanders and planners. Obviously it was not included in the offensive plans of the Allies, but Germany was now on the defensive and the possibility indeed probability, of final defeat could lead to desperate measures on the assumption that the enemy had nothing to lose.

Anti-gas equipment was bulky and an administrative encumbrance, both from the point of view of the man who had to carry a respirator and wear it in battle, and the supplying service which had to provide and maintain the equipment.

In a combined operation against strong opposition these factors were important, and there was a natural though unacceptable reluctance to face facts and "grasp the nettle". Finally the decision had to be made by General Montgomery who, with characteristic precision, laid down the emergency reserves which the RAOC would hold to cope with the introduction of chemical warfare by the enemy.

This policy struck a proper balance between complete defensive preparations, which would have seriously hampered the operation, and no precautions, which would have enabled the enemy to defeat the Allies by the judicious use of chemical warfare on a small scale. In the end the threat never materialized, but the supply and storage of anti-gas equipment was an insurance premium which the RAOC had to pay.

Another unit to be committed early was 1 Ordnance Maintenance Company. It was to deal with the RAOC task of holding and handling stores and ammunition at roadhead or railhead and was under Second Army Command. 4 Ordnance Maintenance Company was also in the Order of Battle but was not due to be deployed until a later stage in the campaign.

Flexibility in the stores supply system was provided by the introduction of Forward Trailer Sections. These were semi-mobile units on similar lines to those formed in the Middle East for the advance from Alamein. There were four of these units scaled for different roles.

14 FTS was scaled to meet the needs of L of C units for MT spares. There were of course many of these units and there was no Ordnance Field Park organization to serve them as in the case of formations. The FTS carried out this function and thus relieved the AODs of a heavy

burden of detailed issues which might have hampered the service to the fighting formations.

15 FTS was scaled to meet the special requirements of three tank Brigades.

16 FTS was scaled for the special requirements of the Canadian Corps and was intended later to support the First Canadian Army.

17 FTS was scaled for the requirements of the Guards Armoured Division, 11th Armoured Division (Sherman tanks) and 15th Division. The momentum of the pursuit depended on the armour being kept on the move, and this FTS was scaled to provide additional spares for this purpose.

The Ordnance Field Park organization was comprehensive and consisted of four Corps OFPs, ten Divisional OFPs and nine independent Brigade OFPs. Divisional support was in two parts. The Divisional OFP which always accompanied the Division was a small unit holding the immediate requirements of the Division, but the Corps organization was divided into the Corps Troops OFP and a number of divisional sub-parks. These were scaled to provide backing for each division in the Corps. When a division was moved from one Corps to another its divisional sub-park moved to the new Corps.

VEHICLES

Vehicle units were phased in according to the plan for the supply of replacement vehicles, and in accordance with the agreed principle that the men must be at the receiving end before the vehicles arrived.

Owing to the need to make full use of shipping space all load carriers were to carry stores, such as unaccompanied AF G1098 (unit) equipment.

There was also a plan to use some of the men from the vehicle companies which were in the later phases of the build-up to accompany replacement vehicles, assist in the off-loading and then return in the ships to the United Kingdom.

AMMUNITION

There were six BADs available for the operation, and also four independent ordnance ammunition companies the initial task of which was to reinforce the ammunition sections of the OBDs.

It was realized that as the Armies advanced a succession of dumps would be left behind them and that these grounded stocks must be effectively maintained and recorded. This control had been lacking in earlier campaigns owing to the failure to recognize that Ordnance units were necessary for that purpose and significant quantities of ammunition were "lost". For OVERLORD 6 ammunition rail/roadhead units and 21 forward ammunition maintenance sections (FBASs) were provided in addition to similar Canadian units. For ammunition repair there were 7 mobile ammunition repair units and 1 field ammunition repair factory.

Ancillary Units

LAUNDRIES

Corps and Divisions had their Mobile Laundries and Bath Units, these being followed by Army and L of C MLBUs as the armies advanced. In the base a Base Laundry and two Base Hospital Laundries were provided.

INDUSTRIAL GAS

Main requirements were for oxygen and acetylene cylinders for REME and RE workshops and other users. It was realized that filled cylinders would have to be supplied initially. At about D + 30 Army Industrial Gas Units were to be phased in followed by Base Industrial Gas Units at about D + 60.

OFFICERS' SHOPS

Originally the stocks consisted of "packs" of stores on a scale the austerity of which fairly reflected the conditions in the United Kingdom at the time.

Naturally the manning of these shops was not a matter of high priority in the planning of a combined operation on the scale of OVERLORD, and existing manpower resources in 21st Army Group were considered sufficient for this purpose.

In the end these shops developed on a considerable scale. The earlier reinforcements were obtained from the staff of the OBDs after these units handed over to 17 AOD. They found their new task very different and in many ways more trying than that for which they had been so carefully selected and trained.

When Brussels was occupied an Officers' Shop was created there on a grand scale, doing thousands of pounds worth of business a day, in eleven languages, with ancillary services of tailoring, hairdressing, shoe shine, etc. Ration cards had to be used to control issues. There was no shortage of competent civilian staff.

This, however, is anticipating events.

PREPARATION AND TRAINING

Hitherto many units had been hurriedly formed and sent to theatres of war without sufficient training in their particular role or the opportunity to "shake down" as units. Although all arms of the service were affected by this situation, which was due to changes of operational plan, the

RAOC was liable to suffer most because administrative decisions must follow operational decisions. Therefore there is less time for action. But full advantage was taken of the long period of preparation for OVERLORD.

Early in 1943 the appointment of a Deputy Controller of Ordnance Services (DCOS) was created. His branches were concerned with the RAOC Field Force Organization, training of RAOC units for war and their fitness for war.

Units were subject to a comprehensive report on their efficiency, covering not only their technical standard but also weapon training, tactics, unit administration in the field, physical fitness and various tasks normally the province of other arms such as mine lifting and the erection of Romney huts for depot covered accommodation.

Thus the RAOC units for OVERLORD were very highly trained and versatile. They needed to be. It would be hard to find a greater contrast than that between OVERLORD and the move of the BEF to France in September 1939 when the RAOC base installations in support of the Army had to be manned by a scratch collection of civilians in uniform with only a handful of Regulars to guide them.

Many exercises were carried out to test the system of maintenance of the force and useful lessons were learnt. Exercises were on a large scale and simulated war conditions as closely as possible thus providing a real test of the feasibility of plans, which were altered where necessary as a result.

A very useful ammunition exercise tested the planning figures of tonnage per man. This was an endurance test as it was realized that units would be handling ammunition for very long periods without a break and that planning figures based on fresh men working for short periods would be unrealistic.

Wet-shod exercises were thorough and realistic. They tested all aspects of the assault and beach maintenance, RAOC units participating to the full.

The Close Theatre Maintenance system of demand and indent clearance was fully tested at Greenford.

The War Office, CODs, 21st Army Group and Second Army were continuously involved in the problem of scaling and packing stores for Landing Reserves and Beach Maintenance Packs.

Frequent changes at short notice of equipment dependencies presented the greatest difficulty. There was an extraordinary variety of equipment available to 21st Army Group, including a good deal of American material, and these changes were due to the efforts which were being made to find the ideal equipment for each phase of the operation. Imagination and ingenuity ran riot in the equipment of that unique formation 79th Armoured Division, which collected all the "funnies".

New devices were coming in all the time and each change of equipment required rescaling and repacking of the spares to maintain the formation.

These changes also affected the weight and bulk of the consignments. Shipping space was at a premium, all arms were in competition, and stowage plans had to be carefully worked out by the experts.

It was particularly difficult to apply a tonnage cut to Ordnance Stores. A Landing Reserve was indivisible as it represented a minimum scale, packed in a particular way in multi-item cases. A tonnage reduction could only be made in the bulk items such as blankets or stretchers, and these were the stores which experience had shown to be needed most.

A tremendous amount of calculating, recalculating and bargaining was needed and this imposed a great strain on the planning staffs. In some respects the long period available for planning only added to the strain because the changes in the Order of Battle and other basic factors continued right up to the late stages in the planning. The strain on the Central Depots which had to react to the plan was also great because they could not be told the reasons for the many adjustments to the plan. They had to work very late hours and leave was suspended for months. It is always frustrating to have to do a task again several times, and to maintain a high degree of speed and accuracy in those circumstances is extremely difficult.

BMPs, scaled and packed on a Divisional basis, proved to be too cumbersome and an unsound basis for maintenance when several Divisions were operating from the same beachhead. At an early date these packs would be concentrated in 17 AOD, which would supply the whole force, and dispersion by Divisional packs did not make sense. These Divisional packs had previously proved to be an embarrassment in North Africa where repacking had been necessary eventually.

This disadvantage was quickly spotted in 21st Army Group and repacking of BMPs on a vehicle and equipment basis was requested. In this respect BMPs resembled normal maintenance shipments with the number of locations for each item reduced to a minimum.

On the other hand important features in this system of beach maintenance, which were common to Landing Reserves, were retained. Cases were limited in size and weight to facilitate manhandling. The cases could be stacked so as to be used as bins, with the contents list pasted inside the lid. The location index system of accounting and location was used. In this way requirements of covered accommodation were reduced to a minimum and there was no need to unpack stores, which could be issued straight from the cases. Such a system was essential for a temporary depot operating close to the beach in an opposed landing.

Many special scalings were required. Among these were Signal Officer in Chief Reserves (SOCR) which were for special signal projects, the Ordnance Stores element of RE Works and Transportation requirements (these were stored by the users in the zone of operations), and "bricks" of accommodation stores.

An innovation which later proved its value was "survivors kits". These were sent in with Landing Reserves. Each consisted of a kit-bag containing a complete outfit of clothing and equipment—everything a soldier needed to put him back into battle after being shipwrecked.

Units landed with assault scales of equipment and it was necessary to bring them up to full scale later on. The scheme was to phase in "unaccompanied AF G1098s" to 17 AOD, these equipments being identified so that units could go to the depot and draw the balance of their equipment.

Large units were not sent over complete but phased, the less urgently required elements, e.g. returned stores companies of AODs being held back until later.

WATERPROOFING

All vehicles required to be waterproofed and whereas the technique and equipment were well known for the standard types, OVERLORD was the breeding ground for many new and strange types of vehicle the waterproofing of which required to be worked out and tested. Then the equipment had to be produced and distributed to the units holding the vehicles in time for the work to be done. For some vehicles a satisfactory system of waterproofing was not devised until rather late in the day, and a further delay occurred while the special stores were produced. This matter had to be given attention at the highest level and the necessary waterproofing was carried out in the nick of time.

MOUNTING THE FORCE

The preparation and marshalling of the British, Canadian and American forces for the invasion of Europe was a massive administrative achievement worthy of a separate book and only an outline of the arrangements, so far as they affect the RAOC, can be given here.

In general, formations were initially concentrated within a distance of 100 miles of their points of embarkation. When called for embarkation units proceeded in the first place to marshalling areas where they were broken down into ship or craft loads. They might have to stay several days in the marshalling area, depending on the availability of shipping. The assault forces were actually concentrated in the marshalling areas, and did not pass through concentration areas.

The smooth working of this complicated process was greatly assisted by the publication of a 21st Army Group Preparatory Administrative Order, issued to every unit in the order of battle. It gave units all the information required to prepare themselves for the operation, enabling them to act intelligently on the many orders which they received from time to time. Second Army also issued to all units relevant extracts from their administrative orders.

Each unit reached a stage before embarkation when it was immobilized because vehicles had been waterproofed or taken away for shipment separately, unaccompanied unit equipment was packed separately, and so on. In the marshalling areas units lost their identity, the troops being organized into "craft loads". It was therefore necessary to provide a "hotel service" to administer the troops confined to the various camps.

It was important for the RAOC to have the means of making last-minute replacements of unit equipment, and depots were established in the marshalling areas to enable this to be done. A scale of stores, vehicles and ammunition for these depots was worked out. This scale proved insufficient as certain items such as mine detectors, mortars, small arms and watches had already been replenished several times by D−3. The scale was then increased.

A procedure for the return, in returning craft, of inflatable lifebelts was necessary as there were not enough for issue to each man and they had to be re-issued at marshalling areas for use in the later convoys. The scale of reserves of waterproofing material for concentration and marshalling areas also had to be worked out.

Formations produced final deficiency lists for stores to be collected from CODs by road. This was necessary to ensure that all units were as fully equipped as possible but it gave a tremendous burden of detailed issues to the already overworked CODs. Inevitably there was large-scale duplication as some of these stores were already on the way to units and others were drawn additionally from the marshalling area depots.

THE ASSAULT

The landings on the coast of Normandy took place in the early hours of June 6th 1944. In spite of a 24-hour postponement due to bad weather, complete tactical surprise was achieved.

The RAOC units which landed on D-Day were six OBDs, two independent Ordnance Ammunition Companies, two Port Ammunition Detachments and one Port Ordnance Detachment.

All beaches came under fire but the assault forces moved inland and sufficient space for initial beach maintenance was cleared with only minor delays. The worst beaches on the Second Army front were those in SWORD sector which came under artillery fire from batteries to the east of the River Orne. This also prevented clearance and use of the Caen–Ouistreham canal. Enemy shelling, which was eventually to force the abandonment of the SWORD beaches, continued unceasingly, but the gallantry and hard work of all ranks ensured that the beach played an effective part in the build-up and consolidation of the beachhead.

The experiences of 11 and 12 OBDs and 44 Ordnance Ammunition Company on SWORD beach illustrate the problems of beach main-tenance in an opposed landing.

11 OBD and half of the ammunition company were scheduled to land on the first tide at Lion-sur-Mer and set up four sector dumps in the gardens of villas about 50 yards off the beach. They had to be ready to

issue ammunition by H + 4 hours. In this period suitable sites had to be found and cleared of mines, and the ammunition which had been landed must be moved to the site and stacked.

Four Landing Craft (Tank) were loaded with ammunition. The first two were due to touch down at H + 2 hours and the second two at H + 4 hours. Meanwhile a reconnaissance party from 12 OBD was to land and reconnoitre the main dump site about a mile inland and south-west of Hermanville. When this was established and stocked (estimated period between H + 16 and H + 24 hours) the temporary dumps would not be replenished and as these dumps were eaten down the men would concentrate at the main site.

Marshalling began on May 28th and was completed by June 1st. The units were split into nine craft serials. The first serials embarked on May 30th and embarkation was complete by June 4th. The first craft serials put to sea on June 5th.

The voyage was uneventful but uncomfortable for the parties in LCTs. Each of these craft carried 200 tons of ammunition, 20 tons of RE stores, five 3-ton lorries, a medical jeep and about 35 troops. Facilities for cooking were primitive and water came in past the landing ramp. The corkscrew motion of the craft was unpleasant for all except the good sailors.

In the early hours of D-Day the craft lay-to while the Navy shelled the shore defences and the assault troops moved in under a heavy smoke screen.

At H + 2 hours the first elements of the RAOC units landed and found the beaches in a fairly chaotic state as the exits were jammed with tanks and it was impossible to move a vehicle.

The beaches were still under shell and small arms fire so the party dug in at the back of the beach to await developments. They spent an hour waiting for the beach to be cleared and had a good view of 105-mm self-propelled guns dealing with the enemy in the houses on the sea-front at 50 yards' range.

Then they were able to get off the beaches to the sites selected for the sector dumps. At this time their first casualty occurred when a Bren carrier ran over a mine, the blast seriously wounding one man and shaking up several others.

The unit then started mine clearance of the sector dumps. In one of these 20 Teller mines were found in an area of about 40 yards square in the first half hour. About 1 in 5 of these were booby-trapped.

The first loads of ammunition were brought in by DUKWS at about H + 4½ hours. Two dumps had been established and a third was being set up along the concrete road of an unfinished housing estate. This dump came under mortar fire from the direction of Colleville-sur-Orne and several Pioneers were wounded, but most of the enemy's shell-fire passed over the unit and fell on the beach or in the sea. Sporadic rifle fire from the houses continued.

Issues of ammunition began almost as soon as the sector dumps were established, 105-mm being the most popular nature. The rest of D-Day was comparatively uneventful from the point of view of enemy attacks on the OBD sites and the build-up continued steadily, the staff of the units working without rest of any sort for the first 48 hours. Enemy aircraft could do little at this stage. On D + 1 eight of them came out of the clouds and immediately five were shot down by AA fire, the remainder falling to RAF fighters within a few minutes. The follow-up parties, to bring the OBDs to full strength, struck bad weather and many of them had to swim ashore. A sergeant of 12 OBD was drowned.

Modifications had to be made to the original plan because pockets of resistance still remained near Hermanville, and the enemy still held Lion-sur-Mer and Luc-sur-Mer between the British and Canadian beaches. It was, of course, essential to deepen the beachhead, and the units which landed first pushed inland as far as possible, leaving the follow-up formations to mop up and to widen the area of lodgement so as to link the various beaches. The optimistic hope that Caen would fall in the early days was not fulfilled and the beachhead remained uncomfortably small and crowded for 2 months.

The ammunition dumps were extended, involving more mine clearance. Areas originally scheduled to hold 300 tons now held 3,000 tons, and the only concession to safety distances was to have distances of about 400 yards between these large dumps.

Snipers continued to be troublesome, not so much in themselves, but because of the fire which they attracted from the Navy. The gunners who manned their 20-mm guns, deprived of the chance to shoot at enemy aircraft which failed to appear, opened fire at the slightest suspicion of movement in the houses on the sea front. These strong points had not yet been cleared. The land rose sharply on the landward side of these houses and this was where some of the dumps were situated. Shell fired at the upper windows often went straight through the house and passed over the sector dumps at about eye level. Luckily no serious damage or casualties occurred, although once or twice grass fires were started.

By D + 2 there were occasional "sneak raids" by isolated aircraft and on this day a Focke-Wolfe got through and bombed the congested area—about 300 yards square—which contained an ammunition dump, an Ordnance stores dump and dumps of petrol and rations. A lucky bomb hit the petrol dump and the flames spread to the ammunition.

Ammunition had to be moved to prevent propagation of the explosion throughout the dump. Shell from the burning stacks was exploding at frequent intervals and Captain Thompson, who took charge of the fire-fighting party, was killed by a shell splinter shortly before the fire was brought under control. The loss amounted to about 400 tons of ammunition and 100,000 gallons of petrol. The fire continued burning for about 6 hours.

The stores detachment of 11 OBD had to do a lot of mine clearance on the site of their sector dump. They located and lifted 80 mines in an area of about 150 square yards.

By D + 4 Lion-sur-Mer and Luc-sur-Mer with other pockets of resistance had been cleared and the main sites were in use.

The OBDs and ammunition companies in the GOLD and JUNO sectors were also operating from their main sites by this date.

CONSOLIDATION AND BUILD-UP OF TROOPS AND EQUIPMENT

The following table indicates the rate of build-up in the congested bridgehead and rear maintenance area:

D Day	*By D + 50 (July 26th and break-out)*
83,000 men	631,000 men
9,000 vehicles	153,000 vehicles
1,900 tons stores	689,000 tons stores

On June 9th the reconnaissance parties of various follow-up units were sent over. These units were 17 AOD, 17 Vehicle Company, 17 BAD and the Ordnance Maintenance Companies (British and Canadian).

It was obviously important to have 17 AOD operating effectively as soon as possible. This would be facilitated if the COO, DCOO and Sub-Depot Commanders were not dispersed and a deliberate risk was taken of sending them all over in the same craft. Unfortunately the ship was torpedoed in mid-Channel and sank. The only survivor was the COO (Colonel T. G. Gore). A second party was formed and sent out four days later with the advance party and between that date and June 23rd the remainder of the unit with 3 Companies of 16 AOD arrived. BMPs for the depot began to arrive on June 14th.

Progressively the load was transferred from the OBDs and by July 2nd the depot had taken the full load and beach maintenance from OBDs ceased. The site for the depot was at Vaux-sur-Aure just off the beach in open fields in the triangle Port-en-Bessin–Bayeux–Arromanches. The site was satisfactory for field storage but difficulties were experienced at first because the area was also occupied by the units of 2 Divisions and a tank transporter column.

A great deal of work had to be done on the depot roads owing to the load of traffic and the bad weather. Construction units of the Royal Engineers did tremendous work but the traffic circuits gave continuous trouble up to the end of the effective life of the depot. There was no enemy interference by day and only minor air activity at night with a few casualties.

The depot, operating from BMPs, received 52,000 tons and issued 10,000 tons in July. In August receipts were 57,000 tons and issues 23,000 tons. At one stage the load on the depot caused an accumulation of indents. The War Office agreed that all outstanding indents should be sent to Greenford under the Close Theatre Maintenance system. This gave the depot a fresh start and thereafter the unit was able to carry the load of maintaining all British and Canadian troops until September 14th, 6 weeks after the break-out, when 14 AOD took over.

Owing to the failure to capture Caen it was impossible to set up an AOD there as originally planned and no suitable site existed. On the other hand 17 AOD could not hope to carry the load in field storage conditions and from Landing Reserves and BMPs indefinitely. The decision was therefore made to construct a depot at Audrieu a few miles short of Caen. The site was still in our own gun lines when work started. The reconnaissance party which had landed on June 28th set to work to plan the depot and the unit was phased in to prepare the site with RE assistance. As the depot did not become effective until after the breakout its activities will be described later.

VEHICLES

The reconnaissance party of 17 Vehicle Company was lost at sea with the rest of the 17 AOD party. However, the first elements of the vehicle company arrived on the planned date of June 13th, but the remainder were delayed for several days by storms in the Channel. Each party brought in the maximum number of reserve vehicles, but the delay in the arrival of men and vehicles hampered the establishment of fully operating vehicle parks.

When the load could be properly estimated it was realized that one vehicle company was not enough, and 16 Vehicle Company was sent as a reinforcement, technical control of all activity remaining with 17 Vehicle Company.

Vehicles arriving at the beach required a good deal of attention before being absorbed into the fit stocks of a vehicle park. They had to be de-waterproofed and serviced. Also in the early days they had to discharge the AF G1098 or other stores with which they had been loaded so as to conserve shipping space. This took time because of the necessity for strict control of movement in the congested rear maintenance area.

The companies remaining in the United Kingdom assisted in the preparation of replacement vehicles for the voyage and in some cases acted as escorts. When this could not be done difficulties occurred. Occasionally, owing to failure to inform Ordnance, there were no drivers to meet craft containing unaccompanied vehicles. Quick turn round of these craft was essential and individuals who had never driven before were employed to unload vehicles. A man was put into the driver's seat, the engine started, first gear engaged and the vehicle precipitated into 3 ft of water. Not surprisingly, this practice tended to add to the number of unfit vehicles.

The site chosen for the vehicle parks was in the 17 AOD area to the south-west of Vaux-sur-Aure. Internal traffic circuits had to be planned to conform with those on the main roads which had not been built to carry the weight of traffic to which they were now subjected. Within the vehicle area there were no roads in the normal sense of the word, only a few lanes or tracks, some semi-metalled but none capable of taking more than one line of traffic.

Although restriction of the bridgehead prevented the selection of more suitable sites, it did enable the Royal Engineers to provide excellent construction service during this period and so movement was maintained. After the breakout the RE services were required elsewhere.

The parks were run by 17 Vehicle Company assisted by about 25 per cent of 16 Vehicle Company, the remainder being fully engaged on ferrying vehicles from beach to park.

AMMUNITION

The ammunition sections of the OBDs and the independent ammunition companies kept supply going until the arrival of 17 BAD on June 11th.

The control of all dumps of ammunition was now assumed by 17 BAD, which was further reinforced by 15 BAD on June 18th, and this depot took over the dumps in 104 Beach Sub-Area. By this time 1 Ordnance Maintenance Company with 4 ammunition roadhead sections and 8 forward ammunition maintenance sections had arrived.

All these units were operating in the congested bridgehead and Second Army took over control of all ammunition stocks. The importance of building up these stocks was obvious. On D-Day alone 6,500 tons of all natures had been landed over the beaches and the daily average over the first 10 days exceeded 8,000 tons. The peak effort was 16,000 tons in 1 day and the maximum tonnage held at the roadheads was 125,765.

On July 12th, 12 BAD arrived and acted as an overflow depot, because stocks had now become unbalanced. An enormous amount of AA ammunition had been phased in at the early stages in anticipation of an air threat which did not materialize. Other natures such as 17-pounder and 75-mm were expended at less than the planned rate.

On the other hand, there was a shortage of 105-mm and 5.5-inch gun, 3-inch mortar and medium machine gun ammunition, which led to the undesirable practice of selective discharge of ships. Later shipments were adjusted in accordance with actual expenditure.

ANCILLARY UNITS

The first mobile laundry and bath units landed on June 18th. The bath sections operated well forward while the laundry sections provided facilities for the hospitals pending the arrival of the base hospital laundries.

An Army Industrial Gas Unit landed on June 24th, earlier than originally planned, thus reducing the number of empty cylinders which had to be sent back to the United Kingdom for filling and re-issue.

GENERAL

By the middle of June a restricted but adequate bridgehead had been established. A roadhead had been formed in the Bayeux area and this developed into the Rear Maintenance Area. The First Key Plan was considerably modified by the delay in the capture of Caen.

The build-up of Ordnance Stores had been very satisfactory from the beginning. No critical deficiencies were reported and the first two shortages notified were toothbrushes and underclothing.

The DOS paid a visit soon after D-Day and was much encouraged by what he saw.

An advanced section of 21st Army Group, which included the DDOS, moved over about D + 15 and was attached to Headquarters L of C. The DDOS L of C was Colonel A. N. C. Varley, who had a similar appointment in North Africa with the First Army. His qualities of ingenuity and initiative were to prove even more useful in this campaign.

Rear Headquarters 21st Army Group began to move in on July 13th and was in control of the base installations by the time of the break-out at the beginning of August.

The total strength of just under 5,000 all ranks was large in the prevailing circumstances. Military headquarters in war (and for that matter government departments at all times) always seem to grow despite the most genuine efforts to keep them within bounds. Apart from Civil Affairs, and other branches whose task, however important, is subsidiary to the main purpose of defeating the enemy, other branches are formed to coordinate control and screen the work of the executive branches, which then have to be enlarged in order to cope with the additional work they are given.

Although the period of attrition continued for longer than was expected the break-out when it did occur was the more effective. The static period of nearly 2 months enabled the bridgehead to be organized and well stocked. The administrative machine was able to meet the demands which were to be made on it. A great deal of work was put into a scheme for the "winterization" of the RMA, and the RAOC was much involved in the supply of material for the installations there. Much of this effort was wasted owing to the rapid advance and early establishment of an advanced base.

THE BREAK-OUT AND PURSUIT TO BELGIUM

The last days of July and the beginning of August marked the end of the period of attrition and the beginning of a rapid advance which cleared most of France and Belgium. General Montgomery confounded the critics who had complained of lack of progress. Although there was a great deal of hard fighting around Caen and in the enclosed "bocage" country, the enemy was forced to expend his effort in a series of unsuccessful counter-attacks in which his armoured forces wasted away. This fighting was concentrated on the eastern flank and the way was paved for a break-through by the Americans to the west.

Through the gap so created the American Third Army under the dynamic General Patton moved irresistibly and with a wide encircling movement caught the German Seventh Army in the Falaise area. Trapped between the Americans to the south and the British Second and Canadian First Armies to the north, the German forces were destroyed. Some remnants managed to escape across the River Seine. In a vigorous pursuit the Americans liberated Paris and advanced towards the French frontier, the British Second Army moved into Belgium, liberating Brussels and Antwerp and approaching the Dutch frontier, while the Canadian First Army successively cleared the Channel ports.

This phase of the campaign came to an end with an attempt to establish a bridgehead over the Rhine by forcing the bridges at Nijmegen and linking up with the 1st Airborne Division which landed at Arnhem. This bold move, which was given the code name of MARKET GARDEN, just failed.

A pause then occurred with most of Belgium in our hands. The ports of Havre, Dieppe, Boulogne, Calais and Ostend were occupied but Dunkirk was still held by the Germans. The port of Antwerp could not be used until the enemy had been driven out of the country on both sides of the River Scheldt and the estuary had been cleared of mines.

THE LOGISTIC PROBLEM

The events which followed the break-out completely transformed the logistic situation. Rapid movement was necessary and for a time the fighting became less intense.

It was now a petrol rather than an ammunition operation, although ammunition must be readily available as soon as the situation showed signs of stabilizing again.

The Second Army established in succession roadheads at Laigle, Beauvais, Brussels, Louvain and Bourg Leopold. Corps stocks were held in FMCs, also formed in succession along the L of C. The transport to carry the stores for these various dumps was obtained by grounding 8 Corps and using its transport for 12 and 30 Corps which were engaged in the pursuit. The daily import tonnage over the beaches was reduced from 16,000 to 7,000. This was possible because of the considerable stocks which had been accumulated during the static period and the shortening of the L of C which would result from the occupation of the various Channel ports. It was thus possible to take a considerable amount of transport from the RMA to augment the resources of the advancing formations.

These necessary measures resulted in Ordnance Stores being given a low priority which led eventually to certain difficulties which are mentioned later.

In the original plan it was expected that, once the enemy realized that he could not drive the Allies into the sea he would make a fighting withdrawal, first contesting the line of the River Seine. The administrative build-up in support of a steady advance of this sort was covered by the existence of certain units such as 15 AOD in the Order of Battle.

But, as at Stalingrad, Alamein and Tunis, the German field commander —under the influence of Hitler's powerful one-track mind—held on too long and was defeated. A rapid retreat followed and intermediate positions could not be held. The only possible place for an advanced base for 21st Army Group was now Belgium.

During the advance units were dependent on OFPs for their requirements of Ordnance Stores. The stocks at roadheads and FMCs were limited by the availability of RASC transport which was further reduced by the low priority given to Ordnance Stores in relation to other commodities. However, something could be done about this. 15 Forward Trailer Section, which had originally been planned to support three tank Brigades, was used as a stores convoy unit, and later on 15 Stores Transit Sub-Depot was deployed at Second Army roadhead to reinforce 1 Ordnance Maintenance Company. This was necessary because stocks of Ordnance Stores had to be built up at roadheads as transport opportunities offered. It was no good waiting for demands and then finding that transport was committed elsewhere.

Although 17 FTS was planned to support 8 Corps, which was now grounded, the nature of its scaling, largely backing for Sherman tanks, made it a useful reserve of urgent fighting stores. The unit was therefore moved well forward in the Second Army area.

VEHICLES

The supply of vehicles now assumed paramount importance. Army vehicle parks moved forward with their formations. Other vehicle parks were located at suitable points along the L of C to control the supply of vehicles being ferried to the Armies. As the speed of the advance increased these staging points changed with disconcerting frequency.

The shortage of RASC transport for the delivery of Ordnance Stores made it essential to employ all replacement vehicles for this purpose. For this and other reasons a turn round of 6 or 7 days was normal in the delivery of replacement vehicles from base to army parks.

Thus the normal occupational disease of RAOC vehicle units, shortage of drivers, was aggravated. The RCOC came to the rescue and 1,500 Canadian Ordnance drivers were sent out from the United Kingdom to assist in the ferrying of stock vehicles. As soon as possible the ports of Ostend and Boulogne were used for the import of vehicles from the United Kingdom and 15 and 17 Transit Vehicle Parks were sent to these ports, but it was some time before the capacity of the Normandy beaches could be dispensed with so far as the needs of the forward troops were concerned.

In October 1944 the DOS decided that the time had now come for vehicle units to be separated from their AODs and he appointed an officer (Colonel T. G. Gore) to control and coordinate their activities. He was called COO—Vehicle Companies and his duties were:

(a) Siting and development of vehicle parks.
(b) Organization for the receipt of vehicles into the theatre, and their deployment in the various parks.
(c) Allocation of staff to meet fluctuating loads.
(d) Technical efficiency of vehicle companies.
(e) Backloading of vehicles to the United Kingdom.

AMMUNITION

We have seen that the problems of a rapid advance on a long L of C had been anticipated by the inclusion in the Order of Battle of a large number of Forward Maintenance Ammunition Sections to deal with grounded stocks in many locations. In addition to the normal roadhead stocks intermediate dumps were formed along the L of C. As soon as the port of Dieppe was opened 3 BAD moved there to handle ammunition for the First Canadian Army.

When the Army reached the Brussels area heavy demands were received for tank and small arms ammunition. Field Artillery ammunition was also scarce and it was necessary to send 112,000 rounds of 25-pounder by air from the United Kingdom.

MARKET GARDEN

This operation involved considerable tactical and administrative risks, which were considered to be justified by the need to exploit success and keep the enemy on the run. It failed because the Germans could still deploy considerable strength on the River Rhine which was a good natural defensive position.

The operation was undertaken at a time when the administrative resources of Second Army were strained to the utmost. By the middle of September the stocks in 6 Army Roadhead were still too low and its location to the west of Brussels was too far back, with the city interposed between it and the forward troops. However, there was no time to form an advanced roadhead before the airborne troops landed at Arnhem on September 17th.

Direct RAOC support of 1st Airborne Division consisted of the ADOS,

Lieutenant-Colonel G. A. Mobbs, 1 other officer and 13 ORs, with an OFP consisting of 1 officer and 12 ORs. A reconnaissance party of 1 officer and 5 ORs was to land on September 17th to find a site for the stores. The remainder were to follow on September 18th, the stores being dropped later on.

The reconnaissance party landed according to plan but soon found themselves engaged in the defence of the northern end of the road bridge. No contact was possible with the main glider party or OFP, and in fact the party fought as Infantry until the end of the operation when they were captured, 4 of the 6 being wounded.

The main glider party landed on September 18th, and as they were unable to make contact with the reconnaissance party the Ordnance Headquarters and OFP were sited in the Divisional Headquarters area. No stores reached the OFP because the dropping zone was not captured and only a fraction of the stores fell in the narrowing bridgehead. Further attempts at replenishment met with little success and like the reconnaissance party the main party and OFP fought as Infantry up to the end of the operation.

Only one RAOC soldier got back across the river. Three men were killed and the ADOS and 13 others were captured. Eight of them were wounded. One glider had its tow-rope cut by anti-aircraft fire and was forced to land in enemy-occupied Holland. The men were helped by the Dutch underground until the area was finally liberated by the Canadians.

The Rear Maintenance Area

THE AODS

The task of maintaining the British and Canadian units with Ordnance stores fell upon 17 AOD from early July, when the OBDs closed down, until September 14th when 14 AOD took over.

This was a long period considering that 17 AOD was only planned as a temporary depot working from Beach Maintenance Packs. It was of course hoped that 14 AOD occupying good covered accommodation in Caen would take over quite soon but this did not happen.

Nevertheless 17 AOD was able to cope, partly because of its accessibility in the limited bridgehead area before the end of July, and partly because the low priority of Ordnance stores for some weeks after the break-out limited the tonnage which could be issued. In the main, however, the depot owed its success to the high standard of training which had been received in the months before the invasion.

14 AOD

The reconnaissance party, arriving on June 28th, found that Caen was still occupied by the enemy. It was not finally captured until July 9th

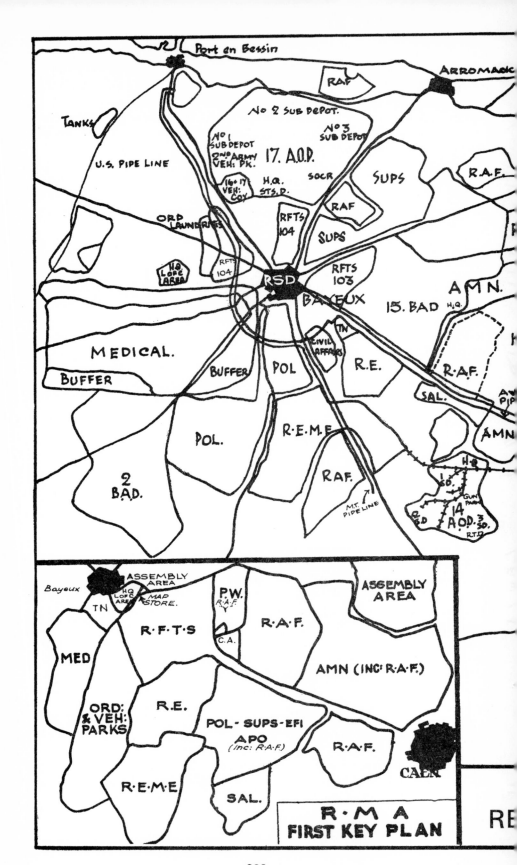

R·M·A
FIRST KEY PLAN

288

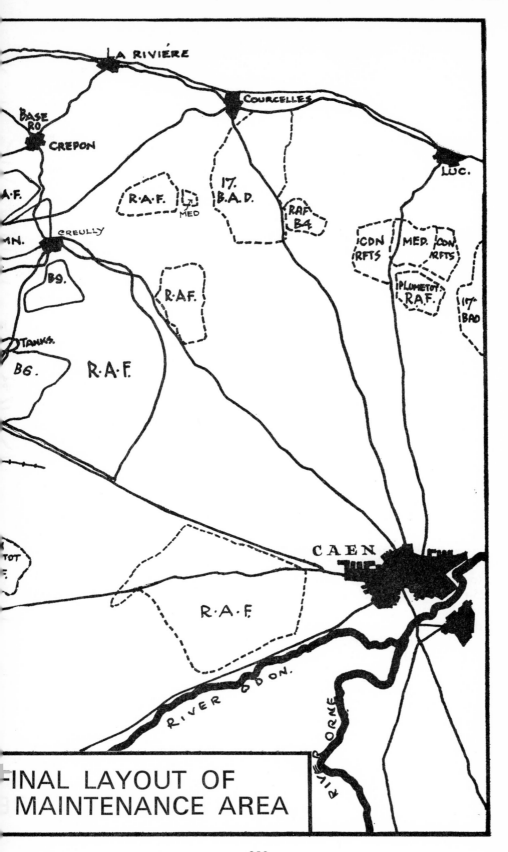

LA RIVIÈRE

COURCELLES

BASE
RO

CREPON

LUC.

A.F.

R·A·F.

17.
B.A.D.

MED

RAF
B4

CREULLY

CDN
RFTS

MED.

CDN
RFTS

MN.

B9.

R·A·F.

PLUMETOT
R.A.F.

17"
BAD

TANKS.

B6.

R·A·F.

TOT

CAEN

R·A·F.

RIVER ODON.

RIVER ORNE.

FINAL LAYOUT OF
MAINTENANCE AREA

and had by then been subjected to such heavy bombing and artillery fire that a suitable site for a permanent depot was unlikely to be obtainable.

In any event the formation of 14 AOD could not be delayed and a new site had to be found and developed. Eight possible locations were inspected and the choice fell on Audrieu, adjacent to the Bayeux–Caen railway and about 9 miles from Caen.

The Royal Engineers were confident that the area could be drained and made fit for use, but experience made the local inhabitants sceptical. However, a decision had to be made and all available sites were unsuitable.

Work proceeded rapidly. The staff of the depot were trained to erect their own Romney hutting, but they also received much useful assistance from the RE experts who advised on the best locations for buildings. By the time that the depot was opened on September 14th, 10 days after the planned date, 178 huts had been erected, roads and railway spurs had been constructed, racking was assembled and 28,000 tons of stores put to stock.

Unfortunately the ship carrying all the depot stock records was sunk and the task of reconstituting the account was a daunting prospect. Heavy and continuous rain in the autumn soon proved that the local estimate of the unsuitability of the sub-soil was correct. The material which had to be used for hardcore broke up and the depot soon became a morass. Officers and men wore thigh boots continuously at work and it was a major problem to move heavy lift stores. Usable tracks for depot transport were difficult to find and maintain. Most of the transport had in any case been taken for use on the L of C and in the Army area.

Manpower was less of a problem. The depot was reinforced by the transfer from 17 AOD of the stores companies of 16 AOD. Considerable numbers of German prisoners were made available and they worked well, although they refused to handle gun barrels, no doubt reckoning that the Royal Artillery was effective enough without their help.

A special problem of re-equipment occurred at this time. Seven Field Regiments had their 105-mm self-propelled equipments replaced by 25-pounders. The self-propelled guns were primarily for the assault role and there was also an acute shortage of 105-mm ammunition which came from American sources. The stores required for this exchange were brought over by a detachment from 15 AOD, and the surpluses from this exchange and from the disbandment of 59th Division were absorbed into 14 AOD.

This was a very big task requiring a special area to be set aside and thorough planning and preparation. The disbandment of 59th Division was not a snap decision but had been planned if events took a certain course. The DOS 21st Army Group had been warned of this possibility and was able to make the necessary arrangements, an excellent example of good staff work. The ADOS of 59th Division was the brother of the

Chief of Staff 21st Army Group which may or may not have had a bearing on the matter.

Some stores were an embarrassment to the depot and no issues were made. Examples were telegraph poles (part of the Signal Officer in Chief's reserve) the need for which was based on an excessive estimate of the disruption of land lines to Belgium by the RAF, and anti-aircraft gun mountings which were scaled for a threat of air attack which did not materialize.

The shortage of road transport made the development of the rail L of C an important matter to 14 AOD. The bridges over the River Seine had been destroyed and until the end of September it was necessary to establish railheads south of the river, a road link across the river and forward movement by rail after that. However, by the end of September the bridge at Le Manoir had been constructed and there was a rail service right through to Brussels. For various reasons the capacity was limited but it did ease the burden on road transport. An air supply service also operated from the airfield at Carpiquet just outside Caen.

The early capture of Antwerp enabled all the preliminary work to be done to establish an AOD there even though the port could not be used for some time. As a result 15 AOD was able to take the load from the beginning of 1945 and 14 AOD was the main supplying depot for the Armies for 100 days only. But although the period was short it was a critical one in the maintenance of 21st Army Group. It is a tribute to the versatility and determination of the staff of 14 AOD that they performed their heavy task successfully in such difficult conditions.

VEHICLES

The area occupied by 17 Vehicle Company could not long survive the removal for other duties of the RE construction unit and it was decided to accept no more vehicles there. Existing stocks were transferred gradually to other parks and the forward areas.

However, until the port of Antwerp was opened, some vehicles must still be brought into the theatre over the Normandy beaches and new sites had to be found. These were very carefully selected, and although only fair weather standings could be found, movement never became impossible even during the winter months.

Piers had now been constructed within the "Mulberry" harbour and waterproofing of vehicles was no longer necessary.

A most efficient transit vehicle park organization was created, and this ensured that vehicles as they arrived in the theatre were properly serviced and passed to vehicle parks in a condition fit for immediate issue.

AMMUNITION

By the time of the break-out there were no less than four BADs—17, 15, 12 and 2—in the Rear Maintenance Area. Most of the serviceable stocks were required in the forward area and movement took place as transport became available. The BADs were also transferred as the advanced base began to take shape and 2 BAD was the first to move to a new site near Brussels at the beginning of October.

A Field Ammunition Repair Factory was established in the RMA. Its main task was to deal with ammunition returned from units after each battle. This ammunition was nearly always unboxed and required 100 per cent inspection before being accepted as fit for issue.

THE ADVANCED BASE

(September 4th to December 31st 1944)

After the failure of MARKET GARDEN it was clear that the Allied forces would have to consolidate and re-group before launching the next phase of the offensive which should be decisive. There was no chance of the war being over before the winter set in.

During this period the landing in the south of France (ANVIL) took place. The American and French forces linked with the Americans 12th Army Group from the Normandy bridgehead. Gradually France was cleared, except for ports on the west coast, and the Armies advanced towards the Rhine.

Meanwhile the first task of 21st Army Group was to clear the Scheldt estuary so that the port of Antwerp could be opened and an advanced base be established in the Antwerp–Brussels area. The next stage was to occupy the country up to the west bank of the Rhine.

The Canadian Army with some British formations under command was given the task of occupying the land on either side of the Scheldt estuary. It was a difficult operation in flat, largely waterlogged country intersected by dykes. Fighting was heavy and prolonged, lasting from early October to November 8th. Mine clearance and other work was necessary before the port could be used. It was opened to coastal shipping on November 26th and to deep-draught shipping on November 28th.

Immediately Antwerp was captured, on September 4th, a reconnaissance party from 15 AOD moved in to find suitable storage accommodation. By this timely action they were able to secure many premises which with very little RE work could be adapted as storehouses and offices. Planning and preparation started at once.

The COO of the depot was Colonel R. J. Volkers. It was clear from the beginning that the depot would be a much larger organization than either of its predecessors in the RMA. The British and Canadian Armies were now at full strength, a full scale L of C organization would develop in Belgium and there would be extensive commitments to the civilian population of Belgium and liberated Holland. The material requirements for the crossing of the Rhine and advance into Germany were bound to be very great.

Within a week Colonel Volkers had found sites for his sub-depots and produced a key plan which was approved by the Base Sub-Area Headquarters at Antwerp. He brought forward his Sub-Depot Commanders and they planned and developed the buildings and areas allotted to them.

Most of the MT Sub-Depot was in locations a mile or so to the south of Antwerp on the Boom road. Stapelaere Factory held "A" vehicle spares and another factory, known as the Camouflage Factory on account of the skilful camouflage which the Germans had put up when they used it for repair of aircraft engines, housed miscellaneous and proprietary items. Tyres were held in a brickworks in the same area. "B" vehicle spares were stored in the Stads magazine, a warehouse in the centre of Antwerp.

The Technical and Warlike Stores Sub-Depot was located in buildings in an area known as the Rivierenhof on the north-eastern side of the town. The Signal Officer in Chief's Reserve was in dockside storage.

Accommodation for the Clothing and General Stores Sub-Depot was found at Malines between Antwerp and Brussels. The locations were served by rail and inland water transport as well as road.

The Stores Transit Sub-Depot was located at the Rampart d'Hoboken in Antwerp. It dealt with the normal through traffic of a transit sub-depot and also coordinated issues from the depot. The site was formerly a German arsenal and attempts had been made to destroy it, so a good deal of cleaning up was necessary.

As soon as the stocks of 17 AOD had been handed over to 14 AOD in the Rear Maintenance Area the unit was available to join 15 AOD which was then re-named 15/17 AOD.

Certain sub-units retained their old identity, for example 17 Stores Transit Sub-Depot was located at Bruges and dealt with all Ordnance stores passing through that port. Its main tasks were the return of repairable assemblies to the United Kingdom and the supply of unaccompanied AF G1098 equipment.

The Returned Stores Depots were split by function. 15 RSD dealt with MT and technical stores and was located in Antwerp. The main task was the identification and conditioning of scarce items which, if serviceable, were returned to stock.

The RSD of 17 AOD dealt with clothing and general stores and was located at Brussels. The organization included a laundry and facilities for the repair of clothing, boots and general stores.

15 Forward Trailer Section, after acting as a stores convoy unit during the pursuit finally functioned as an improvised stores section to the Army Base Workshops in the Antwerp area.

There were many high grade civilians who had lost their jobs under the German occupation and were very keen to accept work in the AOD. Recruiting was carried out by the AOD in Antwerp and Brussels with excellent results. The Army provided a mid-day meal, which was a great incentive as civilian rations had been very poor during the occupation. Thorough training was carried out and depot procedures were written in French.

By the time that the port of Antwerp was opened the depot was already employing 3,900 military and civilian staff and occupied 1,250,000 sq ft of covered and 627,000 sq ft of open storage space. In November 1,300 tons of stores were handled.

The unit was already the size of a Base Ordnance Depot and was considerably dispersed. The sub-depots were self-contained and virtually autonomous and were re-named "depots", which gave a better picture of the degree of responsibility extended to the Lieutenant-Colonels who commanded them.

Until the port of Antwerp was opened stocks for the AOD were gradually moved forward from the RMA and issues from the United Kingdom were sent through Boulogne, Dieppe or Ostend (Havre was allocated to the Americans). During this period 58,000 tons of Ordnance stores passed through the Channel ports.

By the end of November the flow of stores from the RMA, which had practically ceased for lack of transport at the time of the pursuit, was now resumed and inroads were being made into the 65,000 tons, about half of which was required in the Advanced Base. The remainder was required in the RMA or had to be returned to the United Kingdom or was disposed of locally. This task fell to the lot of 14 AOD as the staff of 16 AOD were transferred to reinforce 15 AOD which eventually grew to $3\frac{1}{2}$ times the size of a normal AOD.

The winter started early and proved exceptionally severe. The usual difficulty occurred over the supply of winter clothing and tentage. Shortage of transport prevented it from being sent forward from the RMA when it was first needed, and the supply position in the United Kingdom was bad. However, deficiencies were made up and an increase in scale was approved but not fully up to Scale 1 of *War Clothing Regulations*. Local production was developed and 10,500 rabbit-skin fur coats were issued to the Armies in December.

Although many circumstances favoured the rapid and efficient development of 15 AOD the depot area was subjected to almost daily bombardment by V1s and V2s. The bombardment started in October 1944 and continued right through to March 1945.

VEHICLES

The effect of the pursuit into Belgium and the attempt to break-through to Arnhem caused a heavy wastage in "A" vehicles the replacement of which was a top priority. By September 27th the force was 30 per cent below establishment in tanks. Stocks in the Armoured Replacement Group were down to 15 per cent and depot stocks to 5 per cent.

Urgent action was taken in October to replace these deficiencies and it was arranged that 40 tanks per day would be sent in through Boulogne. Early in November LSTs began to arrive in Ostend and these two ports dealt with the intake of "A" vehicles until Antwerp was opened. Transporters were scarce and much work on the restoration of the railway was necessary so that the clearance of "A" vehicles to units and vehicle parks was difficult.

The shipment of tanks absorbed all the MT shipping lift to forward ports so that "B" vehicles continued to be shipped to the RMA at the rate of 250 a day until Antwerp could be used.

It was not found possible to provide adequate transit vehicle park capacity at the RMA, four Channel ports and Antwerp simultaneously. The large organization already in the RMA was kept going until the flow was transferred to Antwerp. A similar organization was created there and also, later on, at Ostend.

The main areas for vehicle parks were Antwerp and Brussels, separate parks being formed for "A" and "B" vehicles.

Returned vehicle parks now became an important commitment because of the programme of vehicle recovery and the creation of advanced base workshops in the Antwerp area. Holdings in returned vehicle parks became too great for units which had a war establishment of only about 40 men. Some parks held as many as 6,000 vehicles. A high percentage were completely beyond repair and should not have been back loaded.

Ammunition was not removed from AFVs before they were back-loaded and ammunition examiners were borrowed from sub-area staffs to recover and make safe this ammunition. On one occasion two port ammunition detachments were employed full time for a fortnight on this task.

Pilfering of vehicle kits was a major problem at all times. It occurred at every stage from issue in the United Kingdom to receipt by the unit. All sorts of preventive measures were tried, and some improvement resulted but pilfering was never eliminated, except in the case of AFV kits. An Armoured Stores Company was formed and all kits of replacement AFVs were held there. RAOC Kitting Sections were allotted to delivery squadrons.

By the end of 1944 there were 4 separate Vehicle Companies working under the control and coordination of the COO Vehicle Companies.

AMMUNITION

The stocking of 2 BAD in the Advanced Base was slow owing to limited port facilities and the diversion of most road and rail traffic from the RMA to Army roadheads, the first priority being to raise forward holdings to target levels.

When this had been done 2 BAD was rapidly built up to a holding of

75,000 tons. The level was not quite so satisfactory as it might appear. The stocks were unbalanced and there was an acute shortage of field and medium natures.

Early in December 3 BAD moved from Dieppe to the Ostend area.

At the end of the year 17 BAD moved up from the RMA to an area north of Antwerp. Its development was hampered by attacks on the area by V weapons and consequent limitations on the use of Antwerp as an ammunition port.

LAUNDRIES

The inability of divisional laundries to wash large quantities of bulk items such as blankets, coupled with the presence of convalescent depots, reinforcement camps and hospitals in the Army areas made it essential to provide extensive services in the Advanced Base and Army areas.

34 Base Laundry moved to Eindhoven, 4 Base Hospital Laundry was established at Ostend and 2 Base Hospital Laundry at Brussels. 35 Base Laundry moved to Antwerp. Two hundred civilian laundries were placed under contract to serve troops on the L of C in Belgium.

INDUSTRIAL GAS

With the advance into Belgium considerable local resources became available and these were exploited by the various industrial gas units.

1 Base Industrial Gas Unit supervised the work of civilian installations at Caen, Rouen and Lille.

3 Base Industrial Gas Unit did similar work in Brussels, Antwerp, Ghent and Breda.

Although the demand for industrial gases for workshops and inert gas for flamethrowers remained high, existing units were sufficient to meet the requirements and 2 BIGU was not sent out.

PREPARATION FOR THE RHINE CROSSING AND FINAL ADVANCE
(January 1st to March 24th 1945)

The winter campaign involved clearance of the area between the Maas and the Rhine. Before progress could be made Von Rundstedt launched his attack on the American First Army in the Ardennes. The operation lasted from mid-December 1944 to mid-January 1945.

The Americans were caught off balance and the early rapid German advance was a threat to the advanced base in Belgium. The immediate effect was to delay the operations of 21st Army Group and cause a re-grouping of the forces north of the "bulge" under Field-Marshal Montgomery.

Emergency action was taken to replace the losses of equipment which the Americans had suffered. The vehicle depot at Antwerp issued 100 Sherman tanks in 48 hours. It was not a straightforward issue as the

British wireless sets had to be replaced by those of American pattern. Other equipment issued included 25-pounder guns and ammunition and some American natures of ammunition. There was, however, no significant interference with the build-up of the Advanced Base.

The Americans drove the Germans back with heavy loss, and the ultimate effect was to weaken the German resistance to the crossing of the Rhine in the spring.

The clearance of the 21st Army Group front up to the Rhine was carried out in three operations. These were:

BLACKCOCK to clear the area south of the River Roer, which took 12 Corps from January 16th to 26th.

VERITABLE was undertaken by First Canadian Army and 30 Corps. It lasted from February 8th to March 10th and involved heavy fighting in country which had been well adapted for defence by extensive mining and flooding.

GRENADE was an offensive across the Roer, undertaken by the Ninth American Army in conjunction with VERITABLE.

The assault across the Rhine took place on March 24th which gave 14 days' preparation from the time the west bank was cleared, although a great deal of preliminary work was done before that period. By this time the equipment position was really good, armoured units in particular lacking for nothing.

ADMINISTRATION

The first 3 months of 1945 was a period of intense activity for the administrative staff and services. Road and rail communications had to be developed in Belgium and Holland to carry the needs of a tremendous concentration of troops during a period of heavy fighting.

From the RAOC point of view the main problems were:

1. The supply of vast quantities of ammunition both for the fighting in operation VERITABLE and the dumping programme for the Rhine crossing.

2. Development of the AOD and the use of local resources. Clothing, tentage and accommodation stores were extremely important at this stage.

3. Canadian and British formations were transferred from Italy, and these had to be absorbed by an already overloaded administrative organization. Large re-equipment programmes were involved.

4. A re-grouping of administrative resources so as to make Belgium a base for the drive into Germany. This meant that the RMA in Normandy would be closed down and units transferred to the Advanced Base. This was not easy because of the amount of "tidying-up" which was required in the RMA. The low priority of Ordnance stores during the pursuit into Belgium increased the quantity to be transferred before the RMA could be closed down.

THE ADVANCED BASE

The preliminary work on the AOD, before the port of Antwerp was opened, now began to bear fruit.

During January the full load of maintenance was accepted. The programme was First Canadian Army on January 1st, Second British Army on January 10th and L of C troops by January 22nd. The plan worked smoothly. By the end of the month receipts had increased to 83,000 tons during the month and issues to 60,000 tons. The number of items demanded was 191,000.

This was only the beginning for by March items demanded had risen to 469,000. March receipts were 112,000 tons and issues 97,000 tons.

In April the area occupied by the depot was 3,500,000 sq ft of covered and just short of 30 million sq ft of open accommodation. In the same month 140,000 tons were handled. This included the considerable transit and returned stores activity, also the re-stocking of OFPs who were sent to the depot before going forward and were much impressed by this service.

The RAOC strength by April 1945 was 2,500 with 1,000 military labour and 11,000 civilians. The number of item headings in store was 126,000.

Provision branches kept a close watch on issues and, by adjusting the scaled items in accordance with the incidence of demands, ensured that stocks covered fast moving and vital items and that dead stock was avoided.

The experience of other theatres was confirmed here, namely that large receipt transit areas were necessary so that items could be identified and sorted before being put to stock in the correct location. Thus multi-locations were avoided. Quick turn-round of ships and transport was possible without congestion and confusion in the storage area.

V-missile attacks were continuous from October 1944 to the last week in March 1945. This made dispersion an important factor. No less than 5,960 missiles were recorded as having landed and the average number to fall daily per square mile in the greater Antwerp area was 18. The worst day was March 8th 1945 when 120 missiles were reported.

AA units were brought in to deal with the V1 missiles and their requirements were met by a special unit sent over from the United Kingdom and working in conjunction with 14 FTS which had transferred its L of C role from the RMA to the Advanced Base.

The importance of local manufacturing and repair resources to RSDs is shown in the figure of 21,000 tons of clothing and general stores received, sorted, repaired and re-issued at 17 RSD in the month of March 1945. The depot also took on the task of holding and issuing Civil Affairs stores of Ordnance origin.

Early in 1945 Colonel Volkers moved to HQ L of C as a prelude to taking up a Brigadier's appointment in the Far East. His place was taken by Colonel R. C. Hiam, who had previously commanded 14 AOD.

VEHICLES

The main problem of vehicle units in this period was caused by the transfer of units from Italy, operation GOLDFLAKE. "A" and "B" vehicles were sent from Italy to Marseilles and began to arrive on February 20th, but only 50 drivers were available to accompany them.

Reinforcements in the shape of a detachment of 141 Vehicle Park from the RMA were sent to establish a receipts park, pending the arrival of a unit from Italy.

The ferrying of these vehicles across France was an urgent task requiring special arrangements. A vehicle company was formed from the vehicle units in France and Belgium and some reinforcements from the United Kingdom. The men were sent to Marseilles by rail and air. A 7-day turnround was achieved by returning the drivers to Marseilles by air when they had delivered the vehicles.

The additional load was ultimately met by two vehicle parks from the United Kingdom and two from the Mediterranean theatre.

AMMUNITION

There was a very large build-up of ammunition for the crossing of the Rhine. Second Army formed No. 10 Roadhead between the Maas and the Rhine with target stocks of 60,000 tons of ammunition there. In addition to the roadhead activity some ammunition was drawn direct from railhead and dumped at gun positions, while 30 Corps drew 600 tons a day direct from the advanced base.

15 BAD was sent forward to Belgium, bringing the number of BADs in the advanced base up to four. In addition 3 Field Ammunition Repair Factory was moved up to the Advanced Base from the RMA.

SPECIAL TASKS

The units coming under command of Second Army from First Canadian Army had to be re-equipped in the short time available before the Rhine crossing operation.

A special train was sent to Second Army Ordnance railhead and units drew from this consignment controlled stores for which demands had been received at the advanced base only 48 hours earlier. All formations were fully equipped well before D-Day for the operation.

The operation involved 6th Airborne Division securing a bridgehead on the right bank of the river, and, although this formation operated from the United Kingdom, the sea tail had to be re-equipped in the theatre, and special equipment was required.

An Ordnance sub-park was formed for this purpose and was sent over with the special packs from the United Kingdom. Some of the men for this sub-park were found from the theatre.

ORGANIZATION OF THE L OF C

With the break out of the bridgehead, advance into Belgium, and occupation of Brussels and Antwerp the L of C organization took shape. HQ L of C was located at Roubaix. There were two L of C areas, No. 11 covering that part of the L of C within 21st Army Group area which was in Belgium, and No. 12 being in France.

Excluded from these areas were an operational zone for the force investing Dunkirk and a corridor north of the Seine reserved for the American forces which had been allocated Havre as a port. Thus 12 Area was split into a zone covering northern France and a zone south of the Seine which represented an expansion of the RMA. HQ 11 L of C Area was at Malines and HQ 12 L of C Area at Arras.

Within these areas were various sub-areas and garrisons, depending on their size. The policy was to run-down and finally eliminate that portion of 12 L of C Area which was based on the RMA and located south of the Seine. This comprised three sub-areas until early 1945 when it was reduced to an "island" round the RMA, controlled by 5 Sub-Area. The remainder of 12 L of C Area also closed in towards the Somme.

All these processes enabled a greater concentration of military manpower to be effected in the vital area of the Advanced Base.

By the end of hostilities in Europe the RMA had become a garrison, concerned only with tidying up, 12 L of C Area had leap-frogged to take over the extension of the L of C to the left bank of the Maas, and northern France had become a sub-area responsibility. HQ L of C moved to Brussels.

The Ordnance Officers at the various headquarters on the L of C relieved the Ordnance Branch at HQ 21st Army Group of many important duties in connection with local administration so that operations could be given priority. One of the most important duties was the Ordnance aspect of port operation—the work of Port Ordnance and ammunition detachments. The painful lessons of earlier campaigns had now been learnt (only alas to be forgotten after 1945) and close liaison with the Transportation authorities ensured that all necessary sorting was carried out before the onward despatch of consignments of stores and ammunition from the port. Towards the end of the campaign the handling of captured material including "loot" was a real problem.

ORDNANCE SERVICES IN FORMATIONS

DDsOS of Corps and ADsOS of Formations carried out their duties in accordance with the training undertaken before the campaign and the lessons of earlier campaigns.

These lessons had been so well learnt that the work went smoothly and the only significant fault in organization was that ADsOS needed more staff and transport than was allowed on the establishment so that they could keep in hand certain essential reserves. This was necessary when supply was interrupted by shortage of transport and the low priority given to Ordnance stores.

Army troops were considerable in number and required an Army Troops OFP which was improvised from the 59th Divisional OFP for Second Army and 16 Forward Trailer Section for the First Canadian Army.

An important factor was the selection of officers for these appointments. DDsOS of Corps had considerable field experience and had proved that they possessed the right temperament for formation headquarters work. The same largely applied to the ADsOS.

The qualities required were initiative, foresight and the ability to inspire in Commanders and staff officers confidence in the Ordnance Services. The task is far from easy in times of stress and the strain on these officers was not always fully appreciated. They played a most important part in the smooth working of the Ordnance Services in the campaign.

ORDNANCE FIELD PARKS

21st Army Group's OFP organization was based on experience in the Western Desert and was more flexible than that devised at the beginning of the war. Normally divisional OFPs remained centralized and it was rare to detach a Brigade section to act independently.

The avoidance of dispersion was economic in store-holding and enabled full use to be made of storage capacity without sacrificing mobility.

Despite the need for a stores convoy unit, as indicated by experience in the Western Desert and Italy, none was provided in the establishment and improvisation was necessary. This was usually done by employing a sub-park of the Corps Ordnance Field Park and another sub-park was employed to hold the Corps reserves of vehicles and controlled stores.

Some idea of the extent of immediate Ordnance support required for the VERITABLE operation and the Rhine crossing (PLUNDER) may be gathered from the fact that, in addition to Canadian units, there were 10 OFPs or sub-parks employed in VERITABLE and 14 in PLUNDER.

MOBILE LAUNDRY AND BATH UNITS

These Divisional units fully justified their inclusion in the order of battle. They operated well forward and their value in raising morale was universally recognized.

THE FINAL ADVANCE

The crossing of the Rhine went smoothly. This was due to the heavy losses which the Germans had sustained in earlier battles, and also to the very thorough planning and preparation which preceded the operation.

The quantity of stores and ammunition which the RAOC had to supply has already been mentioned, but this included many new and unusual items such as Asdic Echo-Sounding Apparatus, Fluorescent Tape and Panels, Light Floats and Inflatable Lifebelts. The rehearsals used up large quantities of stores which had to be replaced.

The advance after crossing the river was rapid and 6 weeks later, on May 8th, the Germans capitulated. The formations which advanced right through beyond Hamburg to Lubeck were maintained from the advanced base in Belgium.

The usual problem of meeting urgent unforeseeable demands for fighting stores arose. Air freight which was controlled by Supreme Headquarters was not readily available because of the competing requirements of the American Armies and the extensive employment of aircraft to fly home liberated prisoners-of-war. Some RAOC units were grounded so as to form increased stores convoy unit capacity.

An example of the type of action required is provided by the case of certain tanks of a new type which had been issued to 11th Armoured Division. During the advance all these tanks developed a fault which required replacement of the fan belt. The fault had not occurred before. The demand for 200 fan belts was signalled to the United Kingdom. The stores were flown out and transferred to the 11th Armoured Divisional OFP who received them in time to prevent the advance from being held up.

On another occasion some vital items were required. The requirement was telephoned on the "fixed time call" to the War Office, the stores were sent from Old Dalby and reached the unit, which was well forward, in 18 hours. This period included some delay caused by fog.

Casualties were relatively light during these last few weeks and mobile laundries were reinforced from those attached to casualty clearing stations so as to increase the capacity for washing blankets.

More mobile laundries and bath units were sent forward to deal with the needs of liberated prisoners-of-war, displaced persons and the internees of Belsen and other concentration camps. Within 48 hours of the capture of Belsen 304 Mobile Laundry was working there, shortly to be followed by 304, 105, 305 and 310 Bath Sections.

AFTERMATH

The immediate effect of the German surrender was to give the RAOC in 21st Army Group a very large number of new problems.

21st Army Group now became a part of the Army of Occupation. A plan called ECLIPSE had already been produced and this outlined the main tasks to be carried out after the German surrender.

The first thing was to make good wastage and to bring unit clothing up to a peace-time standard of smartness, but this had to be done against a background of shortages, particularly of battledress.

Ammunition had to be collected, concentrated, sorted, inspected and made safe. Enemy ammunition must be taken over and units for this purpose were created from 1 and 12 BADs and certain port ammunition detachments and Ordnance ammunition companies.

A structure of base installations was gradually established in Germany and the advanced base in Belgium was progressively closed down. 14 AOD had completed its task in the RMA and was moved to Hamburg where it became the principle "rundown" organization, receiving surplus equipment from units which were being disbanded or reduced to lower establishment. A sub-depot for clothing and general stores was established at Wehmingen outside Hanover. A very fine, undamaged ammunition depot was found at Liebenau near Nienberg. Suitable sites were found for vehicle depots and parks on airfields and stretches of the autobahn.

While all this work was being done RAOC manpower was considerably reduced by the withdrawal of officers and men under various plans for demobilization, the return home of men who had served overseas for long periods, and the need for reinforcements in the Far East where Japan was still undefeated.

It had been the policy to keep down the ranks of the various Service appointments in 21st Army Group so that the DOS and the DDsOS of the Second Army and First Canadian Army were Brigadiers but other appointments such as DDOS 21st Army Group and COO 15/17 AOD were held at the rank of Colonel. The effect of this policy was that Ordnance and other Service appointments in 21st Army Group were at least one rank lower than appointments of comparable responsibility in other theatres.

The policy was changed for the Army of Occupation and the DOS became a Major-General. Brigadier Denniston returned home at this time and Major-General C. Cansdale took over. Brigadier L. E. Cutforth remained as DDOS.

ROYAL CANADIAN ORDNANCE CORPS

Although this history does not attempt to cover ground outside the activities of the RAOC, no picture of OVERLORD would be complete without mention of the very important part played by the Canadian Army.

The invasion forces included one Canadian Division, and by the time of the break-out 21st Army Group had increased to two Armies, one of which was the First Canadian Army. This consisted of a Headquarters and two Corps. There were three Canadian Infantry Divisions, two Armoured Divisions, two Independent Armoured Brigades and a full establishment of supporting arms and services.

The Army headquarters was staffed and organized so as to be able to absorb British formations under command, and this occurred regularly. In operation VERITABLE 30 Corps was under First Canadian Army command.

On the other hand there was no separate Canadian chain of supply behind the Army. Installations in the advanced base, on the L of C and at ports supporting 21st Army Group were British and supplied all the needs of both Armies. Stores peculiar to the Canadian forces were in the main passed through British installations but they were not pooled and Canadian liaison officers in British depots were able to watch the issue of these items of "continuing Canadian supply". They were also able to assist in ensuring that the system of supply was flexible enough to be adjustable to special situations.

Liaison was also greatly assisted by the "Canloan" scheme whereby certain Canadian officers served in British units. Under this scheme the RAOC benefited by the employment of 51 RCOC officers.

Apart from these arrangements the RCOC establishment in 21st Army Group was confined to the normal formation headquarters staffs and the organic Ordnance units of formations.

The organization closely resembled that of the British Army. The DDOS, Brigadier J. A. W. Bennett, had a good deal of service in England and many friends in the RAOC. He had also been out as DDOS of the Canadian Corps in Italy.

Canadian units were engaged in hard fighting around Caen and in the battle of the "Falaise pocket", but no exceptional difficulties in the supply of Ordnance stores arose owing to the thorough preparation for the operation and the successful build-up of stocks in the adjacent rear maintenance area.

The next task was the rapid advance along the French and Belgian coasts and the capture of the various ports. Here, the Canadian Army faced the same problem of priorities as the Second Army. Brigadier Bennett realized that transport for the supply of Ordnance stores would be at a premium and anticipated the difficulty by increasing the capacity of his OFPs. He obtained additional vehicles and trailers and replaced a number of 3-ton vehicles by 10-tonners. Tank transporters were obtained for the Corps field parks and, suitably adapted, they could carry a great quantity of stores. The additional transport and load-carrying capacity enabled First Army, when the situation demanded, to dump the stocks and release transport for the collection of stores from the RMA. At one time the DDOS had as many as nine dumps along the L of C.

This system was in marked contrast to that which existed in the

Second Army. Broadly speaking Ordnance was self-supporting in transport, leaving the RCASC transport for supplies, petrol and ammunition.

It may be argued that the Canadian system was wasteful compared with the British policy of pooling transport as much as possible. It is possible also that the Canadian Army was lavishly supplied with transport compared with the Second Army, but there is no firm evidence to support this contention. The misuse of transporters is of course only justified if the supply of replacement tanks is not interrupted.

On the other hand the system did successfully cover the difficult period of more than 4 months until the Army could draw from 15 AOD. The self-sufficiency of the Canadian Army in the supply of Ordnance stores at this stage is a tribute to the logistic judgement and persuasive powers of Brigadier Bennett and also to the staff in the Canadian Army who showed an uncommon appreciation of the significance of Ordnance problems.

As the Channel ports were cleared a limited flow of stores, vehicles and ammunition through them afforded some relief to the maintenance from the RMA, but the Advanced Base in Belgium would not be fully effective until the port of Antwerp was cleared and this task fell to the Canadian Army.

This largely amphibious operation took place in conditions which greatly favoured a determined defence. In spite of assistance from the United Kingdom both in troops (52nd Division) and in material, special equipment being flown in, the operation was a logistic nightmare. The ingenuity of the DDOS and his staff was severely tested but all difficulties were overcome.

Once the Scheldt was open the Advanced Base could soon be stocked to maintain both Armies of 21st Army Group, and First Canadian Army was given priority, the target date being January 1st 1945. By then the prolonged strain on the supply system had begun to have a noticeable effect and availability of stores against demands was low.

The opening of 15 AOD produced a rapid improvement which was reflected in the comments from the First Army.

ADOS 3rd Canadian Infantry Division stated that: "Receipts from 15/17 AOD against first 'bulk' submitted have been excellent."

3 Canadian Corps and Army Troops Sub-Park commented: "Our dues out are shrinking fast. . . . The morale of the unit has improved considerably within the past 2 weeks as clerks and storemen, for the first time since the unit mobilized, can see the results of their hard work with dues out being wiped off the cards and stocks beginning to accumulate in the bins."

ADOS 2 Canadian Corps Troops stated: "Due to the increasing flood of stores the percentage of issues has been exceptionally high. Stock of fast moving items in sub-parks has never been higher. It is now the exception when items demanded cannot be supplied. This is due to the efforts of

15/17 AOD. Terrific quantities of stores are passing through the Corps Transit Area."

It was satisfactory for the RCOC to know that the Canadians were the first to benefit from the hard fighting of the First Canadian Army in clearing the Scheldt estuary.

The Canadian Army was to have further heavy fighting in terrible conditions in operation VERITABLE, but by then the advanced base had been firmly established and supply difficulties were never to recur on the same scale.

RCOC units comprised 9 field parks, 8 sub-parks, 9 mobile laundry and bath units, the Canadian Ordnance Maintenance Company and a detachment of the Canadian Central Ordnance Depot.

In addition there were 8 salvage units, salvage being an Ordnance task in the Canadian though not in the British Army.

Cooperation between the RAOC and RCOC in 21st Army Group was always of a very high order and was a major factor in the success of the Ordnance Services.

CONCLUSION

OVERLORD was a dramatic and victorious climax to a war in Europe which had started disastrously 5 years before. It was a massive achievement of organization and logistics. The RAOC in 21st Army Group attained a very high level of efficiency as a result of the long, hard years of experience since the tentative, amateurish days of 1939 in France and 1940 in Norway.

The campaign illustrates the value of thorough preparation and training. The time and material resources necessary for success were available, and this will not often be the case. Moreover, a combined operation on the scale of OVERLORD is extremely unlikely to recur, which reduces the value of the campaign as a guide to the conduct of any war in the future.

CHAPTER TEN

SUBSIDIARY THEATRES

Malaya and Singapore

The story of the campaign in Malaya and the fall of Singapore seems to have all the inevitability of a Greek tragedy. The warning signs of Japanese aggression were just as clear as those which proceeded from Germany and Italy, but they were not heeded. Such defensive measures as were taken did not in any way match the real threat.

When the danger became acute the large civil populations in Hong Kong, Singapore and Burma were totally unprepared and on the whole could only hamper the efforts of the armed services in their fight against odds.

The services themselves were in an almost impossible position. The war in Europe had drawn heavily on the resources of the British Empire. Russia was tending at this stage to neutralize the strength of Germany on land but not at sea or in the air. She posed no sort of threat to Japan.

The British Empire and Holland could not muster sufficient strength at sea and in the air in the Far East to match Japanese resources, but a combination of faulty intelligence, wishful thinking and reliance on the moral effect of American armed forces in the Pacific led to the assumption that Japan had quite enough on her hands with her campaign on the Chinese mainland.

The most highly trained units of the Indian Army had already been absorbed into the campaigns in the Middle East, Iraq and Persia, and their record was second to none, but they had no training in the jungle warfare which would be a feature of any campaign in Burma or Malaya. This was not surprising because Burma, Malaya and Singapore had nothing to do with the Government of India, but were separately answerable to London. The local forces and regular garrisons lacked the numbers, training and armament to cope with any situation more serious than internal security. The only threat which was taken seriously was attack from the sea, and the defences of Singapore were designed for this situation and no other.

As it happened this was playing straight into the hands of the Japanese, whose forces were trained and armed specifically for the campaigns in

South-East Asia on which they embarked. When the Japanese destroyed the American Pacific fleet at Pearl Harbour, this brought the United States into the war against the Axis powers. The British Empire joined forces with the United States and in the long run Germany, Italy and Japan were doomed to defeat. But the Allies were to pay for their earlier errors and negligence by suffering a series of devastating disasters in the next eight months. Our forces in the Far East temporarily lost command of the sea and air, without which success in modern war is not to be expected.

This is the background against which the campaign in Malaya and Singapore in 1942 must be studied, and the RAOC part of the story follows.

SITUATION BEFORE THE OUTBREAK OF WAR WITH JAPAN

The original Ordnance depot for Singapore had been situated on Pulau Brani, a small island in Singapore Harbour. However, in 1937 a new depot which had been built at Alexandra was taken into use. It was within easy reach of the dock area and was rail served. It included bomb-proof magazines to take all types of ammunition up to 15-inch. At the same time new magazines had been constructed at Changi at the eastern corner of the island.

Captain J. G. Denniston had to overcome considerable opposition when he insisted on adequate room for expansion of Alexandra depot. His foresight and determination were vindicated when the number of troops to be maintained was enormously increased in 1940/41. It is not so easy to understand similar opposition to the space for expansion demanded for Kranji Ammunition Depot, as this was built under the threat of war.

Up to the end of 1940 the arrangements for Ordnance supply were comparatively simple, as all units except one Brigade (Mersing defence) had static roles. Each beach defence sector was allocated extra weapons known as "approved armaments" and also beach defence reserves of small arms ammunition. These were held by the units manning the sectors. Replenishment was by second line transport drawing direct from the depot or magazine. The Mersing Brigade was served by an RASC supply column which would hold second line ammunition on wheels.

Although Malaya had been given a low priority for men and stores, it was realized that Singapore might become a base for future operations and every effort must be made to prepare for the expansion which would result. In November 1940 the island of Singapore was formed into an operational organization known as Singapore Fortress, on the staff of which was an ADOS. Ordnance Services in the whole Command were under the DDOS Malaya, Brigadier G. C. Evelegh.

In August 1939 the RAOC consisted of 6 officers and 60 other ranks, apart from workshop staff, the minimum necessary to serve the existing garrison of 8,000. At the end of that month 4,500 Indian reinforcements (Force Emu) arrived with, in support, an IAOC Ordnance Field Depot. This force was ill-equipped for the climate of Malaya.

Force Emu and subsequent reinforcements were on war accounting but the garrison remained on peace accounting until the middle of 1941. A generous scale of accommodation stores was supplied for Force Emu and was used as the basis for future reinforcements. Issues to this scale imposed a heavy strain on existing RAOC resources and later on it was apparent that the scale was much too lavish.

By March 1940 the IAOC detachment was absorbed into the RAOC installations, but this was more than offset by the ordering back to the United Kingdom of 50 per cent of the RAOC staff. At the same time the forces in Malaya received a steady stream of reinforcements. In September 1940, 11th Indian Division (12,000) arrived. They were supposed to bring stores for 7 months but most of the items were to follow and the units themselves were not fully equipped. All other reinforcements from India were in like case.

It was considered that a force of six Divisions was needed to defend the whole Malay peninsula, but in the end only the equivalent of four Divisions were deployed, namely 3 Indian Corps (with headquarters at Kuala Lumpur) consisting of two Indian Divisions and an Australian Division in addition to Singapore Garrison. The Australian Division took over the defence of Mersing, the Brigade thus relieved going into reserve. The L of C from the forward units of 3 Corps to the base at Singapore was 450 miles long.

With the arrival of 2 extra Divisions and many base area and L of C troops, the work of the Ordnance Services rapidly increased. It was decided that, owing to the length of the L of C, it would be necessary to form AODs and AADs in suitable locations on the Malay peninsula. On Singapore island a composite depot was formed for the stocks of stores, vehicles and ammunition. This BOD/BAD was commanded by Colonel R. P. Bridge.

In the peninsula it was decided to form AODs and AADs at Kuala Lumpur, Penang and Valdor. Control of these depots was difficult. There was no conventional L of C organization, and, as the depots were in the Corps area, they came under 3 Corps, who had enough on their hands already. This caused many difficulties as AODs and AADs received no advance information, sometimes no information at all, that a withdrawal was necessary. The same thing happened after the retirement to Singapore island which was divided into small areas under formation commanders. A valuable addition to the Corps strength was Colonel C. Hunt, who was appointed DDOS L of C immediately on his arrival in December 1941.

The depot at Penang was unavoidably in the dock area. An additional AAD was half finished and in use at Bukit Siput.

An Ordnance Field Park was considered essential when it appeared that Thailand might ask for assistance, and one was promised from India, but it never appeared and a small OFP was improvised in a few days and sent up to 3 Corps. The formation of this unit was undertaken by Major C. H. McVittie and Major Lyons and they produced a most efficient OFP. Shortly before the Japanese invasion two small OFPs arrived for the Australian Division.

At Singapore, ammunition storage was increased by a new, large depot at Kranji on the north end of the island, and additional accommodation was acquired to ensure adequate dispersal of stores and vehicles.

Provision was not easy. Technical and warlike stores had to come all the way from the United Kingdom. In 1941 the Central Provision Office at Delhi accepted demands from Singapore for clothing and general stores. A Malaya Provision Officer was appointed on the Command staff to handle policy questions between CPO and Malaya. He was an AQMG with many additional duties and had to delegate most Ordnance questions to a subordinate who had no training in or knowledge of such matters. A trained Ordnance Officer should have been appointed. When a conference was held in Delhi for representatives from Hong Kong, Singapore, Burma and other sources of supply, the Brigadier i/c administration asked Brigadier Evelegh to help the official representative.

The change to war provision imposed a heavy burden on the small European provision staff. Maintenance figures had to be revised to accord with estimated war wastage and reviews were necessary monthly instead of annually.

The British, Indian and Australian forces all worked to different procedures and different scales of equipment, which enormously complicated the supply of stores. RAOC manpower was insufficient for the greatly increased load of work. Local labour was employed but sufficient supervisory staff was not available. Asiatic clerks were employed to a large extent but their standard was not high enough owing to the low wages paid, and they constituted a security risk.

By August 1941 the garrison had increased by nearly 800 per cent to about 60,000. The Base Depot had expanded from 5 officers and 60 other ranks to 9 officers and 140 RAOC other ranks, assisted by 2 officers and about 50 other ranks from the Australian Army Ordnance Corps.

ORDNANCE SERVICES DURING THE CAMPAIGN

The Japanese started the invasion of Malaya on December 8th 1941, the day after Pearl Harbour, by landing in the north at Kota Bahru and within 2 days also crossing the border from Thailand. This was followed by a retreat of over 400 miles carried out in less than 2 months, and in these circumstances it was difficult for the Ordnance Services to function according to plan.

Shortage of aircraft soon lost us command of the air and the sinking of the *Prince of Wales* and *Repulse* followed. This enabled the Japanese to land behind our troops on either coast of the peninsula, and their Army, well trained in jungle warfare, was able to infiltrate between our defended localities, form road blocks and outmanœuvre our troops, who lacked this type of training.

The second and third echelon ammunition was in IAOC hands at the appointed places, ready to hand over to the RIASC of 3 Corps, but their ammunition sections were apparently taken by the staff for other purposes. Daily ammunition expenditure returns were never received at Singapore, but right from the start 3 Corps signalled for train load after train load of all natures of ammunition, normal procedures being ignored. This caused such congestion in the forward areas that many train loads of ammunition had to be returned to Singapore intact, and trains were passing each other going in opposite directions containing the same natures of ammunition. During the retreat 3 Corps formed ammunition dumps at various places down the length of the peninsula, but these often had to be picked up again within 24 hours.

When Kuala Lumpur was evacuated advanced depots for stores and ammunition were opened at the new barracks in Johore. The sites were admirable for the receipt of stocks backloaded from the various depots up country, but no sooner had the depots started to function than the withdrawal to the island took place.

FALL OF SINGAPORE ISLAND

The troops, who had withdrawn from the peninsula, crossed over to Singapore island at the end of January 1942 and the causeway was blown up. The last big party of women and children left Singapore on January 31st.

The topography of the island was such that it could not be defended for long against an enemy who had sea and air supremacy, but little had been done to organize the defences along the narrow and shallow strait which separated the north coast of the island from the mainland.

There were many troops in Singapore but a high proportion were administrative troops, required for their primary role and in most cases insufficiently armed or trained for effective defence of the perimeter against troops of the calibre of the Japanese Infantry. There were also considerable numbers of anti-aircraft and coast defence gunners who had their own weapons to man. It has been noted that the RAOC were so under strength that they were fully employed on issuing stores, vehicles or ammunition and otherwise could only be deployed for local defence.

There were roughly 30,000 men for the defence of the island and they were deployed as follows:

West and north-west coast (Kranji area): Australian Division.

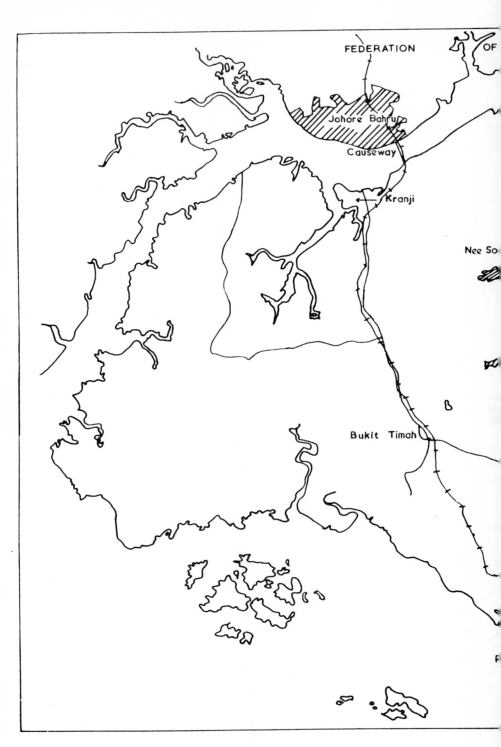

FEDERATION OF

Johore Bahru

Causeway

Kranji

Nee So

Bukit Timah

B

F

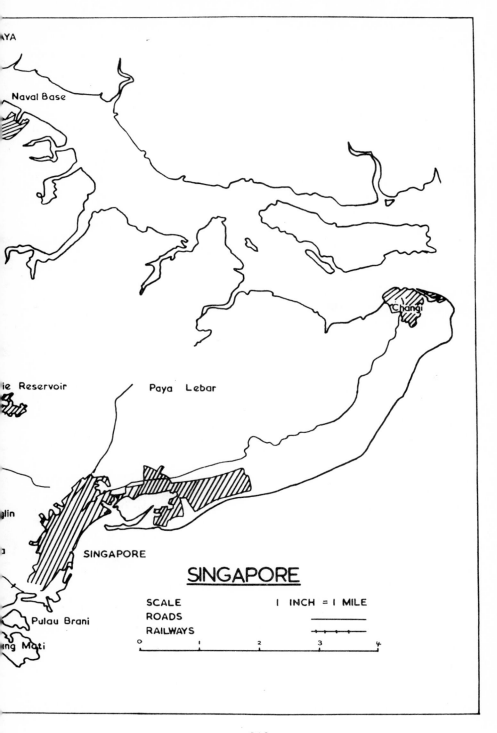

AYA

Naval Base

Changi

ie Reservoir   Paya   Lebar

glin

SINGAPORE

SINGAPORE

Pulau Brani

ng Mati

SCALE	1 INCH = 1 MILE
ROADS	
RAILWAYS	

0   1   2   3   4

North coast (Naval Base area): 18th Division, recently landed after a long sea voyage from the United Kingdom.

North-east coast: Combined 9th and 11th Indian Divisions, elements withdrawn from the peninsula.

South coast: Two British Brigades.

Before the retirement to Singapore island three large ammunition dumps were formed in the Nee Soon area, and another on the Bukit Timah rifle range.

Supply of stores was arranged through RASC Supply Issue Points at each of which an RAOC representative was present. Stores were drawn from the Ordnance Depot at Alexandra in vehicles allocated to the RAOC for that purpose. This arrangement worked well.

The Naval Base was at the north end of the island and could no longer be used. It was well stocked with stores and ammunition, much of which could have been collected and used by the Army, but no plans were made for such an eventuality nor apparently had a "scorched earth" policy been worked out. When it was discovered that the base had been abandoned Brigadier Evelegh set out with a party to see whether he could collect any material the Army might need. The base covered an area of about 4 miles by 2 miles and this had to be searched as information on the types and location of stores was lacking. The magazines were on the waterfront under the eyes of the Japanese the other side of the strait, so collection from them had to be done at night without lights. The Japanese soon hit the large oil tanks which burned for several days and lit up the whole area at night.

On the outbreak of war with Japan arrangements had been made to send stores and ammunition to Singapore which the home authorities had not been prepared to spare while there was no war. These stores arrived in large quantities at a most awkward time as stores and ammunition were being brought back from the peninsula simultaneously.

Ammunition presented the greatest difficulty because the best storage for ammunition was at Kranji, only a mile from the north-west coast. It was necessary to find other areas for the new receipts. There was also transport congestion. There were 1,000 reserve vehicles in the BOD and 500 more were due to arrive any time. The labour situation was critical. Inadequate steps had been taken to recruit labour at a time when it was needed, and now with the enemy bombing and machine-gunning the island from the air, it was difficult to get the men to work. Wages had always been inadequate and now other considerations were paramount.

On February 4th the long-awaited reinforcements in the shape of the 18th Division arrived. With them were 17 officers and 400 other ranks of the RAOC which doubled the strength of the Corps in the island. Unfortunately the Japanese aircraft were able to attack the convoy, and they hit and set fire to the Canadian Pacific liner, *Empress of Asia*. She was grounded and burnt out. Although the troops managed to get ashore all their equipment was lost.

Although the pressure of Ordnance work made it difficult to spare men, Colonel Bridge allocated parties from each company to improve the trenches of the defended localities allotted to them and clear fields of fire. The depots area defence scheme for which Colonel Bridge was responsible provided all-round defence for a large area, 2 miles by 1 mile, and would not have to be manned unless there was a breakthrough by the enemy which placed this area in the front line.

From the point of view of this sector it was felt that things had been stabilized by February 8th. The Japanese had waited for a week after our withdrawal to the island and the longer they waited the better for us. However, disillusion was soon to come. When the Japanese did attack they achieved complete surprise and landed on the north-west shore which was thinly held by the Australian Division. They established a bridgehead and no counter-attacks succeeded in driving them back. The Japanese reinforced success and the island from that moment was doomed.

On February 11th the warning order to man the Depot Area defences was issued. It was recognised that this was a last resort as there would be insufficient staff to issue stores to the troops. However, a skeleton staff was retained to work in the depot. Colonel Bridge established an operational headquarters in the RE office building which overlooked the whole area. The original RAOC staff of the depot were trained in the rifle and light automatic, but the new reinforcements had received insufficient weapon training.

On February 12th it was clear that the enemy had penetrated as far as Bukit Timah, and the Japanese aircraft were to be seen from the depot bombing and machine-gunning. Two Bofors light anti-aircraft guns had been sited in the depot area. They were manned by an Indian unit and in the general confusion one of the detachments left. Some of our men took over the gun, and kept firing it although having no training their marksmanship was poor. But it kept the Japanese aircraft away. During the day the demands for stores increased and men had to be withdrawn from the defences to make issues.

On February 13th the front line had again been withdrawn, to within a mile of the depot defences. A message was received that the Japanese had managed to land tanks on the island and Colonel Bridge improvised tank obstacles covered by fire at each end of the road through the depot.

On this date the enormous stocks at Kranji and the smaller depots at Nee Soon, Bukit Timah, Paza Lebar and Ferdhans College had been captured, and the Changi magazine had been blown up by the Royal Engineers. In every case RAOC men were working until the front line troops had withdrawn behind each depot. They remained at Kranji until the magazine was five miles in advance of our own front line.

315

In the evening orders were received that officers and men of the workshops branch were to be evacuated, leaving Clifford Pier by 2000 hrs. About 200 went, but the majority were captured later on in Sumatra.

Late in the evening orders were received from Brigadier Evelegh to destroy the depot stock in accordance with a plan which had already been prepared. To do this all men except those manning light automatics had to be withdrawn. The storehouses burnt well and it appeared that everything had been destroyed, although there is evidence that the Japanese were able to recover a certain amount of material later on.

On February 14th Colonel Bridge reported to General Keith Simmons at Fortress Headquarters and the unit was placed under the command of Brigadier Williams, commanding 1st Malaya Brigade. His headquarters was on the southern slopes of Alexandra ridge, the opposite side from the depot. The orders were to move three Companies to the Keppel Harbour area and two Companies to the Tiong Bahru area.

The Japanese had captured Mac Ritchie Reservoir, and shortage of water would soon be a serious problem for the large population of Singapore city. The Ordnance Depot companies reinforced the line held by elements of the Loyals, Leicesters and Malay Regiment. All these units were under strength through casualties and sub-units being cut off and captured. There was, however, no further withdrawal, but on February 15th General Percival signed the instrument of surrender.

At the time of the capitulation Alexandra magazine was still in our hands and issues could be made although with difficulty. It was in advance of the headquarters of the front line battalion in that sector. The magazine was not blown up because of its proximity to a hospital which could not be evacuated. Rationing of ammunition had been necessary only in a few natures such as .45-inch sub-machine gun and .5-inch anti-tank rifle.

CONCLUSION

The RAOC did everything possible in disastrous circumstances beyond their control. Apart from the general lessons of the campaign, a peculiar difficulty arose from the existence of three different Ordnance Corps in one small theatre of operations, namely the RAOC, IAOC and RAAOC. There was no good reason why there should not have been a reasonable degree of standardization of organization and procedures between these three Corps before the war.

HONG KONG

It was realized in 1939 that Hong Kong had no strategic significance. It could not be held for long in a war against Japan and it would therefore be a mistake to lock up a large garrison there. On the other hand there was no certainty of a war with Japan and British prestige would suffer a severe blow if we were to abandon Hong Kong without firing a shot. This conflict between the political and military requirements, bearing in mind the critical war situation in Europe, was a most unfortunate dilemma to which there was no obvious solution.

Either Hong Kong had to be made really strong, to ensure prolonged resistance, or it had to be regarded as an outpost, the military forces of which would be expendable and must be kept to a minimum.

In the event an unsatisfactory compromise was reached. Naval and air support could never be strong enough to influence the situation decisively. The military strength was increased numerically but was sadly short of armament, ammunition, vehicles and other vital war material.

The Prime Minister had already advised the Chiefs of Staff at the beginning of 1941 that we must avoid frittering away our resources on untenable positions. He wished we had fewer troops there, but to move any would be noticeable and dangerous.

In spite of this policy a chance of strengthening the garrison without detriment to other commitments, at a time when Japan was becoming more aggressive, seemed to present itself in July 1941. When Major-General C. M. Maltby took over command of the garrison his predecessor, a Canadian, put forward the suggestion that Canada might agree to spare a Brigade Headquarters and two Battalions. This was approved by the Chiefs of Staff, the decision being based on a false appreciation of Japanese intentions and strength, and the impression that an obvious move to strengthen Hong Kong would act as a deterrent. The Battalions were not fully trained operationally and in the end added to the already excessive number of hostages to fortune.

ORDNANCE SERVICES IN HONG KONG

Between September 1939 and June 1940 Hong Kong remained under peace-time conditions. The senior Ordnance Officer, ADOS China Command, was Colonel G. R. Hopkins, who had been COO Didcot until early in the war.

Various moves took place before December 8th 1941 when the war with Japan started and by then, in addition to the ADOS, the main appointments were Lieutenant-Colonel W. J. Smith, COME, Lieutenant-Colonel R. A. P. Macpherson, DADOS, Captain S. G. Burroughs, Ordnance Officer, Captain V. S. Ebbage, Provision and Local Purchase, and Lieutenant M. Hanlon, IOO. Lieutenant-Colonel Macpherson was an officer who had transferred to the Corps from the Royal Scots, taking the Ordnance Officers course not long before the war. The strength of the RAOC Section based on Hong Kong was about 150 Warrant Officers, NCOs and men.

The main Ordnance depot occupied both sides of Queen's Road on the harbour front, the workshops being in the same locality. A small depot was established in Kowloon at Ma Tau Kok, mainly for camp equipment as all camps were on the mainland.

317

Ammunition was held in a recently built, up-to-date magazine at Lyemun, and in the old Naval Magazines at Kennedy Road and Queen's Road. However, as increased armament, particularly anti-aircraft guns, was expected a new 24,000 sq ft magazine was built at Little Hong Kong. This was very well built but too small. Colonel Hopkins requested War Office approval for an extension of 12,000 sq ft but work had not begun when war with Japan broke out.

The workshops were concerned primarily with the inspection of weapons, instruments and radio. They worked closely with the Royal Dockyard, who were equipped to undertake heavy work. In Hong Kong repair of MT was undertaken by the RASC.

Most of the unit mobilization equipment was stored and maintained by the RAOC, not by the units themselves. An additional task was the equipment of the Hong Kong Volunteer Defence Corps, a locally recruited unit initially about 500 strong but constantly expanded and reorganized until it reached a total of 2,500. The unit was supposed to be equipped by the War Office through the RAOC, who issued stores on repayment, but the Hong Kong Government never accepted a charge if they could help it and this placed the RAOC in a rather difficult position. However, no demands were held up and the unit was properly equipped. It was a very efficient and keen unit, with a fine record against the Japanese when the fighting started.

In addition to Hong Kong there were units in Shanghai, Tientsin and Peking, with a training and rest camp at Shanhaikwan. By 1940 the Japanese had occupied a large part of China and early that year the British troops were withdrawn and sent to Singapore.

The Ordnance stores and ammunition still required were brought back to Singapore and Hong Kong. This was not easy as the Japanese were in control and relations with them were bad. It was necessary to bluff the Japanese into agreeing to the removal of thousands of rounds of small arms ammunition from Peking by stating that the mortar ammunition stored with it, which had certainly been damaged by flood water entering the storehouse, was in a highly dangerous condition both to the city of Peking and the Japanese soldiers there.

Hong Kong was on a low priority for arms and equipment and also at the far end of a long supply line. It was therefore most important to make full use of local production. The Chinese manufacturers were found to be adept at producing clothing and general stores in common use. Substitutes for sealed patterns were speedily introduced and the Chinese turned out a high proportion of our requirements of clothing, camp equipment, barrack stores, tentage and personal equipment. The goods were produced without delay, at a very cheap rate, and the quality was excellent. Tools and machinery were imported from Shanghai and a barbed wire factory was set up in Hong Kong.

The Civil Government formed a Hong Kong Civilian War Supply Committee to organize the manufacture and supply of warlike stores to meet requirements formulated by the Far Eastern War Supply Board which sat at Delhi. The Hong Kong committee was under the control of Lieutenant-Colonel R. D. Walker, the civilian manager of the Kowloon and Canton Railway and a Royal Engineer officer of the HKVDC. The work, which was an extension of that already being undertaken by the RAOC local purchase and provision branch, was extremely successful and for some time this small garrison had a greater output than any other country in the Far Eastern Scheme.

The RAOC demanded its requirements from the Supply Committee, having first call on its products. All this initiative and productivity was unfortunate in the long run as the whole concern fell into the hands of the enemy who made full use of it while the supply of raw materials lasted.

With the growing threat of war the Hong Kong defence scheme was reorganized, and Ordnance stores were dispersed to ensure their safety as far as possible. Under this reorganization, RAOC installations were allocated as follows:

1. General stores and an alternative DADOS office at The Ridge. This was a group of private houses which were taken over. They were situated to the north of Repulse Bay.
2. Workshops. Shouson Hill.
3. Camp equipment and anti-gas clothing. Brick Hill.
4. Armament and gun stores. Lyemun Barracks (married quarters).

It was obvious that if the Japanese were to attack Hong Kong everyone would be in the fight, and a special effort was made in 1941 to bring the weapon training of the RAOC up to a high standard, with particular reference to the light machine gun. In 1939 the RAOC Section at Hong Kong consisted of trained Regular soldiers, and these were progressively transferred to more active theatres where their knowledge and experience were needed. Although an important nucleus of Regulars remained in 1941, those who had left were replaced by National Service men, good material but with limited experience in Infantry duties.

Progress was hampered by the usual situation in which the strength of the RAOC lagged well behind the commitments created by the inceased size of the garrison which was preparing for war. This made it difficult to spare men for weapon training without neglecting important Corps duties. It was also necessary to conserve small arms ammunition, but it went rather against the grain to be denied ammunition for training when several thousand rounds had been recovered by the RAOC from under the noses of the Japanese at Peking in 1940. Nevertheless these things had to be accepted and everything possible was done to prepare for the ordeal which lay ahead.

The new magazine at Little Hong Kong was finished in mid-summer 1941 and was soon filled with gun ammunition of which there were receipts arriving during the whole year.

319

There was some anxiety about the reserves of rifles and anti-gas clothing and in fact, there was no response to the demands for these items, owing to the general scarcity at the time, although there was a considerable interchange of cables with the War Office on the subject.

Towards the end of the year various dumps of machine guns, binoculars and other warlike stores were discovered in warehouses in Hong Kong, having been apparently placed there by enemy agents in preparation for the coming war. These items were confiscated and taken into use by the British forces.

In October 1941, when the Canadian contingent arrived the combatant strength of the Hong Kong garrison was nearly 12,000 men. The RAOC strength on December 8th 1941 was 147 all ranks.

THE CAMPAIGN IN HONG KONG

When war broke out on December 8th 1941, stocks of Ordnance stores and ammunition were distributed as follows:

Queen's Road North and South	Bulk stores and some workshops.
Ma Tau Kok (Kowloon)	Blankets and a little ammunition.
Little Hong Kong	
Lyemun	Main ammunition depots.
Upper and Lower Kennedy Road	
Shouson Hill	War-time workshops.
Lyemun (married quarters)	Dispersed essential stores.
Brick Hill	Dispersed stores, chiefly camp equipment.
The Ridge	Dispersed essential stores. Armament and Clothing. Armourers' and instrument workshops.
Kennedy Town Godown	Tentage.

Arrangements were immediately made to establish a Barrack and Hospital Laundry under military control at Stanley Prison, St. Stephen's College, Tung Wah East and Maison Bethanie. Mr. Ramsey, the Manager of the Hong Kong Steam Laundry, was placed in charge and commissioned into the RAOC. After some difficulty the work proceeded satisfactorily. Certain equipment and boilers had to be made in RAOC workshops.

At the same time there was difficulty over Field Bakery ovens which were being repaired under contract. The contractors stopped work but fortunately a large number of Aldershot Field Ovens had been ordered and received. They were a useful substitute.

Within a few days the key position of the Shing Mun Redoubt on the mainland was taken by surprise and the forces there withdrew to Devil's Peak. But it was not long before the order to withdraw to the island followed. All stores and ammunition at Ma Tau Kok were brought back to Lyemun and redistributed from there.

Now the installations on the north side of the island were vulnerable, and were subjected to heavy artillery bombardment and air attack. The Ordnance Depot at Queen's Road was heavily attacked, and left in ruins. The order was given to remove all stores of value and the work continued day and night in difficult conditions under Lieutenant-Colonel Macpherson. Transport was scarce and the local labourers were liable to panic. There were some casualties and finally, after two storehouses had been blown up and another gutted by fire, the work was abandoned and the staff moved to The Ridge, except those from the workshops who went to Shouson Hill.

The magazines at New and Old Kennedy Road still continued to function to the end although bulk explosives were moved out to a safer place. The magazines were under constant shell fire, fortunately without serious effect.

Early on December 13th all troops had withdrawn from the mainland. Units were re-equipped and the Island Defence Scheme was put into operation.

The Lyemun Magazine and Married Quarters now came under heavy fire. Captain Ebbage was in charge of a party which transferred all stores from the Married Quarters to the Ridge. The work was carried out under considerable shell fire, the vehicles being driven by volunteer RAOC drivers. Additional accommodation was obtained from residents on the Ridge and most of the stores were under cover by December 17th, Lieutenant-Colonel Macpherson and Captain Burroughs arrived at the Ridge from Queen's Road on December 14th. Much of the ammunition was brought back from Lyemun to Little Hong Kong, the remainder being handed over to the gunners and held at gun positions.

In the evening of December 15th a bold attempt to swim the Lei U Mun Strait was made by about three Companies with the assistance of small rubber boats and petrol tin rafts. This attack was defeated, all the men being shot in the water and carried away by the strong tide which runs through this narrow strait. L/Cpl Ryan, stationed at Lyemun Magazine, manned a Bren gun at this point on the coast and did great execution.

On the night of December 18th/19th the Japanese landed at a number of points on the coast between Quarry Point and North Point. They moved rapidly inland towards Mount Butler, Mount Parker and the Lyemun Gap. Lyemun was cut off, leaving the Ordnance field installations at the Ridge (stores and DADOS headquarters), Brick Hill (camp equipment), Shouson Hill (workshops) and Little Hong Kong (ammunition).

Unfortunately the Japanese soon overran Jardine's Look-out and occupied Wong Nei Chong Gap. They also advanced by Stanley Gap on

Repulse Bay, thus cutting off Brigadier Wallis's East Brigade and forcing him back towards the Stanley Peninsula.

The Wong Nei Chong Gap was vital to the defence of the island. It was a centre of communications from which roads radiated to all parts of the island. Many counter-attacks were launched in order to retake the Gap and the hills which dominated it.

The Ridge was on the route between Repulse Bay and Wong Nei Chong Gap, both places at which heavy and prolonged fighting took place. On the morning of December 19th a Japanese officer was seen from the depot in the neighbourhood of the Gap, but he and his party were not fired on for fear of hitting the Canadians who were known to be in that area.

Later on fire was opened with two Bren guns on a Japanese unit moving down the road which was cut into the side of the hill at this point. The Japanese could not take cover and suffered heavy casualties. Later still another party suffered a similar fate at the same spot.

At noon the Canadians were seen to be withdrawing, some along the road to Mount Nicholson and some towards Little Hong Kong on foot. The DADOS received a message from Headquarters in which General Maltby gave him permission to set fire to the depot if he considered it necessary.

During the afternoon Captain Atkinson and a party of gunners came into the depot from a location known as Post Bridge. They drew rations and two Bren guns and returned. After dark Major Hunt, RA, and a party of about 100 arrived on their way to attack Wong Nei Chong Gap. Late at night a party of RE, RASC, RAOC and HKVDC arrived under the command of Lieutenant-Colonel Frederick, RASC.

On the morning of December 20th the Ridge was machine-gunned. Colonel Frederick and his party left for Shouson Hill, but soon afterwards they were ambushed, suffered heavy casualties and dispersed. He brought some of them back to the Ridge.

With additional men, approximately 280, the Ridge was prepared as much as possible for defence and the troops were allocated to the various houses, with a proportion of officers in each house. About 1400 hrs there was heavy machine-gun fire from the direction of Wong Nei Chong and the water catchment, causing a number of casualties, 13 seriously wounded and Private Taylor killed. The ADMS was asked to send ambulances and a plan was made to burn the depot and withdraw to Little Hong Kong or on to Aberdeen. This was cancelled when information was received that the Canadians were coming. Two houses were hit by mortar bombs and Lieutenant-Colonel Macpherson received a bullet through the arm when moving from one house to another.

Later on instructions were received from Brigadier Wallis that the Ridge garrison was to be divided into four parties: 8 officers and 80 other ranks to recapture Cross Roads; 8 officers and 80 other ranks to proceed to Middle Spur and storm the water catchment; Lieutenant-

Colonel Frederick and his party to move to Repulse Bay; the balance to burn the depot and withdraw to Repulse Bay.

The parties left at dark. Rations and water were very low. Two ambulances arrived at 1630 hrs and were greeted by the enemy with a hail of machine-gun fire but managed to collect wounded and leave for Stanley after dark. A quiet night in which some stragglers from various units came in.

On December 21st there was considerable activity in the direction of the water catchment. The Japanese were now in positions which commanded all the houses on the Ridge and it was impossible to move from one house to another by day, but fire was returned whenever possible and with some success. Orders were to stay at the Ridge as more Canadians were expected to attack Wong Nei Chong Gap. During the night about 60 Canadians under Major Young arrived but took up positions at "Altamara".

On December 22nd the unit was joined by the Canadians who had been unable to occupy the Gap. Notification was received that if the men could get through to Repulse Bay by midnight it would be possible to move on to Stanley.

However, the Ridge was now under heavy fire from light field guns as well as mortars and machine guns, and although this fire was returned, the position was not really defensible, being commanded on all sides. Casualties began to mount up. Lieutenant-Colonel Macpherson, realizing that the position was hopeless and mindful of the increasing number of wounded men decided to surrender after informing all the houses that those who wished to make the attempt could try to get through to Repulse Bay. It was possible to slip away from some of the houses by day, but in other cases it was necessary to wait until dark. Until it became dark machine gun fire continued and from one burst Lieutenant-Colonel Macpherson received a large wound in the thigh which was probably mortal.

After dark more parties moved away, including one from House No. 1 led by Captain Ebbage. He and QMS Cooper were the only survivors of this party and they moved about in the hills, without food or water for several days, finally being forced to give themselves up on the morning of December 28th, three days after the capitulation.

Some 50 RAOC men remained at the Ridge. A number of these men were killed or died of wounds and a few were killed while escaping. The remainder were captured alive and then killed by the Japanese. A few days after Christmas the ADMS obtained a pass to explore this and other areas in search of wounded. He found that the party had been bound hand and foot with telephone wire and then bayoneted or shot. This was later confirmed by Lieutenant Markey.

This savage action may have been in revenge for the heavy losses caused to the Japanese from this "pocket of resistance". Although the British defence and counter-attacks in this area were somewhat lacking in coordination they made up for it in courage and determination. Colonel Tanaka, commanding the Japanese 229th Regiment, has said that he remained for three whole days on a hill north-west of Repulse Bay Hotel and admitted to heavy losses. The gallant defence of the Ridge was a valuable contribution to this local, if temporary, success.

After the shelling of Kennedy Road and Lyemun, Little Hong Kong held the bulk of the ammunition stocks in the Colony. To begin with it was possible to issue ammunition by day. The bombing raids did no serious damage, and the situation remained satisfactory until the morning of December 20th when it was found that the enemy had penetrated as far as Shouson Hill and Mount Cameron.

Retiring troops, some wounded, had been passing through the depot area. They had been driven out of positions in the Repulse Bay Road and Brick Hill areas, and as the enemy were also on Mount Nicholson and Mount Cameron the magazine was virtually surrounded.

From that day there was heavy fighting in the neighbourhood, the Japanese concentrating on a house on Shouson Hill held by a detachment of the Middlesex Regiment which by skilful defence caused many casualties. However, the enemy eventually established machine gun posts which commanded the Magazine Road, Shouson Hill and approaches. Two lorries and a car attempting to reach the central explosives store were promptly knocked out and it proved impossible to make issues during daylight. Night convoys were introduced and proved successful, meeting surprisingly little interference from the Japanese.

Although the RAOC detachment was twice ordered to withdraw from the magazine to Shouson Hill the men returned again and continued to make issues. A large convoy got through on the night of December 24th. The detachment surrendered when the garrison capitulated on December 25th.

During the first two days of the war workshop machinery was moved to Shouson Hill and the workshop functioned normally until December 19th. Orders were then received to evacuate Shouson Hill and retire to Aberdeen Industrial School. The staff then joined Lieutenant-Colonel Frederick's force for field operations. Early on December 20th the advance party of the workshops staff was ambushed at the junction of Repulse Bay Road and Island Road. The majority were captured though one or two escaped.

The various parties of prisoners from the garrison were eventually concentrated at Shamshuipo on the mainland. A check of RAOC numbers was made at the end of January 1942. There were present 10 officers and 89 other ranks out of 15 officers and 132 other ranks at the beginning of the campaign. The percentage of dead, 33 per cent, was higher than that of any other unit in the Command. They set an example of efficiency and gallantry in the highest traditions of the Army and the Corps.

MALTA

The key position of Malta in the Mediterranean was well understood by both sides. As long as it remained an active British Naval base the operations of German and Italian forces in North Africa were unlikely to prosper.

After the entry of Italy into the war the Axis powers had plans for the capture of Malta, mainly by the use of airborne forces, but Crete was given priority, and the losses in that operation were so heavy that a similar venture was indefinitely postponed. Russia became the main theatre, which absorbed a high proportion of German resources. German forces were sent to the Mediterranean to help Italy, and prevent an Italian collapse, rather than with any idea of launching a large-scale offensive against Egypt and the Suez Canal.

For this it was sufficient to neutralize Malta but the efforts to do so were not always successful. In the last quarter of 1941 only 44,800 tons of enemy equipment were delivered at North African ports out of 123,000 tons sent from Italy, and this had a decisive effect on the result of the CRUSADER operation.

Early in 1942 the situation seemed to favour a more aggressive policy. At the end of 1941, U-boats and Italian frogmen scored notable successes against the Royal Navy in the Mediterranean. Bombing of the island was stepped up and strong naval and air forces were stationed in Sicily and Italy to prevent supplies getting through to the island. The German and Italian staffs set to work on the plan to capture Malta and then drive on to Egypt.

On the British side it was realized that the possession of the Gebel Akhdar and the airfields in that area were necessary for the protection of convoys supplying Malta. The withdrawal early in 1942 to the Gazala position east of the Gebel Akhdar combined with increased Axis naval and air activity enabled convoys to go from Italy to North Africa. After the fall of Tobruk an alternative supply route was available to that port via Crete. Thus the need for the assault on and capture of Malta became less obvious and it was considered by the Germans sufficient to neutralize and blockade the island which might be starved out. In the event Malta held out and remained a valuable forward base for the landings in Sicily and Italy in the summer of 1943.

ORDNANCE SERVICES IN MALTA

The story of Malta in the years from 1939 to 1945 falls into four distinct phases:

1. The preparatory period up to June 1940 when Italy entered the war.
2. The defence of Malta between June 1940 and November 1942, the month which marked the end of the siege.

3. The build-up of Malta as an advanced base for the landings in Sicily and the support of that campaign and the early period of the Italian campaign. This phase lasted until September 1943.

4. Reduction in the size of the garrison and the concentration of stocks of stores and ammunition into the minimum number of locations so as to facilitate the efficient and economic storage of stocks the authorized level of which was by then much reduced.

FIRST PHASE

Shortly before the war a new centralized Ordnance Depot and workshops was approved by the War Office. The buildings were to be sited in open country near the village of Attard, well away from probable target areas, as the only aerodromes at that time were at Hal-Far and Luqa.

The large-scale construction of underground storage was not the policy of any of the three Services, no doubt mainly on account of the high cost.

Work was started on the new site in the summer of 1939, so that when war broke out little progress had been made and the RAOC only had the pre-war depots at Marina Pinto and Ospizio with workshops at Ospizio and Sa Maison. Except for 12,000 sq ft of storage 20ft high under 60 ft of rock at Marina Pinto and some smaller storehouses under rock cover at Ospizio, these installations were above ground. The existing underground storage was used for items of operational importance.

After the outbreak of war, attempts were made to speed up the construction of the new depot, but these efforts were frustrated by lack of steel girders and roof trusses, due from India. This material had not arrived by the time Italy declared war, and it was never possible to make use of this very incomplete site.

It proved fortunate in the end that the new depot at Attard was not finished and occupied by June 1940 as, apart from the concentration of stores and workshop plant, the location became a target through the construction of a new aerodrome at Ta Kali quite close to the site.

The general policy not to construct more underground storage was not applied to ammunition, and War Office approval was given in 1938 for the construction of underground magazines for the existing stocks at Malta and known future commitments. The location was in the rock below and adjacent to the existing ammunition depot at Fort Musta, in open country and well away from probable target areas. All ammunition was underground by the date of Italy's declaration of war.

MANPOWER

In September 1939 the garrison of Malta consisted of a Regular British Infantry Brigade, a Maltese Territorial Infantry Battalion, Coast Defence Artillery and a very limited amount of Anti-Aircraft Artillery, with Services on a small scale.

There was a very small RAOC detachment largely from the workshops branch and a few Warrant Officers and senior NCOs from the Store Branch. There were no RAOC storemen, all such work being undertaken by Maltese civilians. The depots and workshops were very old and located in the crowded harbour areas where labour, in peace-time, was easy to obtain.

The ADOS, Malta, Lieutenant-Colonel B. A. Goldstein, with his COME, Major L. N. Tyler, and their staff were located at Fortress Head-quarters.

Just before Italy entered the war, two Battalions from the BEF France were moved to Malta to increase the garrison.

SUPPLY OF STORES

From the beginning of the war the stocks of stores in Malta were built up to meet the needs of a larger garrison. In May 1940 fourteen ships arrived with 5,000 tons of Ordnance stores and ammunition. Early in June more ships arrived with 9,000 tons of Ordnance stores and ammunition and over 80,000 coils of Dannert wire.

SECOND PHASE

Once Italy declared war Malta was under frequent and often severe aerial bombardment, and was subject to blockade which for long periods was complete. Significant numbers of men and quantities of stores could only be brought in by heavily escorted convoys which frequently suffered severe losses. Inevitably Ordnance commitments increased rapidly and manpower reinforcements lagged well behind the increasing load of work.

A committee was formed by the C in C to study and take action on the storage problems of all three Services and of the Civil Government. Thus at an early date priorities were established, for the safe storage of essential materials and also for the shelter of a large population.

The plan to deal with the increased stocks of Ordnance stores was to disperse them widely in small quantities throughout the island, and this was effective in preventing heavy losses during the siege. At one time there were over one hundred such dispersed storehouses.

The number of combat units, mainly anti-aircraft gunners and Infantry, steadily increased during this second phase until early in 1942, when the invasion of Malta appeared imminent, the garrison had grown to 30,000 from the pre-war figure of 4,000. No RAOC reinforcements arrived until January 1941 and in April 1942 the Corps was 35 per cent below establishment in Clerks and 20 per cent in Storemen.

In January 1941 the appointment of ADOS was upgraded to DDOS (Colonel) and that of COME to ADOS(E), Lieutenant-Colonel. In March 1942 control was transferred from the War Office to DOS Middle East.

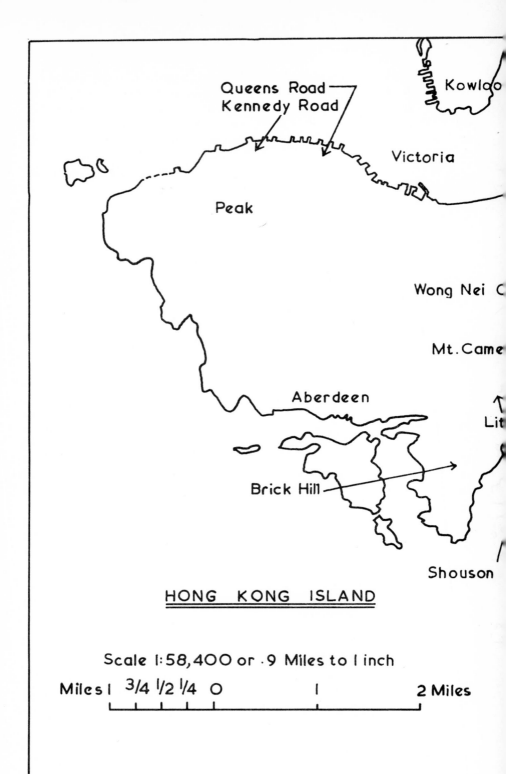

Queens Road
Kennedy Road
Kowloo
Victoria
Peak
Wong Nei C
Mt. Came
Aberdeen
Lit
Brick Hill
Shouson

HONG KONG ISLAND

Scale 1:58,400 or .9 Miles to 1 inch

Miles 1 3/4 1/2 1/4 O   1   2 Miles

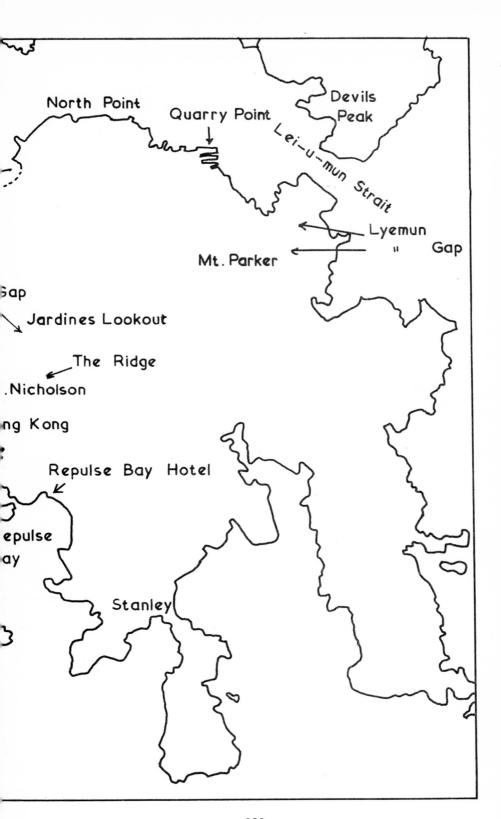

North Point

Quarry Point

Devils Peak

Lei-u-mun Strait

Lyemun
" Gap

Mt. Parker

Gap

Jardines Lookout

The Ridge

.Nicholson

ng Kong

Repulse Bay Hotel

epulse
ay

Stanley

PROVISION AND SUPPLY

Conventional methods of provision and demand on the United Kingdom were in force up to June 1940, and stores in response to these demands continued to arrive up to the end of the year. Unit war equipments were sent out at the same time as the units (mainly anti-aircraft units and general hospitals), but from early in 1941 an increasing shortage of accommodation stores began to be felt.

Local purchase was of little assistance because the resources of the island were negligible. Much was achieved by improvisation in the way of manufacture, modification and repair, using existing equipment.

Frequent cables were sent to the United Kingdom and Middle East, sometimes also to Gibraltar, giving the requirements and priorities of Ordnance Stores. Opportunities of supply varied between cargo ship, warship, submarine and aircraft, although the last two were not often used for Ordnance stores owing to their bulk and the existence of other items of higher priority.

A great deal of calculation and recalculation was necessary owing to the limited and chancy prospects of supply. All requirements, including those for the civil population, had to be centrally coordinated so that when shipments got through they were properly balanced. To take a simple example, it was no good receiving ammunition if there were insufficient guns, or guns with no ammunition, or either if the people were starving.

The various sources of supply were kept informed by cable, or by liaison officer travelling by air, of the vital needs of Ordnance stores, which were at the height of the siege usually anti-aircraft gun parts and ammunition. Thereafter it usually depended on the Royal Navy whether these stores got through.

DISPERSION OF STOCKS

The need for this has already been mentioned and the problem was solved by requisitioning many small buildings scattered all over the island. Eventually there were over one hundred such buildings, many of them concrete-floored garages of about 1,000 to 5,000 sq ft floor space and some schools and halls. In the storage plan some of these buildings were "bulk" and others "detail" storehouses.

Although this dispersion was essential and effective it caused difficulties of control. Transport and petrol were exceedingly scarce and supervisors usually had to visit their storehouses on foot or by bicycle. Replenishment of detail from bulk storehouses often had to be effected by the use of small horse-drawn Maltese carts. These processes were slow but unavoidable. The items held underground were safe but the storage was far from ideal owing to damp and occasional blocking of the entrances by bombing.

The extension of bomb proof storage proceeded rather slowly owing to the limited resources and other higher operational priorities. However, by March 1942 a bomb proof sub-depot had been constructed in the rock at Gargur, and when 70 per cent of the Ospizio depot had been destroyed by bombing the technical stores were transferred to Gargur. Additional bomb proof storage was also constructed at Marina Pinto and Ospizio but this was not completed until the siege was nearly over.

Vital operational items such as anti-aircraft gun barrels were held in locations readily accessible to gun sites by tunnelling into the rock walls of suitable quarries and placing ten to twenty-five barrels in each tunnel.

AMMUNITION

The centrally-held stocks of ammunition were stored underground, as has already been mentioned, but when the fighting started it was necessary to hold considerable quantities in locations which were accessible to the guns, in addition to the ready-use ammunition at gun positions.

To withstand constant attacks from the air and repel a possible invasion this small island required very large quantities of ammunition. The plan of a central holding from which dispersed locations were replenished proved to be entirely sound, and although at times the total stocks fell to a dangerously low level, this was due to intense activity combined with an effective blockade. Although distances in such a small island were not great, the extreme scarcity of transport and petrol emphasized the need for considerable stocks to be held near the guns.

Suitable sites for these sub-depots were places such as St. Edward's College, of which the windows and doorways were bricked up, and various quarries in which huts were constructed of Malta stone with 4-inch and 6-inch concrete roofs. These huts were placed close to the quarry walls, full use being made of re-entrants. Sites were carefully selected and skilfully camouflaged, and each site held only a small tonnage. Thus they did not provide a target for hostile aircraft by day and only a very small quantity of ammunition was lost in the indiscriminate night bombing. The ammunition storage plan and its execution played an important part in the defence of Malta, an island only 90 sq miles in extent, for had the enemy destroyed a significant proportion of the stocks, replenishment would not have been possible.

The capacity of the central depot at Fort Musta was also increased by constructing 6-inch concrete roofs to the moats of the fort and another disused fort known as the Tarja Battery. These moats were very deep and cut into the rock. The existing underground storage at Fort Musta was enlarged by further tunnelling and the capacity nearly doubled. Control of stocks was exercised from the main depot at Fort Musta.

The IOOs and AEs, with their supporting non-technical staff, had a most important task to perform. They carried out almost continuous inspection of ammunition at gun positions and with units, thus ensuring that the ammunition was fit for use and that damaged or suspect ammunition was withdrawn and repaired where possible. When the attacks on Malta were at their height IOOs and AEs were at constant call from gun positions to check the serviceability of ammunition which might have been damaged by near misses from enemy bombs.

Routine inspection of stocks also disclosed faults, the most notable cases being defective .303-inch Mk VIII machine gun ammunition, and several tons of gelignite, in the underground storage at Musta, which was exuding nitro-glycerine.

The following figures of ammunition stocks in Malta are interesting:

	tons
June 1940	1,750
June 1941	8,000
December 1941	13,000
June 1942	6,000
April 1943	16,000
June-November 1943	25–26,000
June 1944	18,000
June 1945	12,000

The stocks in 1941 and 1942 reflect the heavy expenditure and difficulty of replenishment, while those in 1943 indicate the stockpiling for the campaign in Sicily. The maximum quantity in covered accommodation was 13,000 tons.

The staff engaged on Ordnance ammunition duties was as follows:

In the spring of 1940—one part-time IOO and 2 AEs. Mid 1943—4 IOOs, 2 Ordnance Officers, 9 AEs, 25 Ammunition Storemen, 15 Maltese soldiers, supervising some 350 military (working parties of gunners and pioneers) and 150 local civilian employees.

BOMB DISPOSAL

From the time of the declaration of war by Italy until the end of November 1940 the RAOC were responsible for the disposal of all bombs in Malta other than those falling in the Dockyard or on aerodromes.

The method was to notify the DDOS of the approximate location of all unexploded bombs. He then visited the site, where necessary, and decided on the action to be taken and the priority of work.

The task was delegated to the two IOOs. It was arduous and dangerous work, and it often took two days or even longer to dig down through the rock or debris of partly destroyed houses to the unexploded bomb.

Several hundred unexploded bombs were located and disposed of by these two officers—Captain R. L. Jephson Jones, and Lieutenant W. M. Eastman—who were both awarded the George Cross.

At the end of 1940 an RE Bomb Disposal Section was sent out from the United Kingdom, and the RAOC technical ammunition staff were then free to resume their essential task of ammunition inspection and repair.

BOMBING OF ORDNANCE INSTALLATIONS

In Malta all Service installations, including the main Ordnance Depots and Workshops were in the target areas near the harbours and therefore suffered severe damage from bombing. Even the more distant installations were not safe and received their share of bombing and damage.

In January 1942 the whole of the Clothing Group and most of the Barrack and Hospital Stores Group at Marina Pinto were destroyed. Some of the Ordnance staff were buried under tons of stone and debris and it took 6 weeks to dig out the bodies. Fortunately the stocks were well dispersed in the island and issues continued from the sites which were intact. At this time Ospizio was also attacked. The group holding bicycles was destroyed and all the staff injured.

In March and April 1942 the Ordnance installations received their heaviest attacks and most serious losses. The workshops at Ospizio were completely destroyed by bombing over a period of several days. Three-quarters of the depot at Ospizio was destroyed, with considerable loss of general stores and camp equipment, although much of this was recovered several months later.

At St. Andrew's the RAOC Clothing Depot was badly damaged, though without appreciable loss of stocks, and the timber store was burnt out. The new Fire Control Instrument Workshop was destroyed and the main St. Andrew's Workshop severely damaged. The Radio Workshop at Pembroke was wrecked. St. Andrew's was clear of the main target area and was regarded as an evacuation area.

By May 1942 Marina Pinto and Ospizio received further heavy damage and some of the dispersed storehouses were destroyed. Other RAOC buildings to be destroyed were the Sergeants' Mess, troops billets, main cookhouse (hit three times), offices, QM stores and ration stores. However, other units suffered as badly and the RAOC losses may be taken as typical rather than abnormal.

The effect of bombs on the Maltese stone storehouses was to cause the roofs and floors to collapse and the walls to disintegrate leaving a heap of stones and rubble some 40 ft high burying bales, cases and loose articles. The clearance of all this was no easy matter owing to serious shortage of all the means to do the work—labour, transport and handling equipment. The damage done to the roads did not assist the process. Yet it had to be done. The island was under blockade and every item which could be recovered was wanted. Fortunately, owing to the construction of the buildings, fires were rare. A large amount of small arms ammunition was recovered from ships sunk in the harbours or off the coast. About half this ammunition was found to be fit for use.

WORKSHOP SERVICES

Before the war the armament in the island was almost entirely Coast Defence. There was very little Anti-Aircraft Artillery, no mobile artillery and very little MT. There was no industry which could form the basis of static workshops.

Reinforcements of AA Artillery were brought in so that at the outbreak of war there were 50 guns, but the numbers were eventually increased to 400 of all types. Reinforcements of RAOC workshops staff did not begin to arrive until January 1941, but thereafter considerable numbers appeared. Eventually the military staff increased tenfold and the Maltese workshops staff fivefold, full use being made of volunteers.

The small pre-war general workshop grew to four large static workshops, dispersed throughout the island, each self-contained for power supply. In such a small area mobile workshops were unnecessary. As was to be expected during the blockade of Malta, the supply of spares to maintain equipments was uncertain and a great deal of improvisation was necessary. Much local manufacture had to be undertaken, and in this great assistance was given in HM Dockyard by the Admiral Superintendent.

When static anti-aircraft guns were installed, and there were over 70 of them, they had to be dismantled in HM Dockyard after arrival and then reassembled and erected on the site, as there were no transporters on the island.

The 250 AA guns and several hundred heavy and light machine guns were continuously in action during air raids, and were subject to greater wear than was experienced anywhere else during the war. The heavy bombing also did considerable damage to guns and fire control instruments. The task of keeping these in action was the most important one undertaken by the RAOC Workshop Services and involved much work "on site" by travelling teams of Armament Artificers. It was no easy matter to get to the scene of the trouble along roads damaged or blocked by bombing. Sometimes horse-drawn transport had to be used owing to the shortage of MT and petrol.

The workshop staff were under very great strain during the worst of the bombing, as they were working almost continuously and had very little sleep, but their efforts were rewarded by the number of guns kept in action. It was exceptional for more than 5 per cent of the AA Artillery to be out of action at any one time.

The RAOC worked closely with the RAF and Royal Navy in the design and manufacture of special instruments in Gun Operating Rooms for the fighter and anti-aircraft defence of Malta. RAOC workshops were responsible for linking HMS *Terror*, a monitor, into both the anti-aircraft and coast defence systems of the fortress, the 15-inch guns being "tied into" the coast defences.

The coast of Malta was defended by several hundred concrete machine gun posts. The RAOC workshops designed and produced a special mounting for all these posts. It would take either the Vickers or Bren gun, and one could be changed for the other in a matter of seconds.

A small underground workshop was built and in it vital machinery was installed, but no more could be done with the limited tunnelling resources which were engaged on projects of a higher operational priority. All workshops suffered heavy damage from bombing and the peace-time shop at Ospizio was completely destroyed.

When REME was formed in 1942 the RAOC Workshops staff were transferred to that Corps. This occurred towards the end of the siege.

CONVOYS

When the Luftwaffe returned to Sicily in December 1941, the sailing of convoys to Malta became increasingly hazardous. In March 1942 a convoy of four merchant ships from the Middle East was continuously attacked. Only two ships reached the Grand Harbour and they were both heavily bombed there before they could unload their cargo. One of these ships, the SS *Talbot*, tied up close to the wharf opposite the Marina Pinto depot. It contained a good deal of ammunition and was burning fiercely. The Royal Navy therefore decided to sink the ship in the shallow water where she lay.

After this event the Military Docks Directorate was given all military resources in the island to unload cargo as soon as a convoy arrived and clear the stores immediately to dispersal areas away from the harbour. Ordnance stores were then collected from these "field dumps" by staff from the Ordnance Depots and taken to their correct location. As a result of these measures no Ordnance stores were lost afterwards through ships being bombed in harbour.

LOCAL DEFENCE BY RAOC

The RAOC were responsible for the local defence of their installations and surrounding areas, under the Infantry commander of the sector in which they were located. This included action against parachutists. They also manned AA light machine guns at all depots and workshops during air raids, firing at low-flying hostile aircraft. The Corps manned a 4-inch land-mounted naval gun at the depot at Marina Pinto, for defence inside the Grand Harbour against seaborne attack.

END OF THE SIEGE

The advance of the Eighth Army from Alamein and the Allied landings in French North Africa brought the end of the Siege of Malta, which occurred when a large convoy got through late in November 1942. By then all stocks, including Ordnance Stores, were at a very low level.

THIRD PHASE

During the blockade the small number of ships which got through carried mainly food and ammunition. From November 19th to December 31st 1942, 125 merchant ships and 30 tankers discharged their cargos in Malta as compared with 11 merchant ships and one tanker between mid-October 1941 and the end of the siege.

In the 6-week period after the end of the siege the Ordnance depots were stocked up from scratch to a higher level than had originally been planned, as the level of reserves was increased. Thus the raising of the siege gave no relief to the RAOC staff, so far as pressure of work was concerned, although bombing had ceased. During this period they worked continuously, on a 16-hour shift system.

The DOS Middle East was now able to exercise direct control over Ordnance activity in Malta and the depot was reorganized on standard AOD lines with the normal sub-depots, laundry and returned stores depot.

The sub-depot at Sa Maison was rebuilt as an MT depot. The Christian Brothers Education School, which had been used as a "dispersal" depot during the siege, was now reorganized to hold MT detail stores. In the same way St. Edward's College, which had held some ammunition and general stores, was used for Command stocks of clothing and equipment. The RAOC billets near Attard were converted to hold stores for issue to four general hospitals. It was now possible to extend the underground storage at Marina Pinto and an officers shop was opened near Valletta. Now that bombing had ceased, reconstruction and new construction proceeded at a great pace.

SUPPORT OF OPERATIONS AGAINST SICILY

Malta was the assembly area for a significant part of the Eighth Army in the assault on Sicily.

Accommodation stores had to be provided for the camps for this large force, and, although units were supposed to be equipped to full war scale before arrival, some deficiencies were inevitable and these were made up from Malta depot stocks. Altogether 30 tented transit camps were required for the Eighth Army units and three general hospitals were equipped to deal with casualties from Sicily.

It was originally planned that all waterproofing of vehicles would be carried out in North Africa. At the last minute it was decided that the vehicles of units staging in Malta would be waterproofed there. The kits were hurried over from the Middle East and REME staff sent to supervise the work. Nearly 500 vehicles were waterproofed of which 150 required repair first. The repairs were carried out in REME workshops, Malta, and for this a special scaling of spares had to be supplied urgently as Malta was not scaled for many of the vehicles. DADOS Malta obtained most of these items from 500 AOD in Tripoli and then flew on to the Middle East to arrange for the balance to be flown to Malta from the BODs there. During this period a 48-hour air supply service of urgently required stores was arranged from the Middle East, an Air Detachment of 510 Stores Convoy Unit being established at Luqa airfield to assist.

As regards ammunition, the staff at Fort Musta was 6 officers and 35 other ranks, sufficient for Malta Garrison and for the small additional reserves and transit stocks of 1,000 tons planned for the Sicily campaign. However, in May 1943 advice was received that larger quantities would be passed through the island, the final figure being 6,200 tons. The original site at Marsascala, even though enlarged, was inadequate and another was laid out. During June 6th, 172 tons were received in these two sites. The Port Ordnance Detachment sent to Malta from the Middle East to assist in transit work contained no ammunition staff and the ammunition depot bore the brunt of handling the largely increased stocks. This ammunition was a reserve, not normal maintenance, but in the event 3,000 tons were issued, to meet urgent requirements during the campaign —three times the original planned reserve.

Other duties in support of the Sicily campaign were the holding of a reserve of oxygen and acetylene cylinders, the provision of a 12-hour laundry service for hospital ships passing through Malta and the storage, packed specially for urgent issue, of a reserve of Controlled Warlike Stores.

Provision was also made for up to 100,000 casualties and survivors. Special clearing points were established on the beaches and camps were equipped for reception of the casualties. Happily casualties were relatively light but one camp was used for survivors from the airborne assault, who were re-equipped there.

After the occupation of Sicily a few issues of clothing and general stores were made to the Eighth Army for the early stages of the campaign in Italy, but gradually Malta dropped out of the picture and the Port Ordnance Detachment and Air Detachment of the Stores Convoy Unit were withdrawn.

FOURTH PHASE

The Garrison of Malta was reduced to the equivalent of an Infantry Brigade, with anti-aircraft, coast defence and ancillary units with a large and somewhat unpredictable commitment for "common users". Surplus stocks of Ordnance Stores were eaten down by issuing to the BODs which were forming in Italy or by backloading to the Middle East.

It had been necessary to disperse stocks widely as a measure of protection against bombing, but this danger had now passed and in the first 3 months of 1944 a start was made on concentrating the residual stocks so that the depot could be operated efficiently with a much reduced staff. Stores were brought in from outside locations to St. Edward's College, and in the following 3 months the MT Group was transferred from the Christian Brothers School to Sa Maison. The Poor House Laundry was closed down. In early 1945 the technical stores were removed from rock storage at Gargur and this sub-depot concentrated at Marina Pinto.

Late in 1944 Malta again reverted to the control of the War Office except that provision and stock control came under the Central Ordnance Provision Office, Middle East.

CONCLUSION

Malta was the only British island fortress which successfully withstood a siege during the war, and it was also the only colony in which conscription was introduced. The loyalty and fortitude of the population were very properly recognized by the award of the George Cross to the island.

The RAOC had to face unique problems of maintenance and repair under heavy bombing. They attained a high and well-deserved reputation for efficiency and devotion to duty, particularly in the maintenance and repair of anti-aircraft equipment, the supply of ammunition and bomb disposal.

EAST AFRICA

Kenya and Tanganyika were not peace-time Army stations. Only small Colonial forces were maintained. They were not expected to operate outside the colony and were not trained for modern war. They had no mechanical transport and no Ordnance Services.

The Italian conquest of Ethiopia brought a change in the situation. With Italian Somaliland there was now a large area of Italian colonial territory impinging on the Sudan and Kenya. In the event of war with Italy, Kenya would be in danger of invasion, but in more favourable circumstances would form a useful base for an attack on Ethiopia and Italian Somaliland.

In September 1939 an ADOS was sent out from the United Kingdom and the East Africa Army Ordnance Corps (EAAOC) was formed. The total strength on formation was 4 Officers, 2 Warrant Officers, 3 Sergeants and 14 Asiatics and 38 Africans.

Apart from unskilled labour the scope for dilution was limited. Most of the Africans available for recruitment at that time were uneducated and unable to read the markings on the cases or identify the stores, the novelty of which constituted an irresistible temptation to pilfering.

No time was lost in requisitioning buildings, and although the manufacturing resources of the theatre were small, contracts were placed for uniforms and tentage. The railway workshops manufactured 16,000 land mines and spares for small arms and mortars.

The first AOD was opened in December 1939 at Nanyuki. During the first 5 months of 1940 the Ordnance Services had the task of building up their own organization while at the same time equipping and mobilizing units. Two LADs were formed and an Ordnance Field Park was located at Kitale railhead in Kenya.

Progress in the early days might have been quicker if a skeleton RAOC staff had been sent out. As it was, only the ADOS had previous experience. There was no agreed source for the provision of stores. Rifles, ammunition and some general stores were obtained by placing demands, at first without authority, on India.

Earlier liaison with the South African Mobile Field Force on Ordnance matters would have assisted joint planning and operation. Permission to purchase stores from South Africa was not granted until January 1940.

In June 1940, at the time of the capitulation of France and the entry of Italy into the war, the South African Mobile Field Force began to arrive in Kenya, with its associated Services. They worked closely with the EAAOC in stores and ammunition depots.

In August 1940 the head of the Ordnance Services was upgraded to DDOS, and by the end of the year a BOD had been formed at Nairobi with AODs at Nanyuki and Mombasa. After the arrival of 2 officers and 22 other ranks in November 1940 there were no further reinforcements from the United Kingdom until March 1942.

This small organization was called upon to form a base from which the forces under General Cunningham advanced into Abyssinia from the south to liberate that country. Immense distances were covered over country in which roads worthy of the name hardly existed. AODs were formed as the advance proceeded, and three Ordnance Field Parks were maintained in addition to various mobile workshops and ammunition dumps. Staff and stores were despatched long before the place where they were required to form a depot had been captured. For example 5 South African Brigade was refitted at a few days' notice for its transfer by sea from Mombasa to Berbera in British Somaliland in time for its reappearance in the Abyssinian highlands at the appropriate moment.

At the end of the campaign, in addition to a BOD and BOW at Nairobi and a BAD at Mitubiri, the following Advanced Ordnance Depots had been formed.

Location	*Distance from Base*
Kenya	
Gilgil	81 miles, road or rail
Nanyuki	130 miles, road or rail
Mombasa	324 miles, road or rail
Uganda	
Jinja	435 miles, road or rail
N. Rhodesia	
Lusaka	2,290 miles, rail, lake steamer, road, rail

Location	Distance from Base
British Somaliland	
Berbera	1,655 miles road (more by sea)
Italian Somaliland	
Mogadishu	884 miles, road
Afgoi (Ammunition)	900 miles, road
Ethiopia	
Diredawa	1,740 miles, road
Addis Ababa	2,030 miles, road

Two mobile forward ammunition sections and eight mobile workshops were formed.

The length of the L of C and state of the roads, combined with the shortage of transport, made it necessary to hold a month's supply grounded at intervals of about 200 miles. The climate varied from the extreme heat of Somaliland to severe cold and heavy rain in the highlands.

The Ordnance strength for this operation was 58 officers (including 12 South Africans), 90 British and 180 South African NCOs and 580 Asiatics and Africans.

Early in 1942 East Africa became an independent Command and formed a base from which 11th East African Division was mobilized, sent to Burma, and supplied thereafter.

The creation of this base caused overloading of the BOD. Temporary shelters of wood and tarpaulin were constructed for the additional stores, which provided protection but hampered identification and speed of issue. In the late summer of 1942, with the formation of REME, the workshop duties were transferred to the newly formed EAEME, and vehicle parks, previously operated by the EAASC were taken over. Local resources were further developed by establishing a paint factory, a clothing factory and a boot factory (at Nakuru). Soap and leather were supplied to the Middle East. A new BAD was built at Gilgil in 1943. It had a capacity of 35,000 tons of ammunition.

After the Abyssinian campaign when East Africa was being developed as a base, it became possible to recruit Africans with sufficient aptitude to be trained as tradesmen. English-speaking Africans were trained as Clerks and Storemen so that some reduction in European manpower was possible.

The arrival of a draft of ATS clerks in March 1943 was a most valuable reinforcement and the Ordnance strength at the end of that year was:

Officers	159
British other ranks	810
ATS	116
Africans and Asiatics	4,308

During the war the DDsOS in East Africa Command were, in succession, Brigadiers J. W. Gaisford, H. R. Primmer and C. W. Bacon.

MADAGASCAR

The occupation of this island was undertaken in the summer of 1942 to forestall any possible action by the Japanese. The force sailed from the United Kingdom and contained RAOC elements consisting of an Ordnance Beach Detachment, and elements to form small AODs.

The first landing was at Diego Suarez on May 6th 1942. Little opposition was encountered and the OBD was established as the nucleus of a stores depot and ammunition depot. Further landings were made at Majunga and Tamatave at each of which a small depot was formed. But they were closed down when the capital, Tananarive, was captured and an AOD was formed there. The original force was then withdrawn for service elsewhere and the island was occupied and administered by troops from East Africa and South Africa.

Diego Suarez became the AOD for the island supplied from East Africa base, and Tananarive depot was closed down. The concentration of this load on the Diego Suarez depot coincided with a very high sickness rate and for a short time the depot was almost out of action, but a system of reliefs from the mainland was adopted and the sickness rate fell. The depot finally closed a month after the end of the war.

There was some difficulty over the maintenance of vehicles. The original force had British vehicles and spares for them continued to arrive after the force and its vehicles had moved on. The troops from East Africa had a mixed lot of vehicles and maintenance was not automatic. Time was necessary to gather the requisite information and ensure adequate stock levels of the right stores, and meanwhile the shortage of MT spares was serious.

WEST AFRICA

The West African Command embraced four separate colonies, three of which were encompassed by French territory. There was no land communication between any of these colonies. They were:

Gambia (4,100 sq miles). Few roads and no railway. Dangerously near Dakar, a Vichy-controlled port we had failed to capture.

Sierra Leone (27,900 sq miles). Few good roads. One railway to the interior. A defended port at Freetown.

Gold Coast—now Ghana (91,800 sq miles). A large colony with some roads, a railway which did not go far inland. No harbour. Capital Accra.

Nigeria (372,000 sq miles). The largest colony with roads, railways and a good harbour at Lagos.

Before the war there was no Ordnance organization in West Africa Command except for a handful of men. There was a coast defence battery at Freetown but otherwise military requirements were met by the West African Frontier Force, consisting of native units with British officers and senior NCOs, administered by the various Colonial Governments, who purchased their equipment through the Colonial Office.

When war broke out it immediately became clear that West Africa was very significant both as a source of supply and as a focal point in Empire communications. Exports essential to our war economy included manganese, tin, bauxite, cocoa, palm oil, ground-nuts and timber.

However, the area was in no immediate danger of attack and it was not until the end of 1940 that GHQ West Africa Command was formed. The senior Ordnance appointment was ADOS and the RAOC assumed responsibility for the supply of Ordnance stores, equipments and ammunition to all units in the Command including the Royal West African Frontier Force. In January 1942 the senior Ordnance appointment was upgraded to DDOS (Colonel).

Apart from the geographical difficulties and the lack of communications and other facilities, certain other problems hampered the creation of an efficient Ordnance organization. There was a serious lack of covered storehouse accommodation and port facilities were very poor. It was very difficult to recruit suitable labour and the more intelligent men had to be selected, taught English and trained in storehouse procedures. All this took time, but eventually the RAOC establishment was diluted to the ratio of 1 in 14, no mean achievement.

The climate—high temperature and humidity—caused rapid deterioration of stores unless special steps were taken to preserve them. There was widespread prevalence of rust, woolly-bear, teredo worm, fungus and mildew. Stores could not be unpacked and held loose in bins without risk of early deterioration, and it became a rule that stores were not unpacked until required for immediate issue. Preservation was a continuous and heavy commitment. Normal methods were useless, for example the bristles of brushes might be completely covered with naphthalene dust but were nevertheless rapidly eaten by moth and other insects.

The idea of having one BOD for the whole Command was considered but was dropped because of difficulties of inter-communication and it was decided to have Nos. 1 and 2 BODs in Nigeria, No. 3 in the Gold Coast, No. 4 in Sierra Leone and No. 5 in Gambia.

With the capitulation of France, and the consequent threat from Vichy-controlled French North Africa, the flow of Ordnance stores and ammunition to the Command increased. The danger of air attack, lack of accommodation and lack of harbours enforced the wide dispersion of depots, but this hampered their efficient and economical working.

The intake of stores to the Gold Coast was assisted by the building of a jetty, harbour, docks and an aerodrome at Takoradi, which also became a base for the transport of stores across Africa from west to east, thus saving the long haul round the Cape.

BADs were for the most part well sited and planned. Small sheds (100 tons capacity) were sited at safety distances of 100 yards. Many were traversed.

In a further reorganization of depots in mid-1943 the opportunity was taken to re-number the depots to avoid duplication and confusion. For example there was a 5 BOD in the Middle East and another in Gambia. It was therefore decided to use the 300 series for depots in West Africa Command, the final organization being:

> 301 BOD and 301 BAD. Nigeria.
> 302 BOD and 302 BAD. Gold Coast.
> 303 BOD and 303 BAD. Sierra Leone.
> 304 BOD and 304 BAD. Gambia.

The total storage space in BODs was 797,000 sq ft covered and 1,131,000 sq ft open. In BADs the total space was 201,000 sq ft.

Storehouse buildings needed as much attention and repair as the stores they contained. Few buildings were proof against tropical rain after two or three years. Those with concrete floor and walls, and a slate roof were best.

The small number of RAOC officers and other ranks were slightly reinforced and RASC personnel were transferred to the BODs when the Corps took over the supply of RASC vehicles and spares in 1942.

Civilian labourers were hard-working but on the whole unreliable storemen. This was largely due to the language problem. There were scores of dialects and it was necessary to use Hausa as a sort of "lingua franca", much as Urdu was used in India. It was also necessary to teach many of them basic English. Clerks of an adequate standard were almost impossible to obtain in Sierra Leone and Gambia. Those colonies had to rely on African Other Ranks posted from Nigeria or the Gold Coast. A West African Army Ordnance Corps (WAAOC) was formed, trade tests being based on those used in the RAOC.

After the landings in French North Africa in 1942 the threat to British West Africa was removed. It was therefore decided to despatch overseas one West African Division with corps increment and base troops. This was the first mobilization task faced by the Ordnance Services in the Command, and useful lessons had been learnt when a second Division (82nd West African) was mobilized later on. The Ordnance Field Parks were formed from staff drawn from the BODs.

For reasons of stock control it was necessary to centralize the provision work for all stores in the four BODs except MT spares. The central provision office was at GHQ.

At the end of the war the strength of the Army Ordnance Services in West Africa was:

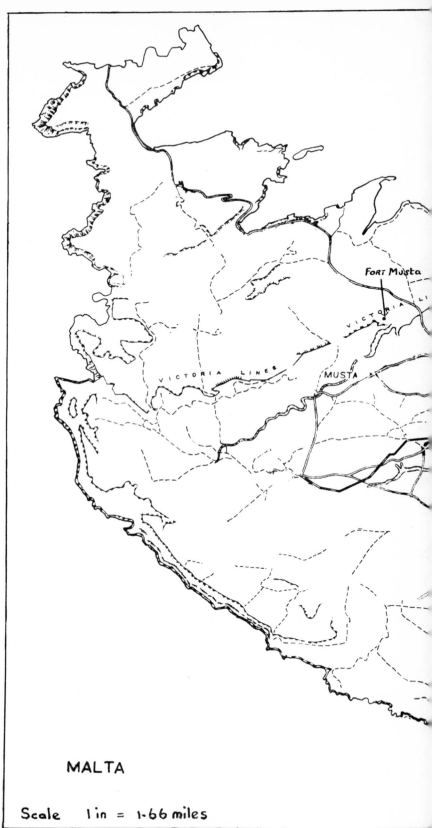

MALTA

Scale 1 in = 1·66 miles

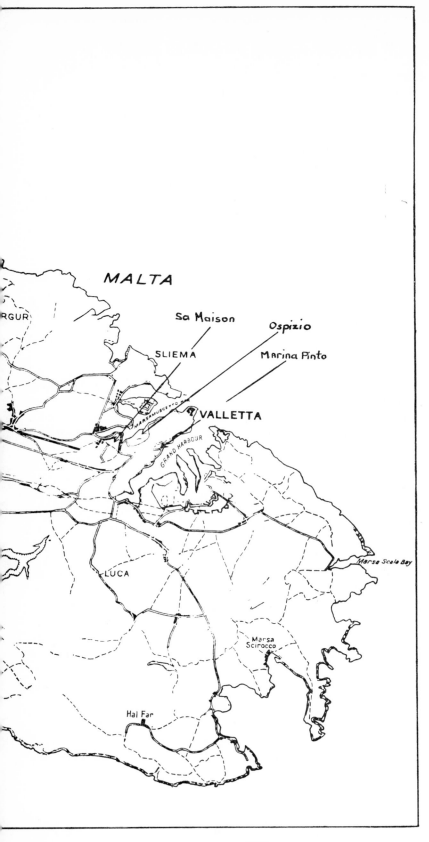

MALTA

RGUR

Sa Maison
Ospizio
SLIEMA
Marina Pinto
MARSAMUSCETTO
VALLETTA
GRAND HARBOUR

Marsa Scala Bay

LUCA

Marsa
Scirocco

Hal Far

British officers	79
British other ranks	344
African other ranks	3,096
Civilians	2,500

PERSIA AND IRAQ COMMAND

The theatre of operations based on the Persian Gulf was subject to constant changes, depending on the fluctuating political and strategic situation. At the beginning of the war this was not an active theatre. It was a British sphere of influence and from the military point of view the RAF were firmly established, although the lack of land forces made this control somewhat tenuous.

In the first half of 1941 the situation changed. The German successes in the Eastern Mediterranean, and the propaganda which accompanied them, encouraged the dissident elements under Rashid Ali and the revolt in Iraq occurred. These operations and the suppression of the revolt have already been described. From the RAOC point of view the dual control caused difficulties.

GHQ Middle East not unreasonably wanted India to take over full responsibility, and at this time such an arrangement was possible. However, Middle East Command was given responsibility and, as has been seen, a small force was despatched from the Middle East. But Indian Army formations were mainly responsible for the suppression of the Rashid Ali revolt and the subsequent operations in Persia.

Iraq again came under the Middle East Command and in 1942 a new threat was created by the rapid advance of the German Armies into the Caucasus. General Auchinleck was in the difficult position of looking both ways. The threat of attack through Palestine and Iraq was always present in his mind, and periodically he found it necessary, when operations went against us in the Western Desert, to move out and take command of the Eighth Army.

After the withdrawal to the Alamein line it was decided that the GOC in C Middle East must be relieved of his dual responsibility. By then General Auchinleck had been moved to India. The decision to form a separate Persia and Iraq Command (PAIC) was undoubtedly sound, but it was made too late, when the need for such an organization was rapidly diminishing. It should also be noted that after the beginning of 1942 the Indian Government and armed forces were fully committed with operations in South-East Asia, and could hardly exercise any influence in Persia and Iraq.

Once the threat from the Caucasus had been removed the threefold purpose of PAIC was:

(a) to form a base for the supply of vehicles and stores to the Russians via Persia;

(b) to protect the oilfields in the area;
(c) to form a base for the supply of equipment to South-East Asia Command for the war against Japan.

In the event these tasks never developed to a significant extent. For the first a special agency was formed. The second posed no serious problem. The sudden collapse of Japan prevented the full development of the third task.

Thus, in the end, the administrative services in the Iraq base were engaged mainly in tidying up the residual confusion of earlier campaigns, and finding reinforcements for theatres of greater operational significance. As the climate at the Persian Gulf end of Iraq is one of the worst in the world, and air-conditioning was not installed in the British camps, it was no easy matter to maintain morale in these conditions and the fact that this was achieved is a tribute to the personality and leadership of those in command of the RAOC units in the later stages of the war.

ORDNANCE SERVICES IN PERSIA AND IRAQ

The first Ordnance units in Iraq were from the IAOC. No. 2 BOD on Indian war establishment had the normal three sub-depot and returned stores depot organization, but was a very small unit, equivalent in strength to a headquarters and one Ordnance stores company RAOC. A permanent site was found at Shaiba in May 1941, but it was not until October 1941 that the erection of storehouses was begun.

Conditions were very difficult. Day temperatures rose to 125 degrees in the shade, the only protection was in tents and there were frequent sand storms lasting 6 hours at a time. The unit had no lifting equipment, no racking and no bins, which had to be improvised from packing cases and petrol tins. There was no timber for use as dunnage. Local labour was unobtainable in the early days and all handling of stores had to be done by this small Ordnance unit with occasional help from detachments of Indian Infantry when they could be spared.

In time reinforcements were sent out. Plans were made for the establishment of AODs at Nussayab, 50 miles south of Baghdad, Ahwaz. Mosul and Kirkuk, but none of these plans matured and in the end nothing larger than a railhead ordnance depot was formed at any of these places.

Later on, British troops were sent out and the units at Shaiba were built up to a full-scale RAOC BOD and BAD by February 1943. The depots were scaled to support a force of 16 Divisions, but after the successful campaigns in North Africa and the removal of the threat to the Caucasus, there was no more likelihood of a force operating from the Persian Gulf and the task became one of sorting stocks and back-loading surpluses. This necessary but somewhat uninspiring work was carried out with great energy and efficiency under the control of Colonel

W. F. Snook commanding the BOD and Lieutenant-Colonel Jones (IAOC), commanding the BAD.

NORTH AMERICA

At the beginning of the war the United States were neutral. For this and financial reasons the U.S.A. were not at first considered as an important source of warlike stores. Canada at that time did not manufacture warlike stores, relying on Britain to supply her forces.

The isolation of Great Britain after the fall of France completely transformed the situation. First "Cash and Carry" and then "Lease Lend" greatly facilitated the use of American material resources. The need for Canada to step up war production was also abundantly clear.

In 1941 a small British Army Staff under Brigadier H. R. Kerr was formed at Washintgon to coordinate the procurement of stores from North American sources. In July 1941 two RAOC officers and four NCOs were sent out to form the nucleus of the Ordnance Branch of the BAS.

From the beginning many difficulties were encountered. The provision of maintenance spares was unsatisfactory. We naturally required spares scaled at war wastage rates but the Americans, not being at war and lacking war experience, saw no need to alter their existing scales and no proper machinery existed for recording details of issues and deficiencies in shipments.

Stores were exported by the shipping section of the British Purchasing Commission, whose records were found to be inadequate and unreliable.

The War Office and theatres of war were not given full information of the state of supply of Ordnance stores from North America. American documentation, catalogues and nomenclature were entirely different from those in the British system and also failed in many respects to meet the requirements of the user in war.

The BAS was a liaison headquarters and had no authority to give instructions to the United States or Canadian Government Agencies or Army Supply Corps, and there was no depot on the Continent into which stores ordered through the British Purchasing Commission could be moved and from which shipment to the United Kingdom or war theatres could be controlled.

Although a knowledge of British Ordnance procedure was important, it was also essential to acquire a full understanding of the methods and procedures used by the various supply organizations in North America, and to our representatives these seemed strange and complex at first.

The original BAS Ordnance staff spent the first 2 months making essential contacts with American Supply agencies, depots and arsenals, and so paving the way for a larger group which sailed in September 1941.

This group, headed by a DDOS, Colonel C. G. Reynolds, consisted of RAOC Officers, Warrant Officers and NCOs, who covered all aspects of Ordnance work including ammunition and engineering. One of the officers was to be an AQMG on Brigadier Kerr's staff. The party sailed on board a small and ancient ship, the S.S. *Baltrover*, and, after an uneventful 3-week voyage, landed at Halifax and moved on to Washington. On arrival there the AQMG was told that he was to move forthwith to Ottawa and establish a branch of the BAS there.

Meanwhile the Ordnance branch settled down to tackle the many outstanding problems in detail. There was a great fund of goodwill towards Great Britain and admiration for her determined fight against odds, but at this time most Americans were determined that their country was not going to be dragged into the fight.

Hard-headed American business men, who prided themselves on their toughness, did not take kindly to any criticism from British Army officers, even though they were disguised as civilians. Any request for a change in procedure, however slight, might be regarded as ignorant and carping criticism asking for a "Take it or Leave it" response. Patience was needed, but it was not easy for those who had been in France at the time of Dunkirk or in London during the Blitz to be patient when the situation demanded urgent action.

Two months later the Japanese attacked Pearl Harbour and the situation changed completely. The Americans were now in the fight. They wasted no time on vain regrets but got down to the business of war with typical drive and determination. North America now grew rapidly into a major source of supply for the Allies, and at the same time the Ordnance Branch of the British Army Staff grew in size and significance.

Eventually the complete organization in the United States was as follows:

Washington Headquarters. Controlled all BAS Ordnance functions in North America. Responsible for liaison with the headquarters of the various U.S. Army Supply Corps and collaboration with other British Missions, and BAS branches. Organized in sections corresponding to the War Office provision branches. A technical publications branch was included. Its task was to obtain and distribute to overseas theatres North American technical publications, also to distribute British publications to BAS branches and British Missions in North America.

Detroit Office. Primarily responsible for "A" and "B" vehicle spares. Opened when the U.S. Ordnance Corps transferred control of these items from Washington to Detroit.

Philadelphia Office. Responsible for controlling the export of ammunition. Opened when the corresponding Division of the U.S. Ordnance Corps was moved from Washington to Philadelphia. The Office also included an Engineer and Signals Technical Section to work with the U.S. Signal Corps.

New York Office. This was a shipping agency in touch with the American War Forwarding Corporation and the British Ministry of War Transport.

Ordnance Outstations. British Ordnance Officers and NCOs were stationed at the main American depots and arsenals which were the sources of supply of stores and ammunition for British and Dominion use.

The main functions of the Headquarters, which eventually had 14 sections, were shipping and progress, statistics, scales, spare parts procurement, demands from war theatres, and accounts and documentation.

METHODS OF PROCUREMENT

There were three methods of procurement which followed one after the other. The first was by purchase on a "spot" or contractual basis. Following depletion of British dollar reserves and the passing of the Lease-Lend Act supplies were obtained by requisitions submitted to the Office of Lease-Lend Administration. Presidential approval for all requisitions was required and initially the process was cumbersome. After the entry of the United States into the war the requisition system was largely superseded by assignment, that is monthly allocations of American production made by the Munitions Assignment Committee.

British representation on the Munitions Assignment Committee was provided by the Assignments and Requirements Branch of the BAS. This was a staff branch but BAS (Ordnance) supplied all the necessary briefing for stores of their concern.

CONTROL AND PROGRESS OF EXPORTS

After the entry of America into the war the BAS was given authority which previously had to be exercised through the British Purchasing Commission. Now, at last, the organization truly represented the War Office and could act as a direct link between the War Office and North American sources of supply.

The transfer of authority assisted the correct linking of spares and accessories with main equipments. It permitted supervision of packing and marking by outstation representatives. It also made possible the creation of comprehensive records covering all details of orders and consignments of spare parts to each destination. A regular exchange of information with the War Office and theatres was established regarding availabilities and exports.

PROVISION OF MAINTENANCE SPARE PARTS

It was found almost impossible to obtain agreement to definite scales. At first the policy was to produce main equipments to the exclusion of spare parts, owing to the urgent need for main equipments and the influence of manufacturers who did not appreciate the war-time requirement for spares and suffered no penalty for failing to produce them.

Maintenance of North American equipments was based on an automatic shipment programme which was frequently changed. Consignments were constantly late and were sometimes over 50 per cent deficient.

The arrangement finally agreed for most equipments was that 12 months' spares would accompany the equipment and future requirements would be met by regular Replenishment Demands from each theatre, supplemented by Urgent Interim Demands in an emergency. This avoided the wasteful automatic supply of unwanted items.

The problem of deficiencies continued to be serious and BAS (Ordnance) maintained a record on an IBM punched card machine from which "settlement" lists were prepared and submitted to the U.S. War Department. However, issues continued to be unsatisfactory until late in 1943. The system of "All Time Buys" in which immediate export was made of all available spare parts proved satisfactory for "A" vehicles and certain other equipments.

CATALOGUING AND PUBLICATIONS

With the rapid expansion of American war production it proved impossible to establish a standard system of cataloguing and this complete lack of uniformity caused considerable difficulty. Different systems were superimposed one on another. New systems were introduced without any attempt to supersede or even complete the previous system. The position had to be accepted while the war lasted.

BAS (Ordnance) dealt with this problem by producing Master Parts Indices, as used in the RAOC, covering equipments of U.S. origin. The MPI listed and cross-referenced all part numbers used for a given item. The BAS Technical Branches, formed in Washington, Philadelphia and Detroit prepared North American MPIs and amendments to them and distributed them to all theatres. Other technical publications were also produced and distributed by these branches, by which a complete technical library was maintained.

CANADA

Industry in Canada represented considerable war potential. The focal points were the industrial areas of Ontario near Toronto, and the factories in Montreal, though there were of course other important centres. Steps to exploit these resources for war production were taken early and a strong Ministry of Supply inspection team was sent out from Great Britain, its headquarters being at Ottawa.

Canada formed her own Ministry of Supply known as the Department of Munitions and Supply and at National Defence Headquarters the equipment side of the business was handled by the MGO, at that time a civilian, Mr. Victor Sifton, a man of considerable influence.

Fords, Chrysler and General Motors all had factories in Ontario, so that the production of vehicles was considerable from the beginning, but other industries had to be converted for war purposes. The workshops of the Canadian Pacific Railway and the Canadian National Railway in Montreal were heavy shops, readily convertible for the production of tanks, and various other industrial concerns were turned over to the production of guns and ammunition.

With this combination of civil industry and a military inspectorate sent out from the United Kingdom, Canadian war production got off to a good start, but the question of storage, supply and distribution had received less consideration. The civilian view prevailed—that stockpiling was to be avoided as it merely multiplied inventory costs, and reputable shipping agencies existed which could deliver the goods direct to the customer. An intermediate Ordnance organization to receive military equipment from production, store it until it could be moved and then send it suitably packed, marked and documented to the appropriate theatre of war, was considered totally unnecessary—a fifth wheel to the coach.

The Canadian Government had not asked for a branch of the BAS to be established in Ottawa, and when Brigadier Kerr sent his AQMG up there in October 1941, attached to the British Ministry of Supply Inspectorate, he was anticipating an early realization of the need for such an organization.

In fact the need for ample storage facilities was already making itself felt. German submarines were very active, and shipping had already been sunk in the Gulf of St. Lawrence. The shipping of equipment from North America was considerably delayed by the need to form convoys and find escorts, so that the large number of crated vehicles and assemblies from the automotive industry in Ontario was building up and there was no place to store them. These crates were stacked along the railway tracks awaiting shipment but the packing was not such as to withstand the rigours of a Canadian winter.

The first task of the AQMG was therefore to advise, from comparable experience in Britain, on the size, layout, organization and facilities of an Ordnance depot to hold all this Canadian war production.

At first the Canadian authorities were inclined to look for existing buildings for requirements which were expected to disappear after the war and the warehouses at the Empress of Britain wharf at Wolfe's Cove, Quebec, were examined and pronounced suitable for development as a depot.

This proposal was violently opposed by the Transport Controller, Mr. Lockwood, whose views carried considerable weight. Montreal was the gateway to Canada and he insisted that the main Ordnance depot must be sited in the neighbourhood. The decision was therefore made to build a depot which was planned at Longue Pointe in Montreal and has since become the "home" of the RCOC. This was the beginning of the construction of a complex of depots for stores and ammunition throughout Canada.

Parallel with this problem another difficult situation arose. The Angus Works of the CPR in Montreal had contracted to produce the hulls of Valentine tanks. The engines, armament and ammunition were to be produced elsewhere. However, Lord Beaverbrook used his influence to increase the number of tanks being sent to Russia by shipping complete Valentine tanks direct from Montreal and also arranging for tanks to be sent from America, although she was not yet in the war.

This involved many new tasks against time. Engines had to be obtained and fitted. Associated stores and maintenance spares had to be scaled, provided and packed. Weapons had to be fitted in the tank, appropriate small arms for the crew provided and ammunition for all weapons supplied. Stowage had to be planned and tried out. Preservation for the long sea voyage was necessary. Handbooks and spare parts lists had to be translated into Russian. The Russian Mission in Washington (AMTORG) paid frequent visits to Montreal. The head of the mission, M. Korovin, was a trained engineer and a good linguist. He was most appreciative of the work done.

The British Army Staff, Ottawa, gave a good deal of assistance in these activities, but credit for a remarkable achievement of versatility and engineering skill goes to the management and staff of the Angus Works. They gave an early indication of the tremendous potentiality of Canadian war production.

As the need for the BAS, Ottawa, came to be realized the branch came first under the wing of the DMS and was then transferred to the offices of the MGO in National Defence Headquarters. The main activity was in the Ordnance field, involving supply, storage and despatch of stores, but there were also S&T, and Movements sub-branches.

Although the branch was under Brigadier Kerr it was largely autonomous because it operated in a different country and the problems differed in detail. The Canadians naturally did not welcome anything that gave the impression of control from Washington. The same applied to control from London (the War Office). These were of course entirely reasonable views, and as long as they were understood the British Army Staff received the most active cooperation and help. Indeed, throughout North America the hospitality was almost overwhelming to those who had but recently left a blacked out and austerity conscious Britain.

Of course in many matters, such as Assignment, the BAS Headquarters had an important coordinating function.

A Montreal section of the BAS was opened later on, when the ammunition control section of the DMS moved there from Ottawa. There were also BAS representatives attached to the staff of Longue Pointe depot in Montreal.

Before the arrival of the BAS branch in Ottawa the War Office, acting on production forecasts from the DMS, issued distribution and marking

14+

instructions direct to them. This was not very satisfactory because the forecasts were often over-optimistic and the effect on operational planning was harmful. Moreover the staff of the DMS and factories were not conversant with Ordnance store markings and errors occurred. Also the stores had to be marked as they came off the line, without reference to available shipping opportunities. While consignments were awaiting shipment usually in the open, progress and control were impossible.

The difficulty was solved by passing all instructions through BAS Ottawa, who were in close touch with the DMS branches. They could see that marking instructions were understood and keep the War Office informed of the state of production. When Longue Pointe depot was opened in 1942 it absorbed the stores from production. Preservation, packing, marking and issue were done from there. Thus effective progress and control was re-established, although this took time.

For the first year BAS, Ottawa, consisted of a handful of officers and senior other ranks. As it became involved in the control of exports to British forces, and more information in detail was required concerning the rapidly increasing volume of Canadian production, the staff was considerably increased to meet these needs.

In August 1942 the Ordnance Officer, who as an AQMG, formed the branch in Ottawa, requested to be moved to a theatre of war. General Kerr granted this request and the officer returned home, to be appointed DDOS at Allied Forces Headquarters in the TORCH operation. He was replaced by an infantryman who, although a very able staff officer, lacked the experience of Ordnance work which the nature of the task seemed to demand.

LIAISON VISITS

Communication by letter and cable was not of itself sufficient to ensure the satisfactory transaction of the enormous amount of business between North America and the United Kingdom or war theatres.

To an increasing extent liaison visits to North America took place and proved invaluable. They provided first-hand information of user reaction to the method of supply of stores from North America—scaling, packing, marking, documentation, advance information, and so on. Unsatisfactory features were speedily corrected, and the visits greatly strengthened the hand of the BAS staff by confirming the views which they had been trying to "sell".

Visits by BAS officers to overseas theatres also proved of great value, and at the top level a number of visits by General Williams served to emphasize special aspects of the situation, and bring home to the top management in industry and the armed services the tremendous importance of North American production to the British war effort.

General Williams inspected all BAS branches in the United States and Canada, and spoke to leading industrialists. In one visit he was particularly concerned to explain the type of packing which experience in North Africa and elsewhere had shown to be necessary. He found that the importance of efficient preservation was fully understood but that the need to establish the identity of each part by its number, and retain this identification by labelled cartons or other means, was not at first appreciated.

COMMAND

The first DDOS, BAS, Washington, was Brigadier C. G. Reynolds. He was succeeded in 1943 by Brigadier G. P. U. Hardy, who, when he went to Donnington towards the end of the war, handed over to Brigadier Abel Smith.

RAOC IN THE INDIA BASE

The Ordnance depots and workshops in India were designed to meet the needs of the Army in India in peace and to support the minor operations which were periodically undertaken on the North-West Frontier.

Defence of the eastern frontier was considered unnecessary. The jungles and hills of Assam provided a formidable natural barrier, and beyond that were Burma and Malaya, independent of India but British spheres of influence and, therefore, valuable as buffer states.

Communications tended to follow the lines of the great river systems of the Ganges and Indus. Strategic roads were designed to serve forces on the North-West Frontier. The main concentrations of troops were in the United Provinces, the Punjab and North-West Frontier Province (as they were then known), and the majority of depots and arsenals were to be found in these areas.

Some years before the war the idea of merging the IAOC with the RAOC was considered and discarded, and there was therefore no central coordination of the development of the two Corps, with a common purpose. Some exchanges were effected however and in 1939 the DOS India was an RAOC officer, Brigadier W. McN. Verschoyle-Campbell.

The Government of India, like the rest of the Allies, was unprepared for the catastrophic turn of events in 1942. The Ordnance Services faced an almost impossible task. Seriously understaffed, and with their depots at the wrong side of a country twenty times the size of Great Britain, they had to supply an Army withdrawing across the north-west frontier of Burma after the fall of Rangoon and establish depots as far forward as possible in most unsuitable conditions of terrain and climate. The supply of stores to these depots was seriously hampered by the limitations of narrow gauge railways, designed to serve tea plantations, frequent river transhipments and an exceptionally heavy monsoon. Nevertheless Ordnance Field Depots, AODs and AADs were established and most of them remained in operation until the end of the war, a remarkable achievement in the circumstances.

In these early days of the war against Japan the enemy dominated the Bay of Bengal. This made east coast sites unsuitable for base installations. It was only possible at this stage to develop existing installations which were too far to the west but which could be supplied through the ports of Karachi and Bombay. It was not until September 1943, after the Allied Command had re-established control of the Bay of Bengal that the firm decision to form the India Base to support the re-conquest of South-East Asia was made.

In India, sanction for depot construction could normally be obtained only after its necessity had become a physical reality. Apart from the delays in obtaining the necessary approval and the lack of resources in an undeveloped country, the construction of Ordnance installations necessarily received a lower priority than airfield and other urgent expansion. Logistically the key to victory at Imphal and Kohima, and in Burma, was air supply and the loss of equipment through bad storage conditions, though considerable, was the lesser evil.

Other features were also unsatisfactory. The excessive load on the Indian railways prevented local manufacturers from clearing their stores and a system of scattered "holding" depots was introduced. It became necessary for central depots to receive all stores, so that they could be checked, identified, packed and issued to the field depots in Assam and the Arakan. This system was also applied to stores received from the United Kingdom.

The decision to finish the war in Europe before concentrating on the elimination of the Japanese was strategically sound, but it led to a feeling, in the Fourteenth Army, that they were "forgotten" when in fact considerable supplies were being sent out from the United Kingdom.

Unfortunately these Ordnance Stores did not always arrive at the "sharp end" as soon as they should have. First they went to Bombay. Then they were moved by rail to a central depot such as Delhi. There they were unpacked, checked and re-packed for issue to the fighting formations. After that, owing to the indifferent communications, some time elapsed before the stores were in the hands of the troops fighting the Japanese.

VISIT OF COS

Towards the end of 1943 General Williams went out to India. He was much concerned at two aspects of the situation:

1. The apparent lack of touch between the command in the field and the Ordnance Services in India. Unless the DOS India was given the opportunity of visiting formations and seeing whether their needs were being met, he could not do his job.

2. The delays in delivering to the fighting troops stores which had been issued from the United Kingdom, though in many cases they could ill be spared. Largely through unnecessary double handling

they seemed to get lost for months in the intricacies of the Indian communications system.

He found that work had already been started on three depots on the east coast:

1. No. 3 Reserve Base at Panagarh north of Calcutta. This involved the construction of 560,000 sq ft of covered accommodation for all types of Ordnance stores and ammunition, with additional open storage for vehicles.
2. No. 4 Reserve Base at Avadi near Madras, involving 450,000 sq ft of covered accommodation for all types of Ordnance stores except ammunition with additional open storage for vehicles.
3. No. 5 Reserve Base near Vizagapatam, consisting of 250,000 sq ft of transit storage for ammunition.

This distribution was intended to be a form of insurance against Japanese interference with traffic along the east coast, but this danger had now passed.

General Williams, who received full cooperation and assistance from everyone, was able to visit all the main locations in the India Base. He was invited by the C in C India, General Sir Claude Auchinleck, to address a large audience at Delhi and explain the problem and its solution as he saw it from the lessons learnt in earlier campaigns in Europe. In his address he stressed the importance of keeping senior Ordnance Officers fully in the operational picture so that they could anticipate the requirements for the supply of Ordnance stores and ammunition.

Another point was that ammunition, clothing, tentage and accommodation stores could be dispersed as planned but that other general stores, warlike stores and MT spares must be concentrated and their distribution centrally controlled because of their scarcity. He advised their concentration at Avadi (re-designated 206 Indian BOD). Panagarh became known as 205 Indian BOD, holding clothing and general stores.

The inspection, checking, modification, etc., of stores in Indian CODs was unnecessary for stores received from the United Kingdom. These had already been efficiently packed, preserved, identified and documented in the issuing depots and could be sent direct to the proposed new Indian BODs at Avadi and Panagarh, thus saving a great deal of time.

General Williams noted the difficulties which the IAOC faced in operating their depots in India. Chief of these were the shortage of officers with adequate experience, the lack of modern office and storehouse equipment and the shortage of British other ranks. Telephone and teleprinter communication with depots was quite inadequate and this led to avoidable delays.

He recommended the adoption of the Red Star system for the issue of new engine assemblies, the cases of which would be used for the return of the replaced repairable assemblies under the Green Arrow system. He

357

also explained the carton packing of spares which was now standard in the European war theatres, and which guaranteed protection and permanent identification of the store. He pointed out the need for linking ancillary stores permanently with their main equipments, and unpacking and inspecting these main equipments for issue as far forward as possible.

On the storage of ammunition he mentioned the safety distances which had proved adequate in Europe and which were a good deal less than those in force in India. Thus storage space, transport and time would be saved. All these and many other recommendations were accepted and General Williams undertook to send a number of selected officers from the United Kingdom who had experience in operating depots on the lines mentioned.

RAOC SUPPORT

It was in the supply of MT and Technical Stores that RAOC knowledge and experience could be of the greatest assistance, and therefore the story of 206 IBOD at Avadi, Madras, gives the best picture of the RAOC contribution to final victory against Japan.

The depots at Feltham (MT) and Greenford (Technical Stores) had been developed to provide Main Base support for the OVERLORD operation, and they were a natural source of supply of senior officers with the type of training and experience required to establish and operate the depots in the India Base.

Lieutenant-Colonel L. W. Browne, Deputy Commandant at Greenford, was promoted to Colonel and appointed Commandant 206 IBOD and his deputy was Lieutenant-Colonel S. Preston, who had been Deputy Commandant at Feltham since that depot was taken over from the RASC in July 1942.

These two officers were fully briefed by General Williams and were then flown to Delhi—Colonel Browne went straight to Avadi, which was still in the early stages of development, but Lieutenant-Colonel Preston spent 4 months in a temporary appointment at the Central Ordnance Depot for MT spares at Delhi. This gave him valuable experience of depot conditions and problems in India. Avadi was a large Supply Base 20 sq miles in extent, comprising an RAF depot, a REME/IEME workshops, a vehicle depot holding 11,000 vehicles and 206 IBOD. The daily muster rolls showed 62,000 men and there were 125 miles of railway with 700 wagons and 14 locomotives.

206 IBOD had 180 store sheds of Romney pattern in 19 blocks. The depot was well planned with rail-served buildings which were ready before the stores began to arrive. Until standard steel racking arrived in sufficient quantity, wooden racks and bins were designed and manufactured locally, and they served their purpose admirably. From the beginning there was the closest cooperation between the RAOC officers and other ranks and the British and Indian officers, other ranks and civilians of the IAOC.

There were some special problems. The cool, dark buildings proved attractive to snakes, the tyre store being particularly favoured, and this gave added interest to the process of selecting tyres for issue. During the monsoon the depot was flooded and, as the countryside was completely flat, the wide and deep drainage ditches filled up and could not be distinguished from the roads. On one occasion most of the depot transport was ditched and thereafter marker poles were introduced. The volume of clerical work was of course considerable and it was fortunate that Madrassi clerical staff of excellent quality were available in sufficient numbers.

Together with all CODs 206 IBOD prepared landing reserves and beach maintenance packs for the projected operations in Malaya, support of which was the ultimate purpose of the depot. However this task never materialized because of the sudden surrender of Japan in face of nuclear attack.

FURTHER DEVELOPMENTS

Towards the end of 1944 the decision was made to reorganize the groups of depots and other storeholding units which had been established to support the formations on the Assam front and in the Arakan. The smaller depots were to be closed down and two IAODs, 226 at Manipur Road and 223 at Chittagong, were to be enlarged and converted to BODs.

Colonel S. Preston was transferred from Avadi to take over 223 BOD. The task was largely one of "tidying-up" a depot that had been operating in field conditions, and establishing facilities and methods which would enable a greatly increased load to be carried.

The location from which this project was to be launched was Chittagong and it was far from ideal. The depot was in temporary "Basha" accommodation and the climate was appalling, annual rainfall exceeding 300 inches.

To improve the accommodation and facilities new buildings of the Nissen–Romney type were acquired. Construction proceeded at a good speed, the buildings being linked by covered passageways. This rapid progress, assisted by a good deal of self-help from the staff of the depot was an essential preliminary to the creation of efficient storage methods in the buildings.

Steel racking was still scarce but adequate racks and bins were made to the 206 IBOD design and, in the absence of tubular racking, Pierced Steel Planking (PSP), normally used for airfield runways, was acquired and mounted on brick walls to hold the bulkier items.

It was now possible to introduce the latest procedures for location of stores, control and progressing, and Dues Out control on the lines which had been found essential in CODs at home.

The ability to improvise was not lost and was in fact stimulated by the size and urgency of the new task. Bicycle wheels were used in the construction of binners and selectors barrows. The clearance of the old "Bashas" would have been a long and irksome task but someone had the idea of offering them to the coolies for removal as fuel, and the depot staff was treated to the unique spectacle of these erstwhile storehouses walking out of the depot on the heads of teams of coolies on the very day they were dismantled.

Provision was mainly by demand on 205 and 206 IBODs but some items such as "A" vehicle spares were obtained from other depots in India and some packs of "B" vehicle spares for American vehicles were diverted to the depot direct from North America. Clothing was always scarce and a boot repair shop was established in the clothing depot.

The effect of the reorganization was to double the depot output in a period of less than 6 months. The main difficulty was the lack of means to transport the stores to the fighting formations. Much was done by air supply but this also had its limitations. On July 31st 1945, 33 tons of stores were awaiting collection by 7 Rear Airfield Maintenance Organization. On August 8th 1945, 800 tons of stores were awaiting air lift to Burma.

It was necessary to weld together into one team men with widely varying origins and backgrounds. There were British officers and men (RAOC), Indian IAOC officers (both Muslim and Hindu), Indian other ranks of all castes and creeds, African Pioneer Corps (from East and West Africa), with British officers, and local civilian employees of all castes and creeds.

Morale remained high and important factors were that there was a clear objective, progress in the new role was rapid, the Japanese were heading for defeat and the depot was playing an important part in that process.

Early in 1945 Colonel Preston was sent to the United Kingdom and 21st Army Group to select officers for the British BOD to be established in Singapore after the invasion of Malaya, but this mission coincided with the dropping of the atomic bombs on Japan, the plan was changed and instead he took 223 BOD to Singapore.

CHAPTER ELEVEN

THE UNITED KINGDOM BASE

The War Office

We have seen (Chapter 2) that the creation of the Ministry of Supply and the abolition of the appointment of MGO, just before the war, had the useful side effect of rationalizing the organization and duties of the Ordnance Directorate at the War Office. The basic structure evolved in 1939 stood the test of time and, although it expanded considerably to meet the increased load of a world war, its essential features remained.

There were, however, two major changes. The first of these was the transfer of the engineering branches into a separate REME Directorate on the formation of that Corps in 1942. The second was the creation of a Deputy Controller of Ordnance Services (DCOS) with branches to deal with the "domestic" problems of the Corps, its field force organization and training. This development did not occur until March 1943. The absence of such a branch in the early days inhibited the evolution of the best field force organization as there was inadequate machinery for obtaining and studying information from the various operational theatres.

The drive and determination of men like Generals Hill, Williams and Richards had done much to enable the RAOC to recover from the state into which it had fallen before the war. But no amount of determination could provide an early solution to a situation in which the Corps had been reduced to a civilian department with military supervisors so few in number as to be fully occupied on peace-time duties.

This enforced isolation was doubly unfortunate. Because there were no RAOC Regular field force units formed in peace, and because individual and collective training with other arms was almost non-existent, the average commander or staff officer was denied the opportunity of observing and studying Ordnance problems.

Of the many difficulties which the RAOC had to overcome during the war one of the greatest was the fact that to most commanders and staff officers Ordnance work was a complete mystery. Lack of understanding breeds lack of confidence and a reluctance to accept the advice of the expert who is obviously trying to "blind everyone with science". Confusion on the important question of where staff work finished and service work began was inevitable and led to difficulties, already mentioned in the Middle East and elsewhere. It also affected the War Office organization.

The QMG had only recently assumed responsibility for Ordnance Services after a lapse of 12 years and the staff structure which represented the link between him and the Ordnance Directorate had to be evolved to suit the conditions of modern mechanized warfare. Time was so short that the system could only be produced by trial and error.

To begin with the division of responsibility at the War Office on equipment matters between the General Staff and the QMG was far from clear and the confusion tended to spread to headquarters overseas. An example was the direct control by the SD branch of the General Staff of a large range of Ordnance Stores in the Middle East.

At the beginning of the war the QMG was assisted by a DQMG who was supposed to deal direct with the heads of services and also cope with the problems of administrative planning posed by the various campaigns in which the Army was involved. The importance of equipment was soon realized and resulted in the creation of a DQMG (B) to deal direct with the COS, and an administrative planning branch under the QMG was also formed as a result of the administrative failures revealed in the Norwegian campaign.

Towards the end of 1940 the Standing Committee on Army Administration, commenting on the overlapping responsibilities of the General Staff and QMG's department, recommended the abolition of the DSD (W) branch and advocated the appointment of a Director-General of Army Equipment (DGAE) to coordinate the activities of the various branches dealing with equipment. This was really an extension of the investigations before the war which dealt with the increase in work of the engineering branch of the Corps.

To many people in the RAOC it was a disappointment that General Hill was not selected for this appointment. His detailed knowledge of the subject and concern with the future of the engineering branch were important factors in his favour. However, war conditions served to accelerate the decision to form a separate Corps and the post of DGAE was given to a very able officer from outside the Corps.

The directorates concerned were at the time all elements of the RAOC. They were the DOS, dealing with clothing and general stores, the DWS (earlier DOS(W)), dealing with technical and warlike stores and ammunition, and the Director of Mechanical Maintenance (earlier DOS(E) and POME), dealing with the engineering activities of the Corps.

The creation of the appointment of DGAE duplicated in large measure that of COS, and as a result General Hill was retired and the separate appointment of COS was abolished. However, fortunately, the domestic side of RAOC business—field force and depot organization, personnel

Controller[1]

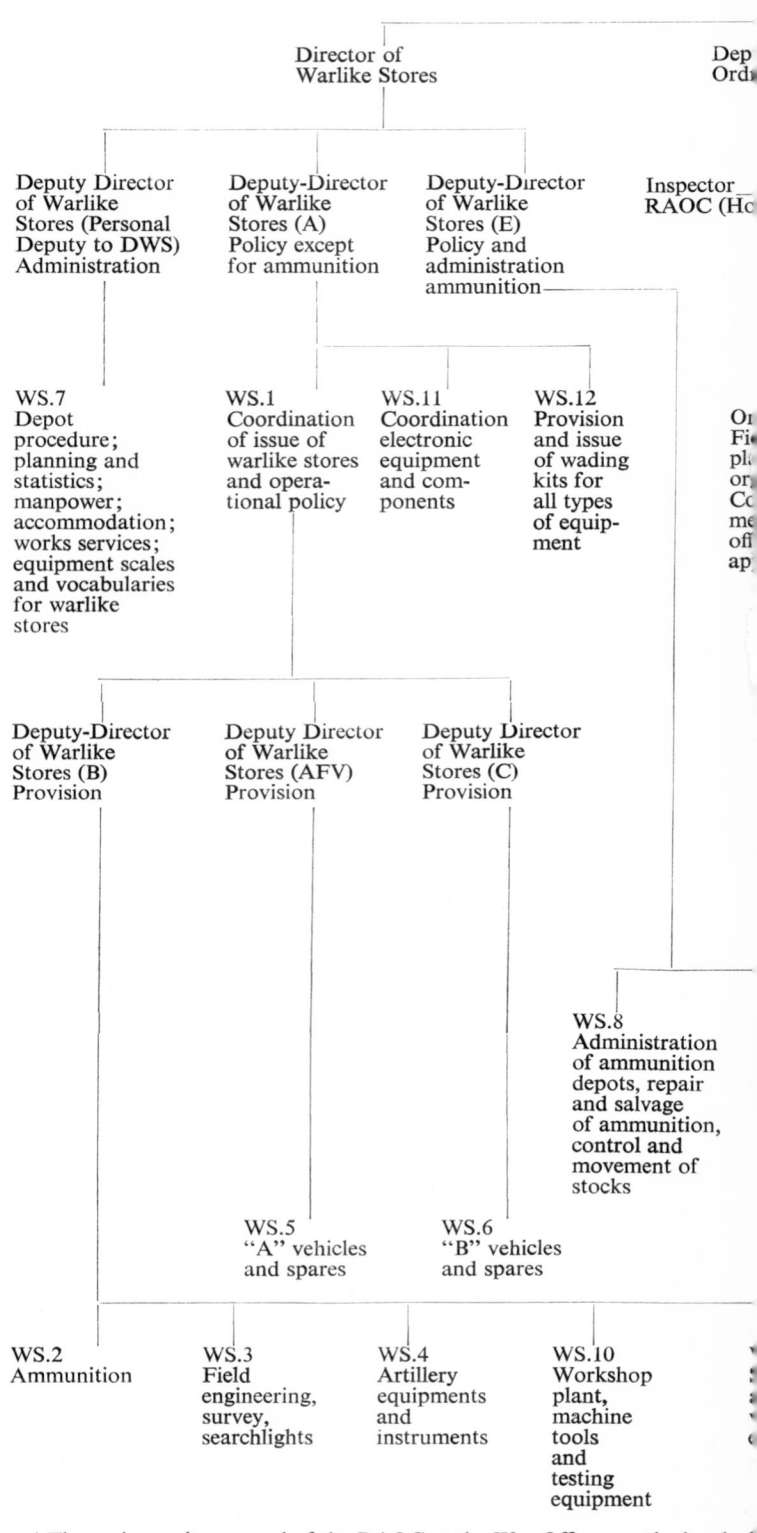

Director of
Warlike Stores

Dep
Ord

Deputy Director
of Warlike
Stores (Personal
Deputy to DWS)
Administration

Deputy-Director
of Warlike
Stores (A)
Policy except
for ammunition

Deputy-Director
of Warlike
Stores (E)
Policy and
administration
ammunition

Inspector
RAOC (Hc

WS.7
Depot
procedure;
planning and
statistics;
manpower;
accommodation;
works services;
equipment scales
and vocabularies
for warlike
stores

WS.1
Coordination
of issue of
warlike stores
and opera-
tional policy

WS.11
Coordination
electronic
equipment
and com-
ponents

WS.12
Provision
and issue
of wading
kits for
all types
of equip-
ment

Or
Fi
pl
or
Cc
me
off
ap

Deputy-Director
of Warlike
Stores (B)
Provision

Deputy Director
of Warlike
Stores (AFV)
Provision

Deputy Director
of Warlike
Stores (C)
Provision

WS.8
Administration
of ammunition
depots, repair
and salvage
of ammunition,
control and
movement of
stocks

WS.5
"A" vehicles
and spares

WS.6
"B" vehicles
and spares

WS.2
Ammunition

WS.3
Field
engineering,
survey,
searchlights

WS.4
Artillery
equipments
and
instruments

WS.10
Workshop
plant,
machine
tools
and
testing
equipment

[1] The senior major-general of the RAOC at the War Office was the head of
appointment of COS was held by DWS.

Ordnance Services[1]

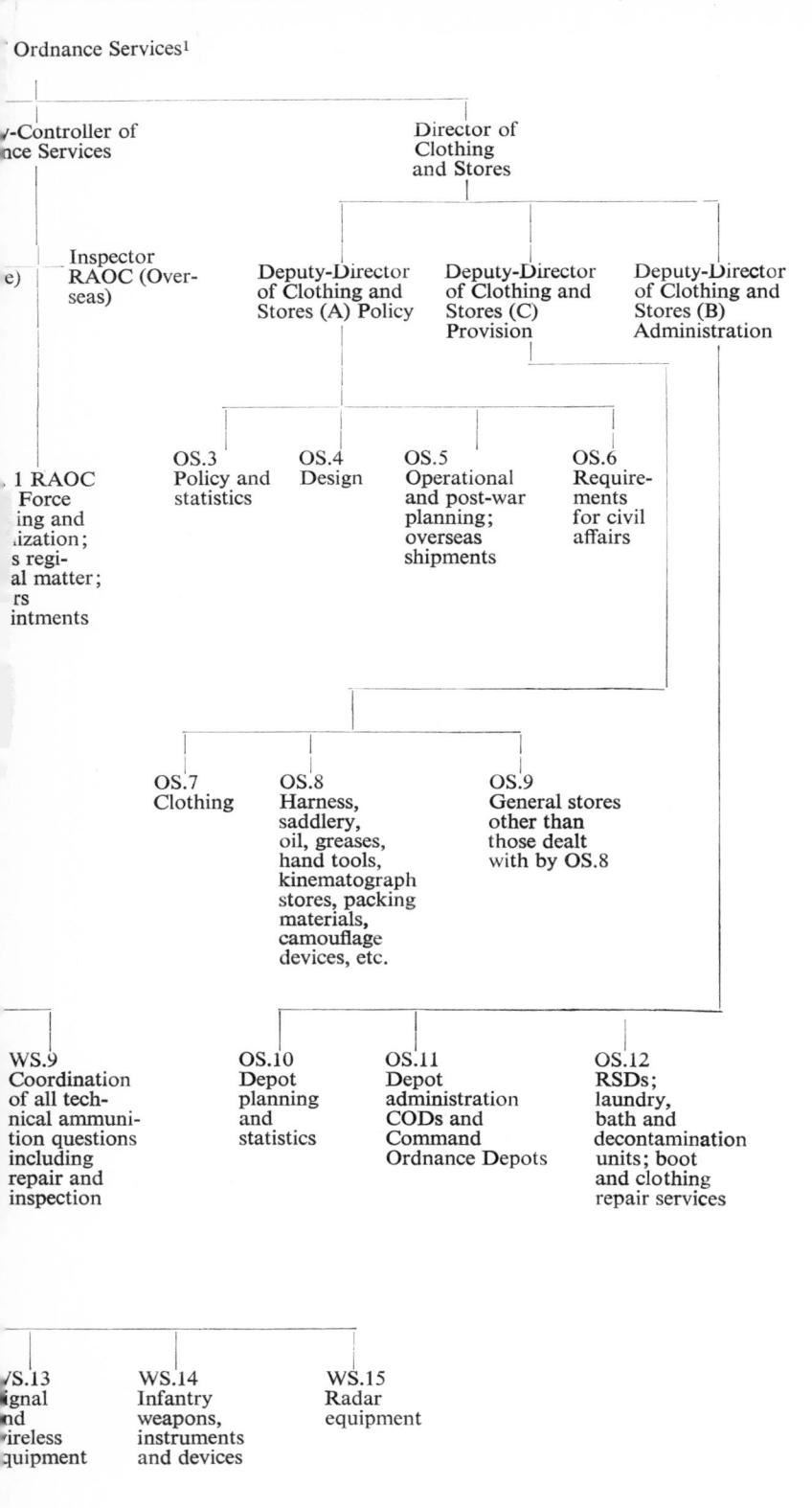

y-Controller of
nce Services

Director of
Clothing
and Stores

e) Inspector
RAOC (Over-
seas)

Deputy-Director
of Clothing and
Stores (A) Policy

Deputy-Director
of Clothing and
Stores (C)
Provision

Deputy-Director
of Clothing and
Stores (B)
Administration

1 RAOC
Force
ing and
.ization;
s regi-
al matter;
rs
intments

OS.3
Policy and
statistics

OS.4
Design

OS.5
Operational
and post-war
planning;
overseas
shipments

OS.6
Require-
ments
for civil
affairs

OS.7
Clothing

OS.8
Harness,
saddlery,
oil, greases,
hand tools,
kinematograph
stores, packing
materials,
camouflage
devices, etc.

OS.9
General stores
other than
those dealt
with by OS.8

WS.9
Coordination
of all tech-
nical ammuni-
tion questions
including
repair and
inspection

OS.10
Depot
planning
and
statistics

OS.11
Depot
administration
CODs and
Command
Ordnance Depots

OS.12
RSDs;
laundry,
bath and
decontamination
units; boot
and clothing
repair services

/S.13
ignal
nd
ireless
quipment

WS.14
Infantry
weapons,
instruments
and devices

WS.15
Radar
equipment

the Corps and, as such, Controller of Ordnance Services. On May 8th 1945 the

administration, etc.—was made the responsibility of the senior director, which was the DWS, Major-General L. H. Williams.

At the end of 1942 the appointment of DGAE was re-named DQMG (AE). By then REME had been formed and a better case existed for a staff branch to coordinate the activities of two important Services. Certain additional tasks such as policy direction on Army Kinematography were added, but these were relatively insignificant.

Towards the end of the war the Q(AE) branches grew and considerably overlapped the Ordnance branches, particularly in the field of provision. This unfortunate duplication of work persisted, and after the war the existence of staff branches doing Ordnance work was severely and rightly criticized by a committee under the chairmanship of General Sir Ian Jacob. Unfortunately no action was taken on its recommendations.

The Ordnance Directorates expanded to meet the greatly increased commitments resulting from the growth of war production and the complexity of modern weapons and equipment.

In March 1941 the DOS(W) became the Director of Warlike Stores and his branches were re-named WS branches. By the end of the war there were 15 of them under six DDsWS. The DOS was re-named Director of Clothing and Stores, the appointment being held first by Major-General C. H. Geake and then by Major-General W. W. Richards. Apart from the network of depots based on Branston and Didcot this directorate was responsible for the technical administration of Command Ordnance Depots in the United Kingdom and had further important responsibilities for laundries and for the recovery and repair of clothing, boots and general stores.

On October 23rd 1942 the appointment of COS was revived. It was not a separate appointment but was held by the senior RAOC director, who was for the remainder of the war General L. H. Williams. He therefore had two hats. When dealing with RAOC matters he wore the COS hat as head of the Corps. In his capacity as Director of Ordnance Services in the field of warlike stores he wore his DWS hat. The creation of the appointment of DCOS has already been mentioned.

The organization of the Ordnance Directorates at the end of the war is in the facing table.

PROVISION

The large War Office organization which has been described was to a great extent engaged on provision duties. Fourteen out of the total of twenty-six branches were provision branches.

For vehicles, ammunition and a considerable range of controlled stores (namely scarce major items of equipment the issue of which was directly controlled by War Office staff branches) the actual calculations were done by the War Office branches. In other cases the calculations were done in Central Ordnance Depots guided by directives from the War Office branches which also provided essential "dependency" information, that is the number of men, vehicles and weapons to be maintained.

This organization was an extension of that recommended by General Williams and adopted before the war. It closely followed civilian practice in which policy, control and guidance emanated from the London office whereas detailed work was delegated to the various local offices. The balance between centralization and delegation depended on circumstances which changed frequently in time of war and the COS was able to make the necessary adjustments. There is a greater need to centralize these activities in war than in peace.

The key to efficiency in this system was the control by one man, the head of the Service, of both the directing or administrative provision branches at the War Office and the executive branches in the depots, and this was made possible by the Esher reforms in 1904. Before that date the Corps had no Director at the War Office and the complete separation of the administrative and executive elements, under different officers, ensured that real efficiency was unattainable.

There were nine provision branches located in the central depots which were the focal storage points for the items concerned.

The branches were:

P1   Signal and wireless stores at Donnington.
P2   MT spares and assemblies at Chilwell.
P3   Artillery equipments and stores at Donnington.
P4   General stores at Didcot.
P5   Clothing at Branston.
P6   Small arms and machine guns at Weedon.
P7   Inert stores and components for ammunition at Bramley.
P8   Machinery at Old Dalby.
P9   Engineer and radar stores at Donnington.

Command Ordnance Depots carried out secondary provision to meet the immediate needs of the Commands in the United Kingdom. Except for a limited amount of local purchase, requirements were met by demands on CODs.

Provision branches in the CODs placed requisitions on the Ministry of Supply. But for main equipments, scarce items and stores of operational importance, war production and distribution was closely watched and controlled by various organizations such as the Munitions Assignments Boards in London and Washington, and the Director-General of Army Requirements at the War Office.

An immense task faced the provision branches in the CODs. As the war continued the range of items to be provided grew. The number of separate item headings mounted fivefold to several hundred thousand.

Every item had a Provision Review Card which was posted by hand. No electronic computer was available to speed up the transaction of posting and provision reviews. The requirements of clerical staff to cope with maintenance calculations alone were very great.

But there was just as much work on initial and scaled issues. These issues were made without demand and it was necessary to calculate the requirement and convert this into issue orders and vouchers so that the stores could be selected and packed. The work was usually done against time and often several times owing to changes of plan.

Examples of such issues are the automatic maintenance packs for every new venture, the calculations of initial maintenance and of associated stores (now known as Complete Equipment Schedules) for each new equipment, and the production of Landing Reserves and Beach Maintenance Packs.

Stock control of important and War Office-controlled stores involved depots in a spate of returns, information having first to be checked and collated. Finally incessant, varied and urgent questions from the War Office had to be answered. Sometimes these questions could not be answered without a good deal of research, and sometimes intelligent guesswork was necessary as the degree of urgency gave insufficient time for precise information to be obtained.

That such questions should be asked reveals a realization of the importance of equipment to an army in modern war. It is, however, easier to ask a question than to provide a prompt and reasonably accurate answer, without which more harm than good would be done. The Ordnance branches at the War Office had, as far as possible, to screen depots from unnecessary questions and also to anticipate the sort of information which would be required and thus give the depot as much time as possible to provide it. The officers in these Ordnance branches required a good practical knowledge of the capacity and capability of their associated COD provision branches, and most of them had worked at the executive level of provision before moving to the War Office.

General Williams paid frequent visits to CODs and was able, by personal observation, to see that the machinery which he had created could withstand successfully the severe and prolonged strain to which it was subjected.

THE HOME THEATRE

The pre-war static organization under rigid War Office control required drastic amendment and expansion to deal with the extraordinary problems of the United Kingdom, particularly in the period 1940 to 1942.

Up to April 1940 military commitments were not heavy. Invasion was not a serious threat and priority was given to the Air Defence of Great Britain. Otherwise the only considerations were the embodiment and maintenance of the Reserve Army, the creation of adequate training capacity for war, and the fitting out and despatch of such expeditionary forces as the circumstances might require. The equipment of the Army depended on the priority given to war production. This may have been high in theory, but in practice, due to the phoney war, there was little sense of urgency for the first 8 months.

The disastrous events in April and May 1940 completely transformed the situation. The whole country was now an armed camp under the imminent threat of invasion. A vast increase in war production was essential to survival and this must be sustained by shipment into the country of essential goods, mainly food, oil and raw materials.

As the danger of invasion receded the importance of the United Kingdom as a base increased. The Home Theatre therefore developed into a basic, static organization, divided into Commands and Districts on which were superimposed Anti-Aircraft Command, Home Forces (an anti-invasion operational command) later replaced by 21st Army Group for OVERLORD, and a separate plan under the code name of BOLERO to provide a base for the American forces forming for operations in Europe. The American forces had their own Services of Supply so in the main the effect of BOLERO on the RAOC was that the Corps had to give up considerable accommodation in the South of England.

We have seen in earlier chapters that the RAOC organization in the Home Commands was designed and manned to meet peace and mobilization commitments only. Before the war RAOC representation at Command Headquarters seldom exceeded six officers and a handful of military and civilian clerks. Commands were not divided into districts. London District and Northern Ireland District were virtually autonomous. Just as control, particularly in financial matters, was over centralized at the War Office, so there was insufficient delegation of powers by Command Headquarters. The important Command Ordnance Depots were located as follows:

Aldershot Command:	The Field Stores and Farnborough.
Southern Command:	Tidworth, Hilsea, Devonport.
Western Command:	Burscough.
Eastern Command:	Colchester, Dover, Chatham.
Northern Command:	Catterick, York.
Scottish Command:	Stirling.
Northern Ireland District:	Kinnegar.

There had been some new construction at Catterick when it was developed as an important military centre, replacing the Curragh. But otherwise the storage buildings and layout in command depots were cramped and archaic.

Most of the officers and men were posted to field force duties at the outbreak of the war, and, on the whole, the civilian staff were elderly. It is not surprising that many of them had great difficulty in making the changes in method and tempo of work which the situation demanded.

The collapse of France, the withdrawal of the BEF and the danger of invasion provided a full measure of shock treatment. Reinforcements were now available from those RAOC units which had returned from France. Both Central and Command Depots played their part in a re-equipment programme against time. Five Divisions were re-equipped in June 1940 and the remaining five during July. This was a fine effort, in keeping with the spirit of the times, but owing to the lag in war production and the loss of equipment in France and Norway, there were many serious deficiencies which could not be made up by the time that invasion might be expected. War Office control of important items was inevitable and essential so that new equipment as it came off the production line could be sent without delay to the unit with the greatest need. A reorganization of the military structure of command and administration in the United Kingdom was necessary.

The Local Defence Volunteers, later named the Home Guard, was formed. This force became a commitment to be clothed and equipped on a limited scale by the RAOC. Although the Home Guard did fine work to the end of the war, it is now almost a forgotten army. But the RAOC has good cause to remember it. The weapons and missiles issued to the Home Guard were of a design which combined ingenuity, simplicity, lethality and unreliability. To this day dumps are found in the most unlikely places. They do not as a rule mellow with age, and it falls to the RAOC to make these missiles safe.

Administratively the War Office controlled the maintenance of the troops at home, and GHQ Home Forces only came into play when an invasion occurred, but this simple concept had to be modified to some extent to give GHQ an over-riding call on all available facilities.

A slight alteration was made in the Command boundaries, Aldershot Command being merged with part of Eastern Command to form South-Eastern Command. Corps Headquarters under the command of Home Forces were regarded as static, and their area of responsibility was designated "Corps District". Areas not covered by Corps Districts were broken down into Districts so that a sound network existed to enable Commands to delegate administrative authority. Large installations remained under War Office control, though such things as the defence scheme were the responsibility of the District in which they were situated.

RAOC representation in this new organization was as follows:

At Command Headquarters:	DDOS (Brigadier)
At Corps District Headquarters:	DDOS (Colonel)
At District Headquarters:	ADOS (Lieutenant-Colonel)
At Sub-District and Area HQ:	DADOS (Major)

COMMAND DEPOTS

In order to provide a good service to the enormous army which formed in the United Kingdom, depot facilities had to be expanded and

367

dispersed. There was little room for expansion in existing depot areas, and dispersion was dictated by the danger of invasion and attack from the air, the limited accommodation which was only obtainable in "penny packets", and the fact that "over-the-counter" service was required for units dispersed all over the country.

It frequently happened that the most unsatisfactory accommodation had to be accepted. The DDOS and his staff had a difficult problem to control, organize and man these scattered depots. It was also necessary, with so many scattered locations, to introduce a system of stock control, and this was done by means of returns submitted to an office in each Command which acted as a focal point for information on stock levels at all locations.

The old peace-time procedure was modified and simplified by the introduction of a Visidex account, a system for progressing transactions and other improvements based on the procedures used at Chilwell.

Stocks in command depots were supplemented by OFPs, workshop stores sections and DADOS dumps (a misnomer for a well-organized little depot of items under DADOS control) in various locations within Commands.

Some idea of the increased activity in Commands is given by the fact that in Southern Command alone, in 1944, 370,000 indents from units were dealt with, some 400,000 tons of stores were handled and the original three depots extended to eighteen.

One effect of BOLERO was that certain depots, notably Hilsea, Tidworth and Coypool, were handed over to the American forces. The civilian staff remained to help run these installations.

COMMAND ORDNANCE SERVICES

The recovery, repair and reconditioning of Ordnance Stores was an important and large-scale activity in war. Returned Stores Depots were set up in all Commands. They were separate from Command Depots which dealt only with serviceable stores.

The RSDs received and sorted all stores. They passed to REME repairable items of their concern, but themselves dealt with the repair of clothing and general stores and the despatch of serviceable and repaired items to the appropriate command depot. The significance of this activity was so great that it was placed under a special branch of the DCS Directorate at the War Office.

The DDOS controlled all boot repair contracts in the Command. He was responsible for allocating contractors to units, notifying standard schedule prices and regulating the release of leather to contractors. In addition to contract repair RAOC boot repair centres were established.

A few WD laundries existed before the war, but as a rule units made their own arrangements by competitive tendering with local laundries.

This arrangement lasted until towards the end of 1940 when laundry contracts were centralized under the DDOS Command in the same way as boot repairs. The service was supplemented by such mobile laundries as were located in the United Kingdom at the time. The Board of Trade established standard laundry prices by means of Statutory Rules and Orders.

Towards the end of the war Civilian Clothing Depots were formed near each military dispersal unit in Commands to supply civilian clothing to men released from the Army. DDsOS Commands were responsible for the administration of CCDs which obtained stocks of clothing from COD Branston.

ANTI-AIRCRAFT COMMAND

Anti-Aircraft Command shared with Fighter Command the responsibility for the air defence of Great Britain. But administratively the units were tied to the home commands, who worked within the policy laid down by AA Command Headquarters.

The units served two masters and lack of a clear dividing line between the responsibility of AA Command and that of Home Commands caused some confusion at first. Eventually the situation was clarified and AA Command was given a greater share of administrative responsibility, but the organization inevitably became something of a "private army".

In the early days AA Command was divided into seven Divisions with a varying number of Brigades in each Division. The number of gun and searchlight units in each Brigade also varied. At the end of 1940 the number of Divisions was raised to twelve and they were grouped into three AA Corps.

In 1943 a further change was made, the Command being organized on a regional rather than a formation basis. The United Kingdom was divided into seven areas each commanded by an AA Group. The Brigades worked directly under the groups and the Corps and Divisional organization was abolished. This was a far more logical arrangement.

The AA Divisions were in no way comparable to Divisions in the field army. They were not of standard size or composition and were sometimes several times as large as field army Divisions. They were not mobile. The RAOC organization at the various headquarters began with a DADOS at each Divisional headquarters. On the outbreak of War AA Command Headquarters had an ADOS with the rank of Colonel. The rank was raised to Brigadier late in 1940.

The Air Defence of Great Britain was one of the few defence activities which had attracted the attention of the Government before the war, and some well-designed installations were built. For Ordnance Stores mobilization storehouses, later named AA Ordnance Depots, were built at suitable places for supplying the various Brigades.

Ammunition was held at gun sites and equipment ammunition magazines (EAMs) from which the gun sites were replenished. There was a considerable number of these EAMs sited in relation to defended areas. The ration of stocks was of the order of 2 days held on site to $2\frac{1}{2}$ days in the EAM.

EAMs were in turn replenished from intermediate ammunition depots (IADs) which drew on Central Ammunition Depots.

The stores and ammunition depots were initially the responsibility of the DADsOS of AA Divisions, but this soon became too big a task for them in addition to their other duties and when AA Corps were formed the RAOC staffs at Corps headquarters were given an establishment big enough to enable them to administer the depots in the Corps areas.

AAODs originally supplied all Ordnance stores to units in AA Command, but at the end of 1941 their range was reduced to technical and warlike stores, clothing and general stores being supplied from Command Ordnance Depots.

The reorganization of AA Command into groups and elimination of the Corps and Divisions did not greatly affect the system of storage and supply of Ordnance stores and ammunition which had long been established on an area basis. Control was changed in that the DDOS of each group controlled the AAODs and EAMs in his area, whilst the DDOS AA Command controlled certain nominated bulk holding depots and IADs.

Rapid developments in fire control and radar occurred which meant that depot stocks were constantly being changed and modified. Ammunition was subject to large-scale re-fuzing programmes as new types of fuze came into service. Important developments were the new mechanical fuze and the proximity fuze which played a useful part in the destruction of V1 missiles.

Towards the end of the war there was a reduction in the activity of AA Command which was extensively used to make up deficiencies in military manpower elsewhere.

MANPOWER

At the beginning of 1936 Britain was not in good shape and morale was very low. This situation was caused by the world economic crisis and the mass unemployment which went with it. Naturally attention was concentrated on national recovery and there was a strong reluctance to becoming involved in international commitments which might hamper this recovery. As a result the peace establishment of the Regular Army bore no relation to possible commitments, and the RAOC was inadequate as a military organization with war potential.

When war broke out the Regular RAOC strength was 727 officers and 5,292 other ranks including trainees and men on probation.

The breakdown of the officer strength was as follows:

Ordnance Officers	155
OEOs	134
Re-employed officers, mainly on administrative work	112
OMEs	261
AOMEs, AIAs and WEOs	65
	727

Of the other ranks 1,763 were in the store branch and the remainder were in the engineering branches.

OFFICERS

Although the numbers showed an increase of about 100 since the time of the Munich crisis, this rate of progress did not match the emergency. Pre-war policies effectively ensured that the number of trained and experienced Ordnance Officers hardly sufficed for the quietest periods of peace-time soldiering so that expansion for war could only be achieved by dilution with men of high potential but little immediate value owing to lack of military and technical training.

On mobilization the Regular contingent was necessarily employed where comprehensive knowledge was needed, and this amounted to appointments in France, with the BEF, and at the War Office in the expanding Ordnance Directorate.

Central and Command Depots and Command Headquarters were left high and dry, most of the higher appointments being initially filled by calling up retired officers who had passed the age for reserve liability and could hardly be expected to provide the drive and up-to-date knowledge required to overcome the inertia of peace-time routine and restrictions. Nevertheless these "repaints", as they were sometimes rather tactlessly described, did excellent work at a critical time.

Reinforcements were found from the following sources:

1. Regular Army Reserve of Officers. There were 152 of these at the outbreak of war. Regular medical examinations were not demanded so that when the time came many of these officers failed to pass the doctor.

2. Territorial Army, comprising 77 Ordnance Officers and 216 OMEs. Most of these were on the strength of units of TA formations. They were keen and good material, imperfectly trained for lack of equipment and opportunity. Some of the senior ranks were too old for active service conditions.

3. Supplementary Reserve of Officers. There were 72, all OMEs.

4. Army Officers Emergency Reserve. A register of good potential RAOC Officer material. Of the 450 on the list at the beginning of the war very few had any military training or experience. The AOER was to prove in time a very valuable source of high class Ordnance Officers.

5. Direct entry. Schemes for increasing the RAOC officer strength by this means were not approved before the war, nor was financial approval obtained for calling up 30 to 40 ex-officers.

The officer structure was a sort of patchwork quilt of improvisation and expediency, making the task of "picking the right man for the right job" immensely difficult.

OTHER RANKS

There were serious shortages and the outlook was gloomy. Even with reserves the situation was very unsatisfactory.

Reinforcements were as follows:

Regular Army Reservists	1,424
Supplementary Reservists (nearly all Section C)	7,703
Territorial Army	6,904
Militia	661

The Regular Army Reserve was divided into four sections, A, B, D and E. Men in Section A had only left the colours within the last year and were in every way fully trained soldiers. Of the RAOC reservists only 15 were in this section. Section E contained older men, with consequent limitations on their employment, but there were only 48 of them.

Thus of the 1,424 Regular RAOC reservists 1,361 were in Categories B and D. The length of time since leaving the colours varied considerably, but the average was probably about 8 years—ample time in many cases to become rusty both physically and technically.

Supplementary Reservists were not such an asset as the numbers seem to indicate. All but 42 were in Section C, which meant that their civilian occupations would fit them to take their place immediately as Army tradesmen. They received no military training, no medical examination during their Reserve service and there were no means of checking that a man was continuing work at that particular trade.

In certain Corps there were some units consisting almost entirely of supplementary reservists. Docks Operating Companies are an example. But in the RAOC these Reservists were individual tradesmen, called up as reinforcements. It was a most inefficient arrangement that there was no check on the standard of each man at his trade. A good deal of extra work and irritation was caused when a man was posted as a shoemaker to an Infantry battalion and had to be replaced because, when he arrived, it was found that he knew nothing about his trade.

The Territorial Army, during the years of stagnation, suffered from the same misfortunes as the Regular Army to an even greater extent. Peace establishments had no scientific basis and were very small in relation to war establishments. There was no reserve. Service units scarcely existed at all, being few in number and token in form.

In March 1939 the Government suddenly decided to double the Territorial Army. There were urgent political reasons for such a step. It was also a splendid gesture to the world that Britain really meant business and would stand no more nonsense from dictators. Unfortunately there was also ample evidence to the contrary and the gesture only served to deceive our friends without deterring our enemies.

As a military measure the scheme was an administrative atrocity to which many of the manpower difficulties of subsequent years can be traced. The balance between arms was even worse than before. Service units were not provided for the new formations and there were no corps or army troops. Existing RAOC units were brought up from cadre form to full war establishment, a badly needed improvement, but there were still far too many units to be provided on mobilization.

The Militia on the other hand was an unqualified success. The numbers were not great because the Military Training Act did not become law until the end of May 1939. But it provided a valuable preliminary exercise in manpower planning, forming the basis for the administration of the National Service Act during the war.

The Auxiliary Territorial Service (now WRAC) came into being shortly before the war. By September 1939 they numbered about 17,000, a small proportion being attached to RAOC units. At Hilsea a small school near the gates of the depot, Hilsea Training College, was taken over for the ATS. They did very useful work in clerical and administrative duties. This was the beginning of a truly magnificent contribution to the work of the Army Ordnance Services throughout the war.

Immediately on mobilization the RAOC strength was suddenly and greatly increased by the decision to draft all volunteers into the administrative corps. The possibility that there would be a very large number of volunteers seemed to have been overlooked, and although no one made the mistake of deliberately discouraging the voluntary spirit, the lack of adequate recruiting machinery for dealing with such numbers was itself discouraging. The deplorable lack of military equipment was known at the War Office, and the decision to double the Territorial Army aggravated the situation. It was therefore a sensible move to divert these volunteers from combat units, who would be without weapons and equipment, to the services who were very short of manpower. Although this caused no little confusion in certain quarters, particularly Hilsea where the majority of volunteers were sent, this was a passing defect which time would cure, and for the RAOC it was a blessing in disguise.

On the first day of the war various Acts of Parliament were passed in order to control the supply of manpower to the armed forces and modify the conditions of service. The most important of these was the National Service (Armed Forces) Act, which introduced conscription and showed that a lesson of the 1914-18 war, the need for manpower control, had been well learnt.

Personnel branches calculated the numbers of men required each month to maintain a regular flow through the training units established for their arm of the service, making due allowance for the numbers joining by voluntary enlistment, a task which was complicated by the wide variation in the time required for basic technical training. This was sound but success depended on a reasonably stable policy both as to the size of the Army and the numbers of volunteers to be accepted. At the outset, policy fluctuated violently and difficulties occurred.

The first phase of the war may be said to have ended in July 1940. This covered mobilization, the Phoney War, the disasters of Norway and France and the regrouping in the United Kingdom to meet a possible invasion and start on the long road to final victory.

By this date the manpower situation of the RAOC had developed as follows:

The officer strength had risen to 3,294. Reinforcements from the Reserve Army had brought the figure to about 1,300 after mobilization and of the remainder no less than 1,400 had been drawn from the AOER. Recruiting of officers from the ranks, through OCTU, and by direct entry with a course at an Officers' Training Unit, did not develop as the main source of supply of RAOC officers until later. For this reason the average age was high—over 40—but this was not of itself a disadvantage in the prevailing circumstances.

The other rank strength grew from just over 5,000 to nearly 23,000 in September 1939, for the reasons which have been described. Thereafter the increase was steady, and by July 1940 the strength was 50,000 which was fully adequate in numbers to meet the needs of the time.

But this is not to say that it was a balanced force. Training, trade structure and numerical distribution were haphazard as a result of the events of the previous 10 months. It could hardly be otherwise and time was needed to ensure that the resources of manpower were deployed and used to full advantage.

Mid-summer 1940 was the only period of the war when available military manpower exceeded commitments. There were few active overseas theatres and drafting was restricted by shortage of shipping. The demand for military manpower to defend the country was insistent. From the RAOC point of view manpower was available for the programme of expansion of depots to hold the increased production of equipment, vehicles and ammunition.

The decision was made in the autumn of 1940 to move the personnel branches from their good, central accommodation in Hobart House,

London, to Cheltenham. This was an unsatisfactory decision. The worst of the bombing of London was already over and communication with the personnel branches was a continuous and vital requirement. There were military branches of the War Office with ample knowledge and experience of the movement and accommodation of large numbers of people. But the task was entrusted to a civil branch which naturally had no experience of this kind of movement. The people of Cheltenham were loyal and patriotic and many of them had relations in the Army, but the move was handled in such a way as to test these qualities to the utmost.

These problems gradually solved themselves, but the main difficulty of communication was never solved, and in the summer of 1942 the branches returned to Hobart House.

Naturally enough the strategic plan on which manpower requirements were based evolved slowly after the changed circumstances of the summer of 1940, and a new Field Force Conspectus was not produced until December of that year. Early in 1941 it became apparent that the manpower resources of the country would be severely strained, and that the allotment between the Services and industry must be strictly controlled.

A system of "ceilings" was adopted. The Army was not allowed to exceed the numbers allotted and intakes were regulated accordingly. The requirements of the Army as a whole, and the balance between the different arms of the service varied with the strategic situation. It was a continuous game of "rob Peter to pay Paul", an increased commitment in one place having to be balanced by reductions elsewhere. With the RAOC dilution was a very important factor and ATS, civilians and, in overseas theatres, locally engaged staff were extensively employed to maintain and increase the capacity of the various depots.

The fluctuations in RAOC other rank strength are interesting and can be illustrated by giving the numbers at the end of each year during which the war was fought.

1939	30,000
1940	62,000
1941	122,000
1942	78,000 (formation of REME)
1943	98,000
1944	115,000
1945	100,000 (demobilization in progress)

Manpower control was not just a matter of allotting the right number of men to each arm of the service. Quality, intelligence and technical skill were important factors. "Selection Testing" was introduced at the time when a man was called up, and men were classified by basic intelligence as well as medical category as a guide to their posting to particular arms of the service.

The principle was carried a step further in July 1942 by the creation of a General Service Corps, into which all intakes were enlisted in the first instance. Primary Training Centres were formed and there recruits underwent 6 weeks basic military training common to all arms and were thoroughly tested. Reports after basic training went to the War Office where the decision on posting to a particular arm was made with considerable knowledge of the suitability of each individual.

This was an improvement on earlier methods, and some such system of manpower control was essential in the context of a world war and acute manpower shortages, but it was unlikely to be popular. It almost eliminated individual liberty of choice. Men were posted where they were most required which was not necessarily where they thought they were most required.

All arms tended to rate their own requirements highest and to insist that only the best men would do for them. It was a valid argument that in the case of the RAOC, the numbers of military could not be kept down unless full use was made of dilution, which meant that all RAOC men must be of supervisory calibre. But there were never enough high grade men to go round and a compromise was inevitable.

Within the Corps the only way to get the best results with the material available was by specialization. At the working level this was done by breaking down the trade structure so that, for example, storemen had the suffix "MT", "Technical", "Ammunition", etc., after their trade to indicate the category in which they had specialized.

In the autumn of 1941 the RD/GD branch was formed to cover the non-trade tasks of military training, such as weapon training and drill instructor, and unit administration. This was but another form of specialization, essential if these important tasks were to be carried out efficiently.

A particular problem arose in the case of the RAOC engineering trades. The writer of a monograph on military manpower during the war has aptly described the Army's search for tradesmen as "the insatiable in pursuit of the unobtainable".

Moreover, the engineering trades were essential to industry in the United Kingdom so that war production could be increased in scope, tempo and efficiency and the Schedule of Reserved Occupations kept many useful men out of the Army.

As in other trades in the RAOC a radical change was necessary in the pre-war pattern. The majority of Army tradesmen in the mechanical and electrical field were trained in the Service itself and enlisted as apprentices at the age of 14 or 15 years. The standard of craftsman was very high and the long period of training produced men with the versatility and skill to deal with the types of engineering problem likely to be encountered on active service. But the numbers were small and there were hardly any reserves of the same calibre having the same type of training.

Light Aid Detachments and Field Workshops were initially built round the Regular Army tradesman and dilution with less highly trained men was introduced progressively without detriment to the standard of technical efficiency.

But Base Workshops, and Central Workshops in the United Kingdom, developed into enormous installations requiring skilled men and providing higher ranks than the field force units. Many armament artificers and other pre-war tradesmen were commissioned and did excellent work in the base workshops.

Specialization was inevitable and trade training and classification had to be adjusted accordingly. This process and the selection of men for the various trades proved to be a difficult problem, particularly in the early days when the methods were not very scientific. Many mistakes were made, and a man who had been a fitter in a tailor's shop was liable to find himself posted as an expert in the repair of mechanical vehicles.

The lack of effective manpower planning for the increase in numbers of techical tradesmen in the Army in war, proved to be a serious handicap, but the achievements of the engineering branch of the RAOC and of REME when that Corps was formed, are all the more creditable on that account.

COMBATANT STATUS

We have seen (Chapter 2) that there was considerable confusion of thought about the non-combatant status of the RAOC. This confusion derived mainly from a failure to define the term "combatant status", which was particularly unfortunate as combat was not a factor and the expression far from being self-explanatory was misleading in the extreme. This led to a general assumption that the Corps was not expected to fight, and consequently a sort of "camp follower" stigma was associated with this false assumption.

The anomaly should have been rectified when the situation of the RAOC was reviewed before the war, but nothing was done. Admittedly there were difficulties as the Corps was in the process of being transferred from the control of the MGO to that of the QMG, but failure to deal with this relatively simple problem reflects little credit on the authorities concerned.

The campaigns in France, Norway and the Middle East clearly indicated the combatant role of the RAOC on active service, and revealed the non-combatant theory as a myth. Some of the more absurd rules were quietly ignored. For example RAOC officers were included on Staff College courses from the beginning of 1941, and before that date a number of staff appointments were held by Ordnance Officers. It was of course a convenient device to break the rules unofficially in war, leaving the letter of the law unchanged so that it could be strictly re-applied at any suitable moment.

By 1941 people were beginning to ask questions to which no satisfactory answer could be given. For example it was not clear why one supply Corps should be combatant and the other non-combatant. Before the war it was easy to ignore, suppress or evade such questions, but now they were being asked by too many people who were sufficiently influential to insist on a straight answer to a straight question.

The result was that Army Order 179 of October 22nd 1941 was published. It read as follows:

"It is hereby declared that all officers, and other ranks of the Royal Army Ordnance Corps are combatant in the fullest sense, and will be so recognized in the future, subject to the following conditions:

1. The provision of *King's Regulations*, 1940, paragraph 189, regarding powers of command will for the present continue to apply.
2. The conditions of service laid down in the Royal Warrant for the Pay, Appointment, Promotion and Non-Effective Pay of the Army will not be altered.
3. Officers of the rank of Colonel and above will not be removed from the Royal Army Ordnance Corps.
4. Major-Generals, Brigadiers and Colonels will wear the scarlet band and Royal Crest on the forage cap and the scarlet gorget patches on the jacket, instead of those at present authorized. Regimental buttons will continue to be worn by Brigadiers and Colonels."

A close examination of the wording of this Army Order shows that by skilful drafting it was possible to retain some of the objectionable elements of the old regulations.

By failing to define the special meaning of the term "combatant status" many people were allowed to retain the impression that the RAOC was not expected to fight hitherto but had that obligation now. Paragraphs 1, 2 and 3 represent qualifying conditions which have nothing to do with combat but are related to the special meaning of "combatant status". Paragraph 4 was not a qualifying condition (except as regards regimental buttons and this has since been changed), but was necessary in order to remove special insignia which would naturally be regarded as a non-combatant label and thus flagrantly contradict the brave opening words of the Army Order.

Whatever its defects this Army Order paved the way to the gradual elimination of the stigma associated with non-combatant status.

NEW PROBLEMS AND THE FORMATION OF REME

In the summer of 1941 Colonel L. E. Cutforth returned to AG 9, in which branch he had been a DAAG just before and in the early months of the war. He replaced Colonel O. A. Walker who had held the appointment of AAG for several years.

There were many new problems. The period of concentration on defence of the country was passing and, as Germany had invaded Russia, Great Britain and the Commonwealth were no longer fighting alone. War production was getting into its stride and North America was gradually becoming an important source of war materials. Great Britain had ceased to be merely a beleaguered fortress and was becoming more and more an important base to sustain offensive operations, the most effective of which would be at first in the Middle East theatre.

An increasing number of new units and drafts were required for service overseas, but there was now a ceiling on RAOC manpower, which limited the numbers which could be supplied from new intakes through training units. Central Ordnance Depots and other large installations were carrying an increasing load as war production developed, and the idea of losing many good men for other ventures was not very enthusiastically received. But a broader view had to be taken and it was necessary for depots to create good methods of personnel management and staff control in addition to improving technical efficiency.

A mobilization centre was formed at Arnold, near Nottingham, and the majority of new units formed there. Later on there was a separate centre for Ordnance Field Parks at Kegworth. Units received their vehicles and scalings at this centre which also provided specialist training in OFP organization and methods in the field.

The Records Office had never fully recovered from the turmoil of mobilization and the move to Leicester in 1940. The unit was overloaded and understaffed. Outstanding work was accumulating at an alarming rate and reorganization was a matter of urgency. The task was given to a trained chartered accountant (Colonel Dyson) and, with the assistance of other selected staff, a proper standard of efficiency was restored.

Personnel branches have a more difficult task than most in having to reconcile the conflicting views of several different authorities. Responsibility for the efficiency of the RAOC rested with the COS. Efficiency must always depend on selection of the right man for the job and the COS was in the best position to know the requirements for each important post and which of the available candidates had the right characteristics for each appointment. But unfortunately there were other important influences which affected decisions on appointments and other personnel matters. On the whole they did little to help and much to hinder the COS and the AAG, AG 9, in their efforts to place officers to the best effect.

AG 9 was of course a branch of the Adjutant-General's Department and the Director of Personnel Administration had the responsibilty for giving effect to the AG's policy. This was all right as long as it was realized that the COS was responsible for the way officers and men in the RAOC did their work, and this was directly related to individual characteristics. Clearly the views of the COS were of paramount importance, but this point was not always appreciated in the AGs department.

Another difficulty was caused by the position of the DGAE. It has already been noted that he had been given, in a rather imprecise way, responsibilities and authority which properly belonged to the COS. This resulted in overlapping and certainly in direct interference in personnel matters, particularly as they affected the engineering side of the Corps. The AAG, AG 9, had to reconcile these conflicting influences in such a way as to enable the COS to carry his heavy responsibilities without endless high level arguments.

The growing importance of the electrical and mechanical engineering side of the Corps had been the subject of a good deal of somewhat ineffective committee work before the war.

Operations in the Middle East revealed the necessity for some re-organization, and the indications were that the work which required to be done or directed by trained engineers should be separated from the supply functions and a new corps formed for this purpose. In practical terms the problem was not quite as simple as that, but its solution was not made any easier by the impact of many powerful personalities outside the Corps. As usual the experts disagreed violently with each other, vested interests and politics were by no means absent, and the principle of "maintenance of the objective" was in danger of being overlooked. It is remarkable in such an atmosphere that a sound, workable decision emerged, and much of the credit must go to the COS, who had the know-ledge and judgement to recognize necessary reform in a welter of quack remedies, and the recently appointed QMG, General Sir Thomas Riddell Webster, who had seen the problems in their practical setting of the Middle East campaigns.

The formation of the Royal Electrical and Mechanical Engineers as a regular and permanent Corps of the Army was authorized by Army Order 70 of May 1942 and the necessary transfers of men to the new Corps were completed by October 1st 1942. All RAOC units with a workshop role were transferred.

The decision had a considerable effect on the RASC, who provided the first DME. Many RASC officers and men with the appropriate qualifications, and some RASC workshop units were transferred to REME.

TRAINING

During the period of peace and retrenchment between the wars training in the British Army was one of the first things to suffer. It became less and less realistic and was regarded in the civilian world as "playing at soldiers", a waste of public money and wanton destruction of "England's green and pleasant land". The attractive image of the Army was main-tained by military tattoos, the Royal Tournament at Olympia and the ceremony of Trooping the Colour. These were splendid events in their way, but it was sometimes forgotten that they contributed little to the creation of an army as an efficient instrument for waging modern war.

In the RAOC training reached an "all time low". Non-combatant status was an excuse for excluding training with other arms of the Service, and establishments were designed to keep the small military staff permanently tied to peace-time duties.

The various courses at Woolwich, Hilsea and Bramley were largely designed to provide the academic qualifications which were deemed to justify the grant of Corps pay. The general view was that an Ordnance Officer became efficient, not because of the 15-month OO's course, which was irrelevant, but as a result of a long period of application of his natural intelligence to peace-time work. This approach was too slow and negative.

Of the other ranks, apprentice tradesmen received a thorough grounding in the work of their trade but Clerks and Storemen covered such a wide field of activity that basic training and trade testing were insufficient unless followed by systematic and continuous training "on the job".

On the whole this type of training was neglected. Depots were over civilianized in the United Kingdom and the handful of young soldiers posted to these units were usually dispersed among civilians to learn from them. This "sit-by-me" type of training could only work if the civilians knew their job, did the work efficiently, could impart the information well and were keen to teach the soldier. It was not often that all these conditions were fulfilled. At Woolwich, which was the central depot for "A" vehicles and guns, a rule was imposed which prevented soldiers from being employed in the depot. Thus the opportunities for soldiers to learn about the storage and handling of these important equipments and their spares were limited.

This was the worst aspect. There were some depots, notably Chilwell, Aldershot and Farnborough, where positive technical training programmes were introduced. Also the opportunities for gaining knowledge and improving efficiency were greater in overseas stations than at home.

A system which was far from satisfactory for the Regular Army provided a poor framework for dealing with an unexpectedly large intake on mobilization. Apart from important basic instruction in drill, weapon training and administration, it was necessary to give intensive technical training with the emphasis on specialization.

It proved necessary to create the following units:

> Officer Cadet Training Unit.
> Officers Training Unit for direct entry commissions.
> Training Battalions for new intakes.

A School with branches to cover:

> Officers War Courses.
> Specialist Stores Training.
> Military Training Courses.
> Ammunition Courses for IOOs and AEs.

Not all these requirements were foreseen at the beginning of the war and the shape of the training organization evolved piecemeal.

The lack of planning for a large-scale war particularly affected the engineering side of the Corps. Initially the supply of officers and men with the required technical qualifications did not present a great problem. Large numbers of men were on the Supplementary Reserve. But these men had received no military training, and they represented a high proportion of the units which were formed at the outbreak of war.

The defects of this system were revealed in the first 8 months of the campaign in France in 1939-40. The BEF was a mechanized army but on the whole the units were not mechanically minded. Vehicles were over-driven and badly maintained so that workshops were overloaded from the beginning. The exceptionally severe winter made the situation worse. Consequently tradesmen had to be concentrated on workshop activity, working very long hours, which left no time for weapon training, drill or military administration. The events of May and June 1940 were particularly hard on these units, and although they emerged with credit, the importance of military training for all units could not be denied and special attention was given to this aspect of RAOC training in the second half of 1940 and in 1941.

It was not until later that the shortage of engineering tradesmen began to make itself felt. A RAOC Artificers School was formed at Arborfield, also an AFV Mechanics School. Potential tradesmen were selected from intakes and given trade courses at the various technical training centres controlled by the DMT.

THE TRAINING ESTABLISHMENT

No training was possible in the first few weeks of mobilization, the residual staff of the Depot and School being fully engaged on administrative duties, dealing with the enormous number of recruits who turned up without warning.

However, training was started as soon as possible. Selected recruits were put through courses in Ordnance duties and procedure at the School of Instruction with a view to employment as instructors in depots and elsewhere. This training, in the absence of any supporting practical experience, may have savoured of teaching the blind to lead the blind, but it was the only possible immediate action which could be taken. Instruction was based on the new *Ordnance Manual (War)* which had not itself been put to practical test. The lessons being learnt the hard way during the Phoney War period in France had not yet been digested and no information was received from that quarter. At the end of 1939 the first Ordnance Officers course was run for Reserve Army officers. Meanwhile "B" Branch at Bramley had started war courses for IOOs and AEs and "G" Branch at Chilwell continued with instruction in MT.

The depot was reconstituted as a Training Establishment with a Headquarters and two Training Battalions (Nos. 3 and 4) which were located at Hilsea and Victoria Barracks in Portsmouth. Towards the end of 1939 an Officers Training Wing was formed at Victoria Barracks and this was the beginning of the RAOC OCTU.

The Commandant of the Training Establishment (Brigadier J. S. Omond) had a wide span of responsibility. He continued to be responsible for the Records Office until it was separated in June 1940. He also had charge of the School of Instruction with its various outstation branches, the ATS unit at Hilsea College, the OCTU, two training battalions and a Boys Training Unit, 600 strong. The first 4 months of 1940 saw these units settling down and beginning to work smoothly.

In May 1940 Colonel Cutforth assumed command of the School of Instruction. He had been on the staff of the School a year earlier and had been transferred to AG 9 from which he escaped for a short spell as ADOS of the ill-fated expedition to Namsos. He arrived at the time of the withdrawal of our troops from Norway and France. Air raids were beginning and invasion was thought to be imminent.

The Portsmouth area was now in the front line and training was constantly interrupted by air raids and invasion scares. Impossible anti-invasion orders were received, based solely on the numbers on the books of the Training Centre and overlooking the fact that a high proportion of the strength consisted of recruits who were only in the unit for 2 weeks. Many were still in plain clothes. Of the remainder 600 were Boys, who were, however, soon transferred to Arborfield on War Office instructions.

In the autumn of 1940 the decision was made to transfer the Headquarters, School of Instruction, Records Office, and one training battalion from Hilsea to the Leicester area. The OCTU also moved and the training battalion in Victoria Barracks moved up to Hilsea.

Various houses were taken over in the area of large villas and this produced accommodation for the Headquarters, School and Records Office. The training battalion found accommodation on the racecourse with one company out at Hinckley. Soon after their arrival the raid on Coventry occurred and this was followed by the first and only air raid on Leicester. There were no casualties in the Training Establishment.

By the end of 1940 the RAOC Training Establishment consisted of a headquarters and the following specialized branches:

A. Ordnance procedures. War Ordnance Officers Courses. Assistant Instructors courses.
B. Ammunition. IOOs, AEs, Ammunition Storemen.
D. Driving and maintenance.
G. MT Stores. Training of Clerks and Storemen and Ordnance Field Park staff.
H. Laundries. Officers and Storemen for Base and Mobile Laundries
R. Regimental Training of officers and other ranks.

Many of these branches were at the parent depots for the particular function. For example B Branch was at Bramley and G Branch at Chilwell. Sub-branches were formed at smaller depots. In 1941, F Branch was formed at Donnington to deal with the storage and handling problems created by the new range of engineer, armament, signal and radar equipments coming into service.

Accommodation was inadequate to meet the growing need, both in the scope of training and the numbers to be trained. However, a steady improvement took place.

In August 1941 Brigadier Omond retired and was replaced by Brigadier F. G. Coleman, who had been an inspector RAOC, with a special responsibility for training, since late 1939. This gave him the opportunity to see the effectiveness of basic training and also the effect of lack of it. He concentrated particularly on War Ordnance Officers courses, regimental courses and training in staff duties, not only to ensure that officers coming into the Corps received a proper grounding before posting to a unit, but also to provide refresher training for the many officers who had been rushed into the Corps in the early days and put to work without any training in military matters or the basic task of the RAOC.

In 1942 it was decided that all primary training in the Army should be uniform and training battalions passed out of control of the Corps and became primary training centres. This relieved the Commandant of the RAOC Training Establishment of any residual responsibility for these units. During 1941 the OCTU moved from Leicester, became No. 26 RAOC OCTU at Foremark Hall near Derby, and ceased to be the responsibility of the Commandant of the Training Centre.

There were, however, certain additional responsibilities. As primary training centres concerned themselves only with all-arms basic training, certain technical subjects, previously taught at the RAOC training battalions, had to be covered separately. No. 1 Clerks and Storemens School was formed at Saltburn-by-the-Sea, Yorkshire, and No. 11 Driver Training Battalion was formed at Halifax, later moving to Market Harborough.

Training at Leicester was not confined to the classroom but included exercises and schemes on the same lines as those at the Staff College.

The following were the main officers courses held at the Training Establishment:

1. *Advanced War Ordnance Officers Course.* This was for senior officers who had reached a high rank in a limited field of employment such as a COD and required to broaden their knowledge.

2. *War Ordnance Officers Course.* This was a very useful course for junior officers who had a certain amount of experience in units. The length of the course varied from time to time, and was up to 7 weeks. Technical training was combined with regimental training.

3. *Officers Initial Technical Training Course.* This was a 4-week course for officers after completion of their OCTU training.

4. *Officers Initial Regimental Course.* Four weeks' training for officers who had received direct commissions. For reasons of age and sometimes service these men did not go through an OCTU and this training was an essential substitute.

5. *Officers Ex-other Arms Courses.* Most of these officers were transferred from disbanded anti-aircraft units towards the end of the war. There was of course a psychological as well as technical problem here. Loyalty to their old Regiment or Corps apart, it is never a pleasing prospect for an expert in one field of activity suddenly to become a "new boy" in another field. Nevertheless these courses proved successful and facilitated the change.

6. *ATS Ordnance Officers Courses.* These courses lasted a month and dealt mainly with technical duties on which ATS officers were employed. They were extremely successful.

In January 1944 Brigadier K. F. Farquarson Roberts took over the Training Establishment from Brigadier Coleman. He held the same views and continued and extended the same policy.

It was perhaps inevitable that technical and regimental training tended to be kept in separate watertight compartments. This could lead to an outlook which conflicted with the principle that a good tradesman in the Army can only be built on a trained soldier foundation.

Special steps were taken, particularly in schemes and tactical exercises without troops, to combine these two forms of training. By then the RAOC field force organization had developed on sound lines and formed a good basis for such training. G Branch, based on Chilwell, extended its activities to instruction in packing and preservation of stores for shipment overseas.

During the war more than 6,000 officers and 250,000 other ranks passed through the Training Establishment and its branches on various courses. The organization made an important contribution to the high standard of efficiency which was attained in all aspects of RAOC work.

TRAINING POLICY

It has been seen that the pre-war situation and that on mobilization prevented much attention being paid to training in the early days of the war. However, the need soon made itself felt and towards the end of 1939 Lieutenant-Colonel F. G. Coleman was sent over from France to get something done. He sponsored the scheme for selecting assistant instructors from the intake at Hilsea, and training them so that they could impart basic technical knowledge to recruits in the training battalions and depots.

This was a period when the conflict between the urgent need to clear outstanding technical work and the military and technical training of new intakes was greater than ever before. The need for basic training had to be proved and this was done by frequent visits to units in which it was explained that the loss of time in training was soon overtaken by the increased efficiency of the trained man.

It had been realized for some time that the Corps should be placed under the DMT for training. Until then the RAOC was not in line with other arms of the Service and was denied facilities available to them. However, this step was not taken until July 1940. Colonel Coleman, who worked under the Inspector RAOC, had to do a great deal of preliminary liaison work with the various War Office Branches to pave the way.

When the decision was finally made RAOC training was the province of a newly formed branch, MT 3, under the DMT. This branch was under an Ordnance GSO II with a GSO III from another arm of the Service initially. The branch dealt with training policy and worked closely with the ADOS (Training) and AG 9. An ADOS (E) (Colonel Kuhne) was appointed as Inspector to deal with the training of the engineering branch of the Corps.

Technical training for the engineering trades was not sponsored by MT 3 but by a separate "technical" branch of the MT Directorate. This branch was not confined to RAOC engineering trades but covered all industrial trades such as plumber, bricklayer, etc. This split in control of RAOC training complicated matters, but on the whole the transfer to DMT control was a great advantage—indeed it was an essential step which should have been taken long before the war.

It was typical of the short-sighted view which prevailed that the OCTU was nearly closed down when there was a temporary glut of officers in the Corps after Dunkirk. Very soon the rapid expansion of the Corps to meet the new commitments led to a great increase in the number of officers accepted on direct commission, mostly from the AOER list. It was claimed that there was no time to go through the OCTU process but basic training was obviously important. Luckily MT 3 discovered that a Cavalry OCTU at Weedon was being closed down and the complete staff, augmented by a number of RAOC officers was immediately available to man a new RAOC Officers' Training Unit. Accommodation was available in a stately home at Rushton Hall, near Kettering, which was taken over and the first course started in a few weeks.

These courses were a great success, and this was mainly due to the enthusiasm and personality of the commanding officer, Lieutenant-Colonel Borwick. As a retired Cavalry officer and Master of the Pytchley Hounds he had little acquaintance with the activities of the RAOC, and the switch from the Cavalry OCTU, for which he was a natural choice, can hardly have been agreeable. But he succeeded in creating the impression that his one ambition was to train officers for the RAOC, and the

Corps owes him a debt of gratitude. From the beginning many officers who came to Rushton Hall for courses were OMEs and the unit became a REME Officers School in 1942.

RAOC OCTU

In the autumn of 1940 the OCTU was moved from Portsmouth to Leicester where it occupied a requisitioned school. The facilities were very poor both for training and accommodation, but in spite of these disadvantages the course was extended to 8 weeks and some basic technical training was included.

In 1941 the unit moved to Foremark Hall. The first commandant was Colonel H. L. Prentis. This was excellent accommodation and the large estate provided ample scope for battle training. The course was extended to 12 weeks, which included a period on the battle course in Wales. Although the course had been extended it was still too short for the programme laid down, resulting in a congested syllabus.

The OCTU attained a high standard and this was largely due to the trouble taken to select suitable officers, warrant officers and NCOs as instructors. After the formation of REME the unit became a combined RAOC/REME OCTU. At the end of the war it was decided that OCTUs would become general purpose and not "special to arm". The RAOC was one of the first Corps to lose its OCTU. The basic technical training of newly commissioned RAOC officers now reverted to the Training Establishment.

THE TRAINING BATTALIONS

The need for creating Training Battalions immediately after mobilization had not been foreseen. This was because the intake of recruits was not expected to exceed the capacity of the depot.

The post-mobilization emergency resulted in the hurried formation of four Training Battalions. These were No. 1 at Woolwich, No. 2 at Chilwell, No. 3 at Portsmouth and No. 4 at Hilsea.

Initially very little military or technical training could be given in these units. All that was possible was to do the necessary administrative work, documentation, kitting and so on—and send the men on to the depot, workshop or other unit according to posting orders received. However, this situation was soon put right as Battalions were brought up to strength with re-employed officers and other ranks, mostly from outside the RAOC. Although many of the staff obtained in this way were somewhat rusty, as their military experience derived largely from the 1914–18 war, they had the enthusiasm and ability to provide the required basic military training. Assistant Instructors were drafted in from the School to give the basic technical training.

This was of course only a beginning and although the best was done in the time and with the resources available, it was realized in the Training Battalions that their product was anything but a fully trained soldier.

Receiving units did not always appreciate the situation, and for a time further training was badly neglected in many cases. This was only to be expected when there was no officer in the Ordnance Directorate at the War Office specifically responsible for training in the Corps.

With the arrival of Lieutenant-Colonel F. G. Coleman at the end of 1940 there was a rapid all-round improvement, but much harm had already been done. Events moved too fast for it to be possible to re-train the enormous number of officers and men who found themselves in units and at work without having received the necessary basic instruction.

No. 1 Training Battalion was at Cambridge Barracks, Woolwich, but after the bombing of Woolwich when Cambridge Barracks was hit, the unit was located partly in Red Barracks and partly in the Royal Military Academy buildings on Woolwich Common. Towards the end of 1941 the unit was moved to Derby.

No. 2 Training Battalion was formed at Chilwell at the beginning of the war and was commanded by Lieutenant-Colonel H. Carter, who had been employed on regimental duty at Chilwell before the war. A large storehouse (Building 176) provided the first accommodation. In September 1940 the Battalion moved out to the Hinckley area. Colonel Carter remained at Chilwell as Garrison Commander and was replaced by Lieutenant-Colonel G. W. Trowsdell.

No. 5 Training Battalion was formed at Chepstow in the summer of 1940, the nucleus of the unit being found from No. 1 Training Battalion.

With the creation of the General Service Corps in 1942 the battalions still remaining ceased to be RAOC units, but some of the staff were transferred to form new technical training units.

Three Clerks and Storemens Schools were formed, but it was soon found that one would meet the needs of the Corps. This was No. 1 CSS at Saltburn-by-the-Sea in Yorkshire. The commander was Lieutenant-Colonel B. D. Hamley, who had previously served as a company commander in No. 2 Training Battalion. The unit remained there until the end of the war when it moved to Hilsea later to become No. 3 Training Battalion and part of the reconstituted RAOC Training Centre.

The course consisted of 4 weeks' technical training after which the men were classified as Clerks or Storemen. Those who showed insufficient aptitude for technical work were classified General Duty. Some 36,000 men passed through the School by the end of the war. The standard of training was high and the School was regarded as one of the best administered units in Northern Command.

CHAPTER TWELVE

UNITED KINGDOM CENTRAL ORDNANCE DEPOTS AND VEHICLE DEPOTS AND AMMUNITION ORGANIZATION

War production and the industrial potential of the nations taking part were far more significant factors in the period from 1939 to 1945 than ever before in the history of armed warfare.

For those forces which depended on the United Kingdom for the supply of equipment, the foundation of the whole system was the complex of Central Ordnance Depots in Britain which received the equipment from production, held the stocks and reserves and issued to all theatres of war.

These depots were War Office controlled, which meant that their growth, activities, manning and methods of operation were directed by the various DWS or DCS branches. In fact the Ordnance Directorates and Central Depots developed concurrently.

Control was not impersonal. General Williams paid frequent visits to Central Ordnance Depots, Vehicle Depots and Ammunition Depots (ammunition coming under the DWS) but gave particular attention to the parent CODs at Chilwell and Donnington. In this way he was able to ensure that work was being done in the way he wanted and that War Office direction was adequate and not misunderstood. His Deputy-Directors and branch officers also visited the depots of their concern and established close links with their opposite numbers.

Colonel A. J. M. Hunt was an invaluable liaison officer with DWS depots. His detailed knowledge of procedures and pleasant personality inspired confidence and he was able to spot where things were going wrong and iron out difficulties with the minimum of friction.

General Williams also used to hold quarterly conferences at which CODs were represented. These were held at the various depots in rotation and they were the means of allocating the load of work and manpower for the immediate future as well as providing the opportunity to emphasize important points of policy.

The same principles applied in the DCS depots except that there was not quite the same personal impact, as in the course of the war the appointment changed three times. The first holder was Major-General K. M. Body (as DOS), followed in succession by Major-Generals C. H. Geake and W. W. Richards (both as DCS). Of course General Williams as head of the Corps and COS was concerned with all units, but he delegated direct control of Clothing and General Stores depots to the DCS.

It has been seen that these central depots, though adequate for the somewhat placid activity which prevailed in peace-time, were not geared to modern, mechanized warfare on a large scale, and a revolution was needed in organization, methods and staffing.

There was a complete lack of standardization in the layout, organization and procedures of the five CODs which existed at the beginning of the war—Branston, Didcot, Chilwell, Woolwich and Weedon.

Although these depots dealt with different classes of store, their organization and methods needed to follow the same general pattern, otherwise their rapid and efficient development would become uncontrolled and chaotic.

The standard methods derived partly from trials carried out at Didcot and Chilwell before the war, and partly from ideas which were introduced as the war progressed. They formed the basis not only for the operation of CODs but for all stores depots in the Corps.

CONTROL AND ACCOUNTING

Each depot had a control office from which issues were initiated. This "control" system, started some years before at Didcot and continued and amplified at Chilwell, was the essential means of establishing priority of issues and of ensuring a steady flow of work through the storehouse. The document for action in the storehouse was the "issue voucher" and under this system it was made out in the control office and not in the storehouse, where an accumulation could cause confusion.

It was also imperative that transactions should be followed through to finality. This was also the task of the control office which, by marking up control sheets, watched the progress of every transaction at each stage.

Issue vouchers were pre-posted on the account before stores were selected for issue. This arrangement had been adopted for clothing several years previously but now came into general use. Perhaps the main advantage over post-posting during the war was that a voucher was not passed to the storehouse for selection when there was no stock of the item. On the other hand there might be large quantities in the receipts bay, not yet entered on the account.

This led to the introduction of Dues Out Control. By this system, vouchers for items not immediately available (Dues Out Vouchers) were held in the storehouse, and every receipt was screened against them. Any receipts which were due out were passed straight to the issues bay and not put to stock. This system, though it caused slight delay in putting stores to stock, was essential in war when urgently required items were submerged among massive receipts in which items not immediately required predominated.

The Visidex system of accounting was adopted universally. It was ideal for the war conditions then prevailing. A simple and compact hand-posting system, it required the minimum training of staff and could be used by clerks of all nationalities in all parts of the world. The use of carbon-backed posting slips enabled a separate check to be made of all entries without the interference caused by checking the account card. In these days of computers this may appear to be a somewhat unsophisticated system, but in the circumstances of the time its merits were undeniable.

Another war-time measure, which was adopted, was the Unified Account. The system of an account on ledgers or machines, supplemented by a storehouse tally, provided checks which ensured the accuracy and precision considered essential in peace. In war the activity was so great that the same degree of precision was neither desirable nor attainable. The old system merely introduced duplication of stock records and the decision was made to transfer the account to the main storehouse where it constituted the only stock record. This became the normal method to which there were few exceptions.

CENTRAL STOCK CONTROL

As the war progressed "shadow" CODs were formed in various parts of the country. This was necessary in order to find accommodation for the vastly increased stocks and also to achieve the necessary degree of dispersion and spread the issue load.

At first shadow depots had their own provision branches, but this system was discarded and provision was concentrated at the "parent" COD (this was the original COD for the range concerned, e.g. Chilwell, Didcot).

Information on stock levels, etc., was conveyed to the parent COD by a simple system of returns so that provision was based on full knowledge of available assets and their location.

COST CONTROL

With such a large organization, spread over the whole country, it was necessary to introduce an instrument of management to ensure the best use of available manpower, particularly when there was a constantly changing work load. Planning staffs of qualified experts in this field were established at the War Office and in central depots and they evolved a system known as Cost Control.

The work load in each function in each depot was measured, using man/hours as a factor. Time tests were taken of the various operations and standards laid down. Management indices were produced and depot efficiency in relation to manpower was recorded. Returns were sent periodically to the War Office and this enabled the deployment of manpower to be watched and adjustments to be made. The planning staffs were trained in time-and-motion techniques and were able to give useful advice to commandants on methods to save labour and increase output.

This was the beginning of the introduction of planning branches into all Ordnance depots, and also of training in these techniques in the RAOC School. When the value of what is now called Work Study was realized in the Armed Services, it is not surprising that the RAOC was found to have used similar methods for some time.

STOREHOUSE METHODS

Before the war somewhat archaic methods were in use in Ordnance depots, and this was mainly due to financial stringency and the fact that the very limited peace-time activity did not require anything more up-to-date. It is true that some new methods had been introduced, notably the standard steel racking and bins at Chilwell, which became and remain to this day the normal method of holding detail stores.

Fortunately the AOER officers, who made up such a high proportion of the management of the central depots, were not inhibited by the peace-time restrictions imposed on the Regular Army, and they had no hesitation in introducing new ideas which they realized were essential to the process of expansion.

The most notable of these were the extensive use of tubular scaffolding to make the best possible use of storage space for bulk while facilitating movement, the introduction of flow packing for speed of issue in detail storehouses and the increasing use of modern methods of materials handling, notably the fork lift truck. All these things have had a lasting effect on storehouse methods in the RAOC.

PACKAGING

The standards of packing and preservation of stores in the Army before the war were very elementary, and the subject continued to be neglected for some time after the war had started because of other more serious considerations.

The North African campaign in 1942 brought matters to a head. The officers who were sent out by General Williams had as one of their main tasks that of seeing whether the stores sent out from CODs were packed and documented in such a way as to make things easy for those at the receiving end in the theatre of war.

They found plenty of room for improvement. Some stores were inadequately preserved against bad climatic conditions, some were in packages which could not stand up to rough handling in transit and others had lost their means of identification. Sometimes all these faults were present.

General Williams immediately started research into the best methods of packaging and by the end of the war standards were very high. RAOC Officers, representatives from industry and the Ministry of Supply and experts from the United States combined to devise the best methods of packaging for all conditions, taking into account the probability that stores intended for one theatre might be diverted to another where the climate was quite different.

The three main factors, of equal importance, were preservation, protection against damage and permanent retention of means of identification. When there were hundreds of thousands of small stores, many of them very similar in appearance, it was extremely easy for an item to lose its identity which meant in fact that it was impossible to discover its part number. This problem was in the end largely solved by the use of cartons which protected the store and also had a label with the part number on it protected by transparent waterproof material. The store remained in the carton until actually required for use.

Investigation into the basic quantity of various items to go into each carton was also undertaken. This carton unit was based on the minimum quantity issued to a unit from a field park. It is now known as the Primary Packaged Quantity (PPQ).

Finally CODs established extensive plant for the preservation of all types of equipment for issue to units operating in the worst climates—in effect the tropics. Hot dip tanks, derusting and cleaning tanks and facilities for complex packing with moisture vapour barriers and the use of a desiccant were installed in all large depots. Large numbers of staff were trained in the various methods of packaging.

HOME INDUSTRY CENTRES

This scheme was extensively used for the carton packing of small items, mainly MT and Technical Stores. Instead of extra staff being brought into the depots the work was taken out to convenient centres of population, schools and so on which were easily accessible. Little training was required for this type of work and it was possible to use a considerable un-tapped source of part-time labour. Home Industry Centres were controlled from the various Central Ordnance Depots.

LANDING RESERVES AND BEACH MAINTENANCE PACKS

These methods of supply have already been mentioned. Their preparation presented many problems to the depots concerned and required a tremendous amount of work in relation to the tonnage of stores involved.

First scales had to be produced. Only essential items for maintenance over the beaches could be included because of the heavy, competing demands for limited shipping space. But there was plenty of scope for argument as to which items were essential and the requirements depended on the order of battle and the details of the operation. No two amphibious operations were alike.

When the scale was settled the stores had to be packed in special cases, robust and waterproof, but not heavy and with rope handles to assist man-handling over the beaches. In the lid of each case was a contents list which could be used as a bin card, marked up when stores were issued. The cases had to be so designed that they could be used as bins.

In addition to this arrangement each Landing Reserve required a Schedule and Location Index. This was in fact a complete list of the contents of the Landing Reserve with, against each item, the serial number of the case or cases in which it could be found.

For various reasons the make-up of a Landing Reserve Set was subject to frequent modification between the date when it was packed and the time when it was finally shipped. With a pack so complicated as a Landing Reserve these changes presented no little difficulty and involved a great deal of hard work, always against time.

MOBILIZATION GROUP

Throughout the war the RAOC had the task of bringing formations and units up to their full scale of unit war equipment for service overseas. Mobilization Groups were formed in most CODs, and each depot assembled the serials laid down for it by the War Office.

This was a special task because it involved holding stores outside the normal depot range. The method of accounting was also abnormal, being against the unit War Equipment Table (AF G1098). Priorities changed frequently and there were always shortages so that the submission of frequent reports and deficiency lists were necessary together with much argument about the "battleworthiness" of the equipment.

The equipment of units for overseas was the concern of the Director of Mobilization and the officer in charge of the mobilization group had to satisfy him as well as the COS, for whom this was but one of many responsibilities. To be in charge of a mobilization group was a thankless and frustrating task, the difficulties of which were not always appreciated. Nevertheless the work, which was of obvious operational importance, was well done, and justifiable complaints were few.

CLOTHING

When Branston was taken over as the Central Ordnance Depot for all Army clothing (except full dress which remained at Woolwich) the covered accommodation amounted to one shed covering 305,000 sq. ft. with some ancillary buildings. A second store shed of 350,000 sq. ft. was built and in use by the beginning of the war. In addition to this construc-

394

tion a six-line marshalling yard was built with branches to the ancillary sheds and the two main storehouses.

Responsibility for the inspection of clothing was transferred from the Ordnance Service to the Ministry of Supply on the creation of that department in the summer of 1939, but the staff and facilities remained at Branston.

Before the war Branston made bulk issues to overseas depots and to Aldershot and Scottish Commands, but issued in detail to other Commands in the United Kingdom. Soon, however, all Commands were placed on the same footing as Aldershot. However, certain special items such as mountain and snow warfare clothing, parachutist clothing and items in short supply continued to be issued in detail from Branston.

The conversion of industry from civilian to military requirements presented less difficulty in the case of clothing than warlike and technical equipment. Moreover, Lord Woolton had streamlined the system of procurement of clothing for the Army. The result was that the accommodation at Branston was found to be inadequate before the end of 1939. Staffing problems also occurred with the removal of supervisory military staff and the calling up of reservists.

The appointment of COO was filled by Colonel C. W. Bacon, who formed the depot initially. Soon after mobilization Colonel F. C. Larmour, who had retired from the Corps in 1937, became Deputy COO, taking over the depot when Colonel Bacon was sent to another appointment.

Early in 1940 an experienced business man and Territorial Army Officer, Colonel (later Brigadier) H. P. Crosland, was appointed COO. He was authorized to pick his own team from which no one was to be posted without his permission. This "top management" did not change for nearly five years, and the arrangement worked well for the supply of clothing.

On mobilization hundreds of lorries appeared on the roads for miles around Branston with unit indents for clothing. It was necessary to comb through the Order of Battle and call units forward according to their priorities. This involved the employment of 12 ATS typists for several days preparing lists and working out issue programmes for the storehouses.

After the bombing of Woolwich in the autumn of 1940 the full dress clothing was transferred from there to Branston for safe keeping. It was of course not issued in time of war, but its maintenance in condition fit for issue after the war was a continuous task for a small team.

The need for expansion and dispersion was soon realized and sub-depots were opened at Dewsbury in Yorkshire and Stalybridge in Cheshire near centres of the wool and cotton trades respectively. The original intention was that these sub-depots would store the new production from the clothing contractors in their areas, but the need for dispersion led to a policy of holding a balanced range of all items of clothing and necessaries in these depots. As an extension of the policy of dispersion new outstation sub-depots were opened at Cambusbarron, near Stirling, Portadown in Northern Ireland and Northolt in the London area.

The first real crisis for Branston was the re-clothing of the BEF after Dunkirk. This occurred simultaneously with the return of such stocks as had been salvaged from the depots in France. It was a non-stop business and issues continued as long as the stocks lasted. Then issues "in lieu", such as canvas shoes for boots, and denims for battledress, were made. Delivery points were established for formations and groups of units so as to facilitate speed of issue.

The next heavy task was the issue of clothing to the Local Defence Volunteers (Home Guard). All these activities were urgent because they were undertaken under the shadow of invasion. At this time overseas issues did not amount to more than one-fifth of the whole.

The Portadown sub-depot was useful at this stage in absorbing the output from the large contracts placed in Northern Ireland. The Conscription Law had not yet been applied there and unemployment was still a problem.

The need for clothing was such that all possible capacity for making up garments had to be used. Control of material from the mills and its diversion to contractors was important and had to be watched so that priority would go to reliable contractors who could guarantee a good output of garments. The problem was not easy when one type of material was used in the manufacture of several garments.

It was not unusual on Fridays for a spate of calls to come in from bank managers asking the depot to approve overdrafts to small contractors to pay weekly wage bills against impending inspection of receipts off their contracts.

As the threat of invasion subsided issues to the Middle East began to build up, although the facilities developed in that theatre made it almost self-supporting eventually.

By the autumn of 1941 the production of Army clothing had reached a peak and so had the capacity of Branston to handle it. This is illustrated by an urgent order for the issue of $3\frac{1}{2}$ million pairs of boots and nearly 3 million yards of greatcoat cloth for Russia. A target of less than a week was set for this gigantic task (most of the cloth was at Dewsbury and Stalybridge) and the work was completed with only a few hours to spare. The achievement was spectacular, but by then the depot had got into its stride and the earlier re-equipment of the BEF was considered to have been a more difficult and hectic business. It was normal to receive sudden requests for extra consignments to fill space in ships. An order to repeat a consignment meant that a ship had gone down.

The need for further expansion was met in a number of ways. In the early days of the war there had been a requirement for the issue of clothing to foreign governments, notably France and Rumania. This was met by placing contracts with Lloyds Packing Warehouses, the largest packers and exporters of cotton in this country. Later on this firm was used as a sub-depot, functioning in the same way as Dewsbury and Stalybridge. It had a peak capacity of nearly 565,000 sq. ft. of covered storage. Temporary accommodation on a small scale was used at Aldershot, Ludgershall and Olympia (London) during 1940 and 1941, and at Sutton Coldfield in 1945.

In August 1943 it was agreed with the Canadian authorities that Branston should take over the clothing sub-depot of the Canadian BOD at Brookwood. This released Canadian military manpower as the depot, which undertook issues to Canadian units, was manned from Branston. This increased the Branston load and also the range which the COD had to handle as many items were of special Canadian pattern, made in Canada, supplied from there in bulk and re-packed in Branston standard packages. In 1944 Branston and its sub-depots occupied 3,335,000 sq. ft. of covered accommodation and 125,000 sq. ft. of open storage.

In the summer of 1942 American troops began to arrive in this country and their Services of Supply established separate depots. Branston gave assistance by the supply of depot equipment and the loan of experienced civilian staff. A certain amount of clothing was produced in this country for the American Army under the reverse Lease-Lend arrangement. Branston undertook the receipt, packing and bulk issue of this clothing to the Americans.

The first Landing Reserves and Beach Maintenance Packs were prepared in 1942 for the operations in Madagascar in May and North Africa in November. The officer largely responsible for this work was Major J. W. Lupton, one of the few Regular officers who remained at the depot. Valuable experience was gained in the operations and changes were made in the size of packages and the system of waterproofing.

Planning for D Day began in 1943 and selected staff undertook the packing programme early in 1944. The bulk of these reserves was enormous and the timetable required the production of no fewer than 246,000 packages, which filled the traffic bays causing temporary congestion and dislocation of the normal receipt and issue flow. The close theatre maintenance system for OVERLORD increased the load of urgent detail issues and special arrangements had to be made.

The importance of avoiding deterioration of clothing in transit was realized at Branston. The main problem was to keep the clothing dry, and the War Office authorized the issue of all clothing in closed railway wagons. It was a fortunate coincidence that one Landing Reserve fitted exactly into a closed wagon.

When the end of the war was in sight the Government decided that the soldier on demobilization would be provided with a free set of civilian clothing and stocks began to flow into Branston in August 1944. Plans were also made for establishing Civilian Clothing Depots near Demobilization Centres. Branston had the task of stocking 18 of these depots which also served men demobilized from the Royal Navy and the Royal Air Force. When war ended with unexpected suddenness in September 1945, the scheme was in readiness and worked very well.

PROVISION

Clothing was a DCS subject and the branch at the War Office was OS 7 working under the DDCS(C). Detailed provision calculations were done at Branston, the branch being known as P5.

As far back as the days of the Royal Army Clothing Department at Pimlico, the central provision of clothing had been entirely civilianized and military staff received no training. It has been seen that Lord Woolton found the system of provision of clothing for the Army to be in something of a groove and war-time pressures showed that a new approach was needed.

The officers appointed to take charge of P5 was Lieutenant-Colonel H. Glanfield. In peace-time he was director of Messrs. Hobson and Glanfield—Military Tailors. He never spared himself in his efforts to create and maintain an efficient provision branch, and produced excellent results.

Theoretically provision of clothing was a simple matter of a scale based on experience being applied to known or forecast strength figures, but in fact there were many difficulties which could not be precisely foreseen.

The proportion of the different sizes required varied in different theatres. For example an Indian Division with a number of Ghurka Battalions would require a higher proportion of the small sizes than a British Division. Divisions were liable to be regrouped at short notice.

Increased wastage due to climatic conditions in, for example, Italy and Belgium made nonsense of the wastage rates on which the provision of cloth had been planned. These and other difficulties could always be solved by over-provision, but here political factors intervened. The civilian population had to be clothed. Conditions were sufficiently austere owing to the priority accorded to the armed forces, and there was unlikely to be support for a proposal that civilian clothing standards should be further reduced in order that the Army might over-insure and possibly accumulate surpluses.

In 1943 the critical manpower shortage in industry combined with raw materials difficulties led to very large arbitrary cuts in production, which automatically threw out of balance the proportion of sizes coming off the production programmes on our behalf in the United States and Commonwealth countries. The Ministry of Supply had the greatest difficulty in getting production restored to something like the old level and in fact for the rest of the war production of clothing was inadequate.

The effect of this calculated risk, if such it can be called, was greatest when 21st Army Group faced a particularly severe winter campaign in Belgium and Holland. A force which had lacked for nothing before D Day and during the summer of 1944 suddenly found itself rationed in the one commodity which should apparently have been the easiest to supply. Traditionally commanders of formations and units tend to combine great attention to the question of the clothing of their troops with a marked inability to understand that its supply presents any problem at all.

It has been seen that the necessary flexibility in the matter of special sizes was achieved in the Middle East, Italy and Belgium by the establishment locally of clothing factories. But the supply of material of the right quantity and quality is a different matter. Deficiencies in this respect cannot be laid at the door of Branston. They had to work to factors provided by the War Office, and a system of central stock control was introduced which gave a complete picture of the distribution of existing stocks. Moreover the recovery of returned clothing was achieved by the system of RSDs in all Commands.

At the War Office the DCS was not a free agent. He had to operate within the framework of Government policy. The policy to reduce production of clothing for the Army was irksome rather than disastrous, but more might have been done to convey to commanding officers the need for the decision and the effect it would have.

It is less easy to understand the decision to go into the reverse-lease-lend business and produce clothing for the American forces at the same time as our own troops were being rationed. The saving of shipping space was always an important consideration but it is unlikely to have been a main factor in this case because a good deal of material had to be imported from America.

As the war progressed quality control in production had to be relaxed in favour of speed of output. Battle dress was produced in a wide variety of shades and it was impossible to guarantee that the blouse and the trousers matched. This was an embarrassment to commanding officers when their troops had to appear on a ceremonial parade alongside their better dressed allies. In any case battle dress was not designed as a ceremonial uniform.

The British Army has always had "hat" trouble, and the complaint was much in evidence in the Second World War. The original hat with battle dress was the Field Service Cap or "fore-and-aft". The cap was of thin khaki material which made a smart appearance almost impossible, and it would not stay on in a wind without the aid of one of the more adhesive types of hair cream. The only advantage was that it was flat and easy to pack.

The beret was found to be an improvement although it had no peak, but very soon the supply of wool ran out and a beret-type cap of cloth was designed to replace it. Although a practical form of headgear it had the disadvantage of making most people who wore it look ridiculous, which was not calculated to raise morale.

Luckily the RAOC is not responsible for the design of Army clothing, but when a new unpopular fashion is introduced the supplier has to try to deal with the complaints of the customer. For example the shortage of metal led to the introduction of plastic cap badges. Some units refused to accept these and a few even contrived to purchase their own metal badges. This shows the importance attached to the effect on unit morale of the supply of these items. It also seems to show that Government contractors did not always have top priority for the supply of raw material.

ACCOUNTING

To avoid unnecessary paperwork and duplication of stock records most depots adopted a system of unified accounting—one stock record in the main storehouse. Such a system could not be used in Branston owing to the volume of receipts of sized garments.

Special sheets were printed detailing a complete size range. Contractors inspection notes usually showed a wide range of garments in sizes and it was quicker to post across the page than on single cards.

At the end of each day the sheets were summarized and extracted to a summary record of each size at all depots. Thus a total physical stock available for issue was known. All issues were pre-posted.

OPERATIONAL ISSUES

To spread the load and meet target dates details were notified by telephone to outstations during the period from midnight to the early hours of the morning. The transaction was confirmed by preparing and despatching Issue Vouchers. The Issue Controller fixed target dates and watched the progress of urgent issues by means of liaison officers in the storehouses.

MANPOWER

The strength of Branston and its sub-depots excluding the Ministry of Supply staff was as follows:

In 1939 there were 21 officers, 100 other ranks and 2,421 civilians at Branston, and 2 officers and 450 civilians in sub-depots. Total 2,994.

In 1945 there were 69 officers, 665 other ranks and 1,451 civilians at Branston, and 17 officers, 189 other ranks and 919 civilians in sub-depots. Total 3,310.

A separate group was formed to deal with the supply of clothing for the Womens Services. This was operated entirely by ATS and was extremely efficient.

The following activity figures illustrate the size of the Branston load:

North African campaign, 1942.

60 Landing Reserves and 16 Beach Maintenance Packs prepared.

North-West Europe, 1944.

87 Landing Reserves and 75 Beach Maintenance Packs prepared. Large issues: 800,000 kit-bags.

400,000 suits anti-gas clothing.
500 tons of winter clothing.
110,000 snow suits (winter 1944).
100,000 yards white calico (winter 1944).
2 million pairs of socks.
430,000 suits of battle dress.

CONCLUSION

Branston operated on efficient business lines throughout the war, after which the senior officers on the staff returned to their pre-war activities. Liaison with the user was left to the staff of the DCS at the War Office. These factors resulted in a self-imposed isolation of Branston with a corresponding lack of outside interference. It is a matter of opinion whether this separation from the rest of the Corps was altogether satisfactory, but the results can be left to speak for themselves.

GENERAL STORES

At the beginning of the war the COD organization for the supply of General Stores consisted of Didcot, with its provision branch, and a sub-depot recently opened at Slaithwaite near Huddersfield.

The term General Stores covers an extraordinarily diverse range of items, many of which are bulky. The reluctance to approve the holding of a reasonable level of war reserves in peace limited the storage commitment, but it also meant that in the event of war an enormous accommodation problem would soon occur.

Some action was taken in anticipation of this commitment. Clothing had already been transferred to Branston. A large storehouse was built with 650,000 sq. ft. of floor space, which experience showed to be a good deal more than the optimum area for one building. A second sub-depot, containing one million sq. ft. of covered accommodation, was built for the storage and issue of camp equipment at Thatcham, near Newbury. This was an excellent sub-depot but it was not ready for use until May 1940.

The organization and layout of Didcot was suited to its role of making bulk issues to Command Depots in the United Kingdom and bulk shipments to overseas theatres. The largely civilian staff lacked experience in dealing with urgent detail issues on a big scale, and it was no easy matter to introduce the necessary degree of flexibility into an organization set in the ways of a long-established routine.

It was essential and inevitable that the expansion of the Didcot organization would develop on the lines of wide dispersion and decentralization. One of the first steps in this direction was to acquire three large sheds within the perimeter of the Central Ammunition Depot at Longtown near Carlisle. Each of these sheds had a floor space of 350,000 sq. ft.

The development of the organization took two forms. There had to be dispersion of stocks into new accommodation throughout the country, leading to geographical grouping under shadow CODs. Then there was the separation of certain specialized stores as the responsibility of nominated depots.

After the opening of Thatcham in May 1940 the programme of expansion was as follows:

November 1940. Outstation sub-depots opened at Maidenhead, Hermitage and Abingdon.

November 1942. Thatcham handed over to the American forces under the Bolero scheme. The consequent re-grouping of stocks was achieved by acquiring more accommodation in the north of the country. The Longtown Depot was re-named Solway and made a shadow COD eventually controlling the Slaithwaite group and other sub-depots in the north. There were 19 of these, varying in size from the 13,500 sq. ft. of covered accommodation at Holmfirth to 398,270 sq. ft. of covered and 45,900 sq. ft. of open storage at Slaithwaite. The total covered accommodation of all depots controlled by Solway was over 3,700,000 sq. ft.

The shadow COD was responsible for the administration and military and technical efficiency of all its depots, but provision was centralized at Didcot and also the associated function of stock control, namely the decision on the distribution of stocks and stock levels throughout the organization.

In the same month Perivale Depot was brought into the Didcot organization as a specialist organization for holding anti-gas stores.

September 1943. At Didcot itself the need for additional storage space was met by the erection of Romney hutting which provided 400,000 sq. ft. of covered accommodation, and by the construction of 250,000 sq. ft. of hard standings. This was an example of self-help, the labour being found from Ordnance resources.

November 1943. Harlesdon Sub-Depot was taken over for cinematograph stores and Crookham for handling mobile laundry equipment.

March 1944. COD Basing was created from a part of the Central Ammunition Depot at Bramley to form a main base depot for the issue of general stores to 21st Army Group under the Close Theatre Maintenance system.

May 1944. Elstree was taken over to hold snow, mountain and jungle warfare equipment.

December 1944. Boughton, near Ollerton in the midlands was taken over from the Americans and used to hold oils, paints and materials handling equipment.

February 1945. Hainault Sub-Depot was opened to deal with the storage and issue of laundry plant.

Elstree and Boughton became shadow CODs each controlling a number of depots on a geographical basis. Where responsibility for a particular group of general stores was transferred from Didcot to another depot in the organization, the provision branch dealing with those stores also moved.

The general stores organization, directed from Didcot, ultimately controlled storage amounting to nearly 8 million sq. ft. of covered and more than 9 million sq. ft. of open accommodation.

EVOLUTION OF METHODS

Until shortly before the war Didcot had been used as an experimental centre for developing up-to-date accounting systems.

The effect of these experiments was to leave the depot with a variety of procedures in operation. Part of the account was on the Hollerith Punched Card system, part on the N.C.R. Machine Account and the remainder on the old hand-posted Tally and Ledger system. The decision was made to adopt as standard for all depots the hand posted Visidex system and Chilwell procedure.

There is no doubt about the wisdom of this decision, but the introduction of yet another procedure at Didcot with little time to train the staff or test the application of the method to the supply of general stores, caused a good deal of confusion at first.

The civilian staff in particular had the greatest difficulty in adjusting to the new procedures, and this may have been partly due to the tradition which rigidly separated the non-industrials who kept the account from the industrials who did the storekeeping.

These factors contributed to serious discrepancies between the stock shown on the Visidex Card and the actual stock held. Many unofficial records were created in the storehouse, which really amounted to the reintroduction of the old Storehouse Tally in another form. This was not necessarily a bad thing as experience has shown the value of a storehouse record for a high proportion of general stores.

In 1942 a measure of decentralization was effected in Didcot by forming three sub-depots, each responsible for a particular range of stores and each self-contained with its own control and accounts branch.

PLANNING

At the beginning of the war this activity was one of the responsibilities of the 0.0. Administration, but with the increasing size and complexity of the organization the need for a separate branch became evident.

A system of cost control was adopted, which compared output with man/hours worked, and collated information on tonnage handled, item headings held, number of postings on the account etc. Appropriate management indices were devised and a picture of activity and efficiency was presented to enable timely action to be taken where necessary.

In due course a comprehensive system of storage control was established. Complete records were kept in Didcot of all accommodation in all depots of the general stores organization. This information was shown in graphic form. Storage requirements were assessed and directions given when contractors were ready to deliver. Forecasts of accommodation requirements were made from analysis of contracts placed.

PACKAGING

The increased usage of timber for packing stores for issue necessitated the establishment of a separate section to hold the stocks of packing cases and also for case recovery and repair. By 1943 a branch had been formed to give the subject of packing continuous study, the most suitable materials, economy, standardization, and the best way of marking packages for identification of the contents.

In 1943 special attention was given to the question of preservation, with particular reference to the problem of long-term storage in adverse conditions of accommodation and climate. Special preservation plant was concentrated at Didcot, where facilities were created for cleaning, degreasing, derusting, drying and preservation of stores. Tropical packing and cartoning of stores was also undertaken.

PRINTING

A Multilith Printing Machine was installed in July 1944. This enabled technical and instructional publications to be printed locally, and in addition Didcot forms, Landing Reserve Location Indices and Contents Lists.

PHOTOGRAPHIC LABORATORY

This laboratory was transferred from Aldershot to Didcot in 1942. The staff consisted of RAOC, ATS and civilians who had been trained in this work in peace-time. The laboratory was employed for the production of military training photographs and lantern slides for lectures. Pictures were taken of new equipment, the latest packing and preservation techniques and so on. After D Day, films were flown over from the Continent, developed and returned within a few hours.

PERSONNEL

The military unit in Didcot at the outbreak of war was No. 4 Section RAOC which was expanded to 60 Training Section in October 1939. This later became 14 Battalion RAOC which remained the military unit at Didcot until after the end of the war. In addition to RAOC there were also considerable numbers of ATS, Royal Pioneer Corps and civilians. In 1943 the strength of the unit was as follows:

RAOC	1,150
RPC	1,000
ATS	850
Civilians	4,410
	7,410

The appointment of COO (later redesignated Commandant) changed more frequently at Didcot than in other main base installations. In September 1939 the COO was Colonel G. R. Hopkins, who was posted to Hong Kong at the end of the year and replaced by a re-employed officer, with a distinguished record in the Corps in the 1914–18 war, Brigadier C. M. Stephen. He was followed in succession by Brigadiers H. R. Shillington, B. C. Lester and B. G. Cox, all Regular RAOC officers.

For much of the war control and coordination of the various CODs and other depots holding general stores had been exercised from the directorate of the DCS at the War Office. Early in 1945 this control was delegated to the Commandant COD Didcot, who became in fact though not in name a commander of the General Stores Organization.

Military Staff requirements at Didcot during the war are illustrated by the programme of construction of accommodation, which was as follows:

Year		Capacity
1940	Durnell's Farm Camp (within depot perimeter)	1,000
	ATS Camp, Station Road	500
1941	Temporary accommodation Vauxhall Barracks	300
1942	Coronet Camp	600
1943	Ryman's Field Camp	600
	Extension Vauxhall Barracks	400
	Extension Coronet Camp	250

Didcot also had to accommodate BODs and other units forming for service overseas.

PROVISION

The branch for the provision of general stores at Didcot was known as P4.

Two main problems presented themselves. The first was the extraordinary diversity within the general stores range, the various categories requiring different treatment. The second problem was that in the important category of accommodation stores capital issues were heavy and could not always be anticipated. Consequently maintenance scales tended to be inflated.

Operational scales could only be worked out from experience. Naturally these scales were unbalanced in the early years of the war and many unwanted items were issued, but by D Day the requirements of 21st Army Group had been calculated with a remarkable degree of accuracy.

The first urgent and heavy task falling upon Didcot was the re-equipment of the BEF on its return from France after Dunkirk and the supply of accommodation stores to staging camps and concentration areas in a country which had suddenly become an armed camp in imminent danger of invasion. Large stocks had been lost in France and stocks in command depots were rapidly depleted.

Later in the war another heavy programme of capital issues had to be undertaken for the camps in the concentration and marshalling areas for OVERLORD. To this was added the provision and packing of 89 Landing Reserve Sets, 75 Beach Maintenance Packs and automatic maintenance shipments for the AODs.

Similar problems on a smaller scale occurred for the forces engaged in the campaigns in North Africa, Sicily and Italy, but in the Middle East and Mediterranean a considerable load was taken off Didcot by the maximum use of local resources and supply from Eastern Group (countries round the Indian Ocean). These theatres drew from Eastern Group nearly all tentage and a high proportion of blankets and textiles, also many of the raw materials for the manufacture of soap and paint.

Some stores were obtained from the U.S.A. on Lease/Lend, but this source was mainly used by laying off demands from the Middle East for direct supply from North America.

As the war progressed it became necessary to introduce first Central Stock Control, covering general stores both in the Didcot organization and in Command Depots, and then Global Stock Control which added the assets in Eastern Group and the Mediterranean Theatre (Central Ordnance Provision Office, Middle East).

This was necessary because provision must be based as far as possible on a knowledge of all assets wherever located. Another factor was that shortages were becoming serious in an increasing range of raw materials and equipment so that maldistribution must be avoided and rationing must be based on the best possible information. Finally the War Office required up-to-date information to plan future operations.

BASING

This depot deserves special mention because of the part it played in the support of 21st Army Group.

The existing transportation facilities at CAD Bramley, and its location in the south of England, made it suitable for conversion in part to a main base depot for general stores. The work was put in hand and the converted portion of the depot was renamed COD Basing in December 1943.

Maintenance calculations were made at Didcot, using the Hollerith Machine and stores were sent in standard packs from Didcot and Perivale so that 21st Army Group units could draw direct from Basing early in 1944.

The establishment approved at the end of 1943 was 800 all ranks but, owing to additional commitments the strength of the unit was increased shortly before D Day to 1,070 all ranks. The Commandant was Colonel A. S. Osborne.

In the period of preparation for D Day unit collection of stores was an important factor. A large car park was created, the layout of the stores and traffic circuits within the depot were carefully planned to assist rapid issues and the control office was linked by telephone with the ADsOS of the various formations. Certain stores were not planned to be held at Basing, and ADsOS were notified of such cases on the telephone so that the vehicles for these stores could be diverted to Didcot.

Storage space presented a difficulty because the need for quick issues and the size of the issue load precluded the most economical use of storage space. The sheds, having been built for ammunition over 20 years earlier, were not ideal for general stores and modifications were necessary to improve access for road vehicles and enable fork-lift trucks to be used. A considerable area was available for outside storage, but it required preparation for use.

By sound planning, good organization and hard work these difficulties were overcome, and the depot was ready by the time it opened in March 1944 to give the required service to 21st Army Group.

Unfortunately considerable difficulties occurred in the initial stocking of the depot. Scales changed frequently and Basing was not always advised of these changes. In February it was necessary to undertake a complete reconciliation between the vouchers notifying automatic issues from Didcot and Perivale to Basing and the actual receipt of stores at the depot.

The original plan, whereby Basing stocks were to comprise maintenance only, was modified to enable the depot to make up deficiencies in unit war equipments, and a further commitment was added when Basing was given the task of assembling and storing the clothing and general stores element of 19 Landing Reserves, and 18 Beach Maintenance Packs.

After D Day all issues from the depot were urgent but the load varied and it was undesirable to keep staff at work for long periods when no demands were being received. A process known as "load phasing" was adopted. The depot existed for one purpose only, to meet demands from 21st Army Group and give a 24-hour service.

The Close Theatre Maintenance procedure, which has been described in Chapter 9, produced a predictable rhythm of work, and it was therefore possible to plan the allocation of staff so that the right numbers of people were available at each point in the flow as the work arrived there.

Indents from 21st Army Group were received daily by air at the Indent Clearing Centre, Greenford. The ICC telephoned to Basing the number of indents being sent and from this information the work programme was calculated, starting at the estimated time of arrival of the indents.

The labour force was divided into six main groups, as follows:

Control
Selection
Packing Day Shift
Traffic Day Shift
Packing Night Shift
Traffic Night Shift

Control was further sub-divided into its various functions, for each of which a separate time phase was calculated.

This arrangement made the best use of manpower, and was good for morale in that it ensured as far as was humanly possible that men were brought into the depot when there was work to do and not otherwise.

However, good administration was necessary and this had to be planned as thoroughly as the work in the depot. Accommodation was re-allocated to fit in with the new grouping, and a complicated programme was devised for the cooking of meals so that each group was served at the most suitable time.

The effect of this shift system on output is illustrated by comparing a day's output in March 1944 and January 1945.

In March 1944, 238 Clerks dealt with 1,922 items in one day. In January 1945, 235 Clerks dealt with 7,357 items in one day.

In March 1944, 442 Storemen handled 90 tons in one day. In January 1945, 746 Storemen handled 372 tons in one day.

From D Day to the end of the war in Europe, Basing met no less than 220,000 indents from 21st Army Group.

D.W.S. DEPOTS

A feature of the stores controlled by the DWS was the great number of item headings, compared with Clothing and General Stores. This complicated the problems of provision, accounting, cataloguing and detailed issues, and multiplied the number of transactions.

Technical and Warlike Stores

DONNINGTON

The plans for transferring these stores from Woolwich to a less vulnerable site have been mentioned in Chapter 2. The place finally chosen was Donnington, a village about 3 miles from Wellington in Shropshire.

The man selected to do the preliminary work was Lieutenant-Colonel C. E. de Wolff, previously ADOS Malta, and he returned to England in March 1939. He first visited leading business and industrial concerns to study the latest methods, and in April he went to Donnington to see the situation on the spot.

Except for the foundations of one shed nothing had been done. Knowing the importance of accommodation for the staff he went to see the Clerk to Wellington Rural District Council and told him that the War Department would require one thousand houses for the civilians to be employed at the depot. Donnington was what would now be euphemistically described as a "development area" and consequently the Council was not accustomed to "thinking big". The proposal was laughed to scorn. However, they finally agreed to build 500 houses with the assistance of the Ministry of Labour. This was the beginning of an estate of some 1,500 first-class houses and shops.

The next problem facing de Wolff was to acquaint the civilian employees at Woolwich with the project. This can hardly have been welcome news to them. Many were prominent in local affairs, several were aldermen and councillors of the Borough Council and all had their roots in Woolwich.

However, by then the seriousness of the international situation was clear. It was a tactful move on the part of de Wolff to take the employees into his confidence, and this gave them time to adjust to the possibility of a change. When the crisis occurred mutual confidence had been established and friction was reduced to a minimum.

The original planning of Donnington was methodical. The process of receipts from the trade and transfer of stores from Woolwich had begun when war broke out in September 1939.

Captain Denham was left in charge while de Wolff left for his mobilization appointment as an ADOS at GHQ in France. He returned to Donnington, with the rank of Colonel in November 1939.

Little progress had been made because it was feared that the transfer of stores to Donnington from an established depot would impede the war effort. Woolwich did not appear to be in immediate danger and it had even been suggested that Donnington should be developed as a sub-depot of Woolwich. However, this gruesome thought did not survive a clear policy statement in December which reinforced the original plan stressing the importance of clearing Woolwich as soon as practicable.

The limiting factor was the rate of construction at Donnington and the contractors were well behind schedule. This was mainly due to the strict control of essential building materials, such as steel and timber, imposed by the Ministry of Supply. General Williams had the greatest difficulty in obtaining release for the minimum requirements of building materials.

The first phase was the construction of Building 1, a heavy-lift building with overhead cranes; Building 2, the main storehouse for Signal and Engineer Stores; and Building 3, the main storehouse for Armament Stores. For various reasons the role of these three buildings could not be changed and it was essential that they should all be completed quickly and at the same time.

Early in 1940 it appeared that Buildings 1 and 2 would be ready for occupation by the early summer, except for the overhead cranes in Building 1. Also the heating and lighting in the sheds could not be installed for some time. It was not desirable that contractors' men should be in the buildings when the stores arrived, but it proved impossible to apply this rule.

At the end of March it was decided that the transfer from Woolwich would be in three main groups, the stores being called forward by Donnington as they could be accepted, and the COO Donnington was given a special planning staff to assist him. Sections were to move complete with the accounting, provision and inspection elements so that a complete working entity would arrive in Donnington, and the minimum dislocation of service would be caused.

The move involved the transfer of some 15,000 tons of stores, and the plan was based on loading railway wagons at Woolwich by vocabulary sections and placing them in the Donnington buildings opposite the section locations. A steady flow of stores from manufacturers into the depot was planned to start on June 14th, but all these schemes were rudely interrupted by the events in France in May 1940.

The danger of enemy action against Woolwich suddenly became real and selected valuable stores were to be transferred immediately. Colonel de Wolff with Captains Daniels, Cornes and Caldwell and Lieutenants Percy, Sims, Gladman, Goffe and Morton moved in on May 31st and were followed by a number of selected key civilians from Woolwich. Ten days later the first consignments of stores began to arrive from Woolwich and by then military reinforcements had come in from Chilwell.

With the fall of France the emergency was such that the carefully prepared plans had to be discarded. Donnington had to accept stores even though the means did not exist to put them to stock tidily or take them on charge. Building 1 provided cover but there was no heating or light. The contractors were still laying the concrete floor of Building 2. As the concrete hardened the stores were moved in.

A further difficulty was caused by the use of Donnington as a depot by the Royal Engineers. Stores for the works services required at Donnington had been collected there, but now large consignments of Nissen huts and other stores no longer needed in France were diverted to Donnington and by the end of July 150 railway wagons for the Royal Engineers were arriving daily and 100 from Woolwich.

The congestion of the railway system throughout the country was acute. At Donnington there was only one marshalling yard and one incoming line from the main track. Consequently wagons were waiting in contractors' yards because they could not be moved. Eventually the LMS Railway complained that 700 wagons were waiting outside Donnington and the Director-General of Transportation decided in August to visit the depot and advise on the best way to clear the congestion. However, the COO turned all officers and men on to the task and 500 wagons were unloaded in 48 hours. This cleared the railway bottleneck, which was the immediate problem but created large stacks of stores which could not be put to stock for lack of storage space.

Similar traffic difficulties did not recur because railway construction proceeded steadily and ultimately, within the perimeter fence of 5½ miles, there were 7 miles of railway line, a "double feed" and two marshalling yards.

By mid-July 4,700 tons of stores had been received from Woolwich and contractors by road and rail, and although many months of sorting, identification, binning and accounting lay ahead, the staff gradually began to get on top of the work.

The two provision branches, P1 (Signal Stores) and P3 (Armament), could not leave their accommodation at Chislehurst and Bromley, respectively, and accompany their stores to Donnington as originally planned. There was no office or living accommodation for the staff and a premature move would have led to chaotic provision.

The actual move took place in September 1940 in two special trains, which also carried the complete provision records. They arrived on a Saturday and started to function on the following Monday. The offices were only just ready. Heating was inadequate and the civilian staff had to be boarded out among the residents of Wellington as living accommodation had not yet been built.

MANPOWER

This was from the beginning an intractable problem. A large-scale transfer of experienced staff from Woolwich was a feature of the original plan, but there were several questions which were significant when the time came to put the plans into effect.

Woolwich might not close down altogether but continue in a somewhat different role. In that case staff would be required both at Woolwich and Donnington and those who lived at Woolwich would be reluctant to move even though the place was a target for enemy bombers. This difficulty did occur and the transfer of some of the staff was delayed as a result. Only established grades could be transferred compulsorily and of the civilian establishment of 1,620 agreed in April 1940, only 507 had volunteered to move to Donnington.

A condition of transfer in the pre-war plan was that accommodation must be available. The original plan for 500 houses was half the ultimate requirement, but difficulty over financial approval was followed, after the outbreak of war, by shortage of materials, and it was not until the end of August 1940 that two houses became available for occupation.

Accommodation was the limiting factor and it was not easy to find in that part of the country. In the main, therefore, transfers were confined to key civilians, such as trained provision staff and supervisory storehouse grades. The hope that unskilled labour would be obtained locally and trained was not fulfilled as the call-up caused a severe shortage of civilian labour throughout the country. When labour was in such demand and the rates paid by the Government compared unfavourably with those obtainable in industry, it was not to be expected that local recruiting would be satisfactory either in quantity or quality. The result was that the manpower gap was filled by military and indeed Donnington became in course of time a military unit with valuable assistance from experienced civilians.

After Dunkirk there was no shortage of soldiers in the United Kingdom, and it was only when the danger of invasion receded and drafts had to be found for overseas theatres that a military manpower shortage began to make itself felt.

General Williams was determined that the development of Donnington was not going to be held up by the lack of manpower, and although great efforts were made to press on with the construction of hutted camps, living conditions for the troops in the winter of 1940/41 were hard, and overcrowding was normal.

The military establishment was not worked out until early 1940, when it was assessed at 1,930 all ranks. The unit was given the designation of No. 1 Armament Stores Section, a misleading name in view of the size of the unit, but it derived from the pre-war use of the word Section for the military element of Ordnance installations. The COO, however, stated that he expected the ultimate military strength to be between 4,000 and 5,000.

So far as construction of camps was concerned there was more discussion than action, and the crisis had arrived at the end of May 1940 before the War Office authorized accommodation for 2,000 men, although a Sandhurst block for a handful of men had been approved and was built. It became known as Venning Barracks.

Until Nissen huts were erected the men had to live in tents, and the first party to arrive was a detachment of 11 officers and 359 other ranks from Chilwell. They were part of 3 BOD which was forming there and they reached Donnington early in June 1940. They were followed by reinforcements from 1 and 2 BODs who had returned from France and this brought the total strength up to 1,000 by mid-July.

By the end of 1940 the total RAOC strength had risen to nearly 2,500 and the garrison, which included considerable numbers of Royal Engineers and Royal Pioneer Corps had attained a strength of 4,900. This was a large command and Colonel de Wolff was promoted to Brigadier in the appointment of Commandant and Garrison Commander.

A second Armament Stores Section was approved in October 1940 and the military organization developed as follows:

1 ASS under Lieutenant-Colonel F. L. Yates (previously commander of 6 OFP in Birmingham) occupied C, D, F and O camps holding 300, 900, 450 and 450 men, respectively.

2 ASS under Lieutenant-Colonel H. J. Impson, The Lincolnshire Regiment, occupied G camp with 900 and M camp with 1,050 men.

In May 1941 these two units were given the more appropriate designations of Nos. 9 and 10 Battalions RAOC.

Events in France and Norway had shown the importance of military training for Service units and had also indicated the difficulty of carrying it out without impeding the primary tasks of supply, transport or repair. This aspect was considered so important, when invasion threatened, that the QMG himself appointed, as Deputy Garrison Commander, Colonel G. de Pass. He was to be responsible for military training and for the Donnington defence scheme.

This arrangement, though correct and inevitable in the circumstances, did not have altogether happy results. Colonel de Pass had served in the Oxfordshire and Buckinghamshire Light Infantry. He was a very keen Infantryman, and he approached his task in a spirit of single-minded dedication which left no room for the essential functions of the RAOC, for which in any case he had no responsibility.

The situation was a delicate one and required something more than a parochial attitude from senior officers, and for some time the Deputy Garrison Commander outranked all officers in the depot except the Commandant.

The effect of the sudden expansion of the Corps was that the new intake had to acquire technical knowledge covering a wide field, be conversant with military administration and discipline, and attain a good standard of basic military training which included drill, weapon training, fieldcraft and elementary tactics. This was knowledge which the Regular officer or soldier gained after many years of training and experience, but there was no time in war for such a programme. The solution lay in specialization.

The officers who worked in the depot were mainly from the AOER. They had the basic qualities and background for the technical work but lacked sufficient basic military training and in some cases had none at all. The OCTU developed after the war had started and the Officers Training Unit at Rushton Hall was not formed until the autumn of 1940. These deficiencies would be put right in time, but meanwhile these officers could only be expected to gain confidence and give of their best if they received leadership, and guidance based on full understanding of the situation.

The regimental officers were nearly all re-employed Infantry officers. They were familiar with the type of work they had to do. Their aim was to convert unpromising material into two highly trained Infantry Battalions fit to take the field at the earliest opportunity. This clearly was a full-time task.

Thus the officers at Donnington fell into two main groups, the RAOC officers who had to run the depot, and the non-RAOC officers who were responsible for military training and administration. These two groups were incompatible.

The RAOC officers, good material but at this stage civilians in uniform, knew that they were responsible for the supply of vital equipment to the

Army, the whole reason for the creation of the depot in the first place. They were inclined to view their responsibilities towards the troops under their command in the same way as a civilian employer regards his employees, and they were happy to hand over the quaint ritual of military administration to those who knew the rules.

The regimental officers had little idea what went on in the depot and were inclined to suspect that the men only went there in order to have an easy time and shirk military training.

There was a serious possibility in times of stress that two factions would develop separated by suspicion and misunderstanding. Brigadier de Wolff had to spend an undue amount of his time reconciling the claims of the two sides of his organization. The troops were the real victims in this situation. They served two masters, and the one least concerned with depot productivity held the disciplinary powers. For short periods Regular RAOC officers were in command of sub-depots, and on these occasions they were able to do something to induce harmony and a broader outlook all round.

In retrospect it seems that it might have been advantageous to integrate the organization throughout by making sub-depot and equivalent commanders responsible for the military training and administration of their own troops, but it is by no means certain that the men immediately available for these appointments had the necessary qualifications. Everyone did his best for the common cause. It was their misfortune not their fault that they had to contend with peculiar difficulties arising from the unprecedented expansion of the Ordnance Services in a short period of crisis. It is only fair to put on record that these difficulties occurred, and that they were successfully overcome.

Donnington was not unique in having these manpower problems, but they were felt less acutely in other depots which existed as going concerns at the outbreak of the war. The officers who helped Brigadier de Wolff to bear the brunt of the early, hectic days of the depot in 1940 were

DCOO: Lieutenant-Colonel C. G. Reynolds

OO Armaments Sub-depot—Lieutenant-Colonel F. S. Weir (transferred from P3)

OO Engineer and Signal Stores Sub-depot—Lieutenant-Colonel V. F. D. Tarrant

Oi/c P1 Provision—Lieutenant-Colonel H. J. C. Hildreth

Oi/c P3 Provision—Lieutenant-Colonel St. J. C. Hooley.

EXPANSION OF THE DEPOT

Before the original three buildings had been completed it was clear that additional building on a large scale would be necessary and this proceeded steadily.

Bulk buildings, similar in size but slightly different in construction to Detail Buildings Nos. 2 and 3, were completed. They were numbered 4,

4B and 5. A second heavy-lift building, the twin of Building 1, was erected. It was named Building 1B. Building 18, the large storehouse originally used for RE stores, was taken over partly as office accommodation and partly for depot stores and equipment. A small building, 18B, was constructed on the traffic spurs. It held first RE stores and later Ordnance stores. Two large provision and control offices were built. Road communications and hard standings were developed. A large workshop was built, but even this proved inadequate and some encroachment of workshop activity into Building 1 was necessary.

DEPOT ACTIVITY

Although the tonnage of stores which came into the depot in the early days was considerable, the stocks were unbalanced and there were serious shortages, particularly of signal stores. The development and production of wireless sets was slower than many other items of Army equipment and, as always, the supply of spares lagged behind that of complete equipments.

The bombing of industrial centres which followed the Battle of Britain aggravated the supply position for a time. As late as the summer of 1941 considerable numbers of No. 18 Wireless Sets were in Building 2 and could not be issued because the factory which produced the valves had been destroyed.

Soon these difficulties were overcome and Building 2 became the most active storehouse in the depot in terms of the number of items received and issued, but the delay in reaching peak issue activity caused by production difficulties gave the depot a chance to recover from the trials of the first year and settle down as a smoothly working organization. Storehouse and accounting procedures were based on those methods which had been tried and proved satisfactory at Chilwell. This worked well because there is considerable affinity between technical and MT stores so far as storehouse problems are concerned.

There was one important difference. At Donnington the main equipments—guns, wireless stations, etc.—were treated as stores, whereas at Chilwell vehicles were handled by a separate organization.

The method of dealing with vehicle kits had been worked out before the war, and although active service conditions introduced new problems, particularly with tank kits, the organization could cope with them.

In the case of technical and warlike equipments the supply, storage and issue of the associated stores had received less attention. Scales were not always adequate and production lagged behind that of the equipment itself. At Donnington the newly formed Technical Branch took this matter in hand. Scales were obtained from the Inspectorates and published by Donnington as Armament, Engineer and Signals (AE & S) Scales, which are now known as Complete Equipment Schedules. Provision, storage, issue and accounting were thus put on a systematic basis.

In 1942 war production in Great Britain had got into its stride. Donnington was filling up, and as the United States had now come into the war and Canadian production had increased considerably, there was a steady flow of stores from North America. Accommodation must be found outside Donnington. Premises at Greenford, on the western outskirts of London, had already been acquired and were used to take stores moved from Woolwich. Greenford now became a shadow COD, controlling stocks in the neighbourhood, including Woolwich which had become a returned stores depot holding equipments for repair locally.

Donnington also had its own outstation sub-depots of which the most important initially were Otley in Yorkshire and Queensferry near Chester. Others followed, including Queniborough, Wem, Barry, and Royston the final total being seventeen.

Up to 1943 the initial organization of the depot into two sub-depots, Armament Stores and Engineer and Signal Stores, had proved satisfactory but the rapid increase in range of the latter made it unwieldy and it was converted into two sub-depots. One held Signal Stores (including Wireless) and the other Engineer (including Bridging and Searchlight) and Radar Stores.

This produced a balanced load so far as receipts, storage and issue were concerned and the organization stood the test of time. It was at times suggested that Radar and Wireless should be in the same sub-depot as the items had a "technical affinity". But this factor is irrelevant to the practical business of storekeeping and at the time Radar Equipment had its own peculiar problems. It was still on the top secret list and special security measures were imposed.

Radar equipments ranged from light weight types of about 3 cwt to heavy trailers weighing up to 40 tons. One was self-propelled, being mounted on an American (White scout car) chassis. There were as many as 500 radar vehicles at a time in Donnington, which was thus brought into the vehicle organization business with all its problems of kitting and servicing apart from the maintenance of the sets themselves. Incidentally this also applied to self-propelled guns which were not transferred to Chilwell until after the war.

The cataloguing, identification and packaging of radar stores was most efficiently done by the manufacturer, and this enormously helped storekeeping. The same cannot be said of engineer stores, particularly in the field of static engines and generating sets. The reason was that these were widely used in industry and the Army obtained what was available as it were "off the shelf". Thus there was no standardization. A very wide range of spares had to be held for the many and various equipments. Quantities of any one item tended to be small. Identification and scaling presented a great problem. There were some 100,000 items in the static engine section alone.

Provision also had to be split and a new branch, P9, was formed taking from P1 the Engineer and Radar items. The branch was commanded by

Lieutenant-Colonel H. C. Daniels (a founder member of the depot) assisted by an experienced civil servant, Mr. J. H. Kennett, and 700 Clerks from P1.

The reorganization involved the conversion of a bulk storehouse, Building 5, into the detail building for the new sub-depot. Some 8,000 tons of stores had to be moved and re-stacked, and 10,000 feet of steel racking re-erected.

Like other CODs Donnington reached its peak of activity in the period from the preparation for D Day to the establishment of an advanced base in Belgium, after which activity eased off somewhat.

The main problems before D Day were the preparation of Landing Reserves and Beach Maintenance Packs, a complex programme of detail issues to make up unit deficiencies, and the preparation of automatic maintenance issues to AODs. In the follow-up phase there was a considerable programme of preparation, waterproofing and issue of artillery equipments to 21st Army Group.

One of the main tasks after D Day was a very heavy programme of issue of AA guns and spares to deal with the V1 attacks on London and south-east England.

At the peak of the depot activity 20,000 cases a day were packed and the weekly tonnage in and out was 15,000.

A good deal of equipment was sent to Russia during the war and this equipment had to be specially treated to withstand arctic conditions. The process included modification of the buffer and recuperator system of guns so that the oil did not clog in the extreme cold. The first two consignments missed the boat because the Soviet Trade Delegation in London sent a representative to check the issue and he insisted on opening all the cases. The Russians, far from being grateful for assistance provided by us and the Americans, were incurably suspicious. In this case a solution was found by having a representative of the Trade Delegation permanently at the depot.

For the first four years of the war there was an acute shortage of weapons and other main items of equipment. Their issue had to be rationed and items on the "Controlled Stores" list had to be released by the War Office. It was irksome for units to see equipments in the depot or in the hands of other units while they had to go short.

A Donnington liaison officer was appointed and it was his task to visit units, go into the question of deficiencies in unit equipment and explain the situation when shortages were unavoidable. When units were being mobilized for service overseas, he attended meetings to agree deficiency lists and returned to Donnington with the necessary information on target dates for vital items. It was essential that units should have confidence in the service Donnington was giving, and that misunderstanding should not occur. That this confidence was obtained was largely due to the efforts of Captain B. Ebel.

FURTHER INCREASE IN STRENGTH

By May 1941 the strength of the garrison had increased to 9,600 all ranks. Eighteen months later the strength of each battalion was about 4,000. In addition there were seven Companies of Royal Pioneer Corps and four Companies of Italian prisoners of war. There were also detachments of RASC, RE and RAMC. The garrison was given several additional commitments and the manpower for them brought it up to a strength of nearly 18,000 shortly before D Day. The more significant of these commitments were a School of Instruction, the RAOC Mobilization Centre and a staging camp at Apley Castle outside Wellington where 21st Army Group units assembled 2 or 3 months before D Day.

THE ATS

The first to arrive were a few Clerks and Storewomen who came in May 1940 and were employed in Building 2, being accommodated in billets. By the autumn a Platoon was formed under an ATS subaltern. Early in 1941 cooks and orderlies took over the RAOC Messes. At the beginning of 1942 a group was formed and was rapidly built up by drafts of 200 each fortnight. They lived in Venning Barracks and in 126 houses on the housing estate. Later they occupied a camp of 80 Nissen huts. By February 1944 the ATS numbered 2,700 and a year later there were just over 3,000, the peak figure.

The ATS proved themselves to be indispensable. They came from all parts of the country and were clerks, shop assistants, factory hands, housewives and girls straight from school. Each Auxiliary working in the depot took a course in Ordnance procedure and many showed great aptitude for the work. Their integration into the organization with RAOC and civilian employees presented no difficulty. They worked as hard as the men, and set a fine example of responsibility and discipline.

CIVILIAN STAFF

It has been seen that Woolwich was manned and run almost entirely by civilians. This created a considerable problem when the depot was moved and expanded rapidly, as progress largely depended on the experienced staff until others could be trained.

A monopoly which ensured that there were no alternative sources of trained staff also imposed considerable obligations and hardships when the crisis occurred. It is greatly to the credit of these civilians that they loyally accepted the new conditions and made a valuable contribution to the creation of a new and eventually far more efficient depot. To them this upheaval came as the end not perhaps of the world but certainly of their world, an ordered, entrenched and predictable existence which they had chosen.

The uncomfortable conditions of billets in the Donnington area combined with long hours of work and often tiresome conditions of travel to and from work were bad enough. But there was also the nagging thought of families left at Woolwich in nightly danger of being bombed, or living as "evacuees", relatively safe but neither happy nor welcome. The number of established civil servants to be accommodated was roughly 1,000 and the total strength, including temporary civil servants and casual labour, amounted to about three times that number.

Brigadier de Wolff and his successors did everything possible to foster the community spirit and help the civilian staff to settle down in their new environment, and when the housing estate was completed there was already an excellent Canteen and Sports and Social Club, behind which was a sports field, secure from encroachment by building or outside storage.

VISITS

As the depot developed it attracted a constant stream of visitors. Representatives from all Allied armies, high business executives and press correspondents, both British and American, went round the depot and studied the organization.

In 1943 Donnington was honoured by a visit from the King and Queen. This was the first time that Their Majesties had been to a large Ordnance installation during the war, and it was arranged by the Bishop of Lichfield, Dr. Woods, who was a friend of the Royal Family and also a personal friend of Brigadier de Wolff. The visit was a great success. The Princess Royal came twice to Donnington to inspect the ATS and Countess Mountbatten visited the depot to inspect the Donnington Division of St. John Ambulance Brigade, which was formed in 1942 and did an enormous amount of good work. It had its own fully equipped ambulance.

CONCLUSION

Donnington, created entirely during the war, became the centre for the provision, storage and supply of technical and warlike stores for the Army. Its development into a modern, efficient organization was achieved in the face of the greatest difficulties. These could not have been overcome without exceptional qualities of leadership, devotion to duty and co-operation. The various elements which made up the community were, to a large extent, inherently incompatible, yet they contrived to sink their differences in the common cause.

Late in the war Brigadier de Wolff moved to an important but less exacting appointment as DDOS on the Lines of Communication in Italy. But by then the main difficulties had been overcome and to him must go the credit for this great achievement. He handed over to a worthy successor in Brigadier G. P. U. Hardy.

General Williams kept a close watch on the development and progress of his Warlike Stores organizations in the United Kingdom, particularly Donnington and Chilwell. He paid frequent visits to Donnington. The knowledge that they were working under "the eye of the master" kept the staff up to the mark, but the visits had a much greater effect in raising confidence and morale. If the COS could find time to visit the depot frequently and give guidance and help, it was obvious that the work must be important and nothing but the best would do.

GREENFORD AND WOOLWICH

By September 1939, as a measure of relief to the storage problem at Woolwich, 632,000 sq ft of covered accommodation has been leased by the War Department at Greenford. This was part of a large industrial estate. Greenford was designated a sub-depot of Woolwich.

By June 1940 stocks included searchlight and engineer stores, radar stores and generating sets. The depot staff consisted only of 3 officers, 3 other ranks and 450 civilians. Soon after this the bombing of London began. In September 1940 the Woolwich sub-depot at Tilbury was badly damaged and it was decided that the stores there would be transferred to Greenford. At the same time Woolwich was heavily bombed and the transfer of stocks from there became a matter of urgency.

General Williams decided that central stocks of technical and warlike stores would be held at Donnington and Greenford in the ratio of 2 to 1. It was also decided that Greenford would be established as a shadow COD, to take the load if Donnington should be bombed and to ensure adequate dispersion of stocks. In the end it was Greenford that was bombed and Donnington was untouched throughout the war.

The first plan was that Greenford should be a bulk dispersal depot but this was soon discarded and it was organized as a fully operating depot; taking its share of bulk and detail issues. Within the United Kingdom the initial issue load covered South Eastern Command and London District. The depot was organized into groups dealing with the receipt, storage and issue of armament, engineer, signal and radar stores. By December 1941 the strength of the unit was: RAOC, 1,700; other arms, 300; civilians, 700.

Woolwich Arsenal at this stage ceased to be an Ordnance Depot and was used solely to hold "stores-in-aid" for the Ministry of Supply.

The development of Greenford was influenced by the decision to create workshops capacity there. The output of the RAOC Workshops at Woolwich was seriously hampered by air raids, the destruction of valuable plant and machinery and the difficulty of moving equipments in and out of Woolwich.

A General Purpose Workshops, RAOC, was therefore established at Greenford, and also a Wireless and Instrument Shop. The latter was supposed to move to Donnington as soon as the workshops there were completed, but in fact the Greenford workshop remained throughout the war and was expanded. The buildings of the Kelvin Construction Company (within the Greenford perimeter) were acquired for this purpose. By November 1941 the staff of the RAOC workshops at Greenford consisted of 192 military and 158 civilians.

It was now necessary to create a central repair organization to receive repairable equipments and arrange centrally a programme of repair on the basis of War Office priorities.

A Central Repair Depot was therefore formed at Greenford and this organization held stocks which could not be repaired locally and also dealt with similar stocks reported from other technical stores depots such as Donnington and Old Dalby. Greenford arranged for these stores to be repaired by the trade or sent to Greenford for repair.

By October 1942 the raids on Woolwich had ceased and it was possible to make use of the facilities again. Consequently the Central Repair Depot (CRD) was moved there from Greenford. Later in the war the Returned Stores Group at Donnington was transferred to CRD Woolwich Dockyard which was so loaded with returned equipments that Moons Garage, Commercial Road, had to be taken over to provide increased accommodation. When this garage was destroyed by a V1 flying bomb in July 1944 the Ministry of Supply handed over Building B35 in Woolwich to the CRD.

Woolwich was a sub-depot of Greenford for the rest of the war. It remained the Returned Stores Depot for the Technical Stores Organization for many years after the war, not being transferred to Donnington until October 1962.

Owing to delays in building accommodation the ATS strength at Greenford remained at one Platoon but in October 1942, the camp was completed and an ATS Group was quickly formed, eventually numbering over 2,000. This released many RAOC men for field force units.

Late in September 1942, Colonel B. A. Goldstein, who had been DDOS Malta throughout the siege, replaced Colonel Johnston-Davies as COO Greenford. He was given the task of preparing Greenford for a special role, in the support of the Army being formed for operations in North-West Europe. The Traffic Branch at Greenford became an important distribution centre for stores issued from Chilwell, Donnington, Old Dalby, Derby, Weedon and Feltham.

The end of 1942 also saw the re-birth of Woolwich Arsenal as a bulk storage sub-depot of Greenford. The year 1943 brought increased receipts of gun equipments, requiring open storage near the depot and at Northolt Racecourse. At one stage Greenford handled 75 per cent of the technical stores issues load. In May 1943 receipts and issues totalled over 14,000 tons as against 5,700 tons in February 1942.

A branch of the RAOC School was established in 1943 for the technical training of ATS before their posting to COD Bicester. Over 1,500 ATS were eventually trained at this school. There was also an RAOC Packaging School at which the latest methods of packing and preservation of Ordnance stores were taught and demonstrated.

In December 1943 the Indent Clearing Centre for the Close Theatre Maintenance of 21st Army Group was set up. It comprised 1 officer and 42 other ranks and was located in a partitioned-off portion of the large Control Office.

Indents from 21st Army Group were flown to Northolt aerodrome and RAOC and ATS despatch riders met the planes and brought the indents to Greenford within 7 minutes. There they were sorted by issuing depots (there were 9 main base depots with a different range of store in each) and the indents were then taken by despatch riders to the appropriate depots for issue of the stores by air or Ordnance Ship through the main base stores transit depot. By this system, in normal conditions, stores were being packed in the main base depot within 12 hours of the despatch of the indent from 21st Army Group.

This scheme was thoroughly tested in a number of realistic exercises before D Day and everyone knew his job. The ICC was capable of dealing with more than 5,000 indents an hour and was continuously manned.

From early July 1944 indents came in daily and the unit operated to the end of the war in Europe. During the bad winter of 1944/45 planes were often forced to land some way from Northolt and the ICC despatch riders were compelled to travel 100 miles or more to collect the indents.

The millionth indent from 21st Army Group was received by the ICC on April 5th 1945. It was mounted, framed and sent to the COS at the War Office. In all 1,104,411 indents were handled by the ICC. The RAOC despatch riders each averaged 1,600 miles weekly and the ATS despatch riders 1,000 miles.

Various other tasks were undertaken at Greenford before D Day. Of these the most important were the packing of Landing Reserves and Beach Maintenance Packs, the build up of Signal Officer in Chief's Reserve (SOCR) for 21st Army Group and special arrangements for units to collect stores to make up deficiencies in their equipment.

The bulk of SOCR was held at Greenford and Northolt Racecourse. Stores poured in during March, April and May 1944. The Royal Signals staff of the Signal Park attached to the depot did invaluable work in testing and carrying out first line repair on this equipment.

Unit collection was a major problem because it became clear that many units in the assault phase of the operation would not have their complete scale of equipment before they were due to move down to the assembly and concentration areas. This situation was partly due to the fact that CODs had not been given priority lists for issues.

Stores to meet deficiencies were sent to Greenford and a programme of unit collection was arranged. Phase I took place in May 1944 and Phase II shortly before D Day. Over the whole period Greenford provided a 24-hour service. There were long queues of vehicles waiting outside Greenford to collect stores and the task was completed on time.

Immediately after D Day, Greenford undertook a programme of preparation and waterproofing of 4,000 artillery equipments required by 21st Army Group.

In June 1944 the depot made 68,000 issues covering no less than 1,021,000 items. The receipt and issue tonnage was over 29,000.

"V" BOMB ATTACKS

Being in the London area Greenford was vulnerable to the V bomb attacks which were launched in the summer of 1944. In August a flying bomb landed near the road between the depot and the ATS camp. A squad of ATS was marching to the depot and they sustained 57 casualties of which 7 were hospital cases. There were 140 alerts at Greenford during this month.

One morning in March 1945 a V1 flying bomb landed on Building 413 and completely destroyed it. This was unexpected as V bomb attacks had practically ceased owing to occupation of the sites, and this was one of the last three flying bombs, which were launched from Holland.

There were 110 casualties, including 14 killed. This bomb passed over the depot, went on for 200 yards and then turned in a half-circle and dived on the depot.

VISITS AND EXHIBITIONS

The organization of Greenford, its accessibility on the outskirts of London, and the fact that between 1943 and 1945 it became a highly efficient, modern depot, made it an ideal place for staging exhibitions and demonstrations of Ordnance work.

General Williams brought round many distinguished visitors including royalty, senior officers of the Allied forces and the chairmen and managing directors of large business organizations. An exhibition of army equipment was established. Its purpose was to demonstrate the size and complexity of equipment required by a formation in modern war.

On July 6th 1943 Her Majesty the Queen and the Princess Royal visited Greenford. The main purpose of the visit was to see the work of the ATS in the depot, and inspect the ATS camp. On May 2nd 1944 HRH The Princess Royal paid a second visit to the depot, spending 7 hours there and taking a great interest in the work of the ATS and their living conditions. These visits were greatly appreciated by the whole staff of the depot, whose morale was raised by the knowledge that the importance and efficiency of their work was recognized.

OLD DALBY

The depot at Old Dalby near Melton Mowbray was originally planned and built early in the war as a Vehicle Depot. However, when it was opened at the end of December 1940 there was a more urgent requirement for accommodation for signal, engineer, armament stores and small arms and the role of the depot was changed.

The design of the depot was not ideal for its new role. It was sited on the slope of a range of hills, with a view to protection from air attack, but the gradient was such as to prevent the sheds from being rail served. The terraced arrangements of the sheds did not assist the movement of stores within the depot.

The initial establishment was 6 officers and 60 other ranks and at first the only storehouses in use were Shed 2 (100,000 sq ft) and Shed 4 (134,000 sq ft).

Towards the end of 1941 the depot had grown to full size as a COD under the command of Colonel R. C. Hiam, who was transferred from Chilwell. A very able business man on the Army Officers' Emergency Reserve, he established Old Dalby as a well-run depot before doing even more notable work with 21st Army Group in command first of 14 AOD in Normandy and then 15 AOD in Belgium.

At the same time a further change in the role was made. Machinery, including that for installation in workshop lorries had been held at Catford and at Paul Camp near Stroud. It was decided to transfer this machinery to Old Dalby and initially 60,000 sq ft of covered accommodation was allocated for the purpose.

Eventually machinery became the main item of equipment at Old Dalby. The policy to hold 20 per cent of Signals and Armament Stores and 25 per cent of stocks of small arms at Old Dalby was initially dictated by the need for dispersion and the stocks were useful for meeting the needs of units stationed in the area. Some issues were also made to units mobilizing in the United Kingdom and to overseas theatres, but this commitment was progressively reduced. Small arms were transferred to Bicester in 1943 and Armament stores to Donnington early in 1945.

In addition to storage for a considerable quantity of machinery, machine tools and test equipment it was necessary to find accommodation for a workshop for fitting out machinery lorries and packing machinery for base workshops.

Storage was also required for vehicles awaiting the assembly and fitting of machinery and for completed vehicles awaiting issue. Originally machinery lorries were held at the VRD at Breedon under Chilwell control, but it soon became clear that Old Dalby required its own vehicle park and a nine-hole golf course at Stanford Park some 10 miles away was requisitioned for this purpose.

The planned capacity of Stanford Park was 1,250 vehicles but the stocks rose to 1,400 in the summer of 1944. It was not until then that any permanent roads were built and the improvised roads of coir matting and wire netting were inadequate in winter.

By the end of 1944 the stocks of vehicles had risen to 2,500 and a second VRD was formed at Caistor. This was 70 miles away but it was used to hold empty vehicles in excess of the capacity of Stanford Park and also all completed vehicles. After 1942 some 10,000 vehicles and trailers were equipped with machinery, kitted up and issued by Old Dalby.

Materials handling facilities in the depot were limited and machinery weighing more than $2\frac{1}{2}$ tons had to be stored in the "heavy-lift" buildings at Donnington. Later Bicester was also used for these heavy items.

Most of the stores held were normal trade items, not made to any Army specification. It was necessary to take what was available and the lack of standardization caused some difficulties as had been experienced at Donnington with static engines.

Shortage of covered accommodation and the need to make extensive use of open storage added to the difficulties of identification and the maintenance of accurate location records.

When REME was formed the RAOC took over the supply and storage of machinery previously handled by the RASC for their own workshops, and in addition to this considerable quantities of "lease-lend" stores were received from America. In November 1944 the depot took over all the machinery held by No. 1 Canadian BOD. By the end of the war the covered storage available for main equipments at the depot was about 260,000 sq ft.

Electronic test equipment posed a problem of packaging because of the fragile nature of most of these stores. Great attention was paid to tropical packing of these items and complaints were few.

The provision branch for machinery, P8, was established at Old Dalby, and also a Technical Branch to deal with the many problems of identification, cataloguing, and the production of machine cards which listed the various items associated with each machine.

At the peak of its activity the depot strength was 4,000 military and 1,000 civilians.

WEEDON

Weedon had been the central depot for small arms for very many years. In construction it was out-of-date. Some of the storehouses were two-storey buildings and the design of buildings and lay-out of the depot hampered the movement of stores and made really efficient storage almost impossible. One of the buildings in the area had been a military prison which had provided the labour for the construction of the depot.

It was obvious that improvements were necessary, and when war threatened some action was taken. Dry rot was prevalent in the double-span roofs of all the main buildings. The defective roofs were removed and replaced by single-span roofs on steel girders, the programme being completed early in 1940.

The internal railway system was altered and a large reinforced concrete platform with roof was constructed in 1939. The platform was wide enough to permit vehicles to run up the ramps at each end to load and unload railway wagons.

The depot had been paved with granite "sets" which had been laid at the time that the prison existed. In 1939 these were removed and replaced by gravel-concrete to provide a smooth surface for the movement of vehicles.

From the transportation point of view Weedon was well placed. It was on a main railway line, and also on Watling Street which has been a main road for centuries. It is sometimes forgotten that there is a very efficient canal system in the Midlands and Weedon was linked with this by a branch canal which served the depot. Some excellent bowling greens, which had been laid to the south of the canal for the depot employees, were sacrificed to provide additional hard standings.

Many years ago Weedon had been used for the storage of ammunition and the "magazines" were converted in 1940 to hold anti-aircraft ammunition and serve as an Intermediate Ammunition Depot for AA Command. A road was built to provide access to Watling Street. In 1942 the IAD was closed down and the storehouses were again used for small arms.

The area adjacent to the depot was used, after the Great War, as the site for the Army Equitation School. Considerable accommodation for officers and other ranks was built, and in addition there were stables, riding schools and a large area for jumping lanes and cross-country riding courses.

After the outbreak of war in 1939 the School was converted into a Cavalry OCTU, but this was closed down in the summer of 1940 and the staff transferred to open up the RAOC Officers' Training Unit at Rushton Hall near Kettering. The facilities of the Equitation School then became available to Weedon, and were invaluable in providing personnel accommodation and also excellent covered and open storage.

At the beginning of the war the supply of small arms to the Army was not a complicated problem. There were few types, consisting of the Rifle No. 1, Rifle No. 3 (Pattern 14), Bren gun, Lewis gun (plentiful but obsolescent), Vickers gun, Boys ·5-inch anti-tank rifle and Pistols ·38 inch and ·45 inch. The heavy and light Besa guns were being introduced to replace the Vickers gun for use in AFVs.

During the war many new types were developed and imported so the work increased in volume and complexity. Stocks had to be dispersed and new sites opened up. The main dispersal site was initially Old Dalby, and later on Bicester, but small sub-depots were formed at brickyards in Long Buckby, Heyford and Northampton (Martin's), also in Northampton at the Old Midland Station St. John Street, Brook Factory and Franklin Gardens Football Grounds.

In the preparations for D Day the detail issue load for 21st Army Group was transferred to Bicester where suitable facilities for a task of this magnitude existed. Weedon continued as a depot for bulk stocks and detail issues other than to 21st Army Group.

After D Day Bicester became the main storage depot for small arms and the provision branch, P6, was moved there from Weedon which became 99 Ordnance Sub-Depot of Bicester.

While the storage space was required Weedon continued in use, but it was inevitable that it would be closed down ultimately in favour of more modern depots, when Army stocks were reduced to peace-time levels.

MANPOWER

Between the wars Weedon was mainly staffed by civilians. In May 1939 the RAOC strength was 5 officers, 3 warrant officers and 4 other ranks.

A training unit was formed in September 1939, but in the crisis of June 1940 the military strength was increased by 2 officers and 110 other ranks transferred from 3 BOD which had been forming at Chilwell. By April 1941 the military strength had been increased to 700. The ATS strength also increased rapidly. It was 94 in June 1940, 165 by March 1941 and about 400 during 1942. The civilian strength before the war was about 200 and during the war it rose to 770.

Early in the war a re-employed retired officer of the Corps, Colonel R. H. McVittie, was appointed COO. He commanded the depot very efficiently for the critical two-year period between February 1940 and the end of January 1942. He was succeeded by Colonel H. T. Bell.

MT VEHICLES AND STORES

Although the Chilwell organization was well established on modern lines when war started it was obvious that considerable expansion would be necessary to meet the needs of a large mechanized Army. Chilwell held the main stocks of "A" and "B" vehicles and their spares, and there were outstation "B" vehicle depots at Handforth, Harlescott and Derby. A vehicle depot at Old Dalby was planned.

The focal point for the receipt, storage and issue of all vehicles, except those for the RASC, was the vehicle reception store (VRS) at Chilwell. The vehicle census was also kept at Chilwell. Although the supply of both vehicles and MT stores was controlled centrally from Chilwell there were virtually two distinct organizations and they are therefore described separately.

VEHICLES

The following table gives an idea of the expansion of the Chilwell Vehicle Organization during the war.

Date	*"A" Vehicles*	*"B" Vehicles*	*Accommodation*
September 1939	700	7,300	VRS and 3 sub-depots.
August 1945	47,000	193,000	58 "B" vehicle reserve depots, 28 AFV depots.

The world-wide holding of vehicles recorded on the Control Census was 44,000 in September 1939 and 1,403,000 in August 1945.

Early in the war the supply of vehicles did not keep pace with the requirements of the Army. Vehicles were kitted and issued soon after arrival in Chilwell and there was little opportunity to build up reserves. Moreover, existing covered accommodation was needed for stores, and in some cases for personnel.

The situation was soon changed by the rapid increase in production from British factories and receipts from America. It was clear that storage in the open would be normal for "B" vehicles and it was eventually accepted for all vehicles. Derby became an MT COD and Old Dalby was turned over to signal stores, armament and machinery.

In January 1941 the first open vehicle depot site was acquired at Castle Donnington Race Track and this became the pattern for subsequent vehicle depots. Sites were chosen for convenience of receipt and issue. Vehicle depots were therefore to be found near factories and Ministry of Supply workshops or near vehicle shipment ports.

Towards the end of 1941 there was a heavy programme of shipment of tanks to Russia by the Arctic route. Special preparation in the way of waterproof sealing and "winterization" was necessary and this was done at Chilwell. The RAOC was responsible for the actual loading and stowage on board ship. Chilwell provided mobile embarkation sections for these duties at the various ports.

The VRS at Chilwell became an "A" vehicle depot which specialized in the kitting and preparation for shipment of tanks. For security reasons, and to ensure that kits did not become separated from the tanks in transit it was normal to box the kit, place it inside the tank and secure it firmly there. A good deal of experimental work was undertaken at Chilwell to find the best way of packing and securing tank kits.

In 1942, at the time of the formation of REME, the dual system of vehicle supply ceased, and the RAOC became the sole supplier, taking over responsibility for RASC vehicles and MT stores.

At the same time the organization previously known as Chilwell Vehicle Reserve Store was renamed "Tanks and Vehicles". Two new branches, Central Vehicle Control (AFV) and Central Vehicle Control (B) were formed at Chilwell. The RASC census records, covering nearly 200,000 vehicles had to be absorbed into the Chilwell "B" vehicle census.

The size and extent of the organization made it necessary to introduce a measure of decentralization of control and five Chilwell MT groups were formed, each group commander being responsible for the administration of all vehicle depots in his group area, to the Commandant Chilwell through the officer in charge of tanks and vehicles. Later on the number of these groups was increased to nine.

Although RASC depots had been taken over with their vehicles, the main depot at Ashchurch was handed over to the Americans under the "Bolero" scheme and other accommodation had to be found for the vehicles.

The new group system was soon tested when in the late summer of 1942 the First Army was mobilized for the campaign in French North Africa. Approximately 35,000 "A" and "B" vehicles, including motor cycles, were issued over a period of about 6 weeks. Not a single adverse criticism was received.

Later in 1942 the need to conserve shipping space led to the decision to send all vehicles "knocked down" and crated. The effect of this decision in the theatres of operations has been mentioned in other chapters. At home it was necessary to form cased-vehicle depots and two were opened at Finningley and Queensferry in November 1942.

In the same month the first open storage depot in the United Kingdom for "A" vehicles was opened at Slough. This was a measure of the rapid increase in the production of "A" vehicles both in Great Britain and the United States, which made continued storage under cover impracticable.

It was found to be an economic arrangement to allot specialized roles to the various VRDs. One category was limited to new vehicles of types in great demand, a second held only part worn vehicles and a third held a broad selection of all types. Each group contained all three categories of VRD.

Apart from the collection of vehicles from factories and their movement to ports for shipment, the vehicle groups were responsible for the movement of vehicles to and from Ministry of Supply Army Auxiliary Workshops (AAWs) and the receipt and issue of vehicles from and to units.

Equipment Branch Detachments were located at factories and workshops to ensure that when fit vehicles were issued their kits were complete to the latest scale.

The Chilwell MT groups were responsible for MT sub-depots and workshops stores sections in their group area, and in this respect had a stores as well as a vehicle function. Each group headquarters had a stores wing to deal with this responsibility.

The closing months of 1943 brought preparations for the invasion of North-West Europe, and the decision to site in the concentration areas "A" vehicle depots to hold stocks of waterproofed vehicles to replace unit casualties and form a general reserve. Sites for these "operational" depots were found at Winchester and Crawley. A depot was also opened at Prestatyn to hold large stocks of specially prepared vehicles in covered accommodation.

Earlier experience of open storage in bad weather underlined the necessity for hard standings and sections of recently built dual carriageway road were requisitioned. In 1943 out of eight new VRDs opened, five were sited on these roads. In the same year six new depots were opened for motor cycles. Two new cased-vehicle depots were opened in the first half of 1943. This was, however, the peak period. Thereafter the rule on shipping all vehicles cased was relaxed and these depots were pro-gressively closed down.

During June and July 1943 five Divisions were brought up to full war establishment in vehicles, more depots were created and others enlarged. In May 1944 the final reorganization into nine groups was effected.

The preparation of vehicles for the assault on Europe was an immense task necessitating an increase in staff of 2,000. Detailed control of VRDs from Chilwell became impracticable. Stock records were decentralized on a group basis and group headquarters nominated the depot from which vehicles were to be issued.

During the period from June to September 1944 vehicles poured down to the embarkation ports. First went 10,000 waterproofed vehicles and these were followed by 24,000 vehicles which did not need waterproofing as by then they could land "dryshod". Issues comprised replacements and reserves. Before D Day over 600 replacement vehicles complete with equipment and ammunition were issued to units of the assault and build-up force.

The waterproofing of vehicles can be taken as a typical task in support of OVERLORD. The number and astonishing variety of vehicles for this operation were unprecedented. Each type of vehicle presented a special problem so that a different set of equipment was needed in each case. The stores then had to be produced and further trials led to im-provements and modifications with consequent alterations in the orders for waterproofing sets.

It was rare for all items to be available in advance so that the work usually had to be done against time and often, owing to the introduction of improved techniques at the last minute, a vehicle had to be de-water-proofed and the work done all over again.

Early in 1944 the War Office stated that the original order for the waterproofing of 1,600 "B" vehicles was to be increased to 2,139. Fresh sites for "operational" depots were necessary and then it was discovered that the waterproofing on the original 1,600 had deteriorated and they had to be done again.

Later the War Office announced that many thousands of reserve water-proofed vehicles would be shipped immediately after D Day, and many of these were modified in course of time. The RAOC staff were insufficient in numbers for this task and hundreds of men from other arms were attached to the operational depots to assist. Working conditions were harsh and many men had to live through the winter under canvas. There were constant delays owing to supplies of waterproofing material being temporarily exhausted. No mistakes were permissible as the success of this amphibious operation depended on the absolute efficiency of water-proofing. The constant anxiety that the work would not be finished in time because of shortage of material added to the strain.

Between May and October 1944 the reserve vehicles were moved to the embarkation ports where they were marshalled into craft loads by the vehicle embarkation parties. During this period 8,624 "A" vehicles were loaded on to landing craft. After September the strain eased and the number of vehicles moved grew less. One new commitment was the issue of "B" vehicles, loaded with food, to civil affairs units.

Vehicles continued to be issued to maintain stocks of reserves in North-West Europe up to the day of the surrender of Germany. In addition a large issue of "A" vehicles was made to the French Army.

Preparations were made for the issue of vehicles and kits to the Far East. Arrangements were made for the "B" vehicles to be specially treated at the contractors' works to withstand tropical conditions and every item was preserved and packed to tropical standards.

After the end of the war in Europe it was realized that the stocks of vehicles would decrease and plans were made for the progressive closing down of depots on the basis of priorities which would accord with the demands of post-war reconstruction.

The organization of the Tanks and Vehicles Department in August 1945 was as follows:

HQ Tanks and Vehicles
Central Vehicle Control (AFV)
Central Vehicle Control (B)   } Located at Chilwell
Equipment Branch
Central Census

9 Chilwell MT Groups
28 AFV Depots
58 VRDs for "B" vehicles, motor cycles and cased vehicles
28 Factory Collection Detachments
17 AFV Embarkation Sections
21 "E" Branch Detachments (at factories, etc., for checking vehicle kits).

THE MT STORES ORGANIZATION

In September 1939 there was a sufficient supply of spares to meet the immediate needs of the Regular Army. The range of items was 98,000. But the expansion of the Army, the rapid increase in the range of vehicles to be held, the existence of considerable numbers of requisitioned vehicles of varying ages and types and the difference between actual and estimated war wastage constituted many new factors which could not be foreseen with precision. Although receipts increased considerably, demand in the early days exceeded supply and it was even necessary to cancel demands from the Middle East which had been outstanding for more than 6 months.

However, the supply situation rapidly improved, and although additional strain was thrown on Chilwell by the re-equipment of the Army after Dunkirk, it soon became clear that increased storage space must be provided in Chilwell as well as new accommodation for stores outside.

Three large buildings in Chilwell, previously used for vehicles, were converted for the storage of MT spares in bulk. In the end only one shed was used for vehicles—Building 174, the "A" Vehicle Shed and Kit Store. Full use was made of the existing space in Chilwell by the erection of tubular scaffolding in storehouses, the construction of temporary shelters, the use of open storage where appropriate, and other devices.

Derby was converted into a shadow COD and Old Dalby was used for MT Stores for a short time before assuming its eventual role of Technical Stores COD.

Additional accommodation was found in disused factories, warehouses, garages and other premises within a radius of 40 miles of Chilwell, and these "relief storage depots" took the overflow from the main depot. In the end there were more than 50 of them.

Depot methods and layout were constantly improved. A system of conveyor belts was introduced into the detail issue storehouse, Building 157, and this speeded up the rate of receipts and issues. Although one detail storehouse was used the depot was organized into three sub-depots, A for "A" vehicle spares, B for "B" vehicle spares and C for miscellaneous and common items. The sub-depots had their own storehouses for bulk.

In 1941 a large relief storage depot was built at West Hallam, approximately 8 miles from Chilwell. This depot was to play an important part in the preparation for the campaign in North-West Europe. It was, however, not road served but decauville rail served which was inconvenient.

Meanwhile a network of outstation sub-depots had been created throughout the country. This became known as the Chilwell MT sub-depots organization. The original purpose, in the context of the crisis after Dunkirk, was to ensure adequate dispersal of MT stores and an over-the-counter service where required. The first of these units were opened at Warminster and Carfin in the autumn of 1940 and part of the vehicle depot at Harlescot was allocated for the storage of major assemblies.

Originally these sub-depots were administered from Chilwell, the men being under the command of OC 7 Battalion RAOC, and apart from certain depots, the size of which warranted the establishment of their own administrative staff, they were attached to local units for pay and rations.

The first stage of the scheme was to build 8 sub-depots with a total of 100,000 sq ft of covered accommodation. By the requisitioning of suitable premises and the erection of Nissen hutting the capacity of the sub-depot organization was increased to 600,000 sq ft by August 1941, 1,500,000 sq ft by the end of 1942 and four million sq ft in October 1944 when there were 37 sub-depots.

In February 1941 a special branch under the Deputy Chief Ordnance Officer Sub-Depots was created at Chilwell to administer the organization and acquire the storage and personnel accommodation for all dispersed sub-units of Chilwell including vehicle depots.

In 1942 it became necessary to decentralize control and the sub-depots were divided on an area basis, roughly equating to the U.K. Command boundaries, each area comprising an MT Group. The DCOO sub-depots was renamed Officer in charge MT Sub-Depots and continued to control technical policy and direct stores activity, although the MT group commanders were responsible to the Commandant Chilwell through the Officer in charge of Tanks and Vehicles, as has already been mentioned.

The stores role of the MT groups evolved in two ways. The sub-depots held a particular range of stores, mainly major assemblies, covers and tubes and tank tracks. For a high proportion of this range they relieved Chilwell of the complete load, being the sole receivers from all sources, stock holders and issuers to all theatres of the items. Each sub-depot was self-contained and self-accounting. Some had special tasks. For example 33 Ordnance Sub-Depot at Spalding dealt with the breakdown of wheel assemblies, the build-up of artillery wheel assemblies and completion with new covers and tubes for shipment overseas. Many of the items were recoverable and issues were made on a one-for-one basis. The replaced assembly or item was then passed, after inspection, to the appropriate workshop for repair.

Tank tracks presented a special problem because of their weight and awkwardness to handle in open storage. It was necessary to have large rail-served sites capable of standing up to the constant movement of cranes. The best depot proved to be at West Hartlepool where two large timber yards at the docks provided over 600,000 sq ft of storage and held 80,000 tons of tracks.

For the Normandy operation the Chilwell Sub-depots prepared for shipment 34,000 assemblies, 20,000 covers and tubes and 8,000 tons of tank tracks. By August 1945 the organization comprised 190 separate premises on covered and open sites and the stocks included nearly 250,000 major assemblies, 750,000 covers and tubes and 150,000 tons of tank tracks.

The other task of the MT groups was to form stores sections to meet the needs of the various workshops established in the country. In August 1945 there were 14 of these stores sections.

The next development in the stores field was the acceptance of responsibility for the supply of RASC vehicles and MT stores in 1942. The large RASC depot at Feltham was converted into a COD and continued to handle MT stores. Soon after this Bicester was built and held stores in both the Donnington and Chilwell ranges.

The distribution of MT stores between the various CODs up to the end of the war was as follows:

Chilwell	Spares for British "A" and "B" vehicles and, until the end of 1943, some spares for American makes.
Feltham	Spares for British "B" vehicles and carriers.
Derby and Bicester	Spares for British and American "A" and "B" vehicles.

433

During the first 3 years of the war the whole issue load was borne by Chilwell and Derby, but from January 1943 the home issue load was divided between Derby, Feltham and Bicester. These depots also undertook issues to overseas theatres of stores which were not held at Chilwell. The Chilwell task included issues to units at home who were mobilizing for overseas service.

The immense task of preparing Landing Reserves and Beach Maintenance Packs for OVERLORD was spread over the four CODs. These packs were then concentrated at Chilwell ready for shipment. They occupied every available stacking area in the depot.

The task continued night and day throughout the winter of 1943–44 and the early spring of 1944, and resources of both manpower and storage space were taxed to the utmost. At the same time heavy issues of units first aid MT outfits were being made to mobilizing units, ordnance field parks and workshop stores sections of formations earmarked for the invasion.

By May 1944 increased shipments of MT spares were arriving from America, and great quantities were being received from home manufacturers.

During the period immediately before D Day the MT sub-depot at West Hallam was given the vital task of preparing and issuing to units the wading and waterproofing equipment mainly for "A" vehicles which was to be fitted to those taking part in the assault landings. Mistakes must be avoided at all costs and staff were trained to identify every item for which they were individually responsible.

The various items of the equipment were made up into complete vehicle kits, some of which included nearly 100 different items. Meticulous care was taken in the sorting, labelling and packing operations, and the packing areas were laid out with the express object of eliminating errors. To ensure that no difficulty in fitting the items of the kit to the vehicle would be ultimately experienced by units RAC men fitted the various items to appropriate specimen vehicles which were brought to West Hallam for the purpose. This experimental fitting was observed by staff of the Inspectorate of Fighting Vehicles who immediately arranged for any modification the need for which emerged at this stage. The size of this task may be judged by the fact that during April and May 1944 West Hallam handled 6,253 tons of stores and 628,000 items of "A" vehicle hardware. Nearly 3,000 lorries were required to collect them.

PROVISION

The system of provision of MT stores established before the war, in conjunction with the Chilwell scales branch, ensured that spares cover for "B" vehicles already in or ordered for the Army was adequate. The increased wastage in war was anticipated by making arrangements for an emergency buy immediately on the outbreak of war, this being done without recourse to complicated calculations or the lengthy process of contract demand and tender. Repeat orders were placed direct on the manufacturer with instructions for production and supply to proceed immediately, any negotiations on price increases taking place afterwards. The basis of the buy was an estimated 6 months' war usage.

The real problems arose from the very rapid expansion of the vehicle fleet, the great variety of makes and types of vehicle brought into the service, the many requisitioned vehicles of varying age and type mostly without spares backing and the steady flow of new vehicles from North America.

Early contracts for British vehicles did not specify that spares were to be delivered concurrently, but as these vehicles were issued immediately to units a serious shortage of spares and assemblies for maintenance soon made itself felt. At the beginning of 1940 new contracts for vehicles specified a percentage of major assemblies to be provided at the same time as the vehicles and gave a target date for the delivery of initial spares estimated at 15 months' war usage. But ordering the spares was one thing. It was quite another to be sure of receiving them. Many manufacturers found it uneconomic to produce spares except for a limited range of fast moving items. Mass production of vehicles was their aim. Unused spares were a liability and requirements would change with the introduction of new models of vehicle.

It was therefore instinctive for manufacturers to give all their attention to the production of vehicles at the expense of spares, and their views were bound to influence Ministry of Supply officials and heads of departments who were under constant pressure to increase the vehicle fleet. The task of changing these preconceived ideas was not easy and General Williams had to use all his powers of persuasion to make people realize that the saving of shipping space was a paramount consideration and that this could only be achieved by providing spares on a scale which would enable all possible maintenance and repair to be done on the spot.

There was little experience to guide the scaling of spares for "A" vehicles and new types were in production. The older types were still in use for training and manufacturers were reluctant to continue the production of spares for these older vehicles. To ease the situation increased powers of local purchase were given, and permission was granted to seek capacity among the general engineering shops of the country.

In spite of all these efforts the provision of spares fell short of requirements. It was difficult to meet demands from overseas theatres and a system of automatic maintenance for all new vehicles being issued was introduced in May 1941. By June of that year vehicles were being received from North America and for them the initial supply of spares was good.

By June 1942 delay in the delivery of spares had increased to as much as nine months after placing of the order. Further commitments in the shape of the maintenance of the First Army in North Africa were im-

435

minent. It was therefore decided to raise the liability period for "A" vehicles to 18 months and "B" vehicles to 2 years, both for initial provision for new vehicles and the maintenance of existing types. This entailed a complete provision review and heavy demands on the trade, but the decision was sound and timely, contributing to the high availability of MT spares later in the war.

When, in July 1942, the RAOC assumed responsibility for the supply of RASC vehicles, the vehicle fleet increased by 110,000 with a corresponding increase in the commitment for supplying MT spares and assemblies. As stocks in the U.K. Base were dispersed among four CODs —Chilwell, Derby, Feltham and Bicester—provision was related to a system of central stock control. A programme of quarterly provision reviews was introduced, each item being reviewed simultaneously in the CODs which held it. At the peak period 355,000 items were covered by this programme of provision and central stock control, but it worked well, ensuring balanced stocks and maximum availability.

Until 1943 the main customer for North American vehicles, which were shipped direct, had been the Middle East theatre. But when preparations for OVERLORD began to develop the flow of these vehicles and their spares into the United Kingdom increased rapidly. The supply of spares, which had been good initially, deteriorated as the promised second year's automatic maintenance either failed to materialize or was deficient of many important items. In July 1943 it was decided that only 1 year's maintenance would be supplied automatically, subsequent requirements being in response to demands placed through British Army Staff, Washington.

In 1944 the steps taken to improve the supply of spares for British makes bore fruit and availability to meet the needs of 21st Army Group was adequate but not excessive. Spares for American vehicles caused some anxiety but after representations had been made to the US War Department the requirements for landing reserves and beach maintenance packs were received in time. The Americans were themselves suffering from serious shortages and their automotive industry was engaged in supplying the considerable and varying needs of all the Allies.

By March 1945 stocks had accumulated in many locations in Africa, the Middle East and elsewhere. A system of global stock control, by means of returns from the various theatres, was introduced. In this way it was possible to make the best use of available assets and pave the way for the process of changing from war to peace.

CHILWELL GARRISON

The nucleus of this organization was the small RAOC section which existed at Chilwell before the war. North and South Camps had been constructed for 600 Militia men but they were not complete when the war started, and soon over 2,000 volunteers arrived. As a temporary measure Building 176 was converted into personnel accommodation.

A Training Battalion was formed at Chilwell but was moved to other accommodation towards the end of 1940 and meanwhile Sandhurst Block was completed. In April 1941 Crusader Camp "A" was ready for occupation. It provided accommodation for 1,000 men. This was followed by Crusader Camp "B" (capacity 600) and Crusader Camp "C" (capacity 500). Finally Cromwell Camp (capacity 1,100) was built.

At the peak period the main units of the garrison were three RAOC Battalions, Numbers 6, 7 and 23, No. 8 Central Workshops REME, and an ATS Group numbering 3,500. No. 23 Battalion was the holding unit for the outstation sub-depots, but under the system of decentralization to MT Groups which was introduced this unit was dispersed. The peak military strength at Chilwell exclusive of ATS, was about 5,000.

The military training, accommodation and administration of this large garrison was the responsibility of Colonel H. Carter, an Infantry officer who had been responsible for military administration at Chilwell before the war. He therefore played a leading part in the development of this enormous training and administrative organization and was Deputy Garrison Commander throughout the war.

THE ATS

The magnificent part played by the ATS in the Ordnance Services during the war has already been mentioned. The Chilwell Group was the largest unit to be formed and by the end of the war numbered about 3,500 at Chilwell and over 5,000 in sub-depots.

The unit undertook the same clerical, storehouse and administrative tasks as in other units, but in addition to this there was an immense amount of work to be done in the Tanks and Vehicles Organization. This involved driving, maintenance, waterproofing, etc.

SOME CHILWELL PERSONALITIES

When Colonel Williams left Chilwell shortly before the war to take up an appointment as a Brigadier at the War Office, he was replaced as COO by Colonel H. C. Whitaker. However, the latter was required for appointments in the field, first in the Norway campaign and later in the Middle East where he created the large central provision office which has already been mentioned.

From that time the top management at Chilwell consisted mainly of Reserve Army Officers, either Territorial Army or AOER. Not only did they organize and develop this organization but also created other new depots in the United Kingdom, North-West Europe and India.

Colonel Whitaker was succeeded by Colonel E. P. Readman. A Yorkshireman, he was commissioned in the 14th West Yorkshire Regiment in

1915, and was later transferred to the South Staffordshire Regiment, serving with them in France. In February 1917 he again transferred to the Heavy Machine Gun Corps which was the nucleus of the Royal Tank Corps. After the war he left the Army but in 1923 he joined the RAOC TA and in April 1939 he was ADOS of 49th Division.

Early in the war he was moved to Chilwell to take over provision. He was appointed Commandant early in 1940 with the rank of Colonel and promoted to Brigadier in September 1940. He was responsible for the development and efficiency of the enormous MT stores and vehicle organization which grew up in the United Kingdom during the war, with a total manpower of over 50,000. In November 1944 he was promoted to Major-General. He commanded the MT organization up to the end of the war.

Although the military and civilian strength was high it was never quite enough to meet the ever-increasing load, and one of General Readman's greatest problems was to make full use of available manpower. He had constantly to watch output in relation to man/hours worked, using the Cost Control system which was introduced into all Central Ordnance Depots.

General Readman's experience in industry combined with the fact that he kept in close touch with the Army between the wars enabled him to cope with the wide variety of problems posed by this enormous organization. It was necessary to select subordinates well, to decentralize freely while retaining control, and to maintain morale and enthusiasm in an organization containing military, ATS and civilians working long hours often in the most trying conditions.

The Tanks and Vehicles Organization was commanded by Brigadier J. W. Mackillop. He joined Chilwell as a subaltern in the provision branch in 1939. He rose rapidly to the control of the branch dealing with "B" vehicle spares and later became Senior Provision Officer with the rank of Colonel. He took over Tanks and Vehicles in August 1943 and was promoted to the rank of Brigadier in July 1944.

Colonel D. H. Warren joined the Corps from the motor industry and soon made his mark in the field of provision. He started work in the scales branch and in 1942 he was in charge of the provision branch dealing with "A" vehicle spares. His final appointment was MT Coordination Officer. He paid many visits to the Mediterranean Theatre, giving invaluable advice and assistance in the establishment of Central Provision in North Africa and the Middle East Scales Branch.

Colonel L. H. McCausland joined the Corps from Tecalemit in 1939. After various duties in the depot he took over MT Stores in 1941 and was responsible for the organization of the storehouses and particularly the detail storehouse, Building 157, to achieve the remarkable tempo of receipts and issues required for the support of 21st Army Group. He became Deputy Commandant in January 1945.

Brigadier D. S. Robinson joined from Dunlops in 1939 and was soon transferred to Derby to convert it into an MT Stores COD. He introduced many new ideas and created a most efficient depot, later moving to Feltham to organize that depot on the same lines. After visits to North Africa and Italy to see RAOC problems in theatres of war, he was appointed Inspector RAOC (Overseas) with the rank of Brigadier, reporting to the COS on all aspects of Ordnance Services in many theatres.

DERBY

The site was originally acquired as a vehicle depot but early in the war the need for finding additional, dispersed accommodation for MT spares was realized. Accordingly Captain D. S. Robinson, who was on the AOER and had joined Chilwell at the outbreak of war, was sent to report on the suitability of the depot to house spares. He reported that the buildings, which were rail and road served, required little adaptation to convert them into an excellent stores depot, and he was given the opportunity to prove his case by being made commander of the new unit.

His team consisted initially of Lieutenants Markham, Hargreaves and Arnold—all AOER officers—and Mr. H. J. Sims, who had been Civilian Stores Superintendent at Chilwell and was later to play an important part in the development and organization of Bicester.

Some 70 civilian employees were recruited through the Derby labour exchange, and the strength of the unit was gradually built up by the transfer of officers and other ranks from Chilwell. The first contingent of reasonable size arrived in July 1940 and they were accommodated in tents near the depot for the next few months. This was the beginning of Sunnyhill Camp. The unit eventually became No. 8 Battalion RAOC.

The men were mostly new recruits who had volunteered at the beginning of the war, and a high proportion came from the main chain stores such as Woolworths, Marks and Spencers and British Home Stores. This was largely a response to a personal letter written by Colonel L. H. Williams, when he was COO Chilwell, to these large organizations pointing out the suitability of the RAOC for men with this type of background.

The officer in charge of military training and administration was Major W. Weston of the Sherwood Foresters and he remained, when the unit grew in size, to command the battalion with the rank of Lieutenant-Colonel. He was the ideal man for the job and maintained a high standard of military efficiency while recognizing the primary importance of the technical work for which the depot existed.

In October 1940 the first group of twelve newly-commissioned subalterns arrived from Chilwell. They came from the same source as the AOER and the volunteer recruits at the outbreak of war.

The ATS component of Derby—first under the command of Senior Commander F. Wynd and later of Chief Commander J. Mann—played a most important part in making the depot a very efficient RAOC organization.

By mid-1942 the total strength of the depot—military, ATS and civilian —was about 8,500. By then the system of shadow CODs had been introduced and, except for central provision and stock control, Derby was autonomous. The Commandants, as they were now called, of these shadow CODs held the rank of Colonel.

The tented accommodation at Sunnyhill Camp was rapidly developed into a permanent war-time camp although for a time some of the troops were housed in a requisitioned orphanage. Later on the barracks of the Sherwood Foresters at Sinfin Lane, a mile or so from the depot, were taken over. They were occupied first by part of No. 8 Battalion and then by the ATS.

The Commandant was fortunate in being able to retain the top structure of "management" of his organization for the first $2\frac{1}{2}$ years of the depot's existence. In this way continuity of control was maintained and team work firmly established.

The storage accommodation was admirable for the purpose for which it was required. The original buildings of the Macintosh Cable Company, all virtually under one roof, covered an area of about 350,000 sq ft, and by the end of 1939 an enormous single shed of 400,000 sq ft had been added for the storage of vehicles. During the life of the depot the covered storage was further increased to a total of 1,250,000 sq ft. It was indeed fortunate that the buildings and facilities, including scope for expansion, were adequate both for the planned load and the enormous increase in work which could not be foreseen. Standard RAOC depot equipment was obtained when it was available, but a fair amount of improvisation was necessary.

Derby, from being a sub-depot holding a limited range of "B" vehicle spares, became a COD holding the full range of spares for "A" and "B" vehicles. In 1940, when the clearance of Woolwich Arsenal became a matter of urgency, Derby was given the task of accepting the MT stores from Woolwich. Inevitably a considerable quantity of obsolete and obsolescent "junk" was included in the Woolwich consignments as the degree of urgency precluded precise scaling, but it was an embarrassment to a new depot which had its own teething troubles.

In addition to the normal duties of a self-accounting COD, Derby was given certain special tasks. These included the scaling, equipping and maintenance while in the United Kingdom of the Canadian Division Field Parks as well as similar work for units of the British Army. The Polish Division was one of the formations based on Derby for MT spares. Derby was also responsible for assisting the American Ordnance Corps to establish a depot at Sudbury, about 7 miles away.

At the peak period of activity Derby was selecting about 125,000 items for issue each week and receiving some 2,500 tons of stores each week from manufacturers at home and in North America.

This was the main MT spares depot for the RASC and acted as a bulk issuing depot to other RASC depots and units. When the decision was made in the summer of 1942 to form REME, the RAOC assumed responsibility for supplying MT vehicles and spares to the whole Army and the RASC task of supplying and repairing their own vehicles lapsed.

It was necessary to merge Feltham into the complex of MT depots forming the RAOC MT Organization in the United Kingdom. The depot was no longer needed in its original restricted role but was required as a shadow COD. It was the only MT COD in the south of England (Bicester still being in the early stages of development), and was particularly well placed to provide main base support for 21st Army Group.

This was a big task, and also urgent because at that time it was hoped that the Allies would land in France in the summer of 1943. General Williams therefore set a period of less than 9 months for the conversion of Feltham into a COD to be complete. General Williams appointed Colonel D. S. Robinson from Derby as the new Commandant COD Feltham.

Colonel Robinson brought with him a number of experienced officers including Lieutenant-Colonel S. Preston, Major L. A. Coates and Mr. H. J. Sims from Derby and Major H. Briers from Chilwell.

The main difficulty was that Feltham was already full of stores but not in the range and quantity required for the new role. Nor was the layout appropriate. The existing staff had not been trained in RAOC methods. The construction of the depot was not ideal for a COD and there were numerous sheds. Plans were made giving a target date for the conversion of each shed in turn. Every item in stock had to be moved.

Fortunately there was no shortage of labour. Within 3 weeks of taking over from the RASC, 300 military were posted in from Greenford in one draft. Large numbers of ATS also arrived and a double shift was started immediately. The greatest problem in the first 3 months was that a general lack of "know how" placed a great strain on supervisors, particularly when there were two shifts in operation every day of the week.

The RASC civilians were a great help as they really knew their MT stores. These men had a strong and very proper loyalty to the Corps which they had served for so long. It is greatly to their credit that they adapted themselves well to the new situation and accepted new loyalties.

The stores held by the RASC on arrival had normally been housed in "cages" in the custody of individual storekeepers. This system was admirable in peace-time conditions and was in fact similar to that used in most RAOC depots between the wars, but it prevented the adoption of a "flow" system essential for fast moving items in war—the type of work for which the depot was being converted.

Eventually the activity figures at Feltham compared well with the other CODs. In the first week after D Day the depot selected and issued 172,000 items.

As elsewhere Feltham sponsored a Home Industries scheme for carton packing. The local Borstal Institution took over a large part of this work, the boys being brought into the depot and working efficiently there alongside secondary school boys.

One night late in the war a V bomb completely destroyed a shed some 80,000 sq ft in extent. The pride and joy of the Depot Fire Brigade—a beautiful red Merryweather fire engine—could not be used as the door of the garage in which it was housed, about 200 yards from the fire, was buckled by the blast. Everyone turned out to fight the fire, including the ATS in their pyjamas. Luckily casualties were minor as there were only a few people in the shed when the bomb struck it.

When the conversion of Feltham was complete Colonel Robinson returned to Derby. He was succeeded by Colonel T. W. Davis, who moved to AFHQ in North Africa towards the end of 1943 and was replaced by Colonel A. Sewell from Chilwell.

BICESTER

Although Chilwell and Donnington had been developed into excellent central depots for MT and technical stores respectively, it became clear that another depot would have to be built, partly because of the enormously increased requirements of the Army for these stores and partly because of the special supply arrangements which would be needed for the Second Front.

The depot must be located in the southern part of England and the layout must permit the fast movement of large quantities of stores. This was the first occasion when the primary purpose of a central depot had not been hampered by other considerations. Branston was a converted pickle factory. Chilwell was originally an explosives factory. Didcot had been built on the cheap and without consideration for the needs of modern war. Donnington, though a modern depot, was not ideally sited owing to the need to provide employment in a "depressed area".

The opportunity was taken to build a depot which was ideal for modern war conditions. The area was, in those days, in the depth of the country, which gave ample room for expansion and dispersion. At the same time it was accessible to two main lines (then known as the London Midland and Scottish and the Great Western Railway), the road system in the area was good and water and power supply was adequate. At that time Bicester was a small market town, but Oxford and Aylesbury were large towns about 12 miles away.

In January 1941 General Williams nominated Colonel G. W. Palmer as the Commandant designate of the new depot and gave him the task of planning its location, layout and construction. He found an office at Steiglers Factory, Beeston, near Chilwell. Two sub-committees were formed, one at Chilwell and one at Donnington. This ensured that information was readily available of the load of MT and technical stores

442

which Bicester would have to handle. It also enabled Bicester to benefit from the lessons which had been learnt in the construction, development and operation of the other two depots.

In the rural neighbourhood of Bicester it was impossible to recruit more than a handful of civilian employees so the unit was from the beginning an all-military establishment.

The depot was divided into two main areas, about a mile apart, one at Arncott some 5 miles on the Thame side of Bicester, the other at Graven Hill between Arncott and Bicester. Five sub-depots were planned, to hold MT, small arms, armament, engineer stores and signal stores, and the first estimate of covered accommodation was two million sq ft.

A good deal of thought was given to the optimum size of storehouses. It was thought that the large buildings of about 300,000 sq ft at Chilwell and Donnington were too big and the final decision went in favour of 100,000 sq ft, and experience has shown that the arrangement of a large number of these relatively small buildings has many advantages. The sheds were built to the latest design so as to minimize risk and damage from fire or enemy action.

Rail and road access was provided to all storehouses and at both ends of the detail storehouses. The lack of adequate transit facilities had caused problems at Chilwell and Donnington. At Bicester there was a large transit shed and smaller separate transit sheds for each sub-depot. Large marshalling yards were also built within the depot area. The floors of the storehouses were built with a very slight gradient sloping down from the receipts entrance towards the issues bay. The design and construction of the storehouses proved to be first class. Clerical functions were to be decentralized to sub-depots and certain detail buildings had an office built on to them with access to the storehouse.

Heavy lift sheds were built and later on a workshops, so that by the time planning was complete the storehouses, ancillary buildings and workshops represented a schedule of requirements of 3,250,000 sq ft of covered accommodation, and further expansion was envisaged in course of time. The site and project were approved by the War Office in May 1941 and Treasury sanction was given in the following month. Colonel Palmer transferred his headquarters to The Cedars, Long Eaton, Nottingham.

Railway construction began within a few days of receiving Treasury sanction for the depot, and this was followed by camp construction for the Royal Engineer and Royal Pioneer Corps units engaged in building the roads, and also for considerable numbers of prisoners of war who provided additional labour.

The first estimate of depot staff was 7,000 all ranks, including 1,700 ATS, and accommodation for them required the building of over 800 huts. By January 1942 the manpower requirement had risen to over 9,000. In December 1941 Colonel Palmer moved his headquarters down to Bicester.

Hard standings and gun parks (rail served at both Arncott and Graven

Hill) had not been neglected and the availability of large concreted areas was an advantage when in April 1942 it was decided to erect 600,000 sq ft of Romney hutting and include a further million sq ft of this construction in the 1943 programme.

The reason for this additional temporary storage was the expected arrival of large numbers of American troops and the Bolero scheme for giving up storage space to meet their needs. Depots retained by us had to be expanded. These Romney huts became known locally as the "Bolero huts".

On August 1st 1942 Colonel Palmer was promoted Brigadier. He was commandant of the depot and commander of what was already a sizeable garrison. In this month also the first receipts and issues of stores were made.

During the autumn of 1942 construction of the depot proceeded at a good speed and stocks were moved in. Bicester was used as a distributing point to other depots of the large stocks of MT stores which arrived from North America at this time. In November considerable stocks of major assemblies were diverted to Bicester and Chilwell.

Manning the depot was achieved by earmarking and training men at other CODs. These men were "on the books" of Bicester and were called in as required. Depot activity grew to such an extent that by May 1943 the garrison strength was over 8,000. The depot was in operation in good time before D Day, June 1944, and played a useful part in the support of 21st Army Group. In this operation its main tasks were as follows:

Waterproofing. Just as West Hallam was the main centre for the waterproofing of "A" vehicles so Bicester carried the main load for "B" vehicles.

Provision of the hardware was undertaken at Feltham and so important was this task that the Commandant Chilwell himself went to Feltham with a small staff to control the provision, progress the production from manufacturers and direct the material to Bicester.

In the depot waterproofing sets were made up, and when these were complete the units concerned were notified and came to collect. This was done on a "type of vehicle" basis, not by complete unit establishments. Enormous parking areas were created in the Bicester area for unit collection of waterproofing equipment and other stores, and a continuous service was given.

Small Arms. The transfer of the detail issue load and the provision branch from Weedon to Bicester has been mentioned elsewhere in this chapter. At this stage Weedon became a bulk holding depot only. Units collected small arms at all hours from Bicester and for a period could take what they fancied without regard to authorized scales or establishments. This was possible because of the astonishing improvement in the supply position since the early days of the war, and, in spite of the priority given to 21st Army Group, there is no indication that other theatres suffered any shortage of small arms in consequence, although some time elapsed before the rigid control by the staff of the issue of these items was relaxed outside the United Kingdom.

American MT Spares. When the supply of these stores became a flood there was no accommodation in other MT depots and Bicester had to take the complete load. These stores arrived in multi-item packs and it was necessary to form a receipts flow line so as to sort and repack them on a single item basis—a process known in those days as "Bombay Binning". This was combined with Dues Out Control so that urgently required stores could be selected at the receipts stage and passed to the issues bay.

The sudden end of the war against Japan prevented Bicester from fulfilling its full war potential, and instead left the depot with an indigestible mass of unwanted waterproofing hardware and American MT spares which required considerable time and effort to clear. Most small arms and the provision branch were returned to Weedon, not because it was the ideal place but because the established civilian staff lived there.

Since the war the depot has had many roles, too many for convenience, but this has indicated that the original concept was sound in all conditions of war and peace. It is in fact the ideal depot for the future.

THE AMMUNITION ORGANIZATION

In September 1939, the RAOC had one Central Ammunition Depot in operation and two others nearing completion. There was no separate ordnance ammunition branch at the War Office. There were only 16 Inspecting Ordnance Officers and 51 Ammunition Examiners directly employed on ammunition duties. Training for war was based on current *Magazine Regulations.*

The mildest description of this situation would be to say that it was quite inadequate to meet the heavy demands which arose immediately on the outbreak of war. At this time, the provision of ammunition was not an RAOC function.

On the declaration of war, the three Base Ammunition Depots (BADs) for the BEF were mobilized at CAD Bramley. Apart from one IOO and three AEs allocated to each of the BADs none of these personnel had more than a perfunctory knowledge of ammunition itself and no experience of its storage, handling and maintenance beyond that provided in *Magazine Regulations.* Part I of this publication did not in any sense apply to active service conditions and Part II conformed rigidly to the teachings of the last war. Instruction given at the School of Instruction at Bramley was painstaking in its efficiency within the scope of the regulations, but personnel were not taught to foresee possible variations under active service conditions, and many lessons learnt in the first few months of the war had to be adopted without hesitation, in order to bring the ammunition organization of the Army up to date.

In November 1939, a new War Office branch was created within the

Ordnance Directorate to take the place of the Master General of Ordnance (MGO) branches which had dealt with ammunition. This new branch was designated "OS2" (later WS2), and its primary function was the provision, distribution and issue of ammunition. It had to undertake, in addition to these tasks, many duties which hitherto were performed by MGO, such as executive action on inspection and examination reports and the issue of technical instructions regarding the inspection, repair and storage of new types of ammunition.

On the evacuation of France in June 1940, a spirit of urgency provided the spur for the complete overhaul and reorganization of the ammunition services. The most pressing concern was the supply of ammunition for the forces deployed to meet the threatened invasion. The permanent ammunition depots—situated at Bramley, Corsham and Longtown—were not suitably placed for this role and could not make rapid issues by road to forces expected to be engaged on or near the East and South-East coasts.

A series of small ammunition depots was, therefore, set up. These depots were located in Eastern, South-Eastern and Northern Command areas and were each designed to hold 5–6,000 tons of ammunition. The need for further expansion soon became evident, since these quantities of ammunition were insufficient for a major action. Some of the depots might be over-run, and the scheme gave rise to an uneconomic use of man-power. Further, provision had to be made for the storage of the very considerable supplies of ammunition that would soon be coming into production. Although the CADs at Bramley, Corsham and Longtown had reduced their stocks by issues to the newly formed operational depots, there was not enough accommodation for this new production which would soon flood into the CADs.

It was realized that, to prepare for this contingency, and to provide for the rapid development of ammunition services generally, additional War Office branches were required, so that direction of policy, and planning for the future, could be conducted speedily on a high level. Two additional War Office branches were, therefore, established in July 1940 under the control of a deputy director; these were OS16 and OS15 (later WS8 and WS9). The responsibilities of these new branches were, respectively, the administration of ammunition services, and the dealing with all technical problems after the ammunition had been received from the Ministry of Supply.

It was also considered necessary to appoint a Chief Inspecting Ordnance Officer to cope with inspection matters, to coordinate the work of Inspecting Ordnance Officers in Commands, to organize routine and special examinations, and to enquire into accidents. The CIOO and his staff were not, however, incorporated in the War Office, although they worked under instructions from the War Office.

The position, therefore, by July 1940, was that three branches had been organized within the Ordnance Directorate at the War Office to direct and organize the future development of ammunition services generally.

The responsibilities of these branches were wide and provided for extensive development in order to keep pace with the quickly growing needs of the Army.

The work of WS2 was confined to provision and allocation of ammunition and in effect it kept a central account of world-wide holdings of ammunition. The supply of ammunition was strictly controlled and allocation of available stocks was made by an Ammunition Allocation Committee which was part of the London Munitions Assignment Board; Assistant Director of Warlike Stores (WS2) and the Secretary of the Assignment Board were joint Secretaries of this Allocation Committee.

Allocation of reserves to the various theatres from production in the United Kingdom, Dominions and U.S.A. were made by WS2 subject only to confirmatory approval at the monthly meeting of the Ammunition Allocation Committee.

In addition to these duties, WS2 was responsible for the detailed planning of initial and follow-up ammunition supply for the North African campaign in 1942, and for the landing in Normandy in 1944. This work of major importance and of immense detail was done in the closest contact with the staffs of First Army and 21st Army Group. The work entailed the tactical stowage of scores of ships and hundreds of landing craft and in the case of 21st Army Group, the pre-loading also of several hundred lorries for the different beaches.

Other responsibilities of this branch were the preparation of staff tables, the calculation of staff requirements, records and statistics of ammunition, and the supply of information for Directors, the Cabinet and the Defence Committee (Supply).

Early in 1940 a provision branch (P7) was established at Bramley for the detailed work of providing inert ammunition components and laboratory equipment: this work had previously been done by another branch (P3) at Woolwich. P7 was, however, in no way concerned with the provision of live ammunition which was entirely dealt with in the War Office.

The immediate problems facing WS8 on its formation were:

(a) How and where to store ammunition for anti-invasion use.
(b) Where to store the vast quantities impending off the production line.
(c) How to obtain and train personnel to man the new field depots to be opened.
(d) Numerous aspects of the administration of these depots, including the provision of storage areas, billets, railway sidings, communications, guards, transport and labour, and the acquisition of land.
(e) To work out new safety instructions for the storage of ammunition in the English countryside since it was clear that the Explosives Act and Home Office Regulations could not apply to the present conditions.

(f) To consider the problem of gas warfare ammunition and to produce regulations for its storage, handling and decontamination.

(This involved close work with the Home Office, county police officials and Regional Commissioners.)

The foregoing problems grew daily, as will be understood from the following statistics covering ammunition stored in the United Kingdom:

	1940	1945
Storage	216,000 tons	2,000,000 tons
Depots	3 CADs	5 CADs
		21 ASDs[1]
RAOC	2,105	13,483
Pioneer Corps Labour	2,400	16,000
Transport	260 tons/lift	2,140 tons/lift
Miles of road storage	116	1,500

[1] Ammunition Sub-Depots

From July 1940, and throughout the war, the whole ammunition service was controlled centrally by the War Office.

NEW DEPOTS FOR STORAGE OF WAR OFFICE STOCKS

An early decision was reached that the small anti-invasion depots which had been hastily formed after Dunkirk should be handed over to the Commands in which they were located, and that a series of larger depots, each organized on the lines of a base ammunition depot, should be created under War Office control. These depots were to be established on a line running roughly up the centre of England, each depot to hold 20,000 tons. The object was to provide reserve holdings for the Armies in South-Eastern, Eastern and Northern Commands. At the same time, other localities were reconnoitred—notably in the West, in Wales and in Scotland—where more field depots could be established for the storage of future ammunition production.

A request was made for financial approval to construct at least three CADs which were to be rail-served and designed on modern principles. As level, flood-free ground was needed, covering 1,000–1,500 acres for each depot, there was strong objection from the Ministry of Agriculture whenever a suitable site was discovered, but eventually one at Nesscliff (Salop) and one at Kineton (Warwick) were selected and approved. CAD Kineton was built by military labour and was completed in 2 years.

The depot at Nesscliff was constructed by the Ministry of Works and Planning and was completed in 3 years. Owing to the difficulty of finding suitable sites to which there was no Ministry of Agriculture objection, Nesscliff was built along 17 miles of the defunct Shropshire and Montgomery Railway which proved awkward to work from a railwayman's point of view.

It was evident that the two new CADs would take some time to construct and, therefore, the formation of field storage depots, which could be opened quickly, became a matter of the utmost priority. These new depots were called "ammunition sub-depots" (ASDs), which was a mistake, as they were independent ammunition depots and in no sense sub-depots of CADs. The error was the cause of much confusion with district and command staffs. The method of selecting the sites is of interest; it was decided that ammunition would be stacked on the verges of country roads and on 30 ft strips of adjacent fields where the verges were too narrow. Ammunition could also be stored in parks and woods, in which roads would be constructed. Each stack was to be 400 cu ft housed in an iron shelter, constructed of 21 sheets of curved corrugated iron easily bolted together by unskilled labour. The number of stacks in a group and the safety distances between groups were based on calculations made at the War Office after modifying existing safety regulations to suit emergency conditions. Localities had to contain two or more railway stations. Ready-made accommodation for troops was to be available in the form of houses and estates which could be requisitioned.

On the basis of these minimum requirements, quarter inch maps of the United Kingdom were closely studied and this was followed by personal reconnaissance of promising localities. If these proved suitable an estate in the centre of the area was chosen as HQ of the ASD, the occupants were tactfully informed and within 5 days personnel were despatched and ammunition began to arrive.

Six such ASDs were opened in July 1940, and 8 more during 1941. Two more opened in 1943, took 3 months before occupation as various branches, committees and other bodies had first to be satisfied each in its own way.

Although requisitioned premises were occupied wherever possible, considerable RE services were always required, public roads had to be closed in some cases and roads were built in woods and parks. Decauville lines were laid in some depots, and in every case the construction of extra railway sidings was planned and carried out.

Expansion of these depots took place as production increased and expenditure remained low, and by 1945 from an initial capacity of 20,000 tons, the holding of the smallest depot had increased to 50,000 tons and of the largest to 180,000 tons. Each occupied 100–120 miles of roads and was served by three or more railway sidings. This method of storing ammunition had the following advantages:

(a) Having selected an area of about 300 sq miles, it was only a matter of days before ammunition could arrive, provided RAOC Ammunition Storemen were available to mark out the stacking roads, and labour was available to prepare the sites and shelters.

(b) Once established with two or more railheads and adequate internal transport, issues could be made with remarkable facility and at very short notice. At peak periods some depots handled more than 2,000 tons a day.

(c) Expansion could be undertaken at any time and with the minimum preparation and work. However, unless a site had a concentration of roads in a small area, expansion beyond 80,000 tons or 100 miles of road frontage involved too large an area for control and administration by one unit.

(d) The use of existing roads and the small easily erected steel shelters for storage reduced enormously the cost of building, and permitted the use of ground which required no work beyond that of spade and shovel. Moreover, the ground and landscape were not permanently defaced.

The disadvantage of these depots was the difficulty of achieving security owing to the evident impossibility of fencing in such large areas. This difficulty was, however, largely alleviated by the war-time patriotic spirit of the public, who were themselves anxious to prevent interference with the ammunition.

ws9

On the formation of the Ministry of Supply, certain War Office branches, including Director-General of Armaments (DG of A) and Chief Inspector of Armaments (CIA) were transferred to that Ministry—a logical move which put all the branches dealing with research, experiment, design and production of ammunition under one unified control.

This, however, left no authority in the War Office to deal with the many and varied technical aspects of ammunition once it was in the hands of the Army. WS9, therefore, became responsible for:

(a) Issuing instructions for the handling and storage of ammunition in the field, which superseded *Magazine Regulations, II.*

(b) Safety regulations in permanent depots at home and abroad.

(c) The policy of inspection, methods of proof, surveillance, repair, rectification, modification and disposal of ammunition.

(d) Mechanization of laboratories and repair plant.

(e) Ammunition publications.

The scope of these publications can be judged by the increase in the number of types and natures of ammunition, which grew from 81 in 1940 to over 700 in 1945. Many types were revolutionary in design and required detail study from the point of view of maintenance and inspection. The study of German and Japanese ammunition became another of the branch's major duties, and it was the subject of special publications.

The inspection of new ammunition became necessary early in 1942, at the peak period of output, when many accidents were traced to faulty assembly or manufacture. A one per cent examination of all new stocks was, therefore, instituted and involved the examination of individual rounds in over 120,000 tons of ammunition.

In the period May 1943–April 1945, 1,695 faults were revealed by this inspection and resulted in the modification or repair of some 210,000 tons of ammunition. The work of rectification was considerable. For example, the 1 per cent inspection of one consignment alone of 25-pounder cartridges disclosed a defect which led to the 100 per cent examination and repair of 80,000 rounds.

The investigation of accidents became of supreme importance. Instructions were issued standardizing the procedure to be followed after an accident to allow a methodical study to be made of the event, and the early issue of precautionary or remedial instructions for the prevention of further accidents of the same type.

Between March 1942 and June 1945 there were 4,660 accidents with ammunition in this country, involving the death of 1,259 soldiers and causing injury to 6,793.

The branch also represented the War Office on inter-service committees, and at conferences of various scientific bodies, it was also the source of information on land service ammunition for the Air Ministry, Admiralty, India and the Dominions.

A vast amount of modification and repair work was undertaken, not only on old ammunition but on new deliveries from the Ministry of Supply. This threw an unexpected strain on IOOs and AEs and it was necessary to arrange with the Military College of Science and with the Training Establishment, RAOC, for double the number of courses at first planned. During the war 31 IOOs Courses and 99 AEs Courses were run, resulting in some 400 IOOs and 1,800 AEs being trained, but nevertheless there always seemed to be a shortage.

In War Office controlled depots, laboratories and repair factories were expanded. The CADs each employed about 80 soldiers and 100 to 130 ATS on repair work. The amount of ammunition modified in Ordnance depots was 320,000 tons and some of the largest tasks undertaken were modifications to 5,500,000 3-inch trench mortar bombs, 2,000,000 rounds of 3·7-inch AA and 2,000,000 rounds of 25-pounder. To plan this work and allot priorities, a Committee was formed which met once a month, allotted tasks to each depot and progressed work systematically.

When the War Office organized the second phase of ammunition supply by establishing ASDs of 20,000 tons capable of vast expansion, the small anti-invasion depots were handed over to Commands. As defence plans expanded there were some 53 of the small operational depots by the end of 1940.

Stocks were based on the equipment of the units located in and defending the various areas, so that much of the ammunition was unorthodox consisting of shell for obsolete weapons such as 13- and 18-pounder guns, cartridges for 12-bore shot guns and many highly dangerous and

451

amateurish devices such as the "Molotov cocktail" (white phosphorus and petrol in commercial soda water bottles).

The War Office allotted to each Command small technical staffs of IOOs and AEs to carry out inspection of the ammunition and instruct the Home Guard Ammunition Officers in its safe storage and handling.

As the threat of invasion receded the Command Depots were used for making training issues, and on this account they handled some 250,000 tons of ammunition during the war.

To cope with the repair and modification of this considerable tonnage Mobile Ammunition Repair Units were formed and allotted to Commands. Thus a great deal of work was done on the spot and the movement of large tonnages to and from CAD repair factories was avoided.

In anticipation of considerable war aftermath tasks of the inspection and disposal of returned, suspect and surplus ammunition, some of these Command depots were converted for this purpose and an Explosives Disposal Unit RAOC was formed with demolition and dumping sections located respectively at Trawsfynnyd in Wales (a pre-war artillery range) and the port of Silloth in Cumberland. The unit disposed of 80,000 tons of ammunition during the war, and formed the basis for the large programme of disposal which continued for many years afterwards.

BOMB DISPOSAL

In the early days of the war the disposal of all unexploded missiles, including enemy bombs, was the responsibility of IOOs and AEs. However, the saturation bombing of London and other towns in the United Kingdom created, in the autumn of 1940, a problem for which we had insufficient trained manpower.

An organization had to be created quickly to deal with the specific task of disposing of enemy bombs in large concentrations and also our own unexploded anti-aircraft shell falling in the same area.

Teams were trained as specialists in this work, which was allocated to the Royal Engineers because most of these bombs were buried and had to be dug out and the available plant for this was already in RE hands.

There was some degree of overlap until sufficient RE bomb disposal teams had been trained or when the bomb was already exposed. Two IOOs received the George Cross in Malta for bomb disposal as has been mentioned elsewhere.

However, in time RE bomb disposal units took over all this important but specialized work in a limited field, and RAOC ammunition technical staff were free to concentrate on the inspection, repair and disposal of all other ammunition for which their comprehensive training fitted them.

MOVEMENT OF AMMUNITION

The RAOC was responsible for the serviceability of ammunition from the time it was received in home depots to the time it was issued to units or to RASC transport for delivery to units.

The ammunition was not, however, on direct RAOC charge at all stages during the long journey from factory to gun, and it was at these times that it was often exposed to treatment which caused undue damage or deterioration.

At ports in the United Kingdom there were Port Ammunition Detachments RAOC, but Q (Movements), at any rate in the early days sometimes failed to employ them for their proper work of checking the handling and stowage of ammunition. For example there was an instance of AFVs being loaded on a flooring of ammunition packages. The same difficulty was encountered at ports overseas, but the lesson was learnt and the team work in the supply of ammunition to 21st Army Group was of a high order.

Central Ammunition Depots

BRAMLEY

Bramley was an old-fashioned depot, vulnerable to attack from the air. The storehouses were large and could only be safely filled to capacity with certain natures of ammunition.

The depot was rail served, and there was no road access to any of the sheds. Some of these defects were remedied in due course, particularly the matter of road construction through the depot, but the best way to increase storage capacity in the United Kingdom was to build new CADs and create field storage depots (ASDs).

Bramley, however, remained the focal point for the Ammunition Organization for several good reasons. There was accommodation for military staff, the School of Ammunition was there and trained civilian staff existed in fair numbers. Bramley became primarily the centre for the technical training of IOOs and AEs, and this is still its main purpose.

CORSHAM

This underground depot was in its infancy at the beginning of the war. It continued to be developed throughout the war. There were three separate areas of caves.

1 Sub-Depot (Tunnel) was the original site, and it was completed in 1942.
2 Sub-Depot (Eastlays) was completed in 1943.
3 Sub-Depot (Monkton Farleigh) was completed in 1943.

All these sub-depots were of course in use some time before their completion. The underground storage area totalled 148 acres and there were 14 miles of conveyor belt in the three sub-depots. The underground siding at Tunnel could take 85 wagons.

Captain P. W. F. Brown was in command of the depot in the early days, and a small amount of ammunition was moved into Tunnel as early as 1938. Monkton Farleigh was opened in March 1939 and Eastlays in 1940. A railway marshalling yard was built at Thingley, some miles from Corsham, using rubble from the excavations at Tunnel, and this was completed in May 1938.

In January 1940 a senior RAOC officer, Colonel A. H. Allen, was appointed COO and remained in command of the depot until July 1945.

The advantages of Corsham were its security from air attack, the excellent storage conditions for ammunition and the concentration of 250,000 tons of ammunition in a relatively small area, which facilitated the movement of large tonnages.

The disadvantages were the need for expensive and elaborate systems of air conditioning and lighting, the introduction of conveyor belts which was necessary but unavoidably led to inflexibility in the handling of receipts and issues, and the somewhat trying conditions of underground working. In addition to the military there were 1,000 civilians who worked on a three-shift-per-day system. Certain natures of ammunition, such as white phosphorus were considered unsafe for underground storage, and for the same reason doubtful or repairable ammunition was barred. This was a disadvantage from the general aspect of ammunition storage although it was a help purely from the Corsham point of view.

The particular features of Corsham dictated its role as a bulk issuing depot, topping up smaller depots in the United Kingdom and issuing ammunition for shipment to overseas theatres. A very efficient control office was established in the depot headquarters on the surface. It was necessary to centralize storage and issue control because the single moving belt could not be used for receipts and issues simultaneously. The peak issue period was from May 14th to July 2nd 1944 when 62,000 tons were issued.

LONGTOWN

This depot, near Carlisle, was started shortly before the war. It was a surface depot the main part of which consisted of "bunker" storage (semi-underground storehouses with earth protection or traverses which covered the roofs) which provided excellent protection from air attack. This system was not used elsewhere in United Kingdom ammunition depots, but the Germans used it extensively.

Other storage was also built and Longtown controlled a miscellaneous collection of permanent and temporary sites established in the neighbourhood at different times. Some large sheds were handed over to the General Stores Organization and formed the nucleus of COD Solway.

One disadvantage of the Longtown site was that it was low-lying land on the fringes of the Solway Firth. The River Esk was apt to overflow its banks and flooding damaged the ammunition. A large bank was built to keep the floods out but it was not at first long enough and water worked round the end. Also it did not prevent seepage in the boggy ground.

Recruiting of civilian employees was very difficult in that area in war time and the establishment was mainly military (RAOC, ATS and RPC). The strength in 1943 was about 3,000.

The depot was commanded for most of the war by Colonel Temple Morris, whose work at the School of Ammunition before the war and in France in the early days has already been mentioned. Needless to say he paid a great deal of attention to technical and military training in the depot.

NESSCLIFF

This was the first CAD to be planned and constructed during the war. The difficulty of obtaining a suitable site has already been mentioned. The location half-way between Shrewsbury and Oswestry was far from ideal, as the River Severn ran through the centre of the area and an unduly dispersed layout could not be avoided.

Construction was the responsibility of the Ministry of Works and Planning. For some reason progress was very slow and the depot took 3 years to complete.

General Williams appointed Colonel B. D. Hurst as Commandant designate of the depot and sent him up there in March 1941 to watch progress. Hurst, an officer of the Royal Engineers, had been in charge of the Army Vocational Training Centre at Aldershot before the war and had a well-deserved reputation for energy and versatility. These characteristics combined with a practical knowledge of constructional work enabled him to keep a disconcerting eye on the work of the contractors. He also turned his attention to the development and improvement of the camp.

The plan envisaged the construction of 164 storehouses and 26 ammunition repair workshops, and the first shed was taken into use in February 1942. The depot finally consisted of nine sub-depots spread over an area of 1,800 acres and holding some 200,000 tons of all natures of ammunition. The peak activity was 2,300 tons in one day and 12,000 tons in one week.

KINETON

This depot was built by military labour and took a year less than Nesscliff to complete. It is at the foot of the Edgehill ridge between Banbury and Warwick, and in fact the depot area covers the place where the Battle of Edgehill, the first battle of the Civil War, was fought. It was the best site so far obtained for a surface CAD and allowed for a relatively compact layout, the only disadvantage being the clay soil of the area.

The depot had 160 sheds and held 150,000 tons of ammunition. The latest ideas in design and layout were introduced but unfortunately in some cases the earth traverses were built up against instead of clear of the walls of the storehouse which caused trouble later on. Other troubles were caused some years later by the hurried war-time construction and installation of lighting and by neglect of maintenance of the buildings, but basically the depot is sound and satisfactory for ammunition storage in peace and war. The depot is rail served to all storehouses, but also has road access to sub-depots.

The first Commandant was Colonel Caruana Dingli, a Regular RAOC Officer, and he was sent up to watch progress from the time the first six sheds were built in July 1942. The first ammunition was received in October 1942 and a year later depot stocks had increased to 80,000 tons.

All this time the inevitable difficulties occurred through the efforts to use the depot while development and further construction was taking place, but Kineton was able to play its part in the support of 21st Army Group.

CONCLUSION

The development of this enormous organization for the supply, inspection and repair of ammunition was one of the greatest achievements of the RAOC in the Second World War.

This was not a question of mere increase in size. The responsibilities of the Corps were greatly extended from the very limited pre-war scope. The handling of suspect ammunition was an extremely arduous and unpleasant task, frequently attended by great risk. The volume of ammunition produced during a world war is prodigious and the circumstances of its production are such that the steps taken in peace-time to ensure safety in storage and handling cannot be applied in war. Calculated risks must be accepted. Two George Crosses and several George Medals were awarded to RAOC men for work on ammunition during the war and other awards of the same decorations have been made since.

Credit for the development and efficiency of this great organization goes to Brigadier V. O. Lonsdale, who was the moving spirit for most of the war, Colonel Temple Morris and Colonel F. M. Day, but they were assisted by many scientists and highly competent technical officers who joined the Corps.

Partly because of the high degree of specialization which was the inevitable result of the rapid expansion of the Corps, and partly because of the nature of the work, the Ammunition Branch of the Corps received relatively little publicity, and perhaps less recognition, both within the Corps and outside, than its achievements deserved. Public Relations is always a controversial subject. There are some who say, misquoting Shakespeare, "Sweet are the uses of Advertisement." Others say that achievements speak for themselves, and can be taken for granted. However, since the war some recognition of the significance of RAOC technical ammunition work has been shown in the fact that the IOO (now an Ammunition Technical Officer) receives Qualification Pay, and the AE (now an Ammunition Technician) is among the highest paid tradesmen in the Army and holds the minimum rank of Corporal.

EPILOGUE

With the surrender of Japan in September 1945 the Second World War was brought to a sudden and dramatic conclusion. The period of 25 years which preceded this event was one of great significance in world affairs, and therefore also in the history of the RAOC, with which this book is concerned.

The British Army was involved in violent changes during this comparatively short time:

1. First there was the aftermath of the Great War, a decade of tidying up.
2. There followed the world depression, a period of six years of stagnation so far as the Armed Services were concerned.
3. Early in 1936 the danger of a Second World War began to make itself felt, but the people were not in the mood to face such an ordeal. The scale and tempo of preparations to meet this threat were not sufficient to act as a deterrent.
4. The climax of the Second World War, 1939 to 1945. This war was three-dimensional (the air had played a relatively small part in the Great War), and technical development was a significant factor in success or failure.

The RAOC, as the main Service of Supply to the Army, was greatly influenced by these rapid changes in policy over such a short period.

The processes of supply are not amenable to sudden change. After a war large surpluses of equipment remain and the Armed Services are expected to "live on their fat" and spend very little money on equipment. But retrenchment is the enemy of progress. Complex modern equipment takes several years to produce, but soon becomes obsolete and relatively useless. These hard facts are not easily recognized by those who hold the purse strings and are concerned with the financial position and prosperity of the country. The "new wine" of modern military techniques does not easily mature in the "old bottles" of obsolete equipment. The Armed Services in peace represent an insurance against war, but the governments of peaceful states do not always see the need to pay the insurance premium, and sometimes find themselves engaged in a war for survival for which they are unprepared. This was the cycle of events in the years from 1920 to 1939, a critical period for the RAOC.

Although the achievements of the Corps in the Great War received a measure of recognition the growing importance of the supply of equipment in modern war was not generally understood and so the Corps responsible for this service was neglected.

Except for the "top management", the Ordnance Services in the United Kingdom were virtually civilianized, the military staff being retained only on a level sufficient to man the peace-time establishments of stations overseas. The military staff were fully employed on these peace-time duties, working longer hours than other units. Thus, although efficient arrangements existed for supplying the Army on mobilization with such equipment as existed, the preparation of the Corps itself for war was seriously hampered by lack of time and opportunity, with other tasks being given a higher priority.

To a certain extent this situation was unavoidable, but the retention between the wars of the "non-combatant" status of the Corps was inexcusable. The designation "non-combatant" was false and misleading, and the complete specialization inherent in this classification effectively isolated the Corps from the rest of the Army.

Training with other arms of the service and attendance on all-arms courses by RAOC officers and men were virtually ruled out. Ordnance Officers were not eligible for Staff College courses. The Corps was unable to influence logistic thought and doctrine in the Army as a whole. The problems in modern war of the supply and repair of equipment and the RAOC field force structure for this purpose were given little serious consideration. When the war started the Army knew little about the RAOC and the Corps had become isolated and introspective.

Such a situation would have been disastrous but for the determination, foresight and knowledge of a few men who controlled the destiny of the Corps in the critical years before and during the war. It was indeed fortunate that men of the calibre of Generals Hill, Williams and Richards were in command during this crisis.

Starting with a nucleus of a few hundred officers and a few thousand men of the Regular and Territorial Army the RAOC developed in little more than four years into an enormous, highly efficient organization of 8,000 officers and 130,000 men.

The main features of the logistic support provided by this organization were:

1. A controlling headquarters at the War Office, the Ordnance Directorate, which dealt with policy, organization of the Corps worldwide, and the provision of stores, vehicles and ammunition.

2. The creation of a United Kingdom Base for the supply of all items of Ordnance concern to all theatres. This organization comprised:

    (a) Covered storage accommodation of approximately 48 million sq ft.

    (b) Open storage of about 50 million sq ft.

    (c) Vehicle accommodation for 250,000 vehicles.

    (d) Open accommodation for ammunition covering 1,600 sq miles.

    (e) Covered ammunition accommodation of 10 million sq ft.

3. A similar though smaller base was created in the Middle East, making full use of local resources.

458

4. The creation of a comprehensive field force organization which provided a reliable and flexible system for the maintenance of a field army. The units were:

    (a) Ordnance Field Parks.
    (b) Forward Maintenance Ammunition Sections.
    (c) Forward Maintenance Stores Sections.
    (d) Mobile Laundry Units.
    (e) Mobile Bath Units.
    (f) Mobile Ammunition Repairs Units.
    (g) Ordnance Beach Detachments.
    (h) Industrial Gas Units.

5. The formation of essential Base and Lines of Communication Units in theatres of operations, e.g. Base Ordnance Depots, Base Ammunition Depots, Vehicle Depots, Base and Hospital Laundries, Base Industrial Gas Units, Port Ordnance and Ammunition Detachments.

6. The creation of a workshops organization for the repair, recovery and manufacture of equipment at the base and in the field. This organization was the basis for the creation of REME in 1942.

7. The creation of a system of packing, preservation and identification of stores which would ensure that they survived the hazards of war-time transportation and handling and storage conditions in all climates and that they would reach the unit in a condition fit for immediate use.

8. The formation of a highly trained technical ammunition branch which inspected, conditioned and repaired our own ammunition and dealt with captured and unexploded enemy ammunition. The branch also undertook the manufacture of certain natures of ammunition such as anti-tank mines. This activity saved many lives, helped give our troops confidence in their ammunition and, through the salvage and repair work undertaken, saved the country considerable sums of money.

The casualties suffered by the Corps during the war amounted to more than 5,000 officers and men.

Some idea of the size of the task is given by the following figures relating to the support of 21st Army Group in North-West Europe:

    (a) Number of different items of equipment packed—350 million.
    (b) Tonnages packed as:

        (i) Landing Reserves   6,000
        (ii) Beach Maintenance Packs   11,000
        (iii) Overseas base reserves   13,300

    (c) Tonnage of ammunition sent in first 2 months—380,000.
    (d) Number of vehicles sent in first 2 months—190,000.

Although a war of the nature and on the scale of the Second World War is unlikely to be fought in the future, the achievements of the RAOC should be recorded if only to show that determination and enterprise will triumph over all difficulties.

There are also many lessons of general application which might be forgotten without a record of these "years of endurance". These lessons are immutable, being in the nature of principles of armed warfare, and the following are most significant:

Unless an Army is at all times fit for war it is useless. The RAOC is an increasingly important element of the Army but will not be able to function if the military strength is unduly reduced and those who remain are fully engaged in peace-time duties. The civilian staff are not alternative to military but complementary to them enabling the soldiers to concentrate on readiness for war. The fact that some of the peace-time activity also provides training for war should not be allowed to obscure the basic principle.

A second lesson concerns operational planning and logistics. General Sir Bernard Paget, commenting on the Norway fiasco, stated, "It has become the habit of the British Army in recent years to assume that whatever the General Staff consider to be politically or operationally desirable is administratively possible". The operational planning in 21st Army Group four years later was in marked contrast to that for the Norwegian campaign. Logistic factors were studied throughout and the RAOC played a full part from the beginning.

A third lesson concerns the place of the RAOC in the Army structure. As long ago as 1904, when the Army Council was created and the War Office reorganized as a result of the Esher Report, the Ordnance Directorate was formed at the War Office with the Staff Branches, QMG 7, 8 and 9, under the DEOS, as the Director was then known. Thus authority and responsibility were not divorced, as had happened previously, and RAOC officers directly influenced policy in their own field, the supply and maintenance of equipment.

Between 1939 and 1945 the same structure remained and was enlarged to deal with the greatly increased and more complex problem of supply in modern war. The powerful Ordnance Directorate at the War Office was able to control RAOC activities and formulate policy on provision, storage, issue and repair of stores, vehicles and ammunition. The obvious point was beginning to be recognized that the best people to handle the staff work of supply were those who had knowledge and experience of the processes of supply of equipment, namely RAOC officers.

Unfortunately these simple lessons are too easily forgotten or obscured in the years of peace. A hard look at existing logistic and organizational concepts in relation to the lessons of the period covered in this history might serve to reveal a few fallacies in some of the latest ideas, and help to ensure a common sense approach to these problems.

HONOURS AND AWARDS

Although this list of honours and awards has been carefully compiled from the best available information, there may be some errors and omissions. The rank shown is that quoted in the *London Gazette* in which the announcement was made.

THE GEORGE CROSS

Capt R. L. Jephson-Jones   Lieut W. M. Eastman

KNIGHTS COMMANDER OF THE MOST EXCELLENT ORDER OF THE BRITISH EMPIRE

Maj-Gen B. A. Hill, CB, DSO   Maj-Gen L. H. Williams, CB, MC

COMPANIONS OF THE MOST HONOURABLE ORDER OF THE BATH

Colonel R. S. Hamilton, CMG, DSO
Colonel H. C. Fernyhough, CMG, DSO
Colonel R. H. McVittie, CMG, CBE
Maj-Gen J. Baker, CBE
Maj-Gen B. A. Hill, DSO
Maj-Gen K. M. Body, CMG, OBE

Maj-Gen W. W. Richards, CBE, MC
Maj-Gen L. H. Williams, MC
Maj-Gen A. R. Valon, OBE, MC
Maj-Gen J. S. Crawford, CBE
Brig C. E. de Wolff, CBE
Maj-Gen C. H. Geake, CBE

COMPANION OF THE MOST EMINENT ORDER OF THE INDIAN EMPIRE

Maj-Gen W. H. McN. Verschoyle-Campbell, CBE, MC

Brig E. McGuinness

COMMANDERS OF THE MOST EXCELLENT ORDER OF THE BRITISH EMPIRE

Brig E. J. J. Britton, DSO
Maj-Gen M. J. H. Bruce
Brig D. Brown
Brig J. S. Crawford
Colonel C. Cansdale, OBE
Brig T. H. Clarke
Brig C. H. Cooper, OBE

Brig G. O. Crawford, OBE
Colonel P. G. Davies, CMG
Colonel N. Douglas, TD
Brig J. G. Denniston
Colonel H. J. Denham
Colonel A. C. H. Eagles, OBE, MC
Brig G. C. Evelegh

18+   461

Maj-Gen C. H. Geake
Colonel W. T. Grimsdale, OBE
Colonel A. F. B. Hopwood
Brig A. W. A. Harker
Colonel G. P. U. Hardy
Brig G. T. W. Horne, OBE
Brig P. W. Kidd
Brig B. C. Lester, OBE
Brig M. Lea-Cox, OBE
Brig V. O. Lonsdale, OBE
Colonel J. J. Mills, OBE
Brig. F. Morris, OBE, MC
Colonel D. McEwan, OBE
Colonel F. Morris, OBE
Colonel H. F. Mackenzie, MBE

Brig M. R. Neale, MC
Brig A. I. Nixon, OBE
Brig J. F. F. Oakeshott, OBE
Brig W. E. C. Pickthall, OBE
Brig G. W. Palmer
Brig H. R. Primmer
Colonel S. Preston
Colonel W. A. Quennell
Brig W. W. Richards, MC
Brig E. P. Readman, OBE
Lt-Col W. T. Sheppard, DSO
Colonel A. N. C. Varley
Brig W. White
Colonel A. J. Wright, OBE
Brig H. C. Whitaker

OFFICERS OF THE MOST EXCELLENT ORDER OF THE BRITISH EMPIRE

Colonel L. H. Aste
Lt-Col C. Arnold-Edwards
Major H. Atherton
Capt H. Badcock, MC
Lt-Col A. R. Brown
Lt-Col J. A. E. Burls
Lt-Col N. Berry
Lt-Col G. W. Briffa
Lt-Col C. P. Brady
Colonel R. F. Barker, MC
Lt-Col R. C. Beach
Lt-Col R. T. Boyes
Lt-Col M. Barnes
Lt-Col L. E. Ball
Lt-Col L. A. Burden
Lt-Col R. V. Blundell
Colonel J. G. Bentley
Lt-Col C. B. Bishton
Colonel E. E. Baker
Colonel A. D. Bateman
Lt-Col E. Bower
Lt-Col R. K. Cullen
Colonel C. H. Cooper
Colonel E. R. Caffyn
Colonel B. G. Cox
Colonel S. F. Clark
Brig. G. O. Crawford
Colonel W. T. Cobb
Lt-Col S. E. Clark
Lt-Col R. Chalkley, GM
Lt-Col H. Charles

Colonel L. E. Cutforth
Colonel J. F. Cottrell
Lt-Col N. E. R. Carroll
Lt-Col G. Chappell
Colonel C. F. Douglas-White, MBE
Major W. G. Drury
Lt-Col F. M. Day
Lt-Col D. D. Dennis
Lt-Col G. Drewry
Colonel T. W. Davis
Colonel W. E. B. Dansie
Colonel C. W. G. Dawson
Colonel A. C. H. Eagles, MC
Lt-Col J. P. Earp, MC
Lt-Col W. Elliott
Lt-Col H. F. Friday
Lt-Col R. H. Ferguson
Lt-Col F. S. R. Foster
Lt-Col G. A. L. Freer
Lt-Col H. A. Fieldhouse
Lt-Col N. A. Fisher
Lt-Col B. A. Goldstein
Lt-Col H. H. Glanfield
Lt-Col J. A. Gibbons
Colonel W. T. Grimsdale
Lt-Col R. C. Gibb
Colonel T. G. Gore
Lt-Col J. T. Goodsir
Lt-Col W. Gray
Lt-Col R. Goldsbrough
Lt-Col J. B. Green

Colonel K. C. Gray
Brig J. R. Grove
Colonel G. C. H. Heron
Colonel H. Howard-Jones
Brig J. H. F. Hitchcock
Lt-Col R. Hayne
Major C. Hopkins
Major J. L. Hume
Brig G. T. W. Horne
Lt-Col J. W. Hayley
Lt-Col W. Hamilton
Brig H. J. C. Hildreth
Lt-Col R. G. Hicks
Lt-Col E. N. Highton
Lt-Col P. R. Hill
Lt-Col J. P. R. Howland
Lt-Col E. A. Horsey
Lt-Col F. D. M. Harding
Colonel R. C. Hiam
Lt-Col A. H. Huddlestone
Lt-Col F. A. Hiney
Colonel A. Heilbut
Colonel A. J. M. Hunt
Lt-Col J. Hall
Lt-Col W. A. Hildred
Lt-Col D. S. Ingman
Lt-Col J. M. Ireland, MBE
Colonel F. A. Ironside
Colonel L. H. Jackson
Lt-Col F. E. Jackson
Lt-Col M. C. Johnson
Capt A. H. Kemp
Lt-Col W. C. Kilvington
Lt-Col W. A. Kenney
Lt-Col C. J. Kinna
Lt-Col G. R. Kerr
Lt-Col R. C. Keymer
Major T. P. Lilly
Lt-Col G. Lillywhite
Lt-Col V. O. Lonsdale
Major B. A. P. Lambert
Brig B. C. Lester
Lt-Col W. E. L. Long
Lt-Col F. Lobley
Lt-Col T. M. Lester
Lt-Col V. A. Lines
Lt-Col B. H. Liggins
Capt W. E. C. Moore
Major C. A. H. Montanaro
Lt-Col G. H. S. Maunder

Lt-Col J. W. McKillop
Lt-Col J. A. Marshall
Lt-Col R. R. M. Mayhew
Lt-Col T. Morris
Lt-Col D. McEwan
Lt-Col F. Morris
Lt-Col G. E. G. Malet
Lt-Col R. E. Moss
Lt-Col L. A. Mahoney
Colonel H. D. Muggeridge
Lt-Col F. E. Manning
Lt-Col V. R. Moll
Lt-Col A. I. Nixon
Lt-Col S. K. Neill
Colonel J. F. F. Oakeshott
Lt-Col J. Orr
Colonel A. S. Osborne
Lt-Col S. W. Owen
Major W. E. C. Pickthall
Lt-Col F. J. Powell
Lt-Col T. A. Perry
Lt-Col W. E. Pavey
Colonel H. H. Philps
Lt-Col W. Perfect
Lt-Col S. G. Purkis
Major E. P. Readman
Lt-Col O. D. Rolland
Lt-Col J. E. Ruddock
Lt-Col C. E. Rusbridge
Lt-Col T. D. Roberts
Lt-Col D. A. K. Redman
Colonel D. S. Robinson
Lt-Col H. O. Robinson
Lt-Col D. J. Russell
Lt-Col E. V. Ranson
Capt G. A. N. Swiney, MC
Major C. F. Sharp
Major F. S. Smith
Major W. A. Stack
Colonel A. O. Samson
Lt-Col W. B. Shine
Colonel L. A. W. Stower, MC
Lt-Col E. J. Smith
Colonel C. Sellars
Lt-Col F. E. Sidney
Lt-Col K. R. Speller
Colonel E. J. Savage
Lt-Col H. E. Sumpster
Lt-Col J. H. Scott
Lt-Col S. G. Slingsby

Brig A. Sewell
Lt-Col A. T. Smith
Colonel J. Southern
Lt-Col P. R. Sandars
Lt-Col E. B. Stewart-Smith
Lt-Col I. N. Tyler
Brig E. Tankard, MC
Lt-Col P. B. Thomson
Lt-Col W. F. Tuson
Lt-Col S. S. Tegner
Lt-Col G. A. Viner
Lt-Col F. B. H. Villiers
Colonel R. J. Volkers
Colonel R. A. Weir

Colonel J. J. Walsh
Lt-Col F. W. S. Walker
Colonel G. C. H. Wortham
Lt-Col A. H. White
Colonel C. P. D. Ward, DSO
Lt-Col A. Wotherspoon
Colonel J. C. Waycott
Lt-Col G. N. Warnock
Lt-Col G. Wray
Lt-Col L. H. Worskett
Lt-Col E. E. Walker, MBE, GM
Colonel D. H. Warren
Colonel D. S. Woolf

THE DISTINGUISHED SERVICE ORDER

Major N. L. T. Darewski

Lt-Col T. G. Gore, OBE

THE MILITARY CROSS

Major J. P. M. Boyd
Lt-Col K. S. Estlin
Major A. H. Fernyhough
Lieut E. C. Farrer
Major F. A. Goodman
Capt R. A. Jacobs

Capt R. V. Knight
Capt F. A. Lowe
Capt J. Nicholson
Lieut F. E. Norris
Capt H. J. C. Robinson

THE DISTINGUISHED CONDUCT MEDAL

Armt QMS S. J. Barton
Pte D. R. Edwards

Pte D. Davidson

THE MILITARY MEDAL

L/Sgt E. G. Brown
Cpl C. H. Carter
Cpl J. Curry
Pte S. Colthorpe
Pte W. Curran
Armr Sgt M. H. Chase
Pte H. R. Daffern
Sgt L. T. Ferris
Pte W. B. A. Gaze
Sgt F. B. F. Greenwood
Pte J. C. Green
Sgt D. W. Ginger
Sgt I. J. Grant
S/Sgt G. F. Hails
L/Cpl J. Hannah
L/Cpl F. M. Hynes

Cpl J. B. Jones
Pte G. A. E. Laming
Sub/Cdr G. E. Melville
Pte T. Nelson
Pte W. J. T. A. Osborne
S/Sgt J. Porter
Cdr R. W. Parker
L/Cpl R. Penny
Sgt L. T. Rowecliffe
Cpl E. R. Stewart
Pte A. W. Sanders
Armt QMS B. E. Sewell
Pte C. R. Studley
Sgt D. M. Smith
Pte G. E. Turner

THE GEORGE MEDAL

Capt R. Chalkley
Capt D. A. S. Martin
Capt F. V. Platel
S/Sgt E. P. Thorner
S/Sgt L. Telford
Capt T. W. Downing
Lieut J. Search

Major E. E. Walker
Major R. W. H. Beaton
Major W. Whittles
Sgt F. W. Pearce
Major G. C. G. Pepper
Sgt J. S. McGowan

THE KING'S COMMENDATION FOR BRAVE CONDUCT

Capt M. O'Connell
Lieut H. N. Cowley
Sgt W. J. Chapman
Pte A. Bateman

Pte H. Bryan
Major K. R. Gray
Capt C. F. Kitchin
Sub/Cdr C. B. McPhee

MILITARY MEMBERS OF THE MOST EXCELLENT ORDER OF THE BRITISH EMPIRE

Major H. C. Andrews
Capt A. K. Ames
Major F. J. N. Ailwood
WO II G. E. Atkins
Cdr A. G. Alford
Lieut E. Atkins
Capt W. H. Airey
Major J. S. Allison
Capt L. Arnott
Sub/Cdr W. T. Anderton
Lieut G. F. Bancroft
Cdr E. W. Buffee
Sub/Cdr E. Bullock
SQMS S. O. Baker
Armt QMS C. E. Briggs
Capt J. D. Berryman
Major E. H. Bax
Capt K. R. Barker
Sub/Cdr H. S. Barris
Sub/Cdr L. A. E. B. Bourlay
Major C. B. Bishton
Major J. P. U. Burr
Lt-Col R. H. Brown, TD
Major R. W. H. Beaton, GM
SQMS K. E. L. Barton
Lt-Col A. K. Brown
Major R. D. R. Bateman
Sub/Cdr A. H. Booth
Major H. A. Brakes
Major W. R. B. Burnett

WO II R. W. Bazzard
Major F. W. G. Barrett
Sub/Cdr L. J. Birt
WO I E. E. Brindle
Major Hon Denys B. Buckley
Major L. E. Baker
SQMS K. Bentham
Major N. E. Britton
WO I W. Budd
Sub/Cdr G. T. Bailey
WO II R. D. Baker
Major S. Bard
Capt W. F. R. Batson
Capt E. Bedworth
WO II K. A. Bill
Major R. W. Beasley
WO II J. C. Blackburn
Major R. N. J. Burgess
Major F. Banfield
Major F. C. Bellamy
Capt F. Bowman
WO I G. L. Budden
Major S. S. Baker
Major D. G. Berry
Sub/Cdr G. L. Bray
Major R. H. Bromley
Major F. Birtwistle
RSM W. Cook
Lieut F. T. Comerford
Lieut R. S. Conner

Capt G. H. Cann
Capt A. Clowes
Capt W. E. Cunnington
Capt W. G. Cleghorn
Lieut W. J. Clifford
SQMS S. Clarke
Sub/Cdr N. G. Cooke
Lt-Col H. E. Caldwell
Sub/Cdr J. Caldwell
Major I. G. C. Cameron
Major W. B. Chapman
Capt A. D. Cheers
Capt W. Cavanagh
Major E. C. Cockrane
WO I R. Cumming
Lt-Col L. G. Cornford
Major L. A. B. Cooke
Cdr E. W. Chamberlain
WO I W. Carradus
WO II J. Cohen
Major J. C. R. Craven
Major W. S. Corken
Major H. B. Cowell
Capt A. D. Costello
Mr. (later Col) G. H. Dawson
SQMS C. Dalglish
Major B. C. Durkin
Capt J. A. Driscoll
Lieut S. J. Driscall
Major G. F. Doran
Armt SM H. D. Dugan
Sub/Cdr J. H. Dudley
Sub/Cdr W. O. E. Dowdall
Lieut R. W. Diggens
Capt G. F. Davey
Capt V. Dunne
Major R. F. Davidson
Major M. H. C. Drewe
Lt-Col L. F. Duval
Cdr L. L. Dolan
Capt F. R. East
Sub/Cdr W. S. Evans
Major G. Edmund-Jones
Major W. J. Elliott
WO I F. N. Emery
Lt-Col A. S. Ellick
Capt V. S. Ebbage, BEM
Sub/Cdr R. C. S. Ford
Capt G. H. W. Fellows
Lt-Col N. H. Finch

Major W. J. French
Sub/Cdr G. W. Foulis
Sub/Cdr L. N. Freeth
WO I W. H. Fausett
Major E. C. Farman
Major W. H. A. Ferns
WO I A. W. Field
Lt-Col W. A. Fordham
WO I F. G. Fuller
Major D. F. T. Farley
Capt J. B. Fisher
Lt-Col A. W. H. Field
Cdr G. Gillam
Cdr F. G. Glover
Major J. W. C. Gillman
Lieut F. C. Green
Capt E. T. Guy
Major G. Goodwin
Cdr W. J. Glazier
Sub/Cdr H. J. Golding
Major D. Graham
Major R. G. B. Greggains
Major R. F. Gingold
Major R. Grimble
Sub/Cdr H. J. Gray
Major L. C. B. Gower
Major R. H. Goodfellow
Major B. W. Grist
Major W. H. J. Gillow
Major D. W. Gooch
WO I H. W. G. Griffiths
Major C. C. Goddard
Capt J. W. Gardiner
WO I J. Gray
Capt A. T. Greenway
Capt G. E. V. Howes
Cdr W. F. Hall
SQMS H. Heald
Major A. E. Heald
Lieut A. J. M. Hunt
Lieut A. Hales
Lieut F. C. F. Horey
Cdr R. A. Hilton
Sub/Cdr W. M. L. Howard
Armt SM A. S. Harley
Lieut E. C. Hollingdale
Major N. M. Harris
Major S. J. Hoyland
Capt L. A. Harrison
Capt J. R. Hill

Capt J. Hayton, BEM
Major E. J. Harris
Major R. H. Heath
Sub/Cdr J. Hasel
Major W. G. Henham
Major C. N. Harding
Major R. Hardwick-Gardiner
Major C. P. Hornby
Major W. L. Holloway
Major G. E. Hubbard
Major E. G. Harris
Lieut A. W. Hawkes
Capt H. T. Humphrey
WO II W. Hutchison
Lieut P. T. Handford
Major R. A. Hume
Major J. M. Ireland
Capt G. D. Izzett
Capt F. C. Johnstone-Hall
Lieut R. E. C. Jennings
Cdr R. C. Jemmett
Major G. T. Johnston-Smith
Major F. L. P. Jones
Sub/Cdr E. N. James
Sub/Cdr W. J. H. Jones
SQMS C. J. Jewhurst
WO I D. Johnson
Major V. C. E. Jones
WO I J. F. Jackson
WO I G. E. Jenkins
WO I K. Jones
Major A. N. Jones
Cdr H. King
Cdr E. H. Kember
Major H. F. S. King
Major K. F. Kinchin
Lt-Col E. J. Kinvig
Major F. T. Kellet
Major E. M. Ketley
Major R. C. Keymer
Capt H. V. Knight
Cdr J. Kane
Sub/Cdr A. Kerr
Major M. O'D. Kerr
Capt F. G. King
Major C. D. Key
Capt A. G. Keast
Capt P. H. Knight
Major R. L. Kenyon
Capt O. Lovett

Sub/Cdr H. Leach
Sub/Cdr G. Ledwidge
Major M. Lockitch
Capt G. B. Lucas
Major C. E. Lane
Sub/Cdr G. D. Lucas
Capt R. H. Latham
Major J. W. Lupton
Major A. Lees
WO I G. W. Lindsay
Major E. J. Longstaff
Sub/Cdr H. A. Miles
Lieut A. U. Mackenzie
Major E. R. Millard
Capt H. F. Mackenzie
Major H. T. May
Capt E. T. Messenger
Capt G. J. Mitchell
Armt SM J. G. Mockford
Lieut H. J. Morrison
Major J. Murray
Capt H. McNeil
Cdr W. D. Moore
Sub/Cdr A. F. Meadon
Lieut L. N. Morris
Major F. L. Manning
Capt G. T. Meadows
Major S. J. Mitton
Major C. P. H. McCall
Lt-Col L. H. McCausland
Major J. N. S. H. Master
Lt-Col F. P. Moore, MM
Major D. J. A. Marfell
Major G. MacDonald
Capt W. Martin
Major K. J. MacKenzie
Sub/Cdr C. McAlister
Major G. R. Marshall
Major A. L. Martin
Lt-Col R. J. Meech
Major I. M. Mills
Capt A. D. Milroy
Lt-Col R. P. Morton
Lt-Col J. J. Marshall
Capt R. J. Merrifield
WO I R. K. Millard
Major H. J. Masters
Major R. O. Milnes
SQMS W. Mitchell
Lieut J. M. Noble

Sub/Cdr N. J. Nealey
Cdr P. N. Nockolds
Major J. Nuttall
Capt A. Napier
Major J. W. Nelson
Major E. J. Norris
Major N. J. Newton
Capt T. W. Overton
WO I E. F. O'Brien
Major S. J. O'Connell
Major P. J. O'Gallagher
Lt-Col N. S. Oxford
WO I N. Oxley
Armt QMS E. E. Parrot
Capt K. Potter
Major L. F. Parker
2/Lieut F. Potts
Sub/Cdr V. H. Pearce
Capt R. J. H. Philp
Major G. H. Phillips
Capt V. Price
Capt J. F. F. Palmer
Major C. H. A. Platten
Sub/Cdr A. E. W. Price
Major J. R. Parsons
Capt L. G. Payne
Major R. H. Pope
Major T. P. Price
Lt-Col E. Parkinson
Lt-Col J. W. Pearce
WO II F. Povey
Major J. H. Preston
Major W. Parker
Major A. H. Parnaby
Sub/Cdr B. J. A. Pearce
Lt-Col G. D. Petts
Major A. H. Pycock
Armt QMS E. Roberts
SQMS S. E. Richardson
Lieut R. Reid
Cdr G. E. Rex
Lieut T. Redfearn
Lieut R. H. Raistrick
Capt E. H. Randell
Major G. R. Rosevere
Lieut W. R. Reed
Capt F. T. Ruse
Capt G. R. Rousell
Major R. J. Rous
Capt G. W. R. Richardson

Capt A. B. Reynolds
Lt-Col G. C. Richardson
Capt W. E. Richardson
Major N. V. Reed
Major F. G. Rudham
Capt D. M. Robson
Major L. S. Rose
Capt J. C. Rawet
Lt-Col P. W. Ricardo
WO I W. J. Rees
Major D. A. Rousham
WO I G. Rushforth
Lieut N. Speller
Major C. H. K. Smith
SQMS H. J. Shrapnel
Capt J. Sedgwick
Lieut F. J. Sargent
Capt F. P. Short
Armt SM D. B. Sturman
Capt F. H. Smith
Lieut A. Stephens
Major S. R. Spicer
Major C. P. Stocker
Lieut H. L. Smith
Capt P. A. Sanders
Sub/Cdr H. J. Smart
Major J. C. R. Sampson
Major E. D. Shaw
Major G. P. A. Shelley
Lt-Col H. J. Sandle
Cdr J. M. Sword
Major J. Snowball
Major G. Stidwell
Capt H. L. Smith
Major R. L. Streather
Major D. W. Searle
WO I J. W. Skeats
Capt B. Smith
Lt-Col H. K. Stanley
Lt-Col F. J. C. Stephenson
Lt-Col W. R. Stubbs
Major R. J. Saunders
Major W. F. d'A. Spencer
Lieut W. Syme
Major M. F. Tully
Capt H. E. Tanner
SQMS M. C. Tarran
Capt J. C. Thetford
Sub/Cdr L. S. Turner
WO II G. Thompson

WO II A. T. Tutchings
Capt W. Thomson
Capt A. J. Tarper
Major E. N. Taylor
Capt W. C. Thomas
Major J. J. Thompson
WO I A. J. Thomson
Lieut F. E. Vigus
Capt G. H. Vooght
Major C. W. Vokings
Major H. M. Vickerman
Armt QMS G. W. Wadley
Lieut R. E. Warry
Armt SM L. J. Walker
Capt D. W. Wilshin
Lt-Col G. H. Way
Major A. L. Wheeldon
Major H. G. White

Major E. Wyatt
Major E. E. Walker, GM
Capt H. Walker
Major H. W. Whittles
Major E. W. Williams
Major R. H. Webb
Major K. R. Woodbine
WO II G. F. Wilks
WO II A. Williams
Lieut H. G. A. Willis
WO I J. Wilmot
Major F. F. Wyatt
WO I D. V. Wyer
Sub/Cdr W. Whitehead
WO I L. G. Wilmshurst
WO I T. G. E. Woods
Capt I. S. Young

THE BRITISH EMPIRE MEDAL

S/Sgt W. H. Allen
L/Cpl A. T. Aston
Sgt K. Ashton
WO I H. E. Albone
S/Sgt C. C. V. Bramble
L/Cpl L. Barratt
CSM G. W. Bridge
SQMS R. G. Bassett
Pte J. Balmforth
S/Sgt V. Beavers
SQMS H. Burns
Cpl J. Briggs
Sgt J. P. Buckley
Pte J. Boyd
Sgt J. A. Brady
Sgt W. Brame
L/Sgt T. J. Brownhill
Sgt O. G. A. Clutton
SQMS L. Coles
S/Sgt J. C. Cheshire
Sgt J. Cross
S/Sgt G. Clarke
S/Sgt T. C. Cleveland
S/Sgt F. J. Cahill
Sgt W. Clarke
S/Sgt W. Challenger
S/Sgt F. E. Dorey
Cpl A. W. Diprose
SQMS L. E. B. Dobell

WO J. T. Donaldson
S/Sgt F. A. Driver
S/Sgt V. S. Ebbage
Cpl E. J. Ellwood
S/Sgt E. Elsmore
Sgt A. W. Ellis
Pte H. E. Frend
S/Sgt W. Fellick
Sgt J. R. Faulding
Pte R. W. Farmer
Cpl A. Fryer
WO I T. P. Flattley
WO I T. Floyd
L/Cpl N. Goodall
Pte H. Gulvin
S/Sgt C. E. Geary
Sgt J. R. R. Grassby
WO I N. Gaskell
L/Cpl W. A. Grundy
S/Sgt F. Green
Pte A. Green
Sgt J. Hayton
Pte B. Hatton
L/Sgt S. G. Hill
Pte J. Hes
Sgt D. Hendry
Sgt T. J. Halls
S/Sgt D. C. Hayes
S/Sgt G. Hurst

S/Sgt H. R. Hurd
Sgt A. N. Harrison
Pte T. A. Ireland
S/Sgt C. J. Jardine
S/Sgt E. D. A. Jones
S/Sgt H. C. Keen
Cpl N. O. Kinshott
WO I J. Kenyon
S/Sgt C. Lockyer
L/Cpl G. Lea
Armt S/Sgt W. H. J. Lillistone
S/Sgt J. Light
L/Cpl T. Lea
Sgt W. B. Leatherbarrow
Cpl H. Liddell
Cpl G. Lambert
S/Sgt N. Landells
Pte W. F. Lock
L/Sgt T. McPherson
Sgt R. L. McIlvride
S/Sgt R. H. Maddocks
SQMS E. A. Morse
SQMS A. G. Morrison
Sgt R. J. Maclennan
SQMS J. McBurney
Pte J. K. Martin
S/Sgt J. Mather
Sgt D. McCann
S/Sgt T. Morton
Sgt J. Mooney
Pte G. V. Nicholson
S/Sgt C. Nowell
Sgt G. W. Newman

S/Sgt J. R. Neilson
Sgt C. A. Payne
Sgt A. Pettit
L/Sgt W. D. S. Paton
Sgt A. E. Porter
S/Sgt W. R. A. Rogers
SQMS H. E. Rollason
Sgt G. B. Robinson
WO II R. W. Robb
Sgt E. Rostron
Sgt R. Rothwell
L/Cpl R. E. Southcott
Cpl D. D. Skinner
Sgt J. H. Stewart
S/Sgt J. P. Savage
Cpl G. Strain
S/Sgt C. J. Smith
Cpl J. E. Shaw
S/Sgt G. E. Smalley
Sgt R. P. Speed
Pte T. P. Slater
Sgt J. Sloan
Cpl J. Salisbury
S/Sgt H. Thomson
S/Sgt J. H. Thornley
Sgt W. T. A. Tyler
Cpl V. Threadgold
S/Sgt W. Worsdell
Sgt H. Wilson
Sgt R. M. West
WO II K. G. Wareham
Pte A. A. W. Weston

Decorations conferred by the President of the United States of America

LEGION OF MERIT

Degree of *Commander:*
Maj-Gen L. H. Williams, CB, MC
Maj-Gen W. W. Richards,
   CB, CBE, MC

Degree of *Officer:*
Maj-Gen C. H. Geake, CB, CBE
Brig V. O. Lonsdale, CBE
Brig A. Abel-Smith
Col C. Arnold-Edwards, OBE
Col J. D. Miller

Lt-Col A. E. Trafford-Owen
Major M. S. Baker
Major E. J. W. Morley
Major E. Westbury
Brig H. J. C. Hildreth, OBE
Lt-Col J. A. Lewando
Lt-Col A. E. Hewlett
Brig M. Lea-Cox, CBE
Brig G. P. U. Hardy, CBE
Lt-Col A. J. M. Hunt, OBE
Lt-Col E. O'Shaughnessey

Honours and Awards

Major E. J. W. Hardy
Brig C. C. Clark

Degree of *Legionnaire:*
Lt-Col P. W. O'Brien, MBE

BRONZE STAR MEDAL

Lt-Col R. M. McCullum

MEDAL OF FREEDOM

Colonel K. C. Gray, OBE
Major the Hon Denys B. Buckley,
   MBE

Lt-Col V. R. A. Cowper
Colonel A. D. Bateman, OBE

Decorations conferred by HM the King of Norway

KING HAAKON VII FREEDOM CROSS

Lt-Col D. McEwan, CBE

KING HAAKON VII FREEDOM MEDAL

Capt L. J. Curd
Capt T. N. Pickett
Capt V. L. Turner
Capt W. D. Morris
WO I G. R. Jenkins, MBE

WO II G. Dawson
SQMS R. H. Beasley
Lt-Col R. K. Cullen
S/Sgt P. Stoller

Decorations conferred by HM the King of Denmark

THE ORDER OF DANNEBROG

Knight:
Lt-Col A. T. Dodd

Knight 2nd Class:
Lieut C. C. Ingram

Conferred by the Government in exile of Poland

ORDER OF POLONIA RESTITUTA 2nd CLASS—KNIGHT

Maj-Gen L. H. Williams, CB, MC

Decorations conferred by the President of the Czechoslovak Republic

MILITARY MEDAL OF MERIT 1st CLASS WITH WAR CROSS (1939)

Maj-Gen W. W. Richards,
   CB, CBE, MC

WAR CROSS (1939)

Capt L. R. Rickaby

MILITARY MEDAL FOR MERIT 1st CLASS

Sub/Cdr K. S. W. Berger

MILITARY MEDAL FOR MERIT, 2nd CLASS

L/Cpl E. J. Martin   L/Cpl R. G. Lumsden
L/Cpl R. C. A. Phillips   Cpl K. Entwhistle

Decoration conferred by the U.S.S.R.

THE ORDER OF PATRIOTIC WAR 1st CLASS

Lt-Col M. D. Smither

Decoration conferred by the King of Egypt

THE ORDER OF THE NILE 3rd CLASS

Major B. C. Lester

Decorations conferred by HM the King of the Hellenes

OFFICER OF THE ROYAL ORDER OF THE PHOENIX

Capt A. T. Casdagli

THE DISTINGUISHED SERVICE ORDER

Major P. R. Clark   Capt A. T. Judd
WO I S. W. Johnson

MILITARY CROSS 3rd CLASS

S/Sgt N. Gaskell, BEM

Decorations conferred by HM the Queen of the Netherlands

THE ORDER OF ORANGE NASSAU WITH SWORDS

Knight Commander: *Knight:*
Colonel H. H. Fitton   Major H. E. Davis
                             Capt J. B. Mitchell

Officer:
Lt-Col W. J. Scragg
Lt-Col C. J. Adshead
Lt-Col D. R. Widdowson
Lt-Col H. S. Futter

GOLD MEDAL OF THE ORDER OF THE HOUSE OF ORANGE

Sgt D. W. Ginger, MM   Sgt A. N. Midgeley

SILVER MEDAL OF THE ORDER OF THE HOUSE OF ORANGE

WO I E. J. Baker

Decorations conferred by the Republic of France

COMMANDER OF THE LEGION OF HONOUR

Maj-Gen Sir Leslie H. Williams, KBE, CB, MC

CHEVALIER, LEGION OF HONOUR AND CROIX DE GUERRE WITH PALM

Lt-Col J. Goodsir, OBE

CROIX DE GUERRE

Capt J. C. Gelardi

BRONZE CROIX DE GUERRE

S/Sgt S. Nuttall

MÉDAILLE DE LA RECONNAISSANCE FRANÇAISE

Major E. C. Farnean, MBE

OFFICER DE L'INSTRUCTION PUBLIQUE

Lt-Col A. G. B. Stewart, OBE

Decorations conferred by HRH the Prince Regent of Belgium

COMMANDER OF THE ORDER OF THE CROWN, CROIX DE GUERRE, 1940, WITH PALM

Maj-Gen Sir Leslie H. Williams, KBE, CB, MC

THE ORDER OF LEOPOLD I, WITH PALM, CROIX DE GUERRE WITH PALM—OFFICER

Col W. A. Kenney, OBE

THE ORDER OF LEOPOLD II WITH PALM, CROIX DE GUERRE WITH PALM

Officer:
Lt-Col R. M. N. Patrick

Companion:
Lt-Col A. C. Lusty
Major W. Mellors
Major K. D. Zerny
Capt H. E. Norris
Capt K. J. Kinder
Capt G. L. Howlett
Capt R. Cox

Croix de Guerre 1940 with Palm:
WO II B. F. G. Cronin
WO II D. R. D'Oyly-Watkins
WO II E. G. Walker
WO II F. McCormick
WO II L. G. Watkins
S/Sgt J. Crombie
Sgt H. Woodward
Pte P. W. Dawe
WO I C. H. Greenway
WO II J. E. West

INDEX